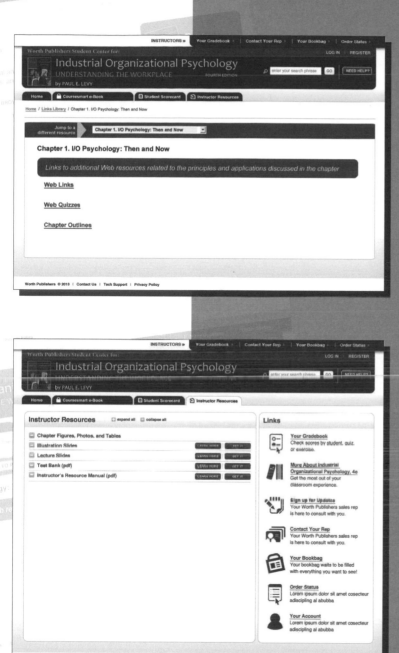

W9-CCT-887

The book companion site for Paul Levy's *Industrial Organizational Psychology*, Fourth Edition, serves students as a free online study guide.

Student resources include:
· Online Quizzes
· Interactive Flashcards
· Web Links

The password-protected instructor's site offers a variety of helpful, easy-to-use presentation, assessment, and course management resources.

Instructor resources include:
· Quizzing Gradebook
· Presentation Slides
· Electronic Figures, Photos, and Tables
· Instructor's Resource Manual
· Link to download CMS course cartridges for Blackboard, WebCT, Desire2Learn, and others

INDUSTRIAL/ORGANIZATIONAL PSYCHOLOGY
Understanding the Workplace

FOURTH EDITION

Paul E. Levy

THE UNIVERSITY OF AKRON

Worth Publishers—New York

Senior Vice President, Editorial and Production: Catherine Woods
Publisher: Kevin Feyen
Acquisitions Editor: Daniel DeBonis
Assistant Editor: Nadina Persaud
Executive Marketing Manager: Katherine Nurre
Marketing Coordinator: Julie Tompkins
Development Editors: Thomas Finn and Cheri Dellelo
Director of Development for Print and Digital Products: Tracey Kuehn
Associate Managing Editor: Lisa Kinne
Project Editor: Helen Song
Media & Supplements Editor: Anthony Casciano
Photo Editor: Ted Szczepanski
Photo Researchers: Hessa Albader and Deborah Anderson
Interior & Cover Designer: Kevin Kall
Production Manager: Sarah Segal
Composition: MPS Ltd.
Printing and Binding: RR Donnelley

Library of Congress Control Number: 2012948907
ISBN-13: 978-1-4292-4229-5
ISBN-10: 1-4292-4229-9

Printed in the United States of America

First printing

Worth Publishers
41 Madison Avenue
New York, NY 10010
www.worthpublishers.com

Dedication

To my University of Akron, Department of Psychology colleagues—past, present, and future—for 25 years they have molded, supported, and humored me in my career journey. I am so much the better for it!

P.E.L.

About the Author

Paul E. Levy was born and raised in Baltimore, Maryland, the youngest of his family's five children. He received his BA in psychology and economics from Washington & Lee University and earned his MA and PhD in industrial/organizational (I/O) psychology from Virginia Tech. A faculty member at The University of Akron since 1989 and Chair of the Department of Psychology since 2005, Dr. Levy has been very involved in the development and training of hundreds of graduate students there. During his tenure, he has also provided many undergraduates with their first exposure to the field of I/O psychology through his Introduction to Industrial/Organizational Psychology course. Dr. Levy's consulting and research interests include performance appraisal, feedback, recruitment, coaching and development, and organizational justice. He has published his scholarly work in many psychology and management journals, including the *Journal of Applied Psychology, Journal of Personality and Social Psychology, Organizational and Human Decision Processes, Personnel Psychology*, and *Academy of Management Journal*. Dr. Levy is married to Sylvia Chinn-Levy and has three sons—Christopher, Sean, and Jared—who have always managed to keep things interesting. Dr. Levy is an avid baseball and basketball fan, youth sports coach, basketball player, and a lifelong fan of the Baltimore Orioles.

Brief Contents

Contents

Preface

Each edition of *Industrial/Organizational Psychology: Understanding the Workplace* has been a unique experience for me. In the first edition, I made every effort to realize the original goals behind writing the book in the first place. In the second edition, I endeavored to further refine our approach to meet the expectations of instructors. For the third edition, I had the opportunity to work with a new publisher, Worth, and placed a greater emphasis on the changing field of industrial/organizational (I/O) psychology. In this fourth edition, I've worked with the publisher to improve the look and design of the text as well as adding new features that should benefit both instructor and student. Yet the reasons I look forward to each revision mirror the reasons why I originally sat down to write the first edition.

I've been teaching Introduction to Industrial and Organizational Psychology at The University of Akron since 1996 and also taught it for a few years at Virginia Tech. I've always loved teaching the course but was never quite happy with the available textbooks; most tend to be quite dry—and a dry textbook for a technical field is not the best combination. My students always had concerns about the textbooks as well, so I wondered if I might make a meaningful contribution to the I/O textbook market.

Therefore, my primary goal for the first edition was to write a textbook that was more interesting, more accessible to students, and a consistently "better read." I worked very hard to produce a book that would engage students, excite them, and, of course, teach them a great deal about the scope of I/O psychology. From the very beginning, what attracted me to this task was the potential to write a book that would draw students into the story of I/O psychology—and that has been my guiding principle for the subsequent editions as well.

Focusing on writing a student-friendly text would have been difficult enough in and of itself. However, my second goal was to also achieve the highest quality in terms of its research orientation. I have been fortunate enough to be a member of one of the finest I/O programs in the country for 25 years; thus, high-quality I/O research is important to me and to my colleagues. So the real task for me was to maintain the rigorous research focus that is critical to understanding I/O psychology—but to do it in a way that students would find interesting and stimulating.

This book was written to serve as the main text in an Introduction to I/O class, which is usually taught at a sophomore or junior level, but I know of quite a few colleagues who have used it in basic or introductory graduate-level courses. It is also more current than most of the other I/O books on the market. Because I also teach separate graduate courses in industrial psychology and organizational psychology, I have to stay current on the research in both areas.

I held fast to the same overriding principles in the design and writing of the fourth edition—to develop interesting, reader-friendly, current, research-based coverage of

I/O psychology. In particular, I revised each chapter based on comments provided informally by colleagues who used the first two editions and on formal reviews submitted by a diverse cross section of I/O psychology instructors from community colleges, four-year schools, and universities with graduate programs in I/O psychology. I attempted to tighten up the writing, expand on the real-world examples, and broaden the coverage to other areas that have emerged more recently on the I/O scene. Another emphasis was on improving the ancillaries available online and also in the book where we added several new and important features.

■ Content and Organization

Industrial/Organizational Psychology, Fourth Edition, is divided into three main sections. The first focuses on the history of I/O psychology (Chapter 1) as well as on the basics of the research process (Chapter 2), including measurement, methods, and statistics. Chapter 1 differs from most other I/O books, however, in its treatment of I/O history because it not only includes history of the development of the field, but also presents important information about how I/O psychologists are trained. Students get a flavor of both how the field develops and how I/O psychologists develop. Chapter 2 is more detailed about the research process than the analogous chapter in other I/O texts. This was a deliberate choice because I believe a basic understanding of correlation, extraneous variables, why they are a problem, and so on, is an essential foundation from which students can build a greater appreciation for more complex topics later in the course.

The second section of the text is built around what we have traditionally called industrial or personnel psychology. The first modification of note here is my emphasis on the importance of job analysis (Chapter 3) throughout. Second, I include a full chapter on criterion measurement (Chapter 4), which most I/O texts roll into the performance appraisal or selection chapters; this material provides the foundation for the rest of the second section and even many elements of the third section. Chapter 5, on performance appraisal, emphasizes the social-contextual approach and has a particular focus on current research in this area.

Another significant modification to the middle section is that the material on selection has been broken down into two chapters. First is a traditional Chapter 6, covering the major predictors used in selection. Chapter 7 focuses on how predictors are used in selection and includes a lengthy discussion of the legal issues involved—an interesting area for students and an important one for the field. Reviewers have always seemed to like this chapter and have noted that I was able to make the difficult material more accessible for students. Finally, the last chapter of this section (Chapter 8) presents a traditional look at training, with an emphasis on issues related to diversity.

The final main section of the text provides an overview of organizational psychology. I strove to make the motivation chapter (Chapter 9) more applied; most other I/O texts tend to present just motivational theories. Chapter 10, on job attitudes, uniquely explores the relationships between predictors (like job satisfaction and organizational commitment) and organizational outcome variables (such as turnover and absence).

The stress chapter (Chapter 11) spends a good deal of time on work–family issues, an extremely important element of work. Violence in the workplace has also become a much-talked-about and examined phenomenon in recent years, and I discuss it within the context of the modern workplace.

Groups and work teams are the focus of Chapter 12, which again starts with basic social psychological work and shows how it has been applied to issues such as self-managing work teams. Leadership is presented in Chapter 13, where theories are categorized as either traditional or contemporary. I also discuss at some length various issues revolving around gender and leadership as well as culture and leadership. The final chapter (Chapter 14) talks about organizational theory and applies these theories, as well as others from earlier chapters, to a discussion of how organizations change and develop. Cutting-edge topics such as knowledge management and continuous learning are also discussed here. This chapter has been commended since the first edition by both instructors and students.

■ New to the Fourth Edition

The first three editions were well received by most of the instructors who used them; those instructors, as well as several other reviewers, were kind enough to send me a good deal of very useful feedback. Their comments, along with the dynamic nature of the field and several of my own ideas, provided the blueprint for a thoroughly revised fourth edition. New references have been added to every chapter, reflecting some of the best new research currently available, and the writing has been tightened up throughout.

A few significant changes have been implemented to strengthen the pedagogy as well. In the third edition, we added a new marginal feature called Technical Tip, which reminds students about technical issues that were introduced earlier in the text. This allows for an easier flow and connection from concepts introduced in one chapter to the application of those concepts in later chapters. This feature was so well received that reviewers asked for more of them, so we've responded by adding new tips throughout the fourth edition. Additionally, the majority of *Practitioner Forum* boxes have been updated either by the original authors or by new Practitioner Forum authors. As always, we worked diligently to provide up-to-date examples and images, including updated Closer Look questions for each photograph.

Critical thinking continues to be a strong emphasis, and in addition to the Critical Thinking Questions we have also included Application Questions at the end of each chapter. We believe that providing both elements to enhance learning at two different levels is a great addition. We also added one more feature that we are quite excited about: Taking It to the Field. In each chapter, we have added a written scenario that asks students to evaluate a problem and then to help solve it in some way. These can be used for discussion in class, as take-home assignments, or as another way for students to gain a better handle on the application of the material. We believe that these will bring together the content of each chapter and allow students to go one step further than just understanding the content by getting some experience problem solving and using the content in an applied situation.

Finally, there are many important changes in each chapter:

Chapter 1
- Includes a discussion of ways I/O psychology can impact the 21st-century workplace.
- Discusses virtual reality in the workplace.
- Expands the discussion of ethics and I/O psychology.
- Attempts to show students how this course and textbook can affect their lives.

Chapter 2
- Provides a better clarification of the characteristics of a good theory.
- Uses tables to differentiate among important concepts.
- Includes a new Practitioner Forum.

Chapter 3
- Presents more information on the O★NET.
- Introduces the notion of job crafting and strategic job analysis.
- Includes a new Practitioner Forum.

Chapter 4
- Reorganizes the section on the criterion problem.
- Includes more discussion about dynamic criteria.
- Presents recent research distinguishing between subjective and objective performance.
- Introduces the idea of group-level OCBs and cultural differences regarding OCBs.
- Includes a new Practitioner Forum.

Chapter 5
- Adds content on the complexity of giving and receiving performance feedback.
- Includes more discussion on performance evaluation of teleworkers.
- Provides a discussion on contemporary rating format issues.
- Considers the role of accountability in performance appraisal.
- Discusses contemporary topics like the feedback environment, feedback orientation, justice, and trust as they relate to performance management.
- Includes a new Practitioner Forum.

Chapter 6
- Includes a new section on Computer Adaptive Testing.
- Includes a new Practitioner Forum.
- Includes the latest research on types of predictors.
- Presents new coverage of situational interviews and behavior description interviews.

Chapter 7
- Introduces the concepts of cybervetting and social media in employee selection.
- Discusses recent research on synthetic validity.
- Provides important legal updates through new cases and cutting-edge issues.

Chapter 8
- Provides updates to workplace diversity management.
- Discusses current trends in sexual harassment training and diversity training.
- Adds content regarding individual differences in trainees and the role of these differences on training effectiveness.
- Provides a cutting edge example of training simulators.
- Expands the section on coaching to include more on executive coaching.
- Includes a discussion, in the Corporate Universities section, about the concept of "third wave," in which the world's industrialized economies evolve into knowledge-based societies.
- Includes new data in the Workplace Diversity Management and Training section.
- Includes a new Practitioner Forum.

Chapter 9
- Includes a new Practitioner Forum.
- Includes new research on VIE theory.
- Includes a new figure to illustrate control system.
- Introduces new coverage of job crafting.

Chapter 10
- Includes new research on the link between culture and performance.
- Includes new research on job satisfaction and turnover.
- Includes a new Practitioner Forum.

Chapter 11
- Includes new coverage of chronic stress versus episodic stress.
- Includes new research on coping with stress.
- Includes expanded coverage of work-family conflict.

Chapter 12
- Includes new section on mental models.
- Includes updated research on punctuated equilibrium models.
- Includes new research on process loss.
- Includes new research on virtual teams.

Chapter 13
- Includes updated research on behavior theories of leadership.
- Includes a new Practitioner Forum.
- Includes new research on LMX theory.
- Includes updated research on ILT theory.
- Includes new research on gender and leadership.
- Includes expanded coverage on emotions and leadership.

Chapter 14
- Includes more and updated examples from business.
- Includes new research on OD.
- Includes a new Practitioner Forum.

■ A Student-Focused Text

A series of pedagogical features aim to make the book more accessible to students and to teach the material in an effective and interesting way. For example, each chapter includes a **marginal glossary,** designed to help students highlight and understand the important terms *as they read* through the book rather than having to go to the end of the chapter to see the key terms and formal definitions. An alphabetical list of these key terms with their page reference numbers is provided at the end of each chapter and a complete glossary for the entire book is also presented at the end of the text.

Second, each chapter includes a set of **Learning Objectives, Critical Thinking Questions**, and **Application Questions.** The learning objectives, found at the beginning of the chapter, show students what the goals of the chapter are up front—that is, they highlight what I want students to understand after having worked through the chapter. The Critical Thinking Questions, found at the end of the chapter, are designed to help students study and to encourage them to think about the material at a deeper level rather than just memorize key points. Finally, the Application Questions are designed to encourage students to work with the material and to consider ways in which the material can be applied to real-world situations.

One of the most innovative (and favorite) features I've included since the first edition is what I've called the **Practitioner Forum,** in which an I/O psychologist practitioner provides a bit of his or her insight and experience in an area relevant to that particular chapter. Readers will find a Practitioner Forum in 13 of the 14 chapters; each one is written by a practitioner who has wonderful experiences and information to share. In trying to keep this feature short and concise, the practitioners have done a terrific job tying their experiences and the situation they describe to the content of the chapter. We believe students will continue to find this feature very interesting.

New to the third edition was a special feature called **Technical Tips.** A good understanding of technical issues such as methods and statistics is useful to fully comprehending the significance of data presented throughout the text, but I find that students often struggle with these technical concepts. For this reason, I decided to incorporate a couple of these marginal notes in each chapter that follows Chapter 2, Research Methods; I actually increased the number of these notes throughout the fourth edition in response to requests for more from users of the text and reviewers. A feature new to the fourth edition is **Taking It to the Field,** which is composed of real-life scenarios or consulting situations where students are provided with information and asked to play the role of an I/O psychologist to solve the described problem. This provides a great opportunity for students to apply what they learn and get a preview of the kinds of problems that I/O professionals commonly address. These scenarios or situations could be used as the basis for written assignments or as the context for interesting and beneficial class discussions.

Also revamped for this edition is the entire **art program.** Virtually all the photos are new, chosen specifically to bring greater clarity to key concepts in their respective chapters. These photos provide visual anchors for the main concepts and aid in students' ability to remember them. **A Closer Look** captions, each in the form of a Critical Thinking Question, further enhance the function of each photo, prompting students to think about the given concept on a deeper—and sometimes more applied—level.

I've also provided a valuable list of **Suggested Readings** at the end of every chapter, along with a very brief summary of each. These readings vary from technical journal articles to very general overviews of the different topics covered in the book. I updated these for the fourth edition where I felt new, important works had been recently published. Complete citations are included to help make it easier for students to pursue additional depth or understanding of I/O information.

Finally, I've also incorporated many **Internet citations,** which provide a wealth of information that would be difficult to access via print media. Each of these sites is an active link as of this writing. Websites like that of the Equal Employment Opportunity Commission (EEOC) and the O★NET, for instance, are great resources for students and serve as a rich source of cutting-edge information.

■ Supplements

All the supplements to accompany *Industrial/Organizational Psychology*, Fourth Edition, can be found or requested at www.worthpublishers.com/levy4e.

Instructor's Resource Manual by Kristie Campana, Minnesota State University—Mankato

The *Instructor's Resource Manual* has been newly updated and expanded to include more extensive tools for instructors than ever before. Each chapter begins with Learning Objectives, a Chapter Summary, and a practical overview of Teaching the Chapter. Suggested Exercises and Assignments provide meaningful ways for students to engage with the material and interact during class. The manual also includes rubrics for evaluating the end-of-chapter features Taking It to the Field and Application Questions. Finally, a Highlighted Study for Discussion offers a summary and analysis of a study of particular relevance to one of the core concepts of the chapter. New and experienced instructors alike will find invaluable support in the *Instructor's Resource Manual*. To download the manual as a PDF, visit www.bcs.worthpublishers.com/levy4e.

Diploma Computerized Test Bank by Kristie Campana, Minnesota State University—Mankato (available in Windows and Macintosh on one CD-ROM)

The *Test Bank* is newly revised and has been expanded to include approximately 90 questions per chapter, including multiple-choice, short-answer, and essay questions. The Diploma software allows instructors to add an unlimited number of questions; edit questions; format a test; scramble questions; and include pictures, equations, or multimedia links. With the accompanying gradebook, instructors can record students' grades throughout a course, sort student records, view detailed analyses of test items, curve tests, generate reports, add weights to grades, and more. This CD-ROM is the access point for Diploma Online Testing. Blackboard and WebCT formatted versions of the *Test Bank* are also available within the Course Cartridge and ePack.

Book Companion Site at www.bcs.worthpublishers.com/levy4e

For students, the companion website serves as a virtual study guide available free of charge 24 hours a day, 7 days a week. Each chapter is accompanied by electronic flash cards and a Web Quiz that students can use to test their knowledge of the chapter. Each quiz is automatically graded upon submission.

For the instructor, the site offers access to the entire suite of supplements for the fourth edition, including the *Instructor's Resource Manual*, all of the figures and images from the book in an electronic format, lecture presentation slides, a quiz gradebook for viewing student Web Quiz results, a link to request a copy of the Computerized Test Bank CD-ROM, the ability to download PDF documents containing all questions and accompanying information included on the Computerized Test Bank CD-ROM, and links to additional tools including course cartridges for Blackboard, WebCT, Angel, Desire2Learn, and others.

Book-Specific Lecture and Art PowerPoint Slides

To ease your transition to *Industrial/Organizational Psychology,* Fourth Edition, a prepared set of lecture and art slides in easy-to-adopt PowerPoint format is available to download from the instructor's side of the book companion site.

■ Acknowledgments

To describe a text as single-authored leaves out so many people whose help, both directly and indirectly, has been a big part of this book's success. While writing this book has been in many ways a labor of love for me, it would have been completely impossible without the help and support of so many friends, family, and colleagues.

I'll start with my current and former graduate students, who have always provided me with the crystal-clear reason why I am a psychology professor. They have been instrumental in helping to shape my thoughts and ideas over the years, and a few have helped with some of the specific tasks associated with the fourth edition. I thank them all, but especially Kelsey Herb and Alison Carr, who were vital to the research process that helped produce the current text.

Next, I must thank all the undergraduates in my Introduction to Industrial/Organizational Psychology class over the years who have experienced this book, in the sense that they lived through the rough drafts via my lectures over the course of each semester. Without their encouragement and favorable response to the class, I would have never considered writing this text.

Third, my I/O colleagues at The University of Akron, with whom I have been so fortunate to have worked over the last 25 years, have contributed in so many ways—from helpful expertise on certain sections, to ideas about how to present information to those key cites from their areas of expertise that often just helped bring sections to life, to just plain-old social support. All of my non-I/O colleagues in the Department of Psychology at Akron have been instrumental in this process as well, by helping me think through ideas, providing resources, and encouraging my efforts.

The authors of the Practitioner Forum features were terrific contributors to the book through their expertise and insight, which is reflected not only in their written contributions, but also in their willingness to pitch in and do so on our sometimes tight schedule. I appreciate the efforts of Douglas Klein, John F. Binning, Deirdre J. Knapp, Elaine Pulakos, Matthew O'Connell, Elizabeth Kolmstetter, Eric A. Surface, Anne Herman, Brian Welle, E. Jeffrey Hill, Tom Ruddy, Jamen Graves, and Laura Heft.

The following individuals served as reviewers at various stages of this project—I was amazed at the level of detail and care they invested in this endeavor. Without their ideas, suggestions, and criticisms, the finished product would be considerably "less finished." Those involved in the fourth edition provided great insight and I am appreciative of their hard work. I can't thank these individuals enough! In particular, I would like to thank Kristie Campana who was not only an insightful reviewer but also an enthusiastic contributor to the pedagogy and supplements for the book.

Michael Amico, *Housastonic Community—Technical College*

William Attenweiler, *Northern Kentucky University*

Pamela Auburn, *University of Houston—Downtown*

Kristie Campana, *Minnesota State University—Mankato*

Kelly Charlton, *University of North Carolina at Pembrooke*

Bryan Dawson, *University of Georgia*

Donna El-Armale, *California State University—Long Beach*

James Farr, *Pennsylvania State University*

Judith Gebhardt, *University of Maryland*

Jennifer Gonder, *Farmingdale State College—SUNY*

Charles Gorman, *Radford University*

Robert Harvey, *Virginia Tech*

Teresa Herckert, *Truman State University*

Paul Herrle, *Community College of Southern Nevada*

Ann Higgs, *Marist College*

Linda Hoffman, *McKendree University*

Keith James, *Portland State University*

Andrea Lassiter, *Minnesota State University—Mankato*

Debra Major, *Old Dominion University*

Karen Marando, *The University of Akron*

Daniel McElwreath, *William Paterson University*

Mary Meisenhelter, *York College of Pennsylvania*

Myungo Moon, *LaSalle University*

Bryan Myers, *University of North Carolina—Wilmington*

Brian O'Leary, *University of Tennessee—Chattanooga*

Joshua Oyekan, *Morris College*

Erin Richard, *Florida Institute of Technology*

Justin Rueb, *University of Wisconsin—Stevens Point*

Charles Samuelson, *Texas A&M Univerisity*

Comila Shahani-Denning, *Hofstra University*

Mark Sibicky, *Marietta College*

Nannette Silverman, *Dowling College*

Arnie Skattebo, *Pennsylvania State University*

Alice Stuhlmacher, *DePaul University*

Harrold Takooshian, *Fordham University*

Liu-Qin Yang, *Portland State University*

I switched publishers for the third edition and have found Worth to be fabulous to work with. Every single individual who has worked on my text has been professional, competent, and fun to work with. Specifically, I would like to thank Charles Linsmeier for bringing me and the project to Worth; his guidance and expertise have been the key to my Worth experience. When Chuck switched to the land of micro and macro (economics), I was fortunate enough to be handed off to Dan DeBonis. He has been a fabulous editor, always encouraging and helping me every step of the way. Cheri Dellelo had wonderful and insightful comments throughout my work on the third edition, and I quickly learned that I could trust her instincts, which lightened the load on me. Cheri continued working with me on the fourth edition, but due to exciting changes in her life, she had to stop working with us part way through. Although Cheri was missed, I was again blessed to be handed off to Tom Finn, who has been a terrific editor and another great source of encouragement with awesome ideas and suggestions. Finally, my appreciation is extended to my friends in production—namely, Sarah Segal, Helen Song, the late Karen Osborne, Tracey Kuehn, Ted Szcepanski, Cecilia Varas, and Kevin Kall; the marketing support from Kate Nurre and Julie Tompkins; the guidance of Nadina Persaud, Anthony Casciano, and Stacy Alexander on the supplement program; and the Worth sales force for having so much confidence in this book. I'd also like to thank Kerry Baruth who is now at Worth, but with whom I worked on my previous versions at Houghton Mifflin—Kerry has always been supportive and someone whom I could trust. Similarly, Jane Potter at Houghton Mifflin shared with me a level of loyalty and integrity that we all should be so blessed to experience from our business partners.

I'd like to thank my extended family, whose faith in me in everything I've ever done has never wavered—that means more to me than they realize. My wife, Sylvia, has continued to put up with me through this long process, as I sometimes juggle more things than seems reasonable—and she has done so with the dignity, class, love, and respect that she has spoiled me with since we first met almost 30 years ago. I could not have done this without her and would not have even tried—in fact, there is very little that I'm able to do without her or her support! Our three boys, Christopher, Sean, and Jared, have provided the immeasurable joy in our lives that we've relied on over and over and over again. There is still nothing I enjoy more than spending time with them and being proud of who they are. One of my graduate students, in the acknowledgments section in her dissertation, thanked me for sharing my family with her for five years—I was touched by that notion because I know that my family is my greatest blessing. I thank God for them and all that He has provided me and I continue to be amazed by His grace.

CHAPTER **1**

SAM EDWARDS/GETTY IMAGES

I/O Psychology: Then and Now

LEARNING OBJECTIVES

This chapter should help you understand:

- How I/O psychologists are trained
- The work of I/O psychologists and how it benefits organizations and employees alike
- The diverse historical trends associated with the development and growth of I/O psychology
- The very important role currently being played by I/O psychology in the changing workplace, as well as the field's great potential to contribute to organizational functioning in the 21st century

For most of us, who we are is in large part defined by what we do. If you were to ask me to describe myself in a few sentences, I would say something like the following:

> My name is Paul Levy. I have been fortunate enough to be married to Sylvia Chinn-Levy for 24 years and have three terrific young boys named Christopher, Sean, and Jared. I am a psychology professor and department chair at the University of Akron, where I specialize in industrial/organizational psychology. I teach both undergraduate and graduate students and do research in the areas of performance appraisal and feedback. I'm a big sports fan (particularly of the Baltimore Orioles), a youth sports coach, and I play basketball and run for exercise.

You can see from this simple example how prominent my job is in my self-description, even though I think of myself as a husband, father, and psychology professor (in that order!). Most of us spend over one-third of our day at work, traveling to and from work, or preparing to go to work. Many individuals bring work home with them or are called into work at night, on weekends, or even in the early morning hours. We have cell phones, BlackBerrys, and iPhones so that our coworkers can reach us when they need to, even if we are at a ball game or a wedding or a concert. Although most of us would concur that family is the most important element in our lives, work is probably a very close second. In this book, I present the world of work from the perspective of I/O psychology and attempt to provide a better understanding of the complexities that are inherent in the interactions between employees and organizations. This chapter introduces I/O psychology by focusing on its history, implications, and trends.

■ What Is I/O Psychology?

industrial/
organizational
(I/O) psychology
The application of
psychological prin-
ciples and theories
to the workplace.

Industrial/organizational (I/O) psychology is the application of psychological principles and theories to the workplace. I/O psychologists study, among other things, the attitudes and behaviors of employees and employers; interpersonal relationships at work; the structure of organizations and organizational policies; the complex processes of motivation and leadership; both individual and organizational performance; the context, culture, and climate of organizations; and the match between people and jobs.

Traditionally, industrial psychology and organizational psychology have been distinguished from each other based on their respective content areas. *Industrial psychology* (sometimes called *personnel psychology*, which shouldn't be confused with *personal* or *personality psychology*) has long been associated with job analysis, training, selection, and performance measurement/appraisal, whereas *organizational psychology* deals with motivation, work attitudes, and leadership, as well as the structure, culture, and processes of organizations. The topics of industrial psychology have traditionally been more technical, focusing on the assessment, measurement, and selection of people into various jobs; organizational psychology's topics tend to include more of the relational elements of the workplace, such as motivation, leadership, employer–employee relations, and job attitudes. In a sense, however, the dichotomy is a false one given the great overlap among the issues involved in each area. Finally, there is no broad line that divides workplace problems into organizational or industrial ones. For instance, a performance problem that might traditionally be defined within the industrial domain (the term *performance* has always been more closely aligned with industrial psychology) is likely to be caused by attitudinal or motivational factors that are traditionally associated with organizational psychology. In addition, most I/O psychologists are trained as exactly that I/O psychologists not as industrial psychologists only or as organizational psychologists only. Nevertheless, I use the distinction here to be consistent with other treatments of the topic and, even more important, to provide a framework for the discussion. I want to reiterate that *I* and *O* are put together into *I/O* for good reason: They are interdependent, related areas that form one applied subspecialty of psychology.

Before tracing the history of I/O psychology, we must consider at length how I/O psychologists are trained and what it is that I/O psychologists do. This background will help you gain a better understanding of what skill sets I/O psychologists possess and what they do in their jobs.

■ How Are I/O Psychologists Trained?

The Society for Industrial and Organizational Psychology (SIOP), Division 14 of the American Psychological Association (APA), is the professional association with which most I/O psychologists affiliate. Most I/O psychologists have obtained a PhD (or a PsyD, which is a similar degree with less research emphasis) from one of the 70 or so I/O psychology programs currently available in the United States and Canada, but there are programs elsewhere in the world as well. For a detailed look at these numerous programs, see *Graduate Training Programs in Industrial-Organizational Psychology and Related Fields* (Society for Industrial and Organizational Psychology, n.d.). The work of I/O psychology can also be done by people without PhDs in I/O (e.g., there are many I/O psychologists with master's degrees), as well as by people without specific training in I/O. Many of those without training in I/O receive their instruction in a graduate program housed in a business school.

SIOP publishes guidelines for doctoral training in I/O psychology, called *Guidelines for Education and Training at the Doctoral Level in Industrial-Organizational Psychology* (Society for Industrial and Organizational Psychology, 1999). These guidelines clearly stipulate that the underlying approach to training I/O psychologists is

scientist/
practitioner
model
An approach
used to train
I/O psycholo-
gists maintaining
that because I/O
psychologists are
both generators
and consumers of
knowledge, training
must be focused
on both theory and
application.

competencies
The skills, behav-
iors, and capa-
bilities that allow
employees to
perform specific
functions.

the **scientist/practitioner model,** which maintains that I/O psychologists are often both the generators of knowledge (scientists) and the consumers of such knowledge (practitioners). Accordingly, doctoral education in I/O psychology must focus on both the theory and applications associated with the various content areas; the dual emphasis on theory and practice is needed regardless of one's career path. Indeed, to be a strong researcher, one needs to understand both the theory involved in the research and how to apply the knowledge that could potentially come from that research.

To effectively teach future I/O psychologists, one must be able to share insights at both a theoretical and an applied level. Similarly, to apply the knowledge in an organization, one must have a theoretical understanding of I/O issues and practices in order to make them work and to enable other employees to understand the potential benefits of the procedures or interventions being implemented.

These guidelines also maintain that the goal of graduate training in I/O psychology is to develop **competencies,** which are the skills, behaviors, and capabilities that allow employees to effectively perform specific functions—or, in this case, to be effective members of the I/O psychology profession. Table 1.1 summarizes the competencies that have been identified as important for I/O psychologists. This comprehensive list is, in reality, only a guide to be used by graduate programs in the training of I/O

Table 1.1 Areas of Competence to Be Developed in Doctoral-Level I/O Psychology Programs

Consulting and Business Skills

Attitude theory, measurement, and change	Job/task analysis and classification
Career development	Judgment and decision making
Consumer behavior	Leadership and management
Criterion theory and development	Organizational development
Ethical, legal, and professional contexts of I/O psychology	Organizational theory
Fields of psychology	Performance appraisal and feedback
Health stress in organizations	Personnel recruitment, selection, and placement
History and systems of psychology	Research methods
Human performance/human factors	Small-group theory and team processes
Individual assessment	Statistical methods/data analysis
Individual differences	Training: Theory, program design, and evaluation
Job evaluation and compensation	Work motivation

Source: Society for Industrial and Organizational Psychology (1999)

psychologists. It is safe to say that no I/O psychologist graduates from school having attained complete competence in every one of these areas, but certainly most graduates have attained some degree of competence in most.

Another issue addressed by SIOP's guidelines is the importance of *diversity* in the training of I/O psychologists. The guidelines point out that, just as science and practice are inherent in each competency, an appreciation of diversity can be applied to each as well. Diversity in this sense refers to an awareness and understanding not only of ethnic, racial, and cultural differences among employees but also of age and gender differences.

Developing competency in the areas outlined by SIOP and graduating with a PhD in I/O psychology usually require at least four to five years of graduate school (following completion of an undergraduate degree). The last portion of this time is spent on a **dissertation,** which is a unique piece of scholarly research; in I/O psychology, it is usually an empirical piece of research. The doctoral student finds a topic of interest and exhaustively reviews the current literature in that area. The student then decides what needs to be done in that area and designs a study to answer a series of research questions, working closely with a faculty member who has some degree of expertise in the topic. Some students choose to attain a master's degree in I/O; this is typically a two-year degree with a bit less emphasis on research training. One of the fastest-growing demands in the field of psychology is for individuals with master's degrees in I/O. In fact, the demand for I/O psychologists (MA or PhD) is expected to increase by 26% between 2008 and 2018 (U.S. Bureau of Labor Statistics, 2010)!

dissertation
A unique piece of scholarly research that is usually the last hurdle before obtaining a PhD.

■ What Do I/O Psychologists Do?

Although I/O psychologists are trained according to the scientist/practitioner model, most choose a career that, in a relative sense, emphasizes either science and research *or* practice. The point here is not that academics don't ever deal with the application of research and theory to the real world, because most do on a regular basis; rather, it's that their emphasis is still on the research and teaching. Similarly, there are practitioners who are also involved in research and establish excellent research reputations by publishing their applied work in scholarly journals, as well as in more practice-oriented journals, but who maintain a focus on the application of I/O to their organizations. Figure 1.1 categorizes I/O psychologists by the various employment settings in which they work. As you can see, a large percentage of I/O psychologists—40%—are employed as professors by universities. These individuals typically teach in psychology or business departments, in addition to doing empirical and theoretical research. Other research-oriented I/O psychologists are employed by research consortia or institutes or by public or private organizations.

Those I/O psychologists who do not work in academic settings devote the majority of their time to applying psychology to the workplace, doing so in consulting firms (24%), private organizations (29%), and public organizations (7%). Many of these practitioners work in the human resource departments of companies in the manufacturing, financial services, telecommunications, and consumer products industries, among others. Among those in the public sector, many work in federal, state, and local government, as well as in the military. (Table 1.2 shows a selection of job titles for

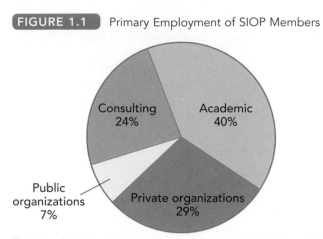

FIGURE 1.1   Primary Employment of SIOP Members

Source: Society for Industrial and Organizational Psychology (2010)

I/O practitioners and Table 1.3 shows a sample of companies that have traditionally employed I/O psychologists.) But what exactly are these I/O psychologists doing?

You got a sense of what I/O psychologists do from the competencies presented in Table 1.1. From this table, it is clear that I/O psychologists have very broad training, but let's get a little more specific and discuss the major areas in which they work. In the ensuing chapters, these areas will be examined in greater detail.

SIOP publishes a pamphlet called *Building Better Organizations* (Society for Industrial and Organizational Psychology, 2006) in which major areas are listed; I will highlight the most significant. First, the area in which more I/O psychologists work than any other is *selection*. Here, experts work on the development and administration of tests used for employee hiring (i.e., selection and placement). An important element in this process is the validation of selection instruments to ensure that they adequately predict job performance. Many I/O psychologists spend a lot of time administering tests to applicants and current employees and then relating those test scores to performance on the job as a way of seeing if the test is a good one. A good test is one in which we can

Table 1.2 I/O Psychologists in the Workplace: Sample Job Titles	
Director of personnel	Compensation analyst
Vice president of personnel	Project manager
Manager of human resources	Senior scientist
Organizational development specialist	Management consultant
Personnel psychologist	Research scientist
Senior consultant	Behavioral scientist

Table 1.3 Companies with Tradition of Employing I/O Psychologists

Procter & Gamble	Johnson & Johnson
United Airlines	Goodyear Tire & Rubber
Frito-Lay	Ford Motor Company
IBM	Dow Chemical
Xerox	S.C. Johnson Wax
AT&T	Wells Fargo

predict who becomes an effective employee in a particular job—that's the true bottom-line goal for organizations. We will examine issues of selection in Chapters 6 and 7.

A second area in which many I/O psychologists work is *training and development*. Companies spend a great deal of time and money on training programs that teach new employees how to do their jobs and more established employees how to do new jobs with new equipment. I/O psychologists develop these training programs. First, they carefully analyze the organization and the job; then they conduct the training program with the company's employees to improve performance on the job; and, eventually, they evaluate the effectiveness of the program. Training will be the focus of Chapter 8.

Organizational development (OD) is a third area of concentration for many I/O psychologists. Experts in this area analyze organizational structures, cultures, and climate and develop interventions appropriate for a particular organization that might make the organization run more effectively. Organizational change is a large part of OD and one that companies are very interested in, given the many changes that are taking place in organizations of the 21st century. We will discuss organizational development in Chapter 14.

A fourth area of emphasis for I/O psychologists is *performance appraisal* (sometimes also referred to as *performance management*). The emphasis here is on developing both individual and organizational measures of performance and using these measures to improve performance. An I/O psychologist might be responsible for developing an appraisal measure, deciding how to implement it, and overseeing its actual administration. Performance appraisal will be discussed in Chapters 4 and 5.

The last area I'll mention is what I call *quality of work life*. The chief concerns for people who work in this area are the measurement and improvement of job-related attitudes, such as job satisfaction and organizational commitment. An I/O psychologist might develop and administer an attitude survey to employees in an attempt to understand what employees like and don't like

▼ **A Closer Look**
How do you think this person's work setting affects her job satisfaction? How might it affect productivity?

ALEX SEGRE/ALAMY

about their jobs. The data from surveys of this kind are often linked to performance; then a plan is devised to improve attitudes by enhancing not only the work climate but also organizational efficiency. Chapter 10 provides a detailed analysis of quality of work life in the context of job attitudes.

Certainly, there are other areas in which I/O psychologists work, such as *consumer psychology and engineering* or *human factors psychology*, but the five areas discussed above account for the largest portion of their work. In the remainder of this text, we will take a much more detailed look at what I/O psychologists do; but first we should examine at some length the history of I/O psychology, for nothing is as relevant to the future as the past.

■ 100 Years of History

Although I/O psychology is often regarded as a newer branch of psychology, its roots actually go back almost to the founding of psychology itself (Lowman, Kantor, & Perloff, 2007). For those interested in a more detailed history of the field, I refer you to a fine resource by Laura Koppes (2007) on the history of I/O psychology. I will use an organizational structure, which breaks down the last 100 years into six periods (Katzell & Austin, 1992). (Refer to the text's website for a detailed timeline of important historical events in the field of I/O psychology.)

Pre–World War I

The initial phase of this history started around the turn of the 20th century and ended with World War I. In 1901, Walter Dill Scott, a professor at Northwestern University and former student of Wilhelm Wundt, was invited by the western advertising manager of a chain of magazines to give a talk at the Agate Club in Chicago on the psychological aspects of advertising. Many refer to the date of this talk—December 20, 1901—as the beginning of business and industrial psychology, or what we now call industrial/organizational psychology. Scott published *The Theory of Advertising* in 1903. Twelve years later, in 1915, the Division of Applied Psychology was established at Carnegie Tech (now Carnegie Mellon University), with Walter VanDyke Bingham as its head, and in 1916 Scott became its first professor of applied psychology.

At about the same time, Hugo Munsterberg (another Wundt student) moved to the United States, continued doing the applied work he had begun in Germany, and published his textbook *Psychology and Industrial Efficiency* (Munsterberg, 1913). It's interesting to note that, as virtually all psychologists at this time were trained as experimental psychologists, Scott, Munsterberg, Bingham, and others with applied interests had to fit these interests in amidst their full-time jobs in experimental psychology (Katzell & Austin, 1992).

Koppes and Pickren (2007) note that many assume that all of this early development in the field of I/O psychology was happening in the United States, but, in fact, this is not true. During these early years, there was more financial and governmental support for the development of the field in Europe than in the United States. According to Moore and Hartmann (1931; cited in Koppes & Pickren, 2007), I/O psychology was developing earlier and faster in Europe (England, Germany, Russia,

Italy, etc.), where centers were established to fund research and bring researchers together to collaborate on common interests with particular research objectives. Interestingly, in the United States, the development proceeded in more of an individual researcher paradigm, whereby lone faculty members spent time conducting their own research—there wasn't much of a coordinated effort to move the field along. In some ways, the contrast between how the field developed in the United States and the rest of world is consistent with how individualistic our society is compared with the rest of the world. This important cultural difference will come up many times throughout the rest of this book as we consider cross-cultural issues in the field of I/O psychology.

World War I Through the 1920s

The second historical phase ranges from the World War I years through the 1920s. This is the period when I/O psychology really came of age and moved out from the hallowed halls of academia into the applied world. During this time, Scott and Bingham established a psychological program under the army's personnel officer. Their staff was responsible for such things as the development of personnel files for military personnel and the creation of performance rating forms. Another group of psychologists led by Robert Yerkes (at that time the president of the American Psychological Association) worked for the government doing selection and placement of military personnel, using their newly developed tools—the **Army Alpha and Army Beta** mental ability tests. These tests, developed as multiple-choice-based intelligence tests that could be administered in groups, differed from the more typical individually administered intelligence tests that existed at the time. It became very clear during this period that those who studied and practiced I/O psychology had a great deal to offer the military—including the ability to administer these and other tests for the screening and classification of people.

Army Alpha and Army Beta Mental ability tests developed by I/O psychologists during World War I that were used to select and classify army personnel.

It was also at this time that I/O psychology began to expand beyond the academic and military realms into government and private industry. I/O psychologists started consulting firms such as the Scott Company (founded by Walter Dill Scott), which worked in the areas of mental ability testing, personnel planning, training, and personnel administration. The Psychological Corporation, specializing in test development, was founded in 1921 and still exists today.

Also in 1921, Bruce V. Moore received from Carnegie Tech what is believed to have been the first PhD in industrial psychology. His is an interesting story, as he rose from assistant professor to become department chair at Pennsylvania State University (the psychology building at Penn State is named after him) and eventually, in 1945, the first president of Division 14 of the APA, which is the section of APA devoted to I/O psychology. While at Carnegie Tech, he was approached by the Westinghouse Electric and Manufacturing Company with a problem: The company could not distinguish very well between new employees who should be directed toward careers in sales engineering and those who were better suited to design engineering (Gilmer, 1981). Moore and others worked on this problem, discovering that these employees were best differentiated on the basis of items that reflected their interests.

ARCHIVES OF THE HISTORY OF AMERICAN PSYCHOLOGY

▲ **A Closer Look**
Testing for selection and classification was an important part of what psychologists did for the military during World War I and World War II. How might knowing the intelligence of military personnel help military leaders make job placement decisions?

This early work by Moore was expanded in later years by Edward Strong (and eventually David Campbell) in what became the *Strong Vocational Interest Blank for Men* (Strong, 1927). In high school, I took a version of this inventory that told me my interests matched up with the interests of those who like to work with people and that teaching might be a good profession for me! And I'm sure that many of you have taken what is now called the *Campbell Interest and Skill Survey* (CISS, n.d.), which guidance departments commonly administer to high school and college students in an attempt to help students identify what careers they might find stimulating.

Frederick Taylor's approach to work motivation, called Scientific Management, became popular in the late 1800s and early 1900s (see Chapter 14 for more discussion of this work). Taylor argued that employees should be rewarded financially for using the best approach to their work and doing their work most effectively. Lillian and Frank Gilbreth built on some of these ideas but with much greater focus on the workers' well-being, which they believed was ignored by Scientific Management.

Lillian Gilbreth received her PhD in psychology (not applied psychology) from Brown University; her dissertation was published as a book, *The Psychology of Management,* in 1914 (Gilbreth, 1914). She was often called the First Lady of Management and the Mother of Scientific Management (Vinchur & Koppes, 2007). Interestingly, she was also the inventor responsible for refrigerator door shelves and the foot-pedal trashcan. The book *Cheaper by the Dozen* (later made into a series of movies) was written by two of her children about their experiences growing up as 2 of Frank and Lillian Gilbreth's 12 children. It's interesting to note that women played an influential role in the development of I/O psychology during this time but that they did so through their roles in industry rather than academia (Koppes, 1997). Along with Lillian Gilbreth, women like Marion Bills and Elsie Bregman made huge contributions to the field through their work at Aetna Life Insurance and the Psychological Corporation, respectively. Koppes suggests that traditional academic positions were limited for these women because academic psychology departments were male-dominated and that industry provided much better opportunities.

The 1930s to Pre–World War II

The defining event of the next historical phase of I/O psychology was a series of experiments collectively referred to as the Hawthorne Studies (see *Timeline for I/O Psychology in the United States,* which can be found on the book's companion website). This period in our history, of course, was marked by the Great Depression, during which unemployment rose to all-time highs and growth in the economy was nonexistent. As a result of these historical trends, our culture became focused less on employee testing and training and more on the human condition (Austin & Davies, 2000).

Table 1.4 Hawthorne Illumination Study			
Description	Manipulation	Expectation	Results
Experiment 1 Test group would work under different light intensities, whereas control group would work under constant light.	Test group experienced three different intensities (24-, 46-, and 70-foot candles), whereas control group experienced no change in light intensity.	Test group would show increased productivity, whereas control group's productivity would remain unchanged.	Test group's productivity increased, but control group's productivity increased by about as much.
Experiment 2 Test group would work under less intense light, whereas control group would work under same light intensity.	Test group's lighting was decreased from 10- to 3-foot candles, whereas control group's lighting did not change at all.	Test group would show a decrease in productivity, whereas control group's productivity would remain unchanged.	Test group's productivity still increased, as did control group's productivity.
Experiment 3 Workers' lighting expectations were the focus of this study.	Workers were led to believe that the lighting was being increased, but in fact it was still the same intensity.	Original expectation was that there would be no effect; but if expectations were really important, then they might affect productivity or other variables.	Productivity remained the same, but workers reported favorable reactions to the increase in lighting. (Lighting, of course, did not increase.)
Experiment 4 Workers' lighting expectations were the focus of this study.	Workers were led to believe that the lighting was being decreased, but in fact it was still the same intensity.	Original expectation was that there would be no effect; but if expectations were really important, then they might affect productivity or other variables.	Productivity remained the same, but workers reported unfavorable reactions to the decrease in lighting. (Lighting, of course, did not decrease.)

The Hawthorne Studies were a series of experiments, some of which examined the impact of illumination on productivity (see Table 1.4), that were conducted at the Western Electric Plant in Hawthorne, Illinois. These experiments highlighted the importance of social relations and employee attitudes, among other things. The remarkable part of the story is that, after observing employees' behaviors, researchers realized that the social and psychological conditions of work were often more important than the physical conditions, such as the amount of illumination (Roethlisberger & Dickson, 1939). One of the interesting findings was that employees reacted positively to being paid attention to—someone taking an interest in them resulted in positive behavior change. We need to keep in mind that, to this point, the history of I/O had read more like the history of "I" alone! In other words, it wasn't until the Hawthorne Studies that team development, supervision, group process, worker morale, and other organizational phenomena played much of a role in the I/O field. As Haller Gilmer (1981), one of the early I/O psychologists, noted in his later years, "Thinking about industrial-psychology problems changed. Simple answers to simple problems were not enough. Questions about motivation, leadership, supervision, and human relations began to emerge" (p. 13). Many view this time period, and the Hawthorne Studies in particular, as marking the birth of organizational psychology.

World War II to the Mid-1960s

Like the previous war, World War II was an important and dynamic time for the development of I/O psychology. Bingham, Scott, and Yerkes were brought back to the military to help match recruits to jobs. Selection, placement, evaluation, and appraisal all largely began during the World War I years, whereas World War II saw a great refinement in terms of the knowledge base and how best to apply the existing knowledge to specific situations. Organizational psychology became a more equal partner with industrial psychology and began to emphasize such areas as organizational dynamics, work groups, and employee morale. Whereas much of the military work initiated during World War I was shut down after that war, World War II work continued as the armed services created centers of research such as the Army Research Institute (ARI) and the Air Force Human Resources Laboratory (AFHRL), where studies are conducted to this day. During the 1950s, many companies, including AT&T, General Electric, Metropolitan Life, and Standard Oil of New Jersey, also established large research groups to do I/O work (Dunnette, 1962).

The number and diversity of universities training students in I/O psychology increased during the same period. New programs were developed at the University of Maryland, Michigan State University, and George Washington University. In addition, several university-based programs were developed that emphasized organizational issues (as opposed to industrial ones), such as the Research Center for Group Dynamics established by Kurt Lewin at the Massachusetts Institute of Technology (Katzell & Austin, 1992). Lewin, chiefly considered a social psychologist, was instrumental in developing theory and methodology in the area of work groups and leadership. His early work still influences modern I/O psychology through its impact on more recent motivational theories such as goal setting and expectancy theory (we'll consider these in Chapter 9). Finally, personnel counseling developed during this time as an outgrowth of the Hawthorne Studies. The focus here was on helping employees deal with personal problems that had the potential to affect their work performance (Highhouse, 1999).

The Mid-1960s to the Mid-1980s

One strong indication of the increasing role of organizational psychology was the fact that, in 1970, Division 14 of the APA changed its name from "the Division of Business and Industrial Psychology" to "the Division of Industrial and Organizational Psychology." Organizational psychology had truly arrived.

On the industrial side, this period saw a great deal of work on selection and performance appraisal. These continue to be two of the largest and most researched topic areas in I/O psychology. One major theme at the time was a concern with ethnic and racial differences on selection tests and the fairness of those tests. This interest emerged as a result of the social, political, and legal climate of the 1960s. As you know, the civil rights movement defined this period; it was a time of great racial tension. Issues of discrimination and fairness permeated society and the workplace. I/O psychology began addressing these issues as well. In Chapters 6 and 7, we will discuss Title VII of the Civil Rights Act of 1964, which was the legal framework for much of this work.

Organizational topics of interest during this period included work motivation, job attitudes, and job characteristics. As we will note in Chapter 9, more than a few of the most popular theories of motivation—including goal setting and expectancy theory—came of age during this period. Indeed, Richard Hackman and Greg Oldham's work on the motivating potential of jobs as a result of their characteristics is among the most cited work in the history of I/O psychology (Sackett, 1994). Similarly, much of the work on job attitudes, such as job satisfaction and organizational commitment (see Chapter 10), was conducted during this time.

These two decades were a time of tremendous growth in I/O psychology. New doctoral training programs emerged at such places as Bowling Green State University (1966), North Carolina State University (1966), and the University of Akron (1965). In 1960, there were about 756 members of Division 14; by 1980 they totaled 2,005 (Katzell & Austin, 1992).

The Mid-1980s to Today

Over the last 30 years, the field of I/O psychology has grown very rapidly, with more work being done in traditional areas such as selection, performance appraisal, motivation, and leadership, as well as in new domains. For instance, the fairness of employment tests—reflecting the legal climate involved in personnel and labor law—has become an even greater focus among I/O psychologists. Cognitive processes, too, are now the focus of much research in the I/O area, reflecting the emergence of this cognitive framework in all aspects of psychology. Historians estimate that, in 1939, there were fewer than 100 I/O psychologists in the world (Katzell & Austin, 1992). That estimate grew to 760 by 1960. In 1992, there were about 2,500 members of SIOP and probably a few hundred more I/O psychologists who weren't members, totaling around 3,000 I/O psychologists. The most recent SIOP data indicate that it has about 3,900 professional members and 3,000 student members (Larry Nader, personal communication, December 2, 2010).

In earlier sections, I highlighted the development of some of the early I/O programs, beginning with Carnegie Tech. The latest SIOP data reveal that today there are more than 70 doctoral programs in I/O psychology or closely allied fields and many others that offer master's degrees. Rogelberg and Gill (2004) note that, between 1986 and 2004, there was an increase in I/O doctoral programs of almost 50% and that master's programs increased by over 200%. There are more than 1,000 professors of I/O psychology today in both psychology departments and business schools around the globe. Bruce V. Moore received the first PhD in I/O from Carnegie Tech in 1921; 1,311 members of SIOP received their doctoral degrees between 1995 and 2003 (Esther Benitez, personal communication, March 15, 2004).

Throughout the approximately 100-year history of I/O psychology, there have been considerable developments in other countries. German psychologists have developed "action theories," which are broad conceptual frameworks within which motivation and performance can be examined. Dutch psychologists have traditionally focused less on management issues and more on broader social responsibilities. French psychologists have played important roles in ergonomics (human factors and the design of the workplace) and intelligence testing. The International Association of Applied Psychology (IAAP), which publishes a well-respected journal called *Applied Psychology: An International Review*, recognized the role of Spanish research in the areas of work efficiency and vocational guidance at its 1994 congress in Madrid. Asian psychologists (chiefly in China and Japan) have approached the study of I/O psychology from a collective mind-set; selection is more about fitting an employee into a company (a collection of people) than about placement in a particular job, and group dynamics plays a more central role than individual differences, which are more likely to be studied and emphasized in the Western world (Warr, 2007b). Whether Americans call it *I/O psychology,* the British refer to it as *occupational psychology,* or Europeans label it *work psychology,* the field has grown, developed, and matured across the globe since its beginnings in the late 19th and early 20th centuries. In addition to being one of the fastest-growing areas within the field of psychology, I/O holds the potential for making a huge global impact on 21st-century society.

■ Current Issues in I/O Psychology

Although the history of I/O psychology presented here seems to reflect a great deal of change over the past century, it is fair to say that this change is just the tip of the iceberg. The 21st century promises to be fast, competitive, and turbulent. Dramatic changes are taking place in the world of work. As American society and the American workplace continue to change, the field of I/O psychology will have potentially more to offer. In a thought-provoking analysis of research trends, researchers have identified 13 areas where they believed research by I/O psychologists could really help organizations become more effective: leadership development, compensation and benefits, executive compensation, work–life issues, retirement of baby boomers, attitudes toward aging, work intensification, talent management, culture transformation, managing change, increasing diversity, globalization, and ethics and ethical leadership (Cascio & Aguinas, 2008). These scholars believe that I/O psychology should be able to improve human welfare in the workplace and inform the important debates about human capital issues that are so crucial to organizations and society at large. Let's look at a few of the more intriguing issues and research topics that promise to be central to organizations in the 21st century.

First, whereas war defined the geopolitical scene of the 20th century, economics will be the defining issue of the 21st century. We hear the term *global competition* thrown about a great deal—and for good reason. Workers and firms in the United States can no longer expect to freely and easily make a profit. Global competition will continue to require us to have a skilled, well-trained, and competent workforce to compare favorably with

© Mike Baldwin / Cornered

MIKE BALDWIN—CORNERED/CARTOONSTOCK.COM

"Three more got laid off today."

▲ **A Closer Look**
What challenges do I/O psychologists face in helping companies that are going through downsizing?

the many, many countries that are now our competitors. Furthermore, mergers and acquisitions will continue to force companies to bridge cultures as American companies such as Dell, Goodyear, and General Electric operate facilities in many different geopolitical settings. How to merge a production facility in Latin America with a parent company in North America is a complex issue. The collective knowledge of the field of I/O psychology has the potential to help in this transition.

Second, new technology has decreased the number of traditional jobs for workers and organizations. At the same time, *downsizing* has occurred at an alarming rate; between 1987 and 1992, more than 6 million employees were laid off (Baumohl, 1993), and in 2005 alone, 1.8 million workers lost their jobs as a result of mass layoffs (U.S. Bureau of Labor Statistics, n.d.). As I write this in May 2012, the United States continues to dig out of its worst recession since the Great Depression. We have empathy, and rightfully so, for those who are laid off due to organizational cutbacks; but the rest of the story is that when these individuals are fortunate enough to be reemployed, it is often at a lower wage rate (Cascio, 1995). Companies are always looking to be more competitive, more efficient, and leaner, but the result is that fewer employees are left to do the work that needs to be done, often being asked to do more for less. I/O psychology is thus important for (1) helping laid-off workers become competitive for other jobs and (2) helping those left behind handle more diverse jobs and sometimes a heavier workload.

Third, the workplace is becoming more diverse in terms of race, gender, age, and ethnicity. This diversity requires much more coordination and sensitivity to "differences" on the part of management and employees. An additional complication is that our workforce is diverse in terms of thoughts, expectations, and culture as well. In fact, some argue that generations develop their own unique cultures such that traditionalists, baby boomers, Gen Xers, and millennials differ significantly in terms of values that develop because of their experiences of different historical events (Doverspike & O'Malley, 2006). Organizations have to recognize and consider how organizational policies and procedures impact these different generations as well as help to ensure reasonable levels of communication between members of these different generations. Education and training regarding diversity among workers have become very important areas for I/O psychologists and will continue to grow in importance in the 21st century.

Fourth, virtual teams, telecommuting, and other technology-related changes have begun to transform the workplace in unprecedented ways; for example, it is estimated that 33 million American employees, about 11% of the U.S. workforce, telecommuted in 2008 (WorldatWork, 2009). A recent review of almost 50 field studies (and over 12,000 employees) found considerable benefits of telecommuting (Gajendran & Harrison, 2007). For instance, telecommuting resulted in perceptions of more autonomy and less work–family conflict. In addition, telecommuting had positive benefits on broader outcome variables such as job satisfaction, stress, and intentions to change jobs. However, although more intensive telecommuting, defined as 2.5 days per week, resulted in favorable work–family benefits, it also led to poorer relationships with coworkers. Research is needed to better understand the causes and potential outcomes of these interesting and growing trends so that organizations can make the best use of these technological and cultural changes.

Finally, ethics in organizations has become an extremely important topic, one commonly addressed in the media since the ethical unraveling of Enron, WorldCom, Pfizer, Arthur Anderson, and other once-respected organizations. A recent review of the literature (Kish-Gephart, Harrison, & Treviño, 2010) proposes and tests a model of unethical choices, with a focus on the antecedents that led to those bad choices. The authors categorize the antecedents according to bad apples (characteristics of people who make poor ethical choices), bad cases (characteristics of the situation surrounding the ethical choice), and bad barrels (organizational climates or cultures that seem defined by poor ethics). The authors provide a great deal of support for the importance of these three types of antecedents and also suggests that we need additional research that looks at how the three categories of antecedents interact in affecting ethical intentions and decisions. They conclude by arguing that companies can use many of the tools of I/O psychology, such as assessment, selection, training, and culture change, to avoid the ethical problems that have become so pervasive in today's organizations.

▼ **A Closer Look**
Many companies are comprised of diverse work groups like this one. What are the advantages and challenges of having a very diverse group of people working together?

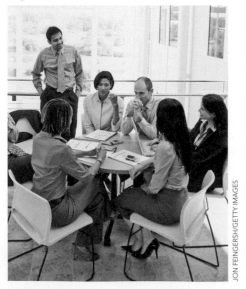

JON FEINGERSH/GETTY IMAGES

■ What Does I/O Psychology Mean to You?

As students, you can use much of what you learn about I/O psychology. For instance, what you learn about motivation can not only be applied to your schoolwork; it can also help you understand why you are more motivated to do certain things rather than others and even more motivated in certain situations. In addition, our examination of stress and well-being may shed some valuable light on your own stress levels, the possible root causes of your stress, and, of course, ways to reduce and better deal with stress in your own life.

Many of you are currently working or are about to enter the workforce. The field of I/O has so much to offer you. You should be able to gain something from every chapter in the book that you can apply to your working life. For example, a better understanding of the role that jobs play in our lives should provide you with a better appreciation for work and its effect on you. Further, how performance is measured at work should provide you with a better understanding of the different dimensions of performance, your boss's perspective on these things, and the value that organizations place on different types of performance behaviors. Additionally, a better understanding of leadership might help you in your dealings with the leaders in your organization, and more knowledge about organizational cultures might aid your perspective when thinking about and examining your own organization.

Because I/O psychology is an applied field, you should find the course material and the textbook to be chock-full of information that you can readily apply to all the domains of your life: school, personal, and work.

■ Summary

I/O psychology, the application of psychology to the workplace, encompasses such diverse areas as performance appraisal, employment testing, organizational development, and motivation. I/O psychologists receive extensive training in a wide range of areas, but their central approach is based on the scientist/practitioner model, which emphasizes both theory and practice. Most obtain an advanced degree such as a PhD. The training is quite intensive and includes a great deal of coursework, practical experience, and research experience. The culmination of the training is usually the completion of a dissertation.

About 40% of I/O psychologists work in academic settings such as psychology departments and business schools, where they teach undergraduate and graduate students and conduct research for the purposes of creating and applying knowledge. The majority of I/O psychologists, however, work outside of academia in the public or private sector, applying what they've learned in graduate school to their particular organization. Many of these I/O psychologists also work for consulting firms that provide services to organizations on a project-by-project basis.

I/O psychology has a rich, albeit relatively short, history. Although its beginnings date to around the turn of the 20th century, its growth as a field emerged with World

War I, when I/O psychologists were employed by the government to train, test, and measure the performance of soldiers. Other historical hallmarks include World War II, the civil rights movement of the 1960s, and the emergence of the global economy in the past 25 years. I/O psychology is positioned to play an ever-increasing role in the constantly changing world of work in the 21st century. In the remainder of this book, we will discuss the various topics and areas in which I/O psychology has, and will continue to have, an impact. You should find a great deal of material that you can apply to your life as a student or employee—the applications of I/O psychology are many, diverse, and useful.

■ Key Terms

Army Alpha and Army Beta (p. 9)
competencies (p. 4)
dissertation (p. 5)

industrial/organizational (I/O)
psychology (p. 2)
scientist/practitioner model (p. 4)

■ TAKING IT TO THE FIELD

One of the more challenging issues facing I/O psychologists is explaining what it is we do. Few people are familiar with the field, and many don't realize how I/O psychology can be useful to a company. Thus, I/O psychologists have to be prepared to educate others in a succinct and polite manner about what I/O psychology is. In addition, I/O psychologists who choose to work in consulting firms have to be persuasive and convince business owners to use their services to help improve their company.

Below is an e-mail from a potential client, Chris. Read the e-mail and then draft a response to Chris that will answer his questions.

Hello—

My name is Chris Covey, and I currently own a restaurant named The Twisted Spoon. My mother started this restaurant almost 15 years ago. After she passed away, I took over the business, and I have been having nothing but trouble from my cooks! First, the cooks don't do a very good job—they come in late, and they leave early. They verbally abuse the servers (who often quit as a result). Sometimes they don't even cook the food properly! Lately, a number of our customers have complained about their chicken and fish being undercooked and their vegetables being overcooked. I have also had to fire a number of our cooks for illegal behaviors. We had one cook who drank on the job and another who was selling drugs out of his car in our parking lot. We're losing a lot of business, and I'm seriously thinking about closing the restaurant and cutting my losses.

I was telling a friend about my problems, and she suggested I contact an I/O psychologist for some help. I looked up your company online, and I am curious about what you do. So, if I hired you, what sorts of things could you help me with?

Thanks for your time.
Chris

Draft a brief, persuasive e-mail to Chris explaining the work your company does and how it might help him with his problems. Keep in mind that Chris is a business owner and so may not be familiar with technical psychological terms.

■ Critical Thinking Questions

1. How has I/O psychology changed since its origins in the early 1900s?

2. How did the military fuel the development of I/O psychology?

3. What tasks might an I/O psychologist perform in organizations?

■ Application Questions

1. Go to www.siop.org and find a university that offers an MA, a PsyD, or a PhD in I/O psychology. Visit that university's I/O psychology page and read about the program. What are some aspects of that program that seem appealing to you? What aspects seem unappealing? If you wanted to apply to this school, what would you need to do?

2. The chapter mentions five main topics that I/O psychologists investigate— selection, training, organizational development, performance appraisal, and quality of work life. Which of these topics seems most interesting to you? Write a question about that topic that you think I/O psychology could answer.

3. The chapter discusses the importance of understanding diversity in the work-place. One currently popular topic is the issue of generational differences. How does your attitude toward work differ from that of people who are older or younger than you (e.g., your parents or children)? What kinds of problems might arise out of those differences?

4. The chapter discusses the scientist/practitioner model. One common problem in I/O psychology is what is called a scientist/practitioner gap; that is, scientists often complain that practitioners don't always use techniques that have empiri-cal support, while practitioners often complain that scientists don't conduct studies that have practical applications in the workplace. What are some steps that the field of I/O psychology could take to ensure that scientists and prac-titioners can benefit from one another's work?

5. Consider a problem that you are facing either at work or at school. How might I/O psychology be able to help you solve this problem?

6. As you probably noticed in reading the chapter, the topics explored by I/O psychology have changed over the years. What topics do you believe are going to be important for I/O psychology to address over the next decade? Why do you think these topics will be so important?

■ Suggested Readings

Arthur, W., Jr., & Benjamin, L. T., Jr. (1999). Psychology applied to business. In D. A. Bernstein (Ed.), *Psychology: Fields of application* (pp. 98–115). Boston: Houghton Mifflin. A nicely written review of I/O psychology in an interesting book about psychology and its diverse subfields.

Cooper, C. L., & Locke, E. A. (2000). *Industrial and organizational psychology: Linking theory with practice*. Malden, MA: Wiley-Blackwell. Leading scholars link the theory underlying core topics in I/O psychology to what happens in "real" organizations.

Earley, C., & Erez, M. (1997). *New perspectives on international I-O psychology*. San Francisco: New Lexington Press. Although the publication date reveals that the perspectives introduced in this book are no longer brand new, this book's illustration of how culture and national origin play important roles in the workplace is still timely and relevant.

Katzell, R. A., & Austin, J. T. (1992). From then to now: The development of industrial-organizational psychology in the United States. *Journal of Applied Psychology, 77*(6), 803–835. A thorough history of the I/O field with an emphasis on the role of the people involved in each time period.

Koppes, L. L. (Ed.). (2007). *Historical perspectives in industrial and organizational psychology*. Mahwah, NJ: Erlbaum. The most comprehensive text ever written on the history of I/O psychology—a must-read for history buffs who are interested in I/O psychology.

Kuther, T. L. (2004). *Your career in psychology: Industrial/organizational psychology*. Belmont, CA: Wadsworth. This book profiles psychologists who have chosen various career paths in I/O psychology.

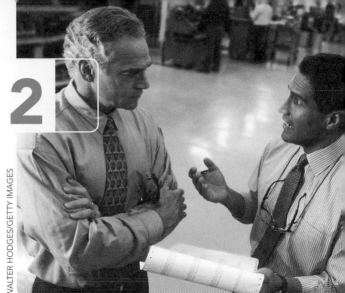

CHAPTER **2**

Research Methods in I/O Psychology

Measurement
Ethics
Statistics
Summary

LEARNING OBJECTIVES

This chapter should help you understand:

- The scientific method and its goals and assumptions
- The importance of theory to science and psychology
- Internal and external validity
- The complex interplay among experimental variables
- How research is conducted, with an emphasis on induction and deduction as well as the five steps involved in the process
- A variety of measurement issues such as reliability and validity
- Basic-level statistics ranging from descriptive statistics to correlation and regression

Suppose that an organization is having a problem with absenteeism such that, on average, its employees are missing about 15 days of work per year. Absenteeism is a very expensive problem for organizations because it slows down production and it costs additional dollars to replace employees who are missing. Suppose further that this company has hired you as an I/O psychologist to help diagnose the problem, provide a potential solution, and implement and evaluate that solution.

First, then, you have to figure out what the problem is. You might do this by interviewing current plant employees, by talking to managers, and by administering surveys. In addition, you might need to look at the organization's absence data and do some statistical analysis to uncover how frequent the absences are, when they tend to occur (e.g., Mondays and Fridays versus days in the middle of the week), and whether they are occurring in certain departments more than in others. Second, you might need to collect some historical data about the company and its absence policy (usually a written policy in the employee handbook) because this may help you to understand the problem better. Third, you might use this information and your expertise in I/O psychology to develop and implement an approach to remedy the problem.

Furthermore, you will need to look at the absence data again a few months after the new approach is under way to see whether absence has decreased. In addition, you might want to survey and interview employees to see if they have noticed any differences since (and as a result of) the implementation of the new approach. At each of these steps in the process, you will need to gather data in order to understand the problem and to evaluate the solution. In this chapter, I will talk about how I/O psychologists gather data and use it to improve their understanding of organizational functioning.

■ What Is Science?

Science is a process or method for generating a body of knowledge. It's important to note that this term refers not to a body of knowledge but, rather, to the process or method used in producing that body of knowledge. Science represents a *logic of inquiry*—a way of going about doing things to increase our understanding of concepts, processes, and relationships. What makes psychology scientific is that we rely on formal, systematic observation to help us find answers to questions about behavior. Science is not about people in white coats in a laboratory, or brilliant teachers in the thought-provoking world of academia, or mind-boggling technological advances; science is about understanding the world in which we live. But scientists are not satisfied with a superficial understanding; they strive for a complete understanding. For instance, the nonscientist may note that employees seem to be more productive when they are allowed to participate in important organizational decisions. The scientist, on the other hand, works at understanding why this is the case, what kind of participation is most important for employees, when participation might not benefit the organization, why it is that participation seems important for some employees but not for others, and so on. In the next section, we will examine the four major goals of science.

> **science**
> A process or method for generating a body of knowledge.

HTTP://XKCD.COM/242

◄ **A Closer Look**
What do you feel is the primary difference between observations made within the scientific realm and those made outside of it?

Goals of Science

There are many different lists of the goals or objectives of science, but I will use the list presented by Larry Christensen (1994) because it is most consistent with my thinking on the subject. First, there is *description,* the accurate portrayal or depiction of the phenomenon of interest. In our example, this is the focus of the nonscientist's approach to understanding—simply noting and describing the phenomenon whereby employees are more productive when given some voice by the organization. But the scientist goes further than this—which brings us to the second goal.

In an attempt to better understand the phenomenon, the scientist focuses on an *explanation*—that is, on gathering knowledge about why the phenomenon exists or what causes it. This usually requires the identification of one or more antecedents, which are conditions that occur prior to the phenomenon. Again, in our example, it may be that giving employees the opportunity to participate in decisions makes them feel needed and important, which leads to or causes increased effort. Of course, as scientists, we realize that almost all behaviors are complex and that there tend to be many causes or antecedents for any given behavior.

The third goal of science is *prediction,* which refers to the ability to anticipate an event prior to its actual occurrence. Accurate prediction requires that we have some understanding of the explanation of the phenomenon so that we can anticipate when the phenomenon will occur. In our example, we may be able to predict an increase in effort on the part of the employees if we know that the company just recently sent out a survey asking for their input on important decisions about medical benefits. Without the ability to predict, we have a gap in our knowledge and are left with very little helpful information that we can provide to the company. In other words, if we have described and explained the phenomenon but cannot help the company predict this behavior in the future, our usefulness is somewhat limited.

The last goal of science is *control* of the phenomenon—specifically, the manipulation of antecedent conditions to affect behavior. Ideally, we'd like to have a sufficiently complete understanding of the phenomenon so that we can manipulate or control variables to increase or decrease the occurrences of the phenomenon. In other words, we'd like to be able to help the company provide the appropriate antecedents so that employees will work harder and perform better. Indeed, by providing employees with opportunities for participation throughout the year, the company should be able to maintain high levels of effort and performance.

In sum, we have attained some degree of scientific understanding only when a phenomenon is accurately described, explained, predicted, and able to be controlled.

Assumptions of Science

In order for scientists to do their work and to make sense of the world, they must have some basic assumptions about the world. First, scientists must believe in *empiricism,* which is the notion that the best way to understand behavior is to generate predictions based on theory, gather data, and use the data to test these predictions. Second, scientists must believe in *determinism,* which suggests that behavior is orderly and systematic and doesn't just happen by chance. Imagine what psychology would be like if its basic assumption was that behavior was a chance occurrence. It would counter what all psychologists believe because it would suggest that we can neither explain nor predict behavior. In effect, if we didn't believe that behavior is orderly, psychology would have nothing to offer society.

The third basic assumption of scientists is *discoverability*, which suggests not only that behavior is orderly but also that this orderliness can be discovered. I'm not suggesting that behavior is so orderly that a psychologist can easily predict what an individual will do at any given moment; if it was that easy, think about how it would change the way you interact with others. For instance, if you knew exactly how a classmate would react to being asked out on a date, you would feel much less stress and be certain that you would never hear the answer "no" (since, in that event, you wouldn't ask the question!). Psychologists do not suggest that behavior is that orderly, only that there is some order to it; so the last major assumption here is that we can experience, examine, and discover—to some extent—that orderliness.

Theories

A **theory** is a set of interrelated constructs (concepts), definitions, and propositions that present a systematic view of a phenomenon by specifying relations among variables, with the purpose of explaining and predicting the phenomenon (Kerlinger, 1986). Fred Kerlinger argues that without an emphasis on theory, science would become nothing more than a simple search for answers, lacking any framework or carefully executed process. It is theory and its accompanying propositions, according to Kerlinger, that allow us to describe, explain, predict, and control the phenomenon under investigation. Even though, as I/O practitioners, our focus may be on conducting research that will help us solve an applied problem, that research should be based on a theory, or its results should be used to help develop new theories and alter existing theories. It's important to realize that theories are as important to applied disciplines like I/O psychology as they are to basic-level scientific disciplines like microbiology.

theory
A set of interrelated constructs (concepts), definitions, and propositions that present a systematic view of a phenomenon by specifying relations among variables, with the purpose of explaining and predicting the phenomenon.

What Makes a Good Theory? As with everything else in science, there are good theories and bad theories. Scientists generally agree that a good theory should meet certain criteria or standards. First, a theory is of little use if it is not *parsimonious*. In other words, the theory should be able to explain a lot as simply as possible. The fewer statements in a theory, the better. If a theory has to have a proposition or statement for every phenomenon it tries to explain, it will become so big as to be unmanageable. Generally, if two theories make the same predictions, the more parsimonious one is the better theory. After all, if people can't understand the theory or use it in their research, the theory will not help advance science by improving their understanding.

The second criterion for a good theory is *precision*. A theory should be specific and accurate in its wording and conceptual statements so that everyone knows what its propositions and predictions are. You might notice a trade-off here between parsimony and precision, but, in fact, scientists try to develop theories that are both simple and precise: Too much of either is a potential weakness of any theory. If the theory is not very precise but instead is wordy and unclear, scientists will not know how to use the theory or be able to make predictions based on it. They would be left in the position of having to try to interpret the theory based on what *they think* it tries to say.

Testability is the third criterion for a theory: If it can't be tested, it can't be useful. Testability means that the propositions presented in the theory must be verifiable by some sort of experimentation. If you have developed a theory that predicts rainfall in inches as a function of the number of Martians that land on the earth per day, you have developed a theory that is untestable (unless you know something I don't know!) and that, therefore, is not a good theory. Notice that I have not said that the theory must be capable of being proven. The reason is that theories are not proven but, rather, are either supported or not supported by the data. We can never prove a theory; we can only gather information that makes us more confident that the theory is accurate or that it is misspecified.

One of the great scientific philosophers, Karl Popper, argued that science is really about ruling out alternative explanations, leaving just one explanation or theory that seems to fit the data (Popper, 1959). He further said that the ultimate goal of a

Table 2.1 Characteristics of a Good Theory		
Characteristic	What Does It Mean?	Why Does It Matter?
Parsimony	The theory explains as much as possible, as simply as possible.	Theories that are too complex are unmanageable and, therefore, not very useful.
Precision	The theory should be as specific and accurate in its language as possible.	If a theory is wordy and unclear, scientists won't know how to test it.
Testability	The propositions in the theory must be verifiable with experimentation.	An untestable theory can't be supported or disconfirmed and is of little use to science.
Usefulness	The theory should be practical and describe or predict an *important* phenomenon.	A theory that only predicts or explains something as trivial as the color of the pen in your drawer isn't of any worth.
Generativity	The theory should stimulate research aimed at testing it.	If a theory never gets tested—that is, if no research follows from it—the theory has no purpose.

scientific theory is to be "not yet disconfirmed." In making this statement, Popper seemed to realize that most theories are likely to be disconfirmed at some point but that it is in the disconfirmation that science advances.

Of course, a theory must also be *useful,* such that it is practical and helps in describing, explaining, and predicting an *important* phenomenon. You may be able to generate a theory about how often and when your psychology instructor is likely to walk across the room while lecturing; but I would wonder, even if your theory describes, explains, and predicts this phenomenon pretty well and is testable, whether anyone really cares. The behavior itself is not important enough to make the theory useful. By this criterion of usefulness, it would be a bad theory.

Finally, a theory should possess the quality of *generativity;* it should stimulate research that attempts to support or refute its propositions. We may develop a theory that seems to meet all the other criteria, but if no one ever tests the theory or uses it in any way, then the theory itself would be of little value.

In sum, science is logic of inquiry, and the primary objective of science is theory building. As a set of propositions about relationships among variables, a theory is developed to describe, explain, predict, and control important phenomena. Theories can be evaluated as to their parsimony, precision, testability, usefulness, and generativity. See Table 2.1 for a useful summary of the characteristics of a good theory. But how do we

◀ **A Closer Look** A slightly different list of the stages involved in the research process. Why are the steps of the research process so important? What would be the impact of not following these steps?

put all of this together and start to conduct research? That will be the focus of the rest of the chapter. First, however, we need to clarify the relationship between theories and data.

Which Comes First—Data or Theory?

Theory and data are of the utmost importance to science and can't be overemphasized. Science uses both theory and data, but individual scientists have disagreed about which should come first and which is more important. Empirical observation, referred to as **induction**, involves working from data to theory. Basically, the argument here is that we must collect data, data, and more data until we have enough data to develop a theory. Others, however, take the opposite approach, known as **deduction**, which involves starting with a theory and propositions and then collecting data to test those propositions. In this case, reasoning proceeds from a general theory to data that test particular elements of that theory— working from theory to data.

In their purest forms, there are problems with both the inductive and deductive approaches to research. Collecting data and then generating theories (i.e., induction) is useless unless those theories are tested and modified as a result of additional data. But generating a theory and collecting data to test its propositions (i.e., deduction) is only a partial process, too, unless those data are used to alter or refute those propositions. The approach taken by most distinguished scientists is one that combines inductive and deductive processes.

Both approaches are depicted in Figure 2.1, which illustrates the *cyclical inductive–deductive model of research*. Note that it doesn't really matter whether one starts with data (induction) or with a theory (deduction)—neither is used exclusively at the expense of the other. If one starts with a general theory (inside path of the figure),

induction
An approach to science that consists of working from data to theory.

deduction
An approach to science in which we start with theory and propositions and then collect data to test those propositions— working from theory to data.

FIGURE 2.1   The Cyclical Inductive–Deductive Model of Research

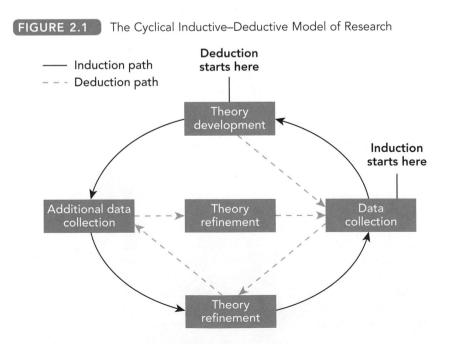

data are collected to test the theory; the data are used to make changes to the theory if necessary; more data are collected; the theory is amended again; and the process continues. If one begins with data collection (outside path of the figure), the data are used to develop a theory; additional data are collected to test this theory; the theory is amended if necessary; even more data are collected; and the process continues.

At least initially, most research tends to be driven by inductive processes. Think about it. Even in research using the deductive approach—theory to data—the original development of the theory was probably based on some data. Hence, induction is an initial part of the process, with an ensuing emphasis on deductive methods. So here, too, we see the cyclical model in action.

By now it should be obvious that there is no perfect way to "do science." However, being aware of the goals of science, the assumptions of scientists, the criteria for good theories, and how induction and deduction feed into each other should help you understand the ways in which the scientific process is best applied. The specific types of research designs and data collection techniques will be discussed soon, but first we need to consider some basic terminology and concepts.

■ Research Terminology and Basic Concepts

To begin to understand what is involved in conducting experiments, you have to know what is meant by drawing a **causal inference** because this is what we typically want to be able to do at the completion of an experiment. Recall my earlier point that we can never prove that a theory is right or wrong; we can only gain confidence in the theory through collecting data that support it. With causality, we have a similar situation. We can never prove a causal relationship between two variables because there may be some other variable, of which we aren't even aware, that's causing the relationship. Thus, our greatest hope is that we have conducted our experiment carefully enough to feel confident about inferring causality from it. We make a causal inference when we determine that our data indicate that a causal relationship between two variables is *likely*. This inability to prove causality explains why psychologists spend a great deal of time working to design their experiments very carefully. Being able to confidently draw a causal inference depends on careful experimental design, which in turn begins with the two major types of variables.

causal inference
A conclusion, drawn from research data, about the likelihood of a causal relationship between two variables.

Independent and Dependent Variables

An **independent variable** is anything that is systematically manipulated by the experimenter or, at the least, measured by the experimenter as an antecedent to other variables. The intention is to determine whether the independent variable causes changes in whatever behavior we are interested in. For example, we might vary the amount of participation that we allow employees in deciding how to do their work: One group might be given no input and simply told how to do its work, a second group might be given some input in deciding how to accomplish the tasks, and a third group might be given complete control over how to do the job. In this experiment, our independent variable would be the degree of participation granted to employees.

independent variable
A variable that is systematically manipulated by the experimenter or, at the least, measured by the experimenter as an antecedent to other variables.

dependent variable
The variable of interest, or what we design experiments to assess.

The **dependent variable** is the variable of interest—what we design our experiment to assess. In short, we are usually interested in the effect of the independent variable on the dependent variable. For example, we might predict that participation (the independent variable) will influence employees' job satisfaction (the dependent variable). In other words, the more opportunities employees are given to decide how to do their own work, the more satisfied they will be with their jobs. If we were to find that this is indeed the case, we would conclude that participation causes job satisfaction. Keep in mind, however, that when I say *causes,* I mean that we are making a causal inference, because we can't be certain that participation causes satisfaction. This shortcut in terminology is typically used by psychologists: We talk about causation when we really mean causal inference. In I/O psychology, common dependent variables include performance, profits, costs, job attitudes, salary, promotion, attendance behaviors, and motivation. Usually, we manipulate the independent variable and measure its effect on the dependent variable.

extraneous variable
Anything other than the independent variable that can contaminate our results or be thought of as an alternative to our causal explanation; also called a *confounding variable.*

Another type of variable is called an **extraneous variable**. An extraneous variable—also called a *confounding variable*—is anything other than the independent variable that can contaminate the results or be thought of as an alternative to our causal explanation. Extraneous variables get in the way and prevent us from being confident that our independent variable is affecting our dependent variable. In our participation–job satisfaction experiment, for example, performance might be an extraneous variable if better performers were given more opportunity for participation. In this case, they may be more satisfied not because of their participation but, rather, because they are getting more organizational rewards as a result of being better performers.

In I/O psychology, we often refer to independent and dependent variables by other, more specific names. Independent variables are frequently called *predictors, precursors,* or *antecedents,* and dependent variables are often called *criteria, outcomes,* or *consequences.* In the selection context, we often talk of predictors and criteria. We use a predictor variable to forecast an individual's score on a criterion variable. For instance, we might say that intelligence is an important predictor of successful job performance. *Predictors* and *criteria* are discussed in much more detail later in the book, but for now it's important to realize that these terms are often used interchangeably with *independent variable* and *dependent variable,* respectively.

Control

Control is a very important element of experimental design. To ensure that we can make a causal inference about the effect of our independent variable on our dependent variable—a matter of internal validity—we need to be able to exercise control over the experiment. In order to confidently draw a causal inference, we must eliminate other potential explanations of the effect. One major way of doing this is to control extraneous variables.

Let's say we're interested in the effect of leadership style on employee performance. To examine this relationship, we could use a survey of employees to measure their leaders' style and then match that up with the performance of individuals who work for each leader. We could then look to see if a particular leadership style results in better employee performance. However, there are many potential extraneous variables in this situation, such as employees' ability or experience. It may be that all the employees who work for the leader with the most favorable style also happen to be the employees with the most ability. Therefore, although it looks as though leadership style leads to a particular level of performance, employees who work for a certain leader may actually be performing well because of their own ability rather than because of the leader's style.

There are various ways in which we can attempt to control for extraneous variables. First, the potentially extraneous variable can be *held constant* in our experiment. For instance, if we think that employees' experience might be an extraneous variable in our leadership–job performance study, we could control for this by using as participants only those employees who have the same amount of job experience—exactly 10 years. In other words, rather than allowing experience to confound our results, we hold it constant. Then, if we find that leadership style and employee performance are related, although we cannot say for sure that style causes performance, we *can* be certain that employee experience is not an alternative explanation. Because all the participants in our study have the same amount of experience, any differences in performance must be due to something else.

A second way in which we try to control for extraneous variables is by systematically *manipulating different levels of the variable*. For example, if we think that gender might be a confounding variable in our leadership–job performance study, we might treat gender as an independent variable and use a more complicated experimental design in which we look at the relationship between leadership style and job performance among female leaders versus male leaders. This would be the opposite of holding the variable constant; here, we make the variable *part of the experimental design* and examine whether it plays a role in affecting the dependent variable. For instance, if we find the same relationship between leadership style and job performance among male leaders as we find among female leaders, then we have successfully ruled out gender as an alternative explanation of our effect.

A third way, though it's too complicated for our present purposes, is to use *statistical control* (see Pedhazur & Schmelkin, 1991). For instance, with statistical techniques such as the analysis of covariance, we can remove or control the variability in our dependent variable that is due to the extraneous variable.

Internal and External Validity

With respect to research, it's important to distinguish the two types of validity associated with research studies from the validity of a test, which is explained later in the chapter. With any experiment, the first thing we are interested in is whether our results have **internal validity**, which is the extent to which we can draw causal inferences about our variables. In other words, can we be confident that the result of our experiment is due to the independent variable that we manipulated, not to some confounding or extraneous variable? Returning to our participation–job satisfaction study, we would have high internal validity if we were confident that participation was the variable that was affecting employees' satisfaction levels. If, however, it was actually the rewards associated with better performance that led to high satisfaction

internal validity
The extent to which we can draw causal inferences about our variables.

COURTESY OF DOUGLAS KLEIN

Douglas Klein
MA, 1989, I/O Psychology, New York University
Principal at Sirota Survey Intelligence
President, Sirota Leadership Advisory

As a practitioner helping companies uncover and overcome obstacles to performance, I have been using field-based research (primarily surveys, but also unobtrusive research methods) for over 20 years. Moreover, reliable, valid, data-driven insights have been fueling strategic decision making in organizations for some time now (although there are still unfortunate examples to the contrary). Gone are the days when successful companies made million-dollar decisions based on unreliable information or management hunches. This is as true for deciding whether to build a new plant as it is for implementing a new leadership development program.

My clients routinely focus on the independent, dependent, and control variables impacting business effectiveness. Recently, a major retailer wanted to understand the relationship between how it led and managed and business results. The hypothesis was that certain leadership and management practices (independent variables) had direct and measurable impacts on business outcomes such as customer satisfaction, employee engagement, operational efficiency, and financial performance (the dependent variables). The company's employee survey data (collected through self-administered surveys) were correlated with existing archival data available for each retail location (e.g., customer ratings, performance metrics, financial performance, turnover, etc.) using a quasi-experimental design. However, we knew that locations in rural areas would have lower financial performance and urban areas would have lower customer service ratings (due to increased volumes), so location-type was used as a control variable. The findings helped this retailer understand why certain locations performed better than others (after controlling for confounding variables) and helped it anticipate future returns on investment in people (and helped it prioritize upcoming spending across a number of potential asset classes).

I/O psychologists help companies recognize the importance of and manage their intangible assets (e.g., people, practices, values, etc.). It is the people who convert a company's tangible resources into business results, so how they are led, valued, managed, and so on plays a huge role in the ultimate success of any organization. Most executives would agree that a weak culture will undermine a sound business strategy every time.

In order to become a successful I/O psychologist providing consultative services, you must understand research theory/methods and statistics and be able to translate learned insights into actions to be taken. A good first step on that path is mastery of the concepts expressed in this chapter on research.

Applying Your Knowledge

1. The first paragraph states that reliable, valid, data-driven insights fuel strategic decision making in large organizations. How do the goals of science align with this business practice?

2. Explain how field-based research, such as surveys and unobtrusive methods, could be helpful in gathering information for business decisions.

3. Toward the end of this feature, the difference between the tangible versus intangible assets of an organization is discussed. How would I/O psychologists be particularly suited to understanding and synthesizing both assets to increase productivity?

---

external validity
The extent to which the results obtained in an experiment generalize to other people, settings, and times.

(as I suggested, these rewards might be an extraneous variable), then we couldn't rule out rewards as an alternative explanation for differences in satisfaction; we would thus have internal validity problems.

The other major type of validity that is important when designing experiments is **external validity**, the extent to which the results obtained in our experiment generalize to other people, settings, and times. Suppose we conduct a study in which we find that those employees who are given specific, difficult goals to work toward perform better than those who are simply told to do their best. We want to be able to say that this effect will generalize to other employees in other companies at other times. Obviously, external validity is extremely important to the development of science; to the extent that we devise studies that are low in external validity, we are not moving science forward. For instance, some criticize I/O research done with student participants as not being generalizable to "real-world" employees. If the work that is done with students does not generalize to employees, it is not very useful for increasing our understanding of the phenomenon under study. (For a different view, see Dobbins, Lane, & Steiner, 1988.)

However, external validity is always an empirical question—that is, a question that can be answered only through experimentation, experience, or observation. We can't simply conduct a study and argue that it is or is not externally valid. Rather, the external validity of this one study is demonstrated by replicating it with different participants, in different settings, at different times. We can also try to use representative samples of the population to which we want to generalize and argue that our results probably generalize to others. However, to be sure, we have to collect additional data.

There is an important trade-off between internal and external validity that often demands the researcher's attention (Cook & Campbell, 1979). As we rule out various alternative explanations by controlling more and more elements of the study to successfully increase our internal validity, what happens to the generalizability of our results? It may decline because, now, a one-of-a-kind situation has been created that is *so artificial* it is not likely to be externally valid. Put more simply, the findings may not generalize to other situations because no other situation is likely to be very similar to the one we've created. So, as we gain control for internal validity purposes, we may lose the potential for external validity.

Of course, if we don't control and rule out alternative explanations, we will not be confident about our causal explanation (internal validity), even if the results have the potential to generalize to other settings and participants. And in any case, if we aren't sure what the results mean, what good is external validity? My point here is that we have to start with internal validity because, without it, our research really can't make much of a contribution to the knowledge in the field. But we also need to balance the two types of validity, as too much control can reduce the extent to which the results are likely to generalize.

A Model of the Research Process

There are various ways to go about conducting a research project, but in this section we will discuss a general approach that should act as a guide for you in developing and conducting your own research. It should also help you understand how research in psychology progresses through various stages. The model is presented in Figure 2.2.

FIGURE 2.2

Stage Model of the Research Process

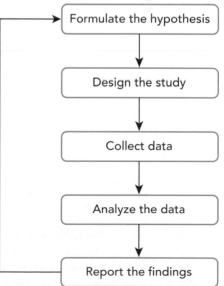

hypothesis
A tentative state-
ment about
the relationship
between two or
more variables.

Usually, the first step in any research project is to formulate testable hypotheses. A **hypothesis** is a tentative statement about the relationship between two or more variables. Hypotheses are most often generated as a result of a thorough review of the literature. Sometimes, however, they arise from the experimenter's own experiences or from a question that has not yet been answered in the published literature. Regardless of how one gets there, hypothesis generation is the first formal step in this process.

The second step involves the actual designing of the study, which we've talked about previously with respect to control, internal validity, and external validity. The two basic choices that need to be made at this stage are who the participants in your study are going to be and what is going to be measured. Although research partici- pants in general can include children, older adults, animals, and people suffering from various disorders, participants in most I/O psychology experiments are either college undergraduates or organizational employees. As for measures, we typically have one or more independent variables and dependent variables.

After the study is designed, it's time to actually go about collecting the data. This can be done in many different ways. Some studies require data collection over more than one time period, whereas others may require the use of more than one group of participants. Some data are collected through face-to-face interactions, other data are collected by mail, and still other data are collected via e-mail or the Internet. We'll talk briefly about some of the more common approaches to data collection in the following sections.

Once the data are collected, the researcher needs to make sense out of them. This is usually done through some sort of statistical analysis, an area in which I/O psy- chologists are well schooled because the field of I/O is one of the more quantitative fields in psychology. I/O psychologists make great use of the various analytic methods that are available. At this stage of the process, the researcher goes back to the original hypotheses and research questions and uses statistical techniques to test those hypoth- eses and answer those research questions.

The last step in the research process is writing up the results. This is the point at which the I/O researcher goes back to the original ideas that were used to generate the hypotheses and describes those ideas and the research on which they were based. The researcher will then present the hypotheses and describe in detail the procedures that were used to carry out the research. The last two sections of the write-up include a presentation of the results and a discussion of what they mean, how they fit into the existing literature, how they help to solve a problem, and what implications they have for organizational functioning.

Ideally, this paper can be published in a journal that is an outlet for research of this type and that allows researchers to communicate their findings to other scholars and practitioners. Sometimes these research reports are presented at national conferences, serve as work toward a student's master's or doctoral degree, or meet the require- ments of a psychology course or an honors curriculum. Whether one is writing up the results of an honors project, a small study done for an experimental psychology class, or a major project to be published in one of the top I/O journals, the process is the same in terms of the steps involved in the research, as well as in the actual written presentation of the research project. For guidelines, see the *Publication Manual of the American Psychological Association* (American Psychological Association, 2009).

■ Types of Research Designs

There are various ways in which studies are designed to answer a particular research question. In this section, we will consider the most frequently employed methods and look at some examples to further your understanding.

Experimental Methods

We have already examined the inductive–deductive cycle of research, as well as the five major steps in the research process. Now we turn to the experimental methods that the researcher can employ in order to answer particular research questions. **Experimental methods** are characterized by two factors: random assignment and manipulation. Table 2.2 presents a learning aid to help you better understand how different methodologies and data collection techniques can be applied to the same research problem—namely, the effect of training on individual employee performance.

    Random assignment refers to the procedure by which research participants, once selected, are assigned to conditions such that each one has an equally likely chance of being assigned to each condition. For instance, if we were interested in measuring the effect of training on job performance, we would want to randomly assign participants to training and no-training conditions so as to provide a fair test of our hypothesis. If we assigned all of the good performers to the training condition and found that their performance was better than that of the no-training group, the reason could be that the training group was composed of better performers than the no-training group even before training. In other words, pretraining performance could be an extraneous variable. To control for this and other potential extraneous variables, we use random assignment to conditions.

    The second necessary factor associated with experimental methods is the **manipulation** of one or more independent variables. With experimental designs, we don't just measure our independent variables; we systematically control, vary, or apply them to different groups of participants. In our training–job performance example, we systematically provide training to one group of participants and no training to another. Random assignment and manipulation of independent variables are the keys to controlling extraneous variables, ruling out alternative explanations, and being able to draw causal inferences. In other words, these two techniques increase the internal validity of our experiment. They are the reason that experimental designs almost always have higher internal validity than observational designs.

Laboratory Experiments One type of experimental methodology is the laboratory experiment. Random assignment and manipulation of independent variables are used in a laboratory experiment to increase control, rule out alternative explanations, and increase internal validity. Most laboratory experiments take place in a somewhat contrived setting rather than a real-world work setting. For instance, a colleague and I conducted a study in which undergraduates were presented with some performance information about a fictitious employee and then asked to provide an annual performance review (Makiney & Levy, 1998). We then manipulated additional information by telling one group of participants that peers had rated each employee better than

experimental methods Research procedures that are distinguished by random assignment of participants to conditions and the manipulation of independent variables.

random assignment The procedure by which research participants, once selected, are assigned to conditions such that each one has an equally likely chance of being assigned to each condition.

manipulation The systematic control, variation, or application of independent variables to different groups of participants.

Table 2.2 Data Collection Techniques

The effect of training on individual employee performance can be investigated in many different ways, such as the following:

Methodology/Data Collection Technique	Example
Laboratory experiment	Student participants are randomly assigned to the training condition (experimental) or the no-training condition (control); then performance is measured.
Field experiment	Employees in a manufacturing organization are randomly assigned to the training condition (experimental) or the no-training condition (control); then performance is measured.
Quasi-experiment	All the employees in one department of a manufacturing organization are assigned to the training condition (experimental), and all the employees in another department of the same organization are assigned to the no-training condition (control); then performance is measured.
Naturalistic observation	The researcher watches individuals as they receive or do not receive training and records what they experience as well as the individuals' performance behaviors.
Archival research	The researcher identifies an existing data set that includes whether or not individuals experienced training and also individuals' performance levels.
Survey	Employees are given a questionnaire that asks them how much training they have received at their organization and what their most recent performance appraisal ratings were.

the participants had and telling a second group of participants that the employees had rated themselves better than the participants had. We were interested in the extent to which participants would use this additional information in making a final performance judgment.

The findings revealed that participants paid more attention to the additional peer information than to the additional self-rating information. Because of our random assignment of participants to experimental conditions and our careful manipulation of the additional information (i.e., the self-ratings and peer ratings), we were able to rule out other plausible alternatives and argue that the difference in final judgments was due to different degrees of trust in the sources of the additional information.

Recall the internal validity–external validity trade-off that we discussed earlier. Laboratory experiments give rise to that very problem. Although they are typically very high in internal validity because of the extent to which researchers have control of the laboratory context, their external validity, or generalizability, is often questioned because of the contrived nature of the laboratory setting. In an attempt to counter this criticism in the study described above, my colleague and I invited as participants only those students who were also employed at least part time. In addition, the majority of our participants had real-life experience in conducting performance appraisals. This factor improved the external validity of our study because our participants were much like the population to whom we wanted to generalize. That they had actual real-world performance appraisal experience made the task we asked them to do (i.e., make performance judgments) appear more reasonable, thus increasing external validity. Imposing enough control to maintain high levels of *internal validity,* having realistic scenarios, and using participants who are representative of the working world for *external validity* are important issues in experimental designs.

Field Experiments and Quasi-Experiments

To overcome the problems associated with the artificiality of laboratory settings, I/O researchers sometimes take advantage of the realism of field settings and do field experiments. Here, we still use random assignment and manipulations of independent variables to control for extraneous variables, but we do so within a naturally occurring real-world setting. Admittedly, these experiments are not used a great deal in I/O research because it is difficult to find real-world settings in which random assignment and manipulations are reasonable. Organizations are typically not willing to allow a researcher to come in and randomly assign employees to a training or no-training group because such arrangements could disrupt productivity and organizational efficiency.

A more viable alternative is a **quasi-experiment**, which resembles a field experiment but does not include random assignment (Cook & Campbell, 1979). Quasi-experiments usually involve some manipulation of an independent variable, but instead of random assignment of participants to conditions, they often use *intact* groups. In our training–job performance study, for example, it would be difficult to find an organization that would allow random assignment of individuals to conditions, but it might be possible to assign departments, work groups, or plants to conditions. In this case, perhaps four work groups could be assigned to the training condition and four others to the no-training condition. And to control for potential extraneous variables, we could measure and control for any preexisting differences between the two experimental conditions in terms of experience, gender, performance, attitudes, and so on. Quasi-experiments are very common in I/O psychology because they are more feasible to conduct than field experiments but still allow for reasonable levels of internal validity.

quasi-experiment A research design that resembles an experimental design but does not include random assignment.

JOHN RENSTEN/GETTY IMAGES

▲ **A Closer Look**
Why are observational methods considered correlational designs?

Observational Methods

Studies that employ observational methods are sometimes called *correlational designs* because their results are usually analyzed by correlational statistics, which we will talk about a bit later in this chapter. This kind of research is also referred to as *descriptive* because we focus exclusively on the relationships among variables and thus can only describe the situation. Descriptive studies are not true experiments because they don't involve random assignment or the manipulation of independent variables. In these designs, we make use of what is available to us, and we are very limited in drawing causal inferences. All we can conclude from such studies is that our results either do or do not indicate a relationship between the variables of interest. Although we can use this approach in either the laboratory or the field, it is much more common in the field because it is here that we are usually limited in terms of what we can control.

In consulting with one company, we were interested in the relationship between job satisfaction and performance of the company's employees. To examine this issue, we administered a job satisfaction survey to 200 employees at a company and then measured their performance using their supervisor's rating. Through statistical analysis, we concluded that job satisfaction was related to performance, but we could not conclude that satisfaction causes performance because we had not manipulated satisfaction or randomly assigned employees to satisfaction conditions. Indeed, it might be that performance causes job satisfaction, as the better performers are rewarded for their performance and, therefore, are more satisfied (Lawler & Porter, 1967). The only way we could have actually examined causality in this situation would have been to manipulate job satisfaction—an option that seems both nonsensical and potentially unethical. Can you think of a company that would allow you to come in and make some employees satisfied with their jobs and others dissatisfied so that you could examine the effects of these conditions on performance? Certainly, the company that hired me would not have allowed me to do that. In such situations, we typically use observational methods and draw conclusions about relationships rather than about causality.

Descriptive research can be very important in a couple of ways. First, although we can't infer causality from such research, we can often gather data that describe a relationship or pattern of relationships. These data can then be used to generate more causal hypotheses, which in turn can be examined with experimental designs. Second, in some cases, there is a great deal to be gained by description alone. Recall that description is one of the basic goals of science. Indeed, some important scientific findings are entirely descriptive, such as the Periodic Table of Elements in chemistry. Descriptive research in I/O psychology can be very important as well, such as when we use surveys to measure the work-related attitudes of organizational employees.

This information is certainly useful for employers who may be trying to decide if it is worth implementing a new reward program for their employees. In addition, it can be integral to us as researchers who are trying to enhance our understanding of work processes.

Prediction, you may remember, is another goal of science—and such studies can be very useful in predicting behavior in certain situations. So, although observational research is not as strong as experimental research with respect to inferring causality, it is important for other reasons.

■ Data Collection Techniques

There are various ways in which data can be collected for a research study. In this section, we will focus on some methods of data collection in I/O psychology, proceeding from the least to the most common approaches.

Naturalistic Observation

Perhaps the most obvious way to gather data to answer a research question about a behavior is to watch individuals exhibiting that behavior. We use observation in both laboratory and field settings in which we are interested in some behavior that can be observed, counted, or measured. *Naturalistic observation* refers to the observation of someone or something in its natural environment. One type of naturalistic observation that is commonly used in sociology and anthropology, though not so much in I/O psychology, is called *participant observation;* here, the observer tries to "blend in" with those who are to be observed. The observational technique more often used by I/O psychologists is called **unobtrusive naturalistic observation**, in which the researcher tries not to draw attention to himself or herself and objectively observes individuals.

unobtrusive naturalistic observation An observational technique whereby the researcher unobtrusively and objectively observes individuals but does not try to blend in with them.

For example, a consultant interested in the effect of leadership style on the functioning of staff meetings might measure leadership style through a questionnaire and then observe the behaviors and interactions that take place during a series of staff meetings conducted by various leaders. Note that, although unobtrusive naturalistic observation can be a very fruitful approach for gathering data, the researcher needs to be aware of the possibility that she is affecting behaviors and interactions through her observation. No matter how unobtrusive she tries to be, some people may react differently when an observer is present.

Case Studies

Somewhat similar to naturalistic observation, **case studies** are best defined as examinations of a single individual, group, company, or society (Babbie, 1998). A case study might involve interviews, historical analysis, or research into the writings or policies of an individual or organization. The main purpose of case studies (as with other observational methods) is description, although explanation is a reasonable goal of case studies, too. Sigmund Freud is well known for his use of case studies in the evaluation of his clients, but an I/O psychologist might use a case study to analyze

case studies Examinations of a single individual, group, company, or society.

the organizational structure of a modern company or to describe the professional life of a Fortune 500 CEO. Case studies are not typically used to test hypotheses, but they can be very beneficial in terms of describing and providing details about a typical or exceptional firm or individual. Of course, a major concern with this approach is that the description is based on a single individual or organization, thus limiting the external validity of the description.

Archival Research

archival research
Research relying on secondary data sets that were collected either for general or specific purposes identified by an individual or organization.

Sometimes social scientists can answer important research questions through the use of existing, or "secondary," data sets. **Archival research** relies on such data sets, which have been collected for either general or specific purposes identified by an individual or organization (Zaitzow & Fields, 1996). One implication is immediately clear: The quality of research using an archival data set is strongly affected by the quality of that original study. In other words, garbage in–garbage out. Researchers cannot use a weak data set for their study and expect to fix any problems inherent in it. Indeed, lack of control over the quality of the data is the chief concern with archival research.

This issue aside, archival data sets can be very helpful and, in fact, are used a great deal by I/O psychologists. Available to them are data sets that have been collected by market researchers, news organizations, behavioral scientists, and government researchers. One of the largest and most extensively used in the employment area is the data set containing scores on the General Aptitude Test Battery (GATB), which was developed by the U.S. Employment Service in 1947. It includes information on personal characteristics, ability, occupation, and work performance for over 36,000 individuals. The GATB has received a good deal of attention for many years, and these data were employed in many research studies as well (Doverspike, Cober, & Arthur, 2004).

Certainly, the use of secondary data sets can be very beneficial to researchers in that they do not have to spend huge amounts of time developing measures and collecting data. Going back to Figure 2.2, we find that steps 2 and 3 are already completed for the researcher who embarks on an archival study. In addition, many of the archival data sets available for use were collected by organizations with a great deal more resources than any one researcher would tend to have. Such data may also be richer in that many more variables may be involved than a single researcher would be able to include. A final strength of archival data sets is that they often include both *cross-sectional data,* which are collected at one point in time from a single group of respondents, and *longitudinal data,* which are collected over multiple time periods so that changes in attitudes and behaviors can be examined. Again, given the limited resources of most researchers, these types of data would typically be difficult to obtain.

Surveys

surveys
A data collection technique that involves selecting a sample of respondents and administering some type of questionnaire.

It certainly seems obvious that if you want information from people, one way to gather it is to ask them. This is the very basis of survey methodology. **Surveys** involve selecting a sample of respondents (or participants) and administering some type of questionnaire. They are terrific tools for gathering data on employees' attitudes and beliefs about their organizations, their supervisors, their coworkers, and many other aspects of the world of work. It follows that surveys are probably the most frequently used method of data collection in I/O psychology. I'm certain that you have had at least some experience with surveys. You might have filled one out at a restaurant to rate the quality of the food or service, completed one on the warranty card that came with your new iPod, or answered questions on the telephone about what you watch on TV or what candidate you are likely to vote for and why. Surveys are, quite frankly, everywhere. Chances are that, if you have conducted any experimental research at all (such as an undergraduate research project, an honors project, or an experiment for another psychology class), you used a survey to some extent.

Self-Administered Questionnaires *Self-administered questionnaires* are surveys that are completed by respondents in the absence of an investigator. The primary example is the mail survey, which is mailed or e-mailed to respondents, who complete it and return it to the experimenter. Sometimes, however, we use the term *self-administered questionnaire* to refer to situations in which the respondent fills out the survey in the presence of the researcher (as in research you may have participated in for extra credit in an introductory psychology course). In these situations, the respondent is provided with a written survey that asks a series of questions requir-

▼ A Closer Look
Why are self-administered surveys useful?

Ralphie's

Home of Akron's Finest Burgers!

We are delighted to offer our guests the chance to win a $25 Gift Certificate. Simply fill out this information card and you will be included on our Preferred Guest List

Our goal is to keep our customers happy! Please fill out this survey to let us know how we are doing.

		Lunch	Dinner		
	Excellent	Good	Average	Fair	Poor
Cleanliness	❏	❏	❏	❏	❏
Service	❏	❏	❏	❏	❏
Quality of food	❏	❏	❏	❏	❏
Value	❏	❏	❏	❏	❏
Overall Experience	❏	❏	❏	❏	❏

Anything else you would like to tell us:

_____

_____

Privacy Policy
This information is for the exclusive use of Ralphie's

Monthly Drawing for a $25 Gift Certificate

Last Name: _____ First Name: _____

Email (print clearly) : _____

City: _____ Zip: _____

Birthday: Month: Day:

Anniversary:

Is this your first visit?   YES   NO

How did you hear about us? _____

Join **Our Preferred Guest List** In appreciation of your patronage, we've decided to give our guests a surprise for their Birthday & Anniversary

Sign Up The Whole Family for Birthdays!

Month / Day

Name: _____ / _____

Name: _____ / _____

Name: _____ / _____

Please refer to the back of card to submit your comments.

Server:

RAE GRANT DESIGN

ing responses along some scale of agreement or frequency. This is a very common approach to collecting survey data.

Self-administered questionnaires are also common in field settings, where employees are often asked about their attitudes and beliefs about their jobs and organizations. For instance, job satisfaction is typically measured with a self-administered survey. Aside from the research goals linked to surveys, organizations routinely survey their employees to gather useful information for future organizational planning and decision making, as well as to give employees a voice in company policies. Self-administered surveys are particularly useful for three reasons. First, they are relatively easy to administer. Second, they can be administered to large groups of people at the same time. Finally, they can provide respondents with anonymity, which makes them feel more comfortable and increases the likelihood that their responses will be honest.

On the negative side, with mail surveys in particular, the researcher is dependent on the respondents returning the surveys. These response rates can be quite low. When only a small percentage of the sample completes and returns the survey, conclusions drawn from the data may be very inaccurate. Also, unless the researcher is available during the administration of the survey, respondents cannot easily get clarification on questionnaire items they do not understand. Despite these limitations, however, self-administered surveys are both popular and useful in the field of I/O psychology.

Interviews An alternative to the self-administered questionnaire is the investigator-administered survey, or *interview,* in which the investigator asks a series of questions orally rather than in writing. Interviews are usually conducted face-to-face but sometimes over the telephone. Either way, the process is much the same. Interviews tend to be more time-consuming than self-administered questionnaires because they are usually done one-on-one. Still, there are some clear benefits to this approach. First, response rates tend to be higher, as people are less likely to turn down a face-to-face interview than to throw away a mail survey (Babbie, 1998). Second, ambiguities about what a question means that may arise with mail surveys can easily be resolved in interviews because the interviewer is available to provide answers. In the I/O domain, interviews are commonly used to gather data about employees' attitudes, concerns over the need for more management attention, applicants' skills and abilities, whether or not applicants fit a particular job very well, and employees' promotability.

▼ A Closer Look
What are the benefits of conducting a face-to-face interview instead of a mail survey?

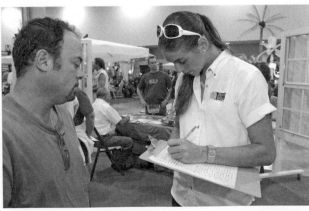

JEFF GREENBERG/ALAMY

Technological Advances in Survey Methodology
Technology seems to play an increasingly larger role in our lives, so it should be no surprise that it also has a widespread effect on the research enterprise

and, in particular, data collection. One innovation in this area is the use of web-based surveys to replace or supplement paper-and-pencil ones. The web has much to offer as a data collection tool because participants can answer survey questions quickly, easily, and on their own time schedule. Researchers are then provided with the survey data electronically in a ready-to-analyze format. Some researchers (Cole, Bedeian, & Feild, 2006) have begun examining whether web-based versions of surveys are equivalent to paper-and-pencil versions—that is, are the measurement properties sufficiently similar that a web-based survey can be used instead of a paper-and-pencil one and vice versa? For instance, do people respond more on the favorable end of the scale when the survey is conducted on the web than when it is conducted via paper and pencil? Although additional research is needed, it appears that well-developed surveys for web administration can be created to be parallel to paper-and-pencil versions and that the two can demonstrate measurement equivalence. That is, the measurement structure, reliabilities, means, and so on are about the same regardless of the form of the administration. These studies suggest that web-based survey administration is proving to be a valuable alternative to paper-and-pencil administration (Leung & Kember, 2005).

Technology is beginning to have another major effect on data collection. **Experience sampling methodology (ESM)** is a data collection approach that captures momentary attitudes and psychological states. Some apparatus is typically used that beeps at times predetermined by the researcher, signaling the participants to answer a series of questions. Recently, personal digital assistants (PDAs) have been used effectively in an ESM approach. The PDA alarm goes off, and then a series of questions asking the participant about his or her feelings, attitudes, emotions, and behaviors appear on the PDA screen. This provides an effective way to measure moment-to-moment attitudes and emotions and has become quite popular among researchers working in the area of emotions (Bono, Folds, Vinson, & Muros, 2007; Dimotakis, Scott, & Koopman, 2010).

For instance, ESM has been used to demonstrate stronger relationships between real-time measures of general affect and affective measures of job satisfaction than between real-time measures of general affect and more traditional cognitive measures of job satisfaction (Fisher, 2000). A recent study used ESM with a sample of cheerleader instructors to measure their emotional states and perceptions of their behaviors on a momentary basis while interacting with cheerleader students (Beal, Trougakos, Weiss, & Green, 2006). The use of this technique allowed the researchers to gain a better view of emotions and behaviors as well as of how individuals regulate those emotions on a moment-by-moment basis (see Chapter 10 for a discussion of emotional regulation).

■ Measurement

We have talked about science, theories, and research design in this chapter, but, although these are all very important to the research enterprise, they are worthless without careful measurement. **Measurement** is defined as the assignment of numbers to objects or events using rules in such a way as to represent specified attributes of the objects (Stevens, 1968). For I/O psychology, this often means that we are quantifying individuals along some attribute. An **attribute** is a dimension along which individuals

experience sampling methodology (ESM)
A technique that allows researchers to obtain repeated real-time reports of phenomena such as moods and emotions through the use of technology such as personal digital assistants (PDAs).

measurement
The assignment of numbers to objects or events using rules in such a way as to represent specified attributes of the objects.

attribute
A dimension along which individuals can be measured and along which they vary.

can be measured and along which they vary. Thus, for instance, we could devise a test of cognitive ability in which job applicants respond to a series of questions or problems, allowing us to *measure* their intelligence; or we could have undergraduates complete a survey of their satisfaction with school, allowing us to *measure* their school-related attitudes. In either case, we are attempting to assign numbers to individuals that indicate how much or how little of an attribute they possess. Ultimately, our goal is to use these measurements or data in our statistical analyses to answer our research questions.

One very important point here is that psychology is very different from other areas such as the physical sciences. For instance, few measurement problems are likely to occur in the measurement of the weight of an object, provided that one has an accurate scale (an inaccurate scale would be a huge problem). However, when we are measuring an employee's attitude about her supervisor, there are many things that can make that measurement inaccurate—many sources of *measurement error*. By this I mean that if the employee had a particularly bad interaction with the supervisor that day, or wasn't feeling well, or was worried about a sick child, the measurement of her attitude might not be accurate or might differ from the measurement of her attitude next week when a whole host of new variables are involved.

Measurement in the behavioral sciences is especially difficult because there isn't an infallible scale, gauge, thermometer, ruler, or calculator that can be used to measure attitudes, beliefs, desires, and behaviors. Thus, when we measure a person's creativity, commitment to the organization, job satisfaction, or motivation, there is greater potential for measurement error than when we measure a person's weight or height. For this reason, we need to be particularly careful in developing our measures. The process of measuring a quality or construct and using it to predict job performance is indeed common in the field; it is also one in which the accuracy of measurement is very important.

Reliability

reliability
The consistency or stability of a measure.

The consistency or stability of a measure is its **reliability**. Three points are relevant in this context. First, keep in mind that if we are going to use a test score as a predictor of on-the-job performance (much like SAT scores are used as predictors of success in college), it is imperative that the predictor be measured reliably. Second, recall that I mentioned measurement error as getting in the way of accurate measurement. Now you should be able to see that measurement error is what renders measurement inaccurate or unreliable. An individual's score on a mechanical comprehension test will not be a perfect representation of the individual's mechanical comprehension; perhaps he missed some questions because he didn't read them correctly, or mistakenly filled in the wrong ovals, or, for that matter, got some questions correct simply by guessing.

There is always some measurement error that causes the person's score to be a less-than-perfect indicator of his mechanical comprehension. The farther that score gets from his actual level of mechanical comprehension, the more inaccurate or unreliable the test is. Third, reliability is extremely important because we cannot accurately predict attitudes, performance, or behavior with a variable that is not measured very well. In other words, reliability provides a ceiling on our prediction accuracy—what we will call *validity* in subsequent sections. First, however, there are a few types of reliability to briefly discuss.

Test–retest reliability reflects the stability of a test over time and is, therefore, often called a *coefficient of stability*. To demonstrate test–retest reliability, we might give our mechanical comprehension test to a group of participants and then administer the same test to the same group six weeks later. Assuming that the participants did not somehow improve their mechanical comprehension in the interim (e.g., by taking a training course or gaining additional job experience), their scores at the first test administration should be about the same as their scores at the second administration. Scores that varied, however, would reflect measurement error, indicating that our measure was not perfectly reliable. Virtually no measure we would use in I/O psychology is perfectly reliable. We can only hope to minimize the error as much as possible so that most of the high (and low) scorers at the first administration are also the high (and low) scorers at the second administration. This outcome would demonstrate acceptable levels of test-retest reliability.

Figure 2.3 shows what seven individuals' pairs of scores on mechanical comprehension might look like when the measure has high versus low reliability. Each line represents one person, and the dots on either end represent that person's score at two

test–retest reliability
The stability of a test over time; often called a *coefficient of stability*.

FIGURE 2.3   Test–Retest Reliability

parallel forms reliability
The extent to which two independent forms of a test are equivalent measures of the same construct; sometimes called *equivalent forms reliability* or *a coefficient of equivalence.*

interrater reliability
The extent to which multiple raters or judges agree on ratings made about a particular person, thing, or behavior.

▼ **A Closer Look**
Here, we see multiple judges rating the same behavior very differently. What kind of reliability problem does this represent?

RAINER HOLZ/ZEFA/CORBIS

different time periods. Notice that when the test has high reliability, the high scorers are the same people across both test administrations but that this is not the case when the test has low reliability.

Parallel forms reliability (sometimes called *equivalent forms reliability*) is often referred to as a *coefficient of equivalence* because it reflects the extent to which two independent forms of a test are equivalent measures of the same construct. In other words, we might want to have two versions of the same test—an approach often used in large, multiple sections of a course to prevent cheating. The important thing is to ensure that the two tests are measuring the same thing. The issue of parallel tests has become very significant in recent years given society's increasing concern that the disabled be treated fairly. We will consider this issue in the context of selection in Chapters 6 and 7, but, for now, note that there are situations in which different tests ought to be developed for applicants or employees who are disabled. Again, we would want to demonstrate that the test for disabled persons is equivalent to the test for nondisabled persons. Similarly, as noted earlier, the use of computerized testing has become popular (Stanton & Rogelberg, 2001). It is important to be able to demonstrate that when measuring, say, cognitive ability, a computerized test is equivalent to a paper-and-pencil test (see the previous section on Technological Advances in Survey Methodology).

An approach to estimating reliability that is similar conceptually to test–retest is what is commonly called **interrater reliability**, which is the consistency with which multiple raters view and thus rate the same behavior or person. This is often relevant in the performance appraisal arena, where we might want to consider how two or three judges rate someone's performance so that we aren't relying on just one judge who may have his or her own biases—we'll consider this kind of situation in more detail in Chapter 5. Interrater reliability is measured in various ways, but many approaches involve examining the correlation between the ratings of two different judges rating the same person. One way to think about this is to conceive of the judges as multiple tests, which makes this kind of reliability somewhat similar to *parallel forms.*

The final form of reliability that we'll discuss is **internal consistency**, which gives an indication of the interrelatedness of the test items. We wouldn't want an item on an IQ test that doesn't seem to fit with the rest of the items because that would suggest that the item is not measuring the same thing as the other items. Internal consistency tells us how well our test items are hanging together. We can estimate internal consistency in two different ways. First, we can split the test in half by odd or even question numbers and see if the even half of the test is equivalent to the odd half—a measure of *split-half reliability*. Second, we can determine whether there is consistency among a set of items by looking at the correlations among all the items—a measure of *inter-item reliability*, referred to as *Cronbach's coefficient alpha* in some situations and *Kuder-Richardson 20* in others (for a more in-depth discussion, see Gatewood, Feild, & Barrick, 2007).

As I've suggested, reliability is very important, and one of our goals should always be to have high reliability. A rule of thumb used by many is that our measures should have reliability levels of at least .70. But because measurement consistency, though important, is not usually our ultimate goal in I/O psychology, we also need to spend some time talking about validity—the extent to which our test measures what we believe it measures and how well it predicts other things. Just as a reminder, you can think of this as a two-step process. First, you have to develop a sound, reliable measure. Second, because you will probably want to use that measure to predict attitudes, performance, or behavior, your focus will turn to validity, our next topic for discussion.

Validity of Tests, Measures, and Scales

The validity of a measure is most precisely considered in terms of **construct validity**, the extent to which a test measures the underlying construct it was intended to measure. A **construct** is an abstract quality, such as intelligence or motivation, that is not observable and is difficult to measure. In a general sense, our test of mechanical comprehension is valid if it really measures mechanical comprehension.

There are two types of evidence that we use to demonstrate construct validity. First, **content validity** is the degree to which a test or predictor covers a representative sample of the quality being assessed. In other words, if you were being tested on Chapters 1, 2, and 3 of this book, a content valid test would be one that covers the entire domain of material presented in those three chapters. Have you ever taken a test that seemed to cover the minor stuff and didn't ask anything about large sections of chapters? You were probably upset about that test and, although you didn't know it at the time, you were upset because the test was *not* content-valid—it didn't fairly and accurately reflect the domain of material in such a way as to be representative of that domain. In an employment setting, performance appraisal measures should be content-valid such that an employee's performance appraisal reflects all the important elements of his or her job, not just one or two.

The second type of evidence that we use to demonstrate construct validity is called *criterion-related validity*. The focus here is on whether the test is a good predictor of attitudes, behavior, or performance. We will discuss this type of validity at greater length in Chapter 7. For now, however, let us simply define the two approaches to criterion-related validity. First, **predictive validity** refers to the extent to which test scores obtained at one point in time predict criteria obtained at some later time. For instance, does our test of mechanical comprehension, when given to applicants, successfully predict their on-the-job behavior once they are hired? In traditional selection situations of this kind, I/O psychologists attempt to develop tests or predictors that companies can use to make employment decisions. The same approach is used for admitting students to college and graduate school: SAT scores and GREs have been shown to

internal consistency An indication of the extent to which individual test items seem to be measuring the same thing.

construct validity The extent to which a test measures the underlying construct that it was intended to measure.

construct An abstract quality, such as intelligence or motivation, that is not observable and is difficult to measure.

content validity The degree to which a test or predictor covers a representative sample of the quality being assessed.

predictive validity The extent to which test scores obtained at one point in time predict criteria obtained in the future.

FIGURE 2.4   Criterion-Related Validity

be predictive of success in college and graduate school, respectively—as have GPAs in both cases (Camara & Kimmel, 2005; Kuncel, Hezlett, & Ones, 2001; Powers, 2004).

Second, **concurrent validity** refers to how well a test predicts a criterion that is measured at the same time that the test is administered. We still want to make the argument that our test predicts a future criterion, but sometimes predictive validity studies are extremely time-consuming and difficult (if not impossible) to conduct, leaving concurrent validity studies as the more viable option. We will discuss the differences between these two approaches in Chapter 7, but I want to emphasize here that both approaches are used to demonstrate that a test is related to a criterion such as job performance. Figure 2.4 depicts a situation in which one cognitive ability test predicts job performance well (high validity) and another does not (low validity). In the case of the high-validity test, those who score well also perform well on the job; those who don't score well also don't perform well on the job. In the case of the low-validity test, however, one's score does not seem all that related to one's job performance.

In the preceding paragraphs, we discussed how criterion-related validity (both predictive and concurrent) is used to demonstrate the construct validity of a measure by showing that it is related to or predicts measures of other, similar constructs. This situation describes **convergent validity**. However, in order to demonstrate that a particular measure is construct-valid, we must also demonstrate that the measure is

concurrent validity
The extent to which a test predicts a criterion that is measured at the same time that the test is conducted.

convergent validity
The degree to which a measure of the construct in which we are interested is related to measures of other, similar constructs.

not related to measures of dissimilar constructs—a matter of **divergent validity**. For instance, if we were developing a new measure of job satisfaction, we would need to demonstrate convergent validity by showing that our new measure is strongly related to other, existing measures of job satisfaction. Divergent validity would be demonstrated by showing that our new measure is not strongly related to measures of organizational commitment, job involvement, and satisfaction with the public school system. The point here is that we can be confident that our new measure is measuring the construct that we intended (i.e., job satisfaction) only if it relates to measures of other constructs in the way that it should, based on the definitions of these constructs.

Convergent and divergent validity can be demonstrated through both predictive and concurrent validation designs, which are discussed in more detail in Chapter 7. In the meantime, Figure 2.5 provides a helpful summary of the major types of reliability and the approaches used to demonstrate construct validity that we've discussed.

divergent validity The degree to which a measure of the construct in which we are interested is related to measures of other, dissimilar constructs.

FIGURE 2.5 Summary of Reliability Types and Approaches to Construct Validity

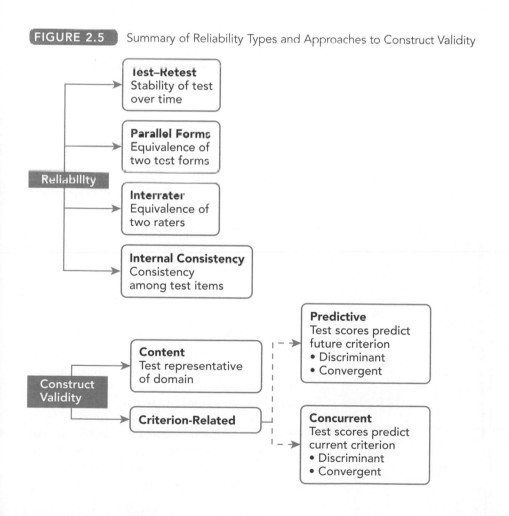

■ Ethics

I/O psychologists and other researchers are expected to maintain a sense of ethics while doing their work. We will discuss ethics throughout the book, as it is a very important aspect of both research and business. We will consider things like ethical reasoning, moral judgment, and ethical behavior. In this section, however, we will introduce the ethical code and focus on the ethics involved in conducting research.

There are various sets of ethical and professional rules and regulations governing the work of psychologists. The chief ethical code for psychologists is the *Ethical Principles of Psychologists and Code of Conduct* of the American Psychological Association (APA). It covers the work of psychologists in research, teaching, clinical practice, and organizational consulting, among other areas. The preamble gives a nice flavor of the code's purpose and goals:

> Psychologists are committed to increasing scientific and professional knowledge of behavior and people's understanding of themselves and others and to the use of such knowledge to improve the condition of individuals, organizations, and society. Psychologists respect and protect civil and human rights and the central importance of freedom of inquiry and expression in research, teaching, and publication. They strive to help the public in developing informed judgments and choices concerning human behavior. In doing so, they perform many roles, such as researcher, educator, diagnostician, therapist, supervisor, consultant, administrator, social interventionist, and expert witness. This Ethics Code provides a common set of principles and standards upon which psychologists build their professional and scientific work (American Psychological Association, 2002, p. 1062).

▼ **A Closer Look**
Why is this scientist's suggestion ethically wrong according to the five principles outlined on this page?

The code consists of five general principles that serve as goals for psychologists:

1. Helping others while doing no harm
2. Establishing relationships based on trust
3. Maintaining high integrity in teaching, research, and the practice of psychology
4. Being fair and just in all professional relationships and actions
5. Respecting the rights and dignity of all people

These general principles should guide the behavior of psychologists in all facets of their professional work.

With respect to research, the ethical code provides some additional stipulations. First, research studies must be approved by the supporting institution, such as a university or hospital. There is typically a mechanism for this approval that involves what is called an Institutional Review Board (IRB), charged with reviewing each

© Mike Baldwin / Cornered

MIKE BALDWIN/CORNERED. DISTRIBUTED BY UNIVERSAL PRESS SYNDICATE.

"Do a double-blind test. Give the new drug to rich patients and a placebo to the poor. No sense getting their hopes up. They couldn't afford it even if it works."

research project and considering ethical and safety regulations. Second, research participants are to be treated fairly and their decision to participate in research is to be an informed one. **Informed consent** requires providing participants with information about the purpose of the study, their right to decline participation, potential risks and benefits to participants, and where to direct questions about the research. Third, psychologists are required to maintain confidentiality of participants' data and sometimes to protect participants' anonymity. Fourth, researchers are ethically bound to avoid the use of deception in research whenever possible. If deception is necessary, researchers are required to debrief participants about the true nature of the deception. Finally, there are ethical requirements for the care and use of animals in research.

■ Statistics

After we collect our data, we need to present them in a way that allows us to draw conclusions about what the data mean with respect to our hypothesis and the research literature. This usually involves a summary of the data, often referred to as *descriptive statistics*. A **statistic** is an efficient device for summarizing in a single number the values, characteristics, or scores describing a series of cases. The first group of statistics we'll discuss are measures of central tendency.

Measures of Central Tendency

Measures of central tendency characterize a *typical* member of the group in that they represent the "best guess" as to the nature of any case chosen at random from the group. They present a way of characterizing the group with just a few relevant numbers. These measures can be very useful in comparing the various conditions or groups in one's study.

Mode The most frequent single score in a distribution is called the **mode**. The following data set reflects the job satisfaction levels of nine employees on a job satisfaction survey that ranges from a low of 1 to a high of 50. What is the mode in this data set?

$$1 \quad 1 \quad 1 \quad 10 \quad 12 \quad 26 \quad 33 \quad 45 \quad 50$$

Clearly, the mode is 1, as it is the most frequent score in the data set. But this example demonstrates why the mode is not usually the best measure of central tendency for describing psychological data: 1 is not the single number we would choose to describe the data set overall. (The mode tends to be useful only in situations involving categorical data, as when we say that the modal religion among Americans is Protestantism.)

Median The score in the middle of the distribution is termed the **median**. In other words, it is the score above which half the distribution falls and below which the other half of the distribution falls—it's the score that cuts the distribution in half.

informed consent
Participants signifying (usually in writing) their willingness and desire to participate in a particular research study after being provided with important and relevant information about the risks, procedures, and benefits of such participation.

statistic
An efficient device for summarizing in a single number the values, characteristics, or scores describing a series of cases.

mode
The most frequent single score in a distribution.

median
The score in the middle of the distribution.

In the data set above, the median is 12. In this example, the median is probably not the best measure of central tendency either, though it seems more descriptive than the mode. One interesting and important feature of the median is that it is not particularly sensitive to extreme scores, meaning that an extreme score in a distribution does not affect the median much, if at all.

mean
The arithmetic average of a group of scores, typically the most useful measure of central tendency.

Mean The most useful measure of central tendency is usually the **mean**, which is the arithmetic average of a group of scores. Almost all inferential statistics that we use are based on it. In our example above, the mean is 19.89—and you can see that this value gives a more accurate picture of the data set than does the mode or median. If you were to pick a single value to describe the data in this simple example, 19.89 would be the best one to choose, as it is more representative than either 1 or 12. One problem with means, however, is that they are sensitive to extreme scores; a single extreme score can have a drastic effect on them. Let's consider another data set. Rather than job satisfaction, let's say that it now reflects the number of days absent in a three-year period among the same nine employees:

$$1 \quad 1 \quad 1 \quad 10 \quad 12 \quad 26 \quad 33 \quad 45 \quad 400$$

Note that only one number has been changed—50 has become 400—but that value is by far the most extreme one, such that the mean is now 58.8 rather than 19.89. Clearly, this one value has a huge effect on the mean. What is the median in our new data set? The median doesn't change; it's still 12 because medians are not sensitive to extreme scores. This suggests that in situations involving extreme scores, a median has some advantages over the mean.

Measures of Dispersion

range
The simplest measure of dispersion, reflecting the spread of scores from the lowest to the highest.

Measures of dispersion inform us about how closely scores are grouped around the measure of central tendency, usually the mean. These are sometimes referred to as *measures of variability* because they provide information about how much the scores vary from one another. In a sense, we can say that measures of dispersion give us an idea of the "spread-outedness" of the data.

variance
A useful measure of dispersion reflecting the sum of the squared differences between each score and the mean of the group divided by the number of total scores.

The simplest measure of dispersion is called the **range**, which is the spread of scores from the lowest to the highest. In our original data set, the range is 49, which is the difference between the largest observed score (50) and the smallest observed score (1). This measure appears in published reports of research, but it is not reported as often as the **variance**, which is recognized as the most useful measure of dispersion. To calculate the variance, the researcher subtracts each score from the mean, resulting in differences that are then squared. The next step is to add these squared differences and divide the sum by the total number of scores, which is usually denoted as N. In our first data set, the variance is 372.11.

standard deviation
A measure of dispersion that is calculated as the square root of the variance.

The third measure of dispersion is called the **standard deviation**, which is the square root of the variance. Returning again to the first data set, we find that its standard deviation is 19.29. We often use this measure because it retains the original metric of the scores. In other words, 19.29 reflects the extent to which employees'

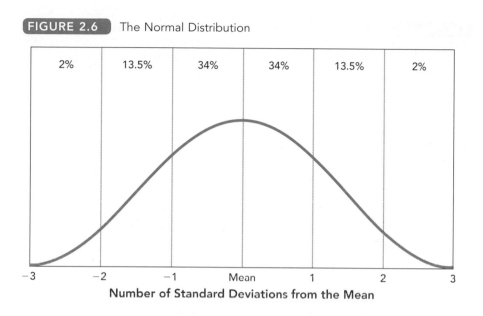

FIGURE 2.6 The Normal Distribution

job satisfaction levels are spread out on a satisfaction scale that ranges from 1 unit to 50 units of job satisfaction. The variance (372.11), on the other hand, is much more difficult to conceptualize because it is in squared units. The standard deviation is very important for our next topic—distributions of data.

Shapes of Distributions

The **normal distribution** is a theoretical mathematical model based on a population of measures that is infinite in size. This distribution is depicted by what appears to be a *bell-shaped curve,* in which most of the observations are clustered around the mean with increasingly fewer observations as we move out along the continuum in either direction. The normal distribution is important in psychology because many psychological variables are distributed in this way. For instance, intelligence, motivation, performance, personal characteristics, and job attitudes are all believed to be normally distributed in the population. Therefore, the properties of the normal distribution take on added significance.

This bell-shaped curve is presented in Figure 2.6, which indicates standard deviation units along the bottom and the percentage of observations that fall within those standard deviation units at the top. In other words, in a normal distribution, 68% (34% + 34%) of the observations in our data fall within 1 standard deviation below the mean and 1 standard deviation above the mean, and about 99% of the observations fall within 3 standard deviations of the mean in either direction. The mean and median have the same value in the normal distribution, indicating that half the observations fall above the mean and half fall below the mean.

normal distribution
A mathematically based distribution depicted as a bell-shaped curve, in which most of the observations cluster around the mean and there are few extreme observations.

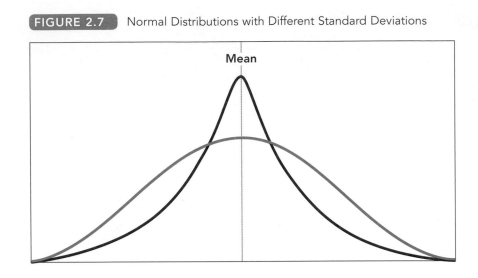

FIGURE 2.7 Normal Distributions with Different Standard Deviations

Figure 2.7 shows two normal curves with different standard deviations. The taller curve has a smaller standard deviation than the shorter curve, but both are normal distributions and the same properties of the normal distribution hold for both.

From the properties of the normal curve and an individual's score, we can determine the individual's *percentile* score relative to the rest of the population. You have all taken some type of achievement test for which a percentile score is given, indicating the percentage of other students in the population who did not score as well as you did. This percentile score is based on the mean, the standard deviation, and the normal distribution. We could apply the same process to the performance of employees at a Fortune 500 company to determine how well, in relation to all employees, a particular employee is performing.

Correlation and Regression

As you undoubtedly are aware by now, I/O psychologists are often interested in the relationship between two (or more) variables. To examine this relationship, we typically use the **correlation coefficient (r)**, which measures the strength of the relationship between two variables. A correlation provides information about the *direction* of the relationship, or its sign, and the *magnitude* of the relationship, or its strength. A correlation can indicate a positive or negative relationship between two variables. A positive relationship is indicated when high scores on one variable reflect high scores on the other variable and when low scores on one variable reflect low scores on the other variable.

For a real-world example of a positive correlation, think of two people on an elevator: As one goes up or down, so does the other. This is a perfect positive correlation. In most of the examples that we've talked about in this chapter, we have hypothesized a positive correlation, as in the relationships between participation and

correlation coefficient (r)
A statistic that measures the strength and direction of the relationship between two variables.

job satisfaction, leadership style and job performance, mechanical comprehension and job performance, SAT scores and school performance, and cognitive ability and job performance. In every case, we predicted that high scores on one variable would be related to high scores on the other variable.

A negative relationship is indicated when high scores on one variable are reflected in low scores on the other variable, and vice versa. Think of two children on a teeter-totter. As one goes up, the other goes down. If one is all the way up, the other must be all the way down. This is a perfect negative correlation. Examples of negative correlations may be a little more difficult to generate at first, but the more you think about the concept, the easier it is to call instances to mind. Here, for instance, are a few negative correlations that we might predict: job satisfaction and the amount of time absent from work, supervisor–subordinate relationships and subordinate resignations, employee sanctions and promotions, and job performance and the number of grievances filed against the employee. In all these instances, we expect high scores on one variable to be related to low scores on the other. We expect satisfied employees to seldom be absent, employees who get along well with their supervisors to be unlikely to resign, employees who are sanctioned by their company to be passed over for promotions, and good performers to have few grievances filed against them.

▼ **A Closer Look**
How does an elevator represent a positive correlation and how does a teeter-totter represent a negative correlation?

BOTH: SYLVIA CHINN-LEVY

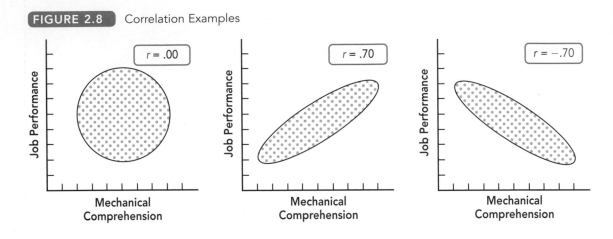

FIGURE 2.8   Correlation Examples

The magnitude or strength of a correlation ranges from 0 to 1, with larger numbers indicating a stronger relationship. It's important to realize that although a correlation can range from −1.0 to +1.0, correlations of −.50 and +.50 have the same magnitude—the only difference being the sign. A scatterplot in which all the data points fall along a straight 45-degree line represents a perfect 1.0 correlation, which is so rare as to be nonexistent in psychology. In the behavioral sciences, correlations among variables are almost never larger than .70. Consider the three scatterplots shown in Figure 2.8. The first, in the shape of a circle, reflects a correlation of 0. This indicates that a high score on the mechanical comprehension test is just as likely to lead to low job performance as to lead to adequate job performance as to lead to superior job performance; in short, there is no relationship between the two variables. The other two scatterplots indicate rather strong relationships—one in the positive direction and the other in the negative direction.

Correlations are relevant for much of I/O psychology because they are intimately involved in prediction. One step beyond computing a correlation among variables is the statistical procedure called *regression,* which allows us to predict one variable from another. Here we calculate how much variance in our criterion variable is accounted for by our predictor variable—a calculation that is based on the correlation between these variables. The percentage of variance accounted for is called the **coefficient of determination**, and it can be computed from the regression as well as from the correlation. In fact, this percentage is actually the correlation squared, commonly expressed as r^2. Returning one last time to our example involving mechanical comprehension as a predictor for job performance, let's measure our employees using a mechanical comprehension test and also measure their on-the-job performance using their supervisors' ratings of their performance. Now imagine that we find a .60 correlation between these two variables, indicating that mechanical comprehension accounts for about 36% (i.e., $.60^2$) of the variance in job performance.

This statistic sounds confusing, and we will spend a little more time on it in Chapter 6; but, basically, it means that some (i.e., 36%) of the differences among

coefficient of determination The percentage of variance in a criterion that is accounted for by a predictor.

FIGURE 2.9 Coefficient of Determination

Mechanical comprehension

Job performance

$r = .60$
$r^2 = .36$

r^2

employees on the performance variable could be predicted by the mechanical comprehension test (not everyone is going to perform at the same level). In other words, knowing an individual's score on the mechanical comprehension test is helpful in predicting that individual's level of job performance. Figure 2.9 describes the relationship between these two variables, using a Venn diagram. As you can see, there is some overlap between mechanical comprehension and job performance. This overlap represents the coefficient of determination. I/O psychology uses correlations and regressions extensively, and we will revisit these throughout the rest of the book.

Meta-Analysis

A recently developed statistical and methodological technique that is widely used in the social sciences has also gained a very strong following in the I/O area. I'm referring here to **meta-analysis**, a methodology that is used to conduct quantitative literature reviews (Hunter & Schmidt, 1990; Rosenthal, 1991). Prior to the development of this approach in the late 1970s, a researcher conducting a literature review on the relationship between, say, job satisfaction and job performance would conduct a *narrative review* consisting of summaries of all the different findings in the literature; however, there was no mechanism for combining these different findings and providing a best estimate of the true relationship between job satisfaction and job performance. With the development of meta-analysis came a way to combine these many findings and thereby *quantify* the relationship between the two variables.

Researchers can use meta-analysis to combine the results from 25, 100, even 1,000 or more studies to arrive at the best estimate of the true relationship. The point here is that statistically combining findings from previous studies is a more accurate way to estimate the true relationship than is focusing on one or two studies that measure this relationship. In the remainder of the book, I present many meta-analytic results as a way of summarizing various findings in the field of industrial/organizational psychology.

meta-analysis
A methodology that is used to conduct quantitative literature reviews.

■ Summary

Research methods are important to I/O psychology—and all scientific endeavors, for that matter—because research conducted without care is unreliable and worthless. But when we are careful to base our theories on data and to use these data to test and revise the theories, the science of I/O psychology can make a meaningful contribution to the world of work. This science is more than just a matter of commonsense predictions and beliefs. Among its goals are to describe, explain, predict, and control human behavior at work. It is also important to realize that theories are the domain not just of basic science but also of applied scientific disciplines such as I/O psychology. In fact, it is only through careful theoretical development, testing, and revision that we can use our knowledge to describe, explain, predict, and control organizational behaviors and environments.

A major goal of most research in I/O psychology is to be able to draw causal inferences about the relationship between two or more variables. Thus, we must design our studies with an emphasis on internal validity, attempting to control for extraneous variables that could provide alternative explanations for our results. In addition to internal validity, we must concern ourselves with external validity, or the generalizability of our findings.

There are many ways in which I/O psychologists go about collecting data, but the survey is perhaps the one most frequently used. Surveys are very useful in gathering information about attitudes and beliefs. Technological advancements such as the Internet have provided new alternative approaches to survey administration. We may also use observational approaches to measure and record frequency or incidents of particular behaviors or interactions. Archival research is a popular approach as well, given our access to the numerous large-scale data sets that have been collected by the government and private organizations. I/O psychologists often combine these and other data collection techniques in any given study to better examine their research questions.

Without reliable and valid measurement, the research conducted by I/O psychologists would have very little to offer. Researchers must work very hard to eliminate sources of measurement error and to ensure that their measures are tapping the constructs that they were intended to tap. There are a few different approaches to estimating reliability, and each is important for demonstrating the soundness of any particular measure. Validity is important as well, but to talk of validity in general is not very helpful, as the term can mean several different things. In I/O, when we speak of the validity of a test or predictor, we are usually referring to the extent to which the test predicts job performance or some other criterion.

After we have collected our data, the next step is to describe and summarize those data using descriptive statistics such as measures of central tendency and dispersion. Because I/O psychologists are usually interested in the relationships among variables and the prediction of one set of variables from another set, correlation and regression are statistical techniques that are very useful to us. Ultimately, we complete our five-step research process with a written report that summarizes the research project.

In the remainder of this text, we will discuss various content areas of I/O psychology and the research that is conducted in those areas, along with their implications for organizational functioning.

■ Key Terms

archival research (p. 40)

attribute (p. 43)

case studies (p. 39)

causal inference (p. 29)

coefficient of determination (p. 56)

concurrent validity (p. 48)

construct (p. 47)

construct validity (p. 47)

content validity (p. 47)

convergent validity (p. 48)

correlation coefficient (*r*) (p. 54)

deduction (p. 28)

dependent variable (p. 30)

divergent validity (p. 49)

experience sampling methodology (ESM) (p. 43)

experimental methods (p. 35)

external validity (p. 32)

extraneous variable (p. 30)

hypothesis (p. 34)

independent variable (p. 29)

induction (p. 28)

informed consent (p. 51)

internal consistency (p. 46)

internal validity (p. 31)

interrater reliability (p. 46)

manipulation (p. 35)

mean (p. 52)

measurement (p. 43)

median (p. 51)

meta-analysis (p. 57)

mode (p. 51)

normal distribution (p. 53)

parallel forms reliability (p. 46)

predictive validity (p. 47)

quasi-experiment (p. 37)

random assignment (p. 35)

range (p. 52)

reliability (p. 44)

science (p. 23)

standard deviation (p. 52)

statistic (p. 51)

surveys (p. 40)

test–retest reliability (p. 45)

theory (p. 25)

unobtrusive naturalistic observation (p. 39)

variance (p. 52)

■ TAKING IT TO THE FIELD

Because I/O psychology tends to rely strongly on empirical data, I/O psychologists must be experts in research design and statistics. One area that I/O psychologists are particularly concerned about is the reliability and validity of measures. In fact, I/O psychologists in consulting firms are often asked for their expertise in understanding how measures work and what measures are best for a certain purpose. Below is an e-mail from Kendall Phillips, the HR manager of the law firm MacLaughlin & MacDougal. She has designed a new selection measure for her firm and needs some feedback from someone who knows more about reliability and validity. Read her e-mail, and provide detailed responses to her questions.

Hello—

    Thank you for agreeing to help me with this measure—I know it's not something you normally do, but with all of the financial challenges facing my company, this is going to be very helpful for us!

    First, let me give you some background: Our firm currently needs to hire a number of administrative assistants. The demands our lawyers place on our administrative assistants are very high; they often yell at them or ask them to do very difficult things in a short amount of time. We have found that one of the best predictors of these assistants staying more than a couple of months is for them to have very low levels of neuroticism. We used to buy a test (called the WIN) that would measure this, but it has gotten too expensive, and so I've started to develop my own measure (I call my test the Neuroticism Assessment Form, or the NAF). To design my measure, I spoke to a few experts in the personality field, looked at some of the items on other tests of neuroticism, and wrote questions that made sense. I asked a number of current administrative assistants to fill out the neuroticism test we formerly purchased as well as the one I am developing. I also have job performance ratings for these administrative assistants. Here's what I've found so far:

- The correlation between their scores on the NAF in July and their scores on the NAF in August is .89.
- The correlation between their scores on the WIN and the NAF is .75.
- The correlation between their scores on the NAF and a test of extraversion is .34.
- The correlation between their scores on the NAF and their performance ratings is .30.

So here are my questions for you:

1. Is my test a reliable measure of neuroticism? If not, what else do I need?
2. Is my test a valid measure of neuroticism? What additional information should I collect, if any?

Thanks again!
KP

Draft a response that clearly answers Kendall's questions. You should indicate what types of reliability/validity she has collected (and whether you think they are adequate) and what types of reliability/validity she has overlooked (and how she can obtain them). Make sure to address <u>all</u> forms of reliability/validity you have learned about.

■ Critical Thinking Questions

1. Describe how you would go about designing and implementing an I/O research project.

2. Compare and contrast the various types of validity.

3. What are some potential instances of *unethical* behavior in I/O psychology? What makes these instances unethical?

■ Application Questions

1. Imagine that a fellow student says to you, "I don't need a study to tell me that lecturing is a bad way to teach students. I know from my own experience that it never works!" How would you convince this student of the value of

research? What might be an example of a study you could conduct to see if this student's belief is accurate?

2. Think about a behavior you have observed among fellow students. What do you think causes that behavior, and what might be a theory you can develop to explain why that behavior occurs?

3. A researcher has been asked to find a way to help construction workers put on their helmets. Describe a survey study she could conduct. What information would she get from that study? Describe an experimental study she could conduct. What information would she get from that study?

4. Reliability and validity are two separate characteristics of a measurement, but they are related. The chapter notes that you must have reliability (consistency) before you can have validity (accuracy). Provide an example of a measure that is consistent but inaccurate.

5. Correlation coefficients can help us understand how two variables are related. What are two variables that might have a strong positive correlation? A strong negative correlation? A correlation of 0?

■ Suggested Readings

American Psychological Association. (2002). *Ethical principals of psychologists and code of conduct.* Washington, DC: Author. This publication provides the ethical rules and guidelines governing the behavior of psychologists.

Babbie, E. (2010). *The practice of social research* (12th ed.). Belmont, CA: Wadsworth. An excellent presentation of research methods that is helpful for both undergraduates and graduate students.

Dillman, D. A. (2007). *Mail and Internet surveys: The tailored design method* (2nd ed.). Hoboken, NJ: John Wiley & Sons. The best treatment of survey methodology available. This book provides lots of hints for improving the quality of survey data.

Lefkowitz, J. (2003). *Ethics and values in industrial-organizational psychology.* London: Psychology Press. A great overview of various ethical issues relevant to I/O psychology; includes research ethics but also covers much broader issues such as the morals and ethics of organizational behavior.

Leong, F. T. L., & Austin, J. T. (Eds.). (2005). *The psychology research handbook: A guide for graduate students and research assistants* (2nd ed.). Thousand Oaks, CA: SAGE. A complete treatment of the research process targeted at new psychology researchers. The best book of its kind, it was written to be useful for both advanced undergraduate and graduate students.

Rogelberg, S. G., Church, A. H., Waclawski, J., & Stanton, J. M. (2005). Organizational survey research. In S. G. Rogelberg (Ed.), *Handbook of research methods in industrial and organizational psychology* (pp. 141–160). Hoboken, NJ: John Wiley & Sons. A nice compilation of chapters focusing on research methodology linked specifically to I/O psychology. This is a useful reference.

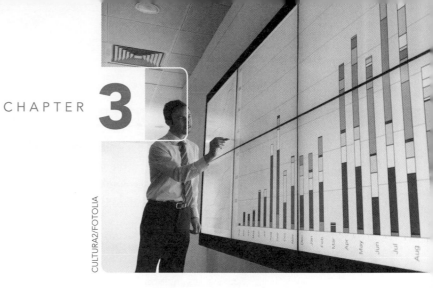

CULTURA2/FOTOLIA

CHAPTER 3

Job Analysis

This chapter should help you understand:

- How important job analysis is to HR functioning
- The common terminology used in the area of job analysis
- How to differentiate between job-oriented and worker-oriented job analysis techniques
- How to conduct a job analysis using the Task Inventory Approach, Functional Job Analysis, Job Element Method, Position Analysis Questionnaire, and Common-Metric Questionnaire
- What's included in the *Dictionary of Occupational Titles* and how it has been improved through the development of the Occupational Information Network (O*NET)
- What a job description is and how it is used in human resource practices
- What job specifications are and how they are used in human resource practices
- The variety of human resource functions for which job analysis is of great importance
- The newly developing role of technology in the analysis of jobs
- The role of job evaluation in setting compensation levels
- The doctrine of comparable worth and the wage gap

The second part of this book centers on *industrial psychology,* or what has been traditionally called *personnel psychology.* Before discussing the major applications of industrial psychology, you must first have an understanding of the foundation for virtually all of this work—job analysis, the focus of this chapter. Think about your own experiences with appraising others' performance. Imagine trying to evaluate their performance without knowing what their jobs or what the outcomes of their work are intended to be. Now picture someone appraising your own performance without knowing the details of the job for which you were hired. Unfortunately, job analysis is often taken for granted by I/O researchers and practitioners, but in this chapter I argue that it is the most important building block for industrial psychology. In order to develop predictors to select and place employees in appropriate jobs, to identify criteria used to evaluate employees' effectiveness, and to identify remedial training needs of particular employees, we must first understand the job. We gain this thorough and comprehensive understanding of jobs through job analysis.

Doing performance appraisals without such knowledge would be like cooking a dish without knowing the ingredients, how to prepare them, or how the dish is supposed to taste. The job analysis provides the recipe—information that is integral to everything else that follows in industrial psychology. Figure 3.1 illustrates how job analysis relates to the major *human resource (HR)* functions that will be covered in this section of the text.

FIGURE 3.1   Framework for Industrial Psychology

■ Some Terminology

Before discussing approaches to job analysis, we must familiarize ourselves with some terms that have very specific meanings within this domain. First in the list are elements. An **element** is the smallest unit of work activity, such as pressing a button to start a machine or turning a key to start an engine. Multiple elements join together to form a **task**, commonly defined as the activity of work that is performed to achieve a specific objective. For instance, among the necessary elements involved in a cab driver taking his passenger to her destination are turning the key, shifting the transmission into "drive," and pressing the accelerator. Collectively, these elements form a task that is the operation of the vehicle. The tasks performed by an individual in an organization define that person's **position**. A **job** is a collection of positions similar enough to one another to share a common job title. **KSAOs** are the knowledge, skills, abilities, and other characteristics that are required for successful job performance (Primoff & Fyde, 1988). They are very important in I/O psychology because they are the basis for much of the work done in employee selection (see Chapters 6 and 7). In short, organizations prefer to hire those employees who possess KSAOs that are likely to make them successful performers. Indeed, this is largely what selection and placement in organizations are all about.

To recap here: The most basic level of work activity is made up of the elements of work, which combine to form tasks, which in turn constitute one's position in the organization; similarly defined positions are what we term a job. Of course, we should be careful to avoid confusing the job and the position with the individuals who occupy them (Harvey, 1991). In other words, job analysis should be focused not on the person who holds the job or occupies the position but, rather, on the job or position itself.

Job analysis is the process of defining a job in terms of its component tasks or duties and the knowledge or skills required to perform them. Job analysis is the basis for the solution to any human resource problem (Brannick, Levine, & Morgeson, 2007).

element
In job analysis, the smallest unit of work activity.

task
A work activity that is performed to achieve a specific objective.

position
An individual's place in the organization defined by the tasks performed.

job
A collection of positions similar enough to one another to share a common job title.

KSAOs
The knowledge, skills, abilities, and other characteristics that are required for successful job performance.

job analysis
The process of defining a job in terms of its component tasks or duties and the knowledge or skills required to perform them.

■ Approaches to Job Analysis

Most procedures in I/O psychology can be conducted in various ways. Job analysis is no exception. Whatever the approach, however, the job analyst needs to consider the purpose of the job analysis when deciding on a strategy. One approach may be more beneficial for a given purpose than a different approach. In this section and the one to follow, we will examine a couple of general perspectives taken in the area of job analysis as well as some specific ways in which job analysis data can be collected.

job-oriented
Referring to approaches to job analysis that focus on describing the various tasks that are performed on the job.

The traditional classification espoused by most job analysis experts over the years categorizes job analysis methods as either job-oriented or worker-oriented (McCormick, 1976). **Job-oriented** techniques focus on describing the various tasks that are performed on the job. These techniques tend to be job-specific because they are based on the particular tasks performed during a particular job. **Worker-oriented** techniques examine broad human behaviors involved in work activities (Gatewood & Feild, 2001). Unlike job-oriented approaches, which focus on very specific levels of tasks, worker-oriented job analyses focus broadly on general aspects of the job, such as the physical, interpersonal, and mental factors necessary for completion of the job and the related worker attributes. In fact, a review and analysis in this area also suggests a third category—hybrid methods. These approaches attempt to gather information about the work and the worker at the same time (Brannick et al., 2007). The distinction between the two traditional categories is not always clear; some job-analytic techniques cross over into the other category (Sackett & Laczo, 2003). Furthermore, one approach is not necessarily better than the other; as a job analyst, you can choose a hybrid approach or any combination of pieces from different job-analytic techniques (Brannick et al., 2007) for whatever purpose is being served by your job analysis.

worker-oriented
Referring to approaches to job analysis that examine broad human behaviors involved in work activities.

■ Job-Analytic Methods

For simplicity's sake, this chapter largely employs the traditional job-oriented and worker-oriented distinction, but it also presents the important results of a hybrid approach employed in the development of the Occupational Information Network (O*NET).

Task Inventory Approach
A job-oriented approach to job analysis in which task statements are generated by experts who are familiar with the job in question.

Job-Oriented Techniques

Job-oriented techniques for conducting job analyses tend to be focused on tasks. (Recall our previous definition of a task as the activity of work that is performed to achieve a specific objective.) One job-oriented approach is called the **Task Inventory Approach**, in which task statements are generated by experts who are familiar with the jobs—**subject matter experts (SMEs)**. These experts may be **incumbents**—that is, people who are currently occupying the job of interest. Or they may be individuals who have expertise or knowledge about the job for some other reason, such as being a supervisor of individuals in that job or an I/O psychologist who has gathered expertise through his or her work. Once a list of task statements

subject matter experts (SMEs)
Individuals who participate in job analyses as a result of their job-related expertise.

incumbents
In job analysis, employees who are currently occupying the job of interest.

FIGURE 3.2 Task Inventory for College Professor

Task Statements	Is task done on this job? Yes or No	Importance of task to job					Relative to other tasks performed on the job, how much time is spent on each of the following tasks?				
		1 Not important at all	2	3 Somewhat important	4	5 Extremely important	1 Much less time	2 Somewhat less time	3 About the same amount of time	4 Somewhat more time	5 Much more time
1. Develops written assignments											
2. Grades exams											
3. Meets with students individually to help them understand things											
4. Lectures to groups of students											
5. Designs research studies											
6. Collects data											
7. Mentors and advises students regarding career issues											

has been generated, this list, which can include hundreds of task statements, is usually administered to incumbents, who put a check next to those statements that describe a task that they do on their job. A sample task inventory for the job of college professor is provided in Figure 3.2. The task statements that are checked as being done on the job are also often rated as to the importance or criticality of the task to the job and the relative time spent on the job doing each task. Together, these pieces of information can provide a thorough analysis, or *picture,* of the job.

In **Functional Job Analysis (FJA)**, a highly structured job-oriented approach developed by Sidney Fine many years ago, data are obtained about *what* tasks a worker does and *how* those tasks are performed. (For a summary of this technique, see Fine, 1988.) Specifically, a series of task statements are developed that are believed to be relevant for the job in question. Incumbents or SMEs rate each of these statements (which are similar to those shown in Figure 3.2) on a series of dimensions. These dimensions are what set this approach apart from the standard Task Inventory Approach.

Functional Job Analysis (FJA) A highly structured job-oriented approach developed by Sidney Fine in which data are obtained about what tasks a worker does and how those tasks are performed.

CORBIS

JOHN HOWARD/GETTY IMAGES

▲ **A Closer Look**
From a Functional Job Analysis perspective, how would a computer technician score on data, people, and things? What would the scores look like for sales jobs?

A picture of the job is generated when these task statements have been rated with regard to *data, people,* and *things*—three factors with which employees in all jobs are assumed to interact. One way to understand a job is to know the extent to which these interactions take place and the complexity of those interactions. This is the focus of FJA. A task focusing largely on *data* requires the employee to use cognitive resources in handling information, ideas, and facts. Tasks that are coded along this dimension range from simple comparisons to more complex synthesizing. The *people* dimension refers to the extent to which the job requires employees to use interpersonal resources such as understanding, courtesy, and mentoring. Tasks coded along this dimension range from simply taking instructions to more sophisticated behaviors such as mentoring. Finally, a task that is linked to the *things* scale requires the use of physical resources and includes the use of strength, speed, and coordination. Tasks coded along this dimension range from the simple handling of things to more intricate and precise operations.

Dictionary of Occupational Titles (DOT)
A tool developed by the Department of Labor in the 1930s that has been used to classify occupations and jobs, consisting of narrative descriptions of tasks, duties, and working conditions of about 12,000 jobs.

In the 1930s, the Department of Labor used FJA to develop the **Dictionary of Occupational Titles (DOT)**, a tool that matches people with jobs. Consisting of narrative descriptions of tasks, duties, and working conditions of about 12,000 jobs, the DOT codes each of these jobs according to the data, people, and things dimensions developed by Fine. The information presented in the DOT is based on years and years of data collected through job analyses. The DOT presents a hierarchical organization of jobs, with nine major occupational clusters at the uppermost level of the hierarchy. Figure 3.3 shows the DOT entry for a faculty member, including labels for the particular parts of the entry. The nine-digit *occupational code* is important in that it uniquely identifies this particular job. The first three digits classify the job with respect to its occupational category. The next three digits identify where the job is classified with respect to data, people, and things; in this example, the digits 227 indicate that the job is high on both data (*analyze*) and people (*instruct*) but low on things (*handle*). This probably fits your preconceived notion of what faculty members do, which is to spend a great deal of time working with data and people but less time manipulating tools, equipment, and so on. The *industry designation* in this case is "education."

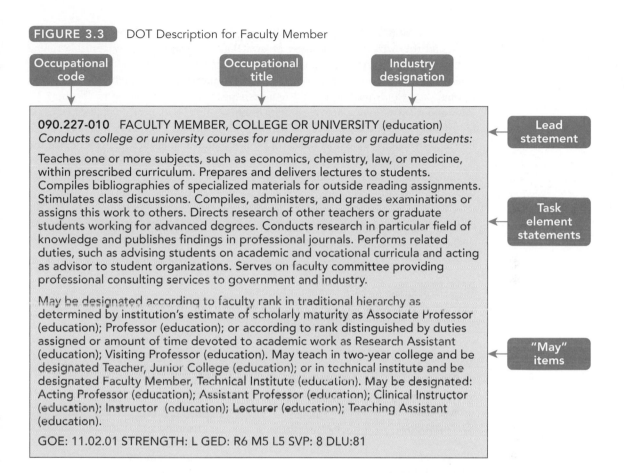

FIGURE 3.3 DOT Description for Faculty Member

Occupational code

Occupational title

Industry designation

090.227-010 FACULTY MEMBER, COLLEGE OR UNIVERSITY (education)
Conducts college or university courses for undergraduate or graduate students:

Teaches one or more subjects, such as economics, chemistry, law, or medicine, within prescribed curriculum. Prepares and delivers lectures to students. Compiles bibliographies of specialized materials for outside reading assignments. Stimulates class discussions. Compiles, administers, and grades examinations or assigns this work to others. Directs research of other teachers or graduate students working for advanced degrees. Conducts research in particular field of knowledge and publishes findings in professional journals. Performs related duties, such as advising students on academic and vocational curricula and acting as advisor to student organizations. Serves on faculty committee providing professional consulting services to government and industry.

May be designated according to faculty rank in traditional hierarchy as determined by institution's estimate of scholarly maturity as Associate Professor (education); Professor (education); or according to rank distinguished by duties assigned or amount of time devoted to academic work as Research Assistant (education); Visiting Professor (education). May teach in two-year college and be designated Teacher, Junior College (education); or in technical institute and be designated Faculty Member, Technical Institute (education). May be designated: Acting Professor (education); Assistant Professor (education); Clinical Instructor (education); Instructor (education); Lecturer (education); Teaching Assistant (education).

GOE: 11.02.01 STRENGTH: L GED: R6 M5 L5 SVP: 8 DLU:81

Lead statement

Task element statements

"May" items

The *lead statement* is always the first sentence of the description itself, followed by a colon. This statement provides the best simple description of the job. The *task element statements,* which come next, describe with more precision what is done on the job to meet the objectives presented in the lead statement. In other words, college professors teach subjects, prepare lectures, stimulate class discussion, and so on, in order to conduct college courses. Finally, the *"may" items* indicate activities that may be done in some organizations by individuals who occupy this job but are not routinely part of this job in most organizations.

The Department of Labor (DOL) has undertaken a new initiative to replace the DOT, which it views as incompatible with the current workplace. This new initiative, known as the Occupational Information Network (O*NET), aspires to identify and describe the key components of modern occupations (Occupational Information Network, 2009). In contrast to the DOT, the O*NET is not based on FJA; rather, it is based on data gathered in various ways, including an initial review of existing literature in the domains of human performance and occupational analysis. Thus, it is categorized as a hybrid approach because it focuses simultaneously on both the work and the worker. This database of over 950 occupations is now available online (http://onetcenter.org), making it much more accessible than the older DOT. In addition to having data on thousands of jobs, it allows individuals to search for occupations through key words relating to skill requirements, and it is connected to *America's Job Bank* and *school-to-work* initiatives in which schools train students to be better prepared for the workplace and to successfully find employment. The greater ease of access (through the Internet) and its focus on both job and worker characteristics make the O*NET a very useful and attractive tool for organizations and I/O psychologists.

Indeed, the O*NET has widespread implications for the world of work and the practice of I/O psychology. The O*NET database of occupational information is based on the O*NET Content Model, which identifies the structure of information stored in the database. The structure, which is presented in Figure 3.4, involves six classes of information: (1) worker characteristics, such as abilities and interests; (2) worker requirements, such as general knowledge and skills; (3) experience requirements, such as past employment

FIGURE 3.4   O*NET Content Model

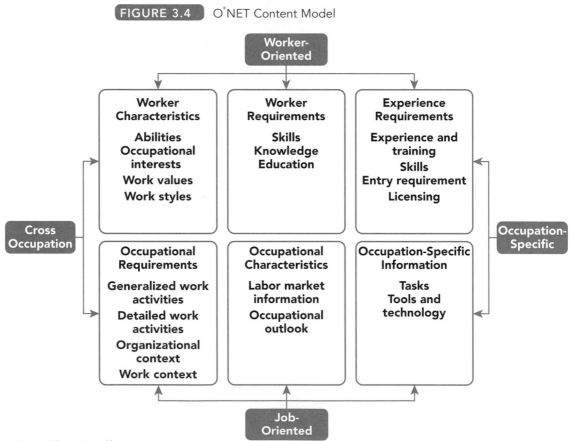

Adapted from http//onetcenter.org.

history, training, or licensure; (4) occupational requirements, such as generalized work activities; (5) occupation-specific information, such as technical information particular to a certain job family; and (6) occupational characteristics, such as labor market and social information. The database is quite useful for career management; for organizational functions like selection, training, and development; and for researchers trying to better understand organizational performance. Counselors, students, human resource professionals, and researchers are among those who benefit from this DOL initiative.

Research on the O*NET has started to emerge over the past 10 years. For instance, one study reports that the O*NET General Work Activities are related to particular employee knowledge, skills, and abilities required for effective work performance (Jeanneret & Strong, 2003) and the work of researchers at the University of Nebraska, Omaha, who have developed and tested a web-based job-analytic technique using the O*NET (Reiter-Palmon, Brown, Sandall, Buboltz, & Nimps, 2006). More recent work has been focused on matching Occupational Interest Profiles (OIPs) from the O*NET with interest-based assessments often used in career counseling (Rounds, Armstrong, Liao, Lewis, & Rivkin, 2008).

Job-oriented approaches to job analysis have been criticized as being potentially too narrowly focused on the tasks for a particular job (Harvey, 1991). Critics say it follows that by focusing microscopically on the tasks of a particular job, we rule out the possibility of making a real comparison across jobs because no job is likely to emerge as similar at such a fine-grained level. In other words, we may miss similarities in jobs because of the high level of technological and behavioral specificity of the tasks and thereby fail to detect more abstract similarities across jobs. Worker-oriented approaches to job analysis address this very problem.

Worker-Oriented Techniques

These job-analytic techniques focus less on the specific tasks done on a job and more on the human characteristics that contribute to successful job performance (Sackett & Laczo, 2003). E. J. McCormick (McCormick, Jeanneret, & Mecham, 1972) provided a very clear distinction between the two types: "The job-oriented concept typically would be reflected by the use of specific task statements. . . . In turn, the worker-oriented concept typically would be reflected by the use of descriptions of reasonably definitive human behaviors of many kinds" (p. 348). Worker-oriented methods of job analysis are more effective than task-focused job-oriented methods if the analyst is interested in comparing across jobs because jobs can then be compared with respect to their reliance on the various talents and abilities of the incumbents.

The **Job Element Method (JEM)** was designed to identify the characteristics of superior workers in a particular job (Primoff & Eyde, 1988). Note that, in this context, the word *element* refers to general work behaviors, not to the smallest unit of work activity as defined earlier. More specifically, job elements in the JEM refer to the KSAOs we talked about earlier. The JEM's aim is to directly connect job analysis to the selection context by identifying the KSAOs that are necessary for successful job performance. The procedure is rather simple. First, SMEs are asked to develop a

Job Element Method (JEM)
A worker-oriented approach to job analysis that was designed to identify the characteristics of superior workers in a particular job.

COURTESY OF JOHN BINNING

John F. Binning
PhD, 1985, I/O Psychology, The University of Akron
Chief Research Officer
The DeGarmo Group, Inc.

The DeGarmo Group specializes in designing and administering preemployment selection tests. One of our assessment tools is the *DeGarmo Personality Inventory* (DPI). The DPI is delivered over the Internet, and job applicant responses are scored and available to client human resource (HR) representatives. What happens between the time an applicant presses the "Finish" button and the HR representative reviews the results is where the real psychological action is!

You will read in later chapters about the Big Five personality factors and how different jobs require different profiles of personality traits. A challenge for HR and talent acquisition professionals is how to determine which personality traits are critical for a particular job. We decided to leverage the vast information available in O*NET to guide the process of determining personality requirements for different jobs.

Our approach unfolds something like this: When an organization wants to hire for a particular job, we find that job in O*NET, and among other information, there are importance ratings for a variety of *work styles*. The work style ratings were determined by having job-knowledgeable people complete job analysis questionnaires about how important the different styles are for different jobs.

The work styles can be interpreted in terms of the Big Five personality factors. For example, one of the O*NET work styles is *Attention to Detail*, and this is relevant to the Big Five factor of conscientiousness. We believe that each work style can be meaningfully

mapped onto Big Five factors, and we have automated this process. For any of the thousands of jobs described in O*NET, we can automatically translate the work style ratings into importance scores on the Big Five factors (or facet subfactors) measured by the DPI. Once we know which DPI scores are important for a job, we have our IT staff write the computational code to score job applicants' responses to determine how well their personalities "fit" the demands of that particular job.

To summarize, when a job applicant presses the "Finish" button, his or her responses are mathematically "crunched" into various personality scores and then given different mathematical weights based on the O*NET information, and a final score and interpretive report are generated indicating how well the applicant's personality matches the specific demands of the job. Client HR representatives then use this information to aid in making hiring decisions. This way we apply the science of job analysis and personality to the needs of various organizations.

Applying Your Knowledge

1. How might the O*NET system be more helpful in job analysis to the DeGarmo Group than the DOT?

2. Given the changing nature of work, why is job analysis so important? How is the DeGarmo Group demonstrating this fact?

3. The DeGarmo Group specializes in trying to match the best applicants to its clients' needs. But what other job-analytic steps are critical for each client organization to take in order to maximize productivity in the hiring process?

comprehensive list of job elements, as well as subelements or employee characteristics that are more specific than the job elements. For instance, one element for a college professor might be "ability to communicate clearly," and subelements within this element might include "can express ideas in an interesting manner to large groups of people" and "able to explain complex issues to students in a one-on-one environment." Once the final list of elements and subelements has been generated, the SMEs are instructed to provide work examples of each. Together, the elements, subelements, and work examples provide a complete picture of the job.

A common criticism of this approach is that the JEM ignores the specific job tasks, making it difficult to demonstrate that a particular element is related to the job (Gatewood & Feild, 2001)—a point that will become clear when we discuss the issues involved in test validation in Chapter 7. This criticism is consistent with other researchers' (e.g., Harvey, 1991) concerns that job analysis needs to remain focused on observables instead of inferring hypothetical worker traits or abilities. However, much of what we do in psychology involves inferences of some sort, so excluding them seems unreasonable. We can resolve this paradox by realizing that an important focus of job analysis is to ensure that when inferences are drawn, they are based on observable work-related data. The job analyst can choose to focus only on work activities or only on worker attributes or on both, which is consistent with the hybrid approach discussed earlier.

Perhaps the best-known job analysis method is the **Position Analysis Questionnaire (PAQ)**, a standardized instrument that focuses on general work behaviors (McCormick et al., 1972). The PAQ consists of 195 items or elements, 187 of which describe general work behaviors, work conditions, and job characteristics. The incumbent employee or SME decides whether each item pertains to the job in question; each one that does is evaluated in terms of various dimensions, such as the extent to which it is used on the job, its importance to the job, and the amount of time on the job that is spent on this behavior. These 187 job elements are organized along six dimensions: information input, mental processes, work output, relationships with other persons, job context, and other job characteristics. Table 3.1 lists these six dimensions, along with two examples of each. A profile of the job emerges as a result of this rather large data collection effort.

Despite its historically widespread use, the PAQ has been the target of at least three major criticisms. First, some data indicate that the reading level of the PAQ is at least college level, if not graduate level (Ash & Edgell, 1975). This is a problem because it limits who can competently do the job analysis and rules out the less educated incumbents in many jobs. Second, the PAQ does not seem well suited for managerial jobs; and, third, the items themselves are too abstract (Harvey, 1993). These criticisms have led other job analysis researchers and practitioners to develop alternative worker-oriented instruments.

The **Common-Metric Questionnaire (CMQ)**, developed by Harvey (1993), is one such instrument. Two basic beliefs about worker-oriented approaches to job analysis are reflected in the CMQ: (1) The instrument must comprehensively describe work activities using a common set of items written at a more behaviorally abstract level than the typical task statements, and (2) the rating scale must have the same meaning across all jobs. The focus here is on describing jobs at a level that allows the descriptions to be compared across jobs, as opposed to describing them so abstractly that differences across jobs are lost.

Think back to such job-oriented approaches as the Task Inventory Approach and Functional Job Analysis. In these cases, the focus is on extremely specific tasks conducted on the job, making it very difficult to uncover any similarities across jobs. But the worker-oriented approaches, best exemplified by the PAQ, may be

Position Analysis Questionnaire (PAQ)
A widely used job analysis instrument that focuses on general work behaviors.

Common-Metric Questionnaire (CMQ)
A newly developed worker-oriented job analysis instrument that attempts to improve the generalizability of worker-oriented approaches through the use of items focused on slightly less general work behaviors.

Table 3.1 PAQ Dimensions and Elements	
Information input	(Where and how does the worker get the information he uses in performing his job?)
Examples:	Use of written materials Near-visual differentiation
Mental processes	(What reasoning, decision making, planning, and information-processing activities are involved in performing the job?)
Examples:	Level of reasoning in problem solving Coding/decoding
Work output	(What physical activities does the worker perform, and what tools does she use?)
Examples:	Use of keyboard devices Assembling/disassembling
Relationships with other persons	(What relationships with other people are required in performing the job?)
Examples:	Instructing Contacts with public, customers
Job context	(In what physical or social contexts is the work performed?)
Examples:	High temperature Interpersonal conflict situations
Other job characteristics	(What activities, conditions, or characteristics other than those described above are relevant to the job?)
Examples:	Specified work pace Amount of job structure

Source: McCormick (1979)

so abstract as to result in the emergence of dissimilar jobs with very similar profiles. For instance, what jobs do you think might emerge with a profile similar to that of police officer? You probably listed things like firefighter, prison guard, and private detective. However, research indicates that one answer is the job of *homemaker* (Arvey & Begalla, 1975). This is probably not one of the jobs you had on your list, but the profiles tend to be similar because both police officers and homemakers are often involved in handling emergencies and troubleshooting. However, I would argue that if the PAQ elements were a little less abstract, these jobs would not emerge as so similar.

The CMQ is computer-based, consisting of 2,077 items that are organized along 80 dimensions. Obviously, one issue with respect to this instrument is its length, but the author reports that over 90% of those who have used the CMQ completed it in less than three hours (Harvey, 1993). A sample question asks whether a particular job involves a skill that requires instruction at a college or university, along with the response scale for that item; the response scale displays the criticality of this particular skill. The items for all 80 dimensions are set up in a similar way. Although rather new, the CMQ has been piloted on over 900 occupations involving over 6,700 positions. Its items are more behaviorally specific than those included on the PAQ, its reading level is much lower, and it is relevant for both managerial and nonmanagerial jobs.

BONNIE KAMIN/PHOTOEDIT INC.

▲ **A Closer Look**
Why are the job profiles of police officer and home-maker so similar according to the PAQ? How would the CMQ address this?

Advances in Job Analysis Practice and Research

Technology has played a role in the development of job analyses, as evidenced by our discussion of the CMQ in the previous section. Other technological advancements have been integral in this area as well. For instance, researchers have demonstrated how to use the Internet to generate job-analytic information via the O*NET (Reiter-Palmon et al., 2006). In their work, they emphasized the use of the web to gather and organize job-analytic information with minimal intervention and guidance. Other researchers have worked to develop metrics, or quantitative rules of thumb, to help with analyzing and using the mass of job analysis data resulting from technological innovation like the O*NET (McEntire, Dailey, Osburn, & Mumford, 2006). They have developed metrics that would allow organizations to make better use of the existing O*NET data. These metrics, or mathematical formulae, can be used with the O*NET database to answer specific questions in the areas of selection, training, and development, for example, who is the best employee for a particular promotion. Given the ever-increasing use of the O*NET database in organizational analysis, the development and use of related metrics hold even greater potential for organizations.

There has also been considerable advancement regarding issues of SME ratings. For instance, two studies have examined the role of personality and motivation in SME job analysis ratings. One investigation examined the potential role of the self-serving bias in affecting job analysis ratings (Cucina, Vasilopoulos, & Sehgal, 2005). The authors argued that SMEs may engage in self-serving behavior when asked to identify which traits are important for the jobs. This would suggest that an SME might weight intelligence, flexibility, and creative thinking as important characteristics for successful employees in their job even though others might more objectively not view these characteristics as terribly important.

In a more sophisticated study testing self-presentation in SME ratings, it was found that SME incumbents tended to endorse ability statements as important for job effectiveness even when those abilities were really nonessential (Morgeson, Delaney-Klinger, Mayfield, Ferrara, & Campion, 2004). Individuals were presenting themselves in a positive light to suggest that, in order to do the job that they currently did, one needed to have a plethora of abilities. Individuals may do this unconsciously and without any real plan to alter the objective job analysis, but the result is job analysis data that are inaccurate—and the implications and potential detrimental effects to the organization are very real. For instance, requiring an ability for a particular job because the job analysis identified it as important makes good sense; however, if the ability really isn't essential for the job, it may lead to many competent individuals not being hired for lack of this ability. Other researchers found that one's attitude toward one's job may bias one's job analysis ratings; this was especially the case for tasks that were objectively coded as discretionary (Conte, Dean, Ringenbach, Moran, & Landy, 2005). By "discretionary," the authors mean tasks like "join and participate in community and social organizations," which may not be required as often as other tasks. It appears that SMEs (in this case, incumbents) allow their attitudes about their own jobs as well as the extent to which the task is required to impact job analysis ratings.

A recent study argues that the appearance of unreliable competency ratings made by incumbents is due to "job crafting" (Lievens, Sanchez, Bartram, & Brown 2010). For instance, in complex jobs that allow incumbents to make choices that allow them more creativity and flexibility, there are more opportunities for these incumbents to exercise discretion and "craft" their jobs in particular ways. Because employees can tweak their jobs, resulting in something that looks quite different from the way the jobs were originally defined, incumbent ratings of competencies may not agree with the competencies from the original job analysis. Results found that 25% of the differences in the two sets of competency ratings appear to be meaningful differences that emerged because of the job crafting (Lievens et al., 2010). That is, incumbents don't see their jobs as the same—even though the jobs were originally defined as the same—because they have crafted their job to be different based on their skills and weaknesses. Variance in incumbent ratings may not be error at all, but rather a reflection of how incumbents view and craft their own jobs. Therefore, organizations might be wise to encourage employees to craft jobs in ways that are consistent with the strategic plan of the organization.

A newer perspective on job analysis is taken by some recent researchers who argue that we need new types of job analyses. Traditional job analyses assume stable jobs, but jobs have a tendency to change and morph into different-looking jobs, leading some to argue for a novel approach to job analysis (Singh, 2008). With the changing of environments in North American organizations, we need more strategic job-analytic approaches in which experts consider not just the current status of

TECHNICAL TIP

In Chapter 2 we talked about variance as a measure of dispersion, or the "spread-outedness" of the scores. Here we are talking about job crafting being responsible for those differences, or variance, in job ratings.

jobs but also how jobs are likely to change and evolve in the future. **Strategic job analysis** is an intentional, systematic process of collecting current and future work-related aspects of a job within the organization's strategic context (Singh, 2008).

■ Defining the Job: Descriptions and Specifications

The basic goal of job analysis is to define the job in terms of its component parts. As noted earlier, job analysis yields three major outcomes: job evaluation, job description, and job specifications. The first of these will be discussed in a separate section. The second outcome, **job description**, is a written statement of what the jobholders do, how they do it, and why they do it (Cascio, 1998). It presents the *task requirements* of the job. The job description typically includes the job title and descriptions of the tasks and machinery involved, and it sometimes includes information about the working conditions and physical environment, social environment, and conditions of employment. Think about the job of college professor and ask yourself what college professors do, how they do it, and why they do it. Upon answering those questions, you might arrive at the following job description, which looks very similar to the DOT entry for faculty member, presented earlier in Figure 3.3:

> College Professor: Teaches college or university courses within a particular curriculum (e.g., psychology, mathematics, history) to classes of undergraduate and graduate students. Prepares and delivers lectures that conform to a predetermined course outline. Stimulates class discussions in smaller informal groups. Evaluates students' knowledge and achievement through reading, writing, and other assignments as well as through examinations that are graded so as to provide feedback. Conducts research in his or her area of expertise and disseminates the findings of that research in appropriate outlets (e.g., scientific journals, books) to further the knowledge in the field. Provides mentoring and advising to students who are seeking academic degrees. Serves on university committees that serve the interests of students, the university, the government, and the community.

The third outcome derived from the job analysis is a description of the *people requirements* that are reflected in the **job specifications** (often called *job specs*). The job specifications delineate the KSAOs deemed necessary to perform the job. Let's return to our college professor example. We've generated a job description, but what would comprise the job specifications or KSAOs necessary to be a successful college professor? Here is one such list:

- Reading and writing at the post-college level
- Advanced knowledge verified by an advanced degree (master's or doctorate)
- Willingness or desire to work with others
- Ability to communicate clearly
- Ability to communicate in an interesting manner
- Methodological and statistical skills
- Mentoring and advising skills
- A deep knowledge/understanding of one's own discipline

strategic job analysis
An approach to job analysis that considers the status of jobs as they currently exist but also factors in how jobs are likely to change in the future as a result of anticipated organizational or industry changes.

job description
As an outcome of job analysis, a written statement of what jobholders actually do, how they do it, and why they do it.

job specifications
An outcome of job analysis delineating the KSAOs deemed necessary to perform a job; often called job specs.

One way to view the relationships among job analysis, job description, and job specifications is to view the job description as stemming directly from the job analysis and the job specifications as being inferred indirectly from the job analysis through the job description. (Look back at Figure 3.1 for this organizational scheme.) For instance, we might use the JEM to develop a picture of the job and to write a job description (like the preceding one) that includes mentoring and advising students who are seeking academic degrees. From the job analysis and this job description, we might infer that successful college professors must have mentoring and advising skills. In short, the job analysis, job description, and job specifications are necessarily intertwined. As you may recall, job analysis should be focused only on observables; inferences about KSAOs from the job analysis should be avoided (Harvey, 1991).

Of course, one of the major purposes of job analysis is to identify KSAOs that can be used in the selection of employees. This process is covered in Chapter 6, but it's worth noting here that even if one limits job analysis to observables that result in a job description, the job analysis and job description must be used to infer job specifications that are of paramount importance for selection and placement. The bottom line is that, as I/O psychologists, we are not simply focused on describing the job; indeed, our longer-term goal is the use of this job analysis information for selection, placement, performance appraisal, and other HR functions.

■ The Many Purposes of Job Analysis

As I suggested earlier, job analysis is the foundation for much of industrial psychology. There are two reasons for this. First, a job analysis is necessary to the success of human resource functions. In other words, without a job analysis, many of the HR functions in organizations would be carried out ineffectively. Second, an increased emphasis on laws associated with the workplace has made it more desirable for companies to use job analyses as their first line of defense when accused of an unfair practice. Table 3.2 presents a few cases in which the existence and quality of a job analysis played a major role in the court's decision. We will discuss legal issues in more depth in the next few chapters; for now, let's consider job classification, an important purpose served by job analysis.

Job Classification

Jobs are often categorized in terms of job families, each of which can then be used as a level of analysis for various personnel decisions. For instance, Word Processing Specialist I, Word Processing Specialist II, and Data Technician I may all be declared parts of a job family called "computer support staff" if the job analyses conducted on each job demonstrated enough overlap to warrant such a designation. If they did, all jobs within this job family would operate under the same benefits package, including number of allowable sick days, number of vacation days, and

---

TECHNICAL TIP

Remember that we talked about the importance of test validity in Chapter 2. In particular, criterion-related validity focuses on whether the test is a good predictor of performance. With the legal cases described here, you can see the practical importance of test validity.

Table 3.2 Legal Importance of Job Analysis to Organizations

Case Description	Legal Ruling
Kirkland v. New York Dept. of Correctional Service (1974): Test used for promotion resulted in many fewer minority promotions than Caucasian promotions. Defendant argued that the test was job-related because it tapped important skills necessary to do the job.	Court ruled that the company had not performed an adequate job analysis, demonstrating that the test items were linked to job performance and that the test was, therefore, not valid to be used for promotion.
Harless v. Duck (1977): A physical test (push-ups, sit-ups, broad jump, and obstacle course) was used in hiring patrol officers, but it resulted in many fewer women hires than men hires. Defendant argued that the test was job related.	Court ruled that the job analysis was adequate for demonstrating that the skills and abilities measured by the physical test were necessary for successful job performance. Thus, the test was deemed reasonable and valid for the hiring of patrol officers.
Adams v. City of Chicago (1996): Sergeant Promotional Test resulted in far fewer minorities promoted than Caucasians, but the city argued that the test was job-related.	Court ruled that the job analysis identified important and relevant skills and abilities that were adequately measured by the Sergeant Promotional Test. Thus, the test was found to be valid for making promotion decisions to the rank of sergeant.

amount of health benefits. In addition, if a company's 2,000 jobs can be grouped into 100 job families, many of the company's personnel practices would be simplified.

Criterion Development and Performance Appraisal

Performance appraisal is certainly one of the most frequent uses of job analysis data. As we will discuss in Chapters 4 and 5, performance appraisal is one of the most important functions performed by human resource departments. Of course, to conduct a useful and fair performance appraisal, organizations must have clearly stipulated goals, objectives, and criteria on which employees can be evaluated. These criteria should come directly from the job analysis. For instance, if college professors are going to be evaluated annually with respect to their success in teaching, the college must be able to demonstrate that teaching is an important part of a professor's job. (This should be an easy thing to do, but it still needs to be verified by the job analysis.) Suppose that I am evaluated based on the reactions of my students to my classes (and, in fact, I am evaluated in this way every semester), but the job analysis done by my school does not demonstrate that teaching is an integral part of my job. This would be neither fair nor appropriate. Here, of course, I would argue that the problem is not with the criteria but with the job analysis, which did not identify an important element of the job. This example, too, demonstrates the importance of doing a thorough and accurate job analysis because the job analysis is used in important ways.

Selection and Placement

There is perhaps no area of industrial psychology for which job analysis is more important than selection and placement (see Chapters 6 and 7). Indeed, a major purpose of job analysis is to help industrial psychologists identify the KSAOs that are necessary for successful performance on the job.

In Chapter 1, I defined *competencies* as the skills, behaviors, and capabilities that allow employees to perform specific functions. Obviously, this definition is very similar to the one I have specified for KSAOs in this chapter. In fact, many experts consider competencies and KSAOs to be the same thing (e.g., Schippmann et al., 2000). Another way to think about this relationship, though, is to view competencies as sets or groupings of specific KSAOs that allow employees to perform specific organizational functions (Reilly & McGourty, 1998). For example, interpersonal communication may be considered a competency. That competency, in turn, may consist of several KSAOs such as (1) the knowledge of different communication styles, (2) the skill to communicate positive and negative feedback to individuals, and (3) the ability to understand what individuals need to hear from their supervisor to increase their motivation.

Competency modeling is parallel to job analysis in that both involve describing jobs in a careful and methodical way so that HR practices can be based on this information (Schippmann et al., 2000). Differences have been observed as well. For example, competency modeling is believed to be more worker-oriented and job analysis more job-oriented (Schippmann et al., 2000). Competency modeling may be a bit broader in focus because it tries to build a full framework for HR functioning by defining the responsibilities, skills, knowledge, abilities, personal attributes, and business challenges that are relevant for a particular organization (see Sanchez & Levine, 2009, for a thorough comparison of the two approaches). A team of researchers suggest using a blended approach that takes advantage of the methodological rigor of job analysis and the organizational strategy involved in competency modeling (Lievens, Sanchez, & De Corte, 2004). This approach, according to the authors, improves the inferences drawn in competency modeling by relying on the step-by-step approach of job analysis. However, the efficiency and success of this blended approach require additional research. Although distinctions exist between the job-analytic approach to identifying KSAOs and the competency modeling approach to building competencies, the two terms are similar enough for our purposes that I will use them interchangeably throughout the text. Please understand, however, that job analysis tends to be a bit more methodologically rigorous and competency modeling tends to consider organizational strategy a bit more.

Let's turn to the world of construction for an example. In doing a job analysis for the job of an architect, we conclude that spatial skills and knowledge of some basic engineering principles are required. Therefore, when screening applicants, we look for individuals who seem to be knowledgeable and skilled in these areas and hire them. This scenario makes sense, but it may also be too simplistic. For instance, we might ignore the part of our job analysis indicating that architects also need to have some drafting (or drawing) skills because they need to be able to develop plans for new buildings. Given this flaw in our process, we may hire knowledgeable and spatially skilled individuals who do not have the drafting skills to put their ideas on paper. In short, because we weren't careful in conducting and interpreting our job analysis, we may have made costly personnel decisions. Does this cost our company money? It sure does, and it also may cost individuals their jobs.

Job Design and Redesign

Job analysis may sometimes uncover problems with a particular job that the organization may want to address. For instance, interviews with incumbents may reveal that some of the current equipment used on the job needs to be updated because it cannot keep pace with other, newer equipment during the production process. A company may use this information to purchase newer equipment or to redesign the job so that the current equipment will work more efficiently within the process. Alternatively, PAQ or CMQ data may indicate that employees spend far too much time on a particular facet of the job, information that the company may use to initiate a job redesign intervention to make the work process more efficient. We can see that in this area of I/O psychology, job analyses are often used to make alterations in the work process with the intent of making the company run more efficiently.

Morgeson and Humphrey (2006) developed the Work Design Questionnaire (WDQ) as a comprehensive measure of job design to replace the incomplete and narrow existing measures. The WDQ consists of 77 items along 21 dimensions of work characteristics. The 21 work characteristics can be organized into: (1) task characteristics such as autonomy and task variety; (2) knowledge characteristics that reflect traditional KSAOs; (3) social characteristics that include social support and feedback from others; and (4) contextual characteristics, composed of physical demands and work conditions. Results suggest that it is a solid measure of work design that relates appropriately to various elements of the O*NET database. Although still quite new, there appears to be great potential for the use of the WDQ in the area of work design.

Training

In many instances, employees are hired into an organization without all the KSAOs necessary to do every facet of their jobs. Sometimes even highly skilled new employees require training to learn the procedures used in a particular organization (see Chapter 8). Job analysis can be used to identify areas in which training programs need to be developed. Ideally, the job analysis should identify what work behaviors occur on the job so that the human resource department can develop training programs around these general and specific work behaviors. In addition, given that jobs are *dynamic*—in that they change considerably with changes in technology, in the workforce, and in economic demands—job analysis can be used to identify the extent to which job behaviors have changed to match the times. This information can then be used to develop and target training programs for existing employees.

■ Job Evaluation

job evaluation
As an outcome of job analysis, a technique that attempts to determine the value or worth of particular jobs to organizations so that salaries can be set accordingly.

Although we like to think that our job is as important to our particular organization as anyone else's, the reality is that some jobs are more important than others. **Job evaluation** is a technique based on job analysis that attempts to determine the value or worth of particular jobs to organizations so that salaries can be set accordingly. Most of us would agree that the clerk who works in the hospital restaurant makes a less important contribution to the organization than the chief surgeon. Job evaluation is about trying to quantify differences of this sort so that salaries can be set in a fair manner based on the value or contribution of jobs. Because compensation is often the largest budget item in many companies, it has an important effect on profits and, therefore, attracts a good deal of attention from organizational administrators and HR practitioners.

Point System

point system
The most common approach to job evaluation, which involves estimating the value of jobs based on points assigned to various predetermined dimensions.

compensable factors
Dimensions or factors that are used to rate jobs, indicating that employees are compensated based on these factors. Examples include effort, skill, responsibility, and working conditions.

There are various approaches to job evaluation, but I will focus on the one most frequently used: the **point system**. This approach involves estimating the value of jobs based on points assigned to various predetermined dimensions (Milkovich & Newman, 1984). Among the most common of these dimensions—referred to as **compensable factors** to indicate that employees are compensated based on them— are effort, skill, responsibility, and working conditions. The idea here is that jobs requiring more effort and skill, involving more responsibility, and taking place in less desirable working conditions (e.g., outdoors in subzero temperatures versus climate-controlled office buildings) should be more highly compensated than jobs that don't have these characteristics.

The steps involved in conducting a point-system job evaluation are rather simple. First, managers or some other group of SMEs use a job analysis to identify the compensable factors. Second, each job is assigned points by a compensation committee with respect to the degree that each has these compensable factors. Third, the points assigned to each job are summed across the factors to arrive at a total score. Fourth, these points are then used to assign wages, with the goal being to maintain equity so that jobs of greater value are better compensated than those of lesser value. Finally, the scores can be plotted against the current wage for existing jobs, providing a clear picture of whether a job is currently undercompensated, overcompensated, or adequately compensated.

Figure 3.5 shows an example of this kind of plot to determine how jobs within the organization stack up against each other in terms of the factors and compensation.

FIGURE 3.5 Wage Equity and Job Evaluation

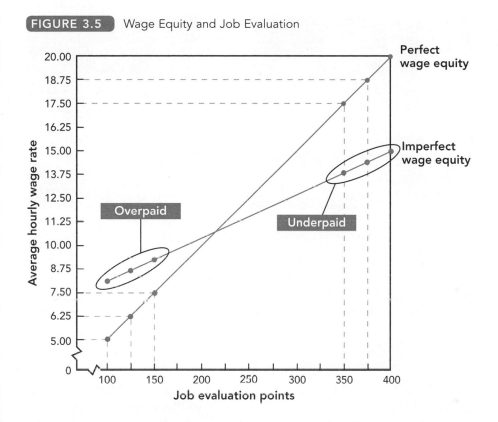

The line marked "perfect wage equity" represents the ideal situation whereby the number of job evaluation points is exactly proportional to the level of compensation. The line marked "imperfect wage equity," on the other hand, is more realistic but much less desirable. As you can see, jobs evaluated at 125 points are overcompensated at $8.75 per hour rather than the expected $6.25 per hour; jobs evaluated at 350 points are undercompensated at $13.75 per hour rather than the expected $17.50 per hour. Clearly, there are compensation issues to be resolved in this particular organization: Some positions are compensated at a higher rate and others at a lower rate than the job evaluation indicates they should be. Yet once organizations have accumulated and examined such data, they can begin to develop ways to bring wages back in line. For instance, jobs that are undercompensated can be targeted for wage increases, whereas those that are overcompensated can be targeted for wage freezes.

So far, this sounds very scientific, and in some ways it is. But as is often the case with I/O psychology, when we move into the applied arena, things are not quite so simple. In the actual labor market, for instance, individuals in jobs with job evaluation scores between 100 and 200 points sometimes have to be "overpaid"; in other words, there are so few people who will take these lower-level jobs that,

▶ **A Closer Look**
What role has
gender played
historically in the
compensation
levels of jobs?
Does gender still
play a role?

to be competitive with other companies, we have to pay higher wages for these jobs than our job evaluation tells us they are worth. At the same time, there may be so many managers interested in upper-level jobs that we can save money by "underpaying" them. Retention of good workers is yet another important issue: We will probably pay what we think is necessary to keep them on the job. In a practical sense, then, companies are likely to use not only job analysis and job evaluation information but also labor market information when setting compensation levels for jobs.

Comparable Worth

It is a long-established finding that women are paid considerably less than men for similar work. In fact, when a field has become dominated by women, as happened with the administrative assistant profession in the twentieth century (for a review, see Lowe, 1987), the rate of pay has decreased. As of 2002, there was a difference of 23% between men's and women's wages (Institute for Women's Policy Research, 2003). This means that, on average, women earn about 77% of what men earn, and this figure has been fairly stable since the mid-1990s, raising concerns about whether women's compensation will ever catch up to men's. The wage gap is smaller, but still sizable (16%), when we consider only starting salaries (Marini & Fan, 1997). A survey of almost 1,000 Harvard graduates found a $10,000 difference in starting salaries of male versus female graduates of the class of 2007 (Hemel, 2007). Further, the wage gap doesn't disappear when we factor in experience, industry, or job; for instance, female administrative assistants earn only 83% of what male administrators earn (Fitzpatrick, 2010).

This issue is a troublesome one, as employees who are doing the same job should be paid similarly regardless of their gender. In fact, the Equal Pay Act of 1963 stipulates that men and women who do work that is *equal* must be compensated similarly. The word *equal* has been interpreted to mean jobs that are the same. But this act does not address the broader issue of gender differences in compensation across dissimilar jobs. For instance, should computer technicians (who are predominantly male) be paid more than executive secretaries (who are predominantly female)? Granted, these jobs aren't the same—but are they equal in terms of their value to the organization? And if they are equal in this sense, shouldn't they be compensated similarly?

A study (Ostroff & Atwater, 2003) demonstrated that compensation is also affected by the gender composition of one's coworkers. In particular, managers (regardless of gender) who work largely with women are paid considerably less than are managers who work largely with men. Apparently, gender issues in compensation extend beyond just the gender of the employees to the gender composition of the work group as well.

These kinds of questions have given rise to the doctrine of **comparable worth**, which maintains that jobs of equal (or comparable) worth to the organization should be compensated equally. This issue has been linked quite closely to gender differences in compensation. Proponents of comparable worth insist that job evaluation should play a larger role, and the market a smaller role, in setting compensation. They argue that the market is biased and that it artificially sets the compensation for female-dominated jobs lower than for male-dominated jobs. They argue that by focusing on job behaviors rather than on job performers, job evaluation decreases the likelihood of gender bias in compensation (Feder & Levine, 2010).

Interest in comparable worth has been growing over the past 20 years. One article, for instance, reviewed the experiences of 8 states that have implemented comparable worth legislation and noted that 45 states have been involved in some pay-equity activities (Gardner & Daniel, 1998). Opponents of comparable worth argue that there is no bias against female-typed jobs and that women can choose whatever jobs they prefer. They encourage women to choose to work in higher-compensated jobs. But the issue of comparable worth is unlikely to be solved quickly or easily, complicated as it is by market factors and historical trends, potential biases in job evaluation, and both real and imagined gender differences. Of course, we have made progress in this area in recent decades, and with careful and fair practices we can continue to improve the financial situation for women who enter the workforce.

comparable worth
A doctrine maintaining that jobs of equal (or comparable) worth to the organization should be compensated equally.

■ Summary

Although job analysis tends to receive little empirical attention, it is among the most important areas of I/O psychology, providing the foundation on which all other HR processes are built. This chapter was largely structured around Figure 3.1, which shows the interrelationships among job analysis, job descriptions, job specifications, job evaluation, and the HR functions that are built on these processes. It should be clear by now that without a carefully designed and executed job analysis, HR practitioners and I/O psychologists would have very little to go on in making HR decisions.

Both job-oriented and worker-oriented approaches to job analysis were presented in this chapter, along with a discussion of different methods within each category. Also discussed were the advantages and disadvantages of each approach, the choice of which should depend on the job analyst's purpose. Some developments in the area of job analysis were considered as well. First, although the DOT has been of great importance to the I/O field for many years, the Department of Labor's current undertaking, the O*NET, should provide more updated, useful, and accessible data on occupations and jobs. Second, the CMQ was presented as one of the newer job analysis instruments with great potential to serve the purposes of worker-oriented job analysis methods while avoiding criticisms regarding reading level and work behaviors that are too general.

Job descriptions and job specifications are derived either directly or indirectly from the job analysis and are directly or indirectly connected to a myriad of HR functions. This chapter provided a brief discussion of the links between job analysis and these HR functions; the remainder of the second part of the text will cover these HR functions at length. Finally, we considered the role of job analysis in job evaluation. The Equal Pay Act of 1963 mandates that individuals who do equal work should receive equal pay, but it does not speak to wage gaps between "male-typed" and "female-typed" jobs. The emergence of the doctrine of comparable worth suggests that organizations and society need to do a better job in setting compensation for jobs while taking gender-based job classes into account.

■ Key Terms

Common-Metric Questionnaire (CMQ) (p. 73)
comparable worth (p. 85)
compensable factors (p. 82)
Dictionary of Occupational Titles (DOT) (p. 68)
element (p. 65)
Functional Job Analysis (FJA) (p. 67)
incumbents (p. 66)
job (p. 65)

job analysis (p. 65)
job description (p. 77)
Job Element Method (JEM) (p. 71)
job evaluation (p. 82)
job-oriented (p. 66)
job specifications (p. 77)
KSAOs (p. 65)
point system (p. 82)
position (p. 65)
Position Analysis Questionnaire (PAQ) (p. 73)

strategic job analysis (p. 77)
subject matter experts (SMEs) (p. 66)
task (p. 65)

Task Inventory Approach (p. 66)
worker-oriented (p. 66)

■ TAKING IT TO THE FIELD

Job analysis is one of the most important activities that I/O psychologists can do. Without a thorough job analysis, it becomes difficult to train, assess, and reward employees. There are many ways to do a job analysis, but one of the more commonly used methods is to interview a job incumbent. Using the guide below, interview someone who works at your college/university and then, using the data you gather, write a worker-oriented job description for that position. You may also refer to the O*NET for ideas about this job, but make sure not to copy any phrases from the O*NET.

Here are some tips for writing effective worker-oriented job descriptions:

- A worker-oriented job description is not about what someone does but rather what KSAOs are necessary to be effective in this position. So focus on characteristics rather than tasks.
- It is best to use bullet points for this assignment because you want your document to be as simple as possible for your reader.
- Each bullet point should begin with a present-tense verb, such as *demonstrates* or *knows*.
- Your description should be no longer than two pages; if you find yourself writing more than that, consider how some categories might be consolidated (e.g., "Knows laws about food safety" and "Follows food safety laws" could be combined into "Knows and complies with food safety laws").
- It is important to avoid vague language. Look at what you are writing and consider whether it provides enough information for a job applicant to accurately determine whether he or she would be qualified for the position.

Here are some possible interview questions:

1. What does an effective _____ look like?
2. What does an ineffective _____ look like?
3. What knowledge does someone need to do this job well?
4. What skills does someone need to do this job well?
5. What abilities must someone have to do this job well?
6. What would make someone a "good fit" for this job?

■ Critical Thinking Questions

1. One use of job analysis is creating job descriptions. Why is it important to have a detailed and accurate job description? What are some possible outcomes of having a job description that is *not* based on a job analysis and does *not* accurately represent the job?

2. Job analysis was an important factor in three court cases presented in this chapter. How is job analysis used in a legal setting? What aspects of a job analysis will make it more likely to hold up in court?

3. As noted in the chapter, some proponents of comparable worth argue that compensation for female-dominated jobs is set lower than for jobs dominated by men. These proponents suggest that more rigorous job evaluations could help close the gap. What are some ways in which job evaluation could be used to more effectively determine fair compensation for male- and female-dominated jobs?

■ Application Questions

1. Find a job ad in the newspaper or online. According to this ad, what are some KSAOs required for that position? Are there any KSAOs you believe might be expected but are omitted from this ad? What might be the consequences of this omission?

2. Consider three potential sources of job information—incumbents, a supervisor, and an I/O psychologist. What are some advantages and disadvantages of using each source for information about a job?

3. Competencies tend to involve broader skill sets than are typically described in a job analysis. One advantage to this approach is that a competency model can generalize to many different roles within an organization. What broad competencies can be used to describe what is necessary to be an effective student in any class, in any college/university? What are some aspects of student competencies that you believe are unique to this specific class?

4. What are some jobs that have a significant need for strategic job analysis? Why is this so?

■ Suggested Readings

Brannick, M. T., Levine, E. L., & Morgeson, F. P. (2007). *Job and work analysis: Methods, research, and applications for human resource management* (2nd ed.). Thousand Oaks, CA: SAGE. This outstanding treatment of job analysis is useful for both researchers and practitioners.

Gatewood, R. D., Feild, H. S., & Barrick, M. (2010). *Human resource selection* (7th ed.). Mason, OH: South-Western College Pub. This is an excellent reference for everything that constitutes industrial psychology, though it is perhaps strongest in its coverage of job analysis and other technical areas.

O*NET Online. (2010). *Build your future with O*NET OnLine!* U.S. Department of Labor. Retrieved December 29, 2010, from http://onetcenter.org/. The U.S. Department of Labor's online database of occupational information provides central characteristics and aspects of both workers and occupations.

Peterson, N. G., Mumford, M. D., Borman, W. C., Jeanneret, P. R., Fleishman, E. A., Levin, K. Y., et al. (2001). Understanding work using the Occupational Information Network (O°NET). *Personnel Psychology, 54,* 451–492. This is a detailed discussion of why the O°NET was needed and how it was developed.

Sackett, P. R., & Laczo, R. M. (2003). Job and work analysis. In W. C. Borman, D. R. Ilgen, & R. J. Klimoski (Eds.), *Handbook of psychology: Industrial and organizational psychology* (Vol. 12, pp. 21–37). Hoboken, NJ: Wiley. This thoughtful, up-to-date review does more than just address technical issues. It synthesizes current knowledge and makes important recommendations.

CHAPTER **4**

BILL PUGLIANO/GETTY IMAGES

Criterion Measurement

As noted in the last chapter, job analysis provides the foundation on which everything in the field of industrial psychology is built. In this chapter, I will talk about the first aspect of this "everything": criteria. Criteria are quite important to industrial psychology because they reflect organizational or individual performance—and, in a competitive market, companies are driven by performance and profits. Thus, I/O psychologists are often hired to help organizations develop criteria, as well as to implement HR processes that are directly linked to those criteria. Criteria are typically dependent variables that provide an indication of success or performance. For instance, when your instructor grades your paper, she uses criteria. When your boss evaluates your performance and decides on whether or not to give you a raise, he uses criteria. This chapter will present the nuts and bolts of criteria—what they are, how they are developed, how they are evaluated, and what they are used for—along with a discussion of the different types.

■ Defining Criteria and Their Properties

Every time you evaluate something or someone, you are using criteria—though you're probably not aware of doing so. We even use criteria to evaluate teams such as a work team or a baseball team (for a more complete discussion of team criteria, see LePine, Piccolo, Jackson, Mathieu, & Saul, 2008). When, for the first time, you walked into your dorm room as a freshman or your office cubicle as a new employee, you very likely wondered whether you and the students in that dorm room or the coworkers in the nearby cubicle would get along. In other words, you wondered whether you would like those people. When you did finally decide that Kristen was a pretty cool roommate, you may have made that decision based on her personality (funny, serious, kind, trustworthy), intelligence (smart about academic things, smart about everyday things), hobbies (enjoys sports, music, movies), hang-ups (dislikes people who are stuck on themselves and people who don't clean up after themselves), and so on. You made your decision based on all of these criteria. Consciously or unconsciously, you defined various criteria that led you to the overall evaluation that Kristen was a cool roommate.

Of course, we don't always make the same decisions. For instance, you may have another roommate, Sarah, who doesn't think Kristen is cool at all. Often, when we disagree in this way, it is because we have different criteria. Different judgments may be involved in determining whether Sarah thinks someone is cool versus whether you think someone is cool. For example, Sarah may think it's important to be involved in community service, which Kristen isn't. In other words, you and Sarah come to different conclusions about Kristen because you are using different criteria. At other times, however, we disagree about things not because our criteria differ but because we evaluate people and things differently on the basis of those criteria. When movie critics disagree about a movie, the disagreement is often based not on different criteria but on how the same criteria are evaluated. For instance, one may think the movie is good because the characters are believable, and the other may think the movie is bad because the characters aren't at all believable. Character believability is an important criterion for both reviewers, but their perceptions about the extent to which the movie scores high on this criterion differ, resulting in different evaluations of the film.

In I/O psychology, **criteria** are defined as evaluative standards that can be used as yardsticks for measuring employees' success or failure. We rely on them not only for appraising employees' performance but also for evaluating our training program, validating our selection battery, and making layoff and promotion decisions. Therefore, if we have faulty criteria, these HR functions would be flawed as well because they depend directly on the adequacy of the criteria. For instance, it seems reasonable to fire an employee because she is not performing at an acceptable level on the performance criterion. However, if that performance criterion is not a good measure of job performance, there is the potential for making a huge mistake by firing someone who may actually be a good worker. In such cases, we leave ourselves vulnerable to lawsuits (we'll talk about legal issues in the workplace in Chapters 5 and 7). Because key organizational decisions will be made directly on the basis of criteria, organizations need to be sure that these yardsticks are measuring the right thing and measuring it well.

In general, the criterion in which I/O psychologists are most interested is **performance** which can be defined as actual on-the-job behaviors that are relevant to the organization's goals. Performance is the reason that organizations are interested in hiring competent employees.

> **criteria**
> Evaluative standards that can be used as yardsticks for measuring an employee's success or failure.

> **performance**
> Actual on-the-job behaviors that are relevant to the organization's goals.

> **TECHNICAL TIP**
>
> In Chapter 2, we talked a bit about interrater reliability, which is the consistency with which multiple judges evaluate the same thing. This is an example of low interrater reliability because the judges—two movie critics, in this case—don't see the movie similarly.

▶ **A Closer Look**
Measuring job performance can be a tricky business. In what kind of work situations do you think measuring job performance is especially difficult?

"Just measuring your job performance..."

Throughout this chapter, I will use the terms *criterion, performance,* and *performance criterion* interchangeably.

Ultimate Criterion

ultimate criterion
A theoretical construct encompassing all performance aspects that define success on the job.

The **ultimate criterion** encompasses all aspects of performance that define success on the job. R. L. Thorndike (1949) discussed this very notion in his classic text *Personnel Selection,* arguing that the ultimate criterion is very complex and not even accessible to us. What he meant is that the ultimate criterion is something we can shoot for, but in actuality we can never completely define and measure every aspect of performance. Doing so would require time and details that simply are not available. As an example, let's say we're interested in defining the ultimate criterion for an administrative assistant's job. Toward that end, we might generate the following list:

- Typing speed
- Typing quality
- Filing efficiency
- Interactions with clients
- Interactions with coworkers
- Creativity
- Written communication
- Oral communication
- Procedural adherence
- Computer skills
- Interactions with supervisors
- Punctuality
- Initiative

This appears to be a fairly complete list, but when I asked two administrative assistants in our psychology department office if they had any to add, they came up with quite a few more that I hadn't thought of, including organizational skills. My guess is that if I gave this list to additional people, they would come up with still other dimensions or subcriteria. The point here is that merely listing all the criteria that define success on the job is difficult enough; *measuring* all of them would be virtually impossible. Thus, the ultimate criterion is a theoretical construct that we develop as a guide or a goal to shoot for in measuring job success.

Actual Criterion

The **actual criterion** is our best real-world representation of the ultimate criterion, and we develop it to reflect or overlap with the ultimate criterion as much as possible. Figure 4.1 illustrates this concept with respect to the administrative assistant job that we discussed earlier. Because we cannot possibly measure every facet of performance that we think is involved in the administrative assistant job and probably could not list everything that would indicate someone's success on the job, we consider only those elements that seem most important and that are most easily measured. Again, as applied psychologists, we need to keep practical issues in mind; we do this by thinking about the time, effort, and cost associated with measuring the different elements

actual criterion Our best real-world representative of the ultimate criterion, which we develop to reflect or overlap with the ultimate criterion as much as possible.

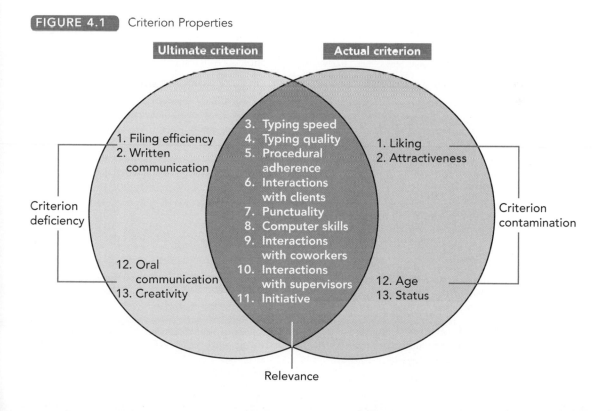

FIGURE 4.1 Criterion Properties

of the criteria involved because these are of great importance to the company with which we are working. In a perfect world, everything that is listed as being a part of the ultimate criterion would be included in the actual criterion, but typically this isn't possible. Thus, our actual criterion includes only those elements of the ultimate criterion that we intend to measure.

Criteria for the Criteria

In this section, we focus on what makes a good criterion. There are many lists of dimensions along which criteria can be evaluated. One of the earliest of these lists features 15 dimensions (Blum & Naylor, 1968). In a classic book, John Bernardin and Dick Beatty (1984) delineate more than 25 characteristics that have been examined as yardsticks for measuring the effectiveness of criteria. For our purposes here, I will highlight what I think are the five most fundamental of these criteria for the criteria (see Table 4.1 for a summary).

Relevance The crucial requirement for any criterion is *relevance*, or the degree to which the actual criterion is related to the ultimate criterion. Relevance reflects the degree of correlation or overlap between the actual and ultimate criteria. In a more technical, statistical sense, relevance is the percentage of variance in the ultimate criterion that can be accounted for by the actual criterion. We would like to see as

Table 4.1 Criteria for the Criteria

Dimension	Definition	Example/Explanation
Relevance	The extent to which the actual criterion measure is related to the ultimate criterion	A measure that seems to capture the major elements of the ultimate criterion; that is, it represents job performance very well
Reliability	The extent to which the actual criterion measure is stable or consistent	A measure that does not give drastically different results when used for the same employees at close time intervals
Sensitivity	The extent to which the actual criterion measure can discriminate among effective and ineffective employees	A measure that consistently identifies performance differences among employees; that is, everyone is not rated the same
Practicality	The degree to which the actual criterion can and will be used by those whose job it is to use it for making important decisions	A measure that can be completed in a reasonable amount of time by a supervisor and does not require excess paperwork
Fairness	The extent to which the actual criterion measure is perceived by employees to be just and reasonable	A measure that does not result in men always being rated higher than women, and vice versa

much overlap between the ultimate criterion and the actual criterion as is practical to achieve. Look at Figure 4.1 and note the nine dimensions in the intersection of the ultimate criterion and the actual criterion. These constitute relevance. The overlap itself thus represents the portion of the ultimate criterion that is tapped by our actual criterion. We want this portion of the Venn diagram to be as large as possible, indicating that our actual criterion mirrors the ultimate criterion fairly well. Relevance in this sense is analogous to validity.

> **TECHNICAL TIP**
>
> *Recall that in Chapter 2, construct validity was defined as the extent to which a test measures the underlying construct that it is intended to measure.*

Two conditions can limit the relevance of a criterion. The first is **criterion deficiency**, which refers to dimensions in the ultimate measure that are not part of the actual measure. A criterion is deficient if a major source of variance in the ultimate criterion is not included in the actual criterion. We want this part of the Venn diagram to be very small. Figure 4.1 shows the criterion deficiency as a list of dimensions that are in the ultimate criterion but are not part of our actual measure—namely, filing efficiency, written communication, oral communication, and creativity. Our criterion is deficient to the extent that these dimensions are not tapped by our criterion measure but are important to the criterion construct. If these particular dimensions are not terribly important to the criterion construct, then our criterion is not very deficient; but, if they are important, then we may have a problem with criterion deficiency.

criterion deficiency A condition in which dimensions in the ultimate measure are not part of or are not captured by the actual measure.

The second condition that can limit the relevance of a criterion is **criterion contamination**, which refers to those things measured by the actual criterion that are not part of the ultimate criterion. This is the part of the actual criterion variance that is not part of the ultimate criterion variance. Criterion contamination occurs in two ways. First, it can be caused simply by random measurement *error.* No matter how carefully we develop a precise and accurate measurement, there is always some error in that measurement—unreliability. This measurement error is random in the sense that it tends to even itself out over time, but any single performance measurement may not reflect true performance. For instance, we might measure performance every six months for two years and find that there are some differences in our four performance measurements, even though true performance (i.e., the ultimate criterion) may not have changed.

criterion contamination A condition in which things measured by the actual criterion are not part of the ultimate criterion.

The second cause of criterion contamination, *bias,* is more troubling given its systematic rather than random nature. Bias is most prevalent when the criteria of interest are judgments made by individuals. It is not unusual for raters to allow their biases to color their performance ratings. For instance, bias would result in criterion contamination if an evaluator, when rating administrative assistants on the dimension of organizational skills, gave a higher rating to those she liked or to those who were more attractive, regardless of actual performance levels. (Two additional examples, age and status, are listed in Figure 4.1.) Sometimes this is done on purpose, while at other times it is unconscious; we will discuss both instances of bias in more detail in the next chapter.

> **TECHNICAL TIP**
>
> *In Chapter 2, we defined reliability as consistency or stability in measurement, but unreliability is always present to some degree because we can't measure these kinds of things perfectly.*

IMAGE SOURCE/GETTY IMAGES

▲ A Closer Look
Your company has only one opening available for a new technical support staff member. On paper, all the candidates in this photo meet the criteria for the job. Can you think of other characteristics individuals might use in choosing which candidate to hire?

Criterion contamination occurs when the measure of the actual criterion reflects things other than what it should measure according to the ultimate criterion. When we are talking about criteria, a criterion is contaminated if it measures something other than what it is intended to measure, such as likability or attractiveness. Contamination is often a problem in the context of performance ratings, which we will discuss at length in the next chapter.

Reliability Although unreliability was mentioned as a potential cause of criterion contamination, its opposite—reliability—is important enough to be listed as a criterion itself. As discussed in Chapter 2, reliability refers to the stability or consistency of a measure. Indeed, an unreliable criterion is not very useful. For instance, suppose that we measured an administrative assistant's typing speed on six successive occasions and found that he typed at 50, 110, 40, 100, 60, and 45 words per minute. Such variability in the criterion measure would lead me to conclude that this particular measure is unreliable. When a measure is unreliable, we can't confidently use it in making important decisions. Another way to conceptualize the situation is to ask if this administrative assistant is a fast typist, as the 110 and 100 words per minute might indicate, or a below-average typist, as the 40 and 45 words per minute might indicate. Because the criterion is unreliable, we simply don't know—and the criterion is thus not useful.

Sensitivity A criterion must be *sensitive* enough to discriminate among effective and ineffective employees. If everyone is evaluated similarly according to the criterion, then it is not very useful. Suppose Goodyear wants to make a series of promotion decisions based on a performance criterion consisting of the number of tire valves produced by each employee in an eight-hour shift. At first glance, this seems a reasonable criterion; but on closer examination, we find that all 100 employees produce between 22 and 24 tire valves per eight-hour shift. In short, there doesn't appear to be much variability in the performance of these 100 employees on this criterion. The criterion isn't sensitive enough to discriminate between effective and ineffective performers, so Goodyear could not reasonably make promotion decisions based on it. (After all, would it make sense to promote those employees who produce 24 tire valves over those who produce 23?)

Yet there are probably other criteria in this situation that *could* distinguish among the employees. Can you think of any? The first one that comes to my mind is quality. Although all 100 employees produce about the same number of tire valves, there may be some serious differences in the quality of these valves. A second criterion, and one that may be even more sensitive, is the amount of waste each employee leaves behind after producing tire valves. Quite a few other alternative measures would work as well.

Every situation is different, of course—but the bottom line is that I/O psychologists work hard to develop sensitive criteria so that confidence can be placed in the criteria on which decisions are based.

Practicality   I have alluded to the importance of practical issues throughout the book thus far, but here the concept of practicality is tied more directly to organizational functioning. *Practicality* refers to the extent to which a criterion can and will be used by individuals making important decisions. Consider the following example. Let's say I spend an extraordinary amount of time conducting a thorough job analysis using the Common-Metric Questionnaire. Then I develop a set of relevant and reliable criteria that have hardly any criterion deficiency or contamination. But there is one problem: The organization's employees choose not to use the criteria on the grounds that they are too difficult to measure and too abstract to be useful. My error here was that I neglected to consider the usefulness or practicality of the measures and failed to work with the organization's management and other employees in the development process. Indeed, criteria must always be relatively available, easy to obtain, and acceptable to those who want to use them for personnel decisions.

Fairness   The last element in my list of criteria for the criteria is *fairness*—in other words, the extent to which the employees perceive the criteria to be just and reasonable. Whereas relevance (along with the interplay of deficiency and contamination), reliability, and sensitivity are rather technical concepts, fairness and practicality have more to do with the human element involved in the use of criteria. Here, the issue is whether the employees who are being evaluated along certain criterion dimensions think that they are getting a fair shake. A criterion that is viewed by the employees as unfair, inappropriate, or unreasonable will not be well received by these employees. This point, of course, has widespread implications for organizational functioning and interpersonal dynamics. For instance, it has been found that employees' perceptions of justice are linked to important organizational criteria such as turnover intentions and customer satisfaction ratings (Simons & Roberson, 2003).

■ The Criterion Problem

You might remember from your introductory psychology class that human behavior is determined by multiple causes, such that it is impossible to point to a particular behavior and demonstrate beyond a shadow of a doubt that the behavior was determined by any one particular cause. Similarly, it is impossible to point to any one performance criterion and argue that it is the perfect measure of performance; performance is simply more complicated than that. In other words, performance (the criterion in which organizations, employees, managers, and I/O psychologists are most often interested) usually includes more than one dimension; some performance criteria are suitable for one type of organizational decision, while other criteria are suitable for a different type of organizational decision. Thus, no one performance criterion fits the bill for all organizational purposes. Given these difficulties, the measurement of performance criteria can be quite complicated. We do not have performance criteria entirely figured out any more than we have human behavior entirely figured out, but, just as we can often predict, understand, and explain human behavior, we can develop, use, and understand criteria in the world of work. However, I will use this opportunity related to our discussion of criteria to present two of the most important elements of the criterion problem.

Multiple Versus Composite Criteria

Most I/O psychologists believe that performance is multifaceted—in other words, that it is made up of more than one dimension. Look back at the list of criteria I presented for the job of administrative assistant; it should be clear that there are many related, as well as potentially unrelated, dimensions of performance for this job. Belief in a multiple-factor model (Campbell, Gasser, & Oswald, 1996)—the view that job performance is composed of multiple criteria—has been common among I/O psychologists for years. However, many experts in the area have noted that studies of criteria-related issues and, especially, examinations of multiple-factor models have been minimal at best (Austin & Villanova, 1992; Campbell, 1990; Campbell, McCloy, Oppler, & Sager, 1993).

Campbell, one of the leaders in this area, has developed an eight-factor model that he suggests should account for performance variance in every job listed in the *Dictionary of Occupational Titles,* or DOT (Campbell, 1990), and now the O★NET. He asserts that although not every dimension will be relevant for every job, every job can be described adequately in terms of a subset of these eight dimensions. (These are listed in Table 4.2, along with definitions and examples.) In addition, he maintains that three of these dimensions—job-specific task proficiency, demonstrating effort, and maintaining personal discipline—are necessary components of every job. There appears to be some empirical support for the dimensions he suggests (Campbell, McHenry, & Wise, 1990). Of course, more research is needed in this area (DeNisi & Pritchard, 2006).

Returning to our administrative assistant example, let's assume that the job has five criteria that are reflective of performance and that each is important and relatively unrelated to the others. Now, when it comes time to hire, promote, fire, lay off, or increase salaries, which criteria will be used to make these decisions? You see, things would be much easier if performance were one-dimensional, because then we could make all these decisions based on the one criterion without any confusion. For instance, if punctuality were the only dimension of performance that mattered, we could easily make hiring and firing decisions based on that one performance dimension. However, because performance is multidimensional, we have to make some tough decisions about which criteria to use or how to combine them for the purposes of HR decisions. This is a part of the criterion problem: Performance is best represented by multiple criteria, but organizations need to make decisions based on one score, number, or combination of these multiple criteria.

There are at least two alternatives for dealing with this criterion issue. Both focus on creating a **composite criterion**, which is a weighted combination of the multiple criteria, resulting in one index of performance. First, if the five criteria are scored on the same scale, they can be combined using equal weighting. Here, they are simply added up to compute one number that represents the performance of each individual. For instance, if each employee is rated on each dimension along a 1–5 point scale, we

composite criterion
A weighted combination of multiple criteria that results in a single index of performance.

Table 4.2 Campbell's Taxonomy of Performance

Performance Factor	Definition	Example
Job-specific task proficiency	Degree to which individual can perform core tasks central to a particular job	An administrative assistant who does word processing
Non-job-specific task proficiency	Degree to which individual can perform tasks that are not specific to a particular job	A plumber who handles phone inquiries and sets up appointments to provide estimates for work
Written and oral communication tasks	Proficiency with which one can write and speak	A military officer who gives a formal talk to recruits
Demonstrating effort	Consistency and persistence in an individual's work effort	A college professor who goes into the office to continue working on her book even though the university is closed due to a winter storm
Maintaining personal discipline	Avoidance of negative behaviors such as alcohol abuse, substance abuse, and rule infractions	An off-duty nurse who avoids excessive alcohol in the event that he is needed in an emergency
Facilitating peer and team performance	Helping and supporting peers with job problems	A journalist who helps a coworker writing a story meet the deadline
Supervision	All the behaviors associated with managing or supervising other employees	A retail store manager who models appropriate behavior, provides fair and timely feedback, and is available to handle the questions of her subordinates
Management/ administration	All the behaviors associated with management that are independent of supervision	A plant manager who gets additional resources, sets department goals and objectives, and controls expenditures

Source: Campbell (1990)

could simply add these up and promote the person based on the highest computed score. But on what grounds do we base this decision? Does it seem appropriate to take these five dimensions, which are largely unrelated, and just add them up and call it performance? Doing so would seem to take us back to the problem that Campbell pointed out—we often mistakenly assume that performance is a single construct (Campbell et al., 1993) when, in fact, it is not.

A second alternative composite criterion can also be created through unequal weighting, whereby some procedure is employed to weight the criteria differentially. For instance, it might make sense to employ only those criterion dimensions that seem especially

Table 4.3 Combining Criterion Dimensions for the Job of Administrative Assistant

Criterion Weights for Promotion to Supervisor	Criterion Dimension	Criterion Weights for Termination Decision
.00	Punctuality	.30
.20	Performance quality	.40
.20	Interpersonal behaviors	.00
.30	Leadership behaviors	.00
.15	Computer performance	.20
.15	Organizational performance	.10

relevant for the particular HR decision that needs to be made and to weight them according to their importance so that the overall weights sum to 1 (see Table 4.3). Note that the way in which the information is weighted is a value judgment made by the organization and that this decision should be based on the organization's goals and on research conducted by the organization (Campbell et al., 1990). Furthermore, the weighting scheme may vary across HR decisions, such that different weights may be employed for making a promotion decision than for making a termination decision about employees.

An example is provided in Table 4.3, which demonstrates how different dimensions might be used depending on the HR decision in question. In this example, the decision to terminate a particular employee would be based largely on such dimensions as punctuality and performance quality, somewhat on computer performance and organizational performance, and not at all on interpersonal behaviors and leadership behaviors. On the other hand, leadership behaviors and interpersonal behaviors would be much more important for deciding to promote this person into a supervisory position, whereas punctuality would be much less important.

Still, unequal weighting does not remove the concern that we have now created an index that is somewhat illogical. Let's say that we combine one's score on organizational performance with one's score on productivity. What is this index? What should we call it? What is the construct that it really measures? Finally, haven't we lost the very thing that we wanted to capture with our measures, the multidimensionality of performance? You can see that combining multiple criterion dimensions is a tricky business.

Given these complexities and concerns, you might think it best to keep the criteria separate; but, of course, this causes problems for making HR decisions because you need to make that one hire/don't hire, retain/fire, promote/don't promote decision based on some number or score. A classic article suggests that the issue becomes one of *purpose* (Schmidt & Kaplan, 1971). Its authors argue that if psychological understanding is the primary goal, then multiple criteria should be examined in light of predictor variables without combining them into a composite. On the other hand, if the primary goal is decision making with an economic focus, the I/O psychologist should combine the criteria into one

COURTESY DEIRDRE J. KNAPP

Deirdre J. Knapp
PhD, 1984, Bowling Green State University
Vice President, Assessment, Training, and Policy Studies Division
Human Resources Research Organization (HumRRO)

Early in my career, I was very lucky to play an important role in seminal research on the criterion domain. This work involved dozens of industrial/organizational psychologists across four organizations and included many of the most renowned academics and practitioners in this field (see discussion of Campbell's work earlier in this chapter).

The project was exciting because a wide array of carefully developed criterion measures were administered across the globe to thousands of soldiers in a variety of army occupations (I was in charge of that part of the project!). The measures included written job knowledge tests; hands-on tests of critical job tasks; peer and supervisor ratings of team, technical, and leadership skills; and ratings of behaviors related to indiscipline and getting along with others. Performance indicators were also retrieved from soldiers' military records. This was a historic opportunity to learn about what it means to "perform."

Considerable effort was made to use the data collected in this project to "model" performance. That is, considering all the scores from all the criterion measures, what performance factors surfaced? The answer has since been corroborated in research on civilian occupations. Six performance factors are relevant to most entry-level jobs:

- Job-specific task proficiency
- Non-job-specific task proficiency
- Written and oral communication
- Demonstrating effort
- Maintaining personal discipline
- Facilitating peer and team performance

Supervisory/leadership and management/administration factors emerge at higher-level jobs.

Most organizations are not able to include all the measures used by the army in this project, nor is it always necessary to examine all possible performance outcomes. Organizations conducting validation studies should first think about what performance factors they want to predict, pick selection tests that would be expected to predict those performance factors, and develop one or more criterion measures that assess the performance factors of interest.

I worked on this project first as an employee of the U.S. Army Research Institute for the Behavioral and Social Sciences and then as an employee at HumRRO (it was a 10-year project). I have continued to use the lessons I learned in much of my work. For example, I've worked with quite a few clients who certify or license professionals in various occupations (e.g., veterinary surgeons, law office managers, physical therapists) and who need valid and fair assessments of job skills. I've also continued to work with the U.S. Army to develop, validate, and implement improved selection procedures.

Applying Your Knowledge

1. How does the army research project outlined here relate to the criterion problem discussed earlier in this chapter?

2. What is the benefit to researchers and practitioners of having this taxonomy of performance?

3. What attempts were made to ensure that the six criteria that emerged from this study were both valid and reliable?

measure and use that as an index of economic success. However, the authors also point out that most applied psychologists should use their weighted composite to make hire/don't hire decisions while at the same time using the multiple dimensions to examine how they relate to various predictors, thereby enhancing the psychological understanding of the performance process and adhering to the scientist/practitioner's ideal—whereby both psychological understanding and applied decision making are important.

Dynamic Criteria

The issue of **dynamic criteria**, measures reflecting performance levels that change over time, has been the focus of much debate in I/O psychology (Austin & Villanova, 1992; Steele-Johnson, Osburn, & Pieper, 2000). This notion may seem unimportant, but let's consider a situation in which an employee performs well for the first 9 months on the job but by the end of 18 months is performing at unacceptable levels. The problem becomes clearer if we consider a selection context in which measures are developed to predict an individual's performance on the job. The measure—say, a measure of intelligence—might predict performance early on in the employee's career (in fact, we believe that it will, which is why we hired the employee based on an intelligence test to begin with), but not over the long haul. In other words, the validity with which our measure predicts job performance deteriorates over time. This, of course, is a big problem for those trying to staff an organization with people who are most likely to be successful on the job. We will address the selection process in greater detail in Chapters 6 and 7, but, for now, just note that the concept of dynamic criteria raises some important issues.

Some I/O psychologists argued that criteria were not really dynamic at all (Barrett, Caldwell, & Alexander, 1985), but this argument was largely refuted by some more recent empirical work (Deadrick, Bennett, & Russell, 1997; Deadrick & Madigan, 1990; Hofmann, Jacobs, & Baratta, 1993) demonstrating that the relative performance of individuals changes over time. In short, the best worker for the first 6 months on the job is sometimes not among the best workers for the next 6 months on the job.

One study demonstrated that National Hockey League players who had become captains of their team (and thus had a new leadership position) also demonstrated significantly better productivity as operationalized by an index of points based on goals and assists (Day, Sin, & Chen, 2004). In other words, performance levels of players (relative levels) changed and appeared to change as a function of new leadership responsibilities. This study was among the first to try to explain dynamic criteria from a motivational/leadership perspective. A more recent study of an entire cohort of European medical students found an interesting relationship between personality variables and GPA scores (Lievens, Ones, & Dilchert, 2009). The results suggested that personality predicts success later in the curriculum much better than it predicts success in classes taken earlier in the curriculum (which tend to be on a more basic level).

The studies cited above certainly suggest that part of "the criterion problem" is reflected in performance changes over time. Predicting performance is all the more difficult when the performance criterion changes. Keep this point in mind when we discuss the various predictors used in the selection of employees in Chapter 6.

■ Distinctions Among Performance Criteria

Among the many different criteria relevant for various jobs are two traditional types of criteria, which I discuss next. After that, I discuss a third criterion type that has received a great deal of attention from I/O psychologists and organizations in the last 15 years—namely, contextual performance.

Table 4.4 Examples of Objective Criteria and Measurement

Criteria	Measurement Examples
Absence	Number of days absent per year; number of incidents of absence per year
Lateness	Number of minutes late per month; number of incidents of lateness per month
Turnover	Percentage of employees who leave the organization over a 12-month period
Accidents	Number of accidents per year; number of workers' compensation claims per year
Grievances	Number of grievances filed per year; number of grievance cases lost per year
Productivity	Number of products produced per day; sales volume in dollars per month
Counterproductive behaviors	Dollars lost in theft per year; number of unlikely events (e.g., arson) per year without a reasonable explanation

Objective Criteria

Objective criteria are taken from organizational records; often based on counting, they are not supposed to involve any subjective judgments or evaluations. They have traditionally been viewed as the "cleanest" criterion measures because they tend not to necessitate making a judgment call about an employee's performance. Objective criteria are also sometimes called *hard* or *nonjudgmental criteria,* reflecting the belief that they are somehow more solid and believable than other types. Table 4.4 presents some examples of often-used objective criteria.

objective criteria Performance measures that are based on counting rather than on subjective judgments or evaluations; sometimes called *hard* or *nonjudgmental criteria.*

Some types of objective criteria are relevant for many different jobs. (These will be discussed in more detail in Chapter 11 when we examine common outcomes of job-related attitudes.) For instance, *absenteeism rate* is often deemed an important criterion by organizations. Related criteria include *turnover rates* and *lateness rates,* which are also used by organizations to evaluate employees and organizational efficiency. Turnover is interesting because, although it generally costs organizations a great deal of money, it can be beneficial to the extent that it involves the replacement of low performers with potentially better performers. Probably the most typical objective criterion is *productivity,* which is usually measured in terms of the number of acceptable products produced in a given time period. This criterion is commonly used in manufacturing plants and assembly lines, where individuals or groups of employees can be evaluated according to how many cars are produced, how many computers are assembled, and so on.

Nonmanagerial jobs lend themselves to objective criteria, but managerial and other higher-level jobs do not. One reason is that most managerial jobs are not based solely on a 40-hour workweek during which the manager punches a time clock; another is that these jobs are not directly linked to a particular item that was produced. Nor are objective criteria appropriate for evaluating college professors, physicians, real estate agents, attorneys, and restaurant managers—with perhaps two exceptions: grievances and counterproductive behavior. The number of *grievances* is a measure of the number of times others have filed complaints about a particular manager. *Counterproductive behavior* is a term that refers to actions, such as theft and sabotage, that reflect the intent to harm the organization in some way.

You may have noted that when I defined objective criteria, I said that these criteria are "not supposed" to require any judgment by others. Indeed, we describe these criteria as objective, and for the most part they are, but they're not completely objective. For instance, a manager can record an employee's absence as being excused, he can record it as being unexcused, or he can fail to record it at all.

On average, objective criteria tend to involve less judgment than do subjective criteria (which we will turn to next). But we need to realize that subjectivity can come into play in virtually all measures of performance. Furthermore, objective criteria can be limited by unexpected factors or situational constraints. For instance, a production employee may not produce at her usual level because her machine has been malfunctioning frequently, thus slowing down her production. The objective criterion would not likely take this into account, but a supervisor could consider it in rating her performance. Performance ratings are typically considered subjective measures of performance, but the subjectivity in this instance is probably a good thing.

Subjective Criteria

subjective criteria Performance measures that are based on the judgments or evaluations of others rather than on objective measures such as counting; sometimes called *soft* or *judgmental criteria.*

Subjective criteria are performance measures that are based on the judgments or evaluations of others rather than on counting. Most published studies on criteria deal with subjective criteria, also called *soft* or *judgmental criteria.* Typical subjective criteria include ratings or rankings of employees by other employees, such as supervisors, coworkers, and subordinates. Of course, these kinds of measures are much more likely to be affected by the biases, attitudes, and beliefs of the raters than are the more objective criteria. On the other hand, they can be an excellent alternative to objective criteria for jobs in which objective criteria don't exist or are insufficient (as in the evaluations of managers). A recent meta-analysis examined the role played by the type of criterion (subjective versus objective) in affecting the relationship between information sharing among team members and team performance (Mesmer-Magnus & DeChurch, 2009). The researchers found a stronger relationship between information sharing and performance when performance was a behavioral measure, such as how much effort was

TECHNICAL TIP

When we talked about correlations in Chapter 2, we said the correlation coefficient was an index of magnitude or strength of relationship. In this example, you can see that magnitude differences can be driven by various factors, such as elements of measurement.

put forth; they argue that this is because the behaviors were more under the control of the team members than were results measures, such as sales or profit. As this study suggests, research results can vary as a function of the type of criterion used. As you will see in the next chapter, we tend to rely largely on subjective criteria, although we may work very hard to make them as objective as possible.

Contextual Performance

Important work in the area of contextual performance has attempted to expand the criterion domain to include more than just the traditional objective and subjective criteria (Borman, 2004). **Task performance** encompasses the work-related activities performed by employees that contribute to the technical core of the organization (Borman & Motowidlo, 1997), while **contextual performance** encompasses the activities performed by employees that help to maintain the broader organizational, social, and psychological environment in which the technical core operates (Motowidlo, Borman, & Schmit, 1997). Slightly different renditions of the concept known as contextual performance are *organizational citizenship behaviors (OCBs)* and *prosocial organizational behaviors (POBs)* (Borman & Motowidlo, 1997).

Up to this point, we've focused largely on task performance. An administrative assistant is rated high on task performance if he types quickly and answers phones efficiently, but he is rated high on contextual performance (OCBs or POBs) if he demonstrates enthusiasm, helps his coworker with a problem that she may be having, and works hard to support his organization. Perhaps we can view the basic distinction as one between what is required in the way of on-the-job behaviors (task performance) and other behaviors that are specifically of value to one's workplace and coworkers (contextual performance). I think of contextual behaviors as reflective of employees who go that extra mile rather than putting forth only what is required or expected of them.

There are many different categorical schemes for the dimensions of contextual performance. One such scheme divides these multiple dimensions into five categories (Borman & Motowidlo, 1997). The first pertains to individuals who work with extra enthusiasm and effort to get their jobs done; the second, to those who volunteer to do things that aren't formally part of their jobs, sometimes taking on extra responsibility in the process; the third, to those who help others with their jobs (reflecting what some researchers call sportsmanship or organizational courtesy); the fourth, to those who meet deadlines and comply with all the organization's rules and regulations (reflecting civic virtue or conscientiousness); and the fifth, to those who support or defend the organization for which they work (as when they stay with the organization through hard times or "sell" the organization to others).

Researchers have done extensive work on contextual performance, differentiating it from task performance and arguing for its inclusion in the domain of performance criteria (Hoffman, Blair, Meriac, & Woehr, 2007). They suggest three major distinctions between task performance and contextual performance. First, task activities vary a great deal across jobs (think of the job descriptions for a plumber and for a musician), but contextual behaviors tend to be similar across jobs (a plumber can help a colleague just as much as a musician can). Second, compared with contextual activities, task activities

task performance The work-related activities performed by employees that contribute to the technical core of the organization.

contextual performance Activities performed by employees that help to maintain the broader organizational, social, and psychological environment in which the technical core operates.

are more likely to be formally instituted by the organization as items on a job description or performance appraisal form. Third, task activities have different antecedents. One important study, for example, demonstrated that cognitive ability was more strongly related to sales performance (task activities) than to OCBs such as volunteerism and, similarly, that a personality measure of conscientiousness was more strongly related to OCBs than to sales performance (Hattrup, O'Connell, & Wingate, 1998).

Researchers argue for the inclusion of contextual performance as part of the criterion space, suggesting that these criterion elements can be differentiated from task performance (Podsakoff, Whiting, Podsakoff, & Blume, 2009). Some scholars have begun to propose selection instruments that predict the likelihood of employees exhibiting OCBs (Allen, Facteau, & Facteau, 2004). Although this work is still in the early stages, it suggests the potential for making hiring decisions based in part on a prediction that certain individuals are more likely to exhibit OCBs than are others.

One framework proposes that OCBs result in favorable relationships among coworkers, which serve as "social capital," and that this capital then affects the organization's performance and effectiveness (Bolino, Turnley, & Bloodgood, 2002). Some scholars have begun to view OCBs as a group-level phenomenon. A recent study of work groups found that relationship conflict and task conflict among group members had negative effects on traditional group task performance; however, task conflict such as disagreements about how best to approach the task increased group-level OCBs and relationship conflict decreased group-level OCBs (Choi & Sy, 2010). However, a recent meta-analysis of 38 studies conducted in the last 10 years that focused on group-level OCBs and performance found a positive relationship between OCBs at the group level, such as group members' ratings of OCBs, and group performance, such as group sales performance or profit margin (Nielsen, Hrivnak, & Shaw, 2009). Furthermore, they reported that group-level OCBs improved social processes (e.g., coordination and communication) within teams.

You may recall from the historical review of I/O psychology in Chapter 1 that industrial psychology was developed within a measurement framework, resulting in a rather narrow conceptualization of performance as productivity—a measurable outcome. Many now argue, however, that an expansion of the criterion space is more consistent with the modern organization. This more expansive view of performance criteria is illustrated in Figure 4.2.

It has become clear with recent research that OCBs are relevant and

FIGURE 4.2 Expansion of the Criterion Domain

important across various cultures and international business contexts. For instance, researchers have developed a model of performance criteria for **expatriates**—employees who are temporarily working and residing in a foreign country. This model includes contextual performance dimensions such as initiative, teamwork, and interpersonal relations (Mol, Born, & van der Molen, 2005). In a Belgian sample, researchers demonstrated that traditional structures or forms of OCBs that have been identified in U.S. samples hold reliably well in this international context (Lievens & Anseel, 2004). However, a recent study of 269 Portuguese men and women working in 37 different companies found that justice-related antecedents of OCBs were perceived differently than is typically the case among North American workers (Rego & Cunha, 2010). Specifically, the authors found that interactional justice—particularly on the interpersonal dimension—was more important to the Portuguese employees than it tends to be in the United States. Furthermore, these interpersonal concerns were also more strongly related to OCBs and specific OCB dimensions like interpersonal harmony, personal initiative, and conscientiousness than were informational and distributive justice concerns. The authors argue that these results reflect the fact that Portugal's culture is less assertive, higher on power distance (i.e., it is accepted that power is not shared equally), and more collectivistic (i.e., a focus on the group and loyalty to the group) than that of the United States. As the work of I/O psychologists continues to become more global as a function of the increasing globalization of business and industry, we will likely see additional research with an international focus being conducted.

We have been talking about OCBs as purely positive behaviors; however, some researchers argue that OCBs can actually have negative effects on organizational functioning and the employees exhibiting those behaviors (Bolino & Turnley, 2005; Bolino, Turnley, & Nichoff, 2004). For instance, these researchers argue that employees focused on exhibiting OCBs may sometimes become overloaded and tend to report extreme role responsibilities, job stress, and work–family conflict. In a very interesting study, researchers showed that both a lack of helping behaviors and an excess of helping behaviors have a detrimental effect on team performance when the tasks are independent (Bachrach, Powell, Collins, & Richey, 2006). This study indicates that helping behavior can get in the way of team performance in certain circumstances.

Counterproductive work behaviors (CWBs) are considered to fall within contextual performance and include those behaviors that somehow harm or detract from the organization, such as theft, sabotage, abuse of others, and withdrawal behaviors (Spector et al., 2006). That OCBs and CWBs are only moderately negatively correlated and seemingly related to different antecedents suggests that these two constructs are quite different from each other, not just the opposite ends of the same construct (Spector, Bauer, & Fox, 2010; Spector & Fox, 2010). In fact, a couple of studies have suggested that CWBs are more strongly related to organizational and individual performance than are OCBs (Dunlop & Lee, 2004; Rotundo & Sackett, 2002). Not only have researchers reported that not all CWBs stem from the same precursors (Spector et al., 2006), but they have also found that sometimes the same people may exhibit both OCBs and CWBs (Spector et al., 2010). The importance of CWBs has been highlighted by research that has shown

expatriates
An employee who is temporarily working and residing in a foreign country.

counterproductive work behaviors (CWBs)
Any behaviors that bring, or are intended to bring, harm to an organization, its employees, or its stakeholders.

PAUL BARTON/CORBIS

▲ **A Closer Look**
This person is
helping her col-
league even
though such
activity does not
fall under her job
responsibilities.
Does this action
fall under task
performance or
contextual per-
formance? How
does it relate to
"social capital"?

these behaviors to have strong negative effects
on business unit performance and productivity
(Dunlop & Lee, 2004).

In expanding the criterion to include contextual
performance, we should examine how various predictors are related to the various criterion dimensions. Borman and his colleagues' performance
model includes two different performance dimensions (task performance and contextual performance) along with two categories of determinants
or predictors of these two performance dimensions
(cognitive ability variables and personality variables).
They report some empirical support for their
notion that personality variables are better predictors of contextual performance and that
cognitive ability variables are better predictors of task performance (Motowidlo et al., 1997).
Indeed, without looking at *both* dimensions of performance, we would likely have a serious
criterion deficiency problem and fail to understand how various predictors map onto the
different criteria.

■ Summary

Traditionally, I/O psychologists have emphasized predictors at the expense of criteria.
But this is less the case now that more and more scientists and practitioners have recognized the great importance of developing valid criteria and understanding their role
in organizations. Consistent with this observation is the fact that all the HR functions
to be discussed in the remainder of the text depend completely on adequate criteria.

In this chapter, the criterion problem was discussed at length and identified as a
potential stumbling block to advancing research in I/O psychology. The measurement
of performance criteria is as complex as it is important, which is why we speak of
the criterion problem. Nevertheless, we are making progress in the process of presenting generally accepted definitions of criteria, examples of criteria, and evaluative
standards for criteria, such as relevance, reliability, sensitivity, practicality, and fairness.
The ultimate criterion and the actual criterion were defined and discussed, and the
traditional view of criteria was explained in detail; also discussed were more recent
concerns about the impression that this view can give about the nature of criteria. An
actual criterion that does not cover a representative sample of the ultimate criterion
was described as deficient, and one that measures things other than what is in the
ultimate criterion was described as contaminated.

In discussing the criterion problem, I highlighted two major issues that contribute
to that problem. First, I considered the debate regarding multiple criteria versus a
composite criterion and suggested that even though, from an applied perspective, a
decision needs to be made based on some score or number, the variety of information
that comes from using multiple criteria must not be ignored. Performance is surely

multidimensional, and multiple criteria are needed to measure it well. Campbell's work in the area of performance modeling and approaches to criteria was highlighted as providing a model for how to proceed in this arena (Campbell, 1990; Campbell et al., 1993). Second, I presented the common belief that criteria are dynamic. This belief is reflected in the relative changes in an individual's performance over time; issues of measurement and prediction were also considered in this context.

Finally, I examined the differences between objective and subjective criteria while considering various examples of each (e.g., measures of productivity, absenteeism, and lateness), as well as supervisor ratings of employees' performance. (The latter are discussed in the next chapter.) In addition, I presented a newer component of performance criteria called contextual performance and considered a great deal of recent research in this area identifying the various antecedents of contextual performance and considering this new line of work within an international context. Lastly, counterproductive work behaviors were also discussed as behaviors that have a negative impact on the organization and other employees.

■ Key Terms

actual criterion (p. 95)
composite criterion (p. 100)
contextual performance (p. 107)
counterproductive work behaviors
   (CWBs) (p. 109)
criteria (p. 93)
criterion contamination (p. 97)
criterion deficiency (p. 97)

dynamic criteria (p. 104)
expatriates (p. 109)
objective criteria (p. 105)
performance (p. 93)
subjective criteria (p. 106)
task performance (p. 107)
ultimate criterion (p. 94)

■ TAKING IT TO THE FIELD

Measuring performance is a particularly challenging issue in I/O psychology. It can be especially challenging for jobs where it is difficult to determine exactly what should be measured and whether a measured criterion truly assesses performance. Even seasoned I/O psychologists wrestle with this issue from time to time.

Below is an e-mail from a client presenting you with some challenges related to defining and measuring criteria. Stacia Mattson, who works in the HR department at Collini's Gardening Service, is having some problems. Read the e-mail, and provide critiques and suggestions for Stacia.

Greetings—
   Thank you for agreeing to advise me on some tricky issues we've been having at Collini's Gardening Service. We have about 30 gardeners working throughout several regions in Georgia. Currently, we are trying to devise a way to evaluate our gardeners so that we can give our top performers year-end bonuses. Right now, we are considering using the following measures of performance:

> - Number of plants that die under the gardener's care for the year
> - Number of houses the gardener visits per week
> - Satisfaction ratings from the gardener's customers
>
> Could you please critique these measures? In addition, do you have three more suggestions for how we might assess gardener performance that I can bring to my committee as potential options?
>
> Regards,
> Stacia

■ Critical Thinking Questions

1. Overall criteria are standards used to assess performance. In addition to grades, what are some criteria that could be used to assess the performance of college students? What does *performance* mean for a college student?

2. We know from the text that the ultimate criterion is theoretical, whereas the actual criterion is our best attempt at capturing the ultimate criterion. What are some implications of having *little* overlap (relevance) between an ultimate criterion and an actual criterion? What would this mean for an organization that is trying to assess the performance of its employees?

3. I/O psychologists are split on the dynamic nature of criteria: Some believe that criteria *are* dynamic, while others disagree. What exactly are dynamic criteria? How could this notion of dynamic criteria be applied to assessing the performance of college students?

4. The evaluation of subjective—as opposed to objective—criteria includes some degree of human judgment. As a result, the evaluation of subjective criteria can be prone to the evaluator's own attitudes and biases. What are some examples of subjective criteria? How might an evaluator's attitudes influence his or her assessment of an employee's performance?

■ Application Questions

1. Consider some of the ways your performance as a student is evaluated (e.g., exams, papers, projects). What might be some examples of criterion deficiency (i.e., what are some aspects of student performance that are not well assessed using these types of measures)? What might be some examples of criterion contamination (i.e., what are some aspects students might be judged on that are not relevant to student performance)?

2. In the United States, there is a great deal of debate about how to distinguish good teachers from poor teachers in public schools. Some people advocate using student scores on standardized tests to determine which teachers are doing well. Other people advocate using student ratings of teachers. What are some pros and cons of each approach?

3. What are some examples of contextual performance that you might have engaged in at your job or in your classes? When were you most likely to perform those behaviors?

4. Imagine that you have a subordinate who has shared something negative about one of his clients using social media (e.g., on Twitter or Facebook). Do you believe this behavior is a part of performance that should be considered during his performance review? Why or why not?

■ Suggested Readings

Austin, J. T., & Villanova, P. D. (1992). The criterion problem: 1917–1992. *Journal of Applied Psychology, 77*, 836–874. This is the most thorough published review on the historical use of criteria in organizations. The article contains a great deal of valuable information, but it isn't an easy read.

Campbell, J. P. (1990). Modeling the performance prediction problem in industrial and organizational psychology. In M. D. Dunnette & L. M. Hough (Eds.), *Handbook of industrial and organizational psychology* (2nd ed., Vol. 1, pp. 687–732). Palo Alto, CA: Consulting Psychologists Press. This presentation of Campbell's work on modeling performance provides a good overview of his theoretical ideas, along with some empirical findings.

LePine, J. A., Erez, A., & Johnson, D. E. (2002). The nature and dimensionality of organizational citizenship behavior: A critical review and meta-analysis. *Journal of Applied Psychology, 87*(1), 52–65. This article provides a good overview of contextual performance and different ways in which that type of performance has been conceptualized and assessed over the years.

Lievens, F., Buyse, T., & Sackett, P. R. (2005). The operational validity of a video-based situational judgment test for medical college admissions: Illustrating the importance of matching predictor and criterion construct domains. *Journal of Applied Psychology, 90*(3), 442–452. As part of a trend to incorporate other criteria into the admissions process for medical schools, this study examines the use of noncognitive criteria, such as interpersonal skills.

Penney, L. M. & Spector, P. E. (2008). Emotions and counterproductive work behavior. In N. M. Ashkanasy & C. L. Cooper (Eds.), *Research companion to emotions in organizations* (pp. 183–196). Northhampton, MA: Edward Elgar Publishing. This chapter provides an outstanding overview of counterproductive work behavior and especially focuses on the antecedents leading to counterproductive behaviors. There are many engaging chapters in this book on other topics as well.

Podsakoff, N. P, Whiting, S. W., Podsakoff, P. M., & Blume, B. D. (2009). Individual- and organizational-level consequences of organizational citizenship behaviors: A meta-analysis. *Journal of Applied Psychology, 94*(1), 122–141. This recent quantitative summary of the research related to organizational citizenship behaviors is written by some of the leaders in the field.

Rotundo, M., & Sackett, P. R. (2002). The relative importance of task, citizenship, and counterproductive performance to global ratings of job performance: A policy-capturing approach. *Journal of Applied Psychology, 87*(1), 66–80. This well-done empirical piece shows how these various performance measures can be combined to make overall ratings for personnel decisions.

Schmidt, F. L., & Kaplan, L. B. (1971). Composite v. multiple criteria: A review and resolution of the controversy. *Personnel Psychology, 24,* 419–434. This article provides a detailed and critical examination of the debate about using composite versus multiple criteria for measuring success.

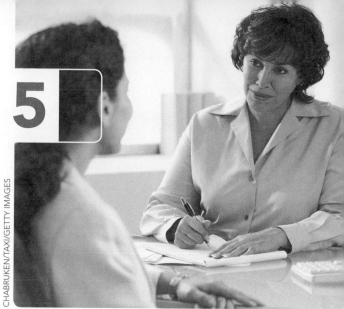

CHABRUKEN/TAXI/GETTY IMAGES

CHAPTER **5**

Performance Appraisal

The process of evaluating employees' performance—performance appraisal—is the focus of this chapter. Having our performance appraised is something we've all experienced at one time or another. Of course, we may not have fond memories of our fathers telling us that we didn't weed the vegetable garden well enough or of our Psychology 100 professor telling us that our test scores so far gave us only a C in the course. The types of performance appraisal just described are examples of negative appraisals. But sometimes we did a nice job mowing the lawn or writing a term paper—instances in which we probably received positive appraisals.

There are many domains in which we are held accountable for our performance, but in this chapter we will talk specifically about the role of performance appraisal in organizational life—in which it plays a very important role indeed. In this domain, **performance appraisal** is defined as the systematic review and evaluation of job performance, as well as the provision of performance feedback. However, as you'll soon see, performance appraisal is a lot more interesting than that definition makes it sound.

performance appraisal
Systematic review and evaluation of job performance.

■ Uses of Performance Appraisal

Performance appraisal is one of the most important processes conducted in organizations. It has many purposes, of which the three most significant are discussed here. First, performance appraisals are used to make important *personnel decisions,* such as who gets promoted, fired, demoted, or laid off; who gets a large raise, a small raise, or no raise at all; and so on. In efficient organizations, these decisions are not made haphazardly; they are made on the basis of performance appraisal data.

Second, performance appraisals are used for *developmental purposes.* Employees are informed of their performance strengths and weaknesses so that they can be proud of what they are doing well and can focus their efforts on the areas that need some work. On the whole, organizations benefit when employees perform better, and performance appraisal data are used to help employees become better performers. In addition, organizations are interested in seeing their employees advance within the company to other important jobs—an outcome that performance appraisal can facilitate. For example, an employee may be told that she needs to improve her interpersonal skills so that she will be eligible when the next promotion becomes available.

A third purpose of performance appraisal is what I'll call *documentation* of organizational decisions—a purpose that has recently evolved out of personnel decisions and the growing area of personnel law. Now that companies are very aware of the possibility of being sued over personnel business decisions, managers are increasingly using performance appraisals to document employees' performance patterns over time. In cases in which employees are fired for inadequate performance, the organization—if it has kept careful track—can point to detailed accounts of the employees' inferior performance, making it difficult for them to claim that they were fired without just cause. (We will discuss legal issues in performance appraisal later in this chapter.)

On the other hand, performance appraisals that are not carefully developed and implemented can have negative repercussions for both the

"It's one of the advantages of having your own business."

▲ **A Closer Look** Performance can be measured in many different ways. How has your performance been measured or recognized in any jobs that you've had, and what made that process useful for you?

organization and its employees. For instance, a poorly conceived appraisal system could get the wrong person promoted, transferred, or fired. It could cause feelings of inequity on the part of good employees who erroneously receive smaller raises than bad employees. It could lead to legal suits in which the company has a very weak defense for why a particular individual was not promoted. Also, it could result in disgruntled employees who decrease their effort, ignore the feedback, or look for other jobs. Even customers are poorly served when an ineffective appraisal system causes employees to operate at less than their peak level of efficiency. Indeed, an ineffective performance appraisal system has widespread implications for everyone involved with the organization, which is why performance appraisal has received so much research attention (for reviews, see Levy & Williams, 2004; Murphy & Cleveland, 1995). A good performance appraisal system is well received by ratees, is based on carefully documented behaviors, is focused on important performance criteria, is inclusive of many perspectives, and is forward looking with a focus on improvement.

■ The Role of I/O Psychology in Performance Appraisal

I/O psychologists play a significant role in the area of performance appraisal. They are often hired to help develop and implement performance appraisal systems. I/O psychologists have measurement expertise, as well as a background in both human resources and organizational psychology—areas of knowledge that are integral to successful performance appraisals. Many companies have I/O psychologists in their HR departments who are responsible for what is known as **performance management**, a motivational system of individual performance improvement (DeNisi & Pritchard, 2006). This system typically includes (1) objective goal setting, (2) continuous **coaching** and feedback, (3) performance appraisal, and (4) developmental planning. The key points here are twofold: These four components are linked to the company's goals and objectives, and the system is implemented on a continuous cycle rather than just once per year. Some research has proposed that when an organization is profitable, it is typically more willing to reinvest in human resource practices like performance management, which then impacts employees, supervisors, and the organization itself (den Hartog, Boselie, & Paauwe, 2004). Remember (see Figure 3.1) that performance appraisal stems directly from the job analysis. Performance criteria are identified by the job analysis and used as the central element of the performance appraisal system. Without a careful job analysis, we would likely end up with unimportant or job-irrelevant criteria and appraising performance on the wrong criterion dimensions.

Researchers who specialize in performance appraisal pursue research questions like the following: (1) What is the best format or rating scale for performance appraisals? (2) To what extent do rater errors and biases affect the appraisal process? (3) How should raters be trained so that they can avoid these errors and biases? (4) What major contextual variables affect the appraisal process? (5) How important is the organizational context or culture in the appraisal process? (6) What factors affect how ratees and raters react to performance appraisal? In addition to addressing such questions, I/O psychology, as an empirically based applied discipline, attempts to use basic psychological principles to help organizations develop and implement motivating, fair, accurate, and user-friendly appraisal systems.

Sources of Performance Ratings

Performance feedback can be generated and delivered by various sources. Traditionally, supervisors were charged with conducting the performance appraisal and delivering the performance feedback. This top-down approach continues to be very popular, and it is quite common for an organization to include this type of appraisal as part of the performance management process. However, there are other, more contemporary approaches for the use of feedback sources, with multisource feedback being the most prevalent.

performance management
A system of individual performance improvement that typically includes (1) objective goal setting, (2) continuous coaching and feedback, (3) performance appraisal, and (4) development planning.

coaching
One-on-one collaborative relationship in which an individual provides performance-related guidance to an employee.

Multisource Feedback This method, sometimes called **360-degree feedback** (Fletcher & Baldry, 1999), involves multiple raters at various levels of the organization who evaluate and provide feedback to a target employee. As presented in Figure 5.1, these multiple sources typically include subordinates, peers, supervisors, clients or customers, and even self-ratings.

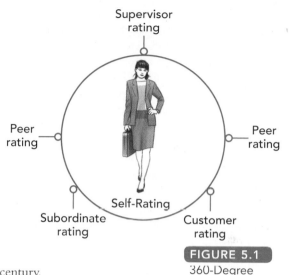

These systems are becoming increasingly important to the modern organization in terms of performance assessment and management (Hoffman, Lance, Bynum, & Gentry, 2010). Many companies—such as Home Depot, Procter & Gamble, General Electric, Intel, and Boeing, among others—are using them for a variety of purposes that are consistent with both greater employee expectations and the more sophisticated organizations of the 21st century.

FIGURE 5.1
360-Degree Feedback

Three basic assumptions are held by advocates of 360-degree feedback systems. First, when multiple raters are used, the participants are happier because they are involved in the process—and this calls to mind the importance of participation alluded to earlier. Second, and perhaps more important, when multiple raters from different levels of the organization rate the same target employee, the idiosyncrasies (and biases) of any single rater are overcome. For instance, if my supervisor doesn't like me and rates me severely for that reason, additional ratings from other individuals that aren't severe should overcome my supervisor's rating and highlight the possibility that there may be a problem with that rating. Third, multiple raters bring with them multiple perspectives on the target employee, allowing for a broader and more accurate view of performance. For instance, who is best able to evaluate my teaching performance? Certainly not my department chair, who *never* sees me in the classroom. Rather, the best judges are my students (some would call them "customers"; see Schneider, Hanges, Goldstein, & Braverman, 1994)—which is why many universities require student ratings of teaching performance in all classes. These are sometimes called **upward appraisal ratings** because they refer to ratings provided by individuals whose status is, in an organizational-hierarchy sense, below that of the ratee (Atwater, Daldman, Atwater, & Cartier, 2000).

Although 360-degree feedback has been used in organizations for a few decades, research efforts to understand it have only recently begun to catch up with practitioner usage. For instance, one study demonstrated that lack of agreement among raters regarding a particular ratee is sometimes not error but a result of the role played by the raters themselves (Salam, Cox, & Sims, 1997). Another study showed that contextual factors such as supervisory style and feedback environment were more important than personality variables in terms of their effect on attitudes about 360-degree feedback (Funderburg & Levy, 1997). A survey of employees found that upward appraisals produced more favorable outcomes and fewer negative ones than peer appraisals

360-degree feedback A method of performance appraisal in which multiple raters at various levels of the organization evaluate a target employee and the employee is provided with feedback from these multiple sources.

upward appraisal ratings Ratings provided by individuals whose status, in an organizational-hierarchy sense, is below that of the ratees.

(Bettenhausen & Fedor, 1997). To this point, the majority of empirical work on 360-degree feedback has focused on measurement properties of the ratings, such as the extent of agreement among rating sources (Levy & Williams, 2004). However, consistent with this chapter's theme of focusing on the social context of appraisal is a list of recommendations to follow for implementing 360-degree feedback: This list includes (1) being honest about how the ratings will be used, (2) helping employees interpret and deal with the ratings, and (3) avoiding the presentation of too much information (DeNisi & Kluger, 2000).

Goodyear employs a 360-degree feedback system that consists of four main tools: (1) a 360-Degree Development Questionnaire, which is administered to multiple rating sources and measures 13 skill dimensions, such as leadership and business acumen; (2) a 360-Degree Feedback Report, which provides the results of the ratings from the various sources, as well as some summary information about ratees' strengths and weaknesses; (3) a Development Workbook, which helps employees work with and understand the Feedback Report; and (4) a Development Guide, which provides suggested readings and activities to improve skills in the targeted areas.

What does the future hold for 360-degree feedback? The frequency with which it's used in organizations suggests that it will continue to play an important role. Recent research suggests that the following important issues will continue to attract attention: construct validity of ratings, determinants of multisource ratings, such as rating purpose, as well as liking, personality, and the effect of multisource ratings on employee attitudes and development.

New Challenges in Telework and eHR

Another recent trend in organizations is the increased frequency of **telework** (see Chapter 11), employees working from home or some other location, a practice that is growing rapidly (Golden, Barnes-Farrell, & Mascharka, 2009). This telecommuting results in altered forms of communication. Many employee–employee and employee–supervisor interactions don't take place face-to-face but via e-mails, phone calls, faxes, text messages, conference calls, and so on. This suggests that supervisors doing performance appraisal must rely on indirect sources of performance information instead of direct interactions and on-the-job observations. Recent research has demonstrated that when provided with both direct and indirect performance information, supervisors rely more on direct performance information (Golden et al., 2009). Supervisors' tendencies to downplay the indirect information that is frequent in telework suggest potential room for performance appraisal errors and ineffectiveness.

Some recent research sketches out a series of hypotheses related to electronic HR systems (Stone & Lukaszewski, 2009). These systems are simply the electronic tools used to access HR data, record HR data, and carry out HR functions like performance appraisal. Hypotheses that should be tested include the extent to which individuals will use face-to-face information more than information from an eHR system, whether individuals will be less favorably disposed to eHR systems, and whether these reactions to eHR systems will spill over into attitudes toward the organization and employees (Stone & Lukaszewski, 2009). Telework and eHR are

telework
Working arrangements in which employees enjoy flexibility in work hours and/or location.

FIGURE 5.2   Graphing Rating Scale for "Following Procedures"

1	2	3	4	5	6	7
Below Expectations			Meets Expectations			Exceeds Expectations

rapidly increasing and are expected to continue into the future, suggesting the need for additional research regarding performance appraisal in these contexts.

Rating Formats

When it comes time for an evaluator to appraise someone's performance, he or she typically uses some type of rating form. There are quite a few options here; in this section, we will discuss the ones most frequently employed.

Graphic Rating Scales
Graphic rating scales are among the oldest formats used in the evaluation of performance. These scales consist of a number of traits or behaviors (e.g., dependability), and the rater is asked to judge how much of each particular trait the ratee possesses or where on this dimension the ratee falls with respect to organizational expectations. Today, graphic rating scales usually include numerical/verbal anchors at various points along the scale, such as "1/below expectations," "4/meets expectations," and "7/exceeds expectations," and the score is whatever number is circled. Graphic rating scales are commonly used in organizations due, in part, to the ease with which they can be developed and used. Figure 5.2 provides an example of a graphic rating scale—in this case, one that appraises the extent to which employees are "following procedures."

Behaviorally Anchored Rating Scales
Behaviorally anchored rating scales, or BARS (Smith & Kendall, 1963), are similar to graphic rating scales except that they provide actual behavioral descriptions as anchors along the scale. An example of a 9-point BARS for a nuclear power plant operator's tendency to "follow procedures" is shown in Figure 5.3.

BARS are perhaps best known for the painstaking process involved in their development (see Smith & Kendall, 1963). This process can be summarized as taking place in five steps (Bernardin & Beatty, 1984). First, a group of participants—such as employees, supervisors, or subject matter experts (SMEs)—identifies and carefully defines several dimensions as important for the job ("follows procedures," "works in a timely manner," etc.). Second, another group of participants generates a series of behavioral examples of job performance (similar to the items in Figure 5.3) for each dimension. These behavioral examples are called **critical incidents**. Participants are encouraged to write critical incidents at high-, medium-, and low-effectiveness levels for each dimension. In Figure 5.3, for example, "Never deviates from the procedures outlined for a particular task and takes the time to do things according to the employee manual" represents high effectiveness, whereas "Takes shortcuts around established procedures at every opportunity" represents low effectiveness.

critical incidents
Examples of job performance used in behaviorally anchored rating scales or job-analytic approaches.

FIGURE 5.3   Behaviorally Anchored Rating Scale for "Following Procedures"

Third, yet another group of participants is asked to sort these critical incidents into the appropriate dimensions. During this *retranslation* stage, the goal is to make sure that the examples generated for each dimension are unambiguously associated with that dimension. Usually a criterion, such as 80%, is used to weed out items that are not clearly related to a particular dimension: If fewer than 80% of the participants place the critical incident in the correct dimension, the item is dropped. A fourth group of participants then rates each remaining behavioral example on its effectiveness for the associated dimension. This rating is usually done on a 5- or 7-point scale. Any item with a large standard deviation is eliminated because a large standard deviation indicates that some respondents think the item represents effective performance, whereas others think it represents ineffective performance—obviously, a problematic situation. Fifth, items that specifically represent performance levels on each dimension are chosen from the acceptable pool of items, and BARS are developed and administered.

This very deliberate and thorough development process is both the biggest strength and the biggest weakness of BARS. Usually such a detailed process involving at least four different groups of participants results in a useful and relevant scale. However, the costs in both time and money are too high for many organizations, so they often employ a simple graphic scale instead.

Checklists   Checklists are another popular format for performance appraisals. Here, raters are asked to read a large number of behavioral statements and to check off each

FIGURE 5.4 A Weighted Checklist

	Computer and Information Systems Manager	
Check Box (if applicable)	**Behavioral Descriptor**	**Scale Score**
☐	Effectively manages backup and computer help systems	+8.5
☐	Consults with users, vendors, and technicians on a regular basis	+6.7
☐	Stays abreast of technology advancements	+4.4
☐	Maintains 40 hours per week in the office	+1.5
☐	Doesn't anticipate likely problems	−1.2
☐	Pays little attention to financial details	−2.4
☐	Rarely provides leadership to his/her work group	−4.6
☐	Isn't able to implement necessary changes	−6.7
	TOTAL SCORE:	

behavior that the employee exhibits. One example from this category is the *weighted checklist,* which includes a series of items that have previously been weighted as to importance or effectiveness; specifically, some items are indicative of desirable behavior, whereas others are indicative of undesirable behavior. Figure 5.4 presents an example of a weighted checklist for the evaluation of a computer and information systems manager.

In a real-life situation, the scale shown in Figure 5.4 would be modified in two ways. First, the items would be scrambled so as not to be in numerical order; second, the scale score column would not be part of the form. To administer this type of scale, raters would simply check the items that apply; in our example, the sum of items checked would be the computer and information systems manager's performance appraisal score. Note that as more and more of the negative items are checked, the employee's summed rating gets lower and lower.

Forced-choice checklists are also used by organizations, though not as frequently as weighted checklists. Here, raters are asked to choose two items from a group of four that best describe the target employee. All four appear on the surface to be favorable, but the items have been developed and validated such that only *two* are actually good discriminators between effective and ineffective performers. The purpose of this approach is to reduce purposeful bias or distortion on the part of raters. In other words, because all the items appear favorable and the raters don't know which two are truly indicative of good performance, they cannot intentionally give someone high or low ratings.

One drawback to this approach is that some raters don't like it because they feel as though they've lost control over the rating process. How would you feel if you had to choose two statements that describe your poorly performing subordinate, but all four statements seem positive? An appraisal format has recently been developed that appears to reduce the bias sometimes associated with other approaches, but without the negative

TECHNICAL TIP

The formula N(N −1)/2 can be used to calculate the total number of comparisons. For example, whereas 3 employees would involve 3 comparisons, 10 employees would involve 45!

reactions on the part of the raters. Borman and his colleagues have developed the Computerized Adaptive Rating Scale (CARS), which, although in its infancy, seems to be more sound from a measurement perspective than are other approaches; it also provides more discriminability—that is, the scale does a better job of differentiating between effective and ineffective performers (Borman et al., 2001; Schneider, Goff, Anderson, & Borman, 2003).

Employee Comparison Procedures The final category of rating formats, *employee comparison procedures,* involves evaluation of ratees with respect to how they measure up to or compare with other employees. One example of this type of format is *rank-ordering,* whereby several employees are ranked from best to worst. Rank-ordering can be particularly useful for making promotion decisions and discriminating the very best employee from the rest. A second example, *paired comparisons,* involves the comparison of each employee with every other employee. If a manager has only three employees to evaluate, this isn't too difficult a task. (Think about doing this for each of your instructors this semester—comparing each to every one of the others.) However, as the number of ratees increases, so does the complexity of the task. Although this method is one way to arrive at a "clear winner" among employees, it obviously becomes very cumbersome as the number of employees grows.

A third example is called *forced distribution.* Here, raters are instructed to "force" a designated proportion of ratees into each of five to seven categories. A similar procedure is grading on the normal curve, whereby teachers assign grades based on meeting the normal curve percentages (i.e., 68% of the grades assigned are Cs, 13.5% are Bs, 13.5% are Ds, 2.5% are As, and 2.5% are Fs). Sometimes organizations require supervisors to use the same sort of procedure, resulting in the categorization of one-third of the subordinates as average, one-third as below average, and one-third as above average (see the *Time* article by Greenwald, 2001). This is often done because performance ratings are tied to raises and, with a limited pool of money for raises, the company wants to make sure that not too many employees are rated as eligible for a raise and to potentially remove inferior employees from the organization.

To appreciate how employees might feel about this approach, think about how you would feel if your psychology instructor told you that you were to be graded on a normal curve. In other words, if you had an average of 95 in the course but 3% of your classmates had an average of 96 or better, you would *not* receive an A because only 3% can get As. Needless to say, forced distribution is not a popular approach among ratees, whether students or employees, but it is currently being used by as many as 20% of Fortune 500 companies, such as General Electric, 3M, Texas Instruments, and Hewlett Packard (Meisler, 2003). However, some very public lawsuits over the use of these systems have created a controversy regarding the extent to which underrepresented groups tend to be disproportionately ranked in the low category. Companies such as Ford and Goodyear (both the targets of legal proceedings) have discontinued their use. You can continue to follow these issues in the popular press.

Contemporary Trends in Rating Formats Although there has been less research and less written about rating formats in recent years, there are a couple of interesting contemporary trends. First, while there are many rating formats and most are quantitative in nature (i.e., performance is rated in terms of numbers), most of these formats include narrative comments (e.g., your performance on this dimension is above average, but you need to enhance your administrative skills) in some way. It is only recently that researchers have begun examining these narrative comments. Some work has found that supervisors' and subordinates' comments are considerably clearer than the comments from peers (Gillespie, Rose, & Robinson, 2006). A recent conceptual paper proposes a framework for the use of narrative comments in the performance appraisal process (Brutus, 2010) and identifies important characteristics, such as the specificity or breadth of the comments as well as the processes that raters and ratees employ in the use of these narrative comments. This paper provides a framework that can be used to help structure a research program focused on gaining insight into the significance of these and other important characteristics of narrative comments.

Finally, additional outside-the-box thinking has resulted in the use of Feedforward Interviews (FFIs) for performance appraisal (Kluger & Nir, 2010). This idea is borrowed from appreciative inquiry (see Chapter 14), a part of the positive psychology movement. The FFI is proposed to replace the traditional performance appraisal interview and to facilitate positive change by focusing on employees' strengths, rather than weaknesses, and also to enhance the relationship between the rater and ratee. While promising, there is currently no empirical research on the effectiveness of the FFI, so further research is needed before I could recommend this approach.

An Evaluation of the Various Alternative Methods Since the 1950s, perhaps no area in performance appraisal has received more research attention than rating type or format. Even in recent years, research has looked at how personality and format may impact performance ratings (Yun, Donahue, Dudley, & McFarland, 2005) as well as how providing ratings via e-mail versus face-to-face meetings impacts the process (Kurtzberg, Naquin, & Belkin, 2005). However, because no single format appears to be clearly superior to the others (Landy & Farr, 1980; Murphy & Cleveland, 1995), I will make no attempt to argue for one. Instead, Table 5.1 provides a summary of the advantages and disadvantages of the four major types discussed here. You can use this to decide for yourself which format you would use to evaluate your employees; in some cases, your choice would depend on the situation. Note, however, that currently companies most often use a graphic rating scale with various behavioral anchors— basically a hybrid of a graphic rating scale and a BARS.

Rating Errors

Evaluating another individual's performance accurately and fairly is not an easy thing to do; moreover, errors often result in this process. An understanding of these errors is important to appreciating the complexities of performance appraisal.

Table 5.1 Summary of Appraisal Formats		
	Advantages	Disadvantages
Graphic rating scales	1. Easy to develop 2. Easy to use	1. Lack of precision in dimensions 2. Lack of precision in anchors
BARS	1. Precise and well-defined scales—good for coaching 2. Well received by raters and ratees	1. Time and money intensive 2. No evidence that it is more accurate than other formats
Checklists	1. Easy to develop 2. Easy to use	1. Rater errors such as halo, leniency, and severity are quite frequent
Employee comparison methods	1. Precise rankings are possible 2. Useful for making administrative rewards on a limited basis	1. Time intensive 2. Not well received by raters (paired comparison) or ratees (forced distribution)

Research in cognitive psychology has shed considerable light on how the human brain processes information while making decisions. This research has provided I/O psychologists with valuable information that has been applied to the performance appraisal process.

Cognitive Processes In a typical company situation, once or twice a year supervisors have to recall specific performance incidents relating to each employee, somehow integrate those performance incidents into a comprehensible whole, arrive at an overall evaluation, and, finally, endorse a number or category that represents the employee's performance over that period. Furthermore, this has to be done for each of 6 to 12 different employees, and perhaps more! With the trend toward flatter organizations, the number of subordinates for each supervisor is increasing steadily, making the task that much more difficult.

Although more complex *cognitive-processing* models of performance appraisal have been developed (see Hodgkinson & Healey, 2008; Landy & Farr, 1980), all such models are consistent with the scheme depicted in Figure 5.5. This figure includes two examples of potential error or bias that may come into play at each of the steps shown (see the left and right columns). The first step in this model is the *observation* of employees' behaviors. In many situations, this is done well; the rater may observe a large portion of the ratee's behavior, as when a grocery store manager observes his subordinates' performance every day. In other situations, however, raters are unable to observe ratees' performance directly. For instance, professors are often evaluated by

FIGURE 5.5 Cognitive-Processing Model of Performance Appraisal

The Rater May:
Miss important behaviors

Not label information well enough for storage

Not store some relevant information at all

Not be able to retrieve relevant information

Make a poor decision based on the only available information

The Rater May:
See what he or she wants to see

Label information incorrectly

Store the wrong information

Retrieve irrelevant information

Come to a biased conclusion because he or she likes the ratee

Observe behavior

Encode information about behavior

Store information

Retrieve information

Integrate Information

their department heads, even though the department heads have little opportunity to view the professors engaging in job-related tasks like teaching.

Second, the observed behavior must be *encoded,* which means that the behavior must be cognitively packaged in such a way that the rater is able to store it. If an observed behavior is encoded incorrectly (e.g., an adequate behavior is somehow encoded as inadequate), the appraisal rating will be affected at a later time.

Third, after encoding, the behavior must be *stored* in long-term memory. Because it is unreasonable to expect that anyone could perfectly store all the relevant performance incidents, some important incidents may not get stored at all.

Fourth, when the appraisal review is being conducted, the stored information must be *retrieved* from memory. In many situations, the rater cannot retrieve some of the important information, leading to an appraisal rating that is based on an inadequate sample of behavior. Also, since performance reviews are difficult and time-consuming, it's not unusual for raters to retrieve irrelevant information and use it as the basis for the performance rating. Think about doing a review of your subordinate's administrative assistant—someone with whom you have very little interaction. In doing this review, you would certainly get input from your subordinate; but later, when doing the final evaluation, you might recall a memo from your subordinate that explained an expensive mix-up in her office in terms of scheduling conflicts. You may consider this when doing the administrative assistant's evaluation (after all, it makes sense that he would be in charge of scheduling), even though you don't know whether this mix-up was his fault. For that matter, he may have been the one who caught the problem and saved the company money. If you stored irrelevant information, you may unwittingly use it later in making a performance judgment.

Finally, the rater has to *integrate* all this information and come to a final rating. If the rater has done a good job of observing, encoding, storing, and retrieving relevant performance information, the integration step should be relatively easy. However, sometimes raters let attitudes and feelings cloud their judgments. If your boyfriend, girlfriend, spouse, or even a close acquaintance worked under your direct supervision, could you be objective in arriving at a performance judgment that would be used in a promotion decision? You'd like to think that you could, but many of us probably couldn't. This is one reason that many companies frown on hiring both members of a married couple or, if they do hire them, make sure to limit their workplace interaction. In one case that I know of, the U.S. military accepted a married couple—two attorneys—into the army as captains, guaranteeing that they would be posted to the same geographical region; but the military also guaranteed that the couple would not be assigned to the same base, thereby avoiding potential problems with favoritism and bias.

I/O psychologists have been developing ways to help raters avoid the cognitive errors involved in performance appraisal for the last 25 years. Let's consider some of the most common of these errors.

halo
The rating error that results from either (1) a rater's tendency to use his or her global evaluation of a ratee in making dimension-specific ratings for that ratee or (2) a rater's unwillingness to discriminate between independent dimensions of a ratee's performance.

Halo One error that has received a great deal of attention is called **halo**. Halo results from either (1) a rater's tendency to use his or her global evaluation of a ratee in making dimension-specific ratings for that ratee or (2) a rater's unwillingness to discriminate between independent dimensions of a ratee's performance (Saal, Downey, & Lahey, 1980). Halo effects can be positive or negative. A retail manager may evaluate a salesclerk as being very good at connecting with potential customers because she knows that the clerk is very good at keeping the shelves neat and stocked even though competence on this dimension doesn't really indicate that he is competent in dealing with customers. The manager has generalized her evaluation of this clerk from one dimension to another. Similarly, I may assume a student is not going to do well in my class because he hasn't done well in his physics classes.

▼ **A Closer Look**
What is the difference between halo and true halo?

IMAGES.COM/CORBIS

The early research in this area assumed that all halo was error. However, some people are competent across *all* dimensions—leadership, communication skills, motivating employees, completing paperwork, and so on. Traditionally, I/O psychologists noted high correlations across ratings on these dimensions and concluded that there was a great deal of halo error. However, from a hiring standpoint (see Chapters 6 and 7), organizations tend to target those applicants they believe will be "good at everything." And, indeed, there are employees in all organizations who do seem to be good performers on all performance dimensions. The point here is that some halo results from accurate intercorrelations among performance dimensions (see Goffin, Jelley, & Wagner, 2003; Murphy & Jako, 1989; Murphy & Reynolds,

1988)—what we call **true halo**. Thus, we no longer view all halo as error.

Rating errors such as leniency, central tendency, and severity (discussed below) are categorized as **distributional errors** because they result from a mismatch between actual rating distributions and expected rating distributions. In other words, the grouping of ratings is much farther toward one end of the distribution or much closer to the middle than what we assume the true distribution to be. Performance is one of those qualities that we expect to be distributed "normally."

> **TECHNICAL TIP**
>
> *We discussed the normal distribution in Chapter 2, pointing out that many qualities like intelligence and normal personality characteristics are distributed in a bell-like shape, with most of the data in the middle and much less of the data in the extremes of the distribution.*

Leniency Raters commit the error of **leniency** when (1) the mean of their ratings across ratees is higher than the mean of all ratees across all raters or (2) the mean of their ratings is higher than the midpoint of the scale. In other words, if your boss rates her employees higher than all the other bosses rate their employees, or if she gives ratings with a mean of 4 on a 5-point scale, she would be described as a lenient rater. Raters may be lenient because they like their employees or want to be liked. They may think that giving everyone favorable ratings will keep peace in the workplace or that doing so will make them look good as supervisors who have high-performing subordinates. In fact, in a laboratory study examining leniency effects, researchers found that when raters were held accountable to their supervisors (as well as ratees), they were less lenient in their ratings than when they were held accountable only to the ratees (Curtis, Darvey, & Ravden, 2005). This surely has implications for how organizations might want to structure performance appraisal processes.

As with halo, we need to be careful in assuming that distributional errors are really errors. Indeed, it is possible, perhaps likely, that some supervisors really do have better employees or work groups than others, resulting in more favorable ratings that are accurate rather than lenient. For example, the airline chosen as the best in the nation with respect to service should show higher performance ratings for its service employees than other airlines. So what might appear to be the result of leniency among the evaluators of this airline would in fact be the result of accurate evaluation. Research also suggests that personality can have an impact on one's tendency to be lenient. Specifically, individuals categorized as "agreeable" have been shown to be more lenient than those categorized as "conscientious" (Bernardin, Cooke, & Villanova, 2000).

Central Tendency Raters who use only the midpoint of the scale in rating their employees commit the error of **central tendency**. An example is the professor who gives almost everyone a C for the course. In some cases, the raters are lazy and find it easier to give everyone an average rating than spending the extra time necessary to review employees' performance so as to differentiate between good and poor workers. In other cases, the raters don't know how well each of their subordinates has performed (perhaps because they are new to the work group or just don't see their employees' on-the-job behavior very often) and take the easy way out by opting for average ratings for everyone. Some research suggests that central tendency error is

true halo
Halo that results from accurate inter-correlations among performance dimensions rather than from rating error.

distributional errors
Rating errors, such as severity, central tendency, and leniency, that result from a mismatch between actual rating distributions and expected rating distributions.

leniency
The rating error that results when (1) the mean of one's ratings across ratees is higher than the mean of all ratees across all raters or (2) the mean of one's ratings is higher than the midpoint of the scale.

central tendency
The tendency to use only the midpoint of the scale in rating one's employees.

sometimes a result of the rating scale itself and that simpler semantic differential scales (e.g., ranging from "effective employee" to "ineffective employee") result in a considerable amount of this bias (Yu, Albaum, & Swenson, 2003).

Of course, a given work group or department may be populated largely by average employees. In fact, the normal distribution suggests that most employees really are average, so it is reasonable to have a large percentage of employees rated as such. At times, then, central tendency is a rating error; at other times, though, it simply reflects the actual distribution of performance, which is largely centered around "average."

Severity Less frequent than leniency and central tendency is the rating error of **severity**, which is committed by raters who tend to use only the low end of the scale or to give consistently lower ratings to their employees than other raters do. Some supervisors intentionally give low ratings to employees because they believe that doing so motivates them (you will see when we get to Chapter 9, on motivation, that this strategy is not likely to work), or keeps them from getting too cocky, or provides a baseline from which new employees can improve. For some, severity represents an attempt to maintain the impression of being tough and in charge—but what tends to happen is that such raters lose, rather than gain, the respect of their subordinates.

Some work groups include a larger number of low performers than other work groups, so low ratings from the supervisor of such work groups may be accurate rather than "severe." Thus, although we don't see these terms in the literature, we could speak of true leniency, true central tendency, and true severity in much the same way as we speak of true halo. For any given situation, though, it is difficult to determine whether the ratings are affected by rating errors or are an accurate reflection of performance.

The chief problem stemming from distributional errors is that the ratings do not adequately *discriminate* between effective and ineffective performers. In such cases, the majority of ratees are lumped together in the bottom, middle, or top of the distribution. This general problem is often referred to as *range restriction* because only a small part of the scale range is used in the ratings. The difficulty for the organization is that it intends to use performance rating information for personnel decisions such as promotions, raises, transfers, layoffs, and other terminations; but if all the employees are rated similarly (whether as a result of central tendency, leniency, or severity), the ratings do not help in making these personnel decisions. For instance, if everyone is rated in the middle of the scale, who gets promoted? If everyone is rated very favorably, who gets the big raise? If everyone is rated as ineffective, who gets fired?

Employee morale is also affected by nondiscriminating ratings, in that employees who believe they are good employees will feel slighted because their reviews are no better than those of employees whom they view as much less effective. Think about this: Have you ever been passed over for a promotion, only to discover that the person who was promoted, though less deserving than you, was rated similarly to you? You likely experienced feelings of *injustice,* which may have affected not only your subsequent on-the-job performance but also your attitude. These additional implications of nondiscriminating ratings will be discussed in more detail in Chapters 10 and 11.

severity
The tendency to use only the low end of the scale or to give consistently lower ratings to one's employees than other raters do.

Other Errors Many other rating errors are discussed in the literature, but I will touch on just three more. One is *recency error,* whereby raters heavily weight their most recent interactions with or observations of the ratee. A supervisor who, in rating his subordinate, largely ignores nine months of superior performance and bases his evaluation on only the past three months of less-than-adequate performance is making a recency error. This is similar to the somewhat misguided belief in organizations that all that matters is the question "What have you done for me lately?"

Another error of note, called *first impression error* or *primacy effect*, is the opposite of recency error. Here, raters pay an inordinate amount of attention to their initial experiences with the ratee. A construction foreman may think back to that first day when the new electrician helped out on the site at a crucial time and use this as the basis for his evaluation of the electrician while largely ignoring some major performance problems over the past few months. First impressions tend to be heavily weighted in our everyday lives, as when we form friendships with people with whom we just seem to "hit it off" from the very beginning; they are also used, sometimes ineffectively, in performance appraisal.

Finally, there is the *similar-to-me* error, which occurs when raters tend to give more favorable ratings to ratees who are very much like themselves. We know from social psychology that people tend to make friends with and like being around people who are much like themselves. An old English proverb states: "Birds of a feather flock together." A similar effect occurs in performance appraisal situations, resulting in more favorable ratings of employees similar to the rater than of those dissimilar.

Rater Considerations

We've talked at length about characteristics of the rating—that is, formats and errors. In this section, we consider important performance appraisal elements that revolve around the rater—namely, rater training, rater goals, and rater accountability.

Rater Training We have just discussed some of the common errors that raters make in evaluating the performance of others. An important question asked by I/O researchers and practitioners alike is whether rater training can reduce such errors and improve the rating process (Hauenstein, 1998; Schleicher, Day, Mayes, & Riggio, 2002). There are two main types of rater training in the performance appraisal area. One, known as **Rater Error Training (RET)**, was originally developed to reduce the incidence of rater errors (Spool, 1978). The focus was on describing errors like halo to raters and showing them how to avoid making such errors. The assumption was that by reducing the errors, RET could increase accuracy.

As suggested early on in the development of this approach, however, RET can indeed reduce errors, but accuracy is not necessarily improved (Bernardin & Pence, 1980). In fact, studies have shown that accuracy sometimes *decreases* as a function of reducing error (e.g., Bernardin & Pence, 1980). How can this be? Well, recall our discussion of halo. When raters are instructed not to allow for halo, they are in effect being taught that there is no relationship among performance dimensions and that their ratings across dimensions should not be correlated. But, in many cases, there is

Rater Error Training (RET) A type of training originally developed to reduce rater errors by focusing on describing errors like halo to raters and showing them how to avoid making such errors.

true halo, and the ratings *should* be correlated. Thus, rater training may have reduced the correlation across dimensions that we used to assume was error, resulting in artificially uncorrelated ratings that are now inaccurate.

A second type of rater training, called **Frame of Reference (FOR) Training**, was designed by John Bernardin and his colleagues to enhance raters' observational and categorization skills (Bernardin & Beatty, 1984; Bernardin & Buckley, 1981). Bernardin's belief was that to improve the accuracy of performance ratings, raters have to be provided with a frame of reference for defining performance levels that is consistent across raters and consistent with how the organization defines the various levels of performance. In other words, for a fast-food employee, on the dimension of cleanliness, all raters must know that, on a 5-point scale, a 5 would be indicated by the following behaviors:

> Table top is wiped down in between runs of burgers. Ketchup and mustard guns are always placed back into their cylinders and never left sitting on the table. Buns are kept wrapped in plastic in between runs of burgers. Floor around production area is swept at least once per hour and mopped once in the morning and afternoon. All items in the walk-in refrigerators are placed on the appropriate shelves and the walk-ins are organized, swept, and mopped periodically.

FOR training attempts to make that description part of all raters' performance schema for the level of "5/exceptional" performance. The hope is that by etching this performance exemplar in the raters' minds, the training will render each rater better able to use it consistently when observing, encoding, storing, retrieving, and integrating behaviors in arriving at a final rating. The goal is to "calibrate" raters so that a score of 5 from one rater means the same as a score of 5 from any other rater. Popular procedures for FOR training have since been developed (Pulakos, 1984, 1986). In these, raters are provided with descriptions of the dimensions and rating scales while also having them read aloud by the trainer. The trainer then describes ratee behaviors that are representative of different performance levels on each scale. Raters are typically shown a series of videotaped practice vignettes in which individuals are performing job tasks. Raters evaluate the stimulus persons on the scales; then the trainer discusses the raters' ratings and provides feedback about what ratings should have been made for each stimulus person. A detailed discussion ensues about the reasons for the various ratings.

Research has consistently shown that FOR training improves appraisal accuracy (Sulsky & Day, 1994). A couple of recent studies have suggested that combining FOR training with *behavioral observation training (BOT),* which focuses on teaching raters how to watch for certain behaviors and avoid behavioral observation errors, may improve the recognition or recall of performance behaviors (Noonan & Sulsky, 2001; Roch & O'Sullivan, 2003). One current concern, however, is that very little field data are available on the FOR technique. Most of the research showing that FOR training improves accuracy has been conducted with students in laboratory settings (see Uggerslev & Sulsky, 2008). The next step is to find a way to bring FOR training research into more organizational settings, but doing so requires some modification to the rather expensive and time-consuming process. Stay tuned as current research tries to accomplish just that.

Frame of Reference (FOR) Training
A type of training designed to enhance raters' observational and categorization skills so that all raters share a common frame of reference and improve rater accuracy.

Rater Goals and Accountability The effect of rater goals/motivation, along with accountability related to the appraisal process, is also quite important and has been the focus of considerable recent research. Raters may have different goals for various reasons. For instance, a particular rater may want all of her subordinates to be rated above a certain level or to have developed in particular areas. These kinds of goals or objectives may affect the ratings provided or the rating process in general. Sometimes this is reflected in raters "bending the rules" or making performance-based judgment calls to enhance individual or organizational performance (Veiga, Golden, & Dechant, 2004); at other times, these goals are reflected in how the rating process is implemented.

Mero and his colleagues have demonstrated that raters who were held accountable to various goals/objectives, such as rating accurately or rating leniently, actually provided ratings consistent with those goals (Mero & Motowidlo, 1995). One step further, it was shown that certain types of raters are more affected by accountability pressures than are others (Mero, Guidice, & Anna, 2006). For instance, raters who are high on conscientiousness tend to be strongly affected by accountability pressures, which is reflected in a felt need to justify one's ratings, some anxiety about the task, and higher-quality performance ratings.

These researchers have also found that the accountability effect was altered as a function of the status of the audience and the manner of being held accountable (Mero, Guidice, & Brownlee, 2007). For example, raters who expected to be held accountable for their ratings in a face-to-face meeting with a high-status session administrator were more accurate raters than were those who anticipated justifying ratings only in writing. Finally, Wong and Kwong (2007) demonstrated a clear relationship between rater goals and rating patterns. When raters were asked to maintain harmony within the work group, they increased their mean ratings and tended not to discriminate between ratees.

Contemporary Performance Appraisal Research

For many years, practitioners and researchers believed that rating scale formats were integral to the success of performance appraisal systems and that *accuracy* should be the chief goal of any performance appraisal system. Because of these two common beliefs, much of the early research in this area focused on the context of performance appraisal as it related to rating formats and rater errors. Format and error research has taught us a great deal about the processes and errors involved in arriving at a performance judgment. However, performance appraisal is not a stand-alone process that can be examined in isolation but, rather, a complex process that takes place in a very rich and sophisticated social-psychological climate, or **context**. Hence, the remaining sections of this chapter will focus on contemporary issues that better emphasize that context (see Levy & Williams, 2004; Murphy & Cleveland, 1995).

The Importance of the Social-Psychological Context Many experts have suggested a more direct research focus on the context in which the appraisal takes place, arguing that this context colors the entire appraisal process. The context

context
The social-psychological climate in which performance appraisal takes place.

in which performance appraisal takes place includes not only the social and legal climates in which the organization exists but also the political and emotional climates and cultures within the organization itself (Ferris, Munyon, Basik, & Buckley, 2008).

These context-related topics include an examination of (1) the use of employees' reactions to the appraisal rather than *accuracy* as a criterion for evaluating performance appraisal systems, (2) how the relationship between the supervisor and subordinate affects performance appraisal, (3) the role of organizational politics in the appraisal process, (4) the importance of trust in the appraisal process, (5) the use of multiple feedback sources rather than just the supervisor's feedback in the appraisal process, and (6) the value of providing employees with knowledge about the appraisal system and the opportunity to participate in the appraisal process. This list represents just a small sampling of the context issues at the core of current performance appraisal research (see Levy & Williams, 2004, for a complete review). With our movement away from an emphasis on formats and errors, we are beginning to increase our understanding of the process itself and to apply that understanding to the use of appraisals in organizations. The next few sections will consider some of this new context-based research.

Reaction Criteria Traditionally, performance appraisals were evaluated with respect to how "accurate" they were, in the sense of being free from errors. But as you now know, there are problems with accuracy and error measures. As early as 1984, researchers suggested that future appraisal research should begin to move beyond psychometric criteria due to the measurement problems inherent in that approach and instead focus on *qualitative criteria* (Bernardin & Beatty, 1984) and *reaction criteria* (Cawley, Keeping, & Levy, 1998). Both phrases refer to the role played by raters' and ratees' reactions in the appraisal process (Hedge & Teachout, 2000; Keeping & Levy, 2000).

One research focus has been the potential importance of raters' and ratees' favorable responses to the appraisal system or process (e.g., Findley, Giles, & Mossholder, 2000). In fact, until this past decade, the relative lack of research attention directed toward reaction criteria instead of psychometric and accuracy criteria led researchers to refer to reaction criteria as one class of "neglected criteria" that might be critical in evaluating the success of an appraisal system (Murphy & Cleveland, 1995). It seems reasonable to expect that subordinates' reactions to appraisal systems would have just as much impact on the success and effectiveness of an appraisal system as the more technical aspects of the system. Indeed, researchers have suggested that reactions are usually better indicators of the overall viability of an appraisal system than are narrower psychometric indices such as leniency or halo (Bernardin & Beatty, 1984). After all, one may develop the most technically sophisticated appraisal system, but if that system is not accepted and supported by employees, its effectiveness will ultimately be limited. Indeed, due to the changing nature of performance appraisals and organizations, worker attitudes toward performance appraisal may play an increasingly important role in appraisal processes as the procedures and systems continue to develop (Hedge & Borman, 1995).

Despite the relative neglect of reaction criteria, several studies have attempted to investigate various appraisal characteristics that elicit or at least contribute to positive employee reactions. For instance, it has been demonstrated that for a sample of bank tellers, appraisal satisfaction was affected by both appraisal characteristics (e.g., frequency of appraisals) and organizational variables (e.g., employees' understanding of their jobs). Furthermore, bank tellers who reported a positive relationship with their supervisors and a low amount of ambiguity about their roles in the organization were more satisfied with the appraisal system (Dobbins, Cardy, & Platz-Vieno, 1990).

One study demonstrated that subordinates reported less anger and higher perceptions of justice when supervisors provided justification for their ratings (Tata, 2002). Furthermore, we have seen that performance appraisals viewed as unfair by subordinates have tended to be related to ratees' emotional exhaustion (Brown & Benson, 2003). This research has great implications for appraisal in organizations because it suggests that organizations and supervisors can do certain things to increase the likelihood that employees will respond favorably to the performance appraisal process—namely, provide frequent performance feedback and relevant job-related information to employees.

The Supervisor–Subordinate Relationship

The relationship between supervisors and subordinates has been discussed in terms of *leader–member exchange (LMX) theory,* which emphasizes the idea that supervisors have different types of relationships with different subordinates (Engle & Lord, 1997; see also Chapter 13). Performance appraisal research has virtually ignored the role of leader–member exchange in subordinate reactions to the appraisal process (Wexley & Klimoski, 1984), but LMX is important in this connection. For instance, a study found that employees of a telephone company who experienced a high level of LMX with their supervisors were rated high in terms of performance regardless of objective performance indicators, whereas those who experienced a low level of LMX received performance ratings that matched their objective level of performance (Duarte, Goodson, & Klich, 1993). In short, the relationship that an employee has with his or her supervisor plays a role in the performance appraisal process.

A recent study demonstrated that the frequency of communication between a subordinate and supervisor interacts with LMX to affect performance ratings. A positive LMX relationship led to favorable ratings when there was also frequent communication, but ratings were less favorable even with a positive LMX when there was little communication (Kacmar, Witt, Zivnuska, & Gully, 2003). This is an excellent example of the connection between the context in which the appraisal takes place and the outcome of the appraisal process. The implication in this case is that understanding the appraisal process within

▼ **A Closer Look**
The relationship between supervisor and subordinates, sometimes called LMX, is very important for organizational functioning. How do theory and research related to LMX help us understand the performance appraisal process?

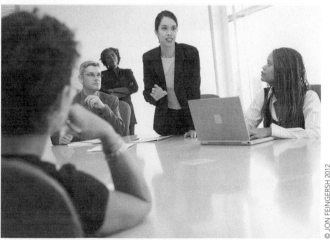

© JON FEINGERSH 2012

a work group requires an understanding of the relationships among those involved because these relationships affect the appraisal process.

Organizational Politics Organizational politics—"deliberate attempts by individuals to enhance or protect their self-interests when conflicting courses of action are possible"—helps delineate the context in which performance appraisal takes place (Longenecker, Sims, & Gioia, 1987, p. 184). Because organizations are political entities, politics plays a role in all important organizational decisions and processes, including performance appraisal (Longenecker et al., 1987). It's important to note that both supervisors and subordinates are affected by the politics of performance appraisal. In particular, Clint Longenecker and his colleagues (1987) have demonstrated through interviews that executives intentionally manipulate appraisals for political reasons (e.g., to send a message to subordinates or to make their own department look good). Research has also indicated that subordinates use *impression management* strategies in an effort to bring about favorable appraisals; in other words, they control their behavior to make a good impression on their superiors (Wayne & Liden, 1995).

Finally, a study of more than 800 employees demonstrated that among those who perceived a high level of organizational politics in their company, the ones who were also high on conscientiousness performed better than did those who were not high on conscientiousness (Hochwarter, Witt, & Kacmar, 2000). It appears that the high-conscientiousness employees were able to overcome the politics and perform well. Thus, to gain a better understanding of the appraisal process in an organization, and to affect that process, one needs to have information about the politics of the organization and the work group. Recent research has begun to examine how perceptions of politics relate to constructs like stress, anxiety, and job morale within a performance feedback context (Rosen, Levy, & Hall, 2006).

Trust and Justice *Trust* in the appraisal process is the extent to which raters believe that fair and accurate appraisals have been or will be made in their organization. Alternatively, if a rater feels that other raters in the organization are inflating their ratings, that rater may do the same. Bernardin and his colleagues developed a scale called *Trust in the Appraisal Process Survey,* or TAPS, to measure raters' perceptions of the rating behavior of the other raters in their department (Bernardin, 1978; Bernardin, Orban, & Carlyle, 1981). They found that raters who scored low on the TAPS were more lenient raters than those who scored high. This finding indicates the importance of trust on appraisal ratings. Trust also seems to be related to employees' acceptance of the appraisal system (Murphy & Cleveland, 1995). In addition, performance appraisal systems that are well received by employees appear to affect employees' trust of top management, suggesting that the performance management system may be an effective tool for enhancing organizational trust (Mayer & Davis, 1999).

In another line of work related to trust issues, researchers have looked at how comfortable raters are with the performance appraisal process (Villanova, Bernardin, Dahmus, & Sims, 1993). In particular, Peter Villanova and his colleagues have shown that scores on a scale they call the *Performance Appraisal Discomfort Scale (PADS)* are related to leniency in such a way that those raters who express great discomfort in evaluating others and providing them with feedback also tend to be among the most lenient raters. In other words, not all raters are equally comfortable doing performance appraisals, and the extent to which raters experience discomfort in this setting is likely to affect the quality of the ratings and other elements of the appraisal process (e.g., interpersonal interactions). In their most recent work, Bernardin and Villanova (2005) have taken an important additional step by showing that raters can be trained to be more comfortable doing performance appraisal, resulting in less leniency. Called self-efficacy training for raters, this new approach seems to have great potential for improving the rating process.

We will talk about organizational justice in Chapter 9, but the notion of the fairness or justice of a performance appraisal system is an important one to mention here. A carefully designed, psychometrically sound performance appraisal system has the potential to be effective, but that potential can be limited by the justice perceptions of those organizational members who are involved in the appraisal process. If raters or ratees see the appraisal system as unfair or biased, its psychometric quality will be irrelevant—it won't matter how "good" the system is if people perceive it to be unfair. Recent conceptual work argues that performance appraisal research must be broad in its focus and include diverse aspects of the appraisal system, such as justice-related constructs (Thurston & McNall, 2010). A good deal of performance appraisal research in recent years has focused on justice-related constructs and processes as they relate to performance appraisal. An interesting recent line of work has looked at how a supervisor's implicit person theory (IPT)—the extent to which an individual believes that people can change—impacts performance appraisal. One such research investigation (Heslin & VandeWalle, 2011) demonstrated that supervisors who tend to believe that people can change and develop are perceived by their subordinates as more just in their performance appraisals than are those supervisors who do not believe that people can change. The justice perceptions led to more frequent OCBs and greater commitment to the organization (see Chapter 10). This is a sizable literature and I refer you to some recent work for a more thorough discussion (see Elicker, Levy, & Hall, 2006; Thurston & McNall, 2010) but want to emphasize the important role played by organizational citizens' perceptions of performance appraisal fairness.

Participation One contextual process variable that has received a great deal of attention in the performance appraisal literature is employee participation. Overall, this research suggests an association between allowing employees to participate in the appraisal process and positive employee reactions toward the appraisal system (Cawley et al., 1998). Specifically, as demonstrated by a meta-analysis, there is a strong positive relationship between participation and a host of reactions to performance appraisal, including (1) satisfaction with the appraisal system and session, (2) motivation to improve as a result of the appraisal, (3) belief in the fairness of the appraisal, and (4) belief in the usefulness of the appraisal (Cawley et al., 1998). In short, when employees are allowed to participate in the appraisal process—by completing a self-assessment or expressing their ideas during the appraisal session or interview—they react more positively to the appraisal than when they are not given the opportunity

TECHNICAL TIP

*Remember from Chapter 2 that meta-analyses
are quantitative reviews of research findings. We
use them to draw useful summaries of relationships among variables from many published and
unpublished studies.*

to participate. Here, too, the important implication is that organizations and supervisors have interventions available to them that can improve the quality of the appraisal process—in this case, by giving employees a voice in the process.

Table 5.2 presents the steps to be followed during a performance appraisal interview. Compiled from various sources (primarily Silverman, 1991), these steps make it very clear that the performance appraisal interview should be a participative process that includes substantial input from the employee. This observation is consistent with findings regarding the importance of participation in the performance appraisal process (Cawley et al., 1998), as well as with the change in management style and structure from autocratic to humanistic that has become pervasive in organizations (Meyer, 1991).

Knowledge of the Appraisal System In 1992, Jane Williams and I introduced a construct called *Perceived System Knowledge (PSK)*. The implication of this construct is that employees' understanding of the performance appraisal system is an important contextual variable in the appraisal process. In particular, we have demonstrated that when employees perceive that they understand the appraisal system and its objectives, their own ratings of their performance tend to agree with their supervisors' ratings. In other words, the leniency commonly found in self-ratings (indeed, it's typical for individuals to rate themselves more favorably than their supervisors do) is significantly reduced when employees understand the appraisal system.

In the years since this first study was conducted, my colleagues and I have further demonstrated that managers report higher levels of PSK than do nonmanagers (Williams & Levy, 1995), that PSK is positively related to job attitudes (Levy & Williams, 1998), and that PSK is positively related to appraisal reactions (Levy & Steelman, 1994). This construct is related to the notion of participation and is thus consistent with the move away from the traditional "supervisor calls the shots" approach to performance appraisal. The idea here is that when employees are provided with information about the system, they not only understand the appraisal system better but also feel as though they are an integral part of that system: It becomes *their* appraisal system, not just something handed down to them without explanation by management.

Providing Performance Feedback The performance management cycle is a multistage, longitudinal process that is central to the development of employees and the success of organizations (London & Smither, 2002). The key element to this cycle is the extent to which employees receive and use feedback. This focus on employee development has received a great deal of attention. For instance, London and Smither (2002) have presented a comprehensive model of the performance management process in which the chief outcomes are behavior changes, better performance, increased self-awareness, and increased self-confidence. They propose that these outcomes are affected by constructs such as the employee's own feedback orientation (see Linderbaum & Levy, 2007) or receptivity to feedback, as well as the feedback environment as defined by the organization or work group (see Whitaker, Dahling,

Table 5.2 How to Conduct a Performance Appraisal Interview

Prior to the Interview	During the Interview	After the Interview
1. Supervisor should give employee adequate notice about meeting date.	1. Supervisor should explain the purpose of interview.	1. Supervisor and employee should independently review major responsibilities and objectives.
2. Employee should do a self-appraisal.	2. Employee should summarize accomplishments and needs with respect to major responsibilities.	2. Supervisor and employee should schedule additional meetings to set objectives for the next review period.
3. Supervisor should receive copy of self-appraisal.	3. Supervisor should do same summary as above, but from his or her viewpoint.	3. Supervisor and employee should agree on the organizational link between achieving objectives and receiving organizational rewards (compensation, promotions, etc.)
4. Supervisor should review documentation of performance.	4. Supervisor and employee should discuss whether developmental need exists with respect to each major responsibility.	4. Communication channels between supervisor and employee should remain open throughout the review period.
	5. Supervisor and employee should diagnose the causes of any discrepancy, or "gap," between objectives and actual performance.	
	6. Supervisor and employee should develop action plans to enhance performance on each major responsibility.	
	7. Supervisor and employee should summarize performance on each major responsibility and review agreed-upon action plans.	
	8. Supervisor should compliment employee on accomplishments.	
	9. Supervisor should set time and date for future meetings to discuss responsibilities and performance.	

COURTESY OF ELAINE PULAKOS

Elaine Pulakos
PhD, 1984, Industrial and Organizational Psychology, Michigan State University
President, PDRI, an SHL Company

Despite more than 50 years of research devoted to designing effective performance management (PM) systems, we have yet to uncover the key to delivering PM processes that managers and employees agree work well and add value.

Over the past few years, our organization has devoted considerable energy to unraveling where our research and best practices are missing the boat. We've concluded that the answer lies in too much focus on the formal PM system—rating scales, rating criteria, process steps, and so on—and too little focus on informal but key behaviors that actually drive effective performance.

Research has shown that engagement and performance are associated with several key behaviors, for example, articulating clear expectations, providing regular feedback, taking an interest in employees' well-being, and developing the employees.[1, 2] These positive, day-to-day behaviors comprise the essence of PM and do, in fact, lead to the promised PM outcomes. However, this is not what we get from our formal PM systems. The disconnect results from the fact that our formal systems tend to drive very intermittent, calendar-based events (e.g., setting goals at the beginning of the year, conducting mid- and end-year feedback reviews) rather than effective, ongoing PM behavior that needs to occur daily.

The behaviors that matter most are deceptively simple yet powerful drivers of performance:

- *Vision.* Alignment between employee activities and the organization's mission is critical. While there are formal processes to achieve this (e.g., cascade goals at the beginning of each year), more is actually gained through regular conversations between managers and employees about alignment between the work and the mission.
- *Action.* While setting expectations is core to PM, it is not the annual goal-setting process that drives outcomes. Rather, it is ongoing expectations that are set regularly as work changes and evolves. Ongoing, real-time feedback tied to expectations is also essential for high performance. In most formal systems, feedback is programmed into one or two annual review meetings, which are too infrequent to impact performance. In contrast, feedback that facilitates engagement and performance happens informally in day-to-day conversations as work is performed.
- *Growth.* Formal PM systems usually include an annual development review. However, because 80% or more of learning occurs on the job, it is actually development through ongoing job experience and regular coaching that enhances performance and engagement.

The bottom line is that more emphasis needs to be placed on fostering and sustaining the key PM behaviors as we implement PM systems in organizations—to the point that they become intricately woven into the fabric of the organization's DNA.

[1]From Corporate Leadership Council. (2004). *Driving employee performance and retention through engagement: A quantitative analysis of the effectiveness of employee engagement strategies* (Catalog No. CLC12PV0PD). Washington, DC: Corporate Executive Board.

[2]From Bryant, A. (2011, March 12). Google's quest to build a better boss. *New York Times*, p. BU1.

Applying Your Knowledge

1. Given the increase in global competition for the best personnel, what role can performance management play in giving companies a competitive edge?

2. How do the issues covered in this section on contemporary performance appraisal research inform PDRI's focus on vision, action, and growth?

3. In what ways has technology allowed for easier assessment of informal behaviors on a more frequent basis? In what ways does technology perhaps present challenges to such assessments?

& Levy, 2007). In other words, employees' development is largely a function of their receptivity to feedback and the organization's approach to or emphasis on feedback.

Continuous employee development has been defined as a "cyclical process in which employees are motivated to plan for and engage in actions or behaviors that benefit their future employability on a repetitive or ongoing basis" (Garofano & Salas, 2005, p. 282). In a recent study, it was demonstrated that how participants responded to employee development goals was affected by their personalities (core self-evaluations, which are related to self-efficacy and self-esteem as well as other traits) and other situational and interpersonal variables (Bono & Colbert, 2005).

As noted earlier, feedback accountability plays an important role in both performance management and, in particular, employee development. Research has found that social support is a key determinant of attitudes toward employee development and that organizational social support for development is likely to lead to a feeling of accountability on the part of the employees (Maurer, Mitchell, & Barbeite, 2002). Supervisors who have experienced the support of their subordinates have reported more feedback accountability and greater self-development initiative, suggesting that the social context is an important element of employee self-development (Rutkowski & Steelman, 2005). Let's talk some more about the feedback process.

The Feedback Process Feedback serves an important role in organizations, meeting the needs of employees and employers. London and Smither (2002) highlight the key steps of the performance management cycle. First, employees *attend to the feedback,* which includes anticipating, receiving, and reacting to the feedback. After this initial interaction with the feedback comes the second stage, *processing the feedback,* which includes interpreting, understanding, dealing with, and believing or discounting the feedback. Finally, the last step is *using the feedback,* which involves using the feedback to set goals and to track progress. These three steps are integral to making effective use of feedback; of course, if any of the three steps are ignored or handled ineffectively, this will likely result in feedback-related problems such as misperceptions, anxiety, a lack of understanding, and unwise behavioral choices.

In addition to the important steps of the performance management cycle, we also need to consider qualities or characteristics of the feedback itself if we are to truly understand the process. For instance, what makes for good feedback? What kind of feedback is most effective? A very important study by Kluger and DeNisi (1996) created a stir by arguing that feedback is not as effective and beneficial as we had long thought. They did a meta-analysis of research on feedback interventions and, while showing a positive moderate effect of feedback on performance ($r = .41$), the analysis also revealed that over one-third of the studies showed negative effects and many found no effect at all. The authors fit these results into the historical literature on feedback and argued that we had been misled by this historical literature. They consequently proposed the feedback intervention theory (FIT), which states that feedback is most effective when it is targeted at the task rather than at the self. They have argued that feedback directed anywhere other than to the task (e.g., "You are such a conscientious employee") distracts the individual and pulls resources and attention from the task at hand, which leads to no change in performance or a decrease in performance. This is a popular theory and Kluger and DeNisi have provided some empirical support.

Feedback Environment and Feedback Orientation The culture of an organization serves to constrain or enhance the effectiveness of feedback. The term **feedback environment (FE)** has been proposed to embody that culture while also specifically representing an organization's climate and attitude toward feedback. Research has shown that FE includes such dimensions as source credibility, feedback quality, and feedback delivery, among others. A favorable FE has been linked to satisfaction with and motivation to use the feedback (Steelman, Levy, & Snell, 2004) as well as an interest in seeking feedback. In addition, a positive FE has been tied to high levels of commitment to the organization and OCBs (Norris-Watts & Levy, 2004). Finally, a recent study found that FE affected performance levels through its effects on feedback seeking and role clarity.

Whereas FE is the situational side of the feedback processes, the **feedback orientation (FO)** is the individual-difference side. FO is an individual's overall attitude toward feedback or receptivity to feedback. It includes things like perceptions of the utility of feedback, accountability to use feedback, social awareness through feedback, and self-efficacy in dealing with feedback (Linderbaum & Levy, 2010). The argument is that just as organizations or departments can set or create different feedback environments, individuals can differ in their receptivity to or ideas about feedback. Together, FE and FO seem important in understanding and affecting the feedback process. FO is related to other individual differences such as learning goal orientation, which is the extent to which individuals believe learning and development are possible. In addition, employees high on FO also tend to seek feedback more often (Linderbaum & Levy, 2010) and perform better than those low on FO (Dahling, O'Malley & Chau, in press).

With recent research on FE and FO, we are gathering more and more advanced knowledge about the feedback process. This promises to improve both the employee development and performance appraisal processes in organizations.

Legal Issues in Performance Appraisal

It is illegal in the United States to discriminate in performance appraisals on the basis of non–performance-related factors such as age, gender, race, ethnicity, religion, and disability. In short, no employee can be promoted, demoted, fired, transferred, or laid off on the basis of any of these factors.

In their article on legal requirements and technical guidelines related to performance appraisal, James Austin, Peter Villanova, and Hugh Hindman (1995) make the following recommendations for performance appraisal:

1. Start with a job analysis. Austin and his colleagues especially recommend developing criteria from a documented job analysis.
2. Communicate performance standards to employees in writing.
3. Instead of relying on just an overall rating of performance, recognize that there are separate dimensions of performance that should be evaluated on an individual basis.

---

feedback environment (FE) The contextual aspects of the day-to-day supervisor–subordinate and coworker–coworker feedback process.

feedback orientation (FO) An individual's overall receptivity to feedback.

4. Use both objective criteria and subjective judgments where possible, and ensure that the subjective judgments evaluate job-related behaviors rather than global personality traits.
5. Give employees access to an appeal mechanism.
6. Use multiple raters rather than one rater with absolute authority.
7. Document everything pertinent to personnel decisions. This recommendation can't be emphasized enough, as one never knows who is likely to bring suit and on what basis. The courts have been clear in such cases: If there is no documentation to support the personnel decision in question, the defendant (i.e., the organization that is being sued for discrimination) is likely to lose the case.
8. Where possible, train the raters; if training is not possible, provide them with written instructions for conducting the performance appraisal.

In an extensive review of court decisions between 1980 and 1995, Jon Werner and Mark Bolino (1997) uncovered more than 300 court of appeals decisions related to performance appraisal. Of these, 109 were related to age discrimination, 102 to race discrimination, and 50 to sex discrimination. The authors attempted to determine which factors were most closely associated with judgments made for or against the plaintiffs (i.e., the employees bringing suit against the company). What they concluded was that, in general, the practical recommendations provided in the literature (e.g., Austin et al., 1995; Barrett & Kernan, 1988; Malos, 1998) seemed consistent with the ways in which the courts make these judgments. For instance, judgment was more likely to be made for the defendant when (1) a job analysis was used, (2) written instructions regarding the appraisal process were provided, (3) employees were provided with an opportunity to review their appraisals, (4) multiple raters agreed on performance ratings, and (5) rater training was used. In addition, these researchers found that rating format (e.g., BARS versus graphic rating scales) didn't seem to matter, as this topic never came up in the judges' written decisions.

On the other hand, the court's view of the fairness of the appraisal process was extremely important. Folger, Konovsky, and Cropanzano (1992) refer to this as the *test metaphor* view of performance appraisal. What they recommend, however, is the *due process metaphor* view of performance appraisal, in which the emphasis is on (1) adequate notice, (2) a fair hearing, and (3) judgments based on evidence. Each of these three components of due process—a familiar term in the legal arena—is built around perceptions of justice. In short, courts value the presence of justice in appraisal systems—an observation that supports continued research on contextual variables of this type.

◀ A Closer Look
Reductions in force or layoffs are serious business. What are the potential implications of a careless or thoughtless approach to making and implementing these decisions?

■ Summary

Performance appraisals are used to make personnel decisions, to provide employees with important job-related feedback, and to document employee performance as a way of protecting the organization from potential legal suits. Industrial/organizational psychologists often play an active and important role in the performance management systems of organizations.

Performance appraisals are available in many formats, including graphic rating scales, BARS, checklists, and employee comparison procedures. Each format has advantages and disadvantages (see Table 5.1); none have clearly been identified as the single best approach. The process of appraising an individual's performance is very complex and can result in rating errors such as halo, leniency, central tendency, and severity. Two types of rater training, Rater Error Training (RET) and Frame of Reference (FOR) Training, have been established as potentially useful in reducing these errors and/or improving accuracy.

Contemporary performance appraisal research continues to focus on the social-psychological context in which the appraisal takes place. This research indicates that ratee and rater reactions toward the appraisal process are important in measuring the success of an appraisal system. Also relevant to the appraisal process are the relationship between the supervisor and subordinate, the political climate within the organization, the rater's motivation and accountability, and the degree of trust among raters.

Participation is another integral element in the appraisal process. One interesting development in this area is the 360-degree feedback system, in which employees receive performance feedback from peers, subordinates, supervisors, and clients/customers. Self-ratings are commonly included in this system, especially when the only other participant is the supervisor. Although 360-degree feedback is relatively new, early research indicates not only that many employees like it but also that it has a great deal of potential for improving the feedback process in general. Employee development continues to grow in importance as both employees and organizations recognize the benefits of employee growth and learning. Employee development not only benefits individual workers but also functions as a source of competitive advantage for organizations that encourage and provide opportunities for development.

Adherence to legal guidelines is also critical to the performance appraisal process. Recent work has identified fairness as important not only to ratees but also to the courts, which appear to weight it quite heavily in making judgments for or against plaintiffs.

As we have seen, performance appraisal has widespread implications for organizations because appraisal information is used for such important personnel decisions as promotions, demotions, layoffs, dismissals, and raises. Obviously, invalid performance appraisal information is likely to result in poor organizational decisions. Our understanding of the appraisal process is thus enhanced by our appreciation of the context in which it takes place.

■ Key Terms

central tendency (p. 129)
coaching (p. 118)
context (p. 133)
critical incidents (p. 121)
distributional errors (p. 129)
feedback emvironment (FE) (p. 142)
feedback orientation (FO) (p. 142)
Frame of Reference (FOR)
  Training (p. 132)
halo (p. 128)

leniency (p. 129)
performance appraisal (p. 116)
performance management (p. 118)
Rater Error Training (RET) (p. 131)
severity (p. 130)
360-degree feedback (p. 119)
telework (p. 120)
true halo (p. 129)
upward appraisal ratings (p. 119)

■ TAKING IT TO THE FIELD

Although this chapter primarily discusses rating formats, errors, and training, performance appraisal also depends heavily on appropriately defining the criteria/criterion, as discussed in Chapter 4. Pai Ng, who is the director of institutional research at Blackwood College, is asking for your advice for a new teaching evaluation that she wants students to complete for their professors each semester. Please read her e-mail below and then respond to her questions, carefully considering both the content and the format of her measure.

Hello again

Below you will find the draft of the measure I am planning on trying out this semester. I would like your advice on the current items and any suggestions for additional items. Which items do you feel will be most helpful, least helpful, and why? And do you feel that I'm leaving any items out that would assist in conducting better evaluations? I also have heard about a different rating system known as BARS: What is it, and would this be a good thing to include on our evaluations?

Pai

Blackwood College Teaching Evaluation

Please rate the following:

	Satisfactory		Good		Excellent
Instructor's knowledge about the topic	1	2	3	4	5
Instructor's responses to e-mails	1	2	3	4	5
Instructor's friendliness	1	2	3	4	5
Instructor's use of technology	1	2	3	4	5
Quality of room	1	2	3	4	5
Quality of book	1	2	3	4	5
Quality of assignments	1	2	3	4	5

(continued)

	Strongly Disagree		Neutral		Strongly Agree
I enjoyed this class.	1	2	3	4	5
This class was interesting.	1	2	3	4	5
I would take another class with this instructor.	1	2	3	4	5
I came to this class most days.	1	2	3	4	5
The instructor's grades were fair.	1	2	3	4	5
This instructor should continue to teach at Blackwood College.	1	2	3	4	5

■ Critical Thinking Questions

1. Based on what you have read, design a rater training program that will help supervisors assess the performance of their subordinates as accurately as possible. What techniques will you include? What important variables can impact rater effectiveness?

2. The chapter discusses both performance appraisal and the broader performance management system. How do these two concepts differ? How are they related?

3. Several different rating formats are presented in the chapter. If you were designing a performance appraisal process for an organization, what format or formats would you choose? Why?

4. Multisource feedback is a tool used to obtain feedback from individuals at various levels of the organization. Frequently, the target employee (the one receiving the feedback) selects the individuals who will provide feedback. What are some potential drawbacks of allowing the target employee to select his or her raters? Should the target employee's supervisor be responsible for selecting raters? How else could raters be determined?

5. As CEO of a company, what are some of the important characteristics you would want to build into the feedback environment of your company? Also, what characteristics related to feedback orientation would you look for in new employees?

■ Application Questions

1. Imagine that when using a 360-degree performance appraisal system, an employee receives a rating of 3.5/5 from his supervisor, 4.2/5 from his peers, and 2.25/5 from his subordinates. What might be some reasons for these

discrepancies? What would you recommend that this individual's supervisor do to gain a better understanding of what these ratings indicate about the employee's performance?

2. Imagine that, in order to assign grades on a group project, your professor requires all group members to provide ratings for one another, which he will consider in grading the project. One group member has been particularly troublesome—she has been argumentative, refuses to accommodate other group members' schedules, and completes the bare minimum amount of work. Would you feel comfortable giving her a poor performance appraisal? Why or why not?

3. Once again, imagine that your professor has asked for your feedback on your fellow group members' performance on a project. This time, you have a group member who is very proactive in volunteering and takes an active role; however, even though she tries very hard, she has a lot of trouble understanding concepts introduced in the class; as a result, often the work she does is not usable for the project. Would you feel comfortable giving her a poor performance appraisal? Why or why not?

4. In many work environments, employees can engage in organizational citizenship behaviors (acts that help coworkers or the organization, even though they are not part of their job), such as staying late to work on a project they are not normally a part of or speaking positively about the organization to other people. Should these behaviors be considered in a performance appraisal? Why or why not?

5. Think of a time when you worked with someone who did not perform as well as you believed he or she should. What sorts of things did this person do/not do that led to a poor performance? If you were asked to deliver feedback to this person, what would you say?

■ Suggested Readings

DeNisi, A. S., & Pritchard, R. D. (2006). Performance appraisal, performance management, and improving individual performance: A motivational framework. *Management and Organizational Review, 2,* 253–277. This is a good resource for understanding the ongoing performance management process and moving away from stand-alone performance appraisals.

Farr, J. L., & Levy, P. E. (2007). Performance appraisal. In L. L. Koppes (Ed.), *Historical perspectives in industrial and organizational psychology.* Mahwah, NJ: Erlbaum, 311–327. This chapter provides a review of the historical development of performance appraisal methods and approaches since the beginning of the 20th century.

Ferris, G. R., Munyon, T. P., Basik, K., & Buckley, M. R. (2008). The performance evaluation context: Social, emotional, cognitive, political, and relationship components. *Human Resource Management Review, 18,* 146–163. This excellent follow-up to Levy and Williams (2004) continues the argument for the importance of context in performance appraisal and fleshes out a theoretical framework for additional research and thinking.

Levy, P. E., & Williams, J. R. (2004). The social context of performance appraisal: A review and framework for the future. *Journal of Management, 30*(6), 881–905. This comprehensive review of the performance appraisal research since 1995 places a particular emphasis on the social context of performance appraisal.

London, M., & Smither, J. W. (2002). Feedback orientation, feedback culture, and the longitudinal performance management process. *Human Resource Management Review, 12,* 81–100. This article presents a model of an ongoing performance management process, focusing on the role of feedback therein. The concepts of feedback orientation and feedback environment are also discussed.

Malos, S. B. (1998). Current legal issues in performance appraisal. In J. W. Smither (Ed.), *Performance appraisal: State of the art in practice* (pp. 49–94). San Francisco: Jossey-Bass. This readable and current review of the legal issues involved in performance appraisal is a great place to start for students interested in personnel law.

Mero, N. P., Guidice, R. M., & Anna, A. L. (2006). The interacting effects of accountability and individual differences on rater response to a performance-rating task. *Journal of Applied Social Psychology, 36*(4), 795–819. The authors examine the influences of rater personality and accountability on performance ratings.

Smither, J. W., London, M., Flautt, R., Vargas, Y., & Kucine, I. (2003). Can working with an executive coach improve multisource feedback ratings over time? A quasi-experimental field study. *Personnel Psychology, 56,* 23–44. This study demonstrates the value of working through multisource feedback with a coach and using the feedback to set goals and create action plans for improvement.

CHAPTER **6**

Predictors

CHAPTER OUTLINE

This chapter should help you understand:

■ The definition of a test and how to find existing tests used for personnel selection

■ The differences between various types of tests, such as speed versus power tests, individual versus group tests, and paper-and-pencil versus performance tests

■ The importance of validity coefficients to employee selection

■ Definitions, estimates of validity, and examples of the following types of predictors: cognitive ability (both general and specific) tests, psychomotor tests, personality tests, integrity tests, work samples, assessment centers, biographical information, and interviews

Criteria are central to organizations and I/O psychology, but in a selection context we typically don't have access to criteria and instead must use predictors as proxies or substitutes for criteria.

Think about a large law firm that is in the market to hire a new associate right out of law school. Ideally, the firm would like to have some criterion data on the potential applicants before making a decision about which one to hire. However, criterion data (e.g., number of lawsuits won, number of cases argued in district court, billable hours logged per month, etc.) aren't available on the applicants because they haven't been employed as lawyers yet. You can see the catch-22 in which the firm is entangled: It wants to hire the right person, the one who will do the best job; but without bringing the applicant on board and seeing how he or she will do, the firm has no criterion data with which to make a decision.

This is where *predictors* come into the picture. Predictors are used in place of criteria; in fact, they are used to forecast criteria. In this situation, the law firm might rely on such predictors as performance in law school, performance in mock trials, letters of recommendation from law professors, and tests of cognitive ability. Selection is all about prediction, or forecasting. Available data are used to predict who is likely to be successful on the job so that the individual in question can be hired. Predictors are of great importance because we place so much trust in their ability to model criteria. Just as faulty criteria can result in bad organizational decisions such as firing or promoting the wrong employee, faulty predictors can result in hiring the wrong person or not hiring the right person.

■ Classification of Tests

test
A systematic procedure for observing behavior and describing it with the aid of numerical scales or fixed categories.

A **test** is a systematic procedure for observing behavior and describing it with the aid of numerical scales or fixed categories. Tests are systematic in that they are administered in the same way across groups of people, following some sort of script or listing of procedures. In the broad area of employee selection, tests are used as predictors to forecast performance on the job or some other work–related criterion. Thus, I will use the terms *predictor* and *test* interchangeably in our discussion. This discussion should be of interest to all readers, even those who aren't budding I/O psychologists, because at some point you will need to apply (or already have applied) for a job, a scholarship, or admission to a school. In all these situations, you probably provided the prospective employer, organization, or school with predictor information. Chances are that these predictors were used to forecast your potential criterion performance.

To select or develop predictors, we start—once again—with a *job analysis*. We use the job analysis not only to define the job but also to identify relevant criteria that are important for job success. This information, in turn, helps us to locate, develop, create, or modify predictors that we hope are valid indicators of the criteria. Sometimes we might develop our own tests to tap the KSAOs (knowledge, skills, abilities, and other characteristics) in which we are interested, whereas at other times we might find an established test and modify it or use it in its entirety to tap a particular KSAO. Figure 6.1 shows a graphical representation of how specific tests may be chosen to measure particular KSAOs regarding the job of college professor. These tests are linked directly to the job specifications stemming from the job analysis. The boxes in this figure give examples of specific data that could be used to quantify the KSAOs

FIGURE 6.1 Linking Job Analysis to Specific Measures of KSAOs identified from the job analysis. In addition, one or two examples of the type of predictors that might be useful for each of these specific KSAOs are provided in the figure. For instance, let's look at a specific ability. The job analysis identifies job specifications; in particular, it specifies "communication ability" as an important KSAO. Communication ability can be tapped in a couple of ways. For instance, we can interview candidates and evaluate the communication skills we observe in the interview. In addition to the interview, we could provide candidates with a work sample test in which they are asked to give a lecture on a given topic to a class of undergraduates.

There are some established sources that describe thousands of existing tests, perhaps the best example of which is the *Mental Measurements Yearbook* (Spies, Carlson, & Geisinger, 2010), which has been published annually for over 50 years and provides evaluations of tests in a variety of areas. These evaluations include the psychometric properties, cost, and administration time of the tests, as well as information on how to obtain them.

Computer Adaptive Testing

computer adaptive testing The process through which computer technology is used to identify easier and harder questions for applicants that eventually estimate their true ability level.

A recent trend in testing is the delivery of tests via the computer and sometimes testing that takes place on the Internet. Some computerized tests (e.g., the GRE) are adaptive. **Computer adaptive testing** means that how you score on earlier questions affects the difficulty of subsequent questions. This approach allows for quick and accurate scoring (Educational Testing Service, 2007). If an individual answers an easy question correctly, the next item that is chosen for delivery by the computer is more difficult. If that is answered correctly, another more difficult item follows, but if that is answered incorrectly, then the next question is less difficult than the one the test taker just got wrong. This process is believed to provide more precise measurement and to quickly identify the test taker's ability level through this back-and-forth process that eventually ends at the best estimate of the individual's ability level (for a more detailed discussion, see Farr & Tippins, 2010).

Tests fall into different categories based on their various dimensions. Several of these categories are described in the following sections.

Speed Versus Power Tests

speed test A test containing relatively easy items with a short time limit in which individuals must complete as many items as they can.

power test A test with no fixed time limits and relatively difficult items.

A **speed test** is composed of relatively easy items with a short time limit in which individuals must complete as many items as they can. One example would be a typing test for a word-processing job. Applicants are instructed to type as much of a writing sample as they can in five minutes, and they are scored on the basis of how much they finished and the number of errors they made. A **power test**, by contrast, has no fixed time limit and tends to be more difficult. Test takers are expected to be able to complete all the items on a power test, but not on a speed test. Most college exams are power tests; although the items are somewhat difficult, students are given what is believed to be enough time to complete them all. In our typing example, however, test takers are not expected to have time to type the entire written sample in the five minutes allotted.

Individual Versus Group Tests

individual tests Tests that are administered to one person at a time.

Individual tests are administered to one person at a time and, thus, are very costly in terms of time and money. Though often used for upper-level managerial positions, these tests tend to be avoided at lower levels because of the costs involved. Intelligence tests such as those developed by Wechsler (WAIS-III and WISC-III) are good examples of individually administered tests in which an examiner assesses one individual at a time. (For more information on these tests, see Kaufman, 1994; Kaufman & Lichtenberger, 1999.) Individual tests may take as long as two or three hours to complete and often have to be administered and scored by someone trained specifically on the test in question. More frequently used in organizations are **group tests**, in which many applicants can be tested at one time. These tests are more conducive to employee selection and, thus, more cost effective—especially in situations in which a company may have 50 or more applicants who need to be assessed for only a few job openings.

Paper-and-Pencil Versus Performance Tests

Paper-and-pencil tests are the ones we've all most commonly experienced. In such tests, we respond to questions in a test booklet or by marking computer sheets to be scanned. These questions can take several different forms, including essay, multiple choice, true–false, and short answer. Most cognitive ability tests are of this type. Both the ACT and the SAT are paper-and-pencil tests; so are most of your course examinations. However, computer technology has led to "paper-and-pencil" tests being available in computerized versions. A body of literature has emerged that focuses on the comparability of assessing personality or intelligence via Internet-based versus paper-and-pencil tests (Aluja, Rossier, & Zuckerman, 2007; Meade, Michels, & Lautenschlager, 2007; Potosky & Bobko, 2004).

One study of 157 German high school students looked at reasoning-ability measures delivered on handheld computers, notebook computers, and paper-and-pencil delivery schemes (Schroeders & Wilhelm, 2010) and concluded that the assessment medium played no meaningful role in individual responses. The issue of proctored versus unproctored tests (i.e., the extent to which the testing environment is monitored by someone) has become a hot issue in recent years. The Internet provides a great venue for unproctored employment tests that applicants or candidates can take at their convenience. This, however, raises a series of issues about unproctored testing, those related to software and hardware, test security, identity of candidates, and cheating (Tippins et al., 2006). Interestingly, despite these potential concerns, recent research has supported the use of unproctored tests by demonstrating equivalent predictive validities (Beaty et al., 2011) and not showing elevated scores on personality tests (Arthur, Glaze, Villado, & Taylor, 2010). More research is necessary, but there appear to be some benefits to the use of unproctored Internet-based testing.

Performance tests require the manipulation of an object or a piece of equipment. These

▼ **A Closer Look**
What do you think is being tested in each of these photos?

HASBRO GAMES

FOTOSEARCH

include tests of manual dexterity or psychomotor skills, which we will talk about later in this chapter. Most of us would insist that our surgeons have a certain degree of manual dexterity with the instruments necessary for their surgical specialty. This skill could not be evaluated with a paper-and-pencil test but, instead, would require some sort of performance test. (Does the children's game "Operation" ring a bell?) Similarly, manufacturing jobs and trades such as plumbing and electrical work often require manipulation of objects or pieces of equipment.

■ Types of Predictors

Many kinds of tests are used for selection purposes, and we will discuss several of these in the following sections; but first, let's revisit a couple of concepts. Recall our lengthy discussion of reliability and validity in Chapter 2 and our application of these concepts to *criteria* in Chapter 4. Reliability and validity are just as important for the predictors that we will discuss here. An unreliable predictor will not be successful in predicting job performance.

Imagine a situation in which you are trying to select automobile mechanics by giving them printouts from a diagnostic machine and asking them to use this information to diagnose a car's problem. This makes sense: Diagnostic skills are important (i.e., they are KSAOs) for mechanics and, thus, ought to be used to predict on-the-job performance. However, suppose we don't realize that in about half of the trials, the diagnostic machine is not working properly. An applicant may appear to make the wrong diagnosis about half the time, thus scoring low on this predictor. In other words, her misdiagnoses may be a result of the diagnostic machine's errors rather than her own errors. In this situation, our predictor score would be unreliable and thus not very useful for predicting performance.

When we talk about the validity of a predictor, we are usually thinking in terms of *criterion-related validity*, discussed in Chapter 2. Keep in mind that the sole purpose of predictors in I/O psychology is to predict some performance criterion. Because we don't have access to performance criteria prior to hiring employees, we use predictors as proxies for the criteria—and it is here that criterion-related validity takes on great importance. If a predictor is not related to a criterion, then the predictor serves little purpose. To avoid this problem, I/O psychologists spend a great deal of effort finding, developing, and validating predictors. In this way, organizations can be confident that selecting applicants based on predictor scores will result in the selection of those with the greatest potential to be successful on-the-job performers.

validity coefficient (r)
A correlation that serves as an index of the relationship between a predictor and a criterion, used by selection researchers and practitioners as evidence that a particular test is a valid predictor of a performance criterion.

The correlation is important to selection because it can be used for prediction, which is often the major goal of any selection or testing initiative. In fact, in the context of selection, it has a special name—**validity coefficient (r)**. As an index of the relationship between a predictor and a criterion, it is used by selection researchers and practitioners as evidence that a particular test is a good predictor of job performance. The coefficient of determination can be thought of as the percentage of variance in the criterion variable that is accounted for by the predictor variable. It reflects how well one variable predicts the other. For example, we could use a measure of general cognitive ability to predict job performance, calculate the validity coefficient (i.e., correlation), and square that coefficient (i.e., coefficient of determination) to estimate the amount of variance in a group of applicants' criterion scores that can be accounted for by this group's cognitive ability scores. In other words, we could determine how well measures of general cognitive ability predict individuals' performance on the job, as summarized by the validity coefficient. Let's take a closer look at predictors in the context of cognitive ability.

> **TECHNICAL TIP**
>
> *Remember, from Chapter 2, our discussion about the correlation coefficient as the index of the strength of a relationship. Also, we saw how squaring the correlation coefficient told us how much variance in one variable was accounted for by another variable—the coefficient of determination.*

Cognitive Ability

Tests of *cognitive ability* are among the most frequently used predictors in selection contexts (e.g., employee selection, college admissions) because of the common belief that mental functioning or intelligence is important for most jobs, as well as for success in school. There are two classes of cognitive ability tests, or what are sometimes called *intelligence tests*. The first are general cognitive ability tests and the second are specific cognitive ability tests.

General Cognitive Ability Tests The Wonderlic Personnel Test (Wonderlic, 1984) has been one of the most frequently used measures of cognitive ability for many years. It's even used (with some controversy) to assess the cognitive ability of professional athletes (e.g., NFL and NBA players) and to attempt to predict how these athletes will perform on and off the field (McCann, 2006). Figure 6.2 presents a few examples

FIGURE 6.2 Items Similar to Those Found on the Wonderlic Personnel Test

1. **Focused is the opposite of:**
   a. *scattered*   b. concerned   c. helpful   d. gracious

2. **Automobile is to road as boat is to:**
   a. air   b. tracks   c. *water*   d. gasoline

3. **Which of the following months has 31 days?**
   a. September   b. April   c. June   d. *December*

4. **Which number completes the series: 2, 4, 8, 4, 8, 16, 8,**
   a. *16*   b. 12   c. 8   d. 20

5. **If Bill runs 3 miles in 30 minutes, how many miles will he run in 1½ hours?**
   a. 12   b. 6   c. *9*   d. 8

Source: Goldstein, H. W., Zedeck, S., & Goldstein, I. L. (2002). Is this your final answer? *Human Performance, 15*(1–2), 123–142. Reprinted by permission of Taylor & Francis Group, http://www.informaworld.com.

of items similar to those found on the Wonderlic test (as well as other tests of general cognitive ability). A debate over the importance of general cognitive ability in employee selection contexts continues to rage (Farr & Tippins, 2010; Gardner & Diedrick, 2009; Goldstein, Zedeck, & Goldstein, 2002; Kuncel, Hezlett, & Ones, 2004; Murphy, 2002).

There's a fair amount of evidence suggesting that general cognitive ability accounts for a large proportion of variance in criterion performance (Ree, Earles, & Teachout, 1994; Salgado & Anderson, 2003). For instance, a meta-analysis of various studies in this area indicates that the validity coefficient for measures of general cognitive ability is .53 (Hunter & Hunter, 1984). This means that over 25% of the performance variance in people (i.e., the differences in performance across people) is accounted for or can be predicted by measures of general cognitive ability. It is important, too, to note that general cognitive ability predicts performance similarly across countries such as the United Kingdom (Bertua, Anderson, & Salgado, 2005) and, in general, the European community, where the validity has been estimated at .62 (Salgado et al., 2003). Notice, however, that if 25% or 36% of the criterion variance is accounted for by this measure, 75% or 64% is left unaccounted for. Is it reasonable to ask if we can do better? This question has been discussed for years, and researchers are continually working to determine what other predictors might help account for a greater percentage of the criterion variance, or what is called *incremental validity*. A recent meta-analysis used more sophisticated statistical techniques to support our knowledge that general cognitive ability accounts for up to 25% of the variance in performance (Lang, Kersting, Hülsheger, & Lang, 2010). In addition, this study found that general cognitive ability wasn't always the most important predictor and that specific cognitive ability sometimes plays a more important role in predicting performance.

Specific Cognitive Ability Tests Whereas general cognitive ability tests attempt to predict the likelihood that an individual will perform well in a particular job by measuring the individual's *general* capacity to learn, tests of specific cognitive abilities attempt to predict the likelihood that an individual will do well in a particular job given his or her *specific* abilities. For instance, tests of **mechanical ability** tap comprehension of mechanical relations, recognition of tools used for various purposes, and sometimes actual mechanical skills. The Bennett Mechanical Comprehension Test (Psychological Corporation, 1980) is probably the best known of this type. Sample items from the SRA (Science Research Associates) Test of Mechanical Concepts, another popular test, are presented in Figure 6.3.

A test of mechanical ability would be relevant for such jobs as machine operator, factory worker, and engineer, in which mechanical principles are important. Glance back at the framework of industrial psychology presented in Figure 3.1, and you'll see that two of the three major outcomes of job analysis—job description and job specifications—should tell us whether or not mechanical ability is important for the particular job of interest.

Closely related to mechanical ability is **spatial ability**, a second specific cognitive ability that plays an important role in many jobs. Measures of spatial ability often deal

mechanical ability
A specific cognitive ability involving a focus on mechanical relations, recognition of tools used for various purposes, and sometimes actual mechanical skills.

spatial ability
A specific cognitive ability involving a focus on geometric relations, such as visualizing objects and rotating them spatially to form a particular pattern.

FIGURE 6.3   Sample Items from the SRA Test of Mechanical Concepts

Mechanical Interrelationships

Which one of these stools is most likely to be steady on an uneven surface?

a. one-legged stool
b. two-legged stool
c. three-legged stool
d. four-legged stool
e. six-legged stool

a   b   c   d   e

Mechanical Tools and Devices

This is what kind of saw?

a. compass saw
b. ripsaw
c. pruning saw
d. hacksaw
e. miter saw

Source: Goldstein, H. W., Zedeck, S., & Goldstein, I. L. (2002). Is this your final answer? *Human Performance, 15*(1–2), 123–142. Reprinted by permission of Taylor & Francis Group, http://www.informaworld.com.

with geometric relations, such as visualizing objects and rotating them spatially to form a particular pattern. Jobs for which these types of tests might be relevant include mechanic and architect.

A third specific cognitive ability, **clerical ability**, is relevant for numerous important positions, such as secretary, administrative assistant, bookkeeper, and clerk. Most measures of clerical ability focus on both perceptual speed and accuracy in processing verbal and numerical data (Gatewood, Feild, & Barrick, 2007). The most frequently used test is probably the Minnesota Clerical Test, which was developed in 1933 (Psychological Corporation, 1979). This test comprises 200 items, each of which consists of a pair of numbers or names; the respondent is asked to place a check next to the pairs that are identical. Items similar to those found on the Minnesota Clerical Test are presented in Figure 6.4. An individual's score is the number right minus the number wrong. This is a speed test in which respondents are not expected to get through the entire list of pairs in the time allotted. Performance on the names subtest has been shown to be related to speed of reading and spelling, whereas scores on the numbers subtest are related to arithmetic skills and computations (Gatewood et al., 2007).

The validity of measures of specific cognitive abilities tends to hover around .40 to .50, with some consistency across cultures (for a review of the relevant research, see Gatewood et al., 2007). For instance, Salgado and colleagues (2003) found validity estimates for the European community to range from .35 to .56. One of the most

clerical ability
A specific cognitive ability, relevant for jobs such as secretary, administrative assistant, and bookkeeper, involving a focus on both perceptual speed and accuracy in processing verbal and numerical data.

FIGURE 6.4   Items Similar to Those Found on the Minnesota Clerical Test

INSTRUCTIONS: Please place an "X" on the line between each pair of items that are exactly the same. Do as many as you can in the allotted time.

Comparison of Names

Bekky Huber	_____	Becky Huber
Verna MacDonald	_____	Verna McDonald
Frank Giorno	_____	Frank Giorno
Bel Air, Maryland	_____	Belair, Maryland
Sylvia Chinn	_____	Sylvia Chin

Comparison of Numbers

13574	_____	13574
245693	_____	245663
5193754	_____	5193457
4396207	_____	4396207
8730916375	_____	8739016375

extensive and thorough studies in the selection area in the past 20 years, the Project A study, was conducted in the military and involved over 4,000 enlisted army personnel (McHenry, Hough, Toquam, Hanson, & Ashworth, 1990). Here, the validity coefficients for general cognitive ability and spatial ability predicting core job performance were .63 and .56, respectively. It is clear that both general and specific cognitive abilities are important predictors of job performance across a wide variety of jobs. However, the same large military study also revealed that these two cognitive predictors did not predict a different criterion, incumbents' personal discipline, very well.

As emphasized in the last chapter, the match between the predictor and the criterion is important. No abilities or skills are predictive of all aspects of performance—I/O psychologists have to rely on the job analysis to identify the important KSAOs for predicting particular on-the-job behaviors. A test of spatial ability would not be predictive of my success as a teacher (and it's a good thing or I'd still be looking for work!) but would likely be very helpful in hiring engineers, architects, or cartographers.

emotional intelligence (EI) Ability of a person to deal effectively with his or her emotions and the emotions of others.

A newer and intriguing intelligence construct is **emotional intelligence (EI)**. EI is the ability of individuals to generate, recognize, express, understand, and evaluate their own (and others') emotions, leading to effectiveness in the workplace and their own personal life (Van Rooy & Viswesvaran, 2004). This construct has become very popular in recent years in part because of the success of Daniel Goleman's 1995 book, *Emotional Intelligence* (Semadar, Robins, & Ferris, 2006).

Some empirical research has indicated that EI may be an important predictor of performance at work. For instance, one study (Carmeli & Josman, 2006) found significant correlations between EI and task performance ($r = .47$), altruistic citizenship behavior ($r = .26$), and compliance citizenship behavior ($r = .21$). An interesting study using undergraduate business students (Rode et al., 2007) found that EI interacted with a conscientious personality to effectively predict college GPA, group performance, and public speaking effectiveness. The authors concluded that it's not enough to be high on EI; you have to be motivated as well. This particular combination of ability and personality seems to predict performance well and, thus, suggests implications for organizations trying to select those applicants who are likely to be effective employees. Further, even more recent work has concluded that EI is a better predictor of social interactions with peers than general cognitive ability but that general cognitive ability predicts academic performance best (Song et al., 2010).

Psychomotor Tests

Jobs such as packer, machine operator, computer assembler, and electrician require great hand, arm, and finger dexterity. Other positions, such as air traffic controller, nuclear plant operator, and fighter pilot, require excellent sensory abilities such as superior vision and hearing. Measures of sensory abilities known as **psychomotor tests** are often used in the selection of applicants for such positions. Psychomotor tests evaluate both the speed and the accuracy of motor and sensory coordination. One of the best-known tests of psychomotor ability is the Purdue Pegboard (Mathiowetz, Rogers, Dowe-Keval, Donahoe, & Rennels, 1986), which measures an individual's ability to make controlled movements with the hands, arms, and fingertips. Test takers are placed in front of a pegboard on a table and asked to manipulate pegs, washers, and collars in and around the pegboard.

psychomotor tests
Tests that measure both the speed and the accuracy of motor and sensory coordination.

Traditional vision and hearing tests are also used for selection in jobs where a certain proficiency of these senses is required. The Project A study mentioned previously (McHenry et al., 1990) reported a validity of .53 for a psychomotor test battery predicting core job performance across nine jobs. In addition, John Hunter and Ronda Hunter (1984) reported validities of psychomotor tests averaging about .40 across several jobs—a figure that varied according to the type of job. Combining these data, we find that psychomotor tests predict between 16% and 28% of the variance in job performance. Keep in mind that these percentages are not precise, given the diversity of the psychomotor measures, performance criteria, and jobs investigated.

For a more recent example of psychomotor testing, we turn to a study that examined the incremental validity of a perceptual speed test over general cognitive ability in a sample of warehouse workers (Mount, Oh, & Burns, 2008) whose main job was the unloading of trucks and organizing of shipments. The perceptual speed test required individuals to identify names that exactly matched names they had seen earlier, much as they would when unpacking their shipments and organizing them by food item and restaurant name. Results showed that perceptual speed predicted warehouse performance above and beyond what was accounted for by general cognitive ability. In fact, prediction was improved by 15%!

Because a psychomotor test used for the wrong job would likely result in a validity of zero, a careful job analysis is recommended here also. For instance, a perceptual speed test or the Purdue Pegboard would not likely predict the success of a waitress or an insurance sales agent. But when used for appropriate jobs, they can be very useful tools.

Personality Tests

personality tests
Tests in which numbers are systematically assigned to individuals' characteristics.

About 40% of Fortune 100 companies use personality assessment to screen job applicants—a $500 million industry in the United States, growing by about 10% per year (http://www.psychometric-success.com/personality-tests/personality-tests-understanding-industry.htm). Compared to many of the other predictors discussed in this chapter, **personality tests** have received a great deal of attention from the research community (Barrick, Mount, & Judge, 2001; Hurtz & Donovan, 2000).

The word *personality* refers to an individual's traits—or predispositions to behave in a particular way across situations—and personality measurement involves procedures that systematically assign numbers to such characteristics The most typical measures are self-report questionnaires such as the NEO Personality Inventory (for a review, see Piedmont, 1998), the Hogan Personality Inventory (Hogan & Hogan, 1995), and the Sixteen Personality Factor Questionnaire (for a review, see Schuerger, 1995). Other measures, such as the Minnesota Multiphasic Personality Inventory (MMPI), have been used in employee selection even though scholars have criticized the use of measures for employee selection that were normed, like this one, on a clinical sample and developed for clinical purposes.

Although there are many different personality measures, personality researchers tend to agree that many of them measure the five broad dimensions that make up the Big Five model: openness to experience, conscientiousness, extraversion, agreeableness, and neuroticism. (A helpful mnemonic is to note that the first letters of each dimension spell O-C-E-A-N.) Of all the personality classification schemes, this is the one used most often by practitioners and researchers alike. To give you a feel for Big Five personality measurement, Table 6.1 shows a few items from the International Personality Item Pool (http://ipip.ori.org/ipip/).

A good deal of empirical research suggests that personality measures are valid predictors of job performance (e.g., Barrick et al., 2001; Ones, Dilchert, Viswesvaran, & Judge, 2007) and OCBs (Chiaburu, Oh, Berry, Li, & Gardner, 2011). In fact, this recent meta-analysis demonstrated stronger relationships between openness and agreeableness and OCB than between openness and agreeableness and task performance.

Although it is generally difficult to estimate the size of the validity coefficient between personality and on-the-job performance, meta-analyses estimate that relationship (.23) to be significant (Barrick et al., 2001). Furthermore, conscientiousness (being dependable and hardworking) and emotional stability have been reported to be the best predictors of performance (Barrick et al., 2001). Accordingly, these two dimensions have received the most research attention. Another benefit of the Big Five model is that the factor structure and other relevant structural information as measured by the NEO Personality Inventory (Revised) hold up consistently across cultures (McCrae & Terracciano, 2005).

Some personality researchers argue that estimates such as the .23 noted above are *under*estimates given that, in most studies, specific personality dimensions are not linked to specific criteria. In particular, some have argued (e.g., Hough, 1998) that

Table 6.1 International Personality Item Pool

Extraversion	Am the life of the party
	Start conversations
	Keep in the background (R)*
	Am quiet around strangers
Agreeableness	Am interested in people
	Take time out for others
	Am not interested in other people's problems (R)
	Insult people (R)
Conscientiousness	Am always prepared
	Pay attention to details
	Make a mess of things (R)
	Shirk my duties (R)
Neurotocism (Emotional Stability)	Get stressed out easily
	Worry about things
	Seldom feel blue (R)
	Am relaxed most of the time (R)
Openness (Intellect)	Am quick to understand things
	Spend time reflecting on things
	Am not interested in abstract ideas (R)
	Do not have a good imagination (R)

*(R) indicates that the item's score is reversed before it is used to compute one's total score.
Source: http://ipip.ori.org/ipip/

the five-factor model comprises dimensions that are too broad, adding that prediction will be improved to the extent that specific personality dimensions are used to predict targeted performance criteria such as effort and leadership, personal discipline, and counterproductive behavior. For instance, a recent investigation demonstrated that those high on conscientiousness and low on agreeableness express greater intentions to be an entrepreneur and more success as an entrepreneur as predicted by theories outlined by the authors (Zhao, Seibert, & Lumpkin, 2010). Again, I strongly emphasize that no predictor works for all criteria and that job analysis has to allow for the appropriate match between predictor constructs and criterion constructs (Borman, Hanson, & Hedge, 1997).

One problem with personality tests is that individuals can potentially guess the responses that are likely to result in high scores—we call this *faking*. For instance, most applicants would know how to answer the following question in such a way as to "look good" to the organization: "I often think of ways in which I can outsmart my supervisor—strongly agree or strongly disagree?" It has been argued that the motivation to fake is influenced by demographic characteristics (e.g., age and gender), individual differences (e.g., integrity and manipulativeness), and perceptual variables (e.g., perceptions of others' behavior and perceptions of organizational justice) (Snell, Sydell, & Lueke, 1999). Recent work suggests that about one-third of all applicants fake (Griffith & Converse, 2011) and that these fakers engage in more counterproductive behavior than nonfakers (Peterson, Griffith, Isaacson, O'Connell, & Mangos, 2011) and have lower integrity and self-efficacy (Gammon, Griffith, & Kung, 2011). Some argue that faking reduces the validity of personality measures for selection by 25% (Komar, Brown, Komar, & Robie, 2008) and that selection decisions are seriously affected because faking substantially affects the rank order of candidates, which can lead to the wrong people being hired (Peterson, Griffith, & Converse, 2009).

On the other hand, another study (Hogan, Barrett, & Hogan, 2007) showed that rejected applicants' scores on a personality measure did not improve when they came back six months later to reapply for the job. The researchers reasoned that not being hired the first time would result in motivation to score higher on the personality test the second time around. However, this didn't happen, and these authors argue from their data that faking is not a serious problem in real-world selection contexts. This conclusion may be too strong given other research and data, but it certainly makes clear that we are still unsure of the role that faking truly plays in the selection context.

As is often the case, there are varying opinions about the benefits of personality assessment for employee selection. Some researchers argue that personality is often inaccurately measured, does not make a large enough contribution to the prediction of job performance, and can be easily faked by applicants (Morgeson et al., 2007). In fact, these same researchers go so far as to suggest that, relative to other predictors, personality tests have low validity for predicting overall job performance and recommend not using published self-report personality tests. They conclude that personality constructs are important in understanding work behavior but encourage researchers to identify and develop alternatives to self-report measures.

Integrity Tests

integrity tests
Tests used in an attempt to predict whether an employee will engage in counterproductive or dishonest work-related behaviors such as cheating, stealing, or sabotage; also called honesty tests.

Among the newest tests used in employee selection are **integrity tests** (also called *honesty tests*), which attempt to predict whether an employee will engage in counterproductive or dishonest work-related behaviors such as cheating, stealing, or sabotage. Since 1988, when the passage of the Employee Polygraph Protection Act prohibited the use of polygraphs for most private-sector jobs, integrity tests have taken on a much more important role in selection (Cascio, 1998).

There are two types of integrity tests. The *overt integrity test* attempts to measure both attitudes toward theft and, through admissions on self-reports, actual theft behaviors. Overt integrity tests might ask respondents to report how often they have stolen from previous employers, whether they believe that lying is okay if one doesn't get caught, and the extent to which they perceive theft to be easy. The *personality-type integrity test* measures personality characteristics believed to predict counterproductive behaviors (e.g., risk taking, emotional instability, dishonesty, and irresponsibility). The purpose of these tests is more hidden from respondents than is that of overt tests. One investigation found that test takers perceived overt integrity tests to have greater face validity (i.e., they appear more believable and useful) and predictive validity than do personality-type integrity tests (Whitney, Diaz, Mineghino, & Powers, 1999).

Researchers have found clear empirical support for the use of integrity tests. For instance, when a personality-based integrity test was administered to more than 300 prisoners who had been convicted of white-collar crimes (stealing, bribery, extortion, etc.) and to more than 300 white-collar workers in positions of authority in the working world, they found that these groups scored very differently on the integrity test (Collins & Schmidt, 1993). The authors conceptualized the differences as being reflective of "social conscientiousness"—or a lack of it—such that the prisoners exhibited greater tendencies toward irresponsibility and disregard for rules and social norms than did the working managers. Meta-analyses have reported validity coefficients of .34 and .47 for integrity tests that predict job performance and counterproductive behavior, respectively (for a thorough discussion, see Berry, Sackett, & Wiemann, 2007). However, a more recent, thorough, and sophisticated meta-analysis has found some different results that are quite interesting (Van Iddekinge, Roth, Raymark, & Odle-Dusseau, 2012). Namely, the researchers found smaller coefficients: .15 for performance and .30 for counterproductive work behavior. There are a few factors that may have contributed to these differences. First, this meta-analysis was more selective in evaluating the quality of the research studies before including them in the analysis. Second, when comparing the studies, it was clear that there were stronger effects for studies that were conducted by integrity test publishers than for those conducted by independent researchers. This difference could reflect the fact that the publishers have a vested interest in the validity of the tests and this interest somehow affects the validity coefficients, although the authors report no reason to suspect this. On the other hand, it could be that the studies conducted by the test publishers provide a more accurate picture and the more pessimistic outlook from the independent researchers is actually inaccurate. More research is needed here, but the authors are careful to point out that we don't know the reason for these differences and can only conclude that the validity differs from test publishers to independent researchers, which should make us cautious before drawing inferences from the literature.

Note that the previous discussion of faking on personality tests is relevant here as well, inasmuch as faking also appears to be possible on some integrity tests (Alliger & Dwight, 2000). Researchers have developed a cognitive lie detection procedure that may help organizations screen out (1) employees likely to engage in misconduct and (2) those likely to provide deceptive answers to screening questions, both of which could improve validity (Walczyk, Mahoney, Doverspike, & Griffith-Ross, 2009).

There isn't much research yet on integrity testing in other cultures. We do know, however, that countries high in power distance (i.e., where members of society accept and expect that power will be unequally distributed) are more likely to use integrity tests (Berry et al., 2007). This is probably because these countries are more comfortable with hierarchically centralized power and less concerned about subordinate employees'/applicants' reactions to this approach to screening.

Work Samples

work sample
tests
Tests that attempt
to duplicate perfor-
mance criteria mea-
sures and use them
as predictors, thus
forming miniature
replicas of the job.

Although a cognitive ability test, a vision test, and a personality test may be useful predictors for the position of police officer, none of these tests actually measure on-the job
behaviors; rather, they are used as proxies or replacements for criteria because we don't
have access to criteria at this stage in the selection process. With **work sample tests**, we
take a very different approach: Instead of measuring constructs that we hope will predict
our performance criterion, we try to duplicate the performance criterion measures and
use them as predictors. Work samples are thus miniature replicas of the job. To develop
them, we create smaller standardized tests that measure the actual job performance criteria identified by the job analysis.

In addition to using measures of personality, general cognitive ability, and specific
clerical ability, we may find it useful to develop a work sample test for hiring administrative assistants. In fact, this type of test is typically included in a selection battery for
the administrative assistant position. As an example in an entirely different occupation,
in most academic departments, potential new faculty members are required to present to faculty and students a research study that they have conducted. This approach
serves two purposes. First, it provides an opportunity for the department to evaluate
the applicant's research after hearing him or her present it for an hour or so. Second,
it provides a work sample in the sense that the applicant, if hired, will have to stand
up before a group of students and lecture about topics that are in his or her area of
expertise. This small sample of behavior is our first clue as to how effective the applicant might be as a teacher in the department.

When work samples are carefully developed, they can demonstrate validities as
high as the .50s (Hunter & Hunter, 1984). This means that an individual's performance on a work sample test is a very strong indicator of whether or not this person
is likely to be promoted within the company. One meta-analysis reported a validity
coefficient of .39 across a series of performance criteria (Roth, Bobko, & McFarland,
2005). The results of these reviews make it clear that work sample tests are among the
most valid predictors of criterion performance.

situational
judgment tests
(SJTs)
Paper-and-pencil
test or video
vignette that pro-
vides hypothetical
scenarios for can-
didates to respond
to by choosing the
best alternative.

A specific type of work sample test has regained the attention of I/O psychologists in recent years—namely, **situational judgment tests (SJTs)**. These include
paper-and-pencil tests or video scenarios that measure applicants' judgment in work
settings (Lievens, Buyse, & Sackett, 2005). For instance, applicants might be asked
how they would handle a situation in which an employee seemed unable to understand how to solve a particular problem, and they would have to choose from the
following response options: (1) continue explaining the problem to the employee,
(2) ask someone else to get involved and explain the problem to the employee,
(3) discipline the employee for his or her deficiency, or (4) place the employee in a
remedial training program. Typically, one of these response options would be scored
as the correct answer based on subject matter expert (SME) judgments regarding the
best response. In one study, scores on an SJT predicted both the task performance and
contextual performance of 160 employees (Chan & Schmitt, 2002). Furthermore,
SJTs demonstrated incremental validity over measures of personality, job experience,
and cognitive ability.

In a study of over 1,700 medical school candidates in Belgium, researchers found an SJT to demonstrate incremental validity for predicting overall GPA beyond cognitive predictors (Lievens et al., 2005). The most recent meta-analysis published to date found that SJTs measuring teamwork skills and leadership had strong validities for predicting job performance (Christian, Edwards, & Bradley, 2010). The researchers also found stronger validities for video-based SJTs than paper-and-pencil ones. Furthermore, in an earlier meta-analysis, researchers found situational judgment tests that were developed on the basis of a job analysis to be more valid ($r = .38$) than were those not based on a job analysis ($r = .29$; McDaniel, Morgeson, Finnegan, Campion, & Braverman, 2001).

▲ **A Closer Look**
Why is a driving test considered a "work sample"?

Assessment Centers

The term **assessment center (AC)** refers to an approach or method in which multiple raters (called *assessors*) evaluate applicants or incumbents (called *assessees*) on a standardized set of predictors (called *exercises*). Many large companies employ assessment centers. ACs differ in many ways, but a typical one might have the following characteristics: Twelve to fifteen assessees are involved in the center at any given time. The assessment is done by a team of four to six assessors who do not know the assessees and are likely to be two levels above them in the organizational hierarchy. Almost without exception, multiple methods of assessment are used, such as a measure of general cognitive ability, an interview, and various work sample–type exercises. The overall assessment usually lasts two to three days. The assessors receive at least a half-day of training and often stay a half-day after the assessment is complete to finalize scores and write up reports.

assessment center (AC)
An approach or method in which multiple raters (*assessors*) evaluate applicants or incumbents (*assessees*) on a standardized set of predictors (*exercises*).

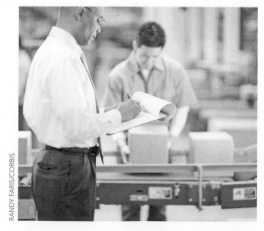

As with much of the testing movement in I/O psychology, assessment centers were developed in the military. They were first created in Germany in the 1930s and later refined during World War II by the British and U.S. military (Gatewood et al., 2007). One important study that employed ACs focused on the career development of young employees as they moved up

◀ **A Closer Look**
Why would you expect an assessment center to be effective in identifying management potential?

through the ranks of AT&T (Bray, Campbell, & Grant, 1974). Data were collected on these young men from 1956 through 1965, and more than 300 of them who were tested in the early years of the AC remained with the company through 1965. The AT&T management progress study is the most extensive study of managerial development ever conducted; it created a rich data set that still provides a wealth of information about the relationships between employees' scores on the various exercises and their career progression. The results of the study are very impressive: Of the 72 men who were not promoted by 1965, the assessors had correctly identified 68 (i.e., 94%) as unlikely to be promoted based on their AC performance.

The United Nations uses ACs to select managers for its worldwide operations (Jackson & Schuler, 2000), and they are also implemented throughout Europe. In the United Kingdom, for instance, a major bank uses them to identify management potential and development needs among upper-level clerical staff. In addition to their widespread use in the private sector, ACs have been extensively employed by metropolitan fire and police departments.

Obviously, an AC is only as effective as the exercises that make it up are valid. In general, considerable evidence suggests that well-established centers are valid predictors for many different performance criteria. The most-cited review of AC validity reports a validity coefficient of .37 for overall AC validity (Gaugler, Rosenthal, Thornton, & Bentson, 1987). More recent reviews found a similar overall relationship and also demonstrated that combining multiple AC dimensions into a composite resulted in a validity coefficient of .45 (Arthur, Day, McNelly, & Edens, 2003; Meriac, Hoffman, Woehr, & Fleisher, 2008). Although the AC dimensions are related to cognitive ability and personality, they improve prediction of job performance above and beyond those predictors (Melchers & Annen, 2010; Meriac et al., 2008). Of course, ACs can also be very expensive in terms of both the time and money involved in assessing employees in a fair and valid way.

Let's now take a closer look at two of the most often used AC exercises: the in-basket and the leaderless group discussion.

in-basket
An individual exercise in which assessees are asked to act as a manager in a particular company with certain issues or ideas that need to be considered and responded to.

In-Basket An **in-basket** is an individual exercise in which an assessee is presented with a scenario, such as being newly hired to replace a manager who has had to leave the company abruptly due to a serious illness. The assessee is also provided with information such as an organizational chart and a description of the company mission, along with the kinds of things that would typically appear in a manager's in-basket, such as memos, letters, requests for information, files on grievances, and employee applications. At that point, the assessee is asked to take the one or two hours that are available prior to hopping on a flight to New York for a board of directors' meeting to review all of the in-basket materials and to respond accordingly with memos, letters, decisions, delegations, interview scheduling, and so on. When the time is up, the assessee is asked to describe (using a checklist or a narrative) all of his or her actions and to present a rationale for each.

Matthew O'Connell

PhD, 1994, I/O Psychology, University of Akron
Executive Vice President & Co-founder
Select International, Inc.

Predicting future behavior is one of the foundations on which I/O psychology was built. Properly designed selection systems allow us to predict a broad range of future behaviors—or, more specifically, the likelihood of those behaviors occurring—with a surprising level of accuracy.

Whenever you talk about prediction, the first thing you need to determine is what you actually want to predict. That may seem like a very simple question, but in my experience it isn't. Job performance is multifaceted. Consider a sales position. A salesperson may be good at selling—that is, meeting or exceeding quotas—but might overcommit the organization's resources, be poor at organizing his or her own time, and fail to follow up with clients. Would that person be a "good hire"? For some organizations the answer would be yes, but for many others it would be no.

That's the reason Select takes a multimethod and multidimensional approach to selection systems, much like a financial advisor looks at an investment portfolio. You wouldn't put all of your money into one stock or even one type of stock. You could strike it rich once in a while, but over the long run your hit rate would be low and you'd have too much volatility. Most of Select's online assessments are multiscale batteries that include a variety of different assessment methods, including personality, situational judgment, applied problem solving, biodata, and interactive simulations. They are combined to create a profile that encompasses multiple competencies. Once we have a sound battery established, we can focus on how best to weight the competencies, establish cutoffs, and so on. That's where determining the criteria that you're interested in predicting becomes critical. It's relatively easy to set up a profile identifying people who learn quickly and are hardworking. But how likely are they to leave within three months? How well do they handle ambiguity and stress? How well do they get along with others and take feedback? How likely are they to do something unsafe? Ultimately, you have to make trade-offs.

Prediction is not only about selecting the most accurate predictors. Prediction also involves putting them together in a cohesive way to ensure consistency and fairness over time. It involves weighting them to maximize the prediction of important outcomes and establishing cutoffs that allow organizations to meet their hiring needs.

Applying Your Knowledge

1. In what ways do assessment centers align with the preferred methods for performance prediction used at Select?

2. In what ways do work samples align with the preferred methods for performance prediction used at Select?

3. Given the difficulty and complexity of making accurate, targeted hiring predictions, do you think that assessment measures would be better at limiting poor hires or better at increasing good hires? Why?

The idea here, of course, is to place the assessee in a set of circumstances similar to those a manager would experience and to evaluate how well he or she responds. Some refer to in-baskets as simulations or even work samples because they mimic actual on-the-job settings. Figure 6.5 presents the background information and instructions presented to participants for an in-basket task that I have used for research purposes. Notice that the instructions have the clear purpose of asking the assessee to take actions and make decisions about how to proceed. This is typical of in-basket exercises.

FIGURE 6.5   An In-Basket Test: The Bradford Consolidated Fund

While working on this exercise, you are to be Pat Chandler, who has just assumed the duties of General Manager for the Bradford Consolidated Fund (BCF) in Bradford, New Jersey. The BCF is a nonprofit organization devoted to charitable enterprises. The Fund is now in the middle of the 2013 annual fund-raising drive. You were recently hired to replace Georgia McKinley, the former General Manager, who was in an automobile accident and had to resign from her position with the BCF.

Today is Sunday, March 15, 2013, the first opportunity you have had to come to Bradford. Your administrative assistant, Harry Stein, has left on your desk a memo along with a number of other items for you to look at and work on during the afternoon. Mr. Stein has also left a list of members of the staff connected with the 2013 fund-raising drive. You will find this on your desk along with some stationery, pencils, paper clips, and so on for your use.

The Current Situation: Your task on this Sunday afternoon is to go through the items, taking appropriate actions as necessary. Keep in mind that you may not finish everything in front of you in the allotted time and it is up to you to decide the order in which to work on the items. You are now actually on the job. Everything you decide to do must be in writing and also recorded on the *Reasons for Actions* form enclosed. Use the stationery provided for memos, letters, lists, and the like. Outline plans or set agendas for meetings you may want to call. Sign papers, if necessary. Wherever possible, clip letters, memos, or notes to the items that they concern.

Behave as though you are actually on the job. Remember, it is Sunday afternoon, March 15, 2013, and you have 30 minutes in the office to get as much work done as you can.

leaderless group discussion (LGD)
A group exercise designed to tap managerial attributes that requires the interaction of a small group of individuals.

Leaderless Group Discussion Whereas an in-basket is an individual exercise, a **leaderless group discussion (LGD)** is a group exercise designed to tap managerial attributes that requires the interaction of a small number of individuals (Gatewood et al., 2007). Typically, a group of five or six assessees are seated at a conference table, surrounded by assessors at the perimeter of the room who observe the interactions. The group is then presented with an issue to resolve. Sometimes each assessee is given a particular role to play, such as the director of one of the departments involved in the issue; at other times, roles are not assigned. But in all cases, no one is assigned the role of leader (hence the term *leaderless*). After the group has been provided with background information about the issue in question and given a fixed amount of time to resolve it, the assessors simply sit and observe the interactions; they do not participate at all. The assessees are typically rated on such dimensions as aggressiveness, persuasiveness, interpersonal skills, communication skills, flexible thinking, and listening skills. Scores on these dimensions are used to predict performance-related criteria.

Biographical Information

The major premise behind the use of **biographical information** for selection is that past behavior is the best predictor of future behavior. Biographical information can be thought of as any information that is descriptive of an individual's personal history. The idea is that if I want to predict how you will respond in a certain situation, one of the best ways for me to do so is to find out how you have responded in similar situations in the past. Those who work with biographical information often go one step further in considering *any* information about a person's history as potentially useful— even information about hobbies or other activities that are not directly related to the job (Mael, 1991). In the selection context, biographical information is typically collected in one of two ways: through an application blank or a biodata questionnaire.

biographical information
In the context of selection, any information that is descriptive of an individual's personal history.

Application Blank

Without a doubt, the application blank is one of the most frequently and widely used selection devices. Whether you are applying for a restaurant job or a faculty position or an executive position at a Fortune 500 company, the chances are good that you will be asked to fill out some sort of application blank. Typically, this form will request historical (as well as current) information such as your educational background, work experience, experience relevant to the job in question, and the names and addresses of previous employers. Most of us have filled out such forms at one time or another. Unfortunately, many companies spend little time developing their application blanks. Some even hand out generic ones, which are available at office supply stores. (Keep in mind that, if these are being used for selection purposes, all the same ethical and legal rules that apply elsewhere to personnel issues apply to the application blank as well.)

The use of generic application blanks suggests that the information the company is asking for has not been developed from a job analysis. But, as we now know, a job analysis is critical. If educational background and work experience are going to be defended as valid predictors of future on-the-job performance, these items have to be backed up by a job analysis. As you can imagine, many companies get themselves into legal skirmishes by using off-the-shelf application blanks rather than developing their own or at least validating the off-the-shelf predictors.

Biodata

Although it may be appropriate to think of application blank information as biographical data, the term **biodata** is usually reserved for the personal history information that is obtained through biographical information blanks (BIBs). BIBs are different from application blanks in that (1) they usually have a multiple-choice, yes–no, or Likert-scale format (the last contains answers ranging from "strongly agree" to "strongly disagree"); (2) they ask questions in much broader areas, such as health, hobbies, family history, interests, and social experience; and (3) they contain many more questions (up to about 150) than do application blanks (typically 10–15).

Table 6.2 presents some items for the job of customer service representative, a person who responds to service complaints or requests from customers over the phone. In the left column of the table are seven predictor dimensions; in the right column are biodata items related to each of those dimensions. In a real-life situation, of course,

biodata
Personal history information obtained through a biographical information blank (BIB) that asks respondents about their attitudes, hobbies, experiences, and so on.

Table 6.2 Biodata Items for the Position of Customer Service Representative

Dimension	Items
Helping others	How often have you helped someone you didn't know by carrying something for them (e.g., boxes, luggage, groceries)?
	How often have you stopped to give aid or called someone to assist a stranded motorist?
Negotiation skills	When you feel strongly about something, how easily can you persuade others to see your point of view?
	As a child, when your parents/guardians originally refused to let you do something, how easily could you convince them to change their minds?
Interpersonal intelligence	In the past, how easily have you been able to judge the moods of your friends, coworkers, or family members?
	In the past, when meeting people for the first time, to what extent were you aware of the kind of impression you made?
Patience	When you have been in a frustrating interpersonal situation, how often have you been able to be patient with the person or persons causing the frustration?
	When asked for travel directions by a stranger, how likely are you to voluntarily repeat them if you suspect the person is confused?
Empathy	To what extent would your friends describe you as sympathetic?
	In the past, how easily have you been able to reach out to or express compassion for someone who was upset?
	In the past, when you've seen a friend or family member upset, to what extent have you actually "felt their pain"?
Extraversion	When socializing with a group of people, how often do you feel the group is relying on you to keep the conversation flowing?
	In the past, how comfortable have you felt in social situations?
Oral communication	While in school, if given a choice, how often would you choose to do an oral presentation rather than a written report?
	In the past, to what extent have you been comfortable in sharing job-related information by having discussions in person?

both the predictor dimensions and criterion dimensions would be developed on the basis of a job analysis. The premise here is that past behavior is a good predictor of future behavior. Thus, for instance, someone with a history of exhibiting patience in socially frustrating situations is likely to respond patiently to customers who are yelling about the lack of quality service they've received from the company. Similarly, someone with a history of helping strangers is not only more likely to be satisfied with a customer service job but also more likely to perform better than someone who has never considered it important or rewarding to help others. In short, biodata items should predict on-the-job performance.

For biodata, the validity evidence is quite consistent: It predicts performance quite well (Allworth & Hesketh, 2000). A review of performance predictors for salespeople reported that biodata was the strongest predictor ($r = .52$) of managerial ratings of sales performance (Vinchur, Schippmann, Switzer, & Roth, 1998). And in more extensive reviews, validity coefficients of .37 (Hunter & Hunter, 1984) and .32 (Schmitt, Gooding, Noe, & Kirsch, 1984) have been reported across a series of criteria, including performance ratings. A great resource for further information is the *Biodata Handbook,* one chapter of which provides a summary of meta-analytic reviews of biodata (Stokes & Cooper, 1994). This chapter makes it clear that biodata consistently demonstrate validities between .20 and .46—these tend to be highest for criteria like supervisory ratings of performance and measures of productivity.

Interviews

As you may have guessed, **interviews** are among the most popular selection devices and are typically used across all job levels. An interview can be defined as a procedure designed to predict future performance based on an applicant's oral responses to a series of oral questions. The rationale is that the person conducting the interview can gather information through such questions that will allow the organization to make accurate predictions of successful job performance. I was a high school student when I experienced my first job interview at a fast-food restaurant, and every job I've had since then was preceded by an interview. I'm sure that most of you have had interviews of some sort, too.

Two major categories of interviews merit special attention. First, the more traditional *unstructured interview* is constructed haphazardly, with no consistency of questioning across applicants. One candidate may be asked what his particular strengths are and why he is interested in the job, while a second candidate may be asked what her particular weaknesses are and whether she's had any experiences that are especially relevant for the job. The unstructured interview process sometimes results in the organization comparing apples and oranges. For this reason, it is generally considered a less useful technique than the structured interview approach.

The *structured interview* consists of a series of standardized job analysis–based questions that are asked of all job candidates. For instance, when interviewing someone for the job of camp counselor, an interviewer might use questions like "What is it about working with adolescents that attracts you?" "What kinds of nature experiences have you had that prepare you for this particular job?" "Which of your strengths match well

interviews Procedures designed to predict future performance based on an applicant's oral responses to a series of oral questions.

with the social and physical requirements of this job?" Each candidate would be asked these questions in the same order, the responses would be noted by the interviewer, and the candidates would receive a score on the interview based on these responses. It is this score that would be used in the selection process. The key to a structured interview is that everyone is asked the same set of questions. This technique not only increases the reliability of the interview process but also allows for a fair comparison among the applicants.

There are two particular structured interview formats that require discussion. First, the **situational interview** focuses on future behavior. Here, the job applicant is presented with dilemmas or situations that are embedded in a work context and asked how he or she would handle the situation (Seijts & Kyei-Poku, 2010). Second, the **behavior description interview** focuses on past behavior—applicants are asked to describe specific ways in which they have addressed various situations in the past. Both situational and behavior description interviews are based on a job analysis, ask consistent questions of each candidate, and use a scoring guide to evaluate the applicant's performance on the interview (Seijts & Kyei-Poku, 2010). Certainly, these features are positively related to the increased validity of the structured interview process.

According to the many reviews of job interview validity conducted between 1960 and 1990, interviews had rather low validity. One well-cited study reported a validity coefficient of only .14 for interviews in predicting supervisor ratings of performance (Hunter & Hunter, 1984). Nevertheless, organizations have continued to use interviews in selection. Among the many possible explanations for this persistence, the most convincing is that the interview is more than a selection device. Indeed, it is a communication process in which the organization gains useful information about the applicant and the applicant gathers useful information about the organization (Cascio, 1998). The interview format may even provide the applicant with a **realistic job preview (RJP)**, which is simply an accurate glimpse of what the job would actually be like. In this way, the applicant can begin to get a feel for the organization's climate, the attitudes among employees, and the interpersonal relationships between subordinates and supervisors.

Since 1990, interview techniques have been refined (e.g., situational and behavior description interviewing) and more sophisticated meta-analytic techniques have been developed (Ganzach, Kluger, & Klayman, 2000). Reviews using these techniques have reported better validity for the employment interview. One meta-analysis found that interviews overall were predictive of job performance ($r = .37$) and, as expected, that structured interviews were more predictive ($r = .44$) than unstructured interviews ($r = .33$; McDaniel, Whetzel, Schmidt, & Maurer, 1994). Another study demonstrated that structured interviews predict performance over and above general cognitive ability and conscientiousness, thus indicating the incremental validity of the interview (Cortina, Goldstein, Payne, Davison, & Gilliland, 2000). These results suggest that interviews can be very useful in employee selection contexts and that practitioners should attempt to use structured rather than unstructured interviews when possible because they are better predictors of job performance criteria.

Of course, some of the biases discussed in the context of performance appraisal (Chapter 5)—including halo error, contrast effects, and similarity effects—may come

---

situational interview An interviewing technique that relies on candidates sharing responses or intentions about job-related dilemmas or situations proposed to them with respect to the new job.

behavior description interview An interviewing technique that relies on candidates sharing examples of past behaviors related to tasks required for the new job.

realistic job preview (RJP) During an employment interview, the presentation of an accurate glimpse of what the job would be like.

into play during interviews as well. For instance, one study demonstrated that interview ratings are affected by nonverbal factors such as physical attractiveness (Burnett & Motowidlo, 1998). However, despite the subjective nature of interview ratings, they tend to be good predictors of on-the-job performance.

One additional point should be made before we leave this topic: Although the employment interview can include many different questions, there are important legal issues involved in deciding what questions *shouldn't* be asked. Table 6.3 contains a list of legally suspect questions that could be challenged in court and used by plaintiffs to allege discrimination; in the next chapter, we will discuss various employment laws that define what organizations can and cannot ask of applicants. Table 6.4 presents validity coefficients for all of the predictors reviewed in this chapter. Notice that general cognitive ability appears to be the best predictor of job performance, followed closely by psychomotor ability, ACs, and biodata. Of course, even these consistent predictors seldom account for more than 25% of the

11-9   e-mail:CLOSETOHOME@COMPUSERVE.COM

© 1998 John McPherson\Dist. by Universal Press Syndicate

Though it was only his second day on the job, employees were already getting bad vibes about the new division chief.

▲ **A Closer Look** How might a personality test or employment interview have prevented this bad selection decision?

variance in a criterion. In one study, for example, researchers examined the extent to which adding predictors to general cognitive ability would help in predicting job performance (Schmidt & Hunter, 1998). What they found was that work sample tests, integrity tests, personality tests, and structured interviews demonstrated incremental validity by accounting for an additional 14% or more of the variance in job performance and that the best two-predictor combination was general cognitive ability and integrity tests (multiple $r = .65$), which together accounted for about 42% of the variance in job performance. One study found that conscientiousness and openness accounted for a significant increment in variance in academic performance beyond that accounted for by intelligence (Chamorro-Premuzic & Furnham, 2008). A new conceptual analysis of existing data across thousands of studies concludes that cognitive ability and personality traits are very important predictors of school, work, and life outcomes (Kuncel, Ones, & Sackett, 2010). The lesson here is that companies and schools should be careful and diligent in choosing which predictors to use in their selection batteries, realizing that using multiple predictors is likely to account for more variance in the criterion and that some predictors tend to be more useful than others in predicting certain criteria.

Table 6.3 Interview Questions That Shouldn't Be Asked

Legally Suspect Questions	Explanation and Alternatives
How old are you? When were you born?	The Age Discrimination in Employment Act (ADEA) does not specifically prohibit an employer from asking an applicant's age or date of birth. However, because such inquiries may deter older workers from applying for employment or may otherwise indicate possible intent to discriminate based on age, requests for age information will be closely scrutinized by the Equal Employment Opportunity Commission (EEOC).
Have you ever been arrested?	Being arrested does not imply guilt of any crime; instead, one could ask if the applicant has been convicted of a felony within the past five years.
Do you plan on having children? Are you pregnant?	An employer cannot refuse to hire a woman because of her pregnancy as long as she is able to perform the major functions of her job. An employer cannot refuse to hire her because of its prejudices against pregnant workers or the prejudices of coworkers, clients, or customers.
Are you a U.S. citizen?	This may lead to discrimination based on national origin. An employer is allowed to ask if an applicant is eligible to work in the United States either as a U.S. citizen or under a government immigration qualification.
Do you have a disability?	Employers may not ask job applicants about the existence, nature, or severity of a disability. Applicants may be asked about their ability to perform specific job functions. A job offer may be conditioned on the results of a medical examination *but only* if the examination is required for all entering employees in similar jobs. Medical examinations of employees must be job related and consistent with the employer's business needs.
Do you have children? What day-care arrangements will be made if you are hired for this job?	It is unlawful to inquire if an applicant has children (an issue that is certainly not job elated). An employer may ask if a candidate has any commitments or responsibilities that might result in considerable absenteeism, but this should be asked of all candidates regardless of gender.
Are you actively involved in the National Association for the Advancement of Colored People (NAACP)?	Requesting preemployment information that discloses or tends to disclosean applicant's race suggests that race will be unlawfully used as a basis for hiring. Solicitation of such preemployment information is presumed to be used as a basis for making selection decisions. Therefore, if members of minority groups are not hired, the request for such preemployment information would likely constitute evidence of discrimination.

(continued)

Have you ever been treated by a psychologist or psychiatrist?

Have you ever been hospitalized? If so, for what?

Please list any conditions or diseases for which you have been treated in the past three years.

How many days were you absent from work due to illness in the past year?

Are you taking any prescribed drugs?

All of these questions are probably illegal under the Americans with Disabilities Act (ADA). It is illegal to ask any preemployment questions about illness.

*Some of this information was adapted from the Equal Employment Opportunity Commission (EEOC) website (http://www.eeoc.gov/).

Table 6.4 Estimates of Validity Coefficients for Common Predictors

Predictor	Validity Coefficient Estimate	Source of Estimate	Description
General cognitive ability	.53	Hunter & Hunter, 1984	Meta-analysis
	.62	Salgado et al., 2003	Meta-analysis
	.48	Bertua et al., 2005	Meta-analysis
Specific cognitive ability	.40–.50	Gatewood et al., 2007	Narrative review
	.35–.56	Salgado et al., 2003	Meta-analysis
	.35–.50	Bertua et al., 2005	Meta-analysis
Psychomotor ability	.53	McHenry et al., 2007	Meta-analysis
	.40	Hunter & Hunter, 1984	Project A data
Personality tests	.30	Tett et al., 1999	Meta-analysis
	.03–.31	Barrick et al., 2001	Meta-analysis
Integrity tests	.34–.47	Ones et al., 1993	Meta-analysis
Work samples	.44	Hunter & Hunter, 1984	Meta-analysis
	.39	Roth et al., 2005	Meta-analysis

(continued)

Table 6.4 Estimates of Validity Coefficients for Common Predictors (*continued*)

Predictor	Validity Coefficient Estimate	Source of Estimate	Description
Situational judgment tests	.34	McDaniel et al., 2001	Meta-analysis
Assessment centers	.37	Gaugler et al., 1987	Meta-analysis
	.38–.45	Arthur, Day, et al., 2003	Meta-analysis
	.28	Hermelin et al., 2007	Meta-analysis
Biodata	.52	Vinchur et al., 1998	Meta-analysis
	.37	Hunter & Hunter, 1984	Meta-analysis
	.20–.46	Stokes & Cooper, 1994	Narrative review
Interviews	.37	McDaniel et al., 1994	Meta-analysis
Structured	.44	McDaniel et al., 1994	Meta-analysis
Unstructured	.33	McDaniel et al., 1994	Meta-analysis

■ Summary

In this chapter, tests were classified in terms of form as well as the predictor type they represent. The most frequently used selection instruments—cognitive ability tests, psychomotor tests, personality tests, integrity tests, work sample tests, ACs, biographical information, and interviews—were discussed in the context of their role in employee selection. The validity coefficients of these selection instruments are listed in Table 6.4. Note that the variability of these coefficients may be due to the diversity of the studies included in the meta-analyses (e.g., Hunter & Hunter, 1984, versus Schmitt et al., 1984) as well as to differences among the predictors and criteria.

We can draw a few general conclusions. First, it is clear that ability measures (e.g., general cognitive, specific cognitive, and psychomotor) are among the most valid predictors of performance criteria in an employment setting. Second, the validity coefficients for personality tests are not as high as those for most of the other predictors included in our review. Third, nontraditional predictors, such as integrity tests, biodata, work samples, and ACs, are consistently valid predictors of on-the-job performance. Finally, structured interviews tend to be better predictors of job performance than unstructured interviews. In Chapter 7, we will discuss the actual selection process, focusing also on the legalities involved in how organizations use these predictors to hire employees.

■ Key Terms

assessment center (AC) (p. 165)
behavior description interview (p. 172)
biodata (p. 169)
biographical information (p. 169)
clerical ability (p. 157)
computer adaptive testing (p. 152)
emotional intelligence (EI) (p. 158)
group tests (p. 153)
in-basket (p. 166)
individual tests (p. 152)
integrity tests (p. 162)
interviews (p. 171)
leaderless group discussion (LGD)
   (p. 168)

mechanical ability (p. 156)
paper-and-pencil tests (p. 153)
performance tests (p. 153)
personality tests (p. 160)
power test (p. 152)
psychomotor tests (p. 159)
realistic job preview (RJP) (p. 172)
situational interview (p. 172)
situational judgment tests (SJTs) (p. 164)
spatial ability (p. 156)
speed test (p. 152)
test (p. 150)
validity coefficient (*r*) (p. 154)
work sample tests (p. 164)

■ TAKING IT TO THE FIELD

One activity that many I/O consultants must address is providing advice to organizations about how to select people for the organization. Because there are many different tools available, consultants must consider what will be reasonable given each client's situation. Pierce Janssen, the CEO of JMF Fireworks Inc., has contacted your boss asking for help redesigning the selection system they use for selecting their pyrotechnicians. Read his e-mail below and provide suggestions for how he might improve his selection battery.

Hello—

Thank you for your help with our selection system—I am looking forward to hearing what you suggest. First, let me tell you a little about the open position. We are looking to hire new pyrotechnicians—that is, the people who are responsible for putting on fireworks shows for a number of clients across the United States. This job entails transporting fireworks to shows, setting them up, programming the choreography, and taking down the setup once the show is completed. In order to do the job competently, pyrotechnicians need the following abilities/characteristics:

- They must be able to lift 80 pounds to shoulder height at least five times per show (the fireworks are quite heavy, and will need to be moved from the truck to the shoot site).
- They need to have good customer service skills (customers will sometimes want to do things that are against regulations; our pyrotechnicians must be effective at being polite but firm so that we follow rules but don't lose customers).
- They must have good attention to detail (small errors can lead to very serious accidents, so our pyrotechnicians need to be careful to not cut corners and to do things by the book).

- They must be cool under pressure (if something goes wrong, they must be able to think quickly and not panic).
- They must also be emotionally stable and not take foolish risks during a shoot.

The last bullet point is fairly well covered by background checks we are required to do by the government. However, we have not always been success-ful in hiring people who fulfill the other four requirements. Right now, here is our selection process:

- Applicants fill out an application blank I picked up at an office supply store that asks about their age, race, and experience.
- Applicants who look good on the application blank are brought in for an interview. We don't really have an HR department, so the managers typically conduct these interviews. I'm not sure what they ask applicants—they pretty much just ask whatever they want to know and go with their gut on whether they think someone will work out well.
- After applicants pass the interview, we send them to a room where we have a bag of sand that weighs about 80 pounds. We have them lift it from the ground and press it over their head five times.

Any suggestions you have about how we can better select pyrotechnicians would be greatly appreciated.

Pierce

■ Critical Thinking Questions

1. What predictors would you use to select a restaurant manager? What is your rationale for including each predictor in your selection battery?

2. Do you think that emotional intelligence is a measurable ability? If so, what is the best way to measure it?

3. What are the advantages and disadvantages of using interviews as a selection measure?

4. Design a new assessment center exercise for use in selecting a CEO.

■ Application Questions

1. Many managers look for indications about how someone behaves outside of an interview and testing context. For example, if a candidate shows up late, is dressed in a sloppy way, or fails to send a thank-you note, the manager may no longer consider that person for the position. Do you think this is a valid predictor of performance? Should managers use information like this in making a hiring decision?

2. There has been some recent debate about looking at job applicants' social media information (e.g., Facebook pages, Twitter accounts). Do you believe it is appropriate for managers to look at this type of information about a candidate? Why or why not?

3. Imagine you are applying for a job and you know the company is looking for a candidate who is very conscientious and extraverted. Do you believe you would be able to fake these traits on a personality test? If so, do you think that personality tests should be used for selection? If not, why do you believe it would be hard to fake these traits on a personality test?

4. Have you ever had a job that was described differently from what it actually turned out to be? What happened? What could the organization have done to better prepare you for the actual job?

5. Some workplaces conduct drug testing to ensure that their employees are not using recreational drugs. Do you agree with this practice? When might this practice be justified?

■ Suggested Readings

Furnham, A. (2008). *Personality and intelligence at work.* London: Psychology Press. This book takes a close look at the role of individual differences at work. It probes the question of whether psychological tests are truly accurate predictors of workplace behavior.

Gatewood, R. D., Feild, H. S., & Barrick, M. (2007). *Human resource selection* (6th ed.). Fort Worth, TX: Harcourt College. This is a solid human resource management text emphasizing job analysis and employee selection.

Guion, R. M., & Highhouse, S. (2006). *Essentials of personnel assessment and selection.* Mahwah, NJ: Erlbaum. This book, written by two distinguished industrial psychologists, focuses largely on criterion measurement and selection, providing a very thorough treatment of the issues involved.

Sackett, P. R., & Lievens, F. (2008). Personnel selection. *Annual Review of Psychology, 59,* 419–450. This article provides a thorough review and analysis of selection methods, assessment techniques, and criterion measurement.

Thomas, J. C. (2004). *The comprehensive handbook of psychological assessment: Vol. 4. Industrial/organizational assessment.* Hoboken, NJ: Wiley. This is part of a four-volume set that wonderfully reviews psychological assessment with sophistication and simplicity. The I/O volume is a great reference, providing a source of tests and data on the tests most often used for assessment at work.

7

JEFF GREENBERG/AGEFOTOSTOCK

Selection Decisions and Personnel Law

This chapter should help you understand:

- The steps involved in validating a selection battery
- Some of the best recruitment strategies used by organizations to recruit individuals to apply for jobs
- The differences between predictive validation and concurrent validation and the steps involved in each
- The importance of cross-validation
- What validity generalization is and how important it has become to I/O psychology
- The three main approaches to selection (multiple cutoff, multiple hurdle, and multiple regression) and the differences among them
- The importance of the utility concept for I/O selection
- The factors that affect the utility of a selection battery (namely, validity, base rate, selection ratio, and cost)
- Important related concepts such as employment at-will, adverse impact, and affirmative action
- What has been rendered illegal by certain U.S. employment laws
- The different forms of sexual harassment
- How the courts seem to be interpreting reasonable accommodation, essential functions of the job, and undue hardship under the Americans with Disabilities Act

In the last few chapters, we have discussed in detail the importance of predictors and criteria in I/O psychology. Recall that Chapter 6 presented a detailed discussion of the common predictors, or tests, that are used in employee selection (see Table 6.4 for a list of those predictors and their validity estimates). In this chapter, we will discuss how an organization might go about using those predictors to select employees.

Let's return briefly to our example from the last chapter, involving the hiring of a new associate by a large law firm. Because the applicants are fresh out of law school, there are no criterion data available, so we will need to use other information to predict performance on the job. How do we go about using these predictors to make hiring decisions? How do we know that our predictors are valid ones? What legal issues come into play in this context of employee selection? For answers to these questions, we need to put together the predictors and the criteria in ways that enable us to do accurate and legal employee selection.

■ A Brief Review

We will talk about selection decisions in this chapter, but first I want to clarify that much of what is discussed here can also be applied to other personnel decisions, such as promotion decisions and decisions about whom to lay off when staff reductions in force become necessary. For instance, we may give employees a promotion test to determine whom to promote into a management job. The same procedures that apply to validating a selection test can be applied to the validation of a promotion test. Accordingly, in this chapter, I present a general process that can be used to make personnel decisions; I use the selection decision as an example because it is very important to organizations and because research and litigation have focused on this type of personnel decision in particular.

Let's say that we all work for a consulting firm called PE Levy & Associates, which has been hired by CS&J Products, a large manufacturing company, to devise, implement, and evaluate a selection battery that is to be used for the selection of *middle-level managers*. A **selection battery** is a set of predictors, or tests, that are used to make employee hiring decisions. In Chapter 6, we discussed the various types of predictors one by one, but note that, in actuality, it is rare for any of these predictors to be used alone. It is much more likely that organizations will employ a *set* of predictors or a battery of tests as a way of predicting criterion performance. Of course, by this time, you know what the first step is. It's the job analysis—the foundation for everything we do in industrial psychology. Thus, we choose a job-oriented, worker-oriented, or hybrid job-analytic technique, as discussed in Chapter 3. From the job analysis, we generate a *job description* and *job specifications,* and from these we develop performance criteria. We should also be sure to consider the "criteria for the criteria" in developing our measures (see Chapter 3).

Using the job analysis—chiefly, the job specifications information—we develop predictors or select predictors from those that already exist. To decide what type of predictors to use, we'll choose among work samples, assessment centers, Biographical Information Blanks, ability tests, interviews, and so on. In this case, because the job is a managerial one, we should seriously consider the use of work samples and assessment centers, as these seem particularly relevant for the job in question. Also, we should opt for multiple tests, as multiple tests would likely increase the proportion of criterion variance that we could account for.

Figure 7.1 demonstrates why a selection battery yields better prediction than a single test. In the figure, the squared correlations between each predictor and the performance criterion vary from .10 to .36. Together, they account for about 55% of the variance in criterion performance (r^2). The validity coefficient for the battery of predictors is about .74 (i.e., the square root of .55). When the predictors are combined in this way, the validity coefficient is a multiple *R*—the correlation between the combination of all the predictors and the criterion. It's clear, based on the validity coefficient (multiple *R* = .74) and the amount of variance accounted for

selection battery
A set of predictors, or tests, that are used to make employee hiring decisions.

> **TECHNICAL TIP**
>
> *Remember that a correlation (r) is used as an index of the relationship between a predictor and a criterion, whereas the coefficient of determination, or the squared correlation (r^2), provides information about how much variance in the criterion is accounted for by the predictor.*

FIGURE 7.1 Selection Battery Example

Assessment center

Work sample

$r^2 = .25$

$r^2 = .36$

$r^2 = .10$

Criterion performance

Interview

Test Battery Multiple R = .74
Test Battery R^2 = .55

($r^2 = .55$), that using a test battery results in better prediction than using any single test in isolation. Notice also that there is some overlap among the predictors, which means that they are slightly correlated. This explains why, if we add up the individual r^2s, we would get .71 rather than .55. The difference between these two numbers reflects the overlap in the predictors. In other words, part of the variance that is accounted for by the work sample test is also accounted for by the assessment center.

Ideally, we want as little correlation among the predictors as possible so that we aren't predicting the same piece of the pie with more than one predictor. In this example, the assessment center is somewhat redundant with the other two predictors. It adds to the prediction, but it makes a smaller unique contribution when you consider its overlap with both the work sample and the interview. If costs were an issue and CS&J Products wanted to use only one predictor, as Figure 7.1 makes clear, using the work sample would be the best choice because it accounts for more variance in the criterion than any other single predictor would. If costs were not an issue, the three predictors as a package would seem to do the best job.

recruitment
The process of encouraging potentially qualified applicants to seek employment with a particular company.

■ Recruitment

Before we can select employees for CS&J, we must get the applicants interested enough in the jobs to apply. **Recruitment**, the process of encouraging potentially qualified applicants to seek employment with a particular company, has often been an ignored element of I/O psychology—but one with widespread implications. We could have a large enough budget to make job offers to five lawyers just coming out of law school, but if the applicant pool is weak and the new lawyers are not qualified, selection doesn't really matter very much.

Many organizations report that they have more challenges related to recruiting than to selection (Ployhart, 2006). There are many ways to entice individuals to apply for jobs. Traditionally, jobs have been advertised through college placement offices, newspaper advertisements, employee referrals, job fairs, and, more recently, Internet ads (Breaugh, Greising, Taggart, & Chen, 2003). Newer work in the recruiting area has begun to enhance our understanding of this process a great deal. For instance, research has shown that recruits use the organization's reputation as an indicator of what they expect their job to be like; this reputation also affects recruits' expectations about the pride they will experience working for a particular company (Cable & Turban, 2003; Collins & Stevens, 2002).

Others (Highhouse, Hoffman, Greve, & Collins, 2002) have demonstrated that organizational values affect recruits' attraction to the organization. They (Lievens & Highhouse, 2003) have also shown that individuals aren't attracted to organizations just because of the job attributes (compensation, work environment, etc.); they also strongly consider their subjective evaluation of the organization (e.g., is it an innovative, cool, prestigious place to work?). In fact, these subjective evaluations appear to be even more important. Research demonstrates the importance of perceived **person–environment (PE) fit** in recruiting (Ployhart, 2006). Individuals seem increasingly interested in jobs and organizations that seem well suited to them. (I introduced the idea of realistic job previews (RJPs) in Chapter 6. You can see how important these RJPs can be for employees and organizations to determine if there is the potential for a good fit.)

The Internet has added a new dimension to recruiting because it reaches an incredibly large audience—one that knows no geographic boundaries (Cober, Brown, Blumental, Doverspike, & Levy, 2000). There have been two elements to this: (1) the general job boards such as Monster.com, Hotjobs.com, and USAjobs.gov, which have broad appeal, and (2) organizations' own employment websites, which focus on attracting recruits for their particular job openings. Some researchers have proposed a model suggesting that applicant attraction is a function of such variables as the aesthetics and usability of the organization's employment website, effective reactions to the website, perceptions of organizational image, and individual applicant differences (Cober, Brown, Keeping, & Levy, 2004). Pieces of this model have been tested, and some of the results suggest that, as predicted, a website's informational content, aesthetic quality, and usability all affect organizational attraction (Cober, Brown, Levy, Cober, & Keeping, 2003; Williamson, Lepak, & King, 2003).

Nowhere is the recruiting and selection landscape changing faster than in the area of **cybervetting**—an assessment of an individual's suitability for a particular job based on information from the Internet (Rose et al., 2010). The popularity of social media has provided an opportunity for organizations to collect information about potential applicants (Preston, 2011). The Defense Personnel Security Research Center (PERSEREC) has taken the lead in reviewing the use of social media in recruiting and selection contexts as well as developing some recommendations specifically for law enforcement agencies.

person–environment (PE) fit
The agreement or match between an individual's KSAOs and values and the demands of a job and characteristics of an organization.

cybervetting
The use of social media as part of background investigations used to make employee selection decisions.

▲ **A Closer Look**
Many organizations now engage in cybervetting. Do you feel it's an efficient and constructive way to get a fuller picture of applicants' job qualifications? Do you feel it's ethical?

However, many of these guidelines may generalize to the private sector as well. Many organizations have quickly learned that the use of social media in recruiting allows them to broaden their potential pool. Job seekers are encouraged to follow companies they find attractive on Facebook, Twitter, LinkedIn, and so on. Talent managers argue that the more people are engaged in the recruiting process, the better. According to Wikipedia, there are over 200 active social media networking sites, and talent managers are constantly using these to contact and engage potential recruits (Lauby, 2010).

Recruiters are also viewing Facebook accounts, personal blogs, and YouTube accounts to get a feel for a candidate's personality and personal behavior. Therefore, people now need to carefully consider how they are representing themselves through these social media sites if they want to be taken seriously for a job.

Informal communication also results in many contacts and, hence, potential job applicants. Often, a company's employees will pass along job information to friends and colleagues, who, in turn, will spread it to other friends and colleagues, greatly increasing the potential applicant pool. This process can be helpful, given that employers tend to be somewhat discriminating about whom they encourage to apply. In this way, informal contacts can help in the screening process. One reason that companies do not want to rely solely on informal contacts is that they could result in discrimination (e.g., if the organization is largely made up of White males, employees' friends and acquaintances are likely to be White males as well); thus, more formal channels are typically used, too. In fact, the more channels that are used to advertise a position, the less likely it is that illegal discrimination will occur, given that increased numbers of culturally and racially diverse people will be aware that the position has become available. (We will spend a great deal of time on legal issues later in this chapter.)

Researchers studying recruiting and racioethnicity (i.e., racial or ethnic differences across people) have proposed a model that describes how culturally distinct group members make decisions about employment at later stages of recruiting, such as during the site visit (McKay & Avery, 2006). One variable that they identify as very important for these racially diverse applicants is the diversity of the community and other available opportunities. They also suggest that some individual difference variables, such as racioethnic identity (i.e., the extent to which an individual's self-concept is defined by membership in a particular racioethnic group), play very important roles. In a companion piece (Avery & McKay, 2006), these scholars provide a framework to help organizations attract female and minority job applicants. This framework is built around organizations demonstrating to applicants that they value and encourage diversity. Both this focus on recruiting more diverse applicants and research that further clarifies the issues and makes recommendations for organizations are likely to continue.

For a thorough review of the recruitment literature and a framework for future research, I recommend that you read Rynes and Cable (2003). For our purposes, however, let's go back to our consulting project and assume that, through varied and appropriate recruitment techniques, CS&J has identified several applicants for its managerial position.

■ The Selection Decision

The focus of the rest of the chapter will be on using a selection battery to decide whom to hire and whom not to hire. Because the work of PE Levy & Associates is based on strong scientific practice and is driven by a strong sense of ethics, prior to recommending any particular selection battery, we set out to demonstrate its validity. There are two general approaches to demonstrating the validity of a selection battery: conducting a *validation study* and *validity generalization*. Let's consider each in turn.

The Process of Test Validation

In this section, we will look more closely at concepts I have introduced earlier—the validity coefficient, predictors, and criteria. We use a validation study to determine the extent to which a predictor or battery of predictors is related to the criterion of interest, such as on-the-job performance. In other words, it is from a validation study that the validity coefficients we've been talking about are derived. There are two approaches to demonstrating criterion-related validity, but both approaches start with the same up front work—and for our consulting gig, we've already done that work. In other words, we've started with a job analysis, which allows us to develop or select both predictors and criteria. The process of validation is how we examine the links between these two sets of variables.

Predictive Validation In our current example, if we were to pursue criterion-related validity through a predictive validation design, we would be asking if scores on the work sample, assessment center, and interview predict performance at CS&J Products.

To demonstrate predictive validity, we would follow these steps:

1. *Gather predictor data on all of the applicants.* In our example, this means running each applicant through a work sample test, an assessment center, and an interview. Each applicant would be scored on these tests, and a composite score would be arrived at by adding the scores or performing some other computation.

2. *Hire some of the applicants to fill the open positions.* Note, however, that these applicants would be hired on the basis of predictors

> **TECHNICAL TIP**
>
> In Chapter 2, we introduced the idea of criterion-related validity, which is the extent to which a test is a good predictor of criteria like job performance. Furthermore, we noted the two types of criterion-related validity—concurrent and predictive. Predictive refers to test scores predicting performance in the future, whereas concurrent shows how well a test predicts performance at the same time.

that are *not* part of our newly developed selection battery. Often this step is implemented by hiring individuals according to the company's current selection system, which is probably quite different from the one we are proposing. By following this rather unorthodox strategy, we are more likely to get individuals hired into CS&J who range from low to high on our new predictors. This outcome is very important for the validation process because if we hired only high scorers on the new predictors, we would not be able to determine whether low scorers were unsuccessful on the job because no low scorers would be in our sample.

3. *After several months, gather performance data that can serve as the criteria for our validation study.* Remember that these criteria are developed from the job analysis and that they are intended to differentiate successful from unsuccessful performers.

4. *Compute a validity coefficient between the predictor score and the criterion score that indicates the strength of the relationship between our predictor and our criterion.* We can compute a validity coefficient for the battery as a whole or for each predictor separately. Likewise, we can compute validity coefficients for each particular performance criterion or for our composite criterion.

Predictive validity studies investigate how effective our predictors are at forecasting the on-the-job performance of applicants. Predictors are measured prior to hiring, and criteria are measured after a few months on the job.

Concurrent Validation

Sometimes predictive validity studies are difficult (if not impossible) to conduct, making concurrent validity studies the more viable option. Predictive validity studies are difficult to conduct because they require selecting employees based on predictors other than those we are intending to validate—and doing so requires two sets of predictor measures. Obviously, this can be expensive in terms of both the dollars involved in the development and administration of the tests and the time spent by applicants and test administrators.

To establish criterion-related validity through a concurrent validation study, we would undergo the following steps:

1. *Collect data on both predictors and criteria from incumbent employees at the same time.* In our example, this means that incumbents would be run through the work sample test, the assessment center, and the interview and that their performance on these predictors would be scored. In addition, performance data would be collected. For instance, we might gather performance appraisal data already in the incumbents' files or ask supervisors and peers to provide performance ratings of these incumbents.

2. *Compute a validity coefficient between the predictor score and the criterion score.* Again, this indicates the strength of the relationship between our predictor and our criterion. We can compute a validity coefficient for the battery as a whole or for each predictor separately. Likewise, we can compute validity coefficients for each particular performance criterion or for our composite criterion.

Table 7.1 Validation Designs		
Element	Concurrent Design	Predictive Design
Participants	Incumbents	Applicants
Predictor measurement	Time 1	Time 1
Criterion measurement	Time 1	Time 2
Selection decision	Made prior to Time 1 and was based on other predictors	To be made between Time 1 and Time 2 and to be based on other predictors
Validity coefficient	Correlation between predictor and criterion	Correlation between predictor and criterion

Table 7.1 presents an overview of each validation strategy. Concurrent validation differs from predictive validation in two major ways: In situations involving concurrent validation, (1) incumbents, rather than applicants, are used as participants, and (2) predictors and criteria are measured at the same time. Although empirical research has not demonstrated many differences between concurrent and predictive validation efforts (Schmitt, Gooding, Noe, & Kirsch, 1984), some I/O psychologists are concerned about the use of concurrent validation because, in their view, incumbents and applicants differ in important ways, such as amount of job experience and potential motivation (Cascio, 1998).

Cross-Validation In cases in which predictive or concurrent strategies are used to validate a selection battery, it is a statistical truth that the validity of that selection battery will always be the highest for the sample on which it was validated. In other words, a given selection battery will likely demonstrate lower validity when employed with a different sample—a phenomenon known as **validity shrinkage**. The statistical explanation for this phenomenon is beyond the scope of this book, but you can find a thorough discussion in Cascio and Aguinis (2004). Here, we consider the general factors involved in our particular situation.

Let's say we find that our selection battery has a validity coefficient (in this case, a multiple R) of .74, as depicted in Figure 7.1. If we use this selection battery with another sample of applicants at the same company, the validity coefficient is likely to be smaller. The key question for the generalizability of our results is "How much smaller?" To cross-validate the selection battery *empirically,* we apply the same predictors and criteria to a different sample at CS&J to see how close the validity coefficient is to the original. Specifically, we generate a regression equation using the original predictor and criterion data. We then plug the predictor scores from the new individuals in the cross-validation sample into this original regression equation to obtain a *predicted criterion score.* Correlating this predicted criterion score with the

validity shrinkage
A statistical phenomenon reflecting the likelihood that a given selection battery will demonstrate lower validity when employed with a different sample.

actual criterion score provides the validity coefficient for the new sample, which can be compared with the validity coefficient of the original sample. Of course, we are hoping for only a small amount of validity shrinkage—maybe .05 to .10. If the validity doesn't shrink very much, we can feel comfortable that the selection battery is still valid and ready for use by CS&J to select employees.

To cross-validate the selection battery *statistically*, we correct or adjust the original validity coefficient for measurement error. But the approach we choose, whether empirical or statistical, is less important than our commitment to estimating the cross-validated coefficient. The best estimate of the validity of a particular selection on battery is the cross-validated coefficient; yet, because it takes a little extra time and effort, this step is frequently skipped in validation projects.

Validity Generalization

validity generalization (VG)
A statistical approach used to demonstrate that test validities do not vary across situations.

Obviously, it takes a great deal of effort, time, and money to demonstrate criterion-related validity using concurrent or predictive approaches. An alternative to this approach that has been gaining in popularity over the past 30 years is called **validity generalization (VG)**. One long-standing belief in the selection area was that test validities varied across situations. If this were the case, the selection battery that PE Levy & Associates developed for CS&J would not likely be valid for another company. Indeed, the work sample we developed would work only for this particular company and this particular situation.

situational specificity
The belief that test validities are specific to particular situations.

The belief that test validities are limited to particular situations is termed **situational specificity**. John Hunter and Frank Schmidt (1990), however, took issue with this belief and developed methods to examine whether validities are truly situationally specific. Their VG technique was both statistically and conceptually tied to the technique of meta-analysis, which they developed in conjunction with this work. Basically, they argued that by using meta-analytic techniques to weight and combine validity coefficients across situations, we can examine whether validities are situationally specific or generalizable across situations. Their conclusion—for which there is a great deal of research support— is that validities do tend to generalize across situations (Murphy, 2003).

Many criticisms and concerns have been raised about the statistical methodology used in VG (Cascio, 1998; Murphy, 2003), and VG is still limited to jobs that are similar to those on which the test was originally validated. For instance, to say that the validity of an in-basket test generalizes is not to say that because it is valid for managerial selection it is also valid for the selection of custodians and ministers, but no test or measure of any construct, regardless of the measure's soundness, is a good predictor for every job (see also *EEOC v. Atlas Paper Box,* 1989).

Another issue regarding VG is that the legal community is often involved in disputes as to whether a particular selection test is legal—an issue we will consider shortly. For now, though, note that, although the courts have traditionally required a validation study to show that a selection battery was valid, in recent years they have viewed VG more favorably, given the caveat that a complete and thorough job analysis is necessary. This job analysis must demonstrate that the job on which the tests were validated is the same as the job for which those tests are being used for selection. In our current example, the implication is that if someone else has validated an in-basket for managerial selection, PE Levy & Associates must be able to show that the CS&J managerial jobs for which we want to use this in-basket are very, very similar to the managerial jobs on which the in-basket was originally validated.

Validation of selection batteries is extremely important not only to organizational performance but also, as we will soon see, to the law that polices our work. There are three main approaches to validation: predictive validation studies, concurrent validation studies, and validity generalization. Each has its strengths and weaknesses, so one's choice should be determined on a case-by-case basis.

A related approach to validity generalization, called **synthetic validity**, has existed for over 50 years but has not sufficiently captured the support of researchers or practitioners to make it as popular as these other approaches. Synthetic validity is based on the notion that job components common across jobs are related to the same KSAs or human attributes (Johnson et al., 2010). Proponents argue for creating large, shared databases of these job components that can be linked to the appropriate KSAs, allowing for selection to occur based on those KSAs and without a local validation study. Some argue that this approach is superior to existing approaches (Johnson et al., 2010), while others find it inferior (Harvey, 2010; Schmidt & Oh, 2010) for various reasons, such as a lack of discriminant validity.

> **synthetic validity**
> Validity that is inferred based on the links between job components and KSAs.

Practical Approaches to Selection

Now that we've demonstrated the validity of our selection battery (including cross validation), we can provide this information to CS&J Products, assuring its executives that our selection battery predicts job performance quite well. CS&J, being a profit-driven company, is interested in achieving two main goals. First, it wants us to provide the names of people who are likely to be successful performers. This is, after all, why it hired us. Second, it wants us to demonstrate that our selection battery is cost effective. We will consider both of these goals in the next few pages, starting with two major approaches to employee selection: multiple cutoffs and multiple regression.

Multiple Cutoffs
The **multiple cutoff approach** is a noncompensatory method of employee selection in which "passing scores," or cutoffs, are set on each predictor. It is considered noncompensatory because applicants, to be eligible for selection, must score higher than these cutoffs on each predictor. In other words, they have to pass each test; scoring well on one test does not "make up," or compensate, for scoring low on another test. Back to our example: In order to be rated as acceptable for the middle-level-manager job at CS&J, applicants have to exceed some minimum level of performance on the work sample test, the assessment center, *and* the interview. An applicant who excels on the work sample and assessment center but bombs on the interview won't be hired—regardless of the importance of the KSAOs (knowledge, skills, abilities, and other characteristics) that the interview was designed to tap.

> **multiple cutoff approach**
> A noncompensatory model of employee selection in which "passing scores," or cutoffs, are set on each predictor.

		Table 7.2 Multiple Cutoff Approach: Cardiac Surgeon			
Applicant	Medical Knowledge Test	Medical School GPA	Interview Score	Psychomotor Test	Total Score
Dr. Pratt	10	8	6	8	32
Dr. Carter	10	10	10	5	35
Dr. Quinn	9	8	8	7	32
Dr. Welby	9	8	7	10	34
Dr. Seuss	6	10	10	10	36
Predictor cutoff	9	7	6	7	

Note: All test scores are on a 1–10 scale, with higher numbers indicating better performance.

Let's say we had two open positions in the cardiac surgery department. If we simply added up the applicants' scores and selected the two highest scorers as our surgeons, we would pick Dr. Seuss and Dr. Carter. However, both of them failed to reach a critical cutoff score. Although they have the highest total scores, they seem weak in very important areas. How about you? Would you hire the two "top" candidates, or would you invoke a multiple cutoff strategy?

Perhaps the strengths of a multiple cutoff approach are best seen when we consider certain types of jobs. For instance, to select cardiac surgeons, we might use a measure of medical knowledge, grades in medical school, an interview, and a psychomotor test involving fine-grained hand work such as cutting and sewing. I won't speak for you, but a multiple cutoff is the way I want my surgeon selected: An incredibly smart and verbally skilled surgeon who shakes uncontrollably with a scalpel in her hand is of no use to me! It is of paramount importance that candidates pass all the cutoffs for the position of cardiac surgeon. Table 7.2 presents the names of five applicants for this position, along with their predictor scores. Look this over and decide whom you would select.

multiple hurdle approach
A rendition of the multiple cutoff approach in which the predictors are administered in a predetermined order and applicants are measured on the next predictor only if they scored above the cutoff on the previous predictor.

One special rendition of the multiple cutoff approach to selection is the **multiple hurdle approach**. As before, passing scores are set on each predictor, and superb performance on one predictor cannot compensate for below-cutoff performance on another predictor. With the multiple hurdle approach, however, predictors are administered in a predetermined order and applicants are measured on a subsequent predictor only if they scored above the cutoff on the previous predictor.

Table 7.3 presents scores for seven applicants on four predictors, as well as the cutoff scores for each predictor. Suppose that we have been hired by CS&J to help it select production line supervisors, and we've identified the relevant predictors as being a cognitive ability test, a personality test, a work sample test, and an interview. The predictors are arranged from least to most expensive because this is typically the way multiple hurdle strategies are conducted. The cognitive ability test can be purchased from a test publisher and administered to applicants in a group, so it is inexpensive in terms of both time and money. But the interview questions probably need to be

Applicant	Cognitive Ability Test (Cutoff = 110)	Personality Test (Cutoff = 55)	Work Sample (Cutoff = 80)	Interview (Cutoff = 18)
Ripken	120	61	88	23
Banks	118	59	76	
Jeter	107			
Tejada	108			
Yount	106			
Belanger	104			
Aparacio	121	40		
	Least Expensive			Most Expensive

Table 7.3 Multiple Hurdle Approach: Production Line Supervisor

developed in-house rather than bought off the shelf, and they are typically done one-on-one—so they may require a great deal of time both to develop and to conduct. Applicants proceed to the next predictor only if they successfully jump the previous hurdle (i.e., by scoring above the cutoff on the previous predictor).

As you can see in Table 7.3, only Ripken, Banks, and Aparacio pass the cognitive ability test. Thus, they go on to the next hurdle. But here only Ripken and Banks pass the personality test. They both go on to the work sample test, on which only Ripken survives to the next hurdle. Ripken also passes the interview and would thus be offered the job. (One thing is sure: You won't have an absence problem if you hire Ripken! Absence will be discussed in Chapter 11.) See the Practitioner Forum for an important example of this approach to selection.

Multiple Regression We briefly discussed regression analysis in Chapter 2, but we need to spend more time on it here because it is an important technique for determining how we use predictor information to make selection decisions. Recall that the validity coefficient is an index of the strength of the relationship between a predictor and a criterion. For our present purposes, however, we are interested in more than just this relationship because the focus of selection is on prediction. Accordingly, we use **multiple regression**, a statistical technique that allows us to estimate how well a series of predictors forecasts a performance criterion. This process can get rather complicated, but I will try to present the basics using the middle-level-manager selection scenario that we've been working with.

First, we use our validation data (let's assume a predictive validity design) to generate a regression equation. We do this by regressing the criterion performance of those applicants who were selected on their predictor scores (work sample, assessment center, and interview). The general form of a multiple regression equation is

$$Y = b_0 + b_1X_1 + b_2X_2 + b_3X_3$$

multiple regression A statistical technique that, when used in the selection context, allows us to estimate how well a series of predictors forecasts a performance criterion.

TRANSPORTATION SECURITY ADMINISTRATION

Elizabeth Kolmstetter
PhD, 1991, I/O Psychology, Virginia Tech
Deputy Associate Director, National Intelligence, for Human
Capital Office of the Director of National Intelligence

In the aftermath of 9/11, Congress passed legislation mandating a new federal agency, the Transportation Security Administration (TSA), to hire and train a federal workforce of more than 50,000 airport security screeners at more than 429 airports nationwide in less than a year. The TSA implemented high standards during all aspects of creating this new workforce, including the recruiting, selection, training, and certification process. A fair, valid, and defensible selection system was the cornerstone of the success of the workforce federalization. Every screener hired went through the same hiring and training process, regardless of airport size or location.

The assessment process was developed and validated following the principles discussed in this chapter regarding a multiple hurdle approach to selection:

1. Application (online or via telephone)
2. Three-and-a-half-hour multiple-choice test: (a) Aviation Security Screener Employment Test (ASSET; personality-based), (b) Screener English Test (SET), and (c) Screener Object Recognition Test (SORT; x-ray image test)
3. Structured interview (in-person)
4. Physical abilities test (i.e., baggage lift, baggage search)
5. Medical evaluation (including tests for drugs, vision, hearing, color vision, orthopedic, cardiovascular, etc.)
6. Background investigation (i.e., credit and criminal checks)

7. 45-hour basic screener training (including classroom training with labs, job knowledge test, x-ray image detection test)
8. 60-hour on-the-job training and initial certification (including formal practical skills evaluation, x-ray image detection mastery test)
9. Annual recertification (job knowledge test, x-ray image detection proficiency test, practical skills demonstration)

In its first year, the TSA processed more than 1.7 million applications, tested more than 340,000 applicants, and hired approximately 50,000 screeners. By implementing a job-related selection process, the TSA ensured that less than 2% of the screeners hired failed the training.

The TSA has been very thorough in the development and validation of this complex selection system, but carrying out this process is done with even greater caution. Test security, training of test administrators and applicant assessors, and quality of test scoring are all issues that involve the expenditure of considerable time by the I/O psychologists and other TSA employees and contractors. Although it takes an incredible amount of work, national security is "high-stakes" employment and a priority for this country. The TSA screener selection program has been very successful in selecting qualified screeners while serving society's needs.

Applying Your Knowledge
1. What are the benefits of the multiple hurdle approach to selection?
2. What other issues are important in the implementation of selection systems?
3. Why should organizations integrate their selection and training programs?

where each X is the individual's score on a specific predictor, each b is the weight for that particular score, Y is the criterion, and b_0 is the intercept (i.e., the point at which the regression line crosses the y-axis). Computing the regression equation with our validation data yields the following result:

$$Y_{predicted} = 1.043 + 1.548 \text{ (work sample score)} + .752 \text{ (assessment center score)} + .320 \text{ (interview score)}$$

This equation indicates the best prediction scheme, based on our validation data, for forecasting any individual's criterion performance. In other words, we use the predictor and criterion data from our validation study to determine the best weights for each predictor in arriving at a predicted criterion score.

Second, we apply that prediction scheme (i.e., the regression equation) to our applicant data to arrive at selection decisions. An example is presented in Table 7.4, which shows the predictor scores for four new applicants, along with their predicted criterion scores derived from the regression equation. These applicants were not part of the validation sample; rather, we are now using the results of the validation to select from our new applicant pool. Specifically, the predicted criterion scores are derived by plugging each individual's predictor score into the regression equation (as presented in the bottom portion of the table). The table clearly shows that Tomlin is predicted to be the best performer.

The final step is to rank-order all the applicants according to predicted criterion scores and then to select from the top until all the open positions are filled. It's important to note that the regression equation creates the best combination of the tests for maximizing the prediction of the criterion. Based on these data, if CS&J had two open positions, we would make offers to Tomlin and Stokes because, based on our validation study, these two applicants are predicted to be the best performers on the job.

There are a few loose ends here. First, the executives at CS&J may have a very good idea of what is acceptable performance for their company. Thus, they may want to set a cutoff score on the predicted criterion. For instance, based on their standards of what is acceptable employee performance, they may decide that the predicted criterion cutoff is 11.00, which means that no matter how many position openings are available, they will not hire anyone whose predicted criterion

Table 7.4 Multiple Regression Approach

Applicant	Work Sample	Assessment Center	Interview Criterion	Predicted
Stokes	3	5	7	11.69
Dulany	4	2	6	10.66
Tomlin	5	5	8	15.10
Blake	2	3	5	8.00

Stokes: $Y_{predicted} = 1.043 + 1.548\ (3) + .752\ (5) + .320\ (7) = 11.69$

Dulany: $Y_{predicted} = 1.043 + 1.548\ (4) + .752\ (2) + .320\ (6) = 10.66$

Tomlin: $Y_{predicted} = 1.043 + 1.548\ (5) + .752\ (5) + .320\ (8) = 15.10$

Blake: $Y_{predicted} = 1.043 + 1.548\ (2) + .752\ (3) + .320\ (5) = 8.00$

TECHNICAL TIP

Of course, as we suggested earlier in this chapter, we would cross-validate the regression equation to make sure that this approach works in more than one context or setting.

score is under 11.00. In terms of our example in Table 7.4 and based on this cutoff, only Tomlin and Stokes would be considered "qualified" to be hired into CS&J Products. Second, it is possible that the executives at CS&J or PE Levy & Associates feel that it is best to set minimum cutoffs on each predictor. This would involve an approach that combines the multiple cutoff technique with the multiple regression technique—for instance, we might set a cutoff of 4.00 on the work sample test. When using the multiple regression, we could still rank-order applicants based on their predicted criterion scores, but, prior to selection, we would check to make sure that the applicants who fall below 4.00 on the work sample test are withdrawn from the applicant pool regardless of their predicted criterion score. In this case, Stokes and Blake would be removed from the qualified applicant pool.

Think back to our cardiac surgeon example. Given the importance of psychomotor skills and medical knowledge, the use of cutoffs on these predictors, as well as a multiple regression approach, would be a very reasonable strategy for the selection of surgeons.

Usefulness of Selection Processes

At this point, we can tell the executives at CS&J that we have developed, validated, and cross-validated a selection battery that will result in successful employee selection. We can present them with a few different ways to use the predictor data in making these employment decisions, such as the multiple cutoff approach, the multiple hurdle approach, the multiple regression approach, or some combination of these. Certainly, they will be pleased with what we have to offer. However, they will probably have one remaining question for us to answer: Is it worth it? The executives at CS&J aren't satisfied with knowing that we have developed a valid selection system for them; they also want to know how much better it is than their current system and how expensive (in time and dollars) it will be to switch to and use this new system. These questions all deal with the **utility** of the selection battery—that is, with how useful and cost efficient it is. We will now spend some time discussing the various elements of the selection process that allow us to answer these questions for the organization.

utility
The degree to which a selection battery is useful and cost efficient.

Decision Accuracy The first element we need to focus on is the accuracy of the selection decision—or, more specifically, the gain in accuracy that is provided by our new selection battery. After all, the whole purpose of our involvement in this project is to improve the quality of the current CS&J workforce by making better employee selection decisions.

Figure 7.2 depicts all possible theoretical outcomes of our selection situation, as represented by Quadrants 1 through 4. In other words, every selection decision can be characterized by whether the person is hired or rejected and whether the person is successful or unsuccessful on the job. (Of course, we won't know about job performance until after the person has been on the job for a while.)

FIGURE 7.2 Decision Accuracy

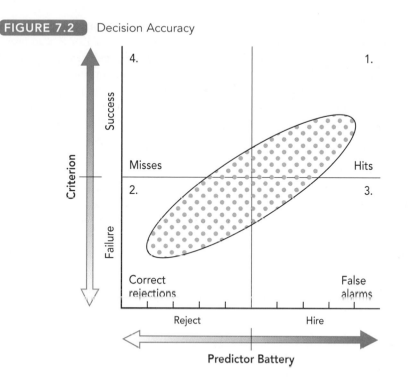

The first two quadrants refer to the accurate selection decisions. Quadrant 1, labeled *hits* (sometimes called *true positives*), represents the number of applicants hired on the basis of our selection system who went on to be successful performers. Quadrant 2, labeled *correct rejections* (sometimes called *true negatives*), represents the number of applicants who were not hired and would have been unsuccessful on the job. (Although this number cannot be accessed from our applicant sample because these individuals are never hired, we are able to gather information about such individuals from the validation sample.) The last two quadrants refer to the inaccurate selection decisions. Quadrant 3, labeled *false alarms* (sometimes called *false positives*), represents the applicants who were hired but proved to be ineffective performers. Quadrant 4, labeled *misses* (sometimes called *false negatives*), represents the applicants we didn't hire but should have hired, as they would have been successful performers. (These individuals, too, can be examined only within the validation sample.)

Companies are often interested in knowing only the outcome of the hiring decisions—that is, whether the hired applicants succeed or fail. This information is provided by the following formula for *decision accuracy for hires*, which reflects the percentage of hiring decisions that are correct:

Quadrant 1/(Quadrant 1 + Quadrant 3)

Certainly, for jobs such as cardiac surgeon, airline pilot, air traffic controller, and nuclear power plant operator, this would be the most relevant measure of decision accuracy. Indeed, I would be willing to reject 10 airline pilots who may have proved to be successful (Quadrant 4), but I would *not* be willing to hire even 1 or 2 who prove to be unsuccessful (Quadrant 3). In other words, in the realm of public safety occupations, misses are preferable to false alarms! Therefore, it seems reasonable to focus only on Quadrants 1 and 3—hits and false alarms—as a measure of accuracy.

In other occupations, however, the number of rejected applicants who would have been successful (Quadrant 4) might constitute important information. For instance, my colleagues and I spend a great deal of time reviewing applications for our doctoral program in I/O psychology. We are certainly concerned about admitting students who prove to be unsuccessful and do not finish the program (Quadrant 3), but we are also concerned about *not* admitting candidates who go elsewhere and do very well, indicating that they may have been very successful in our own program (Quadrant 4). The operationalization for *overall decision accuracy* looks like this:

(Quadrant 1 + Quadrant 2)/(Quadrant 1 + Quadrant 2 + Quadrant 3 + Quadrant 4)

Regardless of how we define decision accuracy, however, the goal of the selection battery is to maximize the number of hits and correct rejections and to minimize the number of misses and false alarms. All else being equal, the utility of the selection battery is demonstrated by the extent to which it does both.

Validity Maximizing hits and correct rejections while minimizing misses and false alarms will occur to the extent that the selection battery is valid. Thus, the first factor that affects the utility of the selection battery is its validity. Figure 7.2 depicts the outcomes of a selection battery with a validity coefficient of about .7. (Compare this figure with the middle panel of Figure 2.8.) Given this degree of validity, the small number of false alarms and misses is not surprising; the selection battery depicted here certainly maximizes the hits and correct rejections. By contrast, Figure 7.3 depicts the outcomes of a selection battery with zero validity, as represented by a circle. (Compare this figure with the left panel of Figure 2.8.) What makes the lack of validity obvious is the same number of hits, correct rejections, misses, and false alarms. In this case, individuals who score high on the battery of predictors are just as likely to be unsuccessful on the job as they are to be successful; those who score low on the battery of predictors are just as likely to be successful on the job as they are to be unsuccessful. Thus, making a selection decision with a battery that demonstrates zero validity is akin to random hiring and clearly provides no utility to the company.

base rate
The percentage of current employees who are successful on the job.

Base Rate The **base rate** reflects the percentage of current employees who are successful on the job. In part, this percentage reflects the quality of the previous selection battery (and, perhaps, is affected by other HR processes such as performance management and training) and provides a baseline against which the new selection battery can be compared. Of course, the organization needs to set a cutoff on the criterion so that the base rate can be calculated. In most colleges, for instance, a 2.0 GPA is thought of as the criterion cutoff, and the percentage of current students who meet that cutoff is considered the base rate. Suppose that 30% of the current employees at CS&J perform at a level that CS&J has decided is acceptable. The baseline would thus

FIGURE 7.3 The Case of No Validity

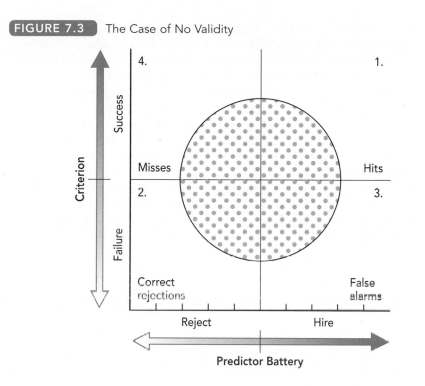

be 30%, and a new selection battery that resulted in an increase in this base rate would be an improvement over the old selection battery. Of course, if CS&J had a base rate of 90%, it is unlikely that we could develop a selection battery to improve on the current one, and the utility of our newly developed selection battery would be low.

Selection Ratio The **selection ratio** is defined as the number of job openings divided by the number of applicants. If CS&J has 20 open positions and 20 applicants, the selection ratio would be 1.00, suggesting that the cost and effort involved in developing and implementing a selection battery are unnecessary because the company would have to hire all available applicants in order to fully staff its organization. On the other hand, if CS&J has 5 open positions and 20 applicants, the selection ratio would be 25% (5/20)—a situation in which the selection battery could prove useful, especially if tough hiring decisions have to be made. Typically, the smaller the selection ratio, the greater the potential utility of the selection battery.

This observation is further evidence of the importance of recruitment for increasing the number of applicants and thus providing organizations with more options. For instance, each year my colleagues and I typically receive about 100 applications for admission into our I/O doctoral program, and we average about 8 open slots. This selection ratio of 8% (8/100) suggests that we have the potential to make better decisions by investing time and money in a complex selection battery than by choosing applicants solely on the basis of their undergraduate GPA or some other easily obtainable predictor.

selection ratio
The number of job openings divided by the number of applicants.

Cost The cost associated with the development and implementation of a selection battery certainly factors into its utility. Even assuming that our selection battery is valid and would improve the workforce dramatically, would CS&J be interested in it if the costs are so high as to be greater than the increased revenue received from hiring better employees? In a dollars-and-cents world, this is really the ultimate comparison in terms of utility for CS&J and thousands of other companies like it.

Of course, cost is important in another way, too. Many organizations are willing to spend thousands and thousands of dollars on a selection battery because, in the long run, it will save them money. Organizations such as the military and the upper reaches of the federal government, where a great deal of money is invested in the training and development of new employees, are especially willing to invest in selection. For example, because it is costly to train an astronaut, the false-alarm rate is very significant. Think of it this way: For every new recruit who is selected to be an astronaut, millions of dollars are invested; thus, a great deal of money would be wasted in the training of someone who fails. This is the reason NASA prefers to invest considerable money up front in the selection system. (We'll talk more about training in the next chapter.)

Putting It All Together Now that we have discussed all the information that comes into play when evaluating the utility of a selection battery, we can look at how this information is combined to estimate this utility.

With a valid selection battery and knowledge of the organization's base rate and selection ratio, it is possible to estimate the improvement that is likely to follow from the implementation of our newly developed selection battery. Keep in mind that we can only estimate this improvement and that we are still making many assumptions about the performance of the newly hired individuals based on their potential. These high-scoring applicants may not perform well on the job for a whole host of reasons. For now, however, we will have faith that our assumptions and calculations are correct.

Tables have been developed that allow us to estimate the improvement in the workforce that will result from the new selection battery. One version of these is known as the *Taylor-Russell Tables* (Taylor & Russell, 1939). Table 7.5 presents a portion of these tables corresponding to base rates of 30% and 70% for various levels of validity and various selection ratios. Suppose that the base rate at CS&J Products is .30 (i.e., 30% of the current employees are performing at, or better than, a level the company views as adequate), the validity coefficient for our new selection battery is .60, and the selection ratio is .40 (i.e., we have 40 openings and 100 applicants). The tables indicate that the predictive efficiency of our new selection battery is .52, which means that with the new selection battery, 52% of the workforce is likely to be successful. Comparing this figure to the current base rate (30%), we see a 22-point improvement in the percentage of successful employees. By contrast, a base rate of .70, a validity coefficient for our new selection battery of .20, and a selection ratio of .30 would yield a predictive efficiency of .78. Comparing this to the current base rate (.70), we see only an 8-point improvement in the percentage of successful employees.

In both of these situations, as a last step, the organization would consider the costs involved in the development and implementation of our new system and ask whether

Table 7.5 A Portion of the Taylor-Russell Tables

Base Rate	Validity Coefficient	Selection Ratio										
		.05	.10	.20	.30	.40	.50	.60	.70	.80	.90	.95
30%	.00	.30	.30	.30	.30	.30	.30	.30	.30	.30	.30	.30
	.10	.38	.36	.35	.34	.33	.33	.32	.32	.31	.31	.30
	.20	.46	.43	.40	.38	.37	.36	.34	.33	.32	.31	.31
	.30	.54	.50	.46	.43	.40	.38	.37	.35	.33	.32	.31
	.40	.63	.58	.51	.47	.44	.41	.39	.37	.34	.32	.31
	.50	.72	.65	.58	.52	.48	.44	.41	.38	.35	.33	.31
	.60	.81	.74	.64	.58	.52	.47	.43	.40	.36	.33	.31
	.70	.89	.62	.72	.63	.57	.51	.46	.41	.37	.33	.32
	.80	.96	.90	.80	.70	.62	.54	.48	.42	.37	.33	.32
	.90	1.00	.98	.90	.79	.68	.58	.49	.43	.37	.33	.32
70%	.00	.70	.70	.70	.70	.70	.70	.70	.70	.70	.70	.70
	.10	.77	.76	.75	.74	.73	.73	.72	.72	.71	.71	.70
	.20	.83	.81	.79	.78	.77	.76	.75	.74	.73	.71	.71
	.30	.88	.86	.84	.82	.80	.78	.77	.75	.74	.72	.71
	.40	.93	.91	.88	.85	.83	.81	.79	.77	.75	.73	.72
	.50	.96	.94	.91	.89	.87	.84	.82	.80	.77	.74	.72
	.60	.98	.97	.95	.92	.90	.87	.85	.82	.79	.75	.73
	.70	1.00	.99	.97	.96	.93	.91	.88	.84	.80	.76	.73
	.80	1.00	1.00	.99	.98	.97	.94	.91	.87	.82	.77	.73
	.90	1.00	1.00	1.00	1.00	.99	.98	.95	.91	.85	.78	.74

Source: Taylor & Russell (1939)

the expenditure is more than offset by the improvement of 22 or 8 percentage points. In addition, even a 5-point improvement for a job like cardiac surgeon would be well worth a hospital's expenditure because it would have such a positive effect on the organization (e.g., improved reputation and fewer malpractice suits), as well as on society at large (e.g., more lives saved). More complex approaches to utility involve estimates of the dollar value of different performance levels, but these are very difficult to calculate. (For a discussion of such approaches and a more sophisticated review and critical analysis, see Boudreau & Ramstad, 2003; Roth, Bobko, & Mabon, 2002.)

In our discussion so far, you have come to understand not only the various predictors in selection but also various techniques used to make selection decisions and ways to evaluate the effectiveness of these techniques. You should thus have a fairly clear idea about how you could use predictor information to arrive at a selection decision and how cost effective this process might be. But the final component in the selection process—legal issues—is equally important. I present these issues specifically within the context of selection because it is here that they have become most relevant;

▶ **A Closer Look**
What role should economics play in making personnel decisions like firings or layoffs?

"*Mr. Herman, you made me laugh and you made me cry, but you didn't make me money.*"

but please note that legal issues apply to *all* personnel decisions, such as performance appraisal ratings used for promotion, layoffs, firings, salary increments, and training (which we will discuss in the next chapter).

■ Legal Issues in Industrial Psychology

It's hard to believe, but, prior to the early 1960s, discrimination in the hiring of employees was *not* illegal in the United States. For instance, it was accepted practice for companies to have "White jobs" for which African Americans were not even considered. As a reaction to this history of discrimination, the Civil Rights Act of 1964 was designed to provide equality of opportunity and equal treatment of all people regardless of "race, color, religion, sex, or national origin." In 1978, the Equal Employment Opportunity Commission (EEOC) published the "Uniform Guidelines on Employee Selection Procedures" (hereafter referred to as the Guidelines), which have been adopted as the legal guidelines for employee selection. In 1987, the Society for Industrial and Organizational Psychology (SIOP) published its *Principles for the Validation and Use of Personnel Selection Procedures* (revised in 2003) to serve as a technical guide for those who work in the field of employee selection, with the caveat that the principles were not intended to be perceived as legal guidelines. These two documents have emerged as a how-to guide for personnel decisions. Both are used extensively by professionals in the field and referred to in court decisions. Much of the content discussed in the remainder of this chapter is based on these documents.

Employment At-Will

employment at-will
A common law doctrine stating that employers and employees have the right to initiate and terminate the employment relationship at any time, for any reason or for no reason at all.

According to the common law doctrine of **employment at-will**, employers and employees have the right to initiate and terminate the employment relationship at any time, for any reason or for no reason at all. This approach to employment began in England and was incorporated into the U.S. legal system during colonial times. However, the interpretation of this idea has changed such that companies are sued each year by employees who claim "wrongful discharge" by their employers.

Although employment at-will is still the default employment condition, there are exceptions, such as the existence or implication of an employment contract that prevents either employer or employee from ending the employment relationship prematurely or "just cause" discharge policies, which provide employees with acceptable reasons for discharge (Dunford & Devine, 1998). Such exceptions continue to grow, leaving the law concerning employment at-will in a state of uncertainty (Roehling & Wright, 2004). The most extensive limitation to employment at-will is federal legislation that renders illegal any employment decisions, such as firings and layoffs, that are based on certain conditions such as race and gender. We will discuss these federal laws shortly, but first we need to look at a few other major concepts.

Adverse Impact

To appreciate the intricacies of employment law as it applies to I/O psychology, you need to understand **adverse impact**. This concept, defined in the Guidelines as the "80% rule of thumb," is the common operationalization of discrimination according to the courts. A selection procedure is said to exhibit adverse impact (i.e., to discriminate) against a group if the selection rate (i.e., the percentage of applicants hired) for that group is less than 80% of the selection rate for the group with the highest selection rate. Usually, but not always, it is a minority group that has been hired at a rate lower than that for Caucasians. For instance, if we hired 60 out of 100 Caucasian applicants (a selection rate of 60%), we would avoid adverse impact if we also hired at least 48 out of 100 African American applicants (i.e., 80% of the 60% rate for Caucasians, or 48%). There are also statistical significance tests that may aid in the more accurate identification of adverse impact beyond the more traditional 80% rule (Roth, Bobko, & Switzer, 2006).

Table 7.6 illustrates two such cases—one in which adverse impact is absent and one in which it is present. Notice that the actual minority cutoff is determined by multiplying the majority rate by 80%. If the minority rate is less than this cutoff, there is adverse impact; if it is at least equal to this cutoff, there is no adverse impact. Although adverse impact is important, its presence alone does not indicate illegal discrimination.

adverse impact
The most accepted operationalization of discrimination, defined in the EEOC Guidelines as the "80% rule of thumb." A selection battery exhibits adverse impact (i.e., discriminates) against a group if the selection rate for that group is less than 80% of the selection rate for the group with the highest selection rate.

Table 7.6 The Absence and Presence of Adverse Impact

Case	Majority Selection Rate	Minority Selection Rate	80% Rule Cutoff	Legal Status
#1	60 out of 100 Caucasians hired (60%)	50 out of 100 African Americans hired (50%)	80% of 60% = $48%	50% > 48%, thus no adverse impact
#2	40 out of 50 men hired (80%)	20 out of 80 women hired (25%)	80% of 80% = 64%	25% < 64%, thus adverse impact

Table 7.7 Steps in an Employment Discrimination Case	
• Plaintiff files a complaint/lawsuit with the courts. • Plaintiff demonstrates a *prima facie* case of adverse impact during the discovery phase of the case. • Motions are filed by both sides, such as the plaintiff's request for organizational data or details about procedures. • Defendant rebuts the adverse impact analysis by showing the statistics to be inaccurate. <div align="center">OR</div>	• Defendant accepts the adverse impact analysis but argues that the selection tests are job related and, therefore, nondiscriminatory. • Plaintiff refutes defendant's statistical reanalysis of the adverse impact data. OR • Plaintiff argues that the selection tests are just a pretext for discrimination and that discrimination is the true motivation for the personnel decision.

To understand this better, let's take a general look at how a discrimination case might proceed (see Table 7.7 for a step-by-step guide).

First, the plaintiff (i.e., the employee who feels discriminated against) must demonstrate a *prima facie* case. In other words, the plaintiff must show, through the 80% rule or some other statistical test, that "on the face of it" the numbers indicate adverse impact. For instance, a Hispanic plaintiff might argue that her not having been hired by a particular company is indicative of a pattern exhibited by this company—a pattern that shows adverse impact against minorities, including Hispanics. The plaintiff would demonstrate this pattern by providing the company's own data showing that the 80% rule has been violated and that minorities are being hired at a rate less than 80% of the rate for the majority group.

Second, the defendant (i.e., the company) may argue against these statistics by showing that the plaintiff is looking at only some of the data, interpreting the data incorrectly, or considering the wrong data. In this case, however, let's say that the company does not dispute the data but instead admits that adverse impact exists. At this point, the company has a few options to combat the charge of illegal discrimination.

The traditional approach is to demonstrate that, despite the presence of adverse impact, the selection battery is *job related* for all minority groups as well as for the majority group. The job relevance of the selection battery is usually established through a validation study, which makes the case that predictors are tapping the KSAOs shown to be important for success on this job. This is one reason validation studies are so important. If the company can show that the selection battery is valid—such that, regardless of ethnicity, race, and gender, those employees who score high on the selection battery are successful on the job and those who score low are unsuccessful—the courts are likely to recognize this case as an example of adverse impact that is *not* illegal.

Rulings and legislation have made it clear that the defendant must show that each test used in the selection battery was job related—it's not enough to show that the bottom-line result was to hire an appropriate percentage of minorities from the pool deemed acceptable (Posthuma, 2002). This is typically referred to as the *business necessity* defense, where the company argues that business cannot be adequately conducted without people of a certain IQ level, personality type, or educational background and that the people in their candidate pool who fit that criteria frequently happen to be more of a particular gender, race, and so on. Finally, the burden of proof shifts back to the plaintiff to refute the defendant's data or argument by somehow showing the defendant's behavior to be a pretext or an excuse for discrimination.

Affirmative Action

Before examining some of the major employment laws, we need to consider a far-reaching concept that is very important in this area: **affirmative action (AA)**. It is employed by many organizations to increase the number of minorities or protected class members (i.e., African Americans, Asian Americans, Hispanic Americans, Native Americans, and women) in targeted jobs. Affirmative Action Plans (AAPs) are not a quota system, although the popular press tends to characterize them in that way. This is not to say that quotas never emerge from or develop in parallel to affirmative action programs. But the important point here is that such programs aim to address the discrimination that has existed in many companies and industries throughout history.

AAPs vary from relatively uncontroversial (as when a company networks with minorities to increase their awareness of job opportunities) to very controversial (as when minorities are hired preferentially). When implemented appropriately, such programs do not result in the hiring of *unqualified* minorities; they may, however, result in the hiring of minority applicants whose qualifications are equal to or perhaps even inferior to those of majority applicants. AAPs have been popular for many years, as evidenced by the inclusion of the following phrase at the bottom of many job advertisements: "This organization is an EEO/AA employer, and qualified minority candidates are encouraged to apply." (EEO/AA stands for equal employment opportunity/affirmative action.)

Much has been written in recent years, in both the popular press and the academic literature, about affirmative action (for a review, see Harrison, Kravitz, Mayer, Leslie, & Lev-Arey, 2006). For instance, some recent studies have examined the stigmatization of AAPs, finding that individuals who benefit from AAPs are sometimes viewed as incompetent (Evans, 2003) and that some people view AAPs as having greater potential benefits to individuals when a justification based on organizational fairness is provided than when it is not (Aberson, 2003).

Perceptions of justice also played a role in a study examining the attitudes of Black applicants toward AAPs. Black applicants viewed an AAP operationalized to show preference for a Black candidate with the same

affirmative action (AA)
A practice employed in many organizations to increase the number of minorities or protected class members in targeted jobs.

▼ **A Closer Look**
Diaz v. Pan Am made it easier for males to be hired as flight attendants. Why is this court ruling important today?

JIM WEST/ALAMY

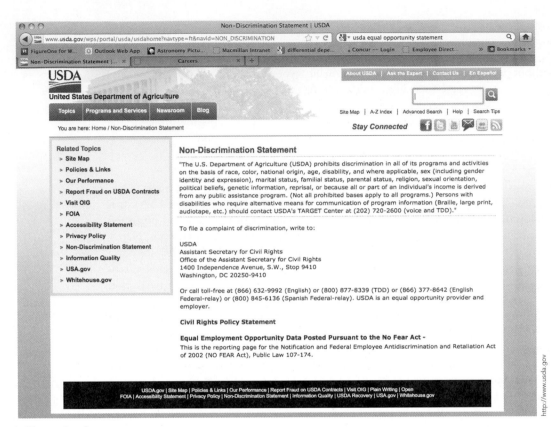

▲ **A Closer Look**
Why do many organizations publicly emphasize that equal employment opportunity is an important principle underlying how they do business?

qualifications as a White candidate as *less fair* than similar plans that emphasized special recruitment of Black candidates or that fostered equity between Black and White applicants (Slaughter, Sinar, & Bachiochi, 2002). More recent research found that Black students perceived race-conscious AAPs, such as preferential hiring, as less just than race-blind AAPs, such as active recruitment of minority applicants (Cropanzano, Slaughter, & Bachiochi, 2005). Researchers also found that various forms of organizational justice affected perceptions of organizational attraction and intention to apply. Other research found that the structure or type of AAP, along with perceiver characteristics and how the AAP was described, interacted to affect attitudes toward AAPs (Harrison et al., 2006).

Two court cases have begun to play a central role in how AAPs are viewed and implemented by organizations. However, both of these cases are about college admissions decisions; thus, it is still unclear to what extent these rulings will affect traditional organizational AAPs. The University of Michigan was sued by two Caucasian males who argued that they were denied admission to the College of Literature, Science, and the Arts because, even though they were both qualified, preference was shown to candidates who were classified as "underrepresented minorities" (*Gratz v. Bollinger*, 2003). The Supreme Court ruled for the plaintiffs, citing an admission policy that automatically distributed 20 points (one-fifth of the points needed to guarantee admission) to every underrepresented minority as too global in form. Ignoring individual differences and qualifications among these minority applicants seemed to go against the purpose inherent in diversity initiatives, which is to consider all that individuals bring to the situation and to choose those who are likely to diversify the educational environment.

The University of Michigan Law School was sued by a Caucasian female who also argued that she was denied admission due to racial preferences (*Grutter v. Bollinger*, 2003). The Supreme Court saw this case very differently and ruled for the university. First, the opinion noted that diversity is a compelling interest for the law school. In other words, the Court said that diversity in graduate education, such as law school, can provide educational benefits to the entire student body and is important; it did not make the same statement regarding the undergraduate admission process (see *Gratz v. Bollinger*, 2003). Second, the Court noted that the law school system, which considered race as a "plus" in the admission process (and did not allocate a fixed number of points based on one's race) and which considered various elements of diversity on an individualized basis, did not make race the defining feature of its decision. A terrific summary of these cases can be found in Gutman (2003).

Three post-*Grutter* lawsuits are worth noting here. First, in *Petit v. City of Chicago* (2003) the Seventh Circuit Court ruled that there is an even more compelling need for diversity in a large metropolitan police force charged with protecting a racially diverse and divided population than there is in a university. Furthermore, it concluded that the city demonstrated this compelling need and met the *Grutter* standard. Second, in *Parents v. Seattle School District* (2007), the issue was about admission and transfer into elementary and high schools in Seattle, Washington. Although the case is very complicated, a few things emerged. The Supreme Court was split down the middle on the legality of comparing the race of a student to the racial composition of the school in relation to the racial composition of the entire district (Gutman & Dunleavy, 2007). Furthermore, the Court ruled that diversity is a compelling government interest, similar to the earlier *Grutter* ruling regarding law school admissions. Finally, any plan that is based on race alone and does not consider individual evaluations of the students will remain illegal, similar to the ruling in *Gratz*. Clearly, *Grutter* and *Gratz* will continue to shape issues of diversity in educational and organizational settings for years to come. The third case is *Fisher v. University of Texas at Austin* (2009), in which the court again supported narrowly tailored AAPs and argued that there is a compelling government interest in achieving diversity in the undergraduate programs at the University of Texas. Although it appears as though the courts are recognizing diversity as a compelling government interest and somewhat open to AAPs that seem focused on meeting the goals of this compelling interest, the *Fisher v. Texas* case will soon be heard by the Supreme Court so the final verdict is surely not in yet.

Table 7.8 presents a list of the major U.S. employment legislation prohibiting job discrimination. These are described in the following sections, along with legal cases where appropriate. Presentation of some recent data prior to a full discussion of the legislation may provide some context. You might find a thorough review of employment discrimination sprinkled with some interesting data very helpful (Goldman, Gutek, Stein, & Lewis, 2006). For instance, the four major statutes (Title VII, ADA, EPA, and ADEA—see Table 7.8) resulted in 88,481 charges filed in 2005. Title VII was responsible for the overwhelming majority of these (55,992), and the Equal Pay Act was responsible for the fewest (978).

Table 7.8 Major U.S. Employment Legislation

Legislation	Year	Description
Equal Pay Act (EPA)	1963	Prohibits discrimination in pay and benefits on the basis of sex for jobs in the same establishment that require equal skill, effort, and responsibility and that are performed under similar working conditions.
Civil Rights Act (Title VII)	1964	Makes it unlawful for an employer with 15 or more employees to discriminate against individuals with respect to hiring, compensation, terms, conditions, and privileges of employment on the basis of race, color, religion, national origin, or sex.
Executive Order 11246	1965	Prohibits job discrimination by employers holding federal contracts or subcontracts on the basis of race, color, sex, national origin, or religion and requires affirmative action to ensure equality of opportunity in all aspects of employment.
Age Discrimination in Employment Act (ADEA)	1967	Makes it unlawful for an employer with 20 or more employees to discriminate against individuals who are 40 years or older with respect to hiring, compensation, terms, conditions, and privileges of employment on the basis of age.
Americans with Disabilities Act (ADA)	1990	Makes it unlawful for an employer with 15 or more employees to discriminate against qualified individuals with disabilities with respect to hiring, compensation, terms, conditions, and privileges of employment.
Civil Rights Act	1991	Amends the 1964 act and the ADA to allow compensatory and punitive damages but places caps on the amounts that can be awarded. Also provides for jury trials in suits brought under these laws.
Family and Medical Leave Act	1993	Allows eligible employees to take job-protected, unpaid leave for up to a total of 12 weeks in any 12 months because of (1) the birth of a child and the need to care for a newborn, (2) the placement of a child with the employee for adoption, (3) the need to care for a family member with a serious health condition, or (4) the employee's own serious health condition.

Equal Pay Act

As we discussed in the section on comparable worth in Chapter 3, the Equal Pay Act (1963) makes it illegal to provide unequal pay and benefits to men and women who are holding jobs that are equal. The disputes that arise regarding this law usually involve the definition of *equal work*. What is and is not equal is decided on a case-by-case basis. For instance, the court ruled in *Brennan v. Prince William Hospital Corp.* (1974) that male hospital orderlies who were assigned the extra duty of turning patients over in bed did not merit additional pay relative to female nurse's aides who were not assigned this one extra duty. The courts have made it clear over the years that there must be sizable and reasonable differences in the work to support different pay for men and women (Gutman, 2000).

There have been important developments in recent years regarding equal pay issues. The Supreme Court ruled against Lilly Ledbetter in *Ledbetter v. Goodyear* (2007), stating that even though Ledbetter had been unaware of the way in which her salary was calculated until years later, the statute of limitations (defined as beyond 300 days) began running at the initial payment many years earlier. This was a controversial decision leaving women no recourse unless they find out about the potential wage discrimination early on in the process (Brody & Grodan, 2010). This led to the 2009 passage by Congress of the Lilly Ledbetter Fair Pay Act, which stipulates that the unfair discriminatory practice occurs every time one is affected by the decision (i.e., each paycheck) and, therefore, that the statute of limitations does not run out. The Ledbetter Act has far-reaching implications beyond the interpretation of the Equal Pay Act and has already played a role in other important cases.

SCOTT J. FERRELL/CONGRESSIONAL QUARTERLY/GETTY IMAGES

▲ **A Closer Look** In 2009, President Obama signed the Lilly Ledbetter Fair Pay Act into law, providing employees more flexibility to file cases asserting that they have been discriminated against with respect to pay. What kind of steps can organizations take to ensure that they don't fall into the trap of paying people differentially based on qualities like age or gender?

Civil Rights Act

From its inception on July 2, 1965, the EEOC has been charged with enforcing the principal federal statutes prohibiting discrimination, and Title VII of the Civil Rights Act of 1964 is the most far-reaching one. The Civil Rights Act of 1991, which modified the 1964 act, deals with issues of monetary damages and jury trials, in addition to clarifying each party's obligation in adverse impact cases. Unless noted otherwise, when I refer to the Civil Rights Act (CRA), I am referring to both laws. In general, the CRA prohibits employment discrimination based on race, color, religion, sex, or national origin, thereby making it illegal to base employment decisions on these factors because such decisions would result in discrimination and "unequal opportunity."

One of the most important cases in this area is *Griggs v. Duke Power* (1971), in which the court ruled that even when a company argues convincingly that it had no intention to discriminate, if adverse impact exists it is incumbent on the company to demonstrate that the selection battery was job related. Cases of this kind are sometimes

disparate impact cases
Cases involving employment procedures that apparently unintentionally discriminate against or unfairly affect a minority group.

disparate treatment cases
Cases involving discrimination that results from intentional differential treatment or behavior.

bona fide occupational qualification (BFOQ)
A characteristic such as one's gender, religion, or national origin that is required or necessary to effectively do the job.

called **disparate impact cases** because they involve employment procedures that apparently unintentionally discriminate against or unfairly affect a minority group. In **disparate treatment cases**, by contrast, the discrimination is intentional and a result of differential treatment. Most cases in personnel law are of the disparate impact variety, in which discrimination emerges as a by-product of employment procedures.

In disparate treatment cases, defendants often must show that a particular sex, religion, or national origin is really required or necessary for the job—a **bona fide occupational qualification (BFOQ)**. But this stipulation is interpreted very narrowly by the courts. Imagine the difficulty of convincing a judge that in order to operate your business, you need to hire only females. In fact, this very issue was addressed in an interesting and classic case, *Diaz v. Pan Am* (1971). Diaz was a man who wanted to be a flight attendant; but because of Pan Am's policy, which favored women to the exclusion of men, he was not selected. Pan Am claimed that gender was a BFOQ and that it was acceptable to hire only women for this job because women provided the intangibles regarding passenger comfort. Think about your most recent flight, and you can probably figure out how this case was decided! The court ruled that the primary function of an airline is to transport passengers safely, and, thus, maintaining safety was the chief job of a flight attendant. A "pleasant environment" is tangential to this primary function; therefore, gender could not be a BFOQ. Even if the "pleasant environment" had been upheld as a primary function, Pan Am would have been in the very difficult position of having to demonstrate that *only* women could provide such an environment—and that would have been difficult to do.

Another interesting take on this issue has been presented by some research on high school athletic directors. Women are not well represented in interscholastic athletics leadership, such as coaching and serving as athletic directors (ADs). A survey study found that women held only 14% of the AD positions across the United States (Whisenant, 2003). Furthermore, in the 2002–2003 school year, 75% of the announced AD openings in Texas required the applicant to also serve as head football coach (Whisenant, 2005). Since no women served as head football coach in the state of Texas, one could argue that women were being discriminated against. The author claims that disparate impact discrimination against women exists and that a BFOQ defense would not be successful if lawsuits were filed over this issue.

In *Griggs v. Duke Power,* the plaintiff, Griggs, was an African American male who had not been hired as a laborer; he presented data documenting adverse impact against African Americans. The defendant, Duke Power, responded by saying that the adverse impact was unintentional, but it lost the case largely because it could not demonstrate the job relatedness of its selection battery, as a validation study had never been done. Think about this case for a minute because it is very, very important. What the court was saying, and this still applies today, is that it is illegal to hire only Caucasians, even when they score better on the selection battery, *if the selection battery has not been demonstrated to predict job performance.* Another conclusion from this decision is that even professionally developed tests can be illegal if the company cannot show that the KSAOs measured by those tests are job related.

In addition to prohibiting discrimination in employment decisions based on race (an issue that certainly receives the most attention in the courts and the popular press), the CRA prohibits discrimination based on *national origin,* such that no one can be denied equal employment opportunity because of ancestry, culture, birthplace, or linguistic characteristics common to a specific ethnic group (EEOC, 2009b). For instance, a company cannot refuse to hire someone because he has an accent unless the company can show that the accent impairs job performance. Since 9/11, the number of claims of discrimination based on national origin has swelled significantly (EEOC, 2009c). The EEOC (2002b) attributes most of that increase to a post–9/11 backlash against Muslims and people of Middle Eastern descent. The EEOC has developed a new website for both employers and employees who have questions about the law regarding discrimination based on national origin as well as a new compliance manual (EEOC, 2002a).

Employment decisions based on *religion* are illegal as well. Furthermore, companies can be required to make reasonable accommodations for individuals' religious practices (EEOC, 2009e). For instance, they may have to provide flexibility in schedules for Jewish employees whose religious practices prevent them from working on the Sabbath if this can be done without undue hardship to the employer.

Protection is also provided to *pregnant women* under the CRA, which stipulates that discrimination on the basis of pregnancy, childbirth, or related medical conditions constitutes unlawful sex discrimination. The bottom line is that pregnant women cannot be treated differently from other applicants or employees with similar abilities (EEOC, 2009d).

Also prohibited by the CRA is **sexual harassment**, which includes such behaviors as unwelcome sexual advances, requests for sexual favors, and other conduct of a sexual nature, submission to or rejection of which affects one's job or creates an offensive work environment (EEOC, 2007). There are two forms of sexual harassment. The first is *quid pro quo harassment,* which refers to situations in which advancement or continuation in a company is contingent on sexual favors. (*Quid pro quo* means "this for that.") This is the blatant kind of sexual harassment that we tend to hear about most often.

The second form is *hostile work environment harassment,* defined by the courts in *Meritor Savings Bank v. Vinson* (1986) as verbal or physical behavior that creates an intimidating, hostile, or offensive work environment or an environment that interferes with one's job performance. Vinson was abused verbally and sexually by her boss at Meritor Savings Bank, and the court ruled in favor of Vinson, arguing that this behavior was both abusive and "unwelcome." Thus, hostile work environment was established as a type of sexual harassment (Cascio, 1998). During Clarence Thomas's Supreme Court confirmation hearing in 1991, Anita Hill, a lawyer employed at the EEOC, where Thomas was her supervisor, raised issues about his sex-related talk, which she alleged created a hostile work environment. Though not a legal proceeding as such, this was certainly the most famous "case" focusing attention on the issue of sexual harassment. Justice Thomas was confirmed by the Senate after a rather long and difficult hearing and still serves on the Supreme Court of the United States.

sexual harassment Behaviors such as unwelcome sexual advances, requests for sexual favors, and other conduct of a sexual nature, submission to or rejection of which affects one's job or creates an offensive work environment.

Federal legislation (i.e., Title VII) does not recognize sexual orientation as a protected class, leaving lesbian, gay, bisexual, and transgender (LGBT) employees without federal protection against workplace discrimination. Many states have elected, however, to provide protection against discrimination for LGBT individuals in the workplace (Berkley & Watt, 2006). As of June 14, 2011, 21 states ban discrimination in the workplace based on sexual orientation and gender identity, and over 100 municipalities in the 29 states without nondiscrimination laws do so as well (National Gay and Lesbian Task Force, 2012.)

Executive Order 11246

Executive Order 11246, enacted in 1965, prohibits job discrimination by employers holding federal contracts or subcontracts on the basis of race, color, sex, national origin, or religion. This piece of legislation is very similar to the CRA but is specifically relevant for federal agencies and those organizations that do work for federal agencies. For instance, universities fall within this legislation if they are a public school or a private school that has contracts with other federal agencies.

▼ **A Closer Look**
In most jobs, individuals cannot be forced to retire at a certain age. What role can BFOQs play with regard to age and employment?

Age Discrimination in Employment Act

Individuals who are 40 years of age or over are protected from discrimination by the Age Discrimination in Employment Act (ADEA), signed into law by President Lyndon Johnson on December 15, 1967. According to the ADEA, it is unlawful to discriminate against a person because of his or her age with respect to any employment-related decision (EEOC, 2009a). In addition, it is illegal to indicate any age preferences or limitations in job ads or notices. Exceptions are possible, but only when the company can demonstrate that age is a BFOQ necessary to the conduct of its business.

JEFF GREENBERG/PHOTO EDIT

EEOC v. Univ. of Texas Health Science Center at San Antonio (1983) is one example of a case in which the court allowed age as a BFOQ exception—specifically, by upholding a maximum age of 45 for campus police officers. In its ruling, the court noted that because the job was dangerous and required individuals to be on the beat alone, an age limit of 45 was a reasonable and safe requirement. Another example is the Age 60 Rule, which states that no commercial airline may employ a pilot or copilot who is 60 years old or older (Sterns, Doverspike, & Lax, 2005). The rationale for these rulings was that age-related decrements in vision and information processing in older individuals hired could lead to safety issues with catastrophic outcomes.

Cleverly v. Western Electric (1979) is a classic example of a typical ADEA case. Cleverly, an engineer, was fired six months before his pension benefits were to become fully vested—despite many years of distinguished service. In any ADEA case, plaintiffs must demonstrate that they (1) are members of the protected class (i.e., 40 or over), (2) were doing satisfactory work, (3) were discharged despite satisfactory work, and (4) were replaced by younger persons (Cascio, 1998). Cleverly was able to meet each of these requirements and was awarded back pay. (Western Electric had even made direct statements to him indicating that he was being let go to make way for young engineers!)

Americans with Disabilities Act

Title I of the Americans with Disabilities Act (ADA), which was signed into law by President George Herbert Walker Bush in 1990 (and took effect on July 26, 1992), prohibits discrimination against qualified individuals with disabilities in employment decisions. To clarify the role played by the ADA in organizations, I will start by defining a few terms. First, according to the EEOC (2005), a person with a *disability* is someone who (1) has a physical or mental impairment that substantially limits one or more major life activities, such as seeing, hearing, speaking, working, learning, and walking; (2) has a record of such an impairment; or (3) is regarded as having such an impairment. However, the law applies not to all disabled employees but only to those who are otherwise qualified for the job in question. By *qualified*, the EEOC means that the person can perform the essential functions of the job—if necessary, with the aid of reasonable accommodations.

Essential functions are tasks that are significant and meaningful aspects of the job. In short, then, it is illegal to deny someone a job because he can't perform tasks that are only tangential to the job. For example, in a company in which heavy lifting is seldom necessary but occasionally useful, the company should be able to make other arrangements when heavy lifting is called for. In those instances, someone with a bad back could still do the essential functions of the job and someone else could do the lifting.

Reasonable accommodations are changes or exceptions made by the employer that would allow the qualified disabled individual to successfully do the job. They include redesigning existing facilities so that they are readily usable by individuals with disabilities (e.g., installing an elevator in a building that does not currently have one); restructuring jobs and schedules to allow disabled persons to perform their jobs; and acquiring equipment, devices, training materials, and qualified readers/interpreters to aid disabled persons. An example in this last category would be voice-activated computer software that allows individuals who have lost the use of their hands to create computer documents without having to type them.

Employers are required to make reasonable accommodations, but only if such accommodations do not impose undue hardship on themselves. This brings us to our final

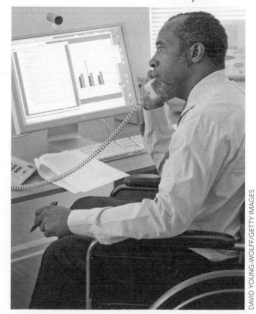

DAVID YOUNG-WOLFF/GETTY IMAGES

essential functions
Tasks that are significant and meaningful aspects of the job.

reasonable accommodations
Changes or exceptions made by an employer that allow qualified disabled individuals to successfully do a job.

▼ **A Closer Look**
Because of the ADA, disabled workers who are qualified for a particular job cannot be rejected for that job because of their disability. How do job analyses and job descriptions affect disabled workers' search for new jobs?

undue hardship
An accommodation for the disabled that would result in significant difficulty or expense given the employer's size and financial resources.

definition: **undue hardship**, an accommodation that would result in significant difficulty or expense given the employer's size and financial resources.

On September 25, 2008, President George W. Bush signed into law the ADA Amendments Act, which became effective on January 1, 2009, and is the first legislative change to the ADA of 1990. The new law describes how individuals are evaluated as to the presence of a disability, clarifies what it means to be regarded as having a disability, and expands the list of major life activities to include things such as caring for oneself, concentrating, and working, as well as major bodily functions (e.g., functions of the immune, digestive, respiratory systems, etc.). Although this has clarified some issues around the implementation of the ADA, there remain other issues regarding the definition of essential functions and reasonable accommodation.

Since 1990, the components of the ADA have continued to be interpreted on a case-by-case basis. For instance, in *Ethridge v. State of Alabama* (1993), the court ruled that Ethridge, a police applicant, could not perform the essential functions of the job due to his limited use of one hand and that no reasonable accommodation existed. The essential function cited by the court was shooting in a two-handed position. In a more recent case, *Rooney v. Koch Air, LLC* (2005), Rooney alleged that he was fired as a result of his disability. Rooney had injured his back on two occasions and eventually resigned after receiving numerous written reprimands for not doing his job. He sued the company, arguing that he had been discriminated against because of his disability. However, the court ruled that he had never demonstrated a disability because he himself had testified that after back surgery he was able to perform all major life activities such as sleeping, bathing, exercising, and performing basic household chores. The district court's decision was affirmed on appeal.

Some argue that the ADA needs to be amended because many impairments do not meet the narrow definition of a disability (Lee, 2003). Furthermore, some recent research suggests that U.S. citizens' views of what constitutes a disability do not match those covered by the ADA (Popovich, Scherbaum, Scherbaum, & Polinko, 2003). Probably the most famous ADA case to date is *Martin v. PGA Tour, Inc.* (1998). Casey Martin was a professional golfer whose right leg was so disabled that when he walked he was placed at significant risk of fracturing his leg. Martin sued the PGA after it refused his request that a reasonable accommodation be made to allow him to use a golf cart on the PGA tour. The PGA asserted that waiving this rule would fundamentally alter the competition and give Martin a competitive advantage. The judge ruled that it was a "gross distortion of reality" to think that providing Martin with a cart would give him a competitive advantage, given his disability and the pain he experiences simply being on his feet. Thus, the judge concluded that the requested accommodation of a cart was eminently reasonable in light of Martin's disability, and this ruling was supported on appeal by the Supreme Court.

Family and Medical Leave Act

The first piece of federal legislation signed by President Bill Clinton was the Family and Medical Leave Act (FMLA) in August 1993, which allowed eligible employees to take job-protected, unpaid leave for up to 12 weeks owing to family-related issues such as the birth of a child, the serious health condition of a family member, or one's own serious health condition. *Serious health condition* is defined as an illness, injury, impairment, or physical or mental condition that involves inpatient care or continuous treatment by a healthcare provider (Franklin, Gringer, & Cohen, P.C., n.d.). In general, the employee has the right to return to the same position or an equivalent position with equivalent pay and benefits at the conclusion of the leave. The purpose of the FMLA is to provide employees with the opportunity to balance their work and family life and to promote the security and economic stability of the family (U.S. Department of Labor, 2009).

California has recently become the first state to pass a paid family and medical leave statute that requires employers to provide six weeks of paid family leave to every eligible employee for each 12-month period. Currently, 11 states have enacted FMLA laws (U.S. Department of Labor, n.d.) that may work in concert with the federal legislation to the benefit of the employee. Employers and employees, though, have raised concerns about the success and effectiveness of the federal legislation (National Coalition to Protect Family Leave [NCPFL], n.d.). It is too complex for our discussion here, but employers have found it difficult to understand and to define what classes of illnesses qualify under the legislation. The confusion and ambiguity have resulted in inconsistency and "intermittent leave," in which employees use the FMLA for, say, three days off from work due to a cold or the flu (NCPFL, n.d.). On the other hand, employees have suffered under the FMLA because many simply can't afford to take 12 weeks off from work without pay. Former Senator Chris Dodd, the author of the 1993 bill, recognized this financial problem and, therefore, introduced the Family Leave Insurance Act of 2007, which would provide paid leave for 8 of the 12 weeks ("Dodd, Stevens," 2007). The bill was reintroduced in 2009 but has not moved through the legislative process; it is expected to be introduced in the 112th Congress again prior to January 3, 2013. On January 16, 2009, revised regulations regarding implementation of the FMLA went into effect. The new recommendations, among other things, provide for extended leave for the families of wounded soldiers, clarify what constitutes serious health conditions, and require enhanced communication between employees and employers regarding these issues. (This balance between work and family life will be considered in more detail in Chapter 11.)

As we have seen, legal issues are tightly linked with employment decisions, especially employee selection. In general, employment laws attempt to ensure *equal employment opportunity* to all individuals. According to the EEOC (2004), it is illegal to discriminate in any aspect of employment such as, but not limited to, the following:

- Hiring and firing
- Compensation, assignment, or classification of employees
- Transfer, promotion, layoff, or recall
- Job advertisements
- Recruitment
- Testing
- Use of company facilities
- Training and apprenticeship programs

- Fringe benefits
- Pay, retirement plans, and disability leave

This is an exciting area that continues to grow and develop. Table 7.8 lists most of the major pieces of employment legislation in existence as of this writing. Because legal work is so driven by court decisions and case interpretations, I suggest that you consult the websites given in the references cited in this chapter for the most recent information on industrial psychology and the law, especially with respect to legal precedent.

■ Summary

Whereas Chapter 6 discussed the many types of predictors used in employee selection, this chapter has presented information about how to use those predictors in making selection decisions. Predictive validation, concurrent validation, validity generalization, and synthetic validation were examined in light of how important they are for employee selection. Recruitment was also discussed as an important precursor to employee selection, and the recent role of social media in this process was examined.

Various approaches to the selection process were discussed, including the multiple cutoff, multiple hurdle, and multiple regression techniques. This part of the discussion provided both a how-to guide and an overview of the differences among these approaches. A lengthy discussion of utility followed; here we noted that if a selection battery is not viewed as useful for an organization, the organization is unlikely to be interested in it. We also looked at two ways in which decision accuracy can be operationalized: decision accuracy for hires and overall decision accuracy. Validity, base rate, selection ratio, and cost were identified as important factors affecting the utility of a new selection battery.

The last half of the chapter was spent on legal issues in industrial psychology. The emphasis was on selection, as it is in this area that legal issues tend to emerge most often. First, we discussed the history of the EEOC. Next, we examined employment at-will, adverse impact, and affirmative action, as these are among the most important concepts one must understand in order to appreciate the context and procedures involved in personnel law. Finally, we considered the major employment laws currently in place (see Table 7.8). Distinctions were drawn between disparate treatment and disparate impact, between *quid pro quo* harassment and hostile work environment harassment, between BFOQ defenses and job-relatedness defenses, and between reasonable accommodation and undue hardship.

■ Key Terms

adverse impact (p. 203)
affirmative action (AA) (p. 205)
base rate (p. 198)
bona fide occupational qualification (BFOQ) (p. 210)

cybervetting (p. 185)
disparate impact cases (p. 210)
disparate treatment cases (p. 210)
employment at-will (p. 202)
essential functions (p. 213)

■ TAKING IT TO THE FIELD

I/O psychologists, while not lawyers, are sometimes asked to provide information about the legality of a hiring process. While this text is not intended to teach you the details of employment law, it is helpful for you to recognize the key problems to watch out for in a selection system. You have been speaking with Mr. Marshall recently regarding some questions he has about his selection system. You have just received the following e-mail from him.

Hello again—

As per our discussion on the phone, I think I would like to get some input from you about whether I need to make any changes to my selection system. Of course, I will also be consulting with a lawyer, but input from you would be very helpful.

Here's the background of my problem:

I own several pork-processing plants. We have roughly 10,000 employees nationally, primarily based in the Midwest. One of the positions that we need to hire for regularly is in the slaughterhouse. Processing the carcasses is physically demanding work, and many people we hire cannot perform the work effectively for very long. Thus, we end up having to fire quite a large number of employees because of low job performance.

Last year, we had 500 Latino American applicants, 200 Caucasian American applicants, and 400 African American applicants. Out of these applicants, we hired 400 Latino Americans, 300 African Americans, and 120 Caucasian Americans. We did not have any Asian American applicants this year.

To be hired, an applicant must pass three selection tests:

1. The applicant must be low on neuroticism. This is because the gore that occurs on the killing floor can be upsetting; we find that people with moderate to high levels of neuroticism typically quit within one week. In fact, we completed a validation study, which indicated that neuroticism and job performance were correlated at −.35.

2. The applicant must be able to pass a physical test by being able to squeeze a rod with a certain amount of pressure for two minutes straight. This is because the workers must move sides of pork all day; unless workers have a basic level of strength in their hands, they will not be able to complete the job over an eight-hour shift. We also find that our physical test correlates .25 with job performance. We have found that Caucasian Americans tend to have less hand strength because they are less likely to have worked in jobs requiring manual labor compared to our African American and Latino American applicants.

3. The applicant must have at least one year of experience in either manufacturing or meat packing. It seems that workers who have done this work before are likely to remain in the organization longer. We find that Latino applicants are much more likely to have experience than any other racial group.

So here are my questions. First, do we have adverse impact? Second, are all three of our selection requirements legally defensible? If any of the processes are not legal, what should I do to make them legal?

Thanks for your help on this!
Regards,
John Marshall

Respond to Mr. Marshall's e-mail. Note that the important part of this assignment is not whether or not you believe Mr. Marshall's system is illegal; rather, it is your reasons for thinking it is (or is not) legal.

■ Critical Thinking Questions

1. How do recruitment and selection fit together?

2. Why is it unheard of for a selection battery to explain 100% of the variance in job performance?

3. Do you believe the major employment laws offer sufficient protection for all workers in the United States? Why or why not?

4. How do performance appraisal and selection complement each other? How are these two very important processes dependent on each other?

■ Application Questions

1. This chapter mentions person–environment fit. When you are looking for a job, what are some cues that indicate an organization is a "good fit" for you? Have you ever been in an organization that wasn't a good fit for you? What happened?

2. Refer to Figure 7.2. Imagine that you are working for a company and a change in federal regulations leads you to require a higher score on the predictor battery. What will happen to the number of false alarms? To the number of false misses? In what other situations might you choose to raise your cutoff score on a predictor battery?

3. How common are BFOQs? Interview five people about their jobs and determine whether someone in a protected class (race, color, religion, national origin, sex, age, disability) would be unable to perform an essential job function.

4. Consider a job you have had. Provide one example of a reasonable accommodation that could be made so an applicant with a disability could do the job. What types of changes do you believe would be unreasonable (i.e., cause undue hardship for the company)?

5. Typically races other than Caucasians are considered to be minorities. Are there any jobs where one might expect a different racial group to be hired more often than Caucasians? In these cases, would you recommend that the organization enact an AAP? Why or why not?

6. In the United States, new mothers are given 12 weeks of unpaid leave. Some countries provide paid maternity leave (e.g., Portugal), paternity leave (e.g., Sweden), or longer periods of unpaid leave (e.g., Japan). What are some advantages and disadvantages of the U.S. policy? What changes (if any) would you make to the U.S. policy?

■ Suggested Readings

Crosby, F. J., Stockdale, M. S., & Ropp, S. A. (Eds.). (2007). *Sex discrimination in the workplace.* Boston: Blackwell. In this multidisciplinary text, a distinguished group of contributors examine causes of and solutions to sex discrimination. Many firsthand accounts from participants in landmark sex discrimination cases are included.

Dipboye, R. L., & Colella, A. (2005). *Discrimination at work: The psychological and organizational bases.* Mahwah, NJ: Erlbaum. More broadly focused than Landy's text (see below), this book explores the various biases that can emerge in the workplace and the implications of these biases.

International Association of Chiefs of Police website (http://www.iacpsocialmedia.org/). This website provides a wealth of information about social media and its growing importance in the world of work—namely, employee recruitment and selection.

Landy, F. J. (Ed.). (2005). *Employment discrimination litigation: Behavioral, quantitative, and legal perspectives.* San Francisco: Jossey-Bass. This book offers a detailed look at fundamental issues in employment litigation.

Outtz, J. L. (2010). *Adverse impact: Implications for organizational staffing and high stakes selection.* New York: Routledge/Taylor & Francis Group. In this volume, leading selection scholars and practitioners tackle the complex issues surrounding adverse impact.

Robinson, R. H., Franklin, G. M., & Wayland, R. (2002). *The regulatory environment of human resource management.* Orlando, FL: Harcourt College. This text presents a nice framework for understanding and interpreting personnel law. A technical presentation is made more user-friendly by many useful examples.

CHAPTER **8**

Training and Development

LEARNING OBJECTIVES

This chapter should help you understand:

- How important training is to both organizations and employees
- How to diagnose an organization's training needs through the use of organizational, task, person, and demographic analyses
- The basic principles of learning that affect training success, such as meaningfulness, practice, overlearning, and feedback
- What makes an organization's learning context conducive to successful training
- Each of the various training techniques, as well as their strengths and weaknesses
- The key elements of transfer of training
- The traditional criteria used in training evaluation, along with a newer perspective on these criteria
- How to design a training evaluation study in a number of different ways
- The increasing importance and prevalence of both sexual harassment training and diversity training

In this chapter, we will discuss the extremely important role of training and development in organizations. Surveys consistently report that over 90% of Fortune 500 companies have some type of formal training program. According to the American Society for Training and Development, U.S. organizations spend $126 billion annually on employee learning and development (American Society for Training and Development, 2011). Firms considered to be on the leading edge of training provide their employees between 40 and 45 hours of training per year. The average training budget for the top 125 companies according to *Training* magazine was $145.5 million (Training Magazine Ranks, 2012).

At a very basic level, we can think of training as being any kind of teaching that is related to one's job—it's about employee development. In previous chapters, we have seen how organizational efficiency is affected by the selection, appraisal, and compensation of employees. This chapter demonstrates how organizational efficiency is also affected by the training of employees.

You might be wondering why training is needed at all if you are careful about your selection system. In other words, if you select high performers, you ought to be able to save a great deal of money on training—because these employees already have the KSAOs (i.e., knowledge, skills, abilities, and other characteristics) necessary to do the job. That logic would be sound if it weren't for a few key issues. First, although a company may hire people who appear to be the most skilled and able of its applicants, they may still need job- or organization-specific training to do the job effectively. For instance, Apple may hire the best and brightest graduates of computer programming departments worldwide, but if those new hires don't know the Apple infrastructure or computer networking system or aren't familiar with the culture, norms, and procedures that are part of the Apple way of doing business, they will not be effective performers until they are trained in these areas.

A second reason training is so important to organizations is that experienced employees must sometimes be *retrained* because of changes in the job or organization. This issue will continue to grow as continued advancements in technology change the nature of many jobs (Zammuto, Griffith, Majchrzak, Dougherty, & Faraj, 2007), making it necessary for employees to keep up with these technological changes.

Third, training is important for the continued development of employees. Experts believe that training programs can lead to increased organizational commitment and job satisfaction, resulting in increased productivity, decreased absenteeism, and less turnover (Jackson & Schuler, 2000). In other words, training and development efforts result in better employees and a more productive workforce.

Although many definitions of training are available in the literature, the following is one that I believe is particularly good: **Training** comprises the *formal procedures* that a company utilizes to facilitate *learning* so that the resultant *behavior* contributes to the attainment of the company's *goals* and *objectives* (McGehee & Thayer, 1961).

■ Assessing Training Needs

Before even beginning to develop a training program, organizations must identify what, if any, training needs exist. Organizations differ greatly in terms of their training needs (Brown, 2002). For instance, some organizations may need training at the management level, while others need it at the nonmanagement level. Some organizations may require rater training (discussed in Chapter 5), while others would benefit from performance training, and still others may need sexual harassment training. A recent development in this area is what some are calling *competency-based training*. (Recall from Chapter 1 that competencies are skills, behaviors, and capabilities that allow employees to perform specific functions.) Organizations that take this approach to training identify what competencies they want all employees to have and then

▲ A Closer Look
Think of a time when you received some sort of training. Was it effective? Why or why not?

training
The formal procedures that a company utilizes to facilitate learning so that the resultant behavior contributes to the attainment of the company's goals and objectives.

develop training programs around those competencies (Holton, Coco, Lowe, & Dutsch, 2006). Those companies that are truly innovative and thought leaders in this area consistently tie training to organizational outcomes (Aguinis & Kraiger, 2009). In this section, we will consider how organizations identify their training needs through four types of needs analyses. (For a thorough treatment of needs analysis, see Goldstein & Ford, 2002.)

Organizational Analysis

Where is training needed in the organization? To answer this question, an organizational analysis is conducted to determine the organization's short- and long-term goals and then to compare those goals to the organization's accomplishments. In this way, the organization can identify which goals aren't being reached, as these areas are likely to be targets for training. I myself have done some training work with a manufacturing company whose organizational analysis indicated that the organization had not been able to achieve one of its important goals—to generate a "team-oriented" relationship among managers and subordinates. The organization believed that a stronger working relationship among supervisors and subordinates would improve productivity. It saw this as a clear need, and I targeted improvement in that area by developing and implementing a training program designed to improve communication among employees, thus creating a shared sense of the organization's purpose and mission.

Organizational analysis should also consider the culture of the organization. Is it an organizational culture that sees training and development as important? If not, this suggests the need to overcome some potential obstacles to training, necessitating careful thought about how best to proceed.

Task Analysis

What duties, tasks, behaviors, and actions need to be improved? At this level, the analysis is much like the job analyses that we have discussed thus far. The organization or consultant examines the task requirements for the successful conduct of each job, specifying exactly what the new employees are going to do on their jobs. By identifying these tasks, the organization can distinguish between those the new employees are able to do immediately upon beginning employment and those for which they will require some training.

Recall that in Chapter 3 we talked about different types of job analyses. The type most often used to determine training needs is a task-oriented job analysis in which subject matter experts (SMEs), such as incumbents or others who are familiar with the job, respond to a series of items in a checklist format. The responses are collected into a summary that serves as the outcome, or result, of the task analysis—a summary that specifically describes the tasks that are completed on the job. For instance, your local telephone company may notice that customers frequently complain that mild windstorms are knocking down their telephone lines and disconnecting their service. After comparing the task analysis and the manner in which telephone line workers were attaching the lines to the house, the company might conclude that the line workers did not know how to effectively perform this task. This is a clear instance in which retraining would be very beneficial.

It's important at this point to note that we talked extensively about job analysis as the foundation for selection. We used job analysis to identify the KSAOs necessary to be an effective employee. In a related vein, we use task analysis here to identify the KSAOs that need to be further developed or refined to allow employees to do their job. One way to think about the relationship between selection and training is to view selection as dealing in the raw materials (i.e., the KSAOs that employees bring to the organization) and training as developing or producing the finished product (i.e., the KSAOs that are developed through training and applied to one's job). Both selection and training deal with **human capital**—the skills, abilities, and experiences of organizational members that provide each organization with its competitive advantage or unique aspects.

human capital
The education, training, and experiences of individual employees that provide value to organizations.

Person Analysis

Who needs the training? A person analysis gets quite specific, focusing on those employees who actually need training. Toward this end, it examines how well all employees are carrying out their job responsibilities and duties. For an example, let's return to our telephone company scenario. The line workers are the employees who have been identified as needing some training; in particular, they need training on attaching telephone wires to houses so that they aren't easily dislodged. Which of the line workers are most in need of this training? If the telephone company has 2,500 line workers but only 500 of them seem unable to grasp this skill, it makes sense to target our training to those 500 employees who appear to need it.

Often, performance appraisal data (see Chapter 5) are used to identify good candidates for training. In addition to traditional performance appraisal ratings, some organizations allow employees to nominate themselves for training in specific areas in which they feel they could further develop as employees. Finally, sometimes organizations will give a test to diagnose employees' strengths and weaknesses and use these test results to indicate who needs additional training. In fact, performance management systems and training programs are often used in concert to develop employees. (We talked about employee development in Chapter 5, and we will talk more about it later in this chapter as well.)

Demographic Analysis

Traditionally, training needs assessment entailed analyses at the organization, task, and person levels. Now, however, scholars and practitioners suggest that needs analysis should also take into account the demographic makeup of the organization (Latham, 1988). Basically, this involves determining the specific training needs of various demographic groups, such as those protected by civil rights legislation. For instance, since the Age Discrimination in Employment Act (ADEA) has made it illegal to discriminate in the selection of employees based on age, many companies recognize that older hires may need training that is not necessary for younger employees. One example is technology training. Many older employees may need such training simply because

COURTESY OF ERIC SURFACE

Eric A. Surface
PhD, 2003, I/O Psychology, North Carolina State University
Co-founder, President, and Lead I/O Psychologist
SWA Consulting Inc.

Learning is critical for organizational success. Needs assessment is the primary tool for aligning learning, assessment, compensation, and policy with performance requirements and business objectives. SWA Consulting Inc. works with organizations to help make a difference in learning and performance by helping to create alignment among requirements, learning, assessment, capability, and performance.

Needs assessment is typically initiated when an organization perceives a need or a gap between desired capabilities and current capabilities. Organizations ask us to help identify and specify the gap and to develop strategies to bridge that gap.

A few years ago, Naval Special Warfare Command (NSW) leaders decided SEAL (Sea Air Land) and SWCC (Special Warfare Combatant-Craft Crewman) personnel needed more foreign-language capability. There was limited foreign-language capability in the force and a heavy reliance on interpreters. Mission analysis demonstrated a need for foreign-language capability, especially speaking. A gap between the current and desired states existed. How could this gap be closed?

There are typically five strategies to resolve a capability gap: (1) select/hire, (2) train, (3) redesign work, (4) outsource, and (5) adapt strategy, mission and objectives. Which of these strategies make sense depends on the situation. Given the constraints of the context, only training and outsourcing (interpreters) were feasible, but outsourcing had demonstrated problems. The NSW leadership decided that all SEAL and SWCC personnel should receive a minimum amount of training in a mission-relevant language focused on developing mission-required

capability, with some personnel receiving advanced training. NSW needed a thorough training needs assessment in order to develop learning objectives, efficient and effective curricula, and valid assessments focused on its mission-related foreign-language requirements.

My company worked with the advisory group, planned the needs assessment, conducted the language-focused task and KSAO analysis, developed learning objectives, created a curriculum plan, and reviewed existing curricula in conjunction with our partner, the American Council on the Teaching of Foreign Languages, and with learning and subject matter experts at NSW. We developed a comprehensive coding system to relate all learning objectives and activities back to mission requirements, allowing for future curriculum updates.

Although this was a very extensive, domain-focused training needs assessment, need assessments can vary greatly in purpose, focus, scope, and methodology. When approaching a needs assessment, judicious flexibility is required because every situation is different. But transferable lessons can be learned from examples such as the one above.

Applying Your Knowledge

1. How do you decide which of the five strategies are feasible and appropriate for addressing an identified capability gap?

2. Why would restricting applicants to those with existing high levels of language proficiency *not* work for an occupation that already has very high selection requirements and a very demanding assessment process?

3. Why was a task and KSAO analysis used to determine the foreign-language requirements?

they grew up during an era when technology was less advanced, whereas younger employees have probably picked up these skills throughout their lives.

Another example is training for employees with disabilities. As discussed in Chapter 7, organizations are legally required to make reasonable accommodations for disabled employees. One such accommodation may be the provision of training that helps these employees do their jobs. Another is the redesign of existing training programs to accommodate disabled employees. For instance, a visual-based management skills training program may have to be altered in such a way that vision-impaired employees can participate in and benefit from it. Trainers must avoid discriminating against employees on the basis of gender, race, physical disabilities, age, ethnicity, and religion—in keeping with the laws, policies, and mission of equal employment opportunity.

■ Learning Context

Before we discuss the various training methods available, we need to describe the learning context because it is so important to the success of any training program. In short, the context, which includes principles of instructional design, basic principles of learning, and characteristics of the trainee and trainer, largely determines the success of a training intervention. In fact, there has been a great deal of focus on *learning organizations*, companies in which there is an organization-wide concern with and valuing of knowledge acquisition and continuous learning (Garofano & Salas, 2005).

Continuous learning is more than just taking lots and lots of courses; it's about learning how to learn. The management guru and scholar Peter Senge (2006) has written extensively about continuous learning, noting that it's about having a personal vision, taking an active role in one's world of work, reflecting on one's experiences, being open to feedback, and making adjustments to how one approaches one's work. Continuous learning organizations make this attitude much easier for employees to embrace.

continuous learning Directed and long-term effort to learn; stems from an intense desire to acquire knowledge and improve results and from participation in activities that facilitate learning.

Instructional Design

Instructional design refers to all activities that are developed and coordinated to support the trainees' learning processes The first important element of instructional design is determining what is to be learned. Learning can take a variety of forms, but generally it can be categorized as cognitive, psychomotor, or social. Another, more sophisticated scheme presents a series of design features, or learning conditions (e.g., providing feedback, informing trainees of goals), that can be mapped to the various categories of learning (Gagne, Briggs, & Wager, 1992). This approach allows an organization to use existing knowledge to build an effective context or environment for the specific learning targeted by the organization. The last element of instructional design is the planned evaluation (Wang & Wilcox, 2006), which, of course, should be part of every training program (see Training Evaluation, later in this chapter).

instructional design A set of events that facilitate training through their impact on trainees.

Principles of Learning

Learning is defined as a relatively permanent change in behavior that occurs as a result of experience or practice (Wexley & Latham, 2002). Therefore, to understand training, which is all about learning, we need a clearer understanding of the principles that enhance the learning process. In academic circles, the research on learning has

learning The relatively permanent change in behavior that occurs as a result of experience or practice.

been chiefly conducted by cognitive, experimental, and social psychologists. As I/O psychologists, however, we try to apply learning principles to the design and implementation of training programs.

In the following sections, we will focus on some of the more general principles that are important to effective organizational training.

Active Learning Learning theory has always argued that learning is facilitated if the learner is active during the learning period. This, of course, is why professors always encourage students to take notes or outline reading assignments, talk to others about the material, and write and rewrite key concepts rather than just read the material over and over again. The suggestions from learning theory about active learning apply very easily to training in organizations as well. One can read about how to conduct a performance appraisal (PA) interview or be provided a list of the specifications for the development of a particular product, but a better way to learn these things is to actually actively practice doing them.

Size of the Unit to Be Learned The question here is whether training should be structured in such a way as to present the whole task or only part of the task in a given training session (Goldstein & Ford, 2002)—a distinction sometimes referred to as *whole versus part learning*. According to learning theorists, it is more effective to practice or be trained on the whole task at one time if the task is highly organized, coherent, and interdependent; however, for a complex task that is easily divided into independent components, a more effective strategy is to be trained on each component separately, moving on to the next component after mastering the previous one.

For instance, let's say that I have just hired a 55-year-old man as my new secretary, that he graduated from secretarial school before personal computers were commonly used in business offices, and that he has been out of the workforce for nearly 20 years. Obviously, I need to provide him with some training on word processing and other computer procedures that I use in my office. Here, it would probably be more efficient to teach bits and pieces of the word-processing software than to try to teach the whole program all at once.

On the other hand, suppose I've hired a new truck driver to deliver my product to the retail establishments that sell it. Assume also that this driver has no experience driving an 18-wheel tractor-trailer, which is the vehicle I want her to use for deliveries. Does it make sense to teach her how to use the clutch first, then the accelerator, then the side-view mirrors? No, because the overall operation of this vehicle requires that the clutch, accelerator, and side-view mirrors be used in concert. Learning them separately would clearly be ineffective. You can see, then, that the way in which material to be learned is structured can play an important role in the success of a training program.

A related structural question is whether the practice of the task should take place all at once or be spread out over time. **Distributed practice** refers to training that is divided into segments, usually with rest periods in between; **massed practice** refers to training that takes place at one time, without breaks. Research has traditionally

distributed practice
Training in which the practice is divided into segments, usually with rest periods in between.

massed practice
Training in which all the practice takes place at one time, without breaks.

shown that, overall, distributed practice is better for learning skills and for long-term retention of those skills. In a recent study of sales employees in Germany, it was found that both massed and distributed practice were effective, but distributed practice was superior (Kauffeld & Lehman-Willenbrock, 2009). However, for practical reasons, many organizations don't make the time for distributed practice; instead, they cram in as much as possible during one eight-hour session (Wexley & Latham, 1991)—an approach that often results in poorly trained employees. According to a meta-analysis of 63 studies, distributed practice is especially effective for tasks that are low in complexity, like psychomotor tasks such as the Purdue Pegboard, discussed in Chapter 6 (Donovan & Radosevich, 1999).

Meaningfulness of Material It makes sense that trainees will be more likely to learn new material if they find it meaningful. Accordingly, organizations should incorporate a few elements into their training programs to make the material more meaningful and relevant for the trainees (Wexley & Latham, 2002). First, the trainer should present an overview of the material, which allows the trainees to better understand the objectives of the training program, as well as its procedures. Second, the material should be presented in a way that trainees can easily understand. This involves using terms, examples, and concepts that the trainees can understand and relate to. One obvious application here is the use of job-relevant examples in the training, such as patient-care issues when training nurses and student-related issues when training schoolteachers. Third, sequencing of the material is important. Trainers should present the material in a logical order. For example, in training air conditioner–repair technicians to replace an air conditioner coil, it makes sense to first demonstrate how to disassemble the unit; next, how to take out the old coil; then, how to install the new coil; and, finally, how to reassemble the unit. Any other order of steps would not be logical and could result in less understanding on the part of the trainee.

Practice and Overlearning You've heard it said that "practice makes perfect." Although true perfection is rarely achieved, this phrase does suggest that practice is important in almost any learning situation. But *how* one practices—that is, the quality of the practice—also affects what one learns. This last point is an important one to make in a training context, as employees who either don't practice or practice in an inappropriate way do not learn very well. We all fall prey to some bad habits in our home lives as well as our work lives. Often those bad habits develop if we fail to practice good habits or continue to repeat a pattern of wrong behaviors. Bad habits—such as when children don't wash their hands after using the bathroom or when UPS drivers lift heavy boxes using just their backs, not their legs—can easily develop from faulty practice. Trainers must be aware of the practice sessions of trainees and make sure they are practicing appropriately because, although practice doesn't really make perfect, "perfect practice" is a near-guarantee of quality performance.

    Overlearning is the process of giving trainees continued practice even after they have appeared to master the behavior, resulting in high levels of learning. You may think this is a waste of time, but, in fact, practicing something so much as to overlearn

overlearning
The process of giving trainees continued practice even after they have appeared to master the behavior, resulting in high levels of learning.

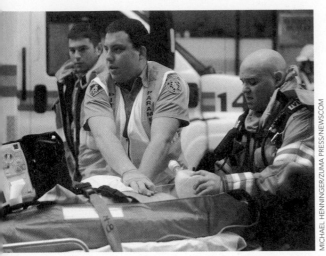

MICHAEL HENNINGER/ZUMA PRESS/NEWSCOM

▲ A Closer Look
Sometimes overlearning can increase the likelihood that a task will be performed more quickly, easily, and effectively. What other job-related tasks might it be beneficial to overlearn?

it increases the likelihood that one will be able to exhibit the behavior quickly, easily, and consistently when called on to do so. Think back to the subject of bad habits. If I stop practicing the use of my turn signal when I drive, eventually I won't be using it at all. However, if I have overlearned this behavior to the point where it becomes second nature to me, I'm likely to use that turn signal forever. The same principle holds true in the workplace. If a secretary is trained to save his document after every page is typed, actually doing so during the training sessions themselves, he is likely to continue this practice because the behavior has been overlearned.

Now let's consider a situation that is truly a matter of life and death. Emergency room (ER) physicians must be trained in such a way that they overlearn certain behaviors because, given the stress and severity of the situations they find themselves in, these behaviors have to be second nature. If a member of my family is rushed to the ER because he can't breathe or his heart isn't pumping, I don't want the ER physician having to think through the steps involved in intubating or defibrillating him—I want these behaviors to be so overlearned that they happen automatically.

Feedback In training situations, it is imperative that participants be given timely and useful feedback about how they are performing. Feedback, also called *knowledge-of-results (KOR)*, serves three purposes in a training context: (1) It provides information that allows trainees to make whatever adjustments may be necessary in their behaviors during training, (2) it makes the learning process more interesting for the trainees and increases their motivation to learn, and (3) it leads to goal setting for improving performance (Wexley & Latham, 2002). Also worth knowing are three important principles regarding how feedback is best delivered to individuals: (1) Feedback works best when it is given immediately following the individual's behavior, (2) immediate and frequent feedback tends to result in the best performance, and (3) both positive and negative feedback have value when delivered in a sensitive yet clear manner. (For an excellent and classic overview of the feedback process, see Ilgen, Fisher, & Taylor, 1979.)

Individual Differences in Trainees

Although the structural elements of the learning context are important, characteristics of the learner are also important, such as the desire for continuous learning. There are three specific characteristics of the learner that deserve some discussion. First, learning is likely to happen only if the learner is prepared to learn—what is sometimes called trainee **readiness**. Sometimes, individuals are incapable of being taught something because they don't have the necessary knowledge, ability, or experiences to allow them to learn.

readiness
Possessing the background characteristics and necessary level of interest that make learning possible.

Second, individuals' beliefs in their ability to be successful in training and in the job—self-efficacy—can play a very large role (Aguinis & Kraiger, 2009). If trainees aren't convinced of their ability to successfully complete the training program and to apply what they've learned at work, the training process is not likely to be effective. A recent meta-analytic review of 89 empirical studies (Blume, Ford, Baldwin, & Huang, 2010) supports this notion.

Third, the motivation to learn is important as well. We will talk at length about motivation in Chapter 9, but, for now, it's important to understand that if employees are not motivated to be trained, the training is almost certain to fail. I could design the slickest multimedia training program ever, making use of nice color videos and computer technology—but if you hate your job and aren't motivated to do any better than you're currently doing, you won't work hard during training, and it's unlikely to have much impact on you. Providing useful, immediate feedback to trainees is one strategy a trainer can use to increase motivation. Another strategy is to demonstrate how the training will pay off for the trainee. This answers the "what's in it for me" question, which is a very reasonable one for the employee to ask. If the trainer can show that, by working hard in training, employees will be able to work more easily, perform better, or enjoy their jobs more, motivation is likely to follow.

Some research has focused on these individual differences in trainees. For instance, some training work has taken a different perspective by encouraging trainees to make errors during training. The rationale is that more exploration (trial and error) may help trainees learn at a deeper level and gain a better understanding of the task at hand. Researchers have found that so-called error training was very effective for trainees who were high in cognitive ability and openness. Those individuals who were high on conscientiousness, however, demonstrated reduced self-efficacy as a result of error training (Gully, Payne, Koles, & Whiteman, 2002).

Others who have focused on the role of individual differences (e.g., Big Five factors) in training success found that those high on emotional stability and openness acquired skills in training at a faster rate (Herold, Davis, Fedor, & Parsons, 2002). They concluded from these and other results that individual differences are useful for predicting training success and that early training success has differential effects on later success, depending on the various levels of these individual differences.

Characteristics of the Trainer

We've seen how the structural properties of the training context, the principles of learning, and individual differences among trainees affect the training process. In some ways, the last piece of the puzzle is a consideration of trainer characteristics. First, Wexley and Latham (2002) suggest that effective trainers establish specific objectives and communicate them clearly to the trainees. Second, trainers should have a solid understanding of how people learn (including the principles of learning discussed earlier) and what role their own approaches or styles can play. Third, communication skills are extremely important. As you might imagine, trainees' attitudes, motivation, and behaviors are likely to be adversely affected by a trainer who communicates in a rigid, closed, negative, and condescending way. Fourth, trainers must realize that different trainees may require a different style or different treatment from the trainer. Although other issues may be important as well, this list provides a good overview of the kinds of trainer characteristics that are likely to be important to training effectiveness.

Transfer of Training

transfer of training
The extent to which the material, skills, or procedures learned in training are taken back to the job and used by the employee in some regular fashion.

Transfer of training is the extent to which the material, skills, or procedures learned in training are taken back to the job and used by the employee in some regular fashion. From the organization's perspective, this principle is integral to the success of the training program. This is the reason that training experts and organizations alike are always concerned about transfer of training (Velada, Caetano, Michel, Lyons, & Kavanaugh, 2007). *Positive transfer* is the organization's goal—the hope is that what is learned in the training program will improve performance back on the job. Sometimes, however, performance declines as a result of training. This outcome is called *negative transfer*.

Irwin Goldstein and Kevin Ford's (2002) classic text on training provides a summary of the literature in this area, as well as some guidelines on how to increase the likelihood of positive transfer. First, trainers should maximize the similarity between the training situation and the job situation. In other words, the training environment should resemble the on-the-job environment as much as possible, an idea that is often called *identical elements theory*. A major cause of negative transfer in many training situations is disparity between these two environments. As an example, let's say we're training employees how to assemble automobile wheels, and we provide all of the materials they need at their workstations, along with an unlimited amount of time to complete the task. However, after these employees successfully complete the training program and get back to their jobs, they find that the materials are not always at their workstations, and, owing to the assembly-line nature of the workplace, they don't have an unlimited amount of time. When the employees try to apply the same procedures they learned in training to the work situation, their performance declines because there isn't enough time to actually use the procedures they learned in training. This is negative transfer.

One study demonstrated that transfer was enhanced when the trainee's actual work situation matched what he or she desired in an ideal work situation (Awoniyi, Griego, & Morgan, 2002). Although not completely parallel to identical elements theory, this finding is certainly related in the sense that the way the relevant situations match up seems important.

Second, providing employees with an adequate amount of active practice is essential for positive transfer. This is especially true for new employees learning new tasks. In such situations, practice to the point of overlearning is a good strategy for enhancing transfer because it helps the new employees do these new tasks correctly, despite the additional stress associated with novel situations. Third, trainers should provide different contexts in which employees can practice the desired behaviors. Practice in different contexts with different stimuli (e.g., wheels of different sizes and parts) increases the likelihood that what is learned in training will generalize to a variety of contexts back on the job. Fourth, the trainers, trainees, and manager should work together throughout this entire process. Fifth, expectations for the trainers, trainees, and manager should be made clear up front. And, finally, trainers need to provide on-the-job maintenance programs that are focused on helping employees to continue their learned behaviors.

Baldwin and Ford's (1988) classic paper on transfer of training proposed a model of the transfer process that emphasized, among the other things just discussed, the importance of social support. It has been demonstrated that social service employees reported a lack of transfer from their training experiences due to heavy workloads, excessive time pressures, lack of reinforcement, and lack of feedback (Clarke, 2002). This led to some discussion about the importance of *transfer climate* (Hatala & Fleming, 2007), which consists of peer and supervisory support for transfer. If trainees don't perceive support for transferring what they've learned back to their jobs, the training is likely to be ineffective. Clearly, these findings suggest that the supportiveness of the work context is important in affecting transfer of training.

A recent meta-analysis found that characteristics like cognitive ability, conscientiousness, and voluntary participation were most strongly related to transfer of training. In addition, both transfer climate and social support (peer and supervisor) were consistently related to transfer. Finally, posttraining self-efficacy and posttraining knowledge demonstrated small to moderate correlations with training transfer (Blume et al., 2010).

■ Training Delivery

Research shows that pretraining interventions aimed at preparing employees for the training that ensues are also important ingredients for effective training (Mesmer-Magnus & Viswesvaran, 2010). These typically involve providing trainees with a preview of the training and strategies that will increase the trainees' capability to make the most of the training.

No book could do justice to all the training techniques that are available to HR practitioners, and we certainly can't cover them all in this one chapter. However, I will talk about a representative sample of the various training techniques organized by type of approach. Before moving on to a discussion of the types of training, it's helpful to know that research also shows that pretraining interventions aimed at preparing employees for the training that ensues are also important ingredients for effective training (Mesmer-Magnus & Viswesvaran, 2010). These typically involve providing information to give trainees a preview of the ensuing training and providing strategies that increase trainees' capability to make the most of the training. First, I will present a few of the more traditional approaches. Second, we'll look at technology-based approaches. Finally, I will conclude with various techniques that are used specifically to develop employees' competencies, including their leadership skills.

DAVID YOUNG-WOLFF/PHOTOEDIT

GIUSEPPI CACACE/AFP/GETTY IMAGES

▲ **A Closer Look**
What elements
of training might
make it more
successful for
transferring back
to the job?

Traditional Approaches

Lecturing One of the oldest and most established training methods is the use of simple lecturing to teach trainees important work-related information. This approach is very economical because many employees can be trained at one time. The effectiveness of this technique varies greatly, depending on the training objectives. Specifically, whereas the lecture approach seems useful for teaching trainees facts or helping them acquire knowledge, it may not be very effective for developing problem-solving or interpersonal skills. Additionally, a lecture with a fixed time limit delivered to a moderately sized group of trainees is not likely to include such important learning principles as active practice, overlearning, and feedback. However, in a meta-analysis of training effects, researchers pointed out that even though the lecture method has a bit of a negative reputation based on perceptions that it is a boring technique, their data strongly supported its effectiveness at teaching many different skills (Arthur, Bennett, Edens, & Bell, 2003).

On-the-Job Training On-the-job training (OJT) is, and has been for years, the most widely used training technique in organizations. Almost all employees are exposed to some form of it. Bosses often ask incumbents to spend some time working with new employees and showing them the ropes. The assumption underlying OJT is that the new employee can learn the job by watching an experienced employee doing the job; by talking with that employee about important elements of the job while he or she performs those job elements; and by working with the actual machines, materials, or raw products that are the focus of the job. With this kind of training, too, success is largely dependent on the skills and motivation of the trainer. Reliance on the trainer can be a weakness of OJT unless the trainer is both skilled at training and motivated.

Some companies do OJT without much thought or preparation—and in such cases, it often fails. In fact, some companies use OJT in place of carefully planned training programs. When new employees report to work, incumbents who happen to be working that shift are asked to work with them—a prime example of poorly designed OJT. In contrast, companies that choose employees to serve as trainers based on their potential to be good teachers, that train the trainers in the proper methods of instruction, that provide incentives for their work as trainers, and that match up trainers with trainees based on their potential to work well together are more apt to have successful training programs (Wexley & Latham, 2002).

Self-Directed Techniques
Self-instructional techniques allow trainees to work at their own pace and to remedy identified weaknesses. *Programmed instruction (PI)* of this variety presents information to the learner while using learning principles to reward and motivate. The first step in programmed instruction is to present material broken down into small elements. Second, these elements are arranged in a logical sequence from simple to complex. Third, following completion of each element, a short test is administered to see if the learners have mastered the material at some criterion level. Finally, the learners are given immediate feedback (KOR). If they answer questions correctly, they are asked to move on to the next stage of the PI. If they answer questions incorrectly, they are given additional information to think about and then asked to revisit those questions until a performance criterion is met.

Programmed instruction is clearly based on many of the learning principles reviewed earlier in the chapter, such as KOR, distributed practice, and reinforcement. One obvious advantage of this approach is that trainees can work at their own pace: Those who are quite skilled don't have to waste time waiting for everyone else to catch up, whereas those who are not as skilled can take as much time as they need. Overall, research indicates that PI techniques result in shorter training times than do other techniques, but PI training groups often do not show superiority in learning or retention as compared with trainees in control training groups (Goldstein & Ford, 2002).

Researchers suggest that the learner control inherent in self-directed programs is counterproductive and makes this method inferior (Bell & Kozlowski, 2002). This control often results in less time spent on-task and the use of poor learning strategies. One study demonstrated that providing self-directed trainees with adaptive guidance during the training process, or simply with information that helps them make more effective learning decisions (i.e., guides them toward what to practice, suggests how best to focus attention, etc.), results in higher levels of knowledge and performance and better transfer. This is certainly an area in which we can expect to see more research, such as the study of medical students that found that self-directed learning with respect to CPR was just as effective as more traditional learning with respect to the quality of chest compressions and ventilations (Roppolo et al., 2011).

Computer-assisted instruction (CAI) stems largely from the PI approach just discussed, but with one difference: Trainees interact with a computer. The computer is the medium through which information is presented and by which their performance is monitored. The computer provides information and then asks questions to determine what the trainees have learned and not learned. Given the computer's storage and memory capacity, both information and questions can be presented on the basis of

physical fidelity
The extent to which the operation of equipment in training mimics that in the real world.

psychological fidelity
The extent to which the essential behavioral processes needed for success on the job are also necessary for success in the training simulation.

▼ A Closer Look
What is the rationale behind using simulators to train astronauts?

NASA

the trainees' responses to previous questions—this is very similar to computer adaptive testing that we discussed in Chapter 6. Thus, fast learners can move through the training program quickly, and slower learners can move at a more deliberate rate with additional practice and tests as needed. Although this individualized approach to training has great potential, careful evaluations of it are lacking.

Virtual Reality Training For virtual reality training, a simulator is designed to be as realistic as possible so that trainees can easily transfer the skills they gain to the real-life situation. For many jobs, it would be too dangerous, costly, and inefficient to train individuals on the actual equipment to be used in the real-life situation (Wexley & Latham, 2002). Training astronauts is one obvious example (you might want to rent the movie *Apollo 13*, where the importance of the flight simulator to space travel is highlighted); it simply isn't possible to send individuals into space to learn how to be astronauts. They need to learn offsite with carefully developed simulators. Virtual reality training places individuals in a situation that is made as real as possible through high technology. Simulators are also instrumental in the training of airline pilots and military fliers, providing repeated practice and individualized feedback without presenting any actual safety hazards. The simulated hazards are made to seem as real as possible, however. In fact, two important determinants of the effectiveness of the simulators used in virtual reality training are their **physical fidelity**, the extent to which the operation of the equipment mimics that in the real world, and their **psychological fidelity**, the extent to which the behavioral processes needed for success on the job are also necessary for success on the training simulation.

One fascinating example of the great potential of simulation training was presented in a recent study of anesthesiology interns and fellows (Bruppacher et al., 2010). Many studies that evaluate the use of simulations use outcomes in training as the focal variable. This study actually measured how well a two-hour high-fidelity simulation, in which the research lab was turned into a replica of a surgical room with all of the various technology and people available, compared to a more traditional two-hour interactive seminar. The results were very clear: With 60 real cardiac patients, those trainees who had participated in the simulation performed much better than did those who had participated in the seminar. Two expert observers (blind to the experimental conditions) watched the trainees wean 60 cardiopulmonary bypass (CPB) patients off anesthesia and then rated their behaviors on an established checklist and an established global skills-rating scale. Although both types of training were effective, the simulation was superior. The authors believe that this type of high-fidelity simulation may be useful for training in other high-stakes clinical settings as well.

Technology-Based Approaches

We have reviewed traditional approaches to training—those that some might call the "tried-and-true" training techniques. In this section, I present three contemporary approaches that employ technology to enhance training delivery.

Audiovisual Techniques Many large consulting firms that specialize in training, such as Development Dimensions International (DDI), have invested extensively in elaborate multimedia training programs. Though not fancy, videos are still quite popular; in fact, they are often used in organizations for behavioral modeling. Audiovisual techniques are believed to be at least as effective as, and often more effective than, traditional live lectures. The flexibility they allow—in terms of reshowing segments, pausing at various segments, repeating earlier segments, and stopping the presentation prior to showing the correct approach—makes them particularly appealing. In fact, some training procedures, such as those involved in a medical operation, would be impossible during a live lecture but quite feasible using audiovisual means (Wexley & Latham, 2002).

▲ **A Closer Look** High-tech presentations, such as this one being delivered by the late Steve Jobs of Apple, are quite common in today's technological age. What are some of the advantages of training that is conducted using multimedia?

Not surprisingly, trainees often report greater interest in and satisfaction with training conducted through multimedia presentations than with training of the live-lecture variety. Even in universities, you will find that instructors often supplement live lectures with multimedia elements. This method of teaching is supported by the belief that students are more interested in and pay more attention to information presented in a multimedia format.

Distance Learning In addition to including video, audio, and computer technologies in workforce training, many organizations make use of the Internet for **distance learning (DL)**, which is the delivery of educational or training materials, usually through electronic means, to people at different locations at the same time. At The University of Akron, we offer our introductory psychology class via distance learning to over 100 high school students per year. This is typically done by broadcasting the on-campus course to other campuses and using technology to allow offsite students to see and communicate with one another as well as the instructor. Perhaps you have taken a class or two via this approach.

Burgess and Russell (2003) summarize the many benefits of DL programs as articulated by various organizations. These include (1) the most efficient use of high-quality instructors and instruction, (2) learners' assumption of more responsibility for personal success, and (3) very clear cost savings. BellSouth reports a potential annual savings of $7 million related to the training of 50 new employees per year using a substantial DL component (Sutton, 2004). Perhaps the latest buzz in this area is around mobile learning, in which handheld devices (e.g., iPhones) are used by employees for learning. The U.S. market for mobile learning products and services approached $1 billion in 2010; as the devices get more sophisticated and the networks get faster, it is anticipated that more and

distance learning (DL) The delivery of material to all participants at the same time even though participants are separated by geographical distance.

more training will be delivered through mobile devices [Ambient Insight, 2011 (http://www.ambientinsight.com/Resources/Documents/Ambient-Insight-2009-2014-US-Mobile-Learning-Market-Executive-Overview.pdf)]. This is certainly an area where I/O psychologists will be focusing more of their research attention in the future.

E-Learning Training delivered via the Internet (e-learning or web-based training) is quite popular. Using an Internet browser, employees at remote sites can sort through, read, and work with information made available by the company. A few benefits of web-based training are worthy of mention. First, it's easy to update and change information because it's stored in one location and transmitted across company intranets or the Internet. Second, the training can be done at work or any other location that's convenient for the trainee. Third, the training can be set up so that trainees can share information with one another via discussion groups, chat rooms, bulletin boards, or even Twitter accounts (Boller 2012).

Research suggests that web-based training is slightly more effective than traditional classroom-based training (Welsh, Wanberg, Brown, & Simmering, 2003). There is also some evidence that trainees react favorably to web-based instruction (Goldstein & Ford, 2002). A study of 47 learners (organizational employees who participated in an e-learning course) found that their computer attitudes were positively related to successful transfer, as were perceptions of the system's usability (Park & Wentling, 2007). A great deal of research seems necessary for organizations to acquire the information they need to make reasoned decisions and choices about the potential for web-based delivery of training and how best to deliver such training.

One of the first studies that attempted to isolate and examine potentially important variables in the e-learning domain specifically investigated learner control, which is the degree of control that trainees are given over instructional elements during training (Orvis, Fisher, & Wasserman, 2009). This laboratory study proposed that learner control (along with personal variables like goal orientation and training motivation) would affect learning through training satisfaction and off-task attention. The researchers argued that if individuals were given control over things such as a play/pause button, text that parallels the video, an interactive outline of themes with additional links, and a pop-up, key points feature that could be turned on or off, they would spend less time off-task, devote more cognitive resources to the training, and be more satisfied with the training. Results indicated that those participants who had more control spent less time off-task taking mental breaks and reported more satisfaction and greater utility of the e-learning process and its content. Further, learner control had a positive impact on learning through these meditational variables. Providing control to learners appears to be an effective way to impact training effectiveness. Additional research will likely explore and identify other important related constructs and techniques.

▼ **A Closer Look**
Why might a company employ e-learning methods to train its employees?

TED SZCZEPANSKI FOR WORTH PUBLISHERS

It seems clear that technology-based training has become the preferred choice for training delivery across large and, to a lesser extent, smaller corporations. In particular, the growth of DL and e-learning is staggering and has become a dominant training delivery method across the United States and other technology-focused countries. Furthermore, there is also a current emphasis on combining e-learning with traditional classroom learning in what is referred to as *blended learning* (Holton et al., 2006). This newer approach provides flexible and user-friendly training programs to a diverse population of employees.

Employee Development–Based Approaches

The techniques we've discussed thus far are general methods that can be used in a variety of jobs. In this section, however, we will consider some techniques that are specifically associated with employee development and leadership skills training. This type of training, in its many forms, has become a huge part of what HR departments do because the development of employees for continued employment and advancement is key to organizations' success.

Orientation Training and New Employee Socialization Though not always treated as a formal training technique, socialization is usually the first element of training that new employees experience. **Organizational socialization** is the process by which an individual acquires the attitudes, behaviors, and knowledge needed to participate as an organizational member (Goldstein & Ford, 2002). This is done both formally and informally. Formally, it may include orientation meetings conducted by the HR staff in concert with line managers, social receptions, policy workshops, and tours of the organizational facilities. (When I was hired into my first academic job, my first formal experience was the new faculty orientation and lunch, during which new faculty were introduced to the administration and to one another.) The socialization process for new employees can be very important in that it determines their first impression of the organization, supervisors, and coworkers. This is also the time when new employees learn the formal and informal rules, procedures, and expectations of the organization or work group.

One study of new-employee training found that employees who experienced an orientation program that focused on the history, values, principles, and structure of the organization were indeed more aware of the goals, values, history, and people of the organization than those who did not experience the training (Klein & Weaver, 2000). They were also more committed to the organization. In a review of the socialization literature, researchers argued that as uncertainty, change, competition, and global expansion increase for both organizations and employees—a trend among most present-day organizations—the need to understand how to effectively manage the socialization process of new employees becomes more critical (Bauer, Morrison, & Callister, 1998).

Coaching Like organizational socialization, coaching is not considered as a training technique in many classic treatments of organizational training. I'm discussing it in this chapter because its focus is on developing employees and helping them to get better at their jobs, which is, in large part, what training is all about. When I talk to

organizational socialization
The process by which an individual acquires the attitudes, behavior, and knowledge needed to participate as an organizational member.

I/O practitioners about the really big issues in their organizations, I invariably find that coaching is one of the first things they mention.

Coaching was introduced in Chapter 5 as a one-on-one collaborative relationship in which an individual provides performance-related guidance to an employee. It is the process by which supervisors provide subordinates with advice and information about current performance and discuss ideas for developing them as employees and setting goals for improving their performance (Whetten & Cameron, 2002). In short, it is a training and motivational technique used to improve performance that serves three functions (Heslin, Vandewalle, & Latham, 2006):

- Guidance: Clearly communicating performance expectations, performance outcomes, and suggestions for improvement
- Facilitation: Helping employees analyze and explore ways to solve problems and enhance performance
- Inspiration: Challenging employees to aspire to and realize their potential

Many organizations invest considerable resources in teaching their managers how to conduct effective and useful coaching sessions. In other words, not only are non-managerial employees trained *through* coaching, managers themselves are also trained *to do* effective coaching.

Some researchers suggest that the feedback orientation of the employee, such as the extent to which he or she welcomes guidance and coaching, interacts with the feedback culture of the organization to determine the effectiveness of coaching (London & Smither, 2002; Steelman, Levy, & Snell, 2004). At least one empirical study (with executives) has shown that coaching has an effect on managerial behaviors such as goals set, amount of feedback shared with subordinates, and extent to which managers ask others for input and ideas. All of these, of course, are important managerial behaviors. Managers in this study who were coached were rated more favorably by subordinates than were those who did not experience any coaching (Smither, London, Flautt, Vargas, & Kucine, 2003).

Executive coaching is similar to coaching as I've described it, except that the coach is typically a consultant external to the organization who develops a coaching relationship with a mid- to high-level executive in the organization. Executive coaching is used to develop executives and improve their skill sets and capabilities to make them more effective leaders. In addition, a common goal of executive coaching is to prepare these individuals to step into an even higher-level executive position within the organization. This practice has grown considerably in the last 10 to 15 years. It has been estimated that the executive coaching market is worth over $1 billion— and this is expected to continue to increase (Liljenstrand & Nebeker, 2008).

Behavior Modeling Because working well with others is so important for managers, developing interpersonal skills is of great interest to organizations. Based on Albert Bandura's (1986) work on social imitation, or social learning theory, behavioral modeling is one technique that seems well suited for improving interpersonal skills. You might recall from your introductory psychology or social psychology class that Bandura did the Bobo doll study in which kids watched adults act aggressively against a blow-up doll and later, when given the opportunity, acted aggressively toward the doll themselves. The theory's main argument is that most social behavior is learned through observation.

Social learning theory has been successfully applied to training for the past 35 years. An especially good example of the use of behavior modeling in organizational training is provided by Gary Latham and Lise Saari (1979), who developed nine training modules to train managers to interact effectively with their subordinates. The modules focused on, for example, socializing a new employee, motivating a poor employee, overcoming resistance to change, and dealing with a problem employee. The trainees met for two hours per week for nine weeks. The training format included (1) an introduction to the topic; (2) a film that demonstrated a manager modeling effective behaviors, which were highlighted in earlier and later films as well; (3) a group discussion of the effectiveness of the model; (4) practice in role-playing the desired behaviors in front of other trainees and the trainer; and (5) feedback from the training class regarding the effectiveness of each trainee's role-play.

Latham and Saari assigned half the supervisors to the training condition and half to a control condition that did not involve the behavior modeling training. (The latter group did eventually receive the training, but not until this segment of the study was completed.) The training resulted in positive trainee reactions, better scores than the control group on a learning test given a few months after the training, and better on-the-job performance than the control group when measured one year later.

Business Simulations
This technique is somewhat similar to the case study approach used in business education. Managers are given a brief introduction that includes some background about a fictitious company, an explanation of a situation, organizational problems, and the organizational goals and then asked to make managerial decisions that subsequently affect the situation and context. These simulations, or management games, are usually set up to be competitive in the sense that managers are organized into teams and the teams develop their own ideas, procedures, and solutions. As decisions are made on a round-by-round basis, they are presented to the trainers, who provide feedback and make alterations to the environment on the basis of those decisions. The next round begins with new and additional decisions to be made by the various teams.

Although the games are designed to model an entire organization, they can often be categorized on the basis of their functional purpose (Wexley & Latham, 2002). Thus, there are many types of management games, such as marketing, finance, production-management, and quality-management games. These games are often well received by trainees because they are interesting to participate in and are perceived as relevant and realistic. They are also effective in helping employees understand the complexities and interdependence of the different departments within organizations. Although there has been little empirical evaluation of management games, some critics argue that trainees often become so interested in the competition that they lose sight of the general principles that the game was designed to teach (Goldstein & Ford, 2002). Of course, as with simulators, the effectiveness of management games is clearly linked to their fidelity—that is, how realistic they are and how well they reflect the KSAOs necessary to do the job.

Corporate Universities Many companies have begun making long-term investments in their workforce through, in part, the development of institutes, or "universities," focused on continuous training and development. These corporate classrooms have modern facilities with up-to-date technology that allows for effective learning and transfer onsite. General Electric began this trend in the 1950s, but substantial development of the corporate university didn't take place until the 1990s (Gould, 2005). Motorola has been at the forefront of this movement and has a campus setting at each major company site worldwide (El-Tannir, 2002). Furthermore, Motorola continues to be at the cutting edge of the movement, having made some progress in taking this corporate university idea to the Internet and extending it to other DL approaches.

Other famous corporate universities include McDonald's Hamburger University in Virginia, Xerox's Document University in Illinois, and the Caterpillar Training Institute in Illinois. As organizations continue to become more focused on continuous learning and the management of knowledge within the company, corporate universities should grow in importance. In fact, one framework suggests that the corporate university be placed at the center of organizational learning because it has implications for knowledge systems, networks and partnerships, learning processes, and people processes (Prince & Stewart, 2002).

The development of the corporate university stems in large part from the societal trend called the Third Wave (Toffler, 1980), in which the world's industrialized economies evolve into knowledge-based societies (Rademakers, 2005). Organizations have begun to recognize the importance of knowledge, learning, unlearning, and relearning at the organizational level and the continuous development of their human capital. Corporate universities have international appeal, too. In China, for instance, they have grown rapidly over the last 10 years, and their focus is often on the use of and management of corporate knowledge (Qiao, 2008). Therefore, corporate universities appear to be one way to enhance the potential for continuous learning.

■ Training Evaluation

Any intervention employed in an organization needs to be evaluated. Unfortunately, training evaluation is often not done because many training practitioners don't have the mind-set necessary to conduct an evaluation, others lack confidence in the success of their training program and are afraid to do an evaluation, and still others won't allocate resources to the evaluation (Wang & Wilcox, 2006). However, a careful evaluation is really the only way that an organization and employees can be certain that the intervention has been effective. Accordingly, I have two objectives in this section: (1) to discuss the criteria used to evaluate training programs and (2) to present a few evaluation designs that are used in these evaluations.

Training Criteria

By this time, you certainly recognize the importance of criteria (see Chapter 4). The criteria for training programs are just as important as the criteria used to evaluate employees or validate selection systems. The "criteria for the criteria" apply here as well. Indeed, the criteria used in the evaluation of training programs, as with all other criteria, have to be relevant, reliable, sensitive, practical, and fair.

Kirkpatrick's Taxonomy By far the most frequently used categorizing scheme of training criteria is based on the work of Donald Kirkpatrick in the late 1950s and early 1960s (for a contemporary view on Kirkpatrick's work, see Giangreco, Carugati, & Sebastiano, 2010). Recognizing that training is a multifaceted endeavor, Kirkpatrick identified four types of criteria to use in the evaluation of training programs (Kirkpatrick, 1976). The first type, **reaction criteria**, has traditionally involved trainees' attitudinal reactions to the training program. These are measured with survey or questionnaire items that tap trainees' feelings about the training. Overall, organizations hope that their training program is liked by the trainees and that the trainees value the experience. However, evaluating a training program at the reaction level is probably not enough to provide solid evidence that the training program has been effective.

The second type, **learning criteria**, reflects how much of the material is actually learned in the training program, as measured by a knowledge test at the conclusion of the training program. The idea here is that because the training program was designed to teach certain material, a test is needed to measure the extent to which the trainees learned that material. Sometimes this knowledge test is given prior to the training program as well as afterward so that trainees' improvement can serve as an index of how much learning occurred. Such learning can be categorized or measured in terms of (1) *cognitive outcomes*, such as amount of knowledge gained; (2) *skill-based outcomes*, such as speed of performance as a result of training; and (3) *affective outcomes*, such as the strength or centrality of trainees' attitudes about the content presented during training (Kraiger, Ford, & Salas, 1993).

The third type, **behavioral criteria**, involves changes that take place back on the job. These are the criteria most closely linked to transfer of training. It should be clear that an evaluation of a training intervention that didn't include measures of behavioral criteria would be seriously flawed because, from the organization's standpoint, learning without transfer is not very useful.

The fourth and final type, **results criteria**, refers to the ultimate value of the training program to the company. Recall that in Chapter 7 we discussed the *utility* of a selection system. Results criteria are the focus of utility for a training program as summed up by the organization's question: "Was the training worth it?" Even if the evaluation indicates that trainees responded favorably to the training program (reaction criteria), learned the material well (learning criteria), and used what they learned to improve their performance on the job (behavioral criteria), the training program is arguably *unsuccessful* if the costs incurred in developing and conducting the training far outweighed the performance improvements. In other words, although the training may appear to have worked in many ways, it still wasn't "worth it" from the organization's perspective.

Note that, as these four sets of criteria are not always related to one another, an evaluation of a training program on the basis of just one or two would probably be insufficient. Indeed, although many training evaluation programs focus exclusively on reaction and learning criteria (sometimes called *internal criteria* because they exist within the training program), doing so is problematic because organizations are often

reaction criteria
In Kirkpatrick's taxonomy, trainees' attitudinal reactions to the training program; along with learning criteria, also called internal criteria.

learning criteria
In Kirkpatrick's taxonomy, criteria that reflect how much of the material is actually learned in the training program; along with reaction criteria, also called internal criteria.

behavioral criteria
In Kirkpatrick's taxonomy, criteria that refer to changes that take place back on the job; along with results criteria, also called external criteria.

results criteria
In Kirkpatrick's taxonomy, the ultimate value of the training program to the company; along with behavioral criteria, also called external criteria.

Table 8.1 Training Criteria Frameworks		
Kirkpatrick's Taxonomy	Augmented Taxonomy of Alliger et al.	Applied to Anesthesia Weaning Study, Bruppacher et al.
Reactions	Reactions: Affective reactions Utility judgments	To what extent was the simulation engaging? How certain are you that the simulation will be helpful in surgery?
Learning	Learning: Immediate knowledge Knowledge retention Behavior/skill demonstration	Ratings of observers regarding knowledge, skills, and behaviors during the simulation
Behavioral	Transfer	Checklist of behaviors transferred to real patients. such as: Restores adequate ventilation Checks cardiac rhythm Determines when pump flow can be stopped
Results	Results	Measurements of patient health after weanings Long-term recuperation Success of procedure

Source: Based on Alliger et al. (1997)

most interested in behavioral and results criteria (*external criteria*), as these are more relevant for the conduct of the organizations' business.

Augmented Framework G. M. Alliger and his colleagues (Alliger & Janak, 1989; Alliger, Tannenbaum, Bennett, Traver, & Shotland, 1997) have worked extensively with Kirkpatrick's taxonomy of criteria. They presented an augmented framework, summarized in Table 8.1, alongside Kirkpatrick's traditional framework; the table also includes some example measures generated to fit our earlier example of weaning CPB (cardiopulmonary bypass) patients off anesthesia. Here, I want to highlight just some of the differences. First, the newer framework recategorizes reactions in terms of affective reactions and utility reactions. *Affective reactions* are the attitudes or feelings that Kirkpatrick referred to in his original conceptualization of reactions, whereas *utility reactions* are trainees' beliefs about the transferability or utility of the training program. Alliger and colleagues suggest that the latter are important elements of training evaluation and different enough from trainees' feelings to be considered separately. Another study also reports empirical support for multiple dimensions of the reactions level, including one dimension called utility reactions (Morgan & Casper, 2000).

Second, Alliger and colleagues recategorized learning criteria in terms of three distinct types: (1) *immediate posttraining knowledge* measures, which resemble the traditional Kirkpatrick criterion and usually refer to multiple-choice tests of knowledge; (2) *knowledge retention* measures, which are similar to immediate posttraining knowledge measures, except that they are administered at a point later than immediately after training and thus give a better indication of the extent to which the information learned during training is retained for some time after training; and (3) *behavior/skill demonstration* measures, which more precisely evaluate behavior in the training context and differentiate it from behavior exhibited on the job. The final change reflected in the augmented framework involved a change in terminology from *behavioral criteria* to *transfer criteria*. Here, too, the intention was to differentiate behavioral changes that take place in training from behavior transfer that takes place on the job.

> ### TECHNICAL TIP
>
> *Effect size, one way that researchers establish the size or magnitude of an effect, allows us to compare effects across studies. For instance, a correlation that ranges from 0 to .29 is a small effect, from .30 to .49 is a medium effect, and greater than .49 is a large effect. In the meta-analysis reported here, the effect size calculated was a d, which is calculated as the difference between the training and the control groups, where effects of .50 are considered medium and .80, large.*

The meta-analysis of Alliger and colleagues reveals, at best, only modest correlations among the various criteria. Affective and utility reactions were correlated more strongly with each other ($r = .34$) than with other criteria, as we would expect. But utility reactions correlated more strongly with on-the-job performance (i.e., transfer) than did affective reactions, immediate learning, or retained learning, suggesting that this new category of utility reactions is more useful for the prediction of job performance than are more traditional criteria such as affective reactions and learning criteria.

Another meta-analysis of about 160 studies is among the first thorough quantitative reviews of training effectiveness to be published (Arthur, Bennett, et al., 2003). A couple of interesting results emerged. First, the effect sizes for training effectiveness across Kirkpatrick's four criteria ranged from .60 to .63, indicating a medium to large effect of training. In other words, whether measuring reaction, learning, behavioral, or results criteria, training clearly works. Second, as noted earlier in this chapter, although the lecture method of training delivery has the reputation of being boring, the data indicate that it is a very effective technique. Thus, perhaps this "low-tech" approach still has much to offer.

Evaluation Designs

Once we have chosen how to specifically measure training effectiveness (at the reaction, learning, behavioral, or results level), we turn to identifying an effective design or experimental methodology to employ. Quasi-experiments are the most viable alternatives for the evaluation of training programs. (Table 8.2 summarizes three such designs.) First, let's say we have four work groups in our organization (all of which are to undergo training at the same time) and we are interested in finding out whether the training results in *changes* in various criteria. For instance, do the trainees know more about the material on which they were trained after participating

TECHNICAL TIP

In Chapter 2, we noted that a quasi-experiment is much like a field experiment, except that, unlike a field experiment, participants are not randomly assigned to conditions. In a quasi-experiment, as in this instance, we can take the people already in a particular group and assign the whole group to the training or control condition.

TECHNICAL TIP

Remember that a control group includes the research participants who do not receive the experimental treatment. We are typically interested in comparing those who received the treatment with those who did not receive it so that we can determine whether the treatment had its intended effect.

in the training program (a question of learning criteria)? Do they perform better on the job after participating in the training program (a question of behavioral or transfer criteria)?

In this situation, we would use what is called a *pre/post design*, which allows us to measure these various criteria prior to training (M_1) and again after training (M_2). The change on these measures (an improvement, we hope) would be indicated by a larger M_2 than M_1 and would reflect the effectiveness of the training program. One weakness with this design, however, is the lack of a control group, which prevents us from drawing a direct comparison between our training participants and others who did not experience training.

Second, let's say we have two work groups that we assign to the training condition and two others that we assign to the no-training condition. This design, often described as a *pre/post design with a control group*, is very similar to the previous design except that it involves a control group. In other words, measures are obtained both prior to and after training, but this time they apply to both the experimental condition and the control condition. In addition, the control group can be provided with some other kind of training, such as an old training program, in an attempt to compare the effectiveness of the old program with the newly designed one. With the addition of a control group, this design is stronger in terms of internal validity than is the previous design because we are able to make not only pre- and postcomparisons ($M_2 - M_1$ versus $M_4 - M_3$ in Table 8.2) but also comparisons between the experimental and control groups ($M_2 - M_4$). If the difference between M_2 and M_1 is larger than the difference

Table 8.2 Training Evaluation Designs

Design	Group	Time 1	Training Intervention	Time 2
1. Pre/post design	Experimental	M_1	Training	M_2
2. Pre/post design with a control group	Experimental	M_1	Training	M_2
	Control	M_3		M_4
3. Solomon four-group design	Experimental I	M_1	Training	M_2
	Control I	M_3		M_4
	Experimental II		Training	M_5
	Control II			M_6

between M_4 and M_3, and if M_2 is greater than M_4, we can be fairly certain that the training program was effective in terms of the criteria that we evaluated.

The third design presented in Table 8.2 is called the *Solomon four-group design*. In terms of internal validity, this is a superb design because it includes two experimental groups as well as two control groups, allowing us to draw *several* useful comparisons. However, it is also very costly in terms of both dollars and resources—precisely because it involves multiple groups, numerous participants, and multiple measures. Thus, although it is a very strong design from a research perspective, organizations find it impractical and are seldom willing to use it for their training evaluation studies.

■ Training and Issues Related to Diversity

Diversity issues related to race, ethnicity, age, and gender have become increasingly important to organizations and employees alike. In this section, two newer areas of training are discussed: sexual harassment and workplace diversity. These are not training delivery techniques or associated with particular elements of a learning context, but are more about skills and knowledge important for contemporary organizations. As the makeup of organizations changes with respect to race, ethnicity, sexual prefer ence, age, and other important personal variables, it becomes paramount for organizations to be aware of these changes and to train and prepare employees for these changes. Training around these skills and knowledge elements is our next topic.

Sexual Harassment Training

As discussed in Chapter 7, sexual harassment is prohibited by the Civil Rights Act and includes behaviors of a sexual nature, submission to or rejection of which affects one's job or creates an offensive work environment (Equal Employment Opportunity Commission, 2007). Sexual harassment has received a great deal of attention over the years because of some very high-profile cases, such as Supreme Court Justice Clarence Thomas' confirmation hearings and the Monica Lewinsky scandal that led to the impeachment trial of President Bill Clinton. Herman Cain's presidential bid in 2012 was derailed by accusations from multiple women about inappropriate sexual language and behavior. Two of the women worked with Cain at the National Restaurant Association, which settled those cases out of court.

In an interesting review (Gutek & Koss, 1993), the consequences of sexual harassment are categorized in terms of three dimensions. First, harassment has widespread implications on *work outcomes*, such as interpersonal relationships at work, an alteration in the direction of one's career, satisfaction with the job, and commitment to the organization. Second, *psychological and somatic outcomes* result from sexual harassment. For instance, it appears that women who are sexually harassed experience reductions in self-esteem, life satisfaction, home satisfaction, and self-confidence, sometimes also becoming angry, hostile, irritable, and depressed. Physical symptoms that emerge as a result of sexual harassment include gastrointestinal problems, teeth grinding, nausea, weight loss, and insomnia. Finally, sexual harassment has negative effects on the *organization* (Gutek & Koss, 1993). Turnover and absenteeism attributable to

ERIC THAYER/GETTY IMAGES

▲ **A Closer Look**
In 2012, Republican presidential hopeful Herman Cain was forced to end his primary campaign after multiple allegations of past sexual harassment surfaced. How should employees proceed if they feel like they have been or are being sexually harassed?

harassment incur direct costs; indirect costs also accrue in the form of low motivation, inability to focus on work, and time spent on reacting to the harassment. Finally, organizations can be torn apart by sexual harassment investigations, resulting in a divided workforce and increased conflict among employees. One study found that 50% of manufacturing and social service employees studied reported experiencing sexual behaviors at work in the previous two years (Berdahl & Aquino, 2009). These behaviors included sexual jokes or stories, the display of sexual materials, and inappropriate touching. Further, experiencing these behaviors at work predicted negative personal outcomes like withdrawal from work and poor psychological well-being.

Because prevention is the best tool against sexual harassment, the Equal Employment Opportunity Commission (EEOC) and other agencies encourage companies to offer sexual harassment training. In fact, many organizations offer such programs, most of which employ behavior modeling through the use of videos (Meyer, 1992). In one study, participants who saw a sexual harassment training film perceived sexually oriented work behaviors as incidents of sexual harassment to a greater extent than did individuals who did not see the film (Blakely, Blakely, & Moorman, 1998). Thus, the authors concluded that the film sensitized the participants to sexual harassment and what constitutes it. In addition, they found that males who had not viewed the film tended to rate items such as "making sexually suggestive remarks or behaviors around a female subordinate" as less sexually harassing than did males who had seen the film and females in both the film training group and the control group. [For further discussion of how men and women view and respond differently to the work group climate for sexual harassment, see Kath, Swody, Magley, Bunk, and Gallus (2009).]

A review of the literature supports these findings, and an empirical study accompanying this review demonstrates the same effect in a large sample of government employees (Antecol & Cobb-Clark, 2003). Overall, these intriguing results suggest that (1) behavior modeling may help some individuals become more sensitive to sexual harassment behaviors and (2) males and females may view behaviors differently with respect to their potential for being sexual harassment. Obviously, a great deal more work is necessary in the area of sexual harassment training, but this is one area in which such work promises to pay huge dividends for organizations and their employees.

Workplace Diversity Management and Training

That demographic changes are affecting the nature of the workforce and are expected to continue to do so is not news to anyone, but data and projections from the Bureau of Labor Statistics present an especially interesting picture in this regard. The segment of the workforce made up of those 55 years of age and older is expected to grow by 46.7% in the 2006–2016 period, which is five times the growth projected for the aggregate workforce (Toossi, 2007). These projections reflect the aging baby boomers who either choose or need to work longer than did earlier generations. This aging workforce creates exciting changes and challenges for HR functions such as training.

The diversity in the U.S. labor force is increasing at an amazing rate, and the outlook for 2016 paints a very different and more colorful picture than we have been accustomed to seeing. For instance, there has been an unprecedented growth in the Latino workforce, as it fulfilled earlier projections by surpassing the African American workforce in 2006. And the Latino workforce is expected to grow by 29.9% in the 2006–2016 period. In addition, by 2016, it is projected that women will make up almost 47% of the workforce; African Americans, 12.3%; and Latinos, 16.4%.

These data trends along with the increasing globalization of organizations result in a very dynamic situation in which organizations must change at a very fast pace to keep up with the changing context in which they exist. This changing nature of the workforce necessitates new HR approaches to managing that workforce. Diversity must become a bottom-line issue if companies are going to be able to compete for— and keep—the best and the brightest. As a result, diversity training has burst onto the scene; estimates indicate that it is now a more than $10 billion a year industry (Von Bergen, Soper, & Foster, 2002). Most government agencies and 60% of Fortune 500 companies provide some type of diversity training (Roberson, Kulik, & Pepper, 2003). Here are a few examples of what some of the more competitive companies are doing with respect to diversity:

1. *Procter & Gamble* (n.d.) reports that "training policy and sensing systems are utilized to reinforce development of an inclusive culture." Among its initiatives are diversity training to equip leaders to both value and nurture differences, policies and practices available to all employees regarding issues of work– family balance, and employee surveys.

2. *Marriott International* (n.d.) has been among the leaders in this area for many years, as evidenced by the diversity training, development, and recruiting programs it began in 1989. The company also created a series of diversity councils to help implement corporate-wide initiatives. Most recently, it created the Diversity Ownership Initiative and now reports over 400 minority- and female-owned hotels, as well as the most diverse appointments to management positions in its history.

3. *Texas Instruments (TI)* (n.d.) continues its reputation as one of America's most forward-thinking organizations regarding issues of technology and diversity. Its diversity vision is both thorough and aggressive. The goal is to "create an environment that recognizes, understands, values, and utilizes the unique skills and abilities of all employees." Since 1989, thousands of TI employees have received diversity training, and more than 25 initiatives have been developed over the years that have resulted in various Diversity Leadership Conferences, a Diversity Network, and Diversity Award Programs.

As you can see from these examples, the most successful companies in the world are focusing on diversity issues by emphasizing recruitment, selection, retention, and training. The last of these categories, diversity training, has three primary objectives: (1) increasing awareness about diversity issues, (2) reducing biases and stereotypes that interfere with effective management, and (3) changing behaviors so that a diverse workforce can be more effectively managed (Hanover & Cellar, 1998).

In an interesting study, over 700 HR professionals were asked a series of questions about diversity practices (Rynes & Rosen, 1995). The researchers found significant relationships between the perceived success of the diversity training and the following variables: (1) diverse top management teams, (2) high priority given to diversity relative to other business issues, (3) top management support, (4) managerial rewards for supporting diversity, (5) presence of a diversity manager, and (6) mandatory managerial attendance.

Although the empirical support for the effectiveness of diversity training has traditionally been quite limited (Rynes & Rosen, 1995), a more recent review provides more favorable evidence for the effectiveness of diversity training (Kulik & Roberson, 2008). For instance, as a result of diversity training, employees have a better understanding of the value of diversity and the organization's diversity goals, better diversity management skills, and more effective diversity-related behaviors (Kulik & Roberson, 2008). Most studies examining the effectiveness of diversity training programs have focused on posttraining learning rather than transfer of learning back to the job. Obviously, the extent to which what is learned in training is applied to work behavior is extremely important. A recent empirical study demonstrated that transfer was predicted by the extent to which skills were learned in training and the favorability of the work environment for use of these new skills (Roberson, Kulik, & Pepper, 2009).

There has been a backlash from some employees about mandatory diversity training programs, the perception being that they advantage nontraditional employees (Kulik, Pepper, Roberson, & Parker, 2007). This has led some companies to make these programs voluntary, but the effectiveness of voluntary programs is still very unclear. An interesting alternative approach to traditional diversity training (and its mixed results) (Chavez & Weisinger, 2008) is the notion of creating a "culture of diversity" within organizations. The scholars who suggest this approach recommend that organizations focus on creating a relational culture in which people feel proud of their uniqueness while still being socially integrated into the larger group. Furthermore, the inclusive culture should be maintained by the organization, but employees must be held responsible or accountable for their learning and development, relying on one another and growing as a result of the uniqueness of others. Finally, they suggest that the organization needs to create an organizational strategy that takes advantage of the multiple perspectives of the various individuals. This notion of a culture of diversity may be helpful in many situations in which diversity training has not worked; it may strengthen the commitment to and understanding of diversity issues in organizations as well.

The effects of organizational diversity on organizational performance have been mixed. Some argue that diverse organizations are not as effective because the heterogeneous groups of employees experience communication, coordination, and conflict problems. Others argue that more diverse organizations are more effective because diversity results in better decision-making strategies and more openness to new ideas. A recent study of government employees addressed these very issues (Choi & Rainey, 2010). In this study of 150,000 federal employees, it was found that racial diversity was negatively related to organizational performance, which is certainly troubling to those of us who believe in the value of diversity. However, there was an important caveat: Diversity management moderated the relationship such that, in agencies where diversity was well managed, diversity had a positive effect on performance. So effective management is a great way to realize the positive effects of diversity in organizations, but diversity that isn't well managed may result in negative effects.

■ Summary

This chapter was structured around five major areas. First, we discussed how organizations are diagnosed with respect to training needs. The organizational analysis identifies where training is needed in the organization, the task analysis identifies which behaviors or duties have to be improved through training, and the person analysis identifies those employees who need to be trained. In addition, demographic analysis may indicate the training needs of particular employee populations.

Second, the learning context and its role in training effectiveness were considered. Some learning principles were defined and then applied to specific training issues. As discussed, these principles can play a critical role in the success of a training program. For instance, we noted that trainees may fail to learn effectively if the material to be learned is too extensive and cumbersome; if the material is not meaningful; if practice is rarely used or done poorly; if the desired behaviors are not overlearned; and if immediate, specific feedback is not provided. We also discovered that the transfer of learned behaviors and skills back to the workplace is contingent on many factors that make up the learning context.

Third, we discussed training delivery methods, categorizing them as traditional, technology-based, or employee development–focused. Many of the most frequently used specific techniques in each category were discussed, along with examples and empirical evidence.

Fourth, we examined the evaluation of training programs. We discussed Kirkpatrick's four levels of criteria (reaction, learning, behavioral, results), as well as the augmented framework presented by Alliger and his colleagues. In addition, we discussed a few commonly used training evaluation designs.

Finally, we spent some time considering a recent trend in the training literature—diversity. In particular, we discussed issues related to both sexual harassment training and general workplace diversity training, with a consideration of the role these play in today's organizations.

■ Key Terms

behavioral criteria (p. 243)
continuous learning (p. 227)
distance learning (DL) (p. 237)
distributed practice (p. 228)
human capital (p. 225)
instructional design (p. 227)
learning (p. 227)
learning criteria (p. 243)
massed practice (p. 228)

organizational socialization (p. 239)
overlearning (p. 229)
physical fidelity (p. 236)
psychological fidelity (p. 236)
reaction criteria (p. 243)
readiness (p. 230)
results criteria (p. 243)
training (p. 223)
transfer of training (p. 232)

■ TAKING IT TO THE FIELD

I/O psychologists draw from many different areas of psychology (e.g., educational psychology, social psychology) in order to design training programs and assess their effectiveness. While the best training designs typically begin with an in-depth understanding of what is lacking in employees that is necessary for good performance, we can often provide solid recommendations based on some general information about employee performance. Read the e-mail below from Imani Dixon, the owner of the Ocho Rios Bar, and provide some suggestions for how she might solve her problem.

Hello—

Thank you for your help with my troubles. Ocho Rios is a bar in Daytona, Florida. We serve regulars most of the year, but around spring break, we get a large number of vacationers, which requires us to add a number of seasonal employees for a few months. Thus, we have to be able to train a large number of servers quickly and cheaply to prepare for the increase in business. I don't have time to spend a whole day training each new employee, so they have to learn on the job.

Right now, new servers shadow another server for two days to learn the menu and how to work the register. Then we allow them to serve during the afternoon, when we are less busy, until they think they are ready to serve drinks at prime time. If we get too many complaints, we fire the server.

We have a number of problems that occur each year. First, the new servers don't always do their job. I discover them smoking, talking on their phones, or talking with other stuff while customers are waiting for fresh drinks. Second, they are not always very friendly to customers. They think their job is just to serve the drinks, but customers who have fun while they are at our bar are more likely to spend money and to come back again. Finally, sometimes I find that a server who has supposedly been trained doesn't know the menu, can't work the register, and messes up orders.

How should I change my training to help these servers learn their jobs? Also, what can I do to eliminate the problems I am having with servers who either forget what they have learned or don't do what they are supposed to do because I am not watching them?

Cheers,
Imani

■ Critical Thinking Questions

1. E-learning is a popular tool for delivering training programs. Organizations tend to favor e-learning because it is easy to update, easy to deliver, and convenient for both the organization and trainee. However, like any training program, e-learning has some disadvantages. What are some disadvantages associated with e-learning? Do you think this type of training works better for some types of jobs than others? Is it a better fit for some types of employees than others?

2. The chapter discusses the notion of *transfer of training*. Why is transfer of training so important? Pretend you are a training coordinator in an auto wheel assembly plant. What steps would you take to enhance transfer of training among your training participants?

3. As discussed earlier in the book, an important part of I/O psychology is the relationship between predictors and criteria. How can you relate training programs and their subsequent outcomes to this idea of predictors and criteria? How would you assess this relationship? What implications does this have for the relationship between selection and training?

4. Economic and labor forecasters suggest that we will soon see an increase in the number of older workers. What implications might this increase have for training programs? Should training programs be adapted to suit the needs of older workers? If so, how? If not, why not?

■ Application Questions

1. Consider some of the different ways you have learned content throughout your college career (e.g., online classes, class activities, lectures). Which methods have you found most effective? Why do you think that is so? What are some things you remember most vividly from some of your classes, and what made them memorable?

2. Imagine that a friend complains that he has been having trouble learning the menu at the restaurant where he works as a cook. He has a copy of the menu, and he looks it over every night right before work to refresh his memory, but he can't seem to keep items and their ingredients straight. What would you suggest he do to help him remember his training?

3. Think of a time when you overlearned something. How did it happen? How did that overlearning come in useful?

4. Talk with another student about a time when he or she was not able to transfer training to the job. What got in the way? What could the organization have done better to help him or her use the training?

■ Suggested Readings

Aguinas, H. & Kraiger, K. (2009). Benefits of training and development for individuals and teams, organizations, and society. *Annual Review of Psychology, 60*(1), 451–474. This current review by two outstanding scholars provides a nice overview of recent trends and problems inherent in the training literature.

Arthur, W., Jr., Bennett, W., Jr., Edens, P. S., & Bell, S. T. (2003). Effectiveness of training in organizations: A meta-analysis of design and evaluation features. *Journal of Applied Psychology, 88*(2), 234–245. This quantitative review of training effectiveness is the most relied-upon resource for drawing inferences about training success.

Chavez, C. I., & Weisinger, J. Y. (2008). Beyond diversity training: A social infusion for cultural inclusion. *Human Resource Management, 47*(2), 331–350. This paper takes a relational approach to diversity and provides some intriguing ideas about how to infuse diversity into organizations.

Goldstein, I. L., & Ford, J. K. (2002). *Training in organizations: Needs assessment, development, and evaluation* (4th ed.). Belmont, CA: Wadsworth. This classic text, although it's relatively old, is very readable and still provides one of the most thorough treatments of the training area.

Kulik, C. T., & Roberson, L. (2008). Diversity initiative effectiveness: What organizations can (and cannot) expect from diversity recruitment, diversity training, and formal mentoring programs. In A. P. Brief (Ed.), *Diversity at work* (pp. 265–317). Cambridge, U.K.: Cambridge University Press. This chapter provides a thorough literature review and analysis about diversity in organizations. The book is a great source for scholarship and useful applications for diversity at work.

Toossi, M. (2007, November). Labor force projections to 2016: More workers in their golden years. *Monthly Labor Review,* pp. 33–52. This is an interesting report on how fast the older labor force is projected to grow as compared with the overall labor force.

U.S. NAVY PHOTO BY MCS 3RD CLASS
CHARLES OKI

CHAPTER **9**

Motivation

CHAPTER OUTLINE

LEARNING OBJECTIVES

This chapter should help you understand:

- The importance of work motivation to organizational psychology
- How the three major categories of motivation theories differ from each other
- The similarities and differences among the various need–motive–value theories of motivation
- How cognitive choice theories emphasize the rationality of human behavior
- The similarities and differences between equity theory and expectancy theory
- How important self-regulatory processes are to work behavior
- The major principles and findings with respect to goal-setting theory
- Why discrepancies are so important to goal-directed behavior
- The widespread use and success of organizational behavior management programs for improving motivation and performance
- How successful goal setting (including management by objectives) is as an applied technique for improving motivation and performance
- What job enrichment approaches have to offer organizations and the various ways in which enrichment can be employed
- The current trends with respect to job crafting and how individuals change and create jobs to better fit their needs and to serve the organization

As discussed in Chapter 1, the Hawthorne Studies in the 1920s and 1930s provided a stable foundation for organizational psychology. Prior to this work, I/O psychology was largely about industrial psychology. The Hawthorne Studies opened the way for researchers to realize that systems of rewards and punishments created by organizations, relationships among workers, organizational norms, and individuals' perceptions of where they fit into the organization were all key elements of the workplace.

As Edgar Schein (1980) noted in his classic book, organizational psychology "is intimately tied to the recognition that organizations are complex social systems, and that almost all questions one may raise about the determinants of individual human behavior within organizations have to be viewed from the perspective of the entire social system" (p. 6). In other words, as organizational psychologists, we cannot study an individual's work behaviors without considering the entire context in which that individual works and lives. **Organizational psychology**, then, can be formally defined as the systematic study of dispositional and situational variables that influence the behaviors and experiences of individuals and groups at work (Lawson & Shen, 1998).

Accordingly, this final part of the text covers the following organizational psychology topics: motivation, job attitudes, stress and worker well-being, group processes and work teams, leadership, and organizational theory and development. As in the

organizational psychology
The systematic study of dispositional and situational variables that influence the behaviors and experiences of individuals and groups at work.

industrial psychology part of the book, much of our discussion will focus on individual performance and organizational effectiveness.

Of all the topics typically considered within the realm of organizational psychology, motivation draws the most interest and attention from scientists and practitioners alike. In fact, it is likely that more journal space over the years has been devoted to work motivation than to any other area of organizational psychology (Steers, Mowday, & Shapiro, 2004). The fact that this topic is especially important to management is evidenced by the following quotes by managers from various companies:

"The workers today aren't willing to put out the extra effort that is required to do a nice job."

"Everybody wants something for nothing—they all want the big pay, nice benefits, and to work in a nice air-conditioned office, but they don't want to work hard for any of those things."

"It's really not that they can't do the work. Most of my workers are pretty competent; they just seem to want to take shortcuts around doing the work—they just aren't motivated."

As an I/O psychologist, I am often asked by organizational managers and executives about what can be done to improve the motivation of their workforce. One theme that I have emphasized throughout this book is the complexity of human behavior at work. This complexity explains why we need to use multiple tests (i.e., a selection battery) for employee selection and why we are fortunate if our battery accounts for 30% of the variance in performance. It also explains why even the most skilled and competent professionals are not always the best performers. Ability is an important predictor of individual performance, but so is motivation. The brightest and most skilled workers in the world will not be successful if they are not motivated to be successful. In this chapter, we take a very detailed look at work motivation.

Among the many definitions of **work motivation**, one that strikes me as particularly useful is to view it as a force that drives people to behave in a way that energizes, directs, and sustains their work behavior (Steers et al., 2004). Work motivation is *energizing* in that it results in the expenditure of effort. It *directs* effort or behavior in a particular way or channels it toward a particular object or place. In other words, having energy is not sufficient to characterize a worker as being motivated; there must also be some direction or purpose to that energy. Finally, work motivation is not fleeting; rather, it *sustains* effort over a period of time. Motivation is an abstract internal concept that cannot be seen, touched, or measured directly. We infer motivation from employees' behaviors; we operationalize it by measuring behavior choice, intensity, and persistence. It is important to note that motivation and performance are different constructs, although many individuals seem to confuse the two. It's not unusual for managers to immediately attribute performance problems to the motivation of the employees involved. As I mentioned earlier, performance is much more

work motivation
A force that drives people to behave in a way that energizes, directs, and sustains their work behavior.

> **TECHNICAL TIP**
>
> *Remember from Chapter 4 that performance is operationalized as actual behaviors on the job relevant to the organization's goals.*

complicated than that. Motivation is an important antecedent of performance, but so are ability, the right equipment, organizational support, and freedom from organizational constraints. For now, we will focus on motivation.

■ Theoretical Perspectives

The following three subsections are based on a framework presented by Ruth Kanfer (1990) that involves three major categories of motivation theories. But before I continue, I'd like to clarify one point of confusion. A happy worker is not always a productive worker. There has been a belief for many years among lay folks that these two constructs are strongly linked, but the relationship between job satisfaction and performance is only moderate in size (Fisher, 2003). I introduce this notion here to simply suggest that motivation and performance are much more complex than we sometimes realize. This complexity will be clear as we discuss the various theories of motivation that follow.

Need–Motive–Value Theories

Approaches to motivation from the need–motive–value perspective emphasize the role of personality traits, stable dispositions, needs, and values. In other words, individuals are motivated to perform a particular behavior as a result of these four factors. The most frequently cited theories of work motivation in this category focus on **need**, a force that organizes perceptions, beliefs, cognitions, and actions, giving rise to behaviors that reduce the force and bring about a steady state (Pinder, 1984). Let's look now at four need–motive–value theories of work motivation.

need
A force that organizes perceptions, beliefs, cognitions, and actions, giving rise to behaviors that reduce the force and bring about a steady state.

Maslow's Hierarchy of Needs
Maslow's theory assumes, in part, that we are all aroused by biological and instinctive needs and that people behave as they do in order to satisfy those needs. For example, an individual who is hungry is experiencing a hunger need; the behavioral pattern that follows that experience of hunger (which may include walking to the refrigerator and grabbing a snack) is exhibited to reduce or satisfy that hunger need. Hunger is one of the physiological needs at the bottom of Maslow's hierarchy of needs (see Figure 9.1). *Physiological* needs are those for food, shelter, and water—the basic needs for existence. *Safety* needs, one level up, are the needs to be free from threat and danger. Then come *love* needs (sometimes called *social* needs), which have to do with our needs for affiliation, belonging, and friendship. The *esteem* needs, at the next level, are those for respect from others, self-confidence, and belief in oneself.

Finally, at the top of the hierarchy is the need for *self-actualization*—the need to fulfill one's potential. Quite a few years ago, the army ran an advertising campaign that included the jingle "Be all that you can be"—this is what I think Maslow meant by self-actualization. A recent analysis (Koltko-Rivera, 2006) of Maslow's later writings concludes that he actually considered a level above self-actualization called *self-transcendence*, which focuses on causes beyond the self, such as social justice, art, and faith.

FIGURE 9.1   Maslow's Hierarchy of Needs

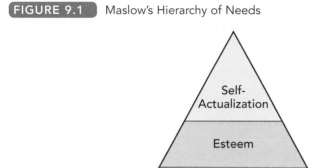

Maslow argued that humans are motivated first by lower order needs and that when these needs are met, higher-order needs become more important as motivators of behavior. Thus, if someone is dying of hunger, the need for food will take precedence over all the other needs above it; but once this need is satisfied, the safety needs become more important, and then the love needs, and so forth up the hierarchy.

One organizational implication of this theory is that different employees are likely to be at different places in the hierarchy, such that no one thing can be assumed to motivate *all* employees. For instance, one employee may be motivated to earn money that he needs right now to pay for his wife's cancer surgery, whereas a second employee may be focused on gaining the respect of her peers because she is at a different stage in her life. The second employee, then, would be motivated to behave in ways that result in her being respected and appreciated by her colleagues—she would be motivated by esteem needs—whereas the first employee would be focused on physiological and safety needs.

This theory of human motivation was popular in organizational psychology during the 1950s and 1960s but has since fallen out of favor because there isn't much empirical support for it. In fact, few empirical tests of this theory have ever been conducted. The reason has to do with the difficulty of testing needs theories—and with the hypothetical nature of needs themselves: We can't see or touch them, or manipulate them, or measure them. This makes it very hard to empirically test whether needs are important causes of human behavior at work. Yet Maslow's theory still remains popular among managers and students of organizational behavior (Payne, 2000; Pinder, 2008).

Alderfer's ERG Theory Whereas Maslow's theory was chiefly rooted in his own clinical observations, Alderfer set out to empirically generate a theory of motivation that focused on the subjective states of need satisfaction and desire. He proposed that satisfaction is an internal state resulting from the attainment of one's goals. Desire is similar to such concepts as want or intensity of need strength. Alderfer developed three categories of needs that somewhat parallel Maslow's five levels. First, there are *existence* needs, analogous to Maslow's physiological and safety needs (e.g., pay and fringe benefits). Second are *relatedness* needs, which correspond to Maslow's love needs and are focused on social relationships. Finally, *growth* needs parallel Maslow's esteem and self-actualization needs. The focus here is on interacting successfully with one's environment through exploration and mastery of it.

One difference between the two theories is that ERG (existence–relatedness–growth) theory suggests that all three categories of needs can operate simultaneously rather than in the sequence suggested by Maslow. Thus, for instance, an employee can be motivated at the same time by existence, relatedness, and growth needs. A second difference is that Alderfer posited a *frustration–regression hypothesis*, which allows for situations in which an individual who is frustrated at a higher level of need then refocuses energy on satisfying a lower-level need. For example, someone who is frustrated over not being able to satisfy her growth needs at work may take a step back and focus instead on continuing to satisfy her relatedness needs.

This hypothesis has a lot of intuitive appeal because it makes sense to think that when we are frustrated over trying to do too much or to be too successful, we can focus instead on maintaining excellence in another way until we are reenergized to resume our attack on the higher-order needs. More research has been done on Alderfer's theory than on Maslow's, but, with few exceptions, it was conducted by Alderfer himself, with very mixed results. Some of his predictions were supported; others weren't.

Herzberg's Two-Factor Theory In the 1950s, Frederick Herzberg and his colleagues (Herzberg, Mausner, & Snyderman, 1959) proposed that the determinants of job satisfaction were different from those of job dissatisfaction. In other words, providing employees with some things will result in job satisfaction and motivation, whereas providing them with other things will result in satisfaction that looks and feels more like neutral affect. This was a rather controversial statement at the time because it suggested that job satisfaction and job dissatisfaction were not at opposite ends of a continuum but, rather, were different constructs entirely.

Two-factor theory suggests that *motivators*—like recognition, interesting work, responsibility, reinforcement for work well done, and potential advancement—are what lead employees to be satisfied with and motivated by their jobs. Motivators have to do with job content: Their presence results in job satisfaction and motivation, but their absence results only in neutrality. *Hygienes*, on the other hand, are related to job context. Examples include supervision, salary, and working conditions. The presence of hygienes results in only a minimal level of satisfaction or neutrality. True job dissatisfaction results from not having hygienes; true satisfaction only results from having motivators.

FIGURE 9.2   Overview of Need Theories

Figure 9.2 shows how Herzberg's two-factor theory of needs maps onto the Maslow and Alderfer theories we've discussed. The implication from two-factor theory should be obvious: To ensure that your workforce will be satisfied and motivated to perform, it is not enough to provide for a reasonable context by altering working conditions and pay. The content of the job, such as interpersonal relationships and recognition for one's contributions to the workplace, must be taken into account as well.

There has been considerably more empirical investigation of this theory than of the other need theories we've discussed, but the results have been mixed. Nevertheless, although this is purely anecdotal, I have heard many practitioners argue (sometimes convincingly) that they see two-factor theory play out before them every day in their organizations. Some, for instance, have dealt with employees whose decent offices and wages prevent them from being dissatisfied but are not sufficient to make them truly satisfied or to motivate them to do their jobs well. Perhaps there is some truth to these anecdotes. Recent interest in the area of positive psychology seems quite consistent with Herzberg's ideas. **Positive psychology** is the study of positive human attributes such as well-being, optimism, creativity, and spirituality. Researchers working in this area find that happiness is more than just the absence of unhappiness and that factors like wealth are unrelated to long-term life satisfaction (Sachau, 2007). Perhaps

positive psychology The study of human strength and well-being rather than weakness and disorders.

Herzberg wasn't so far off after all! We'll look at positive psychology more closely in Chapter 14 when we focus on organizational development.

Job Characteristics Theory In this more contemporary example of need–motive–value theories, the emphasis is on matching individuals to jobs or changing jobs to better fit individuals. In building on Herzberg's earlier work and proposing their *job characteristics theory*, Richard Hackman and Greg Oldham (1980) argued that motivation is determined by the joint effects of individual differences in personality and characteristics of the job; they also developed a model (see Figure 9.3) that explains how jobs influence attitudes and behaviors. Any job, they said, can be described by five *core job dimensions:* skill variety, task identity, task significance, autonomy, and feedback. Jobs vary along these dimensions; some have more of one and less of another. These dimensions influence the three *critical psychological states* that are necessary for motivation.

In particular, jobs that employees perceive as *meaningful* lead them to assume *personal responsibility* for the outcomes they produce; in addition, these jobs are likely

FIGURE 9.3 The Job Characteristics Model

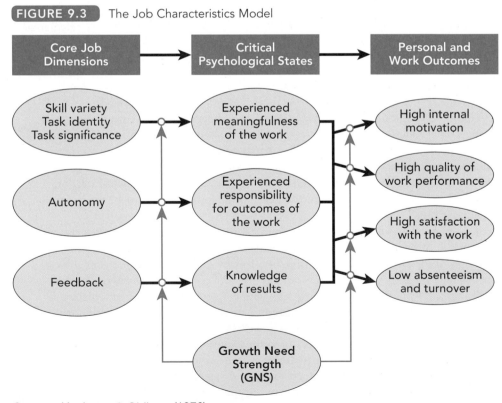

Source: Hackman & Oldham (1976)

to motivate employees to put forth some effort by providing them with *knowledge of the results* of these efforts. Such jobs would be described as having high motivating potential. (Figure 9.3 shows how the five core job dimensions map onto these psychological states.) For instance, employees are more likely to experience meaningfulness if their job requires skill variety (and thus doesn't involve the same old thing every day), provides task identity (such that employees can point to some aspect of their work as being the result of their own efforts), and provides task significance (such that employees' tasks appear to matter to coworkers or others in society at large). The final element of the model concerns the *personal and work outcomes* that follow from the psychological states. These include high internal motivation to work hard and excel, high quality of work performance, high satisfaction with the work, and low absenteeism and turnover.

This model has at least two major implications. The first is that jobs should be designed with the core dimensions in mind. Because positive outcomes are believed to follow from these core dimensions, it seems reasonable to design and redesign jobs to be high on skill variety, task identity, task significance, autonomy, and feedback. (We will talk more about this issue in the section on Applications of Motivational Theories to Organizational Problems.)

Second, some thought should be given to the placement of employees in jobs. Although the core dimensions are arguably positive for most employees, there are likely to be individual differences among them. For instance, autonomy may be much more important to one employee than to another, suggesting that the first employee should be placed in a job involving a great deal of autonomy, while the second employee should be given a job in which he simply follows someone else's direction. According to Hackman and Oldham, **growth need strength**, or the extent to which individuals value or desire fulfilling higher-order needs, moderates the relationships among the variables in the model. For instance, if fulfilling higher-order needs is not an important goal for a particular employee, then meaningfulness of work probably doesn't matter much for that employee.

growth need strength
The extent to which individuals value higher-order needs or desire to fulfill them.

A recent meta-analysis found strong support for the job characteristics model, including the mediational role of experienced meaningfulness of work (Humphrey, Nahrgang, & Morgeson, 2007). Furthermore, 34% of the variance in work performance and 55% of the variance in job satisfaction were accounted for by job characteristics. Most experts would agree that job characteristics play some important role in the motivation of employees. One investigation in the health insurance industry in the United Kingdom looked at a job redesign intervention. The intervention lasted six months and had positive effects on employee well-being through job characteristics like job control, skill utilization, feedback, and participation (Holman, Axtell, Sprigg, Totterdell, & Wall, 2010). It's clear in this study that workplace interventions can affect important outcome variables through their effect on job characteristics.

Job characteristics theory is considered a theory of intrinsic motivation because of its emphasis on personal mastery and control. Another popular theory of intrinsic motivation is Deci's (1975) cognitive evaluation theory, which assumes that individuals adopt either an intrinsic or extrinsic motivational orientation. Ryan and Deci (2000)

MARK RICHARDS/PHOTOEDIT

FANCY/VEER/CORBIS

▲ **A Closer Look**
How do you think these two different working environments might affect someone's work-related motivation?

describe their newer formulation of this theory, self-determination theory, as being focused on specifying factors that explain variability in intrinsic motivation. The theory postulates that social-contextual events (e.g., reception of feedback or rewards) that enhance perceptions of competence improve intrinsic motivation. However, in order for intrinsic motivation to develop, a person must feel that those perceptions of competence are self-determined and attributable to one's own ability or effort.

The theory further proposes a self-determination continuum ranging from amotivation (no self-determination) to intrinsic motivation (total self-determination), with levels of extrinsic motivation in between, each varying in the level of self-determination (Gagné & Deci, 2005). Some researchers have reported that cognitive evaluation theory is especially relevant in describing the motivation of older workers (Claes & Heymans, 2009). The focus groups employed in this study reported that older workers tend to achieve when given more responsibility, more face time with their boss, and greater autonomy. Research in this area continues to examine when and how individuals become intrinsically motivated, as well as when providing external reinforcement reduces intrinsic motivation. This latter phenomenon is called the *overjustification effect* and is illustrated in the following story.

Mr. Warren was an elderly man who lived alone on a dead-end street. All the children in the neighborhood gathered to play at the end of the street every day after school, making a lot of noise outside Mr. Warren's house. One day, Mr. Warren came out of his house and explained to the boys that he loved hearing them having fun outside, and so he would pay them all 50 cents to come back and do it again the next day. The kids were excited, and the first thing they did after school the next day was to gather outside Mr. Warren's house and make even more noise. Mr. Warren followed through on his promise and encouraged the boys to come back again the next day for additional money.

However, when they came back the next few days, Mr. Warren explained that he was running out of money and couldn't pay them as much. The boys weren't very happy, but they came back until one day Mr. Warren only had a dime for them. The boys were very disappointed and their leader, a young boy named Jerry, protested, saying that it wasn't worth their time and they wouldn't be back anymore. The boys left and never played in front of Mr. Warren's house again.

Mr. Warren looks more rested these days since he has returned to getting in his late-afternoon nap every day without interruption!

Cognitive Choice Theories

Cognitive processes involved in decision making and choice are the focus of this next approach to motivation. The assumption here is that people are neither passively driven by inner needs nor controlled by their environment. Rather, people are active decision makers who strive to be rational in choosing what to do, how much effort to exert, and so on. Two such theories are equity theory and expectancy theory.

Equity Theory In the early 1960s, J. Stacy Adams proposed a model of motivation called *equity theory* that focused on social justice. According to this model, behavior is initiated, directed, and maintained by individuals trying to preserve some internal psychological balance (Adams, 1965). Equity theory stemmed in part from the earlier work of Leon Festinger, who developed the theory of cognitive dissonance—a theory that explains how and why we change our behaviors or beliefs to be consistent with other behaviors or beliefs. The idea behind equity theory is that people's perceptions and beliefs about the fairness of their treatment at work affect their motivation, attitudes, and behaviors.

We have all experienced situations at work or at school in which we have felt mistreated. Have you ever thought that you worked too hard on a class project to get only a C, whereas someone else in the class didn't work very hard at all yet received a B? How did you respond? Did you talk to the teacher about how unfair the grading was? Did you stop taking classes from that instructor? There are many ways to respond to situations in which we feel we are not being treated fairly. Let's look at the mechanics of equity theory a bit more closely.

Equity theory is based on the notion that we compare the ratio of what we bring to a situation (i.e., inputs) and what we get out of it (i.e., outcomes) with what others bring to and get out of the same situation. Underlying these comparisons are four main postulates:

1. People strive to maintain a state of equity.
2. When inequity is perceived, a state of tension results.
3. When faced with this tension, people are motivated to reduce the tension.
4. The greater the magnitude of the perceived inequity, the greater the motivation to act to reduce the tension.

In an organizational setting, inputs can include abilities, effort, resources such as money or education level, and anything else employees possess that help prepare them to do their jobs. Outcomes include wages, benefits, feelings of satisfaction, and anything else the employees receive as a result of their inputs. Table 9.1 presents lists

Table 9.1 Potential Inputs and Outcomes	
Inputs	Outcomes
Education	Compensation
Effort	Benefits
Ability	Recognition
Skills	Self-Concept
Knowledge	Experience
Experience	Learning
Diversity	Opportunities
Vision	Satisfaction

of potential inputs and outcomes. Suppose Bill is a market researcher for NBC and works with three other market researchers who are at approximately the same level in the organization. Bill has a master's degree and five years of experience with NBC; he puts in overtime and believes that he works very hard and is quite competent. He makes $69,000 a year but feels that he doesn't get many benefits, accolades for his hard work, or sufficient appreciation. He notices that no one else in his group has a master's degree and that no one else has more than three years of experience. However, all four market researchers make the same salary.

In this situation, Bill perceives inequity because when he compares his input/outcome ratio to that of his coworkers, the ratios aren't equal. He brings more to the job but gets no more than the others. In fact, this is a classic case of inequity, but not because Bill gets less than he deserves; rather, inequity has resulted because, compared with what others have to offer, what Bill has to offer gets him *relatively* less than they get.

Employees can reduce perceived inequity in several different ways. Let's apply a few of these to Bill's situation. The first thing he can do is *change his inputs*. Bill can stop working so hard and avoid working overtime. Of course, with respect to changing inputs, he is limited to altering his effort. He can't suddenly not have a master's degree anymore—this input is relatively fixed. On the other hand, if Bill felt that he was getting more than he deserved, he could reduce the inequity by going back to school and obtaining more training, thereby increasing his inputs.

A second way to reduce perceived inequity is to *change outcomes*. Bill can present his concerns to his boss and ask for a raise, a promotion, additional benefits, more recognition, and so on. Obviously, Bill is dependent on his boss for increasing the outcomes, but he can certainly get the ball rolling by asking for them.

A third way, though perhaps not always a wise one, is to *alter his perceptions*. Bill can attempt to convince himself that his ratio is about the same as his coworkers'. In other words, he can decide that he doesn't really work any harder than they do and that, although he has a master's degree, they have more practical experience from previous jobs than he does. Although this may seem like he's "tricking" himself, this option can be reasonably successful in the short term by reducing the tension that arises from perceived inequity. Whether there are long-term costs associated with this strategy is another matter.

Empirical support for equity theory is generally mixed (Pinder, 1998). According to some studies, when people who are paid on the basis of how much they produce (i.e., on a piece-rate system) feel that their rate of pay is not enough, they tend to produce more but at a lower quality (Mowday, 1991). There is some evidence, though not a great deal, that when individuals believe their hourly pay rate is too low, they tend to reduce their inputs—for example, by reducing their effort (Mowday, 1991). The authors of a meta-analysis on pay satisfaction couched their study in terms of equity theory and discrepancies (Williams, McDaniel, & Nguyen, 2006). They reported that people's level of satisfaction with their pay was determined by the difference between what they were paid and what they felt they should be paid.

One problem with equity theory, however, is its prediction that if individuals believe they are *paid too much*, they will change their inputs to make the situation more equitable. In other words, if you believe you are getting more and better outcomes from your job than those received by your coworkers, all of whom have the same inputs as you, you will be motivated to make this situation more fair either by working harder to *earn your extra outcomes* or by telling your boss that you are being paid too much for what you do. As you can imagine, there isn't much research to substantiate this prediction. Have you ever worked with people who thought they were overpaid and offered to take a cut in pay? Such situations are rare, but studies have shown that inequity in either direction (i.e., getting too little or too much) can lead to burnout (van Dierendonck, Schaufeli, & Buunk, 2001) and negative organizational outcomes (Scheer, Kumar, & Steenkamp, 2003).

A newer construct called **equity sensitivity** has been developed to account for the notion that people differ in terms of their sensitivity to overreward or underreward situations (O'Neill & Mone, 1998). This construct has been quite useful in predicting attitudes and behaviors as a function of various inequitable situations. Depending on how employees score on equity sensitivity measures, they are classified as *benevolents*, who tend to be more tolerant of underreward inequity; as *entitleds*, who always want overreward; or as *equity-sensitives*, who truly desire the state of equity or balance. Some research has shown a relationship between these categories and such factors as job satisfaction, effort, organizational commitment, and turnover (Allen & White, 2002).

Equity theory has served as the foundation for one of the hottest topics in 21st-century organizations—**organizational justice**, the term used to refer to the role of fairness in the workplace. The term was coined by Jerald Greenberg in the 1980s to describe individuals' interest in and concern with fairness-related activities that take place at work. Organizational justice is viewed as a class of motivated behaviors or attitudes that are engaged by different individual and contextual characteristics. Justice perceptions result in both affective and cognitive responses that determine ensuing behaviors.

equity sensitivity An individual difference indicating the extent to which people are affected by overreward or underreward situations.

organizational justice The study of people's perceptions of fairness in organizational contexts.

Adams's (1965) work on equity theory focused on fairness with respect to outcomes, which has become known as *distributive justice*. More recently, researchers and practitioners alike have become interested in *procedural justice*, or the extent to which the procedures and processes used at work are perceived to be fair by employees. An interesting pair of studies recently demonstrated that procedural justice affected task performance through intrinsic motivation (Zapata-Phelan, Colquitt, Scott & Livingston, 2009). Across two studies and varied measures, the researchers found that the use of fair decision-making procedures is one potentially useful way to improve both students' and employees' levels of intrinsic motivation and resulting performance. Finally, a third dimension of organizational justice has received considerable interest in recent years—*interactional justice*, or the way in which decisions and procedures are communicated to employees. This last dimension focuses more on the extent to which individuals are provided information about the rationale and purpose of organizational decisions. In fact, this dimension has been further divided by some scholars and researchers into interpersonal and informational subdimensions. *Interpersonal justice* is the extent to which people are treated with respect and politeness by supervisors or others. *Informational justice* concerns explanations provided to people about decisions or outcomes that provide useful information.

Expectancy Theory One of the most popular theories of work motivation is based on the modern work of Victor Vroom (1964) and stems from the much earlier work of Edward Tolman (see Tolman, 1932). Vroom's expectancy theory includes a model termed *valence–instrumentality–expectancy (VIE)*. The major premise of this model is that people's behaviors result from conscious choices among alternatives and that these alternatives are evaluated with respect to valence, instrumentality, and expectancy. Its basic assumption, to which its critics have objected, is that individuals are rational and make rational decisions. Although the model is called VIE theory, my students have found it more helpful when I discuss the elements in a different order: E–I–V.

We know that rational decision making doesn't always occur, but it certainly does some of the time. **Expectancy** is defined as an individual's belief about the likelihood of achieving a desired performance level when exerting a certain amount of effort. Figure 9.4 presents the VIE model, along with two examples. A student might ask how likely it is that studying three hours for a test will result in getting an A on the test, whereas a computer programmer might ask how likely it is that working 60 hours a week for the next three months will result in performance that is good enough to receive a favorable performance review. Expectancy is sometimes referred to as the effort $\rightarrow$ performance link—a link that should be clear from these two examples.

Instrumentality is the perceived relationship between the performance of a particular behavior and the likelihood that a certain outcome will result from that behavior. This is sometimes viewed as the performance outcome link. In our school example, instrumentality is the extent to which getting an A on the test is likely to lead to other favorable outcomes, such as an A for the course or graduating with honors. In the workplace example, it is the extent to which getting a favorable

expectancy
An individual's belief about the likelihood of achieving a desired performance level when exerting a certain amount of effort.

instrumentality
The perceived relationship between the performance of a particular behavior and the likelihood that a certain outcome will result from that behavior.

FIGURE 9.4 Expectancy Theory: Concepts and Examples

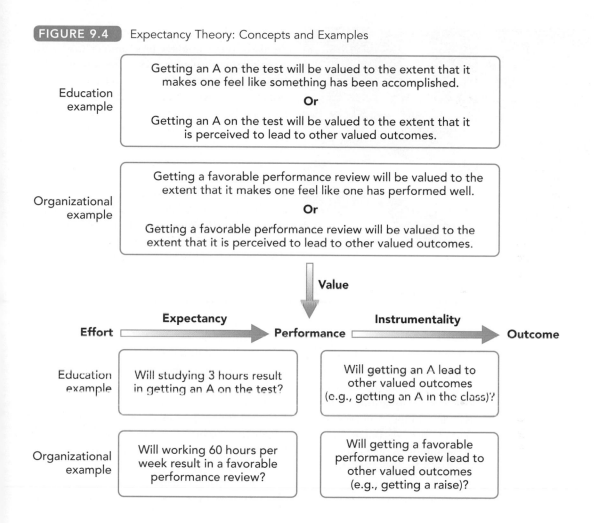

Education example

Getting an A on the test will be valued to the extent that it makes one feel like something has been accomplished.

Or

Getting an A on the test will be valued to the extent that it is perceived to lead to other valued outcomes.

Organizational example

Getting a favorable performance review will be valued to the extent that it makes one feel like one has performed well.

Or

Getting a favorable performance review will be valued to the extent that it is perceived to lead to other valued outcomes.

Value

Effort — **Expectancy** → **Performance** — **Instrumentality** → **Outcome**

Education example

Will studying 3 hours result in getting an A on the test?

Will getting an A lead to other valued outcomes (e.g., getting an A in the class)?

Organizational example

Will working 60 hours per week result in a favorable performance review?

Will getting a favorable performance review lead to other valued outcomes (e.g., getting a raise)?

performance review is likely to result in a pay raise or a promotion. In both examples, instrumentality is reflective of one outcome leading to another outcome.

Valence, which literally means "value," is the expected level of satisfaction to be derived from some outcome. An outcome is positively valued if an individual expects to be satisfied by obtaining it. As Vroom (1964) noted, an outcome is more likely to be valued if other positive outcomes are likely to stem from it. In other words, if one outcome is instrumental for other outcomes, that first outcome is likely to be positively valued.

In our school example, getting an A on the test may be valued in and of itself because it makes a student feel as though she has accomplished something important. In addition, if getting an A on the test is likely to lead to an A for the course (instrumentality), and if getting an A for the course is important to her (value), then getting

valence (value)
The expected level of satisfaction to be derived from some outcome.

DAVID YOUNG-WOLFF/PHOTOEDIT

▲ **A Closer Look**
How is study behavior affected by expectancy, instrumentality, and valence?

an A on the test is positively valued as well. Similarly, our computer programmer may value a positive performance review because it makes him feel that he is doing a good job. In addition, he is likely to value a positive performance review if he believes that the review will result in a large pay raise (instrumentality) and if the pay raise is important to him (value).

Putting all this together, Vroom (1964) suggests that individuals' beliefs about values, instrumentalities, and expectancies interact psychologically to create the motivational force to act in such a way as to bring pleasure and avoid pain. In other words, we tend to do things that make us pleased and proud and not to do things that displease or disappoint us. Motivation is a multiplicative function of these three concepts, which means that if any of the three is 0, there is no motivation. For instance, if getting an A on the test is *valued* and believed to be *instrumental* for obtaining other valued outcomes such as an A in the course, but the student believes that it is completely unrealistic to *expect* that pulling an all-nighter is going to result in getting an A on the test, then she won't pull an all-nighter. Although she perceives high levels of value and instrumentality, her 0 expectancy results in the choice not to exhibit the behavior (i.e., pulling an all-nighter).

A major implication of the VIE model is that if the organization can identify the weak link in the chain, then it can work to rectify it. I chose the performance review example because this is an area in which motivation often breaks down. Although some employees may value a favorable performance review in and of itself, most value it only if it leads to something else. (See Chapter 5 for more details about performance appraisal.) The organization needs to recognize that employees are not likely to exert great effort at work if they don't see the performance review leading to something else of value, such as a pay raise, a promotion, additional benefits, a better job situation, or increased responsibility and autonomy. Indeed, the organization can fix this instrumentality problem by clarifying the links between performance and other outcomes. For instance, the performance review can be used as a basis for important organizational rewards, and employees can be made explicitly aware of this link.

A very intriguing study examined new entrepreneurs to see the effect of VIE constructs on important outcome variables (Renko, Kroeck, & Bullough, 2011). In particular, valence, instrumentality, and expectancy were related to participants' intentions to begin a new firm, but even more interesting is the finding that V, I, and E worked through intentions to impact the sales income and health of the new venture up to 2.5 years later. These results are especially interesting because we know from a great deal of data that most new entrepreneurs exit the start-up process before getting the new venture off the ground—it appears that V, I, and E may be very important predictors of future entrepreneurial success.

A meta-analysis exploring the results of almost 80 studies that tested all or part of the VIE model (Van Eerde & Thierry, 1996) uncovered a few important findings. First, the relationship between the individual VIE components (valence, instrumentality, expectancy) and the work-related out-

> **TECHNICAL TIP**
>
> *We made the point in Chapter 2 that theories are important to the research process. Of course, researchers need to be careful that they are testing their theories appropriately.*

comes is stronger than that between a score that combines the VIE components and the work-related outcomes. Second, many of the studies reviewed were flawed because they examined the model in terms of comparisons between people rather than in terms of predicting how an individual person is likely to behave. The model was developed by Vroom to account for how motivated an individual is to exhibit a certain behavior versus a different behavior—it was not developed to compare one person's motivation to perform a particular behavior with another person's motivation to perform that same behavior.

Finally, the correlations between the VIE components and attitudes/intentions were stronger than those between the VIE components and behaviors (e.g., performance, effort, and choice). Based on these findings, the authors concluded that the VIE components are clearly related to work criteria. VIE theory has since been applied to a diverse set of work-related criteria, such as occupational choices, job choices, decisions to participate in an employee involvement program, strategic decision making (Ambrose & Kulik, 1999), and test-taking motivation (Sanchez, Truxillo, & Bauer, 2000).

Self-Regulation Theories

Self-regulation theories revolve around goal-directed behaviors. The idea here is that motivation is directly linked to **self-regulation**, or the manner in which individuals monitor their own behaviors and make adjustments to those behaviors in the pursuit of goals. Motivation is translated into behavior as a result of self-governing cognitive mechanisms. Unlike needs–motives–values theories and cognitive choice theories, self-regulation theories come into play after a goal has been chosen. They explain how time and effort are allocated across various activities, all of which are directed toward attaining that goal. And whereas the former theories deal with intentions or choices, self-regulation theories deal with *volition*, or will (Kanfer, 1990). That is, given the choice to pursue a particular goal or exhibit a particular behavior, how do we go about pursuing that goal or exhibiting that behavior?

self-regulation
The manner in which individuals monitor their own behaviors and make adjustments to those behaviors in the pursuit of goals.

Goal-Setting Theory
Kurt Lewin's early work on "level of aspiration" (Lewin, Dembo, Festinger, & Sears, 1944) provided the foundation for the most researched and well-established theory of work motivation—goal-setting theory. Largely developed by Edwin Locke, this model suggests that goals affect behavior in four ways (Locke & Latham, 2006). First, goals direct our attention to a particular task or element of a task. Second, goals mobilize on-task effort. In other words, they allow us to focus our effort appropriately to move toward their attainment. Third, goals enable us to be persistent as we strive toward their attainment. Without goals, we would often give up and move

ISTOCKPHOTO/THINKSTOCK

▲ **A Closer Look**
Do you think your
performance
tends to increase
as the difficulty
and specific-
ity of the goal
increase?

on to something else. Finally, goals help us facilitate
strategies that can be used at a higher cognitive level to
move toward their attainment.

Locke and others have conducted empirical research
in this area for over 40 years (for a review, see Locke &
Latham, 2002). This wealth of data has provided us with
a great deal of useful information, but I will summarize
only a few of the major findings. First, people tend to
perform better when they are assigned or choose difficult, specific goals than when they are assigned or
choose easy goals or no goals. Second, the goal-setting
effect—namely, improved performance as a result of
difficult, specific goals—occurs only when individuals accept and are committed to those goals. (For this
reason, providing your employees with a difficult, specific goal that they don't accept and don't care about
achieving will not result in increased motivation or
performance.) Third, feedback about a person's performance in relation to the goal positively affects that
performance.

These three well-supported propositions combine
to produce goal-setting theory's key statement:
*Motivation is enhanced when employees accept and are com-
mitted to specific, difficult goals and when feedback about
progress toward those goals is provided.* This effect has
been found in literally hundreds of studies in both the laboratory and the field, in
both the United States and elsewhere; in addition, it holds true for over 100 different
tasks, as well as for diverse samples along dimensions of race, gender, age, mental ability, and work experience (for a review, see Locke, 1990). More recently, study of the
goal-setting effect has been extended into such areas as group goal setting (Wegge &
Haslam, 2005) and goal strategies of athletes (Senécal, Loughead, & Bloom, 2008).
Goal-setting theory is not only one of the most successful motivation theories in
terms of demonstrating consistent support for its propositions, but it is also among
the simplest. This simplicity (along with its strong results) has made it a favorite technique for HR practitioners who are interested in altering the behavior or effort of
their employees. We will discuss some applications of goal-setting theory a bit later
in the book.

Social Cognitive Theories Social cognitive theories, which gained prominence
in the 1960s, stress the interplay of both behavioral and cognitive elements in motivation. Emerging as a result of dissatisfaction with the way in which behaviorism
ignored the role of cognitive processes in motivation, this approach emphasizes the
cognitive, behavioral, individual, and environmental factors that work together in
determining motivation (Kanfer, 1990).

The most important of these social cognitive theories was developed by Albert Bandura (1986), who views self-regulation as made up of three major components. The first is *self-observation*, which refers to the extent to which we pay attention to specific aspects of our behavior. Because we are limited processors of information, we cannot attend to all dimensions of our behavior; thus, we have to choose which ones will occupy our attention. It is through this process that we are able to monitor our behavior, performance, feedback, and goals to allow for motivational strategies to develop. The second component is *self-evaluation*, which accounts for the attention that individuals devote to feedback processes. Specifically, it is how we evaluate our own performance and effort. Third, *self-reactions* are the internal responses to self-evaluation. Some of these are affective reactions, such as being disgruntled with our performance toward a goal or being overjoyed with the progress that is being made. Others are behavioral reactions, which may involve an increase in effort, a goal shift, or abandonment of the goal altogether.

Another crucial element of Bandura's theory is what he calls **self-efficacy expectations**—that is, individuals' perceptions of their ability to successfully complete a task or attain a goal. Bandura (1986) has argued that strengthening one's self-efficacy enhances motivation to attain a particular goal; other researchers view self-efficacy as being intimately related to the *expectancy* component of VIE theory. Indeed, people do tend to be more motivated to take on a particular task when they feel competent to do that task and expect that they can do it well. Bandura's social cognitive theory specifically views motivation as resulting from the joint influence of self-efficacy expectations and self-reactions to discrepancies between current performance and some standard or goal (Kanfer, 1990). Bandura and Locke (2003) argue that a strong belief in one's performance efficacy or ability is essential to mobilize and sustain the effort necessary to succeed. (For a contrasting view in which self-efficacy is sometimes believed to be negatively related to motivation and performance, see Vancouver, More, & Yoder, 2008.) We form intentions, along with plans and strategies for carrying out our intentions. As self-regulators, we adopt personal standards (i.e., goals) and monitor our actions by self-reactive influence.

In keeping with Bandura's emphasis on self-efficacy, some social cognitive researchers have begun linking motivational principles to other individual-difference variables such as goal orientation (DeShon & Gillespie, 2005). For instance, *learning goal orientation* (i.e., the extent to which individuals approach problems with an emphasis on learning and developing) has been linked to both motivation and affect in the performance of complex tasks; *performance goal orientation* (i.e., the extent to which individuals approach problems with a focus solely on performance) has been linked to motivation and affect in the performance of simple tasks (Steele-Johnson, Beauregard, Hoover, & Schmidt, 2000).

Bell and Kozlowski (2002) have argued that goal orientation, self-efficacy, and ability interact in affecting performance. Specifically, they found that a learning goal orientation was adaptive for high-ability individuals but not for low-ability individuals. Furthermore, high-ability individuals experienced a decrement in performance that was determined by high levels of performance orientation. Finally, Van Yperen

self-efficacy expectations Individuals' perceptions of their ability to successfully complete a task or attain a goal.

▲ **A Closer Look**
How does a thermostat demonstrate the concept of a control system, and what does that have to do with motivation?

and Janssen (2002) found that high job demands felt by those employees who were high on performance orientation and low on learning orientation resulted in low job satisfaction but that the same was not true for those low on performance orientation and high on learning orientation.

Several researchers have proposed and developed *control theory*, which is essentially a social cognitive motivational theory with a negative feedback loop at its core (see Johnson, Chang, & Lord, 2006). The basic premise of control theory is that this negative feedback loop results from the comparison of performance feedback with some goal or standard. If people perceive a discrepancy between the feedback and the standard, they are motivated to reduce that discrepancy in some way. The objective in such cases is to control the situation so that the feedback and the standard match—or, in control theory lingo, to keep the sensed values (feedback) in conformity with the reference value (standard).

Control theory is certainly not limited to the social sciences; in fact, it did not even originate there. Rather, control theory in the social sciences has developed from work done in technical areas such as engineering, which employs the term *control system* to illustrate the process in question. (For criticisms of this approach as too mechanical a description for human behavior, see Bandura & Locke, 2003.) The best example of a control system is a thermostat that operates by sensing the temperature in the room and comparing it with the standard or preset temperature. If the preset temperature is higher than the sensed temperature, the thermostat turns on the furnace to reduce this discrepancy, bringing the sensed temperature (feedback) in line with the preset temperature (standard). Now, what does a thermostat have to do with motivation? A quick look at one of the best-articulated and empirically supported control theories of motivation—developed by Charles Carver and Michael Scheier—will provide an answer. Figure 9.5 presents a simple graphical representation of a control system.

According to Carver and Scheier (1998), most behaviors entail feedback control. Consider the following scenario:

> If your standard for a day's work is to "be productive," how do you decide at day's end whether you've met your goal? You look at the hard evidence of what you've done, and you look at some concrete comparison point (guidelines provided by a work assignment, or perhaps performance of other people engaged in similar activity). In sum, to compare your behavior against an abstract standard, you often seek out concrete information that facilitates the abstract comparison. (p. 32)

This very simple principle has given rise to a complicated but useful theory of motivation. The basics of Carver and Scheier's theory stem largely from earlier work on

FIGURE 9.5 Control System

Adapted from Lord & Levy (1994) in *Applied Psychology: An International Review. Moving from cognition to action: A control theory perspective.*

control theory, but these authors have developed many important related issues that have helped researchers gain a better understanding of motivation. For instance, they have conducted many studies demonstrating that the more self-focused individuals are, the more often they engage the feedback loop and concentrate on comparisons that reveal information about existing discrepancies (Carver & Scheier, 1998). By *self-focused*, the authors mean simply the degree to which individuals focus attention on themselves. Being self-focused, they argue, is more likely than not being self-focused to lead to reactions (both affective and behavioral) that stem from perceiving a discrepancy (when a discrepancy exists) between one's standard and feedback.

The scenario I just borrowed from Carver and Scheier seems quite simple, but their theory points out that the process of gathering, receiving, and interpreting feedback from various sources is quite complex. Think back to Chapter 5, in which we discussed the use of 360-degree feedback in organizations for the purposes of individual development, as well as more formal performance appraisal processes. Obviously, individuals are presented with a wealth of feedback from a 360-degree system, and sorting out and choosing which feedback to use in the feedback loop is a complicated issue. I mention this here only to reiterate that although examples can be simplified to better illustrate control theory and its processes, the theory's operation is, in actuality, much more complex.

For example, control theory has been used to focus on the volitional and intellectual elements of motivation (Diefendorff & Lord, 2003). Researchers have demonstrated that individuals who formed implemental intentions (i.e., specific goals and a plan for acting on those goals) performed better than those who did not, regardless of their particular strategy. However, strategy quality interacted with implemental intentions to result in the best performance. Thus, both volitional and intellectual domains are important parts of the motivational system. In a large-scale review, researchers have recently found that implementation intentions have a sizable effect on goal attainment (Gollwitzer & Sheeran, 2006).

Carver and Scheier (1998) have argued that people are goal-directed and that we use not only goals but also intentions, values, and wishes in our daily lives to move forward. Furthermore, researchers have presented an interesting application of control theory to emotions, explaining the process through which individuals regulate their emotional displays over time (Diefendorff & Gosserand, 2003). However, we don't always reach our goals—and when it appears as though we aren't going to make it, we have an important decision to make: Persevere or throw in the towel? Carver and Scheier suggest that giving up—what they call *disengagement*—is not always a bad thing. Indeed, they argue that it is a natural and necessary part of self-regulation. There are times when a goal is unattainable, and continuing to shoot for it can have serious detrimental effects on one's psychological well-being and ultimate success. But the essential point here is that both continued effort and giving up are necessary parts of adaptive self-regulation. Think about the time you were shooting for an A in a particular class but kept getting Cs on the exams. At some point, revisiting your goal and making an adjustment to it probably helped you move forward (perhaps you passed the course with a B and learned something about yourself in the process). Or imagine a work situation in which you are focused on achieving $10,000 in sales for the quarter, but as the weeks go by, it becomes clear that this goal is unattainable because of a downturn in the economy. Are you better served by continuing to bang your head against the wall or by reevaluating your goal and attempting to move forward toward another reasonable goal?

Hopefully, you see that the answer to this question is to go easy on your head and come up with an alternative goal that is still motivating, resulting in individual and organizational productivity. This holds for supervisors as well in the sense that it can be wise for them to take a step back and help employees readjust their goals downward when that appears to be a reasonable strategy.

■ Applications of Motivational Theories to Organizational Problems

Given that I/O psychology is an applied field with applied goals and issues, the rest of this chapter is devoted to applications of a few of these theories to real-world organizational problems.

Organizational Behavior Management

organizational behavior management (OBM) The application of the principles of behavioral psychology to the study and control of individual and group behavior within organizational settings.

The **organizational behavior management (OBM)** approach to improving motivation and performance in organizations is based in large part on reinforcement theory—particularly operant conditioning, in which desired behaviors are rewarded. OBM can be defined as the application of the principles of behavioral psychology to the study and control of individual and group behavior within organizational settings.

One approach to OBM that has been applied to organizations across the globe is called *applied behavior analysis*, which focuses on the ABC model: A stands for the *antecedents* of the behavior, B stands for the *behavior* itself, and C stands for the *consequences* of the behavior (Wilder, Austin, & Casella, 2009). It is important that the antecedents for desired behaviors be in place within the organization. For instance, employees must have the equipment and training to be able to do the job well. But the consequences are perhaps the most important part of this approach, as they are the rewards that follow the desired behaviors. These can range from seemingly small rewards such as verbal recognition to large rewards such as a salary bonus or additional vacation days. We are beginning to see more work on what is called *pay for*

> **TECHNICAL TIP**
>
> In Chapter 8 we talked at length about the needs analysis that is so necessary to identify specific training needs in an organization. Targeting the behaviors that need to be changed as a part of this behavior approach is quite similar to a needs analysis.

> **TECHNICAL TIP**
>
> Remember that a standard deviation indicates how much spread there is in a set of data. It can also be used to indicate the size or magnitude of an effect. A .5 standard deviation means that the difference in performance between those who use OBM and those who don't is quite sizable.

performance (see Cadsby, Song, & Tapon, 2007; Rynes, Gerhart, & Parks, 2005), which is one direct way to link consequences to behaviors. The better employees perform, the more they get paid. This behavioral approach to the management of human resources can be summarized in five steps (Stajkovic & Luthans, 1997). First, the behaviors that need to be changed are targeted. This step is much like a needs analysis that is done in the area of training. Second, the targeted behaviors are measured so that the organization has a baseline against which to compare behaviors that occur after the intervention. Third, the links between both current rewards and punishments and behaviors are examined. Fourth, the organization intervenes with a program that sets goals concerning the targeted behaviors and links various rewards to the attainment of those goals. Finally, there is an evaluation phase in which the success of the intervention is determined by comparing resultant behaviors with baseline behaviors in terms of the program's goals.

OBM has been used extensively in organizations (Wilder et al., 2009). Let's look at one example in the area of safety improvement, where OBM has been very popular (Grindle, Dickinson, & Boettcher, 2000). An injury prevention model was applied in a large industrial plant to reduce lost time due to injuries and to increase safety behaviors (Sulzer-Azaroff, Loafman, Merante, & Hlavacek, 1990). Three departments with the highest injury rates were identified; the number of employees totaled about 250. The researchers identified behavioral targets for each department and observed behaviors such as safe lifting of heavy materials, use of safety glasses and appropriate safety shoes, immediate clean-up of wet floors, and storage of chemicals in designated areas. In addition, they recorded accident data, including medical visits and lost time due to injuries or accidents.

After implementing the intervention program, which included meetings about safety, weekly safety posters, small rewards and reinforcements, and setting of goals, the researchers noted some drastic improvements. First, safety behavior goals were

CLAYTON SHARRARD/PHOTO EDIT

▲ A Closer Look
In what ways do awards and rewards motivate people?

attained at a rate of over 90% across departments. Second, this period was the best in the history of the company in terms of injury rate and person-hours worked. Third, workers' comments about the program and the improvements were overwhelmingly positive. Results like these are typical of OBM programs, demonstrating the usefulness of this approach in improving motivation and performance behaviors. In fact, a meta-analysis (Stajkovic & Luthans, 1997) reported an average effect of .5 standard deviation on performance (d effect size = .51). What this tells us is that the use of OBM resulted in a sizable performance improvement in the various companies studied.

Goal Setting and Management by Objectives

Goal-setting theory has received considerable attention from practitioners and has been applied across the world in every type of organization imaginable with very consistent success. Let's look at one recent example. Since pizza delivery has become such a huge industry (perhaps nowhere more so than on college campuses!), delivery drivers' safety has become a subject of concern. Pizza deliverers have accident rates that are three times higher than the national average, resulting in fatalities and personal injuries that cost companies millions of dollars (Ludwig & Geller, 1997, 2000). In a 1997 study, pizza deliverers ($N = 324$) from three different pizza stores were observed going out on and returning from deliveries. Observers were stationed in the windows of nearby businesses with a clear view of the streets on which the pizza stores were situated. Three specific behaviors were observed: (1) whether the drivers used their seat belts, (2) whether the drivers used their turn signals when leaving or entering the pizza store's parking lot, and (3) whether the drivers made a complete, slow-rolling, or fast-rolling stop when entering the street from the store's parking lot.

▼ A Closer Look
What role could goal setting play in affecting driving behavior or other safety-related behaviors?

JANIS CHRISTIE/CORBIS

These three behaviors were observed for six weeks to establish a baseline. At this point, deliverers were randomly assigned into a participative-goal, an assigned-goal, or a control condition. Those in the participative-goal group took part in a discussion-based meeting, participative goal setting, and four weeks of group feedback. Those in the assigned-goal group took part in a lecture-based meeting, were assigned a goal (the same goal that was arrived at participatively in the participative-goal group), and underwent four weeks of group feedback. The control group received no intervention at all. The targeted behavior in all three conditions was the percentage of complete stops, and the goal in both goal-setting conditions was 75%.

FIGURE 9.6   Pizza Delivery Results—Intersection Stops

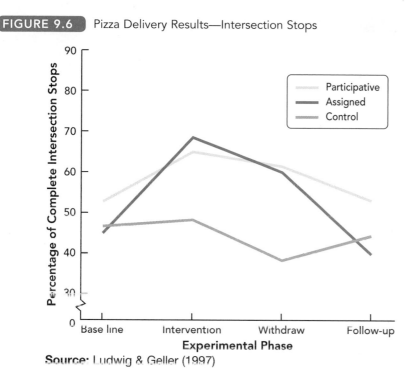

Source: Ludwig & Geller (1997)

Figure 9.6 presents a summary of the observation data for four periods: the six-week baseline phase, the four-week intervention phase, the four-week withdrawal phase (after the feedback posters were removed), and the ten- to eleven-week follow-up phase. The data clearly indicate that both the participative-goal and assigned-goal groups made a larger number of complete intersection stops and that this improvement in safety behavior continued for some time (though for longer in the participative-goal than in the assigned-goal condition).

Interestingly, the observers also coded other behaviors that were not part of the intervention, including seat belt use. (Although seat belt use was observed, it was never mentioned in the meetings, nor was group feedback ever presented on this behavior.) Figure 9.7 presents the relevant data for seat belt use. Here, only participative goal setting seemed to improve safety behaviors and to maintain that improvement—an especially interesting outcome given that seat belt use was not part of the intervention. Apparently, participative goal setting that focused on one particular safety behavior improved other safety behaviors as well. (Similar results were found for turn signal use.) The power of goal-setting programs like this one is very clear: People respond very effectively to feedback that is coupled with difficult, specific goals.

Another practical application of goal setting involves what is called *management by objectives (MBO)*, a managerial technique widely used in the Western world since the late 1950s (Pinder, 1998). MBO dates back to the work of Peter Drucker at both General Motors and General Electric. Drucker's approach to management centered

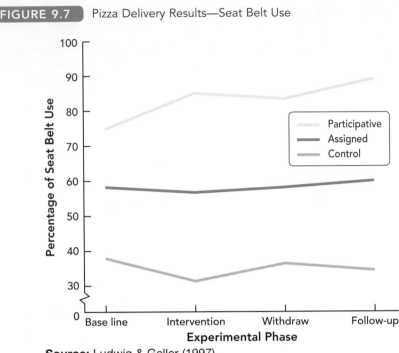

FIGURE 9.7   Pizza Delivery Results—Seat Belt Use

Source: Ludwig & Geller (1997)

on the importance of performance objectives and involves two essential factors: (1) a system for establishing work-related goals and (2) a procedure for assessing a person's performance as compared with those goals.

The MBO process consists of four basic stages. First, managers and subordinates participatively set objectives for subordinates over a specified time period. For instance, they may agree on an increase in sales of 15% over the next six-month period. Second, subordinates develop an action plan, or how-to map, describing the ways in which they intend to achieve those goals. In our current example, it would stipulate the manner in which subordinates will increase sales by 15% and might include a marketing strategy, subgoals for the development of new business contacts, and so on. Third, at the end of the period, managers conduct a performance review that examines the progress made since the last formal meeting, when the objectives were set. Finally, the process comes to a temporary conclusion with the participative setting of objectives for the next period. By "temporary" I mean that this phase is the only one that ends; MBO continues in a cyclical manner with the development of new objectives, action plans, and evaluations over time.

Let's look at an example of an application of MBO. Southern California Edison (SCE) was unhappy with its performance management and motivational system and thus began implementing an MBO program (Moravec, Juliff, & Hesler, 1995). First, it conducted in-depth interviews with employees to gather important data on their attitudes, beliefs, and future outlooks with regard to SCE. This step introduced participation into SCE. Second, consultants were hired to oversee a task force (consisting of 40 employee volunteers) intended to generate some solutions to the performance management problems. The members of this task force encouraged everyone in the organization to add their own perspective to the important issues under discussion.

They concluded that the organization needed a system in which (1) employees (in addition to supervisors) assume responsibility; (2) the focus is on values and future growth, not past problems; and (3) the discussion is not a control tool but, rather, supports a partnership between employees and supervisors. The new MBO system emphasized that supervisors and employees should collaboratively define objectives, develop strategies to attain the objectives, determine ways to measure performance relative to the objectives, and then periodically reevaluate the objectives and adjust them where appropriate. Both supervisors and employees reported that this program had been successful, noting that they felt energized by becoming active participants and appreciated the enhanced openness that had become the culture in the company.

According to a meta-analysis of the MBO literature, 97% of the evaluation studies reviewed found increases in productivity; the mean rise in productivity across those studies with quantitative measures of performance was over 40% (Rodgers & Hunter, 1991). This finding suggests that an organization that was producing 100 units of its product per month prior to an MBO intervention is likely to produce 140 units per month after the intervention. The meta-analysis also revealed that MBO programs tend to result in greater performance improvement when they are supported by upper-level management. This observation is consistent with what we know about most organizational interventions: Support from the top is often necessary for their success. We will see other examples of this in the remainder of the book.

ROBERT GARVEY/CORBIS

▲ **A Closer Look**
Why do more frequent collaborative meetings between management and workers to define goals tend to affect performance and outcomes?

job enrichment
The process of increasing the motivating potential of jobs, often by strengthening the key motivating characteristics identified by job characteristics theory.

Job Enrichment

We have already discussed job characteristics theory, Hackman and Oldham's (1980) model of job design that stemmed from Herzberg's earlier work on two-factor theory. One way in which organizations apply this approach to job design is through job enrichment. **Job enrichment** is the process of increasing the motivating potential of jobs—specifically, by strengthening the key motivating

TECHNICAL TIP

We use different terms for criteria, such as hard versus soft, objective versus subjective, and quantitative versus qualitative. In this case, and as explained in Chapter 4, quantitative measures of performance refer to measures that can be more directly tapped with less likelihood of subjective biases, such as number of units produced, accident rate, sales in dollars, and so on.

characteristics identified by job characteristics theory. Let's briefly look at a couple of organizational interventions along these lines.

Our first example concerns an article about improving the teaching of psychology that argues for the use of job characteristics theory for "course enrichment"— a process similar to job enrichment. The author specifically proposes that the job characteristics model can serve as a theoretical framework for increasing the motivational potential of college courses (Catanzaro, 1997). She suggests that instructors can increase skill variety among students by requiring a wider range of skills through varied written and oral assignments.

For instance, in an I/O course, the instructor could (1) ask students to write about how theories of motivation are used by employers and employees at their place of employment; (2) structure a debate that considers the pros and cons of affirmative action; (3) illustrate task significance through applications of what is learned in class and discussions of their implications for organizations and employees; or (4) give an assignment that requires students to conduct a job analysis of some real job (e.g., interviewing incumbents) or to develop a proposal that outlines a potential selection battery for their current position. Each of the five core job dimensions we discussed earlier (skill variety, task identity, task significance, autonomy, feedback) could be emphasized in the design of such a course in order to enrich its content and increase its motivating potential. A study of over 200 psychology students found that four of these five core dimensions were related to outcome measures such as course motivation, satisfaction, and performance (Bloom, Yorges, & Ruhl, 2000).

Job Crafting

In this chapter I've talked about motivation at work and provided both overviews of general theories and details of precise theories. Among the topics we covered were job design and job enrichment. I'd like to close this chapter by providing some information and ideas about some newer approaches and conceptualizations with respect to jobs. A recent special issue of the *Journal of Organizational Behavior* (Vol. 31, Issues 2–3) was titled "Putting Job Design in Context." This fascinating special issue argued that jobs (and organizations) have changed so dramatically over the past few decades that new questions have emerged with respect to the nature and design of jobs (Grant, Fried, Parker, & Frese, 2010).

job crafting
The process through which employees are allowed to customize, modify, and craft their own job with respect to tasks, responsibilities, and processes.

In the final piece published in this special issue, Oldham and Hackman (2010) write about **job crafting,** in which employees have the flexibility to customize or modify their own job. This is an interesting idea, but we don't know too much about it. They raise some interesting questions. For instance, do the benefits that accrue from job crafting result from the changing of the job or the participation and involvement of employees in making the changes? If the benefits do result from the actual job crafting, what leads to these changes? Why are people more productive and more satisfied after job crafting? Who is more likely to want to participate in job crafting? Who is more likely to follow through with it? What are the characteristics of supervisors who allow and encourage job crafting?

COURTESY OF ANNE HERMAN

Anne Herman
PhD, 2008, I/O Psychology,
University of Nebraska, Omaha
Director and Senior Consultant with Kenexa

This chapter does a great job of outlining the different motivational theories you'll see operating across different aspects of the workspace. Over the past decade, one of the most common areas where many of these theories have converged, and so where many researchers are now focusing, has been in how to create an engaged workforce.

Much of the energy relating to work motivation in organizations is focused on engaging current employees and, to a lesser extent, finding and attracting talent that has the capacity to be engaged. There is a reason for this: There is substantial evidence that organizations that show higher levels of engagement also show better results with respect to customers, financial performance, and employee retention.

Though different engagement models are used, they all include a commitment to and involvement and belief in the organization. Most believe that the state of being engaged results in higher discretionary effort put forth.

Since 2008, many clients and other organizations have asked me if the challenging economic climate is causing lower engagement levels in the workforce. Both my practice experience and research generally show that it is still possible to maintain strong levels of and/or improve employee engagement. Almost all companies have been confronted with significant challenges not seen in the past 50 years. Many organizations have had to make difficult decisions around divesting lines of business, engaging in other types of restructuring, and even examining and taking action on staff redundancies. But it has been possible to continue to cultivate motivated and engaged employees.

The organizations that have been better at keeping workers engaged, and have in many cases also experienced better business performance, did well on three primary critera: (1) They took action on what mattered most to their employees' engagement. (2) Their executive leadership did the best they could to keep employees informed about what was happening (strong communication) and to provide a vision of the future that instilled confidence and was motivating. (3) They created environments where the focus was on the customer, and employees had the tools they needed to fulfill organizational goals.

No doubt we will learn much more about how to engage workers as research continues in this complex area.

Applying Your Knowledge

1. Why do you think engagement is so crucial to an organization's success?

2. How much do you feel people are internally motivated versus incentivized through various leadership and organizational strategies?

3. Of the three criteria outlined above relating to worker engagement and better organizational outcomes, which do think is the most important? Why?

Denise Rousseau has introduced the idea of *idiosyncratic deals* (I-deals) in which employees negotiate with supervisors about their own job conditions and arrangements (Rousseau, 2001). A recent study (published in the same special issue) demonstrated that more successfully negotiated I-deals followed from leader–subordinate relationships characterized as favorable (Hornung, Rousseau, Glaser, Angerer, & Weigl, 2010). Further, the I-deals were related to more favorable job characteristics, greater employee initiative, and more employee engagement. We need a great deal more research on concepts like job crafting and I-deals because there is much more to learn about the nature of jobs in our dynamic work context.

■ Summary

Few topics in I/O psychology have been as thoroughly explored as work motivation. In the first part of this chapter, I presented the most commonly cited theories of work motivation; in the second part, I focused on applications of these theories to organizational problems. Three sets of theories were considered: need–motive–value theories, cognitive choice theories, and self-regulation theories. Although need– motive–value theories are no longer as well accepted by researchers and academics as they were 40 years ago, they are still popular in business settings. First, we discussed Maslow's hierarchy of needs; then we examined two approaches that are related to Maslow's work, ERG theory and two-factor theory. Job characteristics theory and cognitive evaluation theory were also considered in this category, as they clarify the different motivational potentials that are inherent in jobs and people.

Cognitive choice theories, which view motivation and behavior as rational processes rather than as a function of inherent needs or values, were discussed in terms of two important theories: equity theory and expectancy theory. The latter—presented in the context of VIE theory—was described as the most rational theory of them all. Each of its three components was discussed in terms of recent meta-analytic research on expectancy theory. The conclusion drawn was that these three components seem related to motivation, though not always in the multiplicative manner predicted by the theory.

Self-regulation theories were discussed last. In this context, goal-setting theory was presented as one of the simplest and most empirically supported models of work motivation. Social cognitive theories were described as extensions of goal-setting theory that provide potential explanations for why goals are so important to individual motivation and performance. All three sets of theories have received a great deal of attention in the literature, some of which was reviewed in the text.

In the second part of the chapter, I presented applications of motivation theories to organizations. OBM was discussed as a very successful technique (particularly in the area of improving organizational safety) that stems from reinforcement theory. A similar approach was followed with respect to goal setting and management by objectives. There appears to be a great deal of support for these goal-based interventions as well. Finally, I discussed job enrichment and its potential for organizational improvement. In addition, some of the more cutting-edge thinking around job crafting and idiosyncratic deals was presented, and a series of questions was generated that could drive future research.

■ Key Terms

equity sensitivity (p. 267)
expectancy (p. 268)
growth need strength (p. 263)
instrumentality (p. 268)
job crafting (p. 282)

job enrichment (p. 281)
need (p. 258)
organizational behavior management (OBM) (p. 276)
organizational justice (p. 267)

organizational psychology (p. 256) self-regulation (p. 271)
positive psychology (p. 261) valence (value) (p. 269)
self-efficacy expectations (p. 273) work motivation (p. 257)

■ TAKING IT TO THE FIELD

Many companies struggle with motivating their employees—a problem that consultants frequently see among their clients. Thus, it is important to know which theories of motivation have empirical support and how each theory can be applied to an actual situation. One of your clients, Ken Cooper, has been struggling with keeping his employees motivated at Blues Bus Tours, Inc., a small tour company in Nashville. Ken has received some advice from another I/O psychologist, but he would like a second opinion. Read his e-mail, and critique the advice that the other I/O firm has provided.

Hello—

Thanks for being willing to talk with me on such short notice. Recently, our tour guides have been unmotivated—they are coming into work late and putting forth the minimal amount of effort. We've been receiving more complaints from clients, and we're starting to get worried that this will impact our bottom line. However, there simply aren't very many people around who are a good fit for leading tours (it requires that they be away from home for long periods of time, so people with families have some difficulty with the job). So I would rather try to motivate the employees I have than try to replace them. I recently contacted Hollister Consultants, and their I/O psychologist provided me with the following suggestions:

- Tour guides are unmotivated because the job is too complex. According to the job characteristics model, tour guides should have only a few simple tasks that are clearly outlined in an employee handbook, and these tasks should be done the same way on every tour.
- Equity theory suggests that workers who are paid a lot tend to feel guilty and, as a result, will work harder. You should give all the unmotivated tour guides raises to help with this issue.

So what do you think? Should I follow this advice? What might be one other thing I could do to help motivate my employees?

Thanks!
Ken

■ Critical Thinking Questions

1. What on-the-job behaviors would you expect an employee with a high level of motivation to demonstrate?

2. Which theory of work motivation do you personally believe to be the most accurate? Why did you choose this theory over the others?

3. Reflecting on your own work history, how did/do you self-regulate your workplace behavior?

4. Under what circumstances do you think pay-for-performance systems motivate or fail to motivate employees? Why? Please couch your answer in terms of the motivation theories discussed in this chapter.

5. Do you believe that people overall have high or low levels of self-efficacy, or is self-efficacy specific to particular domains?

■ Application Questions

1. Imagine you have a friend who is currently dissatisfied with her job. She feels that she puts a great deal of effort and time into her job yet is passed over for promotions and awards. What would you suggest she do to feel better about her job?

2. Consider a job you held in the past. What were examples of what Herzberg calls motivators? What were examples of hygienes? What were some hygienes that you overlooked or took for granted?

3. Consider the job of a babysitter. How might expectancy theory apply to this job? What is an example of expectancy in this context? Of instrumentality? Of valence?

4. Imagine you have a friend who has decided he wants to do better at his job as a salesman in a retail store. He decides he is going to set a goal for himself: "I will get a promotion within the next three months." What are some problems with his goal? What would you suggest as a more effective goal?

5. Job crafting is a relatively new idea in the field. What are some advantages of allowing employees to customize their own jobs? What are some disadvantages?

■ Suggested Readings

Greenberg, J., & Colquitt, J. A. (Eds.). (2005). *Handbook of organizational justice*. Mahwah, NJ: Erlbaum. This volume, edited by two prominent researchers on the topic, is a great overview of recent thinking about organizational justice.

Latham, G. P. (2007). *Work motivation: History, theory, research, and practice.* Thousand Oaks, CA: SAGE. This is a terrific book by a leading motivational scholar who makes this text very user-friendly.

Latham, G. P., & Budworth, M. (2008). The study of work motivation in the 20th century. In L. L. Koppes (Ed.), *Historical perspectives in industrial and organizational psychology* (pp. 353–382). Mahwah, NJ: Erlbaum. This is a great resource for any psychology history buff; this particular chapter does a thorough job of tracing developments in work motivation.

Latham, G. P., & Pinder, C. C. (2005). Work motivation theory and research at the dawn of the twenty-first century. *Annual Review of Psychology,* 56, 485–516. This is a solid scholarly review of the empirical and theoretical work in the area of work motivation.

Pinder, C. C. (2008). *Work motivation in organizational behavior.* Upper Saddle River, NJ: Psychology Press. My personal favorite! I've used Pinder's earlier book in my classes for almost 15 years and highly recommend this newer version as well. It is a very complete treatment of motivation, written at a level that makes it accessible for undergraduates as well as graduate students.

Steers, R. M., Mowday, R. T., & Shapiro, D. L. (2004). Introduction to special topic forum: The future of work motivation theory. *Academy of Management Review,* 29(3), 379–387. This is the introduction to a special issue on work motivation in one of the field's most respected journals. This paper gives a nice overview of the historical development of work motivation, and the other papers spend considerable time looking to the future and setting a research agenda for the field.

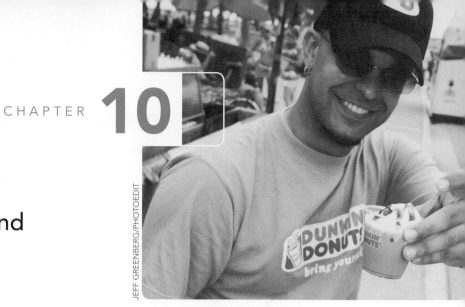

JEFF GREENBERG/PHOTOEDIT

CHAPTER **10**

Job Attitudes: Antecedents and Consequences

CHAPTER OUTLINE

LEARNING OBJECTIVES

This chapter should help you understand:

- The role played by attitudes in predicting behavior
- Why attitudes are sometimes unrelated to behavior
- What job satisfaction is and how it is measured
- What determines a person's level of job satisfaction
- How job satisfaction affects important organizational outcome variables
- The three major components of organizational commitment
- What determines a person's commitment to his or her organization
- How organizational commitment affects important organizational outcome variables
- What types of withdrawal behaviors are important to organizations
- What types of counterproductive behaviors are concerns for organizations
- The role played by emotional labor in organizations
- The effect that perceived organizational support has on employee attitudes and behaviors

Have you ever had a job you didn't like? Did the fact that you didn't like the job affect your performance? Why didn't you like the job? Was it your supervisor, coworkers, the work itself, or the pay that led to your dissatisfaction? Do you say good things to people about your current company, or do you give the impression that you'd rather work anywhere but there? Do you identify with your job, profession, or occupation? In other words, is what you do an important part of who you are, or is it just something you do? All of these questions have to do with job attitudes, which are the focus of this chapter.

Like most of us, you've probably experienced the anger and frustration that come with working in a job you don't like. There's the feeling that you're wasting your time, and each minute of the day seems like an hour. Even routine tasks, which by them-selves should not be so unpleasant, become unbearable. These negative experiences can become so pervasive that their effects trickle into other parts of your life. Before you know it, you're arguing with your spouse or your mom more frequently and running out of patience with your children more quickly. On the other hand, when you really love your job, your thoughts are occupied not with the tasks you have to do at work but, rather, with the opportunities and programs that you get to experience, and you want people to know what you do for a living and why it's the best job in the world.

The difference between a job that we hate and one that we love is very real. In this chapter, we will discuss job satisfaction because this is the attitude that organizations seem most interested in and researchers know the most about. We will also discuss organizational commitment, work centrality, job involvement, perceived organiza-tional support, and emotional labor.

■ Attitudes, Intentions, and Behaviors

In I/O psychology, when we talk of attitudes, we are usually interested in the relationship between attitudes and intentions or behaviors. An **attitude** can be defined as the degree of positive or negative feeling a person has toward a particular person, place, or thing (Fishbein & Ajzen, 1975). As you might imagine, humans have many work-related attitudes. These have to do with supervisors, coworkers, the job environment, the work that is done on the job, and even the amount of respect received on the job.

attitude
The degree of positive or negative feeling a person has toward a particular person, place, or thing.

Why Study Job Attitudes?

Before we delve into job attitudes, it makes sense to understand why such attitudes are important. First, it has long been assumed that job attitudes influence work behavior, which explains why managers and executives are so interested in them. Second, for humanitarian reasons, improving employees' job attitudes is a desirable goal in and of itself. As Edwin Locke (1976) notes, happiness is the goal of life—and making people happy at work should be a goal of organizations. Third, studying job attitudes can help us understand the complexities of our work lives as well as of our nonwork lives. For these reasons and others, researchers and practitioners alike have been, and continue to be, very interested in job attitudes. However, before exploring specific job-related attitudes, we need to examine a popular model of the attitude—behavior relationship.

A Useful Model

The *theory of planned behavior*, as it is known, was developed from an earlier model called the *theory of reasoned action* by Icek Ajzen and his colleagues (Ajzen & Fishbein, 1980; Ajzen & Madden, 1986; Fishbein & Ajzen, 1975). It is a rational choice model much like expectancy theory and equity theory, discussed in Chapter 9 in the context of cognitive choice theories of motivation. These researchers subscribe to the view that people consider the implications of their actions before deciding whether to engage in a particular behavior (Ajzen & Fishbein, 1980). From this perspective, the determinants of an action are one's intentions to perform the action (Ajzen & Fishbein, 1980). Thus, in a sense, predicting behaviors is not that difficult; if we want to predict whether an employee will work hard on a particular project, the most efficient approach is to ask her whether she intends to work hard. All else being equal, there should be a fairly strong relationship between her intention and her behavior.

Because our goal is to understand human behavior, however, just knowing that someone does what she intends to do is not that illuminating. We need to be able to predict the intention as well. This is where attitudes come into play. The theory of planned behavior is useful here because it depicts the relationships among attitudes, intentions, and behaviors (Ajzen & Fishbein, 2005; Ajzen & Madden, 1986). Figure 10.1 presents a simplified version of the model, which clearly shows that

FIGURE 10.1 Theory of Planned Behavior

Adapted from Ajzen & Madden (1986)

attitudes and subjective norms affect intentions, which in turn affect behaviors. A **subjective norm** is an individual's perception of the social pressures to perform or not perform a particular behavior. The theory of planned behavior maintains that a person's intention to act is a function of both the subjective norm for that act and his attitude toward that act. For example, he will intend to meet his deadline if meeting deadlines is the norm at his office and if he has a positive attitude about meeting deadlines. The theory also maintains that his intention to meet the deadline is the best predictor of whether his actions will result in his meeting the deadline.

As shown in Figure 10.1, **perceived behavioral control** is also an important element of the theory. Perceived behavioral control is the individual's belief about how easy or difficult performance of the behavior is likely to be (Ajzen & Madden, 1986). Although an individual may be favorably disposed to a particular act and perceive the social norms as being in favor of the act, she may not perceive that she has any control over performance of the act. For instance, a factory worker may recognize that the norm is to produce 200 units of product per eight-hour shift; she may also want to achieve this level of performance. But if she believes that this action is out of her control because of equipment breakdowns, this perceived behavioral control should be considered when predicting her behavior. In effect, she won't produce 200 units because of a lack of control.

This calls to mind the role played by expectancy in the motivational model known as *VIE theory* (see Chapter 9). You may recall that no matter how valued or instrumental a certain performance level is, if the individual does not believe that a particular amount of effort can lead to that performance level, there will be no motivation to exhibit that level of effort. The theory of planned behavior goes one step further in suggesting that even if an employee has an intention to exhibit the behavior, if she perceives that she can't do so because of a lack of control, she won't.

The work of Ajzen and his colleagues is important as we proceed with our discussion of crucial job attitudes. The theory of planned behavior will

subjective norm
An individual's perception of the social pressures to perform or not perform a particular behavior.

perceived behavioral control
An individual's belief about how easy or difficult performance of a behavior is likely to be.

TECHNICAL TIP

Recall that VIE theory proposes that individuals' behaviors result from conscious choices based on perceptions of value, instrumentality, and expectancy.

become even more useful as we try to make sense of the relationships between job attitudes and job behaviors. We will revisit this theory from time to time as a way of explaining some of the empirical findings in the I/O literature on attitudes and behaviors. Let's turn to the most important of these attitudes: job satisfaction.

■ Job Satisfaction

Job satisfaction is one of the most researched areas of I/O psychology, in part because it has long been viewed as relevant for organizational effectiveness; it is an aspect of the attitude–behavior link discussed earlier, but in an applied setting.

Job satisfaction interests all of us. In fact, we all seem to have an opinion on the subject. Some insist that the key to job satisfaction is money; others claim that it's working conditions; still others believe that it's employee participation. The list goes on and on—and it makes for lively discussions at work and in the grocery store but does not always help us to understand the construct. So let's get a bit more scientific. According to Locke (1976), **job satisfaction** can be defined as a pleasurable, positive emotional state resulting from the cognitive appraisal of one's job or job experiences. The same author notes that job satisfaction stems from our perceptions that our jobs are fulfilling. In other words, we tend to be satisfied in our jobs if we believe that we are getting what we want out of them. Note also that job satisfaction has both an affective component (emotional state) and a cognitive component (the appraisal or evaluation). We will return to this shortly.

> job satisfaction
> A pleasurable, positive emotional state resulting from the cognitive appraisal of one's job or job experiences.

Antecedents

Figure 10.2 presents a framework for studying and thinking about job satisfaction. On the left side of the figure are the antecedents of job satisfaction—the characteristics or factors that lead to job satisfaction. On the right side are the consequences—the outcomes or results of job satisfaction. Below I discuss a sampling of the research in support of these antecedents and consequences, but see the list of suggested readings at the end of the chapter for great places to learn more.

Job Characteristics The first category of antecedents consists of *job characteristics,* which include not only the five core job dimensions postulated by Richard Hackman and Greg Oldham's (1980) job characteristics theory (see Chapter 4) but also workload. The premise here is that one's satisfaction with a job is affected by the structure of the job and what it provides. Look back at Figure 9.3 and you will notice that satisfaction is one of the hypothesized outcomes in job characteristics theory. Research has demonstrated a consistent relationship between employees' perceptions of the characteristics of their jobs and their level of job satisfaction (Spector & Jex, 1991). The more employees perceive that their jobs provide autonomy, task identity, task variety, task significance, and job feedback, the more satisfied they report being with their jobs.

A meta-analysis that reviewed 28 studies found that correlations between the core job dimensions and job satisfaction ranged from .32 (task identity) to .46 (autonomy;

FIGURE 10.2 Framework for Job Satisfaction

Loher, Noe, Moeler, & Fitzgerald, 1985). A more recent study reported that the match between worker preferences regarding such variables as work schedule, shift, number of hours, and organizational staffing policies regarding those same variables was positively related to employee attitudes such as job satisfaction (Holtom, Lee, & Tidd, 2002). Other studies indicate that employees who feel overloaded at work—which often leads to stress—tend to be dissatisfied with their jobs. Furthermore, research has indicated that personality traits such as self-esteem affect job satisfaction through their effects on job characteristics (Judge, Bono, & Locke, 2000). Although stress is also important in this context, we will discuss that in more detail in Chapter 11.

In a look back and to the future, Greg Oldham and Richard Hackman (2010) argue that work design is commonplace in organizations with a continued emphasis on job characteristics. However, as a result of the change from a manufacturing to a service economy, the approach has evolved and will continue to evolve. They propose that the social aspects of work have taken

TECHNICAL TIP

Remember that correlations range in magnitude from −1.0 to +1.0 and the larger the number (in either direction), the stronger the relationship. Positive correlations mean that as one variable goes up, so does the other. Correlations in the .30 to .40 range are considered moderately strong relationships. A correlation above .50 is typically considered an index of a strong relationship.

center stage because of the prominence of social interactions in contemporary work organizations, where product teams, service teams, and technical teams rule the day. They suggest that research on interactions inside and outside the organization, social support, interdependence, interpersonal feedback, and coordination among employees will become the focus of job characteristics and work design initiatives in the 21st century. Thus, it follows that research should also focus on these social aspects of work.

▲ **A Closer Look**
What job characteristics do you notice here that might affect performance?

Individual/Personal Characteristics A

sizable body of research suggests that people have stable characteristics that predispose them to respond positively or negatively to job contexts (e.g., Staw & Ross, 1985). In other words, some people tend to be satisfied with their jobs over the course of their careers, while others tend to be dissatisfied. Barry Staw and Jerry Ross (1985) found moderate correlations between satisfaction measures over time and even saw evidence of this stability in job satisfaction scores when individuals changed jobs. Yet other research has shown that job enrichment and other organizational interventions designed to "improve" jobs still have the potential to raise individuals' levels of satisfaction (Gerhart, 1987; Steel & Rentsch, 1997)

Some researchers in this area have argued that the stability we see in job satisfaction scores over time stems from **affective disposition**, or the tendency to respond to classes of environmental stimuli in predetermined, affect-based ways (Judge & Hulin, 1993). In other words, some individuals respond to the world in a favorable way, while others respond in an unfavorable way. In a recent review that revisits the situation versus disposition debate, researchers concluded that one's affective disposition can strongly impact what is experienced in the workplace, how it is evaluated, and how it is remembered (Staw & Cohen-Charash, 2005).

affective disposition
The tendency to respond to classes of environmental stimuli in predetermined, affect-based ways.

Another group of researchers have taken a slightly different perspective, focusing on genetic differences as an explanation for the stability in job satisfaction. In particular, they argue that genetic factors might influence the way in which individuals respond to their work contexts (Arvey, Bouchard, Segal, & Abraham, 1989). We know that genes affect intelligence, personality, interests, and attitudes—so why not job satisfaction? These researchers used an often-studied group of twins from the Minnesota Study of Twins Reared Apart to examine the extent to which twins who were separated at (or soon after) birth had similar levels of job satisfaction much later in life. They found

TECHNICAL TIP

A longitudinal study is one in which the researcher measures participants on the same variables at numerous points in time to see whether respondents have changed over time. In the Steel and Rentsch (1997) study presented here, the researchers showed that job characteristics predicted job satisfaction later in time even after controlling for job satisfaction earlier in time. Of course, job satisfaction rates at Time 1 and Time 2 were positively correlated, but even with that correlation, job characteristics predicted job satisfaction at Time 2. This is a great way to show the effect of one variable on another even after controlling for another variable.

that the proportion of variance in satisfaction resulting from genetic factors was about 30%, a statistically significant number. Thus, there appears to be some genetic contribution to an individual's level of job satisfaction (Ilies & Judge, 2003).

Some attention has been paid to the idea that individuals with high self-esteem tend to be satisfied with their jobs (Brockner, 1988; Lopez & Greenhaus, 1978). In one study, researchers examined the role played by core self-evaluations in both job satisfaction and life satisfaction (Judge, Locke, Durham, & Kluger, 1998). By *core self-evaluations,* the authors mean the fundamental evaluations we make about ourselves—a concept that includes self-esteem and generalized self-efficacy (Judge, Bono, Erez, & Locke, 2005). Their results strongly support the link between self-esteem (and other core self-evaluations) and both job and life satisfaction. The authors concluded that core evaluations of the self have consistent effects on job satisfaction regardless of the job. In other words, how people view (or evaluate) themselves directly affects how they experience their jobs and their lives. In some research that combines individual differences with job characteristics, studies of students and employees found that individuals high on core self-evaluations tended to choose more complex tasks and were more satisfied with their jobs as a result (Srivastava, Locke, Judge, & Adams, 2010). This research shows very nicely how the interplay of both individual differences and job characteristics likely impacts job satisfaction and, potentially, other outcome variables.

organization-based self-esteem (OBSE)
A measure of how valuable employees view themselves as organization members.

A related variable is **organization-based self-esteem (OBSE)**, which concerns employees' perceptions of their value as organization members (Pierce, Gardner, Cummings, & Dunham, 1989). In other words, OBSE reflects one's degree of work-related self-esteem. It seems reasonable to expect that individuals who view themselves as valuable to the organization would also report higher levels of job satisfaction than would individuals who don't perceive themselves as valuable. This is exactly what researchers found in a study of healthcare workers (Chen, Goddard, & Casper, 2004). OBSE was strongly correlated with job satisfaction ($r = .58$) and even predicted job satisfaction, organizational commitment, and job involvement after first controlling for work locus of control and job self-efficacy.

Social Factors Other antecedents of job satisfaction can be considered social factors; these include interactional and relational variables at work. For instance, employees' relationships with their supervisors and coworkers seem to be important indicators of whether these employees are satisfied with their jobs. Think back to a job that you really liked—one in which you were really motivated to work hard, looked forward to going to work, and never "watched the clock." I've asked many students over the years to do the same; when I then asked them to describe what made the job so great, most started by saying something like, "I had this great boss" or "My manager was a great woman who really knew how to work with people and didn't play head games with us."

Research indicates that job satisfaction is affected by the demographic similarity between supervisors and subordinates (Wesolowski & Mossholder, 1997), by the way in which supervisors assign tasks (Blau, 1999), and by the extent to which subordinates perceive that supervisors have violated their relational expectations (Rosen, Chang, Johnson,

& Levy, 2009). Clearly, the relationship we have with our bosses has an important effect on how we react to our jobs.

Recent research has also shown how individual differences and social factors come together to affect job satisfaction. In a study of 200 Chinese employees, results demonstrated that a proactive personality—a dispositional tendency toward taking personal initiative—led employees to establish high-quality relationships with their supervisors (what Chapter 13 will refer to as leader–member exchange), resulting in high levels of job satisfaction (Li, Liang, & Crant, 2010). Like the study discussed earlier that showed the interplay between individual differences and job characteristics (Srivastava et al., 2010), this research shows how individual differences and social constructs work together. It should be clear that job attitudes like those discussed in this chapter are affected by the meshing of various types of antecedents.

The next thing people with great jobs often tell me is that they like their coworkers. It's nice, they say, to work with a great group of people who pitch in for each other and make work fun. You can look at this from another perspective, too. Think of a job that you really disliked and ask yourself what was so bad about it. Most people will say that the group they worked with was a major reason for their job dissatisfaction because it was not a supportive, helpful, trustworthy, or enjoyable bunch to be around.

Research supports the importance of coworker relations as an antecedent to job satisfaction. One study proposed that organizational restructuring that influences the nature of work interactions affects coworker relationships, which, in turn, affect job satisfaction (Howard & Frink, 1996). Indeed, this study found that after the departments in a few city governments were restructured, attitudes about coworkers predicted job, as well as life, satisfaction. A recent survey of 490 managers reported that 73% of them cited good relationships with coworkers as the key to job satisfaction (Rennie, 2007).

Role variables also affect job satisfaction. If you have ever had a job in which you were not completely sure of your role or function in the organization, you can understand the negative effect that such ambiguity has on job satisfaction. Ambiguity is something that most people feel very uncomfortable with, especially with respect to the expectations associated with one's job.

Another important variable is organizational justice, or fairness, now one of the most investigated concepts in I/O psychology (see Chapter 9). Studies have examined the role of this variable in determining employees' levels of job satisfaction and other work-related attitudes (e.g., Liao & Rupp, 2005). By **organizational justice** I mean simply the role of fairness in the workplace. The question here is whether employees' perceptions of the fairness of policies, procedures, and treatment affect their attitudes, behaviors, and performance. A scale has been developed to measure these perceptions (Donovan, Drasgow, & Munson, 1998). In validating this scale, the authors found that it was strongly correlated with various job satisfaction measures. Even after affective disposition had been controlled for, the justice scale was still correlated with various job satisfaction measures, indicating that justice is an important predictor of job satisfaction regardless of one's affective disposition. Further research has demonstrated that organizational fairness affects job satisfaction through its effect on perceived organizational support and leader–member relationships (Masterson, Lewis, Goldman, & Taylor, 2000; Rhoades & Eisenberger, 2002).

organizational justice
The role of fairness in the workplace.

© WARNER BROS/EVERETT COLLECTION

▲ **A Closer Look**
How would your job attitudes be affected by a boss like the one Colin Farrell played in the movie *Horrible Bosses*? Why?

In sum, employees' levels of job satisfaction are likely to be affected by the quality of the interpersonal relationships they experience at work. These relationships are affected by how well the employees get along with their supervisors and coworkers, as well as by their perceptions of role clarity, organizational fairness, and organizational support.

Growth Opportunities The last group of factors that can affect job satisfaction are what I call *growth opportunities,* such as the employee's perception that there is potential to grow, advance, or be promoted within the organization. The obvious antecedents here include whether someone is paid well, is provided excellent benefits, and is offered the opportunity for advancement. Each of these factors is related to job satisfaction. Pay for performance was discussed as a motivational technique in the last chapter; some research studies show that this motivational approach results in increased job satisfaction (Green & Heywood, 2008). However, a recent meta-analysis shows that pay level was only weakly correlated with job satisfaction (Judge, Piccolo, Podsakoff, Shaw, & Rich, 2010). The authors argued that when individuals get pay increases, they are more satisfied in the short term, but then they revert back to original levels of satisfaction because the new pay level quickly becomes the normal/expected level.

In the next chapter, on work-related stress, we will discuss many issues related to work–family conflict. For now, however, note that the conflict or stress one experiences as a function of valuing both one's family and one's job affects both job and life satisfaction (Bruck, Allen, & Spector, 2002). According to a meta-analysis, work–family conflict was negatively correlated with both job satisfaction ($r = -.31$) and life satisfaction ($r = -.36$; Kossek & Ozeki, 1998). Thus, it appears that employees with high levels of conflict tend to be less satisfied with their jobs (and their lives in general) than are employees with low levels of conflict. Other findings suggest that this relationship is slightly stronger for men than for women and considerably stronger for dual-career than for single-career couples. In addition, the conflict appears to be more strongly related to satisfaction if it is the work domain that is "interfering" with the family domain rather than the other way around. We'll revisit these interesting findings in Chapter 11.

Measurement and Dimensions

We have been discussing job satisfaction without considering the manner in which it can be measured. More important, we have been conceptualizing job satisfaction in a general sense so that the antecedents could be considered separately from the complexities inherent in the measurement process. At this point, however, we need to consider the measurement of job satisfaction from a multidimensional standpoint.

Traditionally, job satisfaction has been assessed at the global level with questionnaire items like "In general, I like my job" or at the facet level with items determining how satisfied employees are with their pay, supervisor, and so on. Both approaches seem reasonable, so the choice may depend on the organization's purpose. But I would also argue that including measures at the facet level provides more fine-grained, or specific, data that can be useful in diagnosing organizational problems and developing organizational interventions.

One of the most frequently used and best-validated measures of job satisfaction is the Job Descriptive Index, or JDI (Kinicki, McKee-Ryan, Schriesheim, & Carson, 2002; Stanton et al., 2002). Developed in the 1960s (Smith, Kendall, & Hulin, 1969), it measures satisfaction along five dimensions (and an overall dimension): satisfaction with the type of work itself, satisfaction with pay, satisfaction with coworkers, satisfaction with promotion opportunities, and satisfaction with supervision. Figure 10.3 presents sample items from each facet, along with a sample item

FIGURE 10.3 Sample Items from the JDI and the Job in General (JIG) Scale

In the blank beside each word or phrase below, write
_1_ for "Yes"
_2_ for "No"
_3_ for "?"

Work on Present Job	**Opportunities for Promotion**
How well does each of the following describe your work?	How well does each of the following describe your opportunities for promotion?
____ Fascinating	____ Good opportunities for promotion
____ Routine	____ Opportunities somewhat limited
____ Satisfying	____ Promotion on ability
____ Boring	____ Dead-end job
Present Pay	**Supervision**
How well does each of the following describe your present pay?	How well does each of the following describe your supervision?
____ Income adequate for normal expenses	____ Supportive
____ Fair	____ Hard to please
____ Comfortable	____ Impolite
____ Bad	____ Praises good work
Coworkers	**Job in General**
How well does each of the following describe the people you work with?	How well does each of the following describe your job most of the time?
____ Stimulating	____ Pleasant
____ Boring	____ Bad
____ Slow	____ Great
____ Helpful	____ Worthwhile

Source: Bowling Green State University, Department of Psychology (2009)

FIGURE 10.4 Sample Items from the JDS

How satisfied are you with this aspect of your job?						
Extremely dissatisfied	Dissatisfied	Slightly dissatisfied	Neutral	Slightly satisfied	Satisfied	Extremely satisfied
1	2	3	4	5	6	7

Pay

☐ The amount of pay and fringe benefits I receive.

Security

☐ The amount of job security I have.

Social

☐ The chance to get to know other people while on the job.

Supervisory

☐ The amount of support and guidance I receive from my supervisor.

Growth

☐ The amount of personal growth and development I get in doing my job.

Source: Hackman, J. R., & Oldham, G. R. (1980). *Work Redesign.* Upper Saddle River, NJ: Pearson. © 1980 by Pearson Education, Inc. Reprinted with permission.

from the overall dimension (i.e., "Job in General"). This scale is so well established that it is often used today to validate and develop other measures of job satisfaction (e.g., Whitaker, 2007).

A scale along similar lines was developed in connection with the Job Diagnostic Survey, or JDS (Hackman & Oldham, 1980), which measures job characteristics (see Chapter 9). This latter scale measures satisfaction as a function of pay, security, social factors, supervision, and growth (see Figure 10.4). There are many other measures of facet satisfaction, but the JDI and the JDS are well known and psychometrically sound.

Overall measures of job satisfaction are plentiful as well. For instance, both the JDI and the JDS include a measure of overall job satisfaction. The JDS measure is presented in Figure 10.5. Another large-scale approach to measuring job attitudes is related to L. H. Lofquist and R. V. Dawis's (1969) theory of work adjustment, which proposes that employees seek to maintain correspondence with their environment. The idea here is that employees want their jobs to fulfill their needs and desires. The Minnesota Satisfaction Questionnaire, which was developed on the basis of this theory, totals 100 items that measure 20 different facets of satisfaction. However, a

COURTESY OF BRIAN WELLE

Brian Welle
PhD, 2004, I/O Psychology, New York University
Manager, People and Innovation Lab
Google

I lead the People and Innovation Lab (PiLab) at Google. We are a group of psychologists, organizational behaviorists, and researchers whose projects include, among other things, the measurement of employees' beliefs, attitudes, opinions, and behaviors.

My team collects and analyzes data to help business leaders and human resource professionals make better decisions that affect Googlers (i.e., employees at Google). In an engineering company like Google, "all" decisions, whether from our sales team, engineers, or human resources, are guided by data. I/O psychologists are like the engineers of HR: We play a pivotal role by collecting, analyzing, and interpreting data for people-related decisions.

We use several methodologies and research tools in the PiLab. One of our most useful tools is surveys, and the best example of these is Googlegeist, our annual employee opinion survey. The Googlegeist survey is sent to all Googlers around the world and provides them the opportunity to tell us about the facets of the workplace that are most important to them: from satisfaction with their jobs, to confidence in their leaders, to perceptions of the company's culture. It also assesses constructs that predict Google-valued outcomes, including the speed and quality of decision making, and innovation. The data we collect through Googlegeist have enabled us to significantly improve our employee development programs, to help our leaders develop and improve, and even to guide business decisions.

Employee opinion surveys are useful tools. They provide a snapshot of people's beliefs and attitudes; however, they are not as good at determining cause-and-effect relationships. We therefore turn to experimental and quasi-experimental research to dive a bit deeper into key behaviors. We have, for example, conducted studies that reveal the best way to motivate retirement-savings behavior and time-series experiments to help Googlers eat healthier.

These examples, from surveys to experiments, illustrate how important psychological research is at Google. Attitudes, opinions, perceptions, and actual behaviors are the foundation for many things that organizations like Google care about, both from a business and an employee well-being perspective. We devote a lot of time to conducting research to understand the perspectives of our employees and using their data to make Google the kind of place where they are proud to work.

Applying Your Knowledge

1. Why does Google use different research methods to gauge employee attitudes versus behaviors?

2. What are some ways in which an organization might benefit from taking the time to assess employee attitudes and perspectives?

3. Based on what you've read about the JDS in this chapter, how does the Googlegeist sound similar? How might it differ?

short form of the scale (with just 20 items) has also been used very successfully for measuring overall satisfaction.

Three versions of the Faces Scale (Kunin, 1955, 1998), which measures the affective component of job satisfaction rather than the cognitive component, are depicted in Figure 10.6 and have also been frequently used to measure overall satisfaction. The Faces Scale can be used in many different situations because it is largely nonverbal and thus easier for verbally unskilled employees to complete. It is easily adapted for measuring various facets of satisfaction as well.

FIGURE 10.5 JDS Measure of Overall Job Satisfaction

Disagree strongly	Disagree	Disagree slightly	Neutral	Agree slightly	Agree	Agree strongly
1	2	3	4	5	6	7

☐ 1. Generally speaking, I am very satisfied with this job.

☐ 2. I frequently think of quitting this job. (R)

☐ 3. I am generally satisfied with the kind of work I do in this job.

☐ 4. Most people on this job are very satisfied with the job.

☐ 5. People on this job often think of quitting. (R)

Source: Hackman, J. R., & Oldham, G. R. (1980). *Work Redesign.* Upper Saddle River, NJ: Pearson. © 1980 by Pearson Education, Inc. Reprinted with permission.

Consequences

Now that we've described job satisfaction, what factors determine it, and how to measure it, we need to consider its consequences for organizations and employees. We return to the theory of planned behavior in considering the role of work-related attitudes in organizations. As illustrated in Figure 10.1, attitude is only one of four variables that are instrumental in the prediction of an individual's behavior. Although we hope that an employee's attitude will strongly predict her behavior, we have to realize that behavior is very complicated and that other important variables will also play a part in the prediction. Hence the old axiom "A satisfied worker is a productive worker" is not always accurate. What if that satisfied worker is incapable of doing what is required on her job? What if, despite her satisfaction, the norm at work is to do just enough to get by? What if her job satisfaction doesn't lead to an intention to work hard because her supervisor doesn't require much effort to give a favorable performance review? In all these situations, despite a high level of satisfaction, this employee is not likely to perform well; the attitude–behavior relationship is thus small or nonexistent. There are many antecedents to behavior other than attitudes. Expecting a strong relationship between attitudes and behaviors might be unrealistic in many situations.

Performance I have just suggested that the satisfied worker may or may not be a productive worker—an outcome that depends on many other variables. Think about this. Have you ever had a job in which you were not very satisfied but still did decent work? For that matter, did you sometimes perform better than others who were much more satisfied than you? Sometimes our performance is not a function of our job satisfaction at all but, instead, is determined by the constraints we perceive at work, the skills we possess to do a particular task, the family obligations that may have distracted us, our misunderstanding of what is expected with respect to particular tasks, our lack

FIGURE 10.6   Three Versions of the Faces Scale

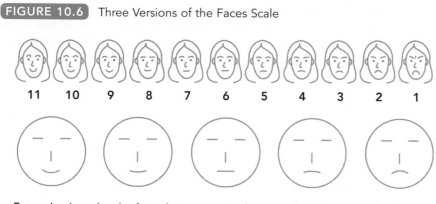

Put a check under the face that expresses how you feel about your **job in general**, including the work, the pay, the supervision, the opportunities for promotion, and the people you work with.

Sources: © 1975 by the American Psychological Association. Reprinted with permission. From Dunham, R. B., & Herman, J. B. (1975). Development of a female Faces Scale for measuring job satisfaction, *Journal of Applied Psychology, 60(5)*, 630; adapted from Kunin, T. (1955). The construction of a new type of attitude measure, *Personnel Psychology, 8*, 65–77. Reproduced with permission of Blackwell Publishing Ltd.

of motivation, and so on. In other words, satisfaction is a good predictor of performance some of the time, but not all of the time; either way, there are always other important predictors involved.

To talk in a general sense about the satisfaction–performance relationship is to ignore all these other potential variables. It's reasonable to do so as long as we keep in mind that these variables exist and that we shouldn't expect an extremely strong relationship between satisfaction and performance. A good general estimate of the relationship (i.e., the correlation) between satisfaction and performance is somewhere around .30 (Judge, Thoresen, Bono, & Patton, 2001). Furthermore, the correlation tends to be stronger for employees in highly complex jobs. A more recent meta-analysis takes a more sophisticated analytic approach and reports a large correlation ($r = .59$) between overall job attitude and work effectiveness (Harrison, Newman, & Roth, 2006). Even the meta-analyses don't always agree due to the particular studies included and the particular focus of the research, but we can reasonably conclude that job satisfaction and performance are moderately correlated.

A new and intriguing study examined the role of culture in the job satisfaction–performance relationship. This meta-analysis of 208 independent studies found that the satisfaction–performance relationship was stronger in those cultures that were high on individualism and low on uncertainty avoidance (Ng, Sorensen, & Yim, 2009). In other words, cultures in which individuals act in accordance with their own desires and preferences (as opposed to those of the collective) and those in which dynamic change is favored (as opposed to having an emphasis on stability) tend to have stronger satisfaction–performance relationships, probably because individuals in these cultures are rewarded for behaving in accordance with their own wishes and believing in their own independence—thus, if satisfied, they perform well.

Another variable to consider is *contextual performance,* also known as *organizational citizenship behavior,* or *OCB* (see Chapter 4). Contextual performance refers to behaviors that are not formally part of one's job description—that is, behaviors that have more to do with social elements at work than with task elements. Research has examined the relationship between job satisfaction and contextual performance as well; in fact, the most studied antecedent of contextual behaviors is job satisfaction. For instance, in a study of machine operators, satisfaction with coworkers, supervision, and pay was significantly correlated with various dimensions of OCB (Lowery, Beadles, & Krilowicz, 2002). Furthermore, in a study of U.S. government employees and various kinds of employees in Saudi Arabia and Egypt, moderate to strong correlations were found between job satisfaction and OCBs (Tang & Ibrahim, 1998). These correlations ranged from .22 to .57, depending on the type of satisfaction and the type of OCBs measured.

Withdrawal Behaviors Performance is one outcome variable of interest to organizations, but withdrawal behaviors are important as well. The three most common withdrawal behaviors are absenteeism, tardiness, and turnover.

We have all missed a few days of work here and there because of illnesses or other uncontrollable events such as a funeral, jury duty, a doctor's appointment, or a child's play or pageant. No one would suggest that employees should come to work every day regardless of illness, personal problems, or other important considerations. The Bureau of Labor Statistics reports that, on average, employees are absent about four days per year due to illness or personal concerns. This doesn't sound like much, but absenteeism costs companies a great deal of money. According to a definitive survey, the cost of absenteeism is at an all-time high, with companies' per-employee direct cost being $789 per year (CCH, 2002). This is really an underestimate because it doesn't include indirect costs like paying other employees overtime to cover for the absent employee. It's hard to determine the total costs incurred, but one source estimates that costs resulting from absent employees caring for aging loved ones alone amount to over $12 billion per year (Bisio, 1999). At the same time, the federal government reports that musculoskeletal injuries like carpal tunnel syndrome account for 62% of all workers' compensation claims, costing $15–20 billion per year, and result in a great deal of absenteeism ("Carpal Tunnel Syndrome," 2005).

FIGURE 10.7 Attendance Model

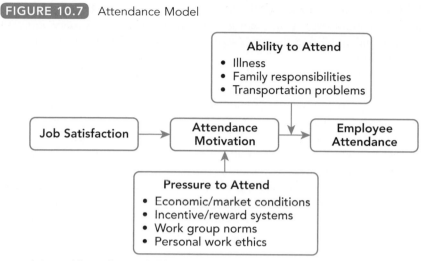

Adapted from Steers & Rhodes (1978)

One survey found that only 33% of unscheduled time off was due to personal illness, which means that there are other explanations for 67% of unscheduled absences; chief among these are family issues and personal needs. A popular model of absenteeism developed by Richard Steers and Susan Rhodes (1978) accounts for some of these alternative explanations. A simplified version of this model is depicted in Figure 10.7. First, notice that *job satisfaction* is an integral variable in the model, but also notice that it is rather far removed from *employee attendance* and that there are many variables in between. Some studies have found low to moderate correlations ($r = -.15$ to $-.25$) between job satisfaction and absenteeism (Hackett & Guion, 1985; Scott & Taylor, 1985), whereas others have demonstrated a stronger relationship. For instance, in a study based on the personnel records of over 300 city employees in Israel, a moderately negative correlation ($r = -.47$) was found between job satisfaction and voluntary absence, which includes everything but excused absence due to sickness or family obligations (Sagie, 1998). Still other studies have reported relationships close to zero (e.g., Goldberg & Waldman, 2000).

Second, notice that in Figure 10.7 the closest predictor to attendance is *attendance motivation*. This should remind you of the work of Ajzen and his colleagues (Ajzen & Fishbein, 2005), who argued that the best predictor of a behavior is the intention to exhibit that behavior. In Ajzen's models, attitude leads to intention, which affects behavior—much like satisfaction leads to attendance motivation, which then influences attendance. Third, notice that attendance motivation is affected by *pressure to attend*. For example, if an individual has very little money and depends on his job to buy food and shelter, then he is unlikely to behave in ways that might cost him his job, such as being consistently absent from work. This individual would experience pressures to attend that might not be experienced by someone who is independently wealthy. Fourth, notice that *ability to attend* takes into account whether employees actually have control over their attendance behavior. (Think back once more to Ajzen's work and you'll find that this variable is similar to the notion of perceived behavioral control.)

In short, attendance motivation is likely to affect attendance behavior only if the employees involved have control over their ability to attend. Consider the case of an employee who is very motivated to attend but needs to stay home to take care of a son who has chicken pox. This inability to attend would affect the relationship between her attendance motivation and her attendance behavior. She doesn't go to work, but it's not because she's unmotivated to attend work. In fact, research on more than 200 employed, married parents has found positive relationships between the number of children under six years of age and absence, and between child-care difficulties and absence (Erickson, Nichols, & Ritter, 2000).

The Steers and Rhodes model of absenteeism makes it very clear that although job satisfaction can be an important predictor of absenteeism, the absenteeism process is much more complicated than that. As discussed in the section on satisfaction and performance, expecting a strong direct relationship between satisfaction and any outcome variable is unreasonable given the complexities of human behavior. A recent study found support for many of the propositions presented in the Steers and Rhodes model, accounting for 46% of the variance in employee absenteeism (Steel, Rentsch, & Van Scotter, 2007) and demonstrating satisfaction to be important.

Much less research has been conducted on tardiness, or lateness (see some recent work by Foust and her colleagues: Elicker, Foust, O'Malley, & Levy, 2008; Foust, Elicker, & Levy, 2006), but some work by Gary Blau (1994) has proved especially interesting. Blau suggests that there are different types of lateness and that one common type, which he calls *chronic lateness,* is significantly predicted by job satisfaction. In his study of hospital employees, he found a $-.39$ correlation between job satisfaction and one's tendency to be chronically late. The Steers and Rhodes model of absence has also been applied to lateness; here, the results indicate that job satisfaction has a small direct effect on attendance but that both motivation to be on time and ability to be on time are important determinants of lateness (Bardsley & Rhodes, 1996).

One last withdrawal behavior is a very important one: turnover, which can have huge cost implications for organizations. Think of some of the major topics discussed thus far. Organizations invest a great deal of time, effort, and money in things like recruitment, testing and selection, training, and performance evaluation. If the employee chooses to leave the company, not only is that money no longer working for the company, but the process must begin again. The Society for Human Resource Management (SHRM) has estimated that it costs $3,500 to replace an employee making $8.00 per hour (Blake, 2006). Other estimates suggest it costs 1.5 to 2.5 times the employee's annual salary to replace him or her (Cascio, 2003).

The average turnover rate in the United States in 2011 was 14.4%, but 29.1% in the hospitality industry (http://www.compensationforce.com/2011/10/2011-turnover-rates-by-industry.html). Of course, the flip side of all this is that turnover can be good for companies if departing employees were ineffective and can be replaced by more

▲ **A Closer Look**
Can you think of a coworker you were glad to see leave the organization? How did your job attitudes change when this person left?

effective ones. This is often the case when employees are fired or when ineffective employees select themselves out of the organization. For our present purposes, however, let's think about situations in which organizations lose employees they would have preferred to keep.

A recent investigation was able to show that employees whose satisfaction levels change also report changes in turnover intentions (Chen, Ployhart, Thomas, Anderson, & Bliese, 2011). The results suggest that one's intent to leave a job changes more as a function of a decrease in satisfaction than as a function of the level of satisfaction. There are broad implications for the importance of tracking attitudes over time; doing so may provide greater insight into employees' attitudes and perhaps even allow organizations to better predict when turnover intentions are likely to increase and become a serious threat to the organization.

Traditionally, researchers have looked at two main antecedents of turnover: (1) perceived ease of movement, or the extent to which employees can find alternative jobs, and (2) perceived desirability of movement, which has largely been operationalized with respect to job satisfaction. In general, a modest relationship has been found between job satisfaction and turnover (Griffeth, Hom, & Gaertner, 2000; Lee, Mitchell, Holtom, McDaniel, & Hill, 1999), with correlations between −.20 and −.30. Figure 10.8 shows a simplified version of Hom and Griffeth's (1991) model. Along one path to turnover, job satisfaction affects the extent to which an individual begins thinking about quitting; a second path leads from job satisfaction to a job search and comparisons of alternatives. Both paths eventually result in a decision to stay or go. A recent study demonstrated that the relationship between job satisfaction and turnover varies as a function of psychological well-being, or PWB (Wright & Bonett, 2007). Namely, the negative relationship tends to be much stronger when people are low on PWB rather than high on PWB.

Indeed, job satisfaction is often integral to the turnover process, but we must also realize that some individuals leave companies because they can't pass up an incredible opportunity elsewhere or because they want to relocate for personal reasons, such as taking care of an ailing parent. In other words, turnover may be less related to the current job than to alternative job opportunities or personal circumstances. For example,

FIGURE 10.8 Modified Model of Turnover

Adapted from Hom & Griffeth (1991)

consider earlier cutting-edge work on turnover, involving what Thomas Lee and his colleagues call the *unfolding model* (Mitchell, Holtom, Lee, Sablynski, & Erez, 2001; Sablynski, Lee, Mitchell, Burton, & Holtom, 2002), in which four different paths to turnover are hypothesized. Along the first path, turnover results from a *shock to the system* (e.g., an unsolicited job offer, a change in one's marital status, a job transfer, a firm merger), and job satisfaction is completely irrelevant. This model provides other turnover paths and some interesting alternatives to traditional beliefs about the turnover process.

A recent empirical investigation extended the work of Lee and his colleagues by successfully categorizing 86% of a sample of accountants into one of the four proposed paths (Donnelly & Quirin, 2006), lending support to the unfolding model. Additional support comes from a recent study that found half the voluntary turnover from a national study was due largely to family reasons or an unsolicited job offer (Lee, Gerhart, Weller, & Trevor, 2008). This study demonstrates the importance of paths to turnover that don't include or emphasize job satisfaction.

Counterproductive Work Behaviors Employees engage in various activities that are detrimental to an organization, including antisocial behaviors and dysfunctional behaviors. Here I use the phrase **counterproductive work behaviors (CWBs)**, defined as any behaviors that bring, or are intended to bring, harm to an organization, its employees, or its stakeholders. Counterproductive behaviors include arson, blackmail, bribery, sabotage, theft, fraud, psychological withdrawal, interpersonal violence, and sometimes absence and lateness (Giacalone & Greenberg, 1997). Frustration is the centerpiece in one model of antisocial behavior (Spector, 1997). It argues that when an employee is frustrated and thus dissatisfied (i.e., when something interferes with his goals or objectives), his potential for antisocial behaviors increases. Recent work has shown that abusive behaviors are driven by anger, whereas withdrawal is more related to boredom and depression (Spector et al., 2006). This work argues that there are some different patterns in antecedents for the various CWBs.

counter-
productive work
behaviors (CWBs)
Any behaviors
that bring, or
are intended to
bring, harm to an
organization, its
employees, or its
stakeholders.

A review of the literature found that young dissatisfied employees were most likely to engage in counterproductive work behaviors (Lau, Au, & Ho, 2003); it has also been demonstrated that individuals low on conscientiousness were most likely to exhibit counterproductive behaviors (Salgado, 2002). More generally, the correlations between job satisfaction and counterproductive behaviors range from $-.10$ to $-.25$ (Boye & Jones, 1997). A recent study of 74 employees found that the effect of hostility on workplace deviance was mediated by job satisfaction (Judge, Scott, & Ilies, 2006). In other words, hostility led to a decrease in job satisfaction, which resulted in more workplace deviance. Although relatively little empirical research has been conducted in this area (because measuring counterproductive behaviors requires "catching" people in the act), the notion that employees' work-related attitudes play a role seems reasonable and is becoming the focus of more research.

In sum, job satisfaction is an important organizational variable. However, although we know a great deal about the antecedents and consequences of job satisfaction, we have probably been guilty in the past of expecting too much from it (Fisher, 2003). That is, we have anticipated very strong relationships between job satisfaction and organizational behaviors. In recent years, however, we have begun to realize the important, but limited, role played by job satisfaction in organizational processes. Our understanding of how satisfaction fits into the bigger picture of organizational and individual functioning continues to grow. The questions that we have asked in the past about the small direct effects of job satisfaction on various outcomes have led the way for research that is now helping to build more accurate models of organizational functioning.

■ Organizational Commitment

Organizational commitment (OC) is the second most frequently studied attitude in the workplace, but it has captured much less attention than job satisfaction. These two attitudes tend to be positively related at a moderate level, with correlations around .30 to .40. However, there has been some controversy over the causal order of these two variables (Kinicki et al., 2002) without a resolution as to which variable causes the other or whether there is a particular causal order at all.

Organizational commitment is broader in scope than job satisfaction given that the target is the "organization" rather than the "job." Furthermore, it is often reported that OC is more stable over time than is job satisfaction, which can fluctuate with daily or even hourly changes at work; OC doesn't fluctuate quite so much. In this section, I will define the various dimensions of organizational commitment and present a brief discussion of some of its antecedents and consequences. In a general sense, workplace commitments can be viewed as bonds or attachments to something related to work (Klein, Molloy, & Cooper, 2009). **Organizational commitment** can be defined as the relative strength of an individual's identification with, attachment to, and involvement in a particular organization. However, to really understand this attitude, we need to consider three components of commitment that have been defined in the literature.

organizational commitment (OC) The relative strength of an individual's identification with and involvement in a particular organization.

Components

In the last 15 years, John Meyer and Natalie Allen have studied organizational commitment more thoroughly than anyone else in the field, so this section borrows extensively from their work (Allen & Meyer, 1996; Meyer & Allen, 1997; Meyer, Stanley, Herscovitch, & Topolnytsky, 2002). Meyer and Allen conceptualize commitment as having three components, and they have developed a measure of each one. Figure 10.9 presents these measures, which are the most frequently used and accepted in the literature (Meyer & Allen, 1997).

The first and most studied component of organizational commitment, **affective commitment**, is characterized by (1) a strong belief in and acceptance of the organization's goals and values, (2) a willingness to exert effort on behalf of the organization, and (3) a strong desire to remain a part of the organization (Mowday, Steers, & Porter, 1979). This component can be thought of as the employee's emotional attachment to the organization. Second is **continuance commitment**, which has to do with the costs that are associated with leaving the organization. This component is sometimes referred to as *sunk-costs commitment* because it concerns attachment to an organization as a function of what the employee has invested in it (Shore, Tetrick, Shore, & Barksdale, 2000). An employee might have high continuance commitment because leaving the organization would cost him a great deal in retirement earnings (high sacrifice continuance commitment) or because he has no other better options (low alternatives continuance commitment). Third is **normative commitment**, sometimes called *moral commitment*, which reflects one's obligation to continue employment with the organization. Individuals who are high in normative commitment tend to believe that they ought to stay with the company regardless of what it offers them.

Antecedents

Figure 10.10 presents a heuristic framework for thinking about and studying organizational commitment. On the left side of the figure, antecedents are grouped into three categories to enhance the understanding of the commitment construct. We will discuss each of these categories in turn.

Organizational Mechanisms Have you ever noticed all the little things that organizations seem to be doing these days to get employees committed to the company? Some organizations have company stores that sell items with the company logo emblazoned all over them (coffee cups, shirts, hats). The use of logos and insignias on merchandise for employees and their children (what "organizational team player" wouldn't want his or her child to have a hat that says Apple or AT&T?) may serve various purposes, but one is clearly to increase the commitment of employees.

No empirical studies have examined the success of this approach thus far, but, speaking for myself, I proudly wear a sweatshirt from Virginia Tech (my alma mater). The same process occurs with respect to organizations. Newsletters can also increase the strength of employees' identification with or involvement in the organization. Hearing about the charity work the company has done, the new employees who have been hired, the employees who are retiring after 30 years of distinguished service to

affective commitment Emotional attachment to an organization, characterized by a strong belief in and acceptance of the organization's goals and values, a willingness to exert effort on behalf of the organization, and a strong desire to remain a part of the organization.

continuance commitment Attachment to an organization as a function of what the employee has invested in it; also called *sunk-costs commitment*.

normative commitment Attachment to an organization that reflects one's obligation to continue employment with the organization; also called *moral commitment*.

FIGURE 10.9 Affective, Continuance, and Normative Commitment Scales

Disagree strongly	Disagree	Disagree slightly	Neutral	Agree slightly	Agree	Agree strongly
1	2	3	4	5	6	7

Affective Commitment

☐ 1. I would be very happy to spend the rest of my career in this organization.

☐ 2. I really feel as if this organization's problems are my own.

☐ 3. I do not feel like "part of the family" at my organization. (R)

☐ 4. I do not feel "emotionally attached" to this organization. (R)

☐ 5. This organization has a great deal of personal meaning for me.

☐ 6. I do not feel a strong sense of belonging to my organization. (R)

Continuance Commitment

☐ 1. It would be very hard for me to leave my organization right now, even if I wanted to.

☐ 2. Too much of my life would be disrupted if I decided I wanted to leave my organization right now.

☐ 3. Right now, staying with my organization is a matter of necessity as much as desire.

☐ 4. I believe that I have too few options to consider leaving this organization.

☐ 5. One of the few negative consequences of leaving this organization would be the scarcity of available alternatives.

☐ 6. If I had not already put so much of myself into this organization, I might consider working elsewhere.

Normative Commitment

☐ 1. I do not feel any obligation to remain with my current employer. (R)

☐ 2. Even if it were to my advantage, I do not feel it would be right to leave my organization now.

☐ 3. I would feel guilty if I left my organization now.

☐ 4. This organization deserves my loyalty.

☐ 5. I would not leave my organization right now because I have a sense of obligation to the people in it.

☐ 6. I owe a great deal to my organization.

Source: Meyer, J. P., & Allen, N. J. (1997). *Commitment in the Workplace: Theory, Research, and Application* (pp. 118–119). Thousand Oaks, CA: SAGE. © 1997 by SAGE Publications. Reprinted with permission.

FIGURE 10.10 Framework for Organizational Commitment

Antecedents

Organizational Mechanisms
1. Socialization
2. Logos, insignias, programs for family members
3. Newsletters
4. Reward systems

Individual/Personal Characteristics
1. Age
2. Job level
3. Stress

Social Factors
1. Coworker relationships
2. Participation and social interaction
3. Role variables
4. Supervisory relationships

Organizational Commitment

Consequences

(+) **Performance**
1. Task
2. Contextual

(−) **Withdrawal Behaviors**
1. Absenteeism
2. Lateness
3. Turnover

(−) **Counterproductive Behaviors**
1. Theft
2. Sabotage
3. Aggression

▼ **A Closer Look** What do companies hope to achieve by providing their employees with merchandise displaying their company logo?

MARK RICHARDS/PHOTOEDIT

the company, the company's goals and objectives over the next five years, and how the CEO is a great champion for the company in the local community can all help to increase employees' commitment to the organization.

Of course, there are more formal mechanisms as well, in the form of reward systems, that give employees trips for positive performance, provide gift certificates for employees of the month, pay for furthering employees' education, and so on. Meyer and Allen (1997) view such mechanisms as leading to affective commitment—specifically, by communicating to employees that the organization is supportive of them, by treating them fairly, and by enhancing their sense of personal importance and competence. Other research, too, has demonstrated that affective commitment is influenced by employees' perception that organizational policies, procedures, and programs are fair (Konovsky & Cropanzano, 1991; Sweeney & McFarlin, 1993). One way an organization can demonstrate support for its employees is by offering flexible work alternatives. For instance, a recent study of 393 employees who telecommute found that the more telecommuting these employees did, the less exhaustion they experienced from their job and the more committed they were to the organization (Golden, 2006).

Individual/Personal Characteristics Examining situational characteristics such as the organizational mechanisms discussed previously would be incomplete without considering individual characteristics as well. Individual employees bring to their jobs many qualities, attitudes, beliefs, and skills—what we often refer to as *individual differences;* these differences are often related to job attitudes such as organizational commitment. In perhaps the largest meta-analysis done in the area of commitment (Meyer et al., 2002), a few individual-difference variables were identified as important predictors of organizational commitment. Across 53 different samples, researchers found a .15 correlation between age and affective commitment, indicating that the older employees are, the more affectively committed they are. This could be the result of more experience or tenure on the job, or it could be that as we age we are increasingly likely to end up in a job that we like and thus we become emotionally attached to it.

In their meta-analysis, the researchers also found a .16 correlation between organizational tenure and affective commitment, suggesting that individuals with more tenure in the organization are more committed to the organization than are individuals with less tenure. Specifically, they discovered a stronger relationship between organizational tenure and continuance commitment ($r = .21$) than between organizational tenure and affective commitment, thus supporting what we know about these two components of commitment: As employees' tenure with an organization increases, their sunk costs—and hence their continuance commitment—also increase.

Social Factors The last category of antecedents revolves around social interactions and relationships. A recent study of 514 solicitors (attorneys) in Hong Kong found that perceptions of justice were related to organizational commitment, but the relationships were mediated through perceived organizational support (Loi, Hang-yue, & Foley, 2006).

Organizational support has been found to be one of the strongest predictors of affective and normative commitment (Meyer et al., 2002). For instance, the extent to which a boss treats employees considerately ($r = .34$) and communicates often and openly with them ($r = .45$) is related to the employees' level of organizational commitment (Mathieu & Zajac, 1990). Role variables are important antecedents of affective commitment, given consistent negative correlations between certain concepts—like role ambiguity (when employees are not sure what is expected of them) and role conflict (when role expectations are inconsistent)—and organizational commitment (Meyer et al., 2002). Organizational justice has been identified as an important predictor of both affective and normative commitment (Meyer et al., 2002), with correlations tending to fall in the .30s.

Consequences

In Figure 10.10, the potential consequences of organizational commitment are divided into three categories—performance, withdrawal behaviors, and counterproductive behaviors.

Performance It is reasonable to assume that any work-related attitude will be more favorably viewed by organizational practitioners if that attitude is directly related to job performance. However, as we noted in an earlier section, expecting strong direct relationships between job satisfaction and performance outcome variables is not reasonable, given the complexity of performance. The same advice holds for organizational commitment: Don't expect a strong direct relationship between commitment and performance. Still, we can try to understand what the empirical data indicate about the relationship that does exist. For instance, in a national sample of almost 300 workers, affective commitment served as an antecedent of innovative performance (Ng, Feldman, & Lam, 2010), suggesting a potentially important role for commitment in organizational innovation.

First, recent studies report correlations between affective commitment and task performance ranging from .15 to .25. Similarly, contextual performance appears to be consistently related to affective commitment in a positive way, less consistently related to normative commitment, and unrelated or somewhat negatively related to continuance commitment (Meyer et al., 2002). Two reviews found a stronger relationship between OC and performance when performance was extra-role (i.e., OCBs) rather than in-role (i.e., task performance) (Meyer et al., 2002; Riketta, 2002). Finally, a study found that even after controlling for procedural justice and job satisfaction, affective commitment accounted for a significant amount of variance in altruistic OCBs (such as helping other employees), suggesting that it might be more important than satisfaction or justice in predicting OCBs (Schappe, 1998). The author of this study concluded that employees' feelings about their organization may manifest themselves in terms of OCBs that are important to organizational functioning.

Withdrawal Behaviors Affective commitment and absence appear to be correlated to a small but significant degree. For instance, one study found a −.18 correlation between affective commitment and the frequency of absence incidents over a 12-month period (Gellatly, 1995). A second study found a −.22 correlation between the affective commitment of bus drivers and the frequency of absence incidents that were under the drivers' control (Hackett, Bycio, & Hausdorf, 1994). Again, think back to the attendance model in Figure 10.7 and recall the many variables other than attitudes that play a part in determining absence behavior; a direct correlation of about −.20 should not be surprising. In fact, the best estimate of the relationship between affective commitment and voluntary absence is −.22 (Meyer et al., 2002). Research indicates that continuance commitment does not appear to be related to absenteeism. Furthermore, so little research has looked at the role of normative commitment that no conclusion can be drawn about its relationship with absenteeism either.

Organizational commitment has a long-standing association with turnover (see Mowday et al., 1979). This association is clear in my earlier presentation of the three characteristics that define a highly committed employee, the last of which is *a strong desire to remain a part of the organization*. By definition, organizational commitment should be negatively related to the turnover process. The meta-analyses vary a bit, but the relationship between affective commitment and actual turnover is approximately −.15 to −.25.

Much stronger correlations (−.40 to −.50) are typically found between affective commitment and intentions to leave a job (e.g., Marique & Stinglhamber, 2011), which is consistent with the theory of planned behavior described earlier. For instance, a study of 316 Belgian employees reported a .57 relationship between affective commitment and intent to quit (Vandenberghe, Bentein, & Stinglhamber, 2004). Interestingly, intent to quit predicted actual turnover very well 18 months later ($r = .38$). Both normative commitment and continuance commitment are significantly and negatively related to withdrawal cognitions as well, but the relationships are smaller than with affective commitment ($r = −.33$ and −.18, respectively). Another study has found similar and consistently strong effects in a Chinese sample (Cheng & Stockdale, 2003). For normative commitment, Meyer and his colleagues have found a similar pattern but weaker relationships, with correlations ranging from −.20 to −.38 (Meyer et al., 2002).

Counterproductive Behaviors Although there has been little research on the role of organizational commitment in counterproductive behavior, there are various reasons to expect a relationship. One model of counterproductive behavior that emphasizes the role of frustration in the process suggests a likely relationship between frustration and a lack of commitment to the organization (Spector, 1997). Other recent work indicates that the values and goals communicated by an organization have a significant effect on the frequency of counterproductive behaviors. Because one important characteristic of an organizationally committed employee is a strong belief in and acceptance of the organization's goals, it follows that commitment ought to be related to the frequency of counterproductive behavior (Dalal, 2005). Indeed, companies that espouse such organizational values as treating employees with fairness, empowering employees, and demonstrating interpersonal cooperation report higher levels of trust than do companies that do not emphasize these values (Boye & Jones, 1997).

■ Additional Job Attitudes

Although job satisfaction and organizational commitment have received by far the most attention from employee attitude researchers, a few other attitudes deserve mention: job involvement and work centrality; perceived organizational support; and emotions in the workplace.

Job Involvement and Work Centrality

Job involvement and work centrality are closely related to each other and to organizational commitment; they also have a long history in I/O psychology. **Job involvement** is the extent to which employees are cognitively engaged in their jobs (Paullay, Alliger, & Stone-Romero, 1994). In extreme cases, employees may become **workaholics**, meaning that they enjoy the act of working (although they may or may not enjoy their particular job; see discussion below) but are obsessed with it and devote great personal time to it at the expense of other important life roles (Ng, Sorensen, & Feldman, 2007). **Work centrality**, on the other hand, is

job involvement
The extent to which employees are cognitively engaged in their jobs.

workaholic
An individual whose high drive to work and high work involvement become so intense that they result in work–life imbalance issues.

work centrality
The degree of importance that work holds in one's life.

defined as the degree of importance that work, in general, holds in an employee's life (Paullay et al., 1994). This attitude usually develops as a result of socialization, reflecting the nature of our individual role models as we grow and mature. One distinction between job involvement and work centrality is that the former focuses on one's particular job, whereas the latter concerns work in general. Although we know less about these two constructs than about the others discussed in this chapter, research continues to illuminate the role they play in organizations.

According to two studies, for instance, job involvement, work centrality, and organizational commitment are moderately intercorrelated, with relationships between .25 and .45 (Hirschfeld & Feild, 2000; Paullay et al., 1994). Based on the relationships among these three constructs, one study of over 300 employees (Hirschfeld & Feild, 2000) concluded that affectively committed employees tend to identify with their work roles (work centrality) and are engaged in their jobs (job involvement). A recent meta-analysis examining the potential effects of work centrality on employee work outcomes demonstrated that work centrality is positively related to salary level, number of promotions, and career satisfaction (Ng, Eby, Sorensen, & Feldman, 2005).

Second, an investigation of over 280 public-sector employees found that job involvement moderated the effect of job insecurity on outcomes such as negative job attitudes, health problems, and psychological distress (Probst, 2000). In particular, job insecurity had stronger effects on these outcomes for individuals who were highly involved in their jobs. This makes a great deal of sense: If you are invested in your job and engaged by it, job insecurity is more likely to lead to negative attitudes and both physical and psychological distress.

Some newer work has also begun to focus on workaholism. Employees who are driven by, involved in, and enjoy their work are termed *enthusiastic workaholics,* whereas more traditional workaholics are driven, involved, and may enjoy the *act* of working but report that they do not enjoy their particular work (Spence & Robbins, 1992). In a sample of over 500 MBA graduates in Canada, enthusiastic workaholics reported higher levels of emotional and psychological well-being than did traditional workaholics (Burke, 2000). This finding suggests that being driven by and heavily involved in your job can have favorable outcomes, provided that you also enjoy your job. However, recent work has found that workaholics in general experience more work–life imbalance and less life satisfaction than do nonworkaholics (Aziz & Zickar, 2006). A newer trend in the research is to hypothesize about and examine the boundaries between work and home and the different ways in which people define them (Kreiner, Hollensbe, & Sheep, 2009). We will consider work–family issues in the next chapter.

Perceived Organizational Support

perceived organizational support (POS) Employees' global beliefs concerning the extent to which the organization values and cares about them.

Perceived organizational support (POS) has been defined by Rhoades and Eisenberger (2002) as employees' global beliefs concerning the extent to which the organization values their contributions and cares about their well-being. A review by these authors of over 70 empirical studies concluded that the major antecedents of POS include fair organizational procedures, supervisor support, and favorable rewards/job conditions, whereas the most strongly related consequences include organizational commitment, increased performance, and reduced withdrawal behaviors (e.g., turnover intentions, tardiness).

For instance, Allen, Shore, and Griffeth (2003) found that POS was strongly related to other attitudes, such as job satisfaction and organizational commitment, but that it also predicted turnover intentions and actual turnover behavior one year later. Another study by two leading researchers in this area demonstrated that supervisors high in POS (i.e., who feel supported by their organization) reciprocate with more supportive treatment of their subordinates, which, of course, has favorable effects on employee attitudes and performance (Shanock & Eisenberger, 2006).

Emotions in the Workplace

In recent years, the role of emotions in the workplace has attracted a great deal of research attention. One topic of interest is generally referred to as **emotion regulation**, or the ways in which individuals monitor their emotions and the expression of those emotions (Gross, 1998).

It is believed that there are two forms of emotion regulation: *amplification,* or faking/exaggerating pleasant emotions, and *suppression,* or hiding displays of felt emotions such as anger or jealousy (Cote & Morgan, 2002). **Emotional labor** is a slightly more specific term, defined as the effort, planning, and control required by employees to express organizationally desired emotions during interpersonal interactions (Morris & Feldman, 1996). Much of the work on the regulation of emotions or on emotional labor has focused on service jobs that emphasize interactions with customers because it is believed that employees in these jobs must constantly regulate their emotions and the expression of them.

Some research suggests that emotional labor is linked to substance abuse, absenteeism, work-related stress, and psychological distress, whereas other research has found these relationships to be weak and inconsistent (Zapf, 2002). One consistent finding, however, is that employees who experience *emotional dissonance*—whose true feelings are different from the emotions they project on the job—experience higher rates of stress (Grandey & Brauburger, 2002). For example, people who tend to see the world in rather rigid and negative ways may experience emotional dissonance as customer service representatives, who are required by their job to be pleasant, helpful, and encouraging. This disconnect between their true feelings and what's required of them at work is likely to lead to stress, burnout, and, ultimately, poor customer service. (See Chapter 11 for a more detailed discussion of stress.)

In an interesting study of employees in the service industry, it was demonstrated that the suppression of unpleasant emotions led to job dissatisfaction, which resulted in strong intentions to quit. On the other hand, the amplification of pleasant emotions led to increases in job satisfaction (Cote & Morgan, 2002).

One particularly fascinating study focused on coffeehouse baristas and service with a smile (Barger & Grandey, 2006). Trained coders observed 220 employee–customer interactions, recording both employee and customer behaviors. They found that the strength of employees' smiles predicted customer satisfaction and customer ratings of service. The authors warn, however, that fake or forced smiles sometimes

emotion regulation The ways in which individuals monitor their emotions and the expression of those emotions.

emotional labor The effort, planning, and control required by employees to express organizationally desired emotions during interpersonal interactions.

RADIUS IMAGES/CORBIS

▲ **A Closer Look**
What role does a server's smile play in your experience as a customer? Does it matter whether the smile is fake or sincere?

backfire, since other research has demonstrated that inauthentic displays of emotion lead to less positive customer impressions (e.g., Grandey, Fisk, Mattila, Jansen, & Sideman, 2005).

The existing work on emotional labor has numerous relevant applications. For instance, emotional dissonance, given its links to stress and burnout, has implications for selection systems that determine how well employees fit into the hiring organization—a factor known as *person–organization fit* (for a comprehensive discussion of this and other "fit" constructs, see Kristof-Brown, Zimmerman, & Johnson, 2005). Not surprisingly, customer service representatives are likely to be more successful at their jobs if their emotional makeup is somewhat consistent with the emotional regulation required in those jobs. A preliminary job analysis conducted by an I/O professional is a vital step in helping to ensure not only person–organization fit but also employee–job fit. Ideally, applicants who believe that people should help themselves and not expect others to help them at all, who don't enjoy interacting with people, and who believe that customers are never right should be screened out by such predictors. Think about it: How many times in the past few weeks have you walked into a store and been "served" by a customer service employee who was clearly unable to do the emotional labor required of that job and really didn't care much about you as a customer? Additional research on emotional labor promises to enhance our understanding of organizations and increase organizational effectiveness.

■ Summary

This chapter is divided into four sections. First, I presented some background information on attitudes, behaviors, and the relationship among them. At the outset, I discussed a popular model of this relationship and then referred to it throughout while trying to make sense of the links between work-related attitudes and organizational outcomes. The work of Ajzen and Fishbein provided a nice foundation for the more work-specific issues that were discussed later in the chapter.

Second, after considering various reasons why I/O researchers and practitioners are interested in job attitudes, I presented a detailed overview of job satisfaction, using Figure 10.2 as a basis for discussion. I cited research dealing with the four main classes of antecedents to job satisfaction: job characteristics, individual/personal characteristics, social factors, and growth opportunities. All of these antecedents appear to make important contributions to employees' levels of job satisfaction. I also discussed a few scales that measure job satisfaction, included examples of those scales, and considered the multidimensional nature of job satisfaction. To conclude this section on job satisfaction, I discussed at length three classes of organizational outcome variables (consequences) that appear to be substantively linked to job satisfaction: performance, withdrawal behaviors, and counterproductive behaviors.

In the third section, I presented Figure 10.10 as a working heuristic for our discussion of organizational commitment. Throughout, I reviewed Meyer and Allen's three-component model: affective commitment, continuance commitment, and normative commitment. I also classified the antecedents of organizational commitment as organizational, individual, or social in nature. Each of these sets of variables seems to have potential effects on organizational commitment. Indeed, recent research in this area demonstrates that performance, withdrawal behaviors, and counterproductive behaviors are all influenced by organizational commitment. Finally, in the context of other work attitudes, I discussed the role played by job involvement, work centrality, perceived organizational support, and emotions in the workplace.

■ Key Terms

affective commitment (p. 310)
affective disposition (p. 295)
attitude (p. 291)
continuance commitment (p. 310)
counterproductive work behaviors (CWBs) (p. 308)
emotion regulation (p. 317)
emotional labor (p. 317)
job involvement (p. 315)
job satisfaction (p. 293)
normative commitment (p. 310)

organizational commitment (OC) (p. 309)
organizational justice (p. 297)
organization-based self-esteem (OBSE) (p. 296)
perceived behavioral control (p. 292)
perceived organizational support (POS) (p. 316)
subjective norm (p. 292)
work centrality (p. 315)
workaholic (p. 315)

■ TAKING IT TO THE FIELD

One particularly difficult part of work is learning how to deliver bad news in a way that preserves an employee's positive feelings and attitudes toward the job. However, because job satisfaction is a well-researched topic, I/O psychologists have many different ways to approach this problem. One of your long-standing clients, Karen Strazinski, manager of River Valley Bank, has recently learned that one of her branches will be closing. She is looking to you to help her strategize how she can salvage morale among workers who will not be laid off.

> Hello—
> Thanks again for agreeing to help me with my problem. I wanted to give you some quick background into the issue at hand as well as the e-mail I have drafted to inform my workers about the branch closure.
> Due to economic issues in the area, we have recently closed our North branch bank. We were able to offer jobs at the South branch bank to a few of our best North branch employees. All other employees received a small severance package.

The problem is with our South branch bank—despite our assurances that their jobs are safe, our employees there are quite demoralized and unmotivated. We've also been noticing more absences and tardiness; in addition, a few of our best employees have left the South branch. I have heard through the grapevine that the South branch employees are afraid they are next on the chopping block. This is not true, and I've told them this. However, the closure of North branch was not handled well, and many of the employees there were blindsided by its closure. I also think that the people who transferred from the North branch after it closed are not helping the situation, as many of them are still upset about losing their original positions.

Right now, I'm pretty frustrated with the lack of performance—I was sad that the branch closed, too, but I still have to do my job! I feel like sending out an e-mail telling them to get over it. What steps would you suggest I take to help improve morale here at River Valley Bank?

Karen

Write an e-mail responding to Karen's problems. Be sure to provide her with specific ways by which she can bolster morale during this difficult time at her company.

■ Critical Thinking Questions

1. Is employees' job satisfaction stable over time, or can it vary? How could an organization modify its work environment in order to increase employees' job satisfaction?

2. How might the varying forms of organizational commitment become manifest in employees' on-the-job behavior?

3. Assume you have been hired by an organization to survey the job attitudes of its employees. Your survey cannot exceed a certain number of items due to concerns that it will take the employees too long to complete. If you only have time to administer valid, reliable measures of *three* job attitudes, which attitudes would you measure and why?

4. Why do you think I/O researchers are paying more attention to emotions in the workplace?

■ Application Questions

1. Compare two jobs you have held and your overall satisfaction with those jobs. Was your satisfaction similar in both jobs? If so, why do you think that is? If not, what affected your satisfaction?

2. It is common in consulting work to encounter managers who believe that job attitudes do not matter—if someone quits, they will just hire another person to replace that person. What might you say to these types of managers?

3. Imagine you have to tell one of your best employees that she will not be getting her expected bonus check this year due to financial problems in the company. What might you tell her to ensure that she will still feel satisfied with her job, even though she will be disappointed about her bonus check?

4. The chapter discusses emotional labor (when employees must fake positive emotions or hide negative emotions). Provide an example in which you had to engage in emotional labor and how that experience made you feel about that situation.

5. If you were to win enough money in a lottery so that you would never need to work again if you didn't want to, would you still work? Why or why not?

■ Suggested Readings

Burke, R. J. (2006). *Research companion to working time and work addiction.* Northampton, MA: Edward Elgar. Contributing authors explore the fascinating and relatively new phenomenon of workaholism.

Elfenbein, H. A. (2008). Emotion in organizations: A review and theoretical integration in stages. *The Academy of Management Annals, 1,* 315–386. Elfenbein provides an excellent overview of emotion in organizations, with particular attention paid to specific job attitudes such as job satisfaction.

Griffin, R. W., & O'Leary-Kelly, A. M. (2004). *The dark side of organizational behavior.* San Francisco: Jossey-Bass. In this edited volume, contributors explore the antecedents and consequences of organizational phenomena such as drug and alcohol use and workplace aggression and violence.

Holtom, B. C., Mitchell, T. R., Lee, T. W., & Eberly, M. B. (2008). Turnover and retention research: A glance at the past, a closer review of the present, and a venture into the future. *The Academy of Management Annals, 2,* 231–274. The foremost researchers on turnover and retention explore the past, present, and future state of research into why employees stay with or leave their organizations.

CHAPTER 11

Stress and Worker Well-Being

RUDI VON BRIEL/PHOTOEDIT

LEARNING OBJECTIVES

This chapter should help you understand:

- The difference between stress and strains
- Why so many Americans are "working scared" and how best to deal with this situation
- How coping skills help individuals handle stress
- Warr's environmental determinants of well-being
- Many of the important issues that are involved in work–family conflict
- The importance of family-friendly employee benefits
- The ways in which companies are helping employees balance their work and family lives with as little stress as possible
- The particular complexities faced by dual-earner couples
- Why job loss is one of the most severe sources of stress that individuals ever experience
- The factors that trigger workplace violence in the United States today

Has something like this ever happened to you?

You wake up in the morning and just don't feel right. You get out of bed and notice that you have a little headache. After your shower, you sit down to eat breakfast and read the morning news, but you can't seem to finish an article—your mind keeps wandering. Before leaving for work, you pull out your calendar and remember that your day includes a meeting with a supervisor who usually asks to see you only when she has a problem with your work, a meeting with a disgruntled subordinate who thinks he should have been promoted but you think should be fired, about four hours of administrative paperwork, and a sexual harassment training session because your department has been guilty of some serious violations in this area.

Or how about something like this? After waking with a headache, probably the result of staying up until 3:00 A.M. studying for two final exams that happen to fall on the same day, you go to the refrigerator to find there's no milk for your cereal. You instead gobble down a Pop-Tart while reviewing your notes for your psychology exam—and suddenly realize that you never got the notes for the day you missed to attend your grandmother's funeral. After unsuccessfully trying to call a couple of friends in the hope of catching a quick glimpse of their notes, you go back to studying and get frustrated because you just can't seem to remember all the definitions that are likely to be on the exam. Finally, you grab your backpack and head for the bus. As you close the door behind you and step outside, your foot sinks into eight inches of snow that you didn't even realize had fallen overnight. It's now 9:00 A.M., and you realize it will take a lot longer to get to class. Making it to your 10:00 A.M. exam will be tight—and your psychology professor makes no exceptions for makeups or tardiness.

These situations involve stress—a word that is often thrown around casually. In this chapter, I will define stress in a more formal way and discuss it as it relates to work. In addition, I consider some modifications that organizations are implementing to reduce the stress that is so prevalent in today's workplaces. The chapter concludes by focusing on one of the most terrifying outcomes of excessive stress—workplace violence.

■ Stress and Strains

Stress refers to any force that pushes a psychological or physical function beyond its range of stability, producing a strain within the individual (Cartwright & Cooper, 1997). In other words, we experience stress when we feel "stretched too thin." The opening scenarios of this chapter presented many examples of stressful events and elements, such as anxiety over a work meeting, the death of a close family member, the prospect of being late for class, and so on. **Strains**, on the other hand, are undesirable personal outcomes resulting from the combined stressful experiences of various life domains (Bhagat, Allie, & Ford, 1995). In other words, stress leads to strains. Employees who are particularly stressed at work may experience sickness, low-quality performance, increased absence, poor communication, and many other strains. An upset stomach, for example, is the strain that stems from the stress of a tight deadline. The short fuse and general crankiness of a worried employee is the strain resulting from the stress of impending layoffs. Let's tease these apart a bit more.

Stress

There are many models of workplace stress. Each has unique elements, but most share several elements as well. Figure 11.1 was developed on the basis of two such models (see Bhagat et al., 1995; Cartwright & Cooper, 1997). Though not perfect, this figure presents a reasonable picture of the sources and outcomes of stress, along with two of the most important coping strategies. In particular, note that the sources of stress are categorized in ways that we have seen elsewhere in the book (e.g., in the Chapter 10 discussion of job satisfaction). Intrinsic factors such as poor working conditions (e.g., low lighting, excessive noise, and poorly designed office space) tend to lead to perceived stress, as do long hours, excessive travel, and lack of control over one's job.

This last factor—lack of control—has been found to play an especially important role in employees' stress levels. According to Robert Karasek's (1990) demand–control model of stress, for example, stress is a function of the psychological demands of work and the amount of decision latitude (i.e., control) that employees are provided (see also Theorell & Karasek, 1996). Since the inception of this model, many studies have demonstrated links between low levels of workplace control and psychological and physical problems such as heart disease, depression, exhaustion, job dissatisfaction, stomach ailments, and absenteeism (reviewed in Karasek, 1990). More recent work has demonstrated links between excessive workload and time pressure (i.e., stress) as well as major depressive and generalized anxiety disorders (Blackmore et al., 2007; Melchior et al., 2007).

stress
Any force that pushes a psychological or physical function beyond its range of stability, producing a strain within the individual.

strains
Undesirable personal outcomes resulting from the combined stressful experiences of various life domains.

FIGURE 11.1 General Stress Model

Sources of Stress

1. Intrinsic work factors
2. Role variables
3. Interpersonal relationships
4. Career development

Organizational stress

Coping Strategies

1. Problem-focused
2. Emotion-focused

Strains

Job-related
1. Low job satisfaction
2. Ineffective performance
3. Lack of motivation
4. Increased absences

Emotion-related
5. Emotional exhaustion
6. Depression
7. Irritability
8. Reduced self-esteem

Physiological
9. Increased illnesses
10. Physiological changes (blood pressure, chest pains, heart rate, etc.)

role
A set of behaviors expected of a person who occupies a particular position in a group.

role ambiguity
A situation that results when role expectations are unclear and employees are thus not sure what is expected of them.

role conflict
A situation that results when role expectations are inconsistent, as when a supervisor sends employees mixed messages about their roles.

Role variables are important as well. A **role** is a set of behaviors expected of a person who occupies a particular position in a group. **Role ambiguity** results when role expectations are unclear and employees are thus not sure what is expected of them. **Role conflict**, on the other hand, occurs when role expectations are inconsistent, as when a supervisor sends employees mixed messages about their roles. For instance, your boss might tell you to be creative and to take initiative—but when you do so, he says that you aren't following company policy. Alternatively, you may get conflicting messages about your role from two different people, such that your subordinate sees your role one way and your boss sees it another way. Needless to say, both role ambiguity and role conflict can lead to workplace stress. A recent study has found that political skill and organizational support can lessen the negative effects of role conflict (Jawahar, Stone, & Kisamore, 2007).

Another source of stress has to do with interpersonal relationships at work. Employees who have bad relationships with their supervisors and coworkers tend to be more stressed than are individuals whose interpersonal relationships are more favorable. If you can recall a stressful job situation that you have experienced, you can also likely recall relationships with your colleagues at that job that were contentious or lacking in trust. It has always been my belief that the people I work with actually have more to do with my stress levels and attitudes toward my job than the job itself does. Indeed, bad interpersonal relationships tend to be stressful regardless of whether they occur in the context of one's job, school, neighborhood, or family.

As noted in an earlier chapter, many people define themselves, at least in part, by what they do. Our jobs and careers are important parts of our lives. Thus, it is very stressful to reach a point where opportunities for additional advancement or job security are lacking. In their aptly titled book *Working Scared,* Ken Wexley and Stan Silverman (1993) argue that the stress, nervousness, and uneasiness associated with the changing nature of work have left many of us working scared: scared of being downsized, fired, or considered less competent—and thus more expendable than

Table 11.1 21st-Century Organizational Changes (Stressors) That Lead to Stress

Organizational Change	Techniques for Dealing with These Stressors
Less supervision: As organizations downsize and cut back, managers have more subordinates—and less time for each.	Develop your own responsibilities and objectives. Seek high-quality feedback from coworkers, supervisors, and subordinates.
Team culture: It's typical for employees today to work in a team environment, and being a team player can be difficult.	Be prepared for and accept empowerment. Improve your communication skills.
Focus on quality: Many employees are learning new methods and approaches to ensure that the organization is doing "quality" work.	Don't wait for training—start learning on your own. Look for ways to improve your work—slowly, but steadily.
Downsizing: Organizations feel the need to get "lean and mean," leaving many employees without jobs and others as layoff survivors.	Be aware of rumors, but don't let them dominate your thoughts. Work hard and creatively to prove your worth to the organization.
Mergers and acquisitions: Companies are buying each other out; the result is very different companies—a situation that affects employees.	Learn as much as possible about the other company. Be prepared and receptive to organizational changes.
Diversity: As the workforce becomes more diverse, employees interact more with coworkers who have backgrounds different from theirs.	Become more aware of your own values and prejudices. Consider the many benefits that come from diversity, including increasing productivity.
International environment: Companies are becoming more international, and employees often find themselves working in a different culture.	Be honest in considering whether an overseas assignment might work for you and your family. Expect six difficult months at first, with serious adjustments necessary on your part.
Innovative pay strategies: Employees are faced with different payment plans, such as gainsharing and bonuses.	Understand the organization's new pay strategy. Ask for periodic performance reviews

episodic stress
Stress resulting from life experiences and situations that varies with those experiences.

chronic stress
Consistent, debilitating stress arising from lifelong experiences that can result in suicide and violence.

burnout
A condition that occurs when employees become so stressed that they experience emotional exhaustion, depersonalization, and a sense of reduced personal accomplishment.

▼ **A Closer Look**
Burnout can be debilitating for people. Do you think that individuals have much control over burnout, or is it more a function of characteristics of the job?

younger and cheaper employees. More recently, we are experiencing an economic recession in the United States unlike any we have seen in decades. We can't glance at a newspaper without learning of major layoffs at one major company or another. In January 2009, Microsoft laid off 5,000 workers, marking the first mass layoffs in the company's 34-year history. Table 11.1 lists eight major areas of change in organizations that have given rise to stress among employees. Because they are sources of stress, these changes are referred to as *stressors* (Wexley & Silverman, 1993). It isn't fun to be working scared, but unfortunately many of us are. We have less supervision than we used to have, we work in environments in which doing more with less is expected of us, and we witness many of our coworkers being "let go" to save the bottom line. Table 11.1 provides some suggestions for dealing with these and other stressors.

One common distinction among types of stress is that between chronic and episodic stress. **Episodic stress** is experienced as a result of particular life situations, such as family issues, changing economic conditions, and so on. Some people suffer from acute episodic stress—they always seem to be dealing with these episodic stressful situations. What we call "worry warts" would fall into this category, as might Type A personalities (www.apa.org/helpcenter/stress-kinds.aspx). On the other hand, **chronic stress** is the constant grinding away that people experience from poverty, dysfunctional families, a hated career, and so on. Chronic stress is more likely to lead to suicide, violence, and many medical disorders; unfortunately, people get used to chronic stress because they've experienced it their whole lives.

Strains

Strains are everywhere in the workplace. A partial list is presented in Figure 11.1, which groups them into three categories: job-related, emotional, and physiological. The first category, job-related strains, can occur, for example, when you have a job that creates a great deal of stress or when you probably aren't terribly satisfied with that job or motivated by it. Indeed, a lack of satisfaction and motivation often leads to low effort, high absenteeism, high turnover, and low productivity or ineffective performance (Cartwright & Cooper, 1997). Stress costs industry over $300 billion per year in the United States, and up to 19% of absenteeism and 40% of turnover are related to job stress (Tangri, n.d.)

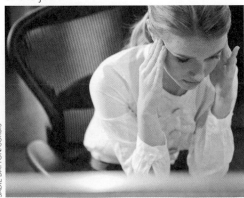

The second category of strains is emotional strains. Stress certainly takes a toll on us emotionally. One clear indicator that I'm stressed at work is that I have much less patience with my children and become irritable. After a particularly stressful day at work, when my kids act up (as all do), I am very quick to lose my temper and seem unable to understand that they are doing exactly what kids their age do. Sometimes employees become so stressed that they experience **burnout,** a condition characterized by (1) *emotional exhaustion,* or being overextended by one's work; (2) *depersonalization,* or a cynical view of others and the work role that often

SADIE DAYTON/CORBIS

results in detachment; and (3) *reduced personal accomplishment,* or the belief that one is no longer very useful or successful at one's job.

Burnout was originally believed to be limited to the helping professions, such as medicine and psychology (Cordes & Dougherty, 1993). Since then, however, it has been recognized as a more widespread phenomenon (Demerouti, Bakker, Nachreiner, & Schaufeli, 2001) and linked to characteristics of jobs (e.g., workload, control, rewards, social relationships, fairness, and values) rather than to dispositions of people (Maslach, 2003). Work-related stress can be so overwhelming that some individuals lose a sense of self or begin to lack self-esteem. In cases of chronic high stress, they may even become depressed. Furthermore, burnout has effects on job performance, organizational commitment, and turnover (Eatough, Chang, Miloslavic, & Johnson, 2011; Jawahar et al., 2007).

The third category of strains is physiological in nature. There is considerable evidence for the role of stress in physical conditions. One study, for instance, found both life stress and work stress to be significant predictors of the frequency of serious illnesses (Bhagat et al., 1995). In the United States alone, over 2,400 people die each day from heart disease (Centers for Disease Control, 2009). Stress plays an integral role in heart disease, and workplace stress is a major culprit. The leading cause of disability in the U.S. workforce are heart disease and stroke (Centers for Disease Control, 2009).

In addition, there is substantial evidence that managers experience a great deal of stress—the level of which has been increasing in recent years (Cohen, 1997). A study of more than 800 upper-level managers reported some interesting results along these lines (Cavanaugh, Boswell, Roehling, & Boudreau, 2000). According to the researchers, stress is either *challenge-related* or *hindrance-related.* Challenge-related stress—which results from time pressures at work, high levels of responsibility, and job overload—is positively related to job satisfaction and negatively related to searching for a new job. In other words, stress related to being challenged at work has positive outcomes for the manager and for the organization. The researchers also found that hindrance-related stress—which results from constraints that interfere with one's work—is negatively related to job satisfaction and positively related to job searching and voluntary turnover. Hindrance-related stress is often due to red tape, organizational politics, and job insecurity. In fact, employees who reported high levels of hindrance-related stress tended to be much less satisfied; they were also much more likely to search for new jobs (Cavanaugh et al., 2000). Clearly, these two types of stress have potentially important differential effects on outcome variables.

Coping with Stress

Stress is clearly a problem for many employees, but fortunately there are coping mechanisms that can help. **Coping** is defined as efforts that help people manage or reduce stress. Some of these techniques are listed in Table 11.1. For instance, to handle the stress that comes with reduced supervision because of cutbacks in managerial positions, employees can develop their own responsibilities and objectives and seek high-quality feedback from coworkers, supervisors, and subordinates.

coping
Efforts that help people manage or reduce stress.

problem-focused coping
A coping style that involves behaviors or actions targeted toward solving or handling the stress-inducing problem itself.

emotion-focused coping
A coping style that involves cognitive, or thought-related, strategies that minimize the emotional effects of stress-inducing events.

Coping mechanisms take two general forms: problem-focused coping and emotion-focused coping. **Problem-focused coping** involves behaviors or actions targeted toward solving or handling the stress-inducing problem itself. One example might be compromising with a coworker on a particular conflict. **Emotion-focused coping**, on the other hand, involves cognitive, or thought-related, strategies that minimize the emotional effects of stress-inducing events. Examples include rationalizing or intellectualizing, looking for the "silver lining," and making the best of a bad situation.

One study suggested that the effectiveness of coping depends on the coping method, the particular stressor, and one's view of oneself (i.e., self-efficacy; Jex, Bliese, Buzzell, & Primeau, 2001). For instance, researchers have shown the coping process to be very complex in situations in which employees have to adjust to an organizational merger over time (Fugate, Kinicki, & Scheck, 2002). An interesting study conducted in Germany and Switzerland found that the extent to which employees used their time away from work to psychologically detach from work was key to protecting their well-being and keeping them engaged at work (Sonnentag, Binnewies, & Mojza, 2010). So the better we use our downtime from work, the less stressed we will be and the fewer strains we'll experience.

A recent study showed that emotional competence (EC) training can improve employee subjective and physical well-being (Kotsou, Nelis, Gregoire, & Mikolajczak, 2011). Emotional competence is the ability to understand, express, and manage feelings. EC has been linked to general well-being as well as work and academic performance. This interesting study of 132 participants found that those randomly assigned to an EC training program—which included group discussions, role-play, and self-observation—showed a significant improvement in EC along with a decrease in perceived and objective stress, a decrease in physical complaints, and improved social relationships (Kotsou et al., 2011). Incredibly, these changes lasted for over a year. Obviously, there is great potential in this kind of intervention as a coping technique.

In addition to coping styles, social support can play a huge role in helping us deal with stress. I'm sure you've experienced this firsthand. It's always easier to handle stress-inducing events or situations if you have others around to provide the kind of support you need. In the workplace, for instance, credible senior-level employees or peers who make an effort to convince you that you can succeed may help you push through stressful situations and rise to the occasion. Quite a few studies have demonstrated the importance of social support in dealing with stress (e.g., Bliese & Britt, 2001; Zellars & Perrewé, 2001). For instance, problem-focused coping along with supervisory support of family-related issues results in a decrease in work–family conflict (Lapierre & Allen, 2006); problem-focused coping results in reduced strain (Searle, 2008). Even family support can contribute to lowering stress at work.

■ Environmental Determinants of Well-Being

As I pointed out in Chapter 1, employment is a central element of our lives. Certainly, some individuals are more apt than others to define and view themselves with respect to their jobs or occupations; but all in all, our work is important to most of us. In his research and writing, Peter Warr takes a very useful approach toward helping

I/O psychologists gain an understanding about work processes. He has spent years developing his model of the environmental determinants of well-being (Warr, 1999, 2007a) and has applied this model to job-related well-being, which is a function of people's feelings about themselves in relation to their jobs (Warr, 1999). Indeed, Warr argues that the workplace is central to mental health. His framework provides a way of further investigating how individuals interact with the workplace.

Warr's 10 environmental determinants of well-being are listed in Table 11.2. The more employees experience these determinants on the job, the less likely they are to experience negative well-being, which, according to Warr, is reflected in anxiety, displeasure, and depression rather than enthusiasm, pleasure, and comfort. Let's consider each of the determinants in turn.

Opportunity for personal control refers to one's ability to control situations and events at work. We have discussed in various chapters (and earlier in this chapter) the importance of participation, freedom to choose, and job autonomy. *Opportunity for skill use* is the extent to which employees are encouraged to use and develop skills. Not having the opportunity to develop their skills can be stifling for employees, resulting in a negative sense of well-being. Employees who enjoy *variety* at work don't do the same old thing each day but, rather, have an assortment of tasks and responsibilities. *Environmental clarity* has to do with whether employees have a clear understanding of current and future expectations, as reflected in the amount and quality of feedback they receive at

Table 11.2 Warr's Environmental Determinants of Well-Being

Environmental Determinants	Links to I/O Theory
1. Opportunity for personal control	Job characteristics theory
2. Opportunity for skill use	Job characteristics theory
3. Variety	Job characteristics theory
4. Environmental clarity	Job characteristics theory
5. Valued social position	Job characteristics theory
6. Externally generated goals	Intrinsic motivation and reinforcement theories
7. Availability of money	Intrinsic motivation and reinforcement theories
8. Physical security	Maslow's hierarchy of needs, ERG
9. Supportive supervision	
10. Opportunity for interpersonal contact	

work. *Valued social position* is the extent to which employees gain prestige or a sense of accomplishment from their work.

Do these first five determinants remind you of anything? Recall that in Chapter 9 we discussed job characteristics theory and the effect of factors like feedback, autonomy, skill variety, task significance, and task identity on certain psychological states, which lead to outcomes such as job satisfaction, high motivation, and high work quality. In this sense, the work of Warr is consistent with job characteristics theory. Table 11.2 lists this theory and others in relation to each of Warr's environmental determinants.

Externally generated goals and the *availability of money* may be familiar from previous discussions about motivation. In this context, goals have to do with task demands; a job that requires very little from employees is not likely to be challenging or stimulating. And although having money doesn't guarantee positive well-being, not having what one considers to be enough money can result in a devastatingly negative sense of well-being. Much the same can be said about *physical security*, which has to do with working conditions and safety.

The last two determinants, *supportive supervision* and *opportunity for interpersonal contact*, deal with the social atmosphere at work. As discussed in previous chapters in the context of interpersonal relationships, having an understanding, supportive, and effective boss is quite important to employees' well-being, as are their opportunities for social interactions with peers, supervisors, subordinates, and customers.

Warr (1999) has reviewed dozens of empirical studies demonstrating the relevance of these factors to well-being in the workplace. For the most part, the more one's job provides these factors, the more positive one's well-being is likely to be. However, where some of these determinants are concerned, there may be a point at which more *isn't* better. For instance, employees tend to be favorably disposed toward jobs that demand a lot from them and provide a good deal of responsibility. However, too many demands and too much responsibility can easily result in overload, stress, and a negative sense of well-being. In fact, jobs that combine very high demands with very low opportunity for control tend to be extremely stressful. Although Warr places considerable emphasis on the environmental (i.e., job-related) determinants of well-being, he also makes it clear that one's job environment and experiences are not wholly independent of other life experiences. We turn now to a discussion of the two most salient elements of individuals' lives, work and family, which appear to be quite closely linked.

■ Work–Family Conflict

Never before has the interplay between work and family been the focus of so much talk at work, at home, in the neighborhood, at places of worship, and, especially, in research labs across the United States. According to one survey, the number-one priority for 78% of all employees is to successfully balance their work and personal lives (Gregg, 1998). In the last 20 to 30 years, the American family has undergone some significant changes that have had widespread impact on organizational life as well. In this section, I consider some of these changes and what they typically mean for today's employees who try so hard to successfully juggle their work and family responsibilities.

Recent models of work–family conflict have begun to examine its bidirectional nature. In other words, family life affects work life, and work life affects family life. The model presented in Figure 11.2 clearly shows that both organizational and personal variables have an impact on work–family conflict and work–family enrichment, which have both organizational and personal outcomes. **Work–family conflict (WFC)** exists when the two domains don't fit well together and results in one role having a negative effect on the other (Hammer, Cullen, Neal, Sinclair, & Shafiro, 2005). **Work–family enrichment** occurs when attitudes and behaviors are believed to have a positive carryover from one domain to the other (Greenhaus & Powell, 2006). Traditionally, this kind of approach has been termed a *spillover model*. Another form of spillover was identified by a recent study that found commuters to perceive greater stress than noncommuters. Furthermore, driving experiences during their morning commute (especially for men) affected their aggression and hostility at work for the rest of the day (Hennessy, 2008). Another recent study, this one conducted in China, found that workers who experienced more work–family conflict tended to drink more alcohol and that this relationship was affected by peer drinking norms and social support (Wang, Liu, Zhan, & Shi, 2010).

An interesting recent study of Israeli workers explored various work-based and family-based coping techniques for dealing with or minimizing *work interfering with family conflict* (WIF) and *family interfering with work conflict* (FIW). The authors showed that different coping techniques seem to work better for different people—in other words, the success of coping strategies may be a function of people and situations (Somech & Drach-Zahavy, 2007). For instance, they found that nontraditional women and

work–family conflict (WFC) A model of work–family relations in which work and family demands are incompatible.

work–family enrichment A model of work–family relations in which positive attitudes and behaviors are believed to carry over from one domain to the other.

FIGURE 11.2 Conceptual Model of Work–Family Interface

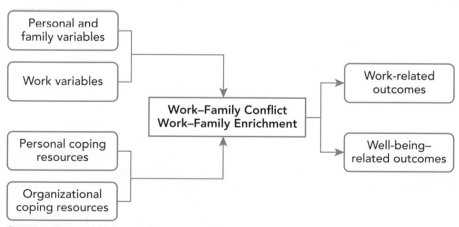

Source: Frone, Yardley, & Markel (1997)

RICK GOMEZ/CORBIS

▲ **A Closer Look**
How do WIF, FIW, and spillover affect employees' relationships with their families?

traditional men deal with FIW conflict by exerting extra effort at work and delegating responsibilities at home. This allows them to focus on their jobs, which are very important to these two groups, while also serving the needs of the family. Vastly different patterns emerged for nontraditional men, who chose to emphasize the family and delegate at work so that work didn't interfere with their family role.

Considerable research support exists for the effects of work–family conflict on both personal and organizational outcomes. For instance, employees with high levels of work–family conflict tend to be less satisfied with their jobs ($r = -.31$) and their lives ($r = -.36$) than their low-conflict counterparts (Kossek & Ozeki, 1998). Furthermore, the spillover is stronger for WIF conflict than for FIW conflict. In addition, a recent and thorough meta-analysis demonstrated convincingly that work domain variables such as job involvement and job stress influence WIF conflict, which impacts family satisfaction (Ford, Heinen, & Langkamer, 2007). On the flip side, family domain variables like family conflict and family stress influence FIW conflict, which impacts job satisfaction.

These interesting results suggest the importance of both work and family and even explain how one might spill over to affect the other and vice versa. However, we need to be wary of our Western bias: Because most I/O psychology research has been conducted in predominantly White Western cultures, we cannot conclude that these findings generalize across other cultures. For example, a recent study (Grzywacz et al., 2007) using in-depth interviews of Latinos employed in the North Carolina poultry-processing industry concluded that these employees experienced little WFC as compared with the studies we've discussed to this point. The researchers argued that this was due to the collectivistic nature of the Latino culture, where hard work is valued and seen as securing one's family's well-being. Little conflict is perceived between work and family because of the value placed on work in service to the family. Latina women did experience more WFC, but much of it was due to the physical demands of their jobs. Other studies have also found other cultural differences in WFC as well as gender differences (e.g., Grzywacz, Almeida, & McDonald, 2002).

The common belief has always been that women give their family roles greater priority than do men, even when comparing men and women with careers outside the home (see Grzywacz et al., 2007). It follows, then, that the career satisfaction of women versus men should be more affected by work–family conflict. Martins, Eddleston, and Veiga (2002) found this to be the case in their survey of more than 1,000 professionals from more than 100 organizations: WFC was not significantly related to career satisfaction for men ($r = -.07$), but it was for women ($r = -.23$). Furthermore, they found that this pattern held up for women at all ages; but for older men, work–family conflict became more important. That is, for men over 40, work–family conflict was significantly related to career satisfaction ($r = -.26$), suggesting that men reprioritize their life domains as they age, making family more central. The authors note that this finding is consistent with early theoretical work suggesting that men are less willing to sacrifice family relationships later in their lives and thus are less tolerant of work–family conflict.

In another interesting study, Baltes and Heydens-Gahir (2003) applied Baltes's *life management theory* to WFC. Basically, they found that individuals who identify and set goals, who develop and refine strategies for achieving those goals, and who are flexible enough to employ alternative approaches when the initial targeted approach isn't working both perceive less job and work stress and report low levels of work–family conflict. It's also important to understand that boundaries help us keep domains separate or allow for some interaction across domains. Some people want very segmented domains with thick boundaries separating them; others want more integrated domains with thin, more permeable boundaries. A model of boundaries involved in WFC has been proposed that emphasizes the match between one's desired boundaries and one's environment (Kreiner, Hollensbe, & Sheep, 2009). Furthermore, this very interesting model proposes four general tactics used to manage our boundaries: behavioral (e.g., using technology), temporal (e.g., blocking off segments of time), physical (e.g., creating a separate work space at home), and communicative (e.g., setting and communicating rules to others). I expect that this model will be tested in future research and used to help us better understand work–home boundary issues.

Earlier, I discussed the importance of social support in relieving stress; this seems particularly important with respect to work–family conflict. A study that surveyed over 400 government employees who were married and/or had children at home found that individuals who develop strong social support networks at work and at home perceive less stress in both their organizational and family lives (Carlson & Perrewé, 1999). A study of 2,100 respondents from the 2002 National Study of the Changing Workforce found that a supportive work–family culture results in less WFC and stress (Voydanoff, 2005).

It seems that work–family research has traditionally focused on WFC, but experts in this area have become increasingly aware that to understand work–family dynamics requires more research on work–family enrichment (Hammer et al., 2005). Although not much research has examined work–family enrichment yet, we do know that it is positively related to physical and mental health, as well as to job and family satisfaction, and that it is negatively related to problem drinking and depression (for similar results and the validation of a newer measure of work–family enrichment, see Hanson, Hammer, & Colton, 2004).

Data from the 2004 Study of Overwork in America indicate that one-third of all U.S. employees are chronically overworked (Galinsky et al., 2004); this leads to lower performance, increased anger, and increased resentment at work as well as personal outcomes such as high levels of stress symptoms, clinical depression, and poor health. Furthermore, employees who are family-centric, or at least prioritize family and work equally, are less likely to be overworked than those who are work-centric (Galinsky et al., 2004).

In a special issue of the *International Journal of Stress Management*, researchers (O'Driscoll et al., 2003) found that organizational and supervisory support for family life were related to key stress and strain variables, suggesting an important role for family-friendly policies in organizations. And, in fact, many companies offer family-friendly programs, or what are often called *work-life supports* (Sahibzada, Hammer, Neal, & Kuang, 2005), to alleviate some of the stress experienced by workers. Some research has found that the extent to which a woman experiences WFC or enrichment upon her return from maternity leave strongly affects mental and physical health and even the likelihood of turnover (Carlson et al., 2011). Table 11.3 provides a list of some of these programs.

Data from 2,810 employees surveyed in the 2002 National Study of the Changing Workforce provide an interesting look at work-life supports (for a summary, see

---

Table 11.3 Work–Life Supports Offered by Organizations

Traditional Benefits	Nontraditional Benefits

Child-care benefits
  Onsite child-care centers
  Informational assistance
  Financial assistance
  Sick-child care
	Convenience benefits
	  Onsite physicians, dry cleaning, postal services, etc.
	  Take-home meals
	  Preferred banking

Elder-care benefits
  Counseling
  Informational assistance
  Geriatric care management
  Financial assistance
	Health promotion benefits
	  Onsite fitness centers
	  Health screening
	  Flu shots
	  Counseling services

Flexible work arrangements
  Flextime
  Part-time options
  Job-sharing
  Telecommuting
	Education assistance benefits
	  Tutoring
	  Tuition reimbursement
	  Scholarships
	  Student loan assistance

Leave/time-off policies
  Maternity leaves
  Family and medical leaves
  Parental leaves
  Educational leaves
	Housing assistance programs
	  Relocation programs
	  Seminars
	  Home-purchase savings accounts
	  Preferred mortgage arrangements

	Group purchase programs
	  Discounts at local merchants
	  Auto-purchase arrangements
	  Group auto and home insurance

Bond & Galinsky, 2006). Fifteen practices/policies (i.e., supports) were identified to define what is meant by workplace flexibility. Many of these are listed in Table 11.3. The researchers found some interesting differences between the availability of these supports for middle-and higher-income employees (i.e., annual income of $40,000 or more) versus lower-income employees (i.e., annual income of $40,000 or less). For instance, whereas 79% of the middle/high-income employees report being allowed some paid time for personal illness, only 39% of low-income employees report the same benefit. Fifty-four percent of the middle/high-income employees report being allowed a few days off without loss of pay to care for a sick child, whereas only 24% of low-income employees report the same support. Forty-five percent of the middle/high-income employees report having the opportunity to take advantage of flextime, whereas only 33% of the low-income employees report the same opportunity.

Combining all 15 components of flexibility, they categorized 30% of the middle/high-income employees as high in overall workplace flexibility, compared with only 10% of the low-income employees; 38% of the low-income employees were coded as low in overall workplace flexibility, compared with 19% of the middle/high-income employees (Bond & Galinsky, 2006).

This analysis by income level suggests that we still have far to go in giving support to those who may be most in need of some workplace flexibility. However, we need to recognize that even things that are generally positive for organizations and employees alike may have a potential downside, too. For instance, a recent study surveyed 454 telecommuters from a high-tech firm. This study found that telecommuting reduced the extent to which work interfered with family (WIF) but *increased* the extent to which family interfered with work (FIW)—and this increase was larger for larger households (Golden, Veiga, & Simsek, 2006). Apparently, for employees who spend considerable time telecommuting from home, there is the potential for the family domain to interfere with work outcomes.

Let's look at a few particularly innovative programs. NRG Insurance is a Seattle company that won a 2006 Alfred P. Sloan Award for Business Excellence in Workplace Flexibility (Families and Work Institute, 2007). This is one of the largest woman-owned brokerage companies in the United States, where all employees are required to work at home one day per week; that way, according to the company owner, they can concentrate better without the phones ringing all around them. All staff members take a three-hour break one Friday afternoon per month and get one month off (a paid sabbatical) every five years.

Another Sloan winner is Intel, which gives all 5,000 employees in a microchip manufacturing plant in Arizona two consecutive months off, fully paid, every seven years. Intel argues that this allows employees to come back rested and recharged, able to throw themselves back into the very demanding world of innovation and creativity. Employees can also tap additional time to further their education—and Intel pays the bill.

Fortune magazine publishes its list of the 100 best companies to work for based on surveys and an audit of the company's culture ("100 Best Companies," 2008). In 2008, Google emerged at the top of the list for the second straight year. A few Google perks

E. Jeffrey Hill

PhD, 1995, Family and Human Development, Utah State University
Consultant, Work and Family Issues, IBM Global Workforce Diversity
Associate Professor, School of Family Life, Brigham Young University

I have worked at IBM for 30 years. In one five-year stretch, I had five different IBM jobs and lived in Washington, Utah, New York, Georgia, and Arizona. I traveled extensively and worked long hours.

I found myself becoming a casual occupant in our home. I missed birthdays, ball games, plays, concerts, recitals, and parent–teacher conferences. I began to worry that I was living to work instead of working to live.

In 1990, I was offered a promotion to do employee surveys for IBM. But the job was in New York and the commute horrendous. I decided to accept the job with conditions. I reasoned with my future boss that I could better design surveys and analyze results through a modem from my home. To my surprise, she agreed to let me try it.

The difference in my life was immediate. Instantly, I gained an hour and a half a day because I didn't have to drive to and from work. I could roll out of bed early with an exciting idea and immediately type it into the laptop.

I became more focused, energized, and productive at work. Without the constant interruptions of coworkers, I was able to deliver higher-quality surveys and analyses in less time. The arrangement worked so well that soon four of my colleagues were working from home as well.

In the mid-1990s, IBM began to implement what was called the "virtual office" in a big way. Soon 25,000 IBMers no longer had dedicated IBM offices but were given laptops, cell phones, and pagers. Controlled research findings were similar to my personal experience. On the work side, telecommuting at IBM was associated with increased productivity, higher morale, greater organizational commitment, and better customer relationships. On the family side, telecommuting was found to have a positive influence on family relationships and well-being.

Sure, it's true that telecommuting works better in some jobs than others. But for me and thousands of telecommuters I have studied at IBM and in other companies, the flexibility alluded to in this chapter has been a positive step toward resolving work–family conflict.

Applying Your Knowledge

1. Discuss Dr. Hill's experience of telecommuting in the context of the benefits described in this chapter.

2. Why is schedule flexibility so important to workers in the 21st century?

3. What are the potential long-term benefits of telecommuting for IBM (or any other company)?

---

include an onsite child-care center, an onsite fitness center, subsidized gym membership, telecommuting, an emphasis on green technologies, options to control projects one works on, choice of departments to work in, and a nondiscrimination policy that includes protections related to sexual orientation and domestic partner benefits for same-sex couples.

Whole Foods Market is a natural and organic food market that employs over 40,000 people in the United States alone. It provides 100% healthcare coverage (only 20 other companies in the list of the 100 best provide this), subsidized gym memberships, a compressed workweek, and telecommuting options, along with same-sex partner benefits and a nondiscrimination policy. These and other benefits garnered them a #16 ranking in 2008. I would encourage you to read through the *Fortune* list,

DILBERT: © SCOTT ADAMS/DISTRIBUTED BY UNITED FEATURE SYNDICATE, INC.

◀ **A Closer Look**
Certainly, most managers have a better handle on the importance of work–family issues than Alice's boss does. In real life, what are the pros and cons of letting employees work from home?

its measurement approach, and the descriptions of what various companies are doing. Think about what factors would be most important to you at this point in your life and perhaps how your values and priorities might change over time.

We now turn to a more detailed discussion of three work–family supports that are being more frequently offered by organizations as well as one work-family trend that continues to grow in importance.

Family-Leave Policies

As discussed in Chapter 7, the first piece of legislation signed into law by President Bill Clinton was the Family and Medical Leave Act (FMLA), which allows eligible employees to take job-protected, unpaid leave for up to 12 weeks because of family-related issues such as the birth of a child, serious health condition of a family member, or one's own serious health condition (see also the new regulations discussed in Chapter 7, which went into effect in January 2009). The United States is actually a late arrival in this respect; many other countries have had formal family-leave programs and laws in place for over 30 years. Nevertheless, many U.S. companies provided some form of family leave to their employees before it was mandated by law; indeed, many states have had family-leave policies for state employees since 1978.

Hungary and Sweden first introduced parental leave in 1967 and 1974, respectively. **Parental leave** was developed to enable employees to combine work and family responsibilities related to child rearing; many countries provide for this type of leave for children up to the age of three and, in some cases, until school age. Belgium has a rather distinctive program: Employees can take a *career break,* with an allowance payable by unemployment insurance, provided that the employer hires an unemployed person to replace the worker on leave.

Although family-leave programs can provide great relief for many employees for whom juggling family and work responsibilities is a major priority and an increasingly complex task, such programs are not without their problems. About 40% of employees taking advantage of the FMLA are forced to cut their leave short because they can't afford to go without pay during the entire leave—and 25% actually borrow money to make ends meet. Some experts in this area are advocating making family leave affordable for the majority of workers who cannot utilize it in its current form. Many other bills have been introduced in Congress to expand the FMLA, but none have worked

parental leave
A program offered by organizations that enables employees to combine work and family responsibilities related to child rearing.

their way through the congressional system yet. The most recent is the Family Leave Insurance Act of 2009, which would amend the FMLA to provide paid leave for 8 of the allowable 12 weeks. Of course, many foresee this kind of law as resulting in huge unemployment costs to employers.

Child-Care Benefits

If you have children and work outside the home, then you know how frustrating it can be to balance your work responsibilities with the care that you want to provide for your kids. Many studies have linked child-care difficulties not only to employee absenteeism, tardiness, productivity, and leaving work early but also to indirect effects on coworkers' productivity (e.g., Erickson, Nichols, & Ritter, 2000; Tetrick, Miles, Marcil, & Van Dosen, 1994). In fact, a general conclusion is that an employee who fills the dual role of full-time employee and parent (i.e., who has a child under 18 living at home) tends to experience lower psychological well-being, decreased life and marital satisfaction, and increased work–family conflict (Sahibzada et al., 2005). Given the effect of child-care problems on employee morale, productivity, and well-being, many companies have begun to give serious attention to child-care benefits and other child-care programs.

Four of these child-care benefits are listed in Table 11.3. Some organizations provide resources that inform employees of other child-care facilities in the area. They may also provide some financial assistance to employees to help cover the high costs of child care. But perhaps the most interesting benefit is the onsite child-care center. This is a popular feature—29 of the 100 best companies to work for in 2008 provide this support. In a survey of employees who worked at hospitals with onsite child-care centers, researchers found that active users of the onsite center were more likely to believe that the center was a good recruitment and retention tool for the company than were those employees not actively using the center (Kossek & Nichol, 1992). Also, those using the center held more positive attitudes toward managing their work and family responsibilities than did those who weren't using the center.

In another example, according to a survey of individuals employed by two companies with onsite child-care centers (Rothausen, Gonzalez, Clarke, & O'Dell, 1998), current, future, and past users of the centers had more positive reactions to the center than did nonusers. In particular, they were more likely than nonusers to report that the centers were associated with recruitment and retention benefits and that they were pleased with the company's support of the centers.

▼ **A Closer Look**
How might the availability of affordable child-care options affect employees' absenteeism, attitudes, and productivity?

YELLOW DOG PRODUCTIONS/GETTY IMAGES

Elder-Care Assistance

Some might say that child care was the family-friendly emphasis of the 1980s and 1990s (Perry-Jenkins, Repetti, & Crouter, 2000), but for the first few decades of the 21st century, the emphasis will most certainly be on elder care. According to a major study by the National Alliance for Caregiving and the American Association of Retired Persons (AARP), there are 22.4 million U.S. households providing care to elderly relatives or friends (Crute, 2007). It is expected that going forward half of the workforce will be caregivers in the very near future (Smith, 2012).

Here is the typical profile of a caregiver: a 46-year-old employed woman who spends about 18 hours per week caring for her mother, who lives nearby. Her mother is 77 years old, lives alone, and has a chronic illness (Timmermann, 1999). Sixty percent of caregivers are women, and over 60% of them work full time. In addition, 45% of today's working caregivers are men. Most problematic is the fact that 41% of the caregivers are caring for children under 18 at the same time they are caring for an elderly parent! The members of this generation of baby boomers (born between 1946 and 1964) have thus been labeled the *sandwiched generation* because they provide care to both their children and their parents and often feel stuck in the middle. Obviously, financing child care and elder care at the same time can be extremely costly, and the enormous stress these caregivers experience often results in health problems of their own.

The statistics are amazing. The U.S. Census Bureau projects that there will be more than 70 million Americans over age 65 by 2030—doubling in the 30 years between 2000 and 2030 (Seaward, 1999). It is estimated that the elderly will make up 20% of the U.S. population by 2030. Furthermore, the fastest-growing subpopulation of the elderly comprises people over 85, who are most likely to be in need of care ("America in 2050," 2012).

Given these demographics, employers have begun to respond to elder-care needs; according to one estimate, over 50% of employers now offer some form of elder-care services, up from 40% in 1998 (Gonzalez, 2004). As more and more employers begin to recognize the importance of elder-care benefits to employees, this percentage should increase considerably (much as the percentage of child-care programs has done). Some recent data are likely to motivate employers to move quickly in this direction: The MetLife Caregiving Cost Study reports that U.S. companies lose between $17 billion and $34 billion annually on lost productivity due to caregiving responsibilities (MetLife Mature Market Institute, 2006). Caring for elderly parents from afar costs companies 15 million workdays per year. The major expenditures include replacement costs for employees ($6.6 billion), absenteeism costs ($5.1 billion), and costs due to workday interruptions ($6.3 billion).

▼ **A Closer Look**
How is the baby boomer generation forcing modern-day companies to evaluate their elder-care benefits?

JOSE LUIS PELAEZ INC./GETTY IMAGES

The most prevalent elder-care services offered by organizations are resource and informational assistance, dependent-care accounts, seminars, counseling, and long-term insurance (Work Options Group, 2006). Some employers have begun reimbursing their employees for elder-care expenses, with a limit on the funds provided, and certain large companies have even established onsite intergenerational day-care centers (e.g., Oakwood Healthcare). Perhaps the fastest-growing benefit is geriatric care management, whereby the employer provides certified professionals to go to an elderly person's home and assess his or her well-being and specific needs (Prudential Financial, Inc.). Furthermore, the professional may also provide an onsite review of an elder-care facility for the employee (Gonzalez, 2004). Other organizations provide long-term insurance for parents, grandparents, and so on (e.g., Cornell University) and 80 hours per year of backup care (e.g., Verizon Wireless).

Experts who work in the areas of family-friendly benefits and elder care argue that caregiving for the elderly directly affects employees' performance, causing them to report late for work, to work fewer hours, and, sometimes, to resign or retire early (Seaward, 1999). Of the 22.4 million individuals who indicated on the AARP survey that they were providing care to an older parent or friend, about half reported that they took time off, came in late, and worked fewer hours because of their caregiving responsibilities. Conversely, employees who don't have to worry about caring for an elderly individual are more satisfied with their jobs as well as more productive (Seaward, 1999). According to Ceridian Corporation, the largest dependent-care resource provider, 16% of employee caregivers leave the workforce to provide full-time care (Gonzalez, 2004).

Empirical work has indeed begun to examine the impact of elder-care responsibilities on workplace functioning. For example, a comprehensive survey was administered to over 400 employees from various organizations across the United States in an attempt to examine organizational responses to employees' growing elder-care concerns (Goodstein, 1995). Among its interesting findings were the following. First, the more female employees there were in the organization, the more likely the company was to be involved in elder-care issues. Second, the more work–family benefits the organization provided, the more likely the organization was to provide elder-care benefits as well. Third, the more the company perceived that elder-care benefits improve productivity, the higher the level of company involvement in elder care. Fourth, and perhaps most interesting, the more the company worked with other companies that emphasized work–family issues, the more likely the company was to become involved in elder care. This last finding suggests that an organization is somewhat affected by the values, attitudes, and benefits associated with its clients and business partners. Finally, a more recent study found that employees who were provided with elder-care benefits reported greater organizational commitment (Singleton, 2001).

Dual-Earner Couples

dual-earner couple
A couple in which both members are employed and maintain a family life.

We turn now to a discussion of dual-earner couples, a trend in the world of work that is clearly and logically linked to work–family conflict. A **dual-earner couple** is one in which both members are employed and maintain a family life. As this topic plays a role in the changing nature of work and the demographic characteristics of the current labor force, let's add a few more statistics to the mix. In 1994, 75% of all women between the ages of 25 and 54 were in the U.S. labor force—a statistic that has stayed fairly constant (U.S. Bureau of Labor Statistics, 2007). In 1996, the percentage of married couples who both worked was more than 60%; by 2002, this number had grown to 78% (Bond, 2002). According to the Census Bureau, only 17% of U.S. households conform to the traditional model of a dad who brings home the wages and a mom who stays home and takes care of the kids.

One motivating factor for women to work in addition to their spouses is that they now make about 81% of what men make—up from 63% in 1979 (Kelleher, 2007). In fact, a survey by Catalyst, a research group that focuses on working women, found that 85% of the respondents listed increased income as the biggest advantage of a dual-earner situation and that 56% noted a lack of time as the biggest challenge (Kate, 1998). In an interview in *Forbes* magazine, Ralph Gomory, president of the Sloan Foundation and former director of the research labs at IBM, provided an interesting take on the notion that everyone is working harder and putting in more hours: "It's not that one individual is working longer so much as that two people are now doing three jobs. In the past, one person did the working job and the other one brought up the family, took care of the home, built a social network or anything else you want to describe in that category. It was never recognized as a job. But it was" (quoted in Machan, 1999).

In other words, for the dual-earner couple there are now two jobs outside the home and one inside. Needless to say, this situation takes more effort and is more difficult. As for the job of taking care of the home and the kids, men still do less than their fair share—even when their wives are working full time. However, according to the University of Michigan Institute for Social Research, American men do over seven hours of housework per week, which is double what they did in 1968. The disparity is much worse in Japan, where a government survey found that husbands in dual-earner families devote less than eight minutes per day to housework, while their income-earning wives spend over three hours on domestic duties (Beck, 1998).

Although little academic research focused on dual-earner couples in the past, interest has increased of late. One study, for instance, looked at the effects of work and nonwork influences on the career satisfaction of dual-earner couples in Hong Kong and found some interesting results (Aryee & Luk, 1996). First, work-related variables

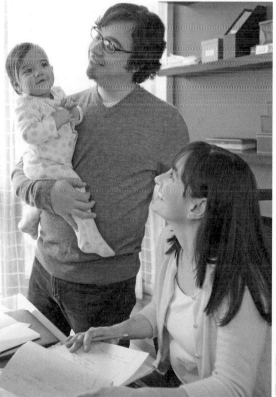

▼ **A Closer Look**
How do role-sharing dual-career marriages differ from conventional dual-career marriages?

GETTY IMAGES

are better predictors of career satisfaction than are nonwork-related variables. Among the predictors for both husbands and wives are supervisor support, the extent to which employees' skills are optimized on the job, and the extent to which employees feel they are an important part of the organization. Second, the only nonwork-related variable that is important to both husbands and wives is satisfaction with child-care arrangements. Given the previous discussion about child-care benefits, this finding makes a great deal of sense. Third—and this surprised the authors—results for both husbands and wives were parallel. In other words, the same variables seemed to be important predictors of career satisfaction for both husbands and wives, indicating considerable agreement about what these partners see as integral to making their dual-earner situation successful.

In a national sample of 234 sandwiched-generation dual-earner couples, Hammer and colleagues (2005) uncovered longitudinal crossover effects regarding both work–family conflict and work–family enrichment. Crossover effects refer to the transmission of stress, strain, and depression from one member of a couple to the other. For instance, they found that husbands' work–family enrichment (i.e., positive spillover) was negatively related to wives' depression one year later; a parallel effect was found from wives' family–work enrichment to husbands' depression. This is the first study to highlight the important role of a dyad member's positive spillover from work to family or family to work in the well-being of the other member of the dyad. An even more recent study of dual-earner parents in the Netherlands found support for a model in which one partner's job demands affect his or her WIF conflict. The resources he or she must channel into the job leave little reserves for home activities; this increases demands on his or her partner at home, affecting the partner's level of FIW conflict and leading to the partner's exhaustion (Bakker, Demerouti, & Dollard, 2008).

Another study has taken a different approach by surveying over 170 career-oriented college women in the United States about their expectations and desires regarding future careers and family life (Hallett & Gilbert, 1997). Participants were limited to those who reported that they envisioned themselves in a dual-career marriage. Based on the responses, the authors classified each student as expecting either a *conventional dual-career marriage,* in which the female maintains primary responsibility for the home and the children while simply adding a career to her responsibilities, or a *role-sharing dual-career marriage,* in which both spouses actively pursue careers and actively involve themselves in the household and parenting.

One interesting finding was that women who expected a role-sharing marriage were significantly more likely than their conventional counterparts to be committed to a lifelong, time-consuming career. They were also higher in self-esteem, suggesting that this attribute allowed them to consider a less conventional option (Hallett & Gilbert, 1997). In addition, having a spouse who would involve himself in managing the household and parenting the children was more important to those women looking for a role-sharing marriage than to those looking for a more conventional dual-career relationship. The authors concluded that many college-educated women today are thinking about their futures in ways quite different from those of earlier generations.

No longer must women choose between a career and a family; today's college-educated women believe that both are possible. Fortunately, many are leading the way in demonstrating how to make this work so that everyone involved can benefit.

I conclude this section on work–family conflict with a quote from Robert Haas, chairman of Levi Strauss:

> We used to think you could separate the soft stuff from the hard stuff—the soft stuff was our commitment to the workforce—and the hard stuff—what really mattered—was getting pants out the door. No more. Now we know you can't get stuff out the door unless your employees are 100% committed and free of home life distractions. And the way you get them there is simple. You do everything you can to help them handle those home life issues. So work and family can co-exist, successfully. (quoted in MacGregor, 1999)

I don't think it's much of a stretch to predict that the companies emerging as future national and world leaders are likely to be the ones that subscribe to the simple but accurate reflections of Mr. Haas. In fact, a close look at today's top-drawer companies suggests that this is already happening. In *Fortune* magazine's "100 Best Companies to Work For," the most important criterion is the extent to which these companies are helping employees balance work and life issues. Its list for 2011 includes some companies you will recognize: Google, Nordstrom, Whole Foods, Microsoft, and Smucker's ("100 Best Companies," 2011).

■ Psychological Effects of Job Loss

Recall that in Chapter 1, when highlighting the reasons why I/O psychology is important and relevant to most of us, I focused on the fact that a large part of who we are is, in some way or another, tied to what we do.

I talked about how being a psychology professor is an integral part of who I am. It affects not only the way I live my life but also my perceptions, beliefs, and attitudes. Is the same true for you? Certainly, some of us identify with our occupation or job more than others; but I really believe that, for the overwhelming majority of us, our occupation is central to who we are. That said, it shouldn't be a surprise to learn that losing one's job is a profoundly stressful event. In fact, research has consistently found job loss to be among the 10 most stressful events in a person's life (Maysent & Spera, 1995). For some, it can be almost as stressful as the loss of a loved one.

Jobs are important to us for various reasons (Cartwright & Cooper, 1997). First, of course, they provide the financial means for living our lives in the manner that we desire. Second, they provide time structure to our day. They determine what time we get up, when we eat lunch, what we do in the afternoon, and when we are available to be home for dinner. If we were to suddenly lose our jobs, this structure would fall apart and leave us unmotivated and without direction. Third, jobs provide an opportunity to use our existing skills and to develop new ones. Without this opportunity, people can become stagnant and bored. Fourth, for most of us, an important feature of our jobs is social interaction with people outside our family. Human beings are social animals, and we all need some degree of social interaction. Our jobs provide an opportunity to interact not only with people who have interests and skills in common but also with those who differ from us in these respects. In other words, at work we have the opportunity to interact with various kinds of people.

Fifth, our jobs help provide a purpose to our lives—in the form of both short-term day-to-day goals and long-term goals regarding career development and advancement. A sense of purpose is crucial; without it, individuals can get stuck "spinning their wheels." Finally, we tend to get a sense of identity and even prestige from our jobs. Being a professor is important to me in part because it is a job that I value and a job that many others in society value—I am pleased with the prestige that goes with being a professor. I didn't choose this profession for that reason alone, of course; but the sense of identity that I receive from my job is very important for my sense of well-being.

The Hard Facts

Whether we call it "rightsizing," "downsizing," "layoffs," or "reductions in force," there's no denying that U.S. corporations have been reducing the size of their work-forces at alarming rates since the late 1980s. From July 1989 to June 1990 alone, nearly 81,000 positions were eliminated in 1,219 U.S. corporations (Schwartz, 1990). Some of the most stable and reliable companies in the world—including United Airlines, DuPont, General Electric, and General Motors—have laid off workers in record numbers. According to one estimate, over 43 million jobs were lost in the United States from 1979 to 1999 (McKinley, Zhao, & Rust, 2000). About 80,000 people lost their jobs because of layoffs in each month of 2004 (Weber, 2004).

For instance, Maytag, the giant appliance maker, laid off over 1,100 employees due to slow sales in the first half of 2004 alone. And in the third quarter of 2008, 1,330 mass layoffs were initiated in the United States, with 218,000 employees separated from their jobs (U.S. Bureau of Labor Statistics, 2008a). A mass layoff is a company action in which at least 50 employees are separated from their jobs. The average size of the layoff during this period was 164 employees, but 48% of the layoffs affected between 50 and 100 employees. Almost 50% of the layoffs were in the manufacturing and construction industries.

Worse still, one study using a very large employment database has reported that U.S. workers are even more concerned about losing their jobs than the data suggest they should be—anxiety about job loss continues to rise (Rudisill & Edwards, 2002; Schmidt, 1999). A perceived lack of career opportunities is related to psychological distress and poor health (Melzer et al., 2010). According to Carol Wilson, a vice president of a firm specializing in employee assistance, when a layoff is announced in a company, 20% of the remaining employees leave the organization either physically or emotionally; another 60% take a "wait and see approach" (Wilson, 2004).

Let's consider some empirical work that looks at how unemployment affects stress levels as well as attitudes and behaviors. First, Sally Grant and Julian Barling (1994) tested a model in which they proposed that the subjective experience of unemployment leads to depression, which leads to negative interactions with one's spouse, which in turn leads to marital dissatisfaction. They found that unemployed individuals' perceptions of time use and negative life events were strong predictors of depressive symptoms. In other words, unemployed individuals who reported that their days lacked time structure and who reported frequent negative life events were also likely to report symptoms of depression, such as a lack of desire to do anything at all and a belief that they were incapable of doing anything valuable. These depressive symptoms in turn predicted negative behaviors such as yelling at, becoming angry with, and being disrespectful toward one's spouse. Finally, these negative behaviors directed toward one's spouse were strongly linked to marital dissatisfaction. This study demonstrates the indirect effects that unemployment can have on behaviors toward one's spouse as well as on marital satisfaction.

In a second study of employees who had lost their jobs as a result of a company closing, coping resources were examined as predictors of distress and reemployment (Gowan, Riordan, & Gatewood, 1999). The researchers operationalized problem-focused coping as job search activity and emotion-focused coping as distancing oneself from the job loss. Their results indicated that the more social support employees had, the better able they were to distance themselves from the job loss. Social support (along with lack of financial resources) also led to job search activities. But employees' ability to distance themselves from the job loss (measured by items like "I remind myself that other people have been in this situation and that I can probably do as well as they did") appeared to be the key variable, as it was negatively related to distress about the job loss and positively related to reemployment.

This study suggests that although stress is likely to follow job loss, coping strategies like getting distance from the event can help to alleviate the stress and make acquiring a new job more likely through more effective interview behavior and more reasonable decisions about job search activities (Gowan et al., 1999).

A third line of research has focused on the stress and pressure involved in being layoff survivors—that is, employees who have survived a layoff but who are left at the workplace to deal with its aftereffects. A review of the literature in this area showed that layoff survivors tend to be less productive, less trusting of the organization and supervisors, more angry and anxious about their futures, and more likely to suffer from low morale and low job satisfaction (Grunberg, Anderson-Connolly, &

▼ **A Closer Look**
How can being laid off affect people's mood, interactions with their spouses, and satisfaction with their marriages?

Greenberg, 2000). In addition, employees' perceptions of the fairness of the process, organizational commitment levels prior to the layoff, and levels of self-esteem affect how survivors respond to the layoffs (see Brockner, Wiesenfeld, & Martin, 1995; Wiesenfeld, Brockner, & Martin, 1999).

One study examined *managers* as layoff survivors, giving careful consideration to procedural justice, organizational commitment, and ensuing managerial behavior (Wiesenfeld, Brockner, & Thibault, 2000). The results from the two studies reported in this article indicated that managers (as opposed to nonmanagers) who perceive injustice in how layoffs are handled tend to report low self-esteem, which seems to be partly a function of their high levels of organizational commitment. They also exhibit less effective managerial behaviors than are necessary in times of organizational change and direct these less effective behaviors toward subordinates, who report a less supportive work environment. A series of studies has also shown perceptions of justice to be very important in determining how employees respond to various organizational changes such as the violation of one's psychological contract (the expectations and responsibilities shared between employees and their employers) and layoffs (Edwards, Rust, McKinley, & Moon, 2003; Kickul, Lester, & Finkl, 2002).

Finally, a new line of research has begun investigating a model of job uncertainty in the downsizing process (Paulsen et al., 2005). This study found that, for a sample of Australian hospital employees whose hospitals were undergoing large-scale restructuring and downsizing, job uncertainty and feelings of personal control were quite low at the anticipation stage of the downsizing, when the environment was most turbulent. The study also found that personal control mediated the negative effects of job uncertainty on both emotional exhaustion and job satisfaction in the anticipation stage and for survivors at the implementation state. Personal control appeared to be less important in the aftermath of downsizing, when the environment became more stable. More research seems necessary to gain a better understanding of the role played by personal control and job uncertainty in this process.

Environmental Determinants—Revisited

I close this section by returning briefly to Warr's environmental determinants of well-being (see Table 11.2). As you may recall, Warr argues that the more employees experience these determinants on the job, the more likely they are to experience positive well-being. Another way to look at the importance of work in our lives is to consider the potential effect that losing one's job has on each of these determinants, along with the more general effect of job loss on overall well-being.

First, work tends to provide people with *opportunity for personal control;* when they lose their jobs, they experience a considerable loss of control, which, in turn, affects their well-being. Second, job loss largely eliminates *opportunity for skill use,* causing some individuals to feel that their skills are being wasted. Third, *variety* is important, and doing the same old thing has a negative effect on job-related well-being. But when one's job is lost, doing the same old thing becomes more the norm than the exception and often involves unappealing activities like standing in unemployment lines and searching the newspaper and Internet for potential jobs. Fourth, *environmental clarity* helps employees define their roles, but without jobs, they lose all sense of their roles and lack environmental clarity altogether. Fifth, the sense of *valued social position* that employees derive from their jobs is damaged when they lose their jobs, thereby affecting their general sense of self-esteem and self-worth.

Sixth, people without jobs tend to lose focus on their *externally generated goals;* because there are no demands placed on them by their jobs, supervisors, or organizations, they engage in little activity or achievement. Certainly, job security provides both *availability of money* and *physical security,* the seventh and eighth factors in Warr's list; but when people lose their jobs, both are gone, creating anxiety-arousing circumstances that affect every facet of their lives. Ninth, *supportive supervision*—a form of social support—is obviously relinquished when a job is lost. The tenth and last determinant of job related well-being is *opportunity for interpersonal contact*—one of the main benefits provided by a job. When employees lose their jobs, they are cut off from the outside world, or at least from a circle of people who were an important part of their lives. For some, a large void is left. For others, interpersonal contact is experienced through job search behaviors, but the quality and depth of that contact pale by comparison to what used to occur at work.

I have reviewed these environmental determinants to demonstrate how significant job loss can be. When we look at Warr's model, what becomes quite clear is how much we actually receive or gain from our jobs. When we lose our jobs, we lose a great deal—more than any of us (including myself) can understand until it happens to us.

The last area we need to cover in this chapter stems in part from our discussion of how damaging job stress can be. In very extreme situations, it can even result in workplace violence.

■ Workplace Violence

Violence in the workplace has become a very important topic for organizations, employees, and researchers. The trends are indeed staggering. According to the U.S. Bureau of Labor Statistics, homicide is one of the leading causes of death among American employees (along with falls and transportation accidents). About 20 employees are murdered each week while working or on duty (LeBlanc & Kelloway, 2002). Of the 5,488 fatal work injuries in the United States in 2007, 839 (15%) involved violence and 610 were homicides (U.S. Bureau of Labor Statistics, 2008b). Retail sales workers are the most frequently assaulted or threatened; indeed, job-related homicides in retail account for almost half of all workplace homicides (many of which occur during robberies).

In July 1993, Northwestern National Life Insurance Company conducted the first comprehensive assessment of fear and violence in the workplace. It surveyed 600 full-time American workers and, in generalizing these data to the U.S. workforce as a whole, uncovered some startling facts. It found that more than 2 million American workers self-reported that during the preceding 12 months they had been victims of physical attacks; 6 million, that they had been threatened; and 16 million, that they had been harassed (Northwestern National Life Employee Benefits Division, 1993).

This amounts to one out of every four full-time U.S. workers between July 1992 and July 1993. Of those individuals who reported being attacked, almost 80% were affected psychologically, 40% found their work lives disrupted by the experience, and 28% were physically injured or sick as a result of the attack. A strong relationship between job stress and workplace violence was also found.

In 2006, 22,430 employees filed formal claims that they had been assaulted at work (U.S. Bureau of Labor Statistics, 2008c). The National Institute for Occupational Safety and Health (NIOSH) lists the following risk factors for the likelihood of being assaulted at work (Biles, 1999):

- Having contact with the public
- Being involved in the exchange of money
- Delivering passengers, goods, or services
- Having a mobile workplace (e.g., taxicab or police cruiser)
- Working with unstable persons (e.g., healthcare, social services, criminal justice settings)
- Working alone or in small numbers

One study developed and validated a measure for identifying the risk for workplace violence by focusing on 28 different job characteristics that have been reported in the literature as being related to workplace violence (LeBlanc & Kelloway, 2002). Along with those characteristics listed by NIOSH, this new measure asks about whether the job involves serving alcohol, caring emotionally or physically for others, disciplining others, handling weapons, or making decisions that influence other people's lives. The study reported significant correlations between 22 of the job characteristics and reports of violence. Furthermore, researchers found that the new scale was more strongly related to violence from individuals outside the organization (e.g., customers) than from those inside the organization (e.g., other employees). Other research has shown that most violence at work is initiated by what are called "organizational outsiders" rather than "organizational insiders" (LeBlanc & Barling, 2004). Finally, researchers have made it clear that even though insider-initiated violence is not as frequent (nor, usually, as deadly) as outsider-initiated violence, it still frequently occurs and has devastating effects for its victims (LeBlanc & Barling, 2004).

Interest in workplace violence has increased only in the past 25 years or so. In fact, prior to the events in Edmond, Oklahoma, in 1986, most Americans weren't even aware of the potential impact of workplace violence. It was at the Edmond Post Office that Patrick Sherrill went on a rampage that resulted in the death of 14 of his coworkers before he took his own life. This event, and others that followed, resulted in the coining of the term *going postal* to refer generically to wild episodes of violence at work. What set Sherrill off isn't completely clear, but we do know that his performance record at work was spotty and that he wanted to get revenge on his shift supervisor, who was his first victim in the onslaught.

▶ **A Closer Look** This 25-year-old man, Wesley N. Higdon, shot and killed five people at a plastics plant in Kentucky where he worked as a press operator, before taking his own life. Why do you think organizational insiders sometimes exhibit violence at work?

AP PHOTO/HENDERSON, KY. POLICE DEPT.

This atrocious crime is the first well-known incident of workplace violence in the United States, and it marks the beginning of the escalating trend toward workplace violence that we just discussed. In recent years, I/O psychologists, social psychologists, organizational development experts, and others have begun a systematic examination of this phenomenon. The remainder of this section briefly highlights the results of their research.

Figure 11.3 presents a profile of the dangerous employee. This profile is consistent with a 1995 study published by the U.S. Department of Justice and the FBI that discovered some interesting trends after reviewing 89 incidents of serious violence in the workplace (Duncan, 1995). First, 97% of the murderers were male, and over 70% were White. Second, the average age of the perpetrators (nearly 40) was a bit higher than that of nonworkplace murderers (under 30). Third, in each of the 89 incidents, a firearm was used to commit the crime. Fourth, almost 90% of the perpetrators were current or former employees. Fifth, many of the perpetrators had a history of psychological or personality disorders and an affinity for weapons. Sixth, they often exhibited warning signs, such as extremely erratic behavior, threats of violence, irrational thought processes, and agitated mood, just prior to the incident.

A useful model along these lines has been developed (O'Leary-Kelly, Griffin, & Glew, 1996). It uses the term **organization-motivated aggression** to refer to attempts by someone inside or outside the organization to cause injury or to be destructive as a result

organization-motivated aggression Attempts by someone inside or outside the organization to cause injury or to be destructive as a result of some organizational factor.

FIGURE 11.3 Profile of the Lethal Employee

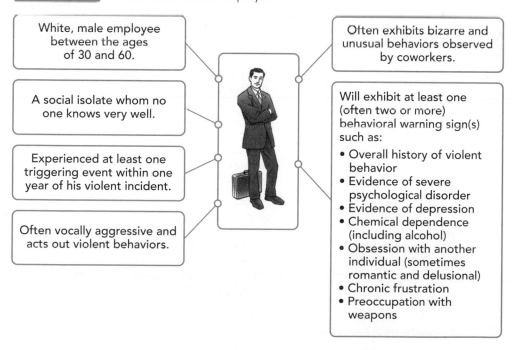

White, male employee between the ages of 30 and 60.

A social isolate whom no one knows very well.

Experienced at least one triggering event within one year of his violent incident.

Often vocally aggressive and acts out violent behaviors.

Often exhibits bizarre and unusual behaviors observed by coworkers.

Will exhibit at least one (often two or more) behavioral warning sign(s) such as:
• Overall history of violent behavior
• Evidence of severe psychological disorder
• Evidence of depression
• Chemical dependence (including alcohol)
• Obsession with another individual (sometimes romantic and delusional)
• Chronic frustration
• Preoccupation with weapons

of some organizational factor; the term **organization-motivated violence** refers to the negative effects on people or property that result from the aggression. Figure 11.4 presents this model of organization-motivated aggression, which demonstrates the importance of both the organizational environment and individual characteristics. Some individuals are clearly more disposed toward violent or aggressive behavior than others (again, see Figure 11.3), but organizations that are rigid, punitive, and aggressive themselves may also encourage aggressive behavior on the part of employees (Tobin, 2001). The model further indicates that the way in which the organization responds to the aggressive behavior moderates the extent to which the aggression results in violence and other negative outcomes.

A second model of organizational aggression extended this earlier work (Martinko & Zellars, 1998). Though extremely complex, it builds on Figure 11.4 by focusing on the individual characteristics. The findings for this second model were grouped into three categories: *reliable findings,* for which sufficient research evidence has verified their accuracy; *tentative findings,* supported by the literature but for which the evidence is insufficient to verify their accuracy; and *propositions,* which are potential findings that need to be tested with future research. The authors' literature review led to four reliable conclusions: (1) High levels of frustrating events in the workplace lead to a greater incidence of aggression and violence; (2) employees who tend to exhibit violent and aggressive behavior also tend to have been rewarded in the past for this pattern of behavior and to have had role models who were violent and aggressive; (3) employees who believe that what happens to them is beyond their control (i.e., those who are high on external locus of control) are more likely than others to respond to negative events in an aggressive or violent way; and (4) males are considerably

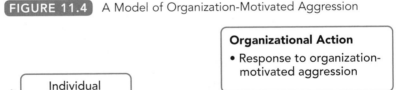

FIGURE 11.4 A Model of Organization-Motivated Aggression

Adapted from O'Leary-Kelly et al. (1996)

more likely than females to be aggressive and violent in the workplace. A recent study found results consistent with this model. For instance, employees' perceptions of how controlling their supervisor was played an important role in creating psychological workplace aggression, such as making disparaging remarks about one's supervisor (Dupré & Barling, 2006).

The literature review has also given rise to a few tentative findings. For instance, a series of seemingly minor frustrations at work may serve as a trigger for aggression (Tobin, 2001). Individuals who exhibit a high degree of negative affectivity—that is, who see their lives and the world around them in an unfavorable light—are more likely to respond to aversive outcomes (e.g., being laid off) with aggressive behavior than are those who exhibit a low degree of negative affectivity. Similarly, individuals who tend to be impulsive are more likely to react to aversive outcomes in violent ways than are those who tend not to be impulsive.

> **TECHNICAL TIP**
>
> *Propositions are typically general statements about two or more concepts. In Chapter 2, we defined a hypothesis as a tentative statement about the relationship between two or more variables. Hypotheses often stem from general propositions and are usually presented in a form that allows them to be tested by scientific research.*

The researchers have developed a series of propositions as well. First, they argue that some aggressive behaviors happen without conscious thought on the part of the perpetrator; in effect, these behaviors are purely emotional reactions to a trigger event. Second, they propose that individuals who are emotionally susceptible (i.e., easily affected by events happening around them) are more likely to perceive workplace incidents as trigger events than are those who are not emotionally susceptible. Third, they suggest that in ambiguous situations, perpetrators may attribute negative outcomes to a general cause such as "management," such that personnel who are most like management are likely to be blamed for the trigger events. An extension of this work has resulted in a very new model proposing that a triggering event is perceived and processed differentially, resulting at times in aggressive behavior (Douglas et al., 2008). This model distinguishes among different cognitive-processing paths that foster different types of aggressive behavior. Empirical tests of this model should be forthcoming.

All these models provide useful summaries of what we know about workplace aggression and violence. But even more important, they provide directions for future work in this area. One final point: We must not assume that all (or even most) aggressive behaviors in the workplace involve fatal physical assaults. In actuality, such incidents often entail subtle, covert, or verbal types of aggression, the majority of which are directed at coworkers rather than at supervisors (Neuman & Baron, 1998). But of course it is the heinousness of the murders and rampages, in combination with the media spotlight, that makes them more salient than more typical incidents such as verbal threats, arguments, paybacks, and assaults among coworkers.

■ Summary

The purpose of this chapter was to discuss stress as it manifests itself in the workplace. I began the chapter with a look at stress, strains, and coping. After defining these important terms and briefly considering stress in general, I presented a model that indicates various sources and outcomes of job-related stress. In the second section, I highlighted

Warr's model of environmental determinants of well-being as a way of thinking about how employees' jobs can affect their well-being. (Later in the chapter the same model was used to show how job loss can result in anguish.)

In the third section, I focused on work–family conflict. Given the importance of this area to both employees and organizations, I devoted a substantial amount of space to discussing it. In particular, I defined work–family conflict and enrichment, presented a conceptual model to demonstrate how work and family interact with each other and related variables, and emphasized the various struggles faced by people who are working and nurturing a family at the same time. I then discussed the benefits that some organizations currently provide employees to help them deal with this conflict—benefits such as family-leave policies, child care, and elder care. Because more and more married people are dual-earner couples, I also considered some of the issues that make this situation stressful and explained how companies can help reduce the stress associated with juggling multiple careers and family responsibilities. Throughout this section, specific companies' work-life supports were highlighted to provide a sense of the many family-friendly benefits and services being offered to help reduce employees' stress.

The last two sections took a darker turn. First, I discussed the psychological effects of job loss in light of the increased number of layoffs at major U.S. corporations and the perceived threat of being laid off experienced by so many employees in the 21st century. Then I presented some incredible statistics indicating the rise of workplace violence. In this context, employees at risk of becoming perpetrators were profiled, some recent research was reviewed, and a discussion was presented of two recent theoretical works that attempt to model the process through which workplace aggression and violence occur.

■ Key Terms

burnout (p. 328)
chronic stress (p. 328)
coping (p. 329)
dual-earner couple (p. 342)
emotion-focused coping (p. 330)
episodic stress (p. 328)
organization-motivated aggression
   (p. 351)
organization-motivated violence (p. 352)

parental leave (p. 339)
problem-focused coping (p. 330)
role (p. 326)
role ambiguity (p. 326)
role conflict (p. 326)
strains (p. 325)
stress (p. 325)
work–family conflict (WFC) (p. 333)
work–family enrichment (p. 333)

■ TAKING IT TO THE FIELD

Work–family conflict is a growing concern among U.S. organizations. There are many practical issues that must be considered when designing programs to help support workers with families. One of your clients, Dutler Accountancy Firm, has reached out to you for some advice on a current problem they are encountering. Read the e-mail from Michael Yurttas, and draft a response with some recommendations.

Hello—

Thank you for taking the time to help me out with this problem.

Dutler Accountancy Firm has historically had quite a bit of difficulty recruiting and retaining female accountants. Part of this is because the field tends to be male-dominated; however, over the past decade, we have put forth a great deal of effort on recruiting and selecting qualified women for many of our positions. However, we seem to be having much difficulty retaining these women.

We recently conducted a focus group with female employees from all levels of the company. From these sessions, it's become evident that our workplace policies are not a good fit for women with families. However, I'm not sure that we can change some of these policies to satisfy our female employees.

Throughout most of the year, we have a typical 9-to-5 workweek. However, during the two months leading up to tax season, our accountants often have to work 60 to 70 hours each week. Of course, we provide them with overtime pay for these long weeks. It became clear during our focus group sessions, though, that women, particularly women with children, do not find this work model effective. Many of our working mothers indicated that the long workdays were wreaking havoc with their child care. Many women also indicated that this timing sometimes conflicted with spring break, which prevented them from joining their families on vacations. Obviously, we can't cut back their hours during this time—the work has to get done, and we have very strict deadlines. It also doesn't make sense to hire more full-time workers—we have enough people at our firm to get the work done when it isn't tax season. In fact, sometimes we don't have enough work during the rest of the year to keep our workers busy.

We would really like to find a way to encourage women to stay with our organization. What suggestions do you have for us?

Sincerely,
Mike Yurtlas

■ Critical Thinking Questions

1. You learned at the beginning of this chapter that stress leads to strains, which are the negative outcomes of stressful experiences. Based on what you read, what are some ways that people can keep stressful experiences from leading to strains? What are some advantages and disadvantages of these coping mechanisms?

2. Some unique employee benefit programs and perks were noted in this chapter. What are some new, innovative benefit programs that you think organizations should consider implementing for their employees? If you were exploring the job market right now, what kind of programs would you look for in your next employer?

3. Dual-earner couples are becoming increasingly common. What are some of the challenges faced by individuals in these dual-earner roles? How might organizations help their employees alleviate, or lessen, some of these challenges?

4. Work–family conflict is an important topic in I/O psychology and an important issue for organizations and their employees alike. A related but lesser-known concern is family interference with work. What do we mean by family interference with work? Is it a bigger issue for some people more than others? Why?

■ Application Questions

1. Consider a recent stressful event you experienced at work. What types of job-related, emotional, and physiological strains did you experience as a result of this event? What are some problem-focused and emotion-focused coping strategies you might have used?

2. Telecommuting is becoming more popular in a number of different companies. Consider your own schoolwork and how productive you are when you are working at home or in your dorm room, compared to when you are in a computer lab or a library. What are some benefits you have found to working at home? What are some difficulties? Given the choice, would you prefer to always work from home or never work from home?

3. Some jobs, such as being a police officer or a social worker, involve a great deal of stress nearly every day. Imagine yourself in such a stressful occupation. What could the organization do to help you feel less stress?

4. Imagine that a friend of yours talks about a coworker who has recently been acting aggressively at work, such as throwing objects when she gets frustrated and yelling at other people. What advice would you offer this friend?

5. Imagine that a friend was recently laid off. He has only been unemployed for a few weeks, but already he is feeling depressed and hopeless about finding another job. What might you do to help him? What advice would you offer him?

■ Suggested Readings

100 best companies to work for. (2011). *Fortune*. Retrieved January 2, 2012, from http://money.cnn.com/magazines/fortune/bestcompanies/2011/full_list/. This very interesting annual report from *Fortune* magazine is a fun read; it provides cutting-edge examples of the workplace supports provided by some of the more progressive companies, both large and small.

American Psychological Association. (2004). *Public policy, work, and families: The report of the APA presidential initiative on work and families.* This report presents cutting-edge knowledge and a thorough summary of the social science research on the challenges faced by working families and their employers. It's a very readable account of what we know and don't know about some very complicated and important issues.

Cartwright, S., & Cooper, C. L. (1997). *Managing workplace stress.* Thousand Oaks, CA: SAGE. This book provides a readable treatment of stress at work and offers approaches and techniques for dealing with stress.

Warr, P. (1999). Well-being and the workplace. In D. Kahneman, E. Diener, & N. Schwartz (Eds.), *Well-being: The foundations of hedonic psychology.* New York: Russell Sage Foundation. Peter Warr is one of the most interesting writers on this topic. The chapter cited here focuses on well-being at work and ties in nicely with Warr's more general models of well-being and health. Accordingly, it serves as a good place to begin reading and learning about how work affects our lives.

Wexley, K. N., & Silverman, S. B. (1993). *Working scared: Achieving success in trying times.* San Francisco: Jossey-Bass. This book by respected I/O psychologists, despite being written more than almost 20 years ago, portrays the state of many 21st-century organizations. A very easy read, it can be used as a how-to book for dealing with workplace stress caused by recent changes in organizations.

CHAPTER 12

Group Processes and Work Teams

© MARK RICHARDS/PHOTOEDIT

This chapter should help you understand:

- How social influence affects group behavior
- Group cohesion and its importance in group processes
- The stages of group development
- The implications for work groups of social loafing and free riding
- The stages of effective decision making
- Why groups don't always make good decisions
- What groupthink is and how it can affect organizations
- Why one current trend in organizational processes is the use of work teams
- How to differentiate among the various types of work teams
- What self-managed work teams are, along with some of the processes involved in their success
- How to measure work-team effectiveness and what factors affect it
- The implications that work teams have for employee selection and placement

At some point during your education, you probably worked with other students on a group project. It may have been a book report in the fifth grade, a science project in the tenth grade, or a term paper in your freshman year of college. Group projects are a common way for students to learn about relevant material, develop interpersonal skills, and achieve goals that may have been more difficult to achieve individually.

Groups are quite prevalent in our day-to-day lives as well. I was a member of a softball team for over 10 years, I participate in various groups at church, and I've done some volunteer work as part of a group. You may have been a member of the Boy Scouts or Girl Scouts, and perhaps you are in a sorority or fraternity. Maybe your parents belonged to the Rotary Club or a neighborhood association. Groups, it seems, have always played a role in people's lives, from playgroups in early childhood to social or service groups in late adulthood. In the years between, people in the workforce encounter various groups in the workplace as well.

Though typically considered a specialty area within social psychology, group processes have been extensively examined by I/O psychologists interested in organizations that use work groups. In this chapter, I deal with the role of such groups in organizations. Specifically, I review some of the basics of group processes, apply them to groups at work, consider what I/O psychologists know about work teams, and discuss the great potential that teams have for transforming organizations.

■ Groups Versus Teams

A **work group** is "an interdependent collection of individuals who share responsibility for specific outcomes for their organizations" (Sundstrom, DeMeuse, & Futrell, 1990). Other definitions, too, emphasize that members of work groups have interrelated goals; in short, a collection of people is not a group unless the individuals share common goals that affect one another. For instance, five people sitting in close proximity on a subway do not constitute a group; but when the subway doors get stuck, they become a group that works together to achieve such interrelated goals as getting the door open, contacting emergency personnel, comforting children who may be scared, and so on. *Formal groups* are subunits that the organization has actually established (e.g., committees, small departments, work crews), whereas *informal groups* develop apart from the official structure of the organization and exist relatively independently of it. Informal groups often emerge among employees who work in close proximity and interact frequently. They may consist of employees who get together for a working lunch, go through training together, or study together for a certification exam.

> **work group**
> An interdependent collection of individuals who share responsibility for specific outcomes for their organizations.

All organizations have both formal and informal groups. Formal groups are discussed at greater length in this chapter, but first we need to recognize how powerful and important informal groups can be. Informal groups serve a variety of functions, including the following:

1. They satisfy social needs such as friendship and companionship.
2. They satisfy security needs in that they make employees feel safe and connected.
3. They facilitate cooperation among employees.
4. They regulate social and task behaviors such that organizational norms and procedures are disseminated.

In the past, researchers drew a distinction between work groups and work teams; they argued that the former consist of individuals who work together but can do their respective jobs without the other members of the group, whereas the latter consist of individuals who are truly interdependent such that they must "work together" to get their jobs done. Many contemporary researchers, however, use these terms interchangeably, arguing that the distinction is unnecessary, sloppy, and not widely recognized (Sundstrom, McIntyre, Halfhill, & Richards, 2000). I myself use both terms to refer to the same idea: *Work groups* were defined at the beginning of the chapter, and *work teams* are discussed later on in the context of organizations, but I do not mean to imply any qualitative difference between the two terms.

▼ **A Closer Look**
Why would passengers on a plane, like this, not be considered a group?

JACK SULLIVAN/ALAMY

■ Social Influence in Groups

Social psychologists spend a great deal of time studying the ways in which groups affect individual behaviors. In this section, we will review some major concepts related to group processes that have traditionally been studied by social psychologists but that I/O psychologists now apply to organizations.

Norms

norms
Shared expectations about appropriate ways of responding in a group.

Norms are shared expectations about appropriate ways of responding in a group. As such, they are guidelines that serve an important organizational function, sometimes by stipulating certain behaviors as off-limits or inappropriate. *Descriptive norms* define what most people tend to do, feel, or think in a particular situation; *prescriptive norms* suggest what people *should* do, feel, or think in a particular situation (Forsyth, 1999). As you might imagine, employees who violate descriptive norms are viewed as unusual or different, but those who violate prescriptive norms are viewed as dysfunctional—that is, bad employees.

Sometimes groups sit down and list their norms; more often, norms develop gradually as group members become more comfortable with their place in the organization—and more comfortable with each other. Norms may also be passed down by employees who were members of the group at an earlier time. New employees, rather than changing existing norms, tend to adapt or adjust to them.

I have had experience with an organization in which the norm was for employees not to use their sick days at all. It was very clear to new employees that unless they had to be hospitalized, they were expected to be present at work; that way, their sick days would accumulate for years and years and would allow them to retire early. However, new employees who did not see the value in carrying over their sick days but preferred to stay home when ill essentially violated a prescriptive norm at this organization, leading at times to interpersonal conflict. A recent model of counterproductive work behavior (CWB) proposes that group norms and other team processes interact with individual-level variables to impact the frequency of CWB (O'Boyle, Forsyth, & O'Boyle, 2011).

Roles

We have discussed roles elsewhere in this text (see especially Chapter 11), but let's take a more formal approach here. First, consider the context of behavior. An individual's behavior is jointly determined by internal forces (e.g., values, attitudes, and needs) and external forces (e.g., social pressure and job requirements). In other words, behavior is a function of both the person and the situation. Kurt Lewin (1951), widely recognized as the leader of the scientific study of groups, put it a bit differently: Behavior is a function of the person and the environment, or

$$B = f(P, E)$$

Second, the term *role concept* is used to describe how people perceive the various situational forces acting on them. For example, my role as a father is composed of what

I think a father is supposed to do and, in particular, what I think *I* am supposed to do as a father. Similarly, my role as a psychology professor consists of how I interpret the expectations and demands of the environment to arrive at what I think I am supposed to do, how I should behave, and what my chief purpose is as a psychology professor.

Third, as defined in Chapter 11, a *role* is a set of behaviors expected of a person who occupies a particular position in a group or organization. The process by which a group or organization establishes distinct roles for various members of the group or organization is called **role differentiation**. This is accomplished through formal job descriptions, rules, and task requirements, as well as by supervisors, subordinates, and coworkers who communicate expectations and beliefs to individual employees. Thus, for example, a computer programmer at Apple knows what her role is not only because it is spelled out in the job description and other formal organizational documents but also because it is defined through discussions and interactions she's had with her supervisor and other computer programmers. A recent study of Major League Baseball teams found that player experience and skills were related to team performance. Further, these characteristics were especially valuable when held by those who occupied the core roles on the team and when the team allocated more resources to the core—here defined as pitchers and catchers (Humphrey, Morgeson, & Mannor, 2009).

role differentiation The process by which a group or organization establishes distinct roles for various members of the group or organization.

Especially when combined with the work stress caused by role conflict and role ambiguity (again, see Chapter 11), role differentiation within work groups can become quite complicated. With this in mind, let's now examine one of the more important dimensions of groups—cohesion.

Cohesion

At some point in your life, you have probably been part of a group in which the members were very close-knit, expressed a unified commitment to the group, and shared similar beliefs about issues relevant to the group. You may also recall that morale was generally high in that group. All of these elements are related to **cohesion**, defined as the strength of members' motivation to maintain membership in a group and of the links or bonds that have developed among the members. Cohesion is seen as (1) both a binding force that pushes members together and a combative force that tries to pull them apart; (2) group unity, or "we-ness," in which group members feel such a strong sense of belonging that they put the goals of the group above their individual goals; (3) a special type of interpersonal attraction; and (4) an aspect of "teamwork" (Forsyth, 1999). Some groups are cohesive because they consist of close personal friends, others are cohesive because the members feel a strong sense of belonging, and still others are cohesive as a result of great teamwork (Cota, Evans, Dion, Kilik, & Longman, 1995).

cohesion The strength of members' motivation to maintain membership in a group and of the links or bonds that have developed among the members.

Cohesion has both positive and negative consequences for groups and organizations. The negative consequences, which are largely related to group decision making, are discussed in a later section. For now, however, I focus on the positive consequences. Most managers, if asked to choose between supervising a cohesive and a noncohesive work group, would quickly opt for the former. Faced with a similar choice, you would probably do the same. What, then, are the positive consequences of cohesion?

First, a great deal of research across athletic, industrial, and educational settings demonstrates that members of cohesive groups report being more satisfied than do members of noncohesive groups (Forsyth, 1999). Think about your own experiences in this regard. I would predict that you have more positive things to say about the cohesive groups you've belonged to than about the noncohesive groups. There tends to be less tension and anxiety in cohesive groups because their members get along, like one another, have similar goals and objectives, and work well together.

Second, group cohesion is positively linked to performance (Kerr & Tindale, 2004). One of the truly great groups of the 20th century was the Disney group that worked together in the early days of Walt Disney's success (Bennis & Biederman, 1997). Creative, hardworking, and cohesive, this group made incredible contributions to the world of animation and film.

Indeed, two meta-analyses support a positive relationship between cohesiveness and performance (Evans & Dion, 1991; Mullen & Copper, 1994). Both meta-analyses identified a series of moderators that affect the strength of this relationship, as did a recent study employing sophisticated virtual laboratory methods. This study found support for the argument that the causal relationship between cohesiveness and performance varies as a function of type of task and type of cohesiveness (Fullagar & Egleston, 2008). The results suggested that social cohesiveness (interpersonal attraction) affects performance on tasks requiring social interaction; however, on tasks that don't require much social interaction, performance impacts task cohesion (task commitment). In other words, when there isn't much social interaction, performance of the task is necessary before task cohesiveness can be developed.

Examples of cohesive work groups are widespread; think of the many work groups depicted on television. Any of the many medical dramas on television, for instance, have routinely presented the emergency-room employees as belonging to a very cohesive group whose members get along well; are committed to one another, the patients, and the hospital; share similar beliefs about medicine and patient treatment; and are clearly motivated to maintain affiliation with the group. Interestingly, some of the storylines of these popular TV shows have been about the conflict that results when someone disrupts the cohesiveness of the group by disagreeing with other group members or violating a group norm.

▼ A Closer Look
How might the status of their interpersonal cohesiveness affect the performance of this team's members?

DAVID M. GROSSMAN/MEDNET/CORBIS

In reality, of course, many work groups are not very cohesive. They consist of employees who don't get along very well, who see things very differently, and who remain affiliated with the other group members only because doing so is part of their job. Research has consistently found task cohesion, as opposed to social cohesion, to be more strongly related to many outcome variables such as team performance (Carless & De Paola, 2000). The role of cohesion is widespread. For instance, in a study of elite ice hockey players, it was discovered that perceptions of team cohesion predicted the tendency to return to the team in the following year (Spink, Wilson, & Odnokon, 2010). Have you experienced both cohesive and noncohesive groups at work, at school, or in social circles? If so, you know that the differences between the two types of groups are striking. But how do cohesive groups develop?

Group Development

Traditionally, theories and models of group development agree that groups pass through various stages as they develop. One model that many group researchers have endorsed is the five-stage version proposed by Bruce Tuckman in the 1960s (Tuckman, 1965; see also Tuckman & Jensen, 1977). We'll examine this model in some detail because it provides a solid general view of group development.

Tuckman believed that groups develop while passing through five stages over time (see Table 12.1). In the first stage, groups go through an orientation period that Tuckman referred to as *forming*; group members spend time getting to know each other. This is followed by a period of conflict called the *storming* stage, in which group members have moved beyond polite conversation and actually begin disagreeing with one another, questioning one another's ideas and beliefs, and openly revealing who they are.

Table 12.1 Tuckman's Five Stages of Group Development

Stage	Group Processes
1. Forming	Members get acquainted.
	Interactions are polite, tentative, exploratory, and sometimes guarded.
2. Storming	Interactions are characterized by disagreement.
	Members question one another more pointedly.
	Some conflict emerges.
3. Norming	Unity is established.
	Members become more cohesive.
	Roles, standards, and relationships develop.
	Trust increases.
4. Performing	Members become focused on productivity and goal achievement.
	Task orientation is high.
5. Adjourning	Roles are terminated.
	Relationships weaken, and members become much less dependent on one another or the group.
	Some degree of stress or tension is likely.

In the third stage, a structure-building stage that Tuckman referred to as *norming*, group members become more cohesive and establish unity among themselves. During the fourth stage, members are focused on productivity, or *performing*. It typically takes a while before a group is productive, occurring after the members have a better feel for one another.

Of course, some groups never make it to this stage. Having stagnated at the norming stage, they fail to reach their potential in terms of productivity. Examples of unproductive groups can be found in numerous studies of combat groups, civic groups, and personal-growth groups. On the other hand, we have all experienced truly productive groups that reached the performing stage. It is exhilarating to be part of a group that grows and matures into a productive arm of society, whether at work, a house of worship, or school.

The final stage involves the dissolution of the group, or what Tuckman called *adjourning*. This stage can be planned for, as when a work group charged with a particular project dissolves because the project is finished. Sometimes, however, groups dissolve due to lack of performance or group members' dissatisfaction. The organization itself may decide that a particular group is no longer successful or useful. At other times, work groups are dissolved for financial reasons, as when group members are laid off or asked to take on more work that necessitates their being pulled out of the group.

Change is stressful regardless of the context, especially when one has spent considerable time as a member of a group, only to see it disband. The stress that accompanies the dissolution of a team was made very clear to me by my oldest son when he was eight years old. He loved playing baseball and soccer in the local recreation leagues; every time the season ended, he became very sad and told me how much he was going to miss his teammates and the fun that comes from working together to score more than the other teams. I always pointed out that he would see the same guys in school, at church, and around the neighborhood, but he would say that it wasn't the same because they wouldn't be a team anymore. Indeed, when we affiliate with others in close situations and work interdependently to achieve a goal, it's hard to accept the end of that relationship.

We need to be careful about generalizing this process to all groups all the time. Some groups may go through the five stages in a different order and spend more time at one stage than at another. Other groups may stop short of making it through all the stages; still others may skip a stage or two.

Gersick's work on models of *punctuated equilibrium* presents an alternative in which groups fluctuate more quickly among these and other stages of development (Gersick, 1989). This model has become extremely popular in describing how groups form, and it's a stark contrast to Tuckman's more traditional linear stage view. This more complex model argues that all groups don't pass through these stages one step at a time. In many instances, groups will oscillate between stages or perhaps even go through them in a different order. According to this model, groups go through inactive periods where very little is happening and then, as a result of time and an awareness of deadlines, a spike in activity occurs and group activity picks up. Sometimes groups adopt a task-focused approach early on, but not much happens until about half their time allotment is gone, and then they shift into gear.

In a recent study of MBA students using a sophisticated business simulation, results showed that a group's business charter or a plan for how the group would operate interacted with performance strategies to determine group performance (Mathieu & Rapp, 2009). What is most interesting for our purposes is that about halfway through the simulation—as would be suggested by the punctuated equilibrium model—the performance of the groups with a low-quality performance strategy declined drastically, while the performance of the groups with a high-quality performance strategy was maintained or began a steady incline. As suggested by the theory, when groups realize they are about halfway through their task, they tend to become more active and therefore to enact their strategies and approaches.

Another approach has been proposed in which groups may actually develop in a way that combines the traditional stage model and the punctuated equilibrium model. Chang, Bordia, and Duck (2003) compared Gersick's punctuated equilibrium model with a stage approach and found that the two models together explain group formation fairly well. They argued and demonstrated that each model is useful when looking at a particular unit of analysis. For instance, the punctuated equilibrium model describes the discontinuous changes in a group's pacing and task activities over time, but a stage model describes the continuous manner in which a group's structure changes over time. So in the 1990s, the pendulum swung away from linear stage models like Tuckman's and toward Gersick's punctuated equilibrium model; but today some researchers (e.g., Chang et al., 2003) and theoreticians argue that it may have swung too far and that the models complement each other in providing a better understanding of group functioning. Future research will continue to explore the various ways in which groups evolve and develop.

Social Loafing

The idea of social loafing was first analyzed and presented in the early 1900s by Max Ringelmann, who noticed that individual effort in a wide variety of tasks often decreased with increases in the size of the group. What later became known as **social loafing** refers to the reduction in individual effort that occurs when people work in groups instead of alone. The point here is not that groups, as a whole, work less hard than individuals but, rather, that individuals, in many situations, work less hard in groups than they do when working alone. Ringelmann and others noticed this effect across a variety of tasks such as rope pulling and clapping.

social loafing
The reduction in individual effort that occurs when people work in groups instead of alone.

Since Ringelmann's early work, social loafing has been empirically demonstrated by additional researchers on such tasks as making noise, working on mazes, writing, swimming, and problem solving. Although there are various explanations for this effect (Pinder, 1998), most researchers agree that people are less likely to "loaf" (1) when they believe that their individual efforts can be identified and (2) when others are going to be personally affected by their effort. Some argue that social

TECHNICAL TIP

Recall that the VIE (valence–instrumentality–expectancy) theory of motivation (see Chapter 9) describes one's motivation to behave in a particular way as a function of the valence of rewards that are likely to come from that behavior, the extent to which the behavior will lead to other positive outcomes, and the expectancy that exhibiting the behavior will lead to the desired outcomes.

loafing is especially pervasive in groups and usually occurs because people don't expect their efforts on group tasks to be as directly tied to valued outcomes as their efforts on individual tasks (Karau & Williams, 1993). You may recognize this explanation as being based on the expectancy theory of motivation.

When Stephen Zaccaro (1984) conducted a study in which students were given the opportunity to "loaf" in groups, he found that social loafing occurred only among group members who were working on a task low in attractiveness. The opposite effect, *social enhancement*, occurred among group members who were working on a task that was high in attractiveness. In the latter case, individuals in larger groups performed better than those in smaller groups. Other research has also demonstrated that social loafing is less likely to occur in cohesive groups than in noncohesive groups (Karau & Hart, 1998; Karau & Williams, 1997); thus, variables other than task attractiveness may affect the likelihood of social loafing in any given situation (Goren, Kurzban, & Rapoport, 2003).

Research has generally supported the idea that North Americans socially loaf more than the Chinese. However, a recent study demonstrated a more complicated relationship. Chinese workers actually performed at a level that matched their coworkers'— this was especially the case in public contexts (Hong, Wyer, & Fong, 2008), where the authors argue that Chinese employees prefer not to stand out. So, while it's true that Chinese tend to socially loaf less than North Americans (probably due to their collectivistic nature, as opposed to the more individualistic nature of North Americans), it's actually more complicated than that.

Group dynamics can get even more thorny. Sometimes, for instance, employees do less than their share of the work but still share equally in the rewards. Known as **free riding**, this situation appears to happen when employees perceive that their efforts are not necessary to group success and rewards. In such cases, other group members become concerned that their coworkers are holding back, at which point they reduce their own efforts to the level they believe is being exhibited by their coworkers. This outcome, called the **sucker effect**, occurs when group members decide they will no longer be played for a sucker and thus reduce their effort—even if it results in failure on the task. Have you ever experienced this in a group project for class? Kerr and Tindale (2004) discuss other complex group effects such as *social compensation*, which occurs when individuals increase their efforts on collective tasks because they don't anticipate much help from their group members. You can see, then, how complicated social processes can become, with potentially far-reaching effects on organizational functioning.

free riding
A situation that occurs when employees do less than their share of the work but still share equally in the rewards.

sucker effect
An outcome that occurs when group members become concerned that their coworkers are holding back, at which point they reduce their own efforts to the level they believe is being exhibited by their coworkers.

■ Group Decision Making

Think about the roles that various groups play throughout the world. We often entrust groups with the greatest responsibilities. Groups run major national and international companies that affect our economy and lives (e.g., boards of directors); groups run universities and colleges that influence our own and our children's education (e.g., boards of trustees); groups decide the fate of our accused criminals and provide the only means of protection for the unjustly accused (e.g., juries); we even entrust our physical health and well-being to groups when faced with serious illness (e.g., surgical teams). Although most of us would agree that as citizens of the United States we live in an individualistic society, we must not lose sight of the importance of groups—especially considering the power and responsibility we hand over to them to make crucial decisions. In this section, we will consider both effective and ineffective group decision making.

Decision-Making Processes

Although no two groups make decisions in exactly the same way, certain elements can be said to characterize most successful decision making. There are various ways to break down these elements (Schilling, Oeser, & Schaub, 2007); I do so by relying on the five steps outlined in Table 12.2.

▲ A Closer Look
What steps go into effective decision making?

Table 12.2 Five Steps to Effective Group Decision Making		
Step	Description	Common Mistakes
1. Diagnose the problem	Group members come to an agreement on the nature of the problem.	Confusing facts with opinions Confusing symptoms with causes
2. Generate solutions	Group interaction is focused on understanding the problem well enough to identify potential solutions.	Suggesting irrelevant solutions Looking at what should have been done rather than looking forward
3. Evaluate solutions	Group members consider each solution in terms of its potential for success and failure.	Failing to consider the potential downside to each solution Attacking the person who proposed a particular solution rather than focusing on the solution itself
4. Choose a solution	Group members come to some agreement on the best solution.	Allowing powerful members of the group to dictate the solution chosen; biasing a particular solution because it's politically correct
5. Develop an action plan and implementation	Group members determine steps to follow in carrying out the decision and monitoring progress.	Preventing some members from being involved even though they were part of the decision process

Source: Adapted with the permission of the Free Press, a Division of Simon & Schuster, Inc., from *Decision Making: A Psychological Analysis of Conflict, Choice, Commitment* by Irving L. Janis and Leon Mann. Copyright 1977 by the Free Press. All rights reserved.

Before any intensive work can be done to solve a problem by making a particular decision, groups must first *diagnose the problem*. Group members must come to some agreement about the nature of the problem, the goals of the group with respect to this problem, and the obstacles the group should be sensitive to and then prepare to overcome. Although at first glance this step in the process appears rather straightforward, research indicates that many groups don't spend enough (or any!) time on it (Forsyth, 1999). Some common mistakes at this stage include confusing facts with opinions and looking for scapegoats. For instance, the members of a salary-equity task force charged with identifying and resolving apparent differences in pay between men and women may mistake as a fact what is merely their opinion—that the pay differences are based purely on skills and experience—and thus distort their perception of the problem.

The second step of effective decision making is to *generate solutions*. This discussion-oriented stage involves communication among group members in which they process the problem and group goals while trying to identify potential solutions. A useful technique here is **brainstorming**, in which all members of a group generate potential solutions without fear of having their suggestions criticized by other members. The purpose is to create an atmosphere in which each group member feels comfortable generating solutions—and, indeed, the group is arguably best served by having a long list of such solutions.

brainstorming
A technique in which all members of a group generate potential solutions without fear of having their suggestions criticized by other members.

One mistake sometimes made at this stage, however, is to raise irrelevant solutions, thereby throwing the group off-task. Another mistake is to rely on "old" solutions rather than remaining open and willing to think creatively about the problem. In general, research suggests that the effectiveness of brainstorming is reduced when (1) members have to wait their turn or are otherwise delayed in their opportunity to share, thus blocking the free flow of ideas (this is called *production blocking*); (2) members are apprehensive about voicing their ideas to the group; and (3) members are more motivated by concern for how "good" they look in comparison with others than by concern for generating viable solutions (Forsyth, 1999).

Several decades of research have shown many instances in which brainstorming results in worse performance than that of nominal groups (i.e., individuals not working together). This performance decrement has been the major criticism of brainstorming. More recent work, however, has begun to challenge these negative findings and provide some solutions for improving the effectiveness of this technique, such as employing a trained facilitator to minimize production blocking (Kerr & Tindale, 2004).

Perhaps the most intriguing solution is the recent development of "electronic brainstorming," in which software allows individuals to type in their ideas without production blocking, with anonymity, and with other group members' ideas available to them at any time on the screen. Some research has demonstrated the superiority of this approach to the use of nominal groups (for a review, see Nijstad, Stroebe, & Lodewijkx, 2003), which may result in greater interest in electronic brainstorming in the future.

The third step, *evaluating solutions*, follows directly from the previous one. Specifically, the group critically evaluates each of the solutions proposed during the brainstorming procedure, accepting those that seem workable and rejecting those that do not. At this point, it's important for the group to consider the worst-case scenario regarding each alternative when deciding whether to eliminate it from further consideration. For instance, if our salary-equity task force decides to explain pay differences in terms of the importance of jobs held by the respective genders, the result could be a worst-case scenario involving angry female employees whose commitment to the organization is compromised. This could then lead to dissatisfaction with their jobs, a decrement in performance, high turnover rates, potential suits brought against the company, and depleted morale.

Choosing a solution from those on the list is the fourth step of the process. After considering the potential benefits and weaknesses of each alternative and eliminating those that are not workable or that would have negative consequences, the group must compare the remaining solutions and pick the best one for implementation. Groups choose solutions in various ways. Forsyth (1999) discusses some common approaches:

- *Delegating:* The group provides information to the chairperson, who makes the decision. (Alternatively, a subcommittee speaks for the whole group.)
- *Averaging individual inputs:* Group members make individual private decisions, which are then averaged to arrive at a group-level decision.
- *Majority rules:* The group votes, and the majority viewpoint becomes the group's choice.
- *Group consensus:* The group members discuss the issue until they reach a unanimous agreement.

Potential mistakes at this stage include allowing those with power to dictate the chosen solution and biasing the benefits and weaknesses to support a "favorite" solution.

Finally, after the decision has been made to enact a particular solution, the group begins to *develop an action plan and implementation* of that solution. Detailed action steps and methods for monitoring and evaluating progress toward the solution are developed. Let's say our salary-equity task force decides to conduct a reevaluation of job classifications and wage scales; toward this end, it must develop a plan that includes timelines, steps in the process, and objectives for each step. After the action plan is ready, implementation begins, with each step monitored and evaluated along the way.

Although success is not guaranteed, consideration of the issues raised in each of the preceding five steps is certainly more likely to result in effective decisions than ignoring such issues. Of course, groups can also undergo these steps with varying degrees of commitment, which explains why some decisions are good ones and others are not so good.

Ineffective Decision Making

The fact that groups are asked to make many of our important decisions doesn't mean they always do it well. Indeed, in American culture we often poke fun at groups, especially committees, through humor—such as the *Cathy* comic strip in this chapter and the several *Dilbert* cartoons throughout the book. Forsyth (1999), for instance, quotes the all-too-common view that "committees consist of the unfit appointed by the unwilling to do the unnecessary." Now perhaps that's a bit extreme, but we have

► **A Closer Look** Does the group in this cartoon exhibit any of the five steps to effective group decision making outlined in Table 12.2?

cathy® by Cathy Guisewite

all had bad experiences as part of a group decision-making effort or been adversely affected by an inadequate group decision-making process.

Process Loss In 1972, Ivan Steiner suggested the following *law of group performance*:

Actual Productivity = Potential Productivity − Losses Due to Faulty Processes

Here, "potential productivity" refers to all the positive things that can come from group work, such as shared responsibilities and the variety of skills brought to bear on a particular problem. At the end of the equation, however, is the category of "losses due to faulty processes," or **process loss**, which refers to any nonmotivational element of a group situation that detracts from the group's performance. For example, coordination problems among group members result in process loss, as when one employee works on her part of a group task without coordinating her efforts with other members who are doing related parts of the task. Actual productivity is adversely affected by process loss, a key element groups need to be aware of so that they can take advantage of the benefits of group processes rather than being limited by potential disadvantages.

A program of research by James Larson and his colleagues (Larson, Christensen, Franz, & Abbott, 1998; Larson, Foster-Fishman, & Franz, 1998) has focused on the factor of shared versus unshared information in terms of its effect on decision making. *Unshared information* is that held by only one group member; *shared information* is that held by all group members. According to these researchers, one reason we entrust important decisions to groups is that we assume a larger pool of relevant information is being brought to bear on the problem. As their studies have shown, however, groups are not particularly effective at pooling unshared information; indeed, group decisions tend to be determined more by shared information.

This finding is ironic, given that the notion of pooling unshared information is one of the assumed strengths of group decision making. Larson and his colleagues argue that to improve the quality of group decision making, the pooling of valuable unshared information should be encouraged (see also Brodbeck, Kerschreiter, Mojzisch, Frey, & Schulz-Hardt, 2002). One technique they suggest is for leaders to employ a "participative" style of leadership. This method has received some qualified

process loss Any nonmotivational element of a group situation that detracts from the group's performance.

support in their research (Larson, Foster-Fishman, et al., 1998), but more work needs to be done regarding how to encourage groups to take advantage of one of their potential benefits—the pooling of unshared information.

The process loss that we see in many group failures often centers on communication problems. Some researchers have argued that process losses often stem directly from not sharing information and arriving at decisions too quickly (Van Ginkel & van Knippenberg, 2009). In addition, problems emerge when group members don't discuss foundational ideas regarding the group task—that is, when they don't discuss how they see the task or their perceptions of what the task requires. Researchers assigned 252 students to groups of three and invited them to work on a cooperative decision-making task dealing with retail stores and a few important marketing and operating decisions (Van Ginkel, Tindale, & van Knippenberg, 2009). They found that group reflection about the nature of the task affected group members' information sharing and elaboration, which in turn affected decision quality. Indeed, communication about task perceptions and reflection on what the task entails are important determinants of effective decision making.

Groupthink

Without a doubt, the most talked-about group decision-making error is **groupthink**, defined by Irving Janis (1972) as a mode of thinking that individuals engage in when the desire to agree becomes so dominant in a cohesive group that it tends to override realistic appraisal of alternative courses of action. In such instances, group members become so focused on sticking together and following through as a cohesive group that their decision making is clouded or biased. Indeed, groupthink has been presented (by Janis and others) as an explanation for various poor decisions made throughout the history of the United States.

An especially compelling example has to do with Japan's attack on Pearl Harbor on December 7, 1941. U.S. military commanders in Hawaii had been provided with a great deal of information about Japan's buildup for this attack; as a group, however, they never really took the situation seriously. They didn't strategically place aircraft carriers in the Pacific, where they could have provided some warning of the attack, and they didn't deem the threat real enough to warrant any military buildup on the part of the United States. Thus, there was absolutely no warning at all until the Japanese bombers were directly overhead, attacking our defenseless ships and airfields (Janis & Mann, 1977).

Although some researchers argue that the empirical data about groupthink are mixed at best and perhaps better characterized as weak (e.g., Park, 2000), others suggest that additional research is needed—both to examine the theoretical variables involved and to expand these variables to include other potentially important constructs (Henningsen, Henningsen, Eden, & Cruz, 2006). Many experts agree, however, that the groupthink construct presents a useful framework for analyzing and combating ineffective group decision making (Mulrine, 2008).

groupthink
A mode of thinking that individuals engage in when the desire to agree becomes so dominant in a cohesive group that it tends to override the realistic appraisal of alternative courses of action.

▼ **A Closer Look**
In what ways does the attack on Pearl Harbor appear to be related to groupthink?

DEPARTMENT OF DEFENSE

FIGURE 12.1 Janis's Model of Groupthink

Antecedents of Groupthink

- Group cohesion
- Isolation
- Strong, biased leadership
- High decisional stress

Symptoms of Groupthink

- Belief in invulnerability of group
- Belief in unanimity of group members
- Pressure on dissenters
- Appointing of a mindguard
- Rationalizing
- Stereotyping
- Self-censorship
- Illusions of morality

Defective Decision Making

Adapted from Janis & Mann (1977), p. 132.

Regarding the *antecedents* of groupthink, what do you think are some of the factors likely to lead to this phenomenon? Not surprisingly, Janis has presented a list of these factors in his model of groupthink (see Figure 12.1). The primary necessary antecedent for groupthink to occur is *cohesion* (Janis, 1982). Members of cohesive groups often feel such a strong sense of belonging that they put group goals above their own individual goals. The implication here is that group members may even avoid expressing a dissenting opinion because they believe group unity to be more important; in this case, group cohesion is problematic.

Groupthink is also more likely in groups that are *isolated* from others. This makes sense, given that isolation from others limits the dissenting opinions that could be shared with the group. *Strong, biased leadership* is another important antecedent of groupthink. Strong leaders have a tendency to "dictate" the direction of the group and even some of its opinions. In your own experience, have you ever tried to get a group to listen to your opinion about something, only to be silenced by the group leader, who had a seemingly solid explanation of why your opinion wasn't relevant? The last antecedent of groupthink is *high decisional stress*, which refers to situations in which a decision needs to be made quickly and the context in which it exists is very important and emotionally charged.

As for the *symptoms* of groupthink, take another look at Figure 12.1, in which eight such symptoms are listed. Limited space prevents me from discussing all of these, but I will mention briefly a few of the more interesting ones. First, in situations involving groupthink, members tend to believe that they are *invulnerable* to harm and *unanimous* in their beliefs. I always think of Watergate as a great example of this; the accounts and interviews of those involved with the Nixon White House—the principal players on the Committee to Reelect the President (CREEP)—make it very clear that these people never considered the possibility that they could be caught, brought down, and damaged, much less that they were doing anything "wrong."

Two other symptoms that seem to go hand in hand with the ones just discussed are *pressure on dissenters* and *appointment of a mindguard*. When groupthink occurs, a great deal of pressure is usually put on members whose opinions seem at odds with those of the rest of the group. In other words, when a group is experiencing groupthink, it is not unusual for dissenters to be coerced through guilt or some other means to "join the rest of the group" and contribute to the unanimity. Related to this is the group's formal or informal appointment of a **mindguard**, a member of a cohesive group whose job is to protect the group from outside information that is inconsistent with the group's views. Obviously, this approach maintains the cohesiveness of the group and keeps it isolated from outside influences that might otherwise negatively affect the perceived unanimity of the group.

Finally, the steps to effective decision making presented earlier (see Table 12.2) should be followed in the hope of eliminating or preventing groupthink altogether. The more carefully the problem is diagnosed, the more tightly focused the group is in identifying potential solutions, the more critically the potential solutions are evaluated, the more carefully a final solution is chosen, the more precisely the action plan and implementation are carried out, and the less likely groupthink is to emerge.

mindguard
A member of a cohesive group whose job it is to protect the group from outside information that is inconsistent with the group's views.

■ Work Teams of the 21st Century

Collaboration, which is an important concept for 21st-century organizations, is reflected in two or more people engaged in interaction with each other who are also working toward a common goal (Patel, Pettitt, & Wilson, 2012). A recent conceptual framework suggests seven major factors of collaboration (context, support, task, interaction process, teams, individuals, and overarching factors) (Patel et al., 2012). In the remainder of this chapter, I will focus on one very important factor of collaboration: teams.

Although I made it clear at the outset that I would use the terms *work group* and *work team* interchangeably, I predominantly use the latter in this last section in order to be consistent with the growing I/O literature. In this literature, work teams are essentially defined as work groups in which the actions of individuals are interdependent and coordinated; each member has a specified role, and the team has common goals and objectives. But regardless of the specifics of the definition, a growing organizational trend that cannot be denied is the steady increase in work teams across every segment of the industrial sector.

Mental Models

Group learning is an important element in the functioning of work teams. Group learning can be viewed as an outcome—a new shared understanding among group members. The process of group learning includes sharing a new understanding, storing it, and being able to retrieve it (Goodman & Dabbish, 2011). This shared understanding is more than just an aggregation of beliefs across people; it is actually a property of the team (Goodman & Dabbish, 2011).

Related to the notion of group learning is a concept called shared mental models. First, a **mental model** is an organized knowledge structure that enhances the interaction of an individual with his or her environment (Mathieu, Heffner, Goodwin, Salas, & Cannon-Bowers, 2000). Mental models allow people to make sense of the world

mental model
An organized knowledge structure that helps an individual make sense of the world around him or her.

COURTESY OF TOM RUDDY

Tom Ruddy
PhD, 1989, I/O Psychology, Bowling Green State University
Vice President of Talent Management and Learning and Development, Becton Dickinson

Much of what you've learned in this chapter about work teams rings true in the real world of corporate America. At Xerox and Siemens, I became familiar with these concepts while implementing empowered teams for over 14 years in over 36 countries worldwide. For Xerox's global customer service organization, the empowered team implementation process consisted of several steps: (1) Form teams (controlling size and composition), (2) understand and communicate the company vision, (3) develop a team mission, (4) define team goals, (5) establish team norms of behavior, (6) clarify team member roles, and (7) document and follow key work processes (e.g., communication, meeting, and work processes).

We used these team start-up steps during team training as a way to get teams up and functioning. We sometimes found that there was a lack of clarity in one of these key areas, which affected the team's success. The completion and monitoring of these process steps would often ensure effective team functioning.

As my own study and observation of over 3,000 teams has demonstrated, team members' ability to follow agreed-upon processes and norms is more predictive of good team functioning than is the extent to which team members "like" each other. While positive personal relationships do not hurt team functioning, such relationships are not necessary or sufficient to create high-performance work teams. My work at Siemens with virtual teams that operate across multiple countries and time zones has highlighted the fact that well-defined processes and behavioral expectations are the critical factor in making teams successful.

Our research data, based on over 16 separate studies on Xerox and Siemens teams, has identified the following critical organizational context factors in team performance: (1) team-based support structures (e.g., team-based incentives, performance feedback systems), (2) management leadership and coaching, and (3) technical resources (e.g., pagers, laptops, real-time communication devices). The presence or absence of these factors has an impact on the ability of teams to develop effective team processes (i.e., the seven start-up steps mentioned previously) and drives performance (e.g., customer satisfaction, employee satisfaction, and expense management).

Applying Your Knowledge

1. Why is team cohesiveness related to tasks more important than general liking among team members?

2. In what ways are Dr. Ruddy's experiences regarding team development consistent with the punctuated equilibrium model?

3. How do virtual teams differ from traditional face-to-face teams with regard to the importance of team processes and organizational context factors?

shared mental models
Organized structures combining the knowledge, beliefs, and understandings of two or more individuals that help coordinate their efforts.

around them—to describe, explain, and predict what's happening in their environment. Individuals need to be able to describe, explain, and predict the attitudes and behaviors of their team members so that effort can be coordinated; this is where **shared mental models** come into play. They are structures that allow team members to use their own knowledge and understanding in choosing behaviors that are coordinated and consistent with their teammates' behaviors (Mathieu et al., 2000).

As you can imagine, shared mental models become very important for high-functioning teams that don't have extra time to discuss issues and situations, are under considerable pressure, and need to work quickly and carefully. These team members need to be on the same page and to understand one anothers' thought patterns and tendencies so they can coordinate their efforts. Studies have found that the extent to which mental models are shared among team members determines team performance through effective team processes such as strategy formation, coordination, cooperation, and communication (Mathieu et al. 2000). Furthermore, a recent study found that individuals are better able to retrieve and rely on team expertise throughout the organization when there is strong communication among the team members (Yuan, Fulk, Monge, & Contractor, 2010)—that is, individuals are more apt to call on others' expertise and understand where expertise lies in the organization when there are strong connections among the minds of team members.

Types of Work Teams

As I/O psychologists began studying work teams more intensively, it became clear that such teams could be grouped into five different categories (Sundstrom et al., 2000). These are summarized in Table 12.3. First, *production teams* are groups of

Table 12.3 Types of Teams

Production teams	Front-line employees producing tangible output
	Often self-managed, self-led, self-directed
	Examples: Electronics assembly units, coal mining crews, candy production crews
Management teams	Corporate executive teams; regional steering committees
	Coordinate other work units under their direction
	Responsibilities include planning, budgeting, staffing
	Examples: Top management teams, military command teams, healthcare teams
Service teams	Attend to the needs of customers
	Serve many customers at one time
	Examples: Flight attendants, hospital emergency units, retail sales groups
Project teams	Created for the duration of a project
	Cross-functional
	Disband at completion of project
	Examples: New-product teams, research units, research and design project groups
Advisory teams	Solve problems and recommend solutions
	Very popular in organizations
	Temporary
	Examples: Quality circles, employee involvement teams, university advisory group to the president

employees who produce the output. They tend to be front-line employees in that they are responsible for production at the front end. Second, *management teams* coordinate workers who report to them as the product is being made, developed, or refined. They aren't on the front line but are instead responsible for the planning, staffing, budgeting, and logistics of work projects. Third, *service teams* consist of employees who work together to attend to the needs of customers. One example of a service team is the group of flight attendants who assist you and other passengers on an airplane.

Fourth, *project teams* are formed to carry out specific projects only and are then dissolved upon project completion. These may also be referred to as **cross-functional teams**, especially when they involve team members from diverse departments of the organization, each with its own function. For instance, a book publisher might assign a particular book to a cross-functional team that will handle all the procedures necessary to get the finished product into stores. Members of this team might include someone from production, marketing, finance, and circulation.

These various team members are responsible for working with one another while at the same time focusing on their individual responsibilities to best serve the company's interest with respect to this one particular book or project. Harley-Davidson, for example, uses cross-functional teams extensively in the production of its motorcycles. Typically, each line of motorcycle is designed, manufactured, and marketed by a specific team consisting of a program manager from the design department and representatives from the departments of manufacturing, purchasing, and marketing (Brunelli, 1999).

Finally, we come to *advisory teams*, sometimes called *parallel teams* because they are developed to work separately from but in parallel to production processes (Sundstrom et al., 2000). A company may have an employee involvement team, for example, or a college may have an advisory group whose chief task is to keep the president informed about morale on campus and other faculty/student issues. Typically, members of advisory teams serve for a limited term, after which they are replaced by new members. A recent book called *The Third Opinion*, by Saj-Nicole Joni (2004), describes advisory team members as external thinking partners who may help the executive deal with a particular problem or with big-picture issues.

In their review of work-team literature published between 1980 and 1999, Sundstrom and his colleagues (2000) reported that 33% of the research focused on service teams, 17% on production teams, 14% on management teams, and 14% on project (or cross-functional) teams. Interestingly, despite the obvious popularity of advisory teams, very few studies have formally examined this newer approach to management and productivity. Future research is certainly called for, given the prevalence of these teams in organizations today. It would be helpful to know how successful these teams are, how they are received by employees, and how they are viewed by upper-level management.

We have just discussed one popular scheme for categorizing work teams (again, see Table 12.3). Another important dimension along which teams differ has also received both popular and scholarly attention—namely, the extent to which work teams are self-managing, self-directing, self-leading, and self-regulating. These terms, which are often used interchangeably, refer to work teams that assume complete responsibility

cross-functional teams
Work teams that are composed of members from diverse departments of the organization, each with its own function; also called *project teams*.

for a final product or an ongoing process (Mohsen & Nguyen, 1999). In short, the **self-managed work team (SMWT)** is responsible for monitoring and controlling the overall process or product, as well as for doling out specific tasks to team members. These teams often schedule their own work, do routine housekeeping, and maintain their own equipment; some may even participate in discussions of budgets, performance appraisals, or training (Sundstrom et al., 2000).

In the 1980s, only about 5% of American organizations used work teams; by 1992, this figure had grown to about 20% (Mohsen & Nguyen, 1999). It has been reported that 72% of Fortune 1000 companies had at least one SMWT in 1999 (Lawler, 2001)—SMWTs are discussed in more detail later. Xerox, Chrysler, Apple Computer, Motorola, Texas Instruments, and Frito-Lay are among the leaders at the forefront of the teams movement. This emphasis on teams reflects the growing realization that the complexity of work in the 21st century requires collaboration. Many different skills and so much knowledge are required that individuals can no longer accomplish certain tasks on their own.

Traditionally, organizations have taken a "command-and-control" approach to operations. Generally, organizations have been viewed as machine-like systems that were all about order, predictability, and control (Ashmos & Nathan, 2002). Some theorizing suggests that in the current global environment of rapid and discontinuous change, the emphasis should be on being flexible enough to change as the organization encounters more complex and varied situations (Henningsen et al., 2006). An alternative way to characterize effective teams is as sensemakers. In this way, teams can help the organization get to know itself, its history, and its future. To serve this purpose, teams need to be flexible, independent, and self-empowered rather than a command-and-control arm of the organization.

SMWTs seem to fit this sensemaking framework quite well. Research has demonstrated that autonomy and empowerment, essential features of these types of teams, are positively related to team effectiveness. Some research has found that empowered teams were not only more productive than less empowered teams but also had higher levels of customer service and more favorable attitudes (Kirkman & Rosen, 1999). Similarly, another study found that, in cases in which team members' tasks were interdependent, autonomy had a positive effect on work-team effectiveness (Langfred, 2000). In other words, when team members were dependent on each other for the completion of their tasks, their autonomy as a team was an important predictor of team success. However, in some instances, SMWTs are not effective in managing themselves. A recent study suggests that conflict among team members can lead to ineffectiveness in SMWTs (Langfred, 2007).

Work-Team Effectiveness

An important question is how to evaluate the effectiveness of work teams. Among the various ways to do so, one of the best is a framework developed by Susan Cohen (Cohen, 1994; Cohen & Bailey, 1997). According to this framework, there are three major dimensions of work-team effectiveness: (1) *team performance*, which concerns how well the team is performing and includes such variables as productivity, quality

self-managed work team (SMWT) A work team that is responsible for monitoring and controlling the overall process or product, as well as for doling out specific tasks to team members.

▲ A Closer Look
Three of the best players in the NBA performed very well in 2011 but didn't succeed in winning a championship; they did, however, win in 2012. What does this situation possibly tell us about the nature of teamwork?

taskwork
Activities, behaviors, or actions that involve the task-oriented aspects of work.

teamwork
Activities, behaviors, or actions that involve the process-oriented aspects of work.

of output, and the degree to which costs are controlled in this process; (2) *attitudes* of team members, which reflect such variables as quality of work life, trust in management, organizational commitment, and job satisfaction; and (3) *withdrawal* behaviors, such as turnover, absence, and tardiness.

Another useful way to think about the effectiveness of teams is to consider two types of behaviors (McIntyre & Salas, 1995): **taskwork**, which involves the task-oriented aspects of work, and **teamwork**, which involves the process-oriented aspects of work. Whereas task-work entails specific individual behaviors or duties that are required for success, teamwork includes the wide range of activities aimed at maintaining and enhancing team performance. Teamwork revolves around communication and coordination among team members, feedback, team cohesion, and norms (Levy & Steelman, 1997). Most team experts argue that both taskwork and teamwork are integral to successful team performance. In other words, if teams are to be successful, it isn't enough for members to fulfill their individual duties; they must also work together toward common goals.

Whether we use the term *teamwork* to describe a great NBA team, the board of directors of General Electric, or the cross-functional groups at Harley-Davidson, the importance of teamwork is clear. Further insights into this area are likely to emerge from research that has begun to examine the level at which team data should be analyzed—for example, at the level of individual perceptions, perceptions aggregated across team members, and perceptions combined across teams at the organizational level.

A second important question concerns the factors involved in increasing work teams' effectiveness. In an extensive review of the literature on work teams, researchers identified five categories of factors that appear to be important predictors of work-team effectiveness: organizational context, group composition and size, group work design, intragroup processes, and external group processes (Sundstrom et al., 2000). Table 12.4 presents some examples of each of these categories.

One category in particular has received considerable attention of late: group composition. A series of studies have built on this notion, paying particular attention to personality traits of team members. For instance, a recent study found that teams with high variability on extraversion and low variability on conscientiousness were the most effective (Humphrey, Hollenbeck, Meyer, & Ilgen, 2011). Apparently, teams will function best if all teammates are conscientious about their work, but only if this is accompanied by significant differences in people's interpersonal styles and other individual differences will we see high-functioning teams. In another interesting study,

Table 12.4 Predictors of Work-Team Effectiveness	
Organizational context	Rewards
	Goals and feedback
	Training
Group composition and size	Cognitive ability of group members
	Personality traits of group members
	Demographic characteristics of group members
Group work design	Member task interdependence
	Member goal interdependence
Intragroup processes	Group cohesion
	Group efficacy or communication processes
External group processes	Communication outside the group
	External interaction patterns

Source: Adapted from Sundstrom et al. (2000)

it was demonstrated that when an individual perceives that his or her team member really needs help with a task—what the literature calls *backup behavior*—the personalities of the helper and the recipient of help play an important role (Porter et al., 2003). For instance, team members higher on conscientiousness delivered more backup to one another, whether it was really needed or not; those high on extraversion secured more backup from others, regardless of their true need for help, than did those low on extraversion.

A recent meta-analysis identified group composition variables as very important to group effectiveness (Stewart, 2006; see also Bell, 2007). In particular, team performance improves when members have high cognitive ability, favorable personality traits, and relevant expertise. The author also found significant relationships between task design variables and team effectiveness as well as between leadership skills of team leaders and effectiveness.

Another recent meta-analysis found that demographic diversity among team members was unrelated to team effectiveness (Horwitz & Horwitz, 2007). However, the authors did find that diversity related to the task, such as expertise and education, was positively related to team effectiveness. Finally, an intriguing analysis of movie production over a 30-year period showed that team diversity with respect to newcomers and old-timers had favorable effects on movie-making innovation (Perretti & Negro, 2007). Certainly, these studies have implications for how organizations will consider diversity in constituting work teams in the future.

■ Current Trends

Sundstrom and his colleagues (2000) suggested that the use of work groups or teams would continue to expand in the areas of service, production, and project completion. They also suggested that work teams would continue to become more fluid; in other words, the teams would be assembled in such a way as to make use of various people, including employees from other units and other companies. Today, some organizations use teams as a way to link or partner with other organizations. The definition, development, and use of teams will continue to evolve as organizations find new and interesting ways to make use of them. Let's look at a couple of those new and interesting uses of teams.

Virtual Teams

With the increase in telecommuting and electronic work, the use of virtual teams promises to expand (Zaccaro & Bader, 2003). Virtual teams are composed of members who work in different cities or countries and communicate via e-mail, fax, web pages, and videoconferencing. Such team members may be working on the same sales account or for the same client but rarely do so face-to-face. Increases in creativity and innovation are believed to be positive outcomes of virtual teams (Martins & Shalley, 2011).

There is the potential for virtual teams to be very effective. One major advantage is that team members can communicate, collaborate, and create regardless of their location, time zone, weather, and so on. Face-to-face meetings are not necessary to keep projects moving along. Communication is obviously central to this process, and the organization must be certain to establish guidelines and rules regarding communication along with the necessary resources to allow for effective communication and collaboration.

Most larger organizations today employ virtual teams to some extent (Hertel, Geister, & Konradt, 2005), and it is not just a U.S. phenomenon; virtual teams are popular in Europe and other parts of the world. Some recent theoretical works suggests that the degree to which a team functions on a virtual basis stems from contextual features, such as organizational boundaries; temporal dynamics, such as time pressures; and task–media–member compatibility, such as synergy among members' abilities and available technologies (Kirkman & Mathieu, 2005).

Various dimensions have been identified as requirements for categorizing a team as virtual; at a minimum, virtual teams must use computer-mediated communication, and most experts agree that they should also be geographically dispersed (Johnson, Bettenhausen, & Gibbons, 2009). Furthermore, teams can be categorized on a virtuality dimension from almost completely face-to-face communication to almost completely computer-mediated communication. In

▼ A Closer Look Often videoconferencing is used to link team members across the globe. What are some of the complications that might arise in these situations?

B BUSCO/GETTY IMAGES

other words, there are gradations of virtuality, with some teams being somewhat virtual and others being mostly virtual (Berry, 2011).

A recent study of employed MBA students found that compared to all other groups that used less computer-mediated communication, those who used computer-mediated communication at least 90% of the time reported lower levels of positive affect, task effectiveness, and affective commitment (Johnson et al., 2009). The authors conclude that there is a tipping point—when about 90% of communication is computer-mediated—where virtual teams become less effective. Another way to view this finding is that even a small amount of face-to-face time may further enhance the performance of virtual teams.

Team Member Selection

One other trend worth discussing has to do with selecting employees to work in a team environment. Think back to Chapters 6 and 7, which discussed the various predictors and procedures used for hiring employees. As you might recall, the selection process always begins with a job analysis to identify what tasks are done on the job (job description) and what knowledge, skills, abilities, and other characteristics (KSAOs) employees need to have in order to do the job successfully (job specification). We also talked about the use of ability tests, personality tests, work sample tests, and so on as techniques for predicting how effective or successful particular individuals are likely to be in a particular job. Given this background and review, what additional kinds of information might we want to know about applicants prior to hiring them into a job that exists within a team-based environment? I certainly wouldn't want to hire onto a production team someone who is highly self-involved and cannot or will not get along with others. In short, it makes sense from a selection standpoint to consider applicants in light of their desire and ability to work in a team environment.

Some earlier work began examining this issue, which has now become an important and growing trend in the team area. For instance, a laboratory experiment in which students worked together on group decision-making tasks found that work-team performance was predicted by students' preferences for and attitudes about working in teams, as well as by their perceptions of group confidence and ability (Jung & Sosik, 1999). The authors of this study argued that group preference appears to be a stable individual disposition and thus can be used to select individuals for group membership, increasing the likelihood that those selected will be suitable for and will perform well in team-based work environments.

Another study examined the mental abilities and Big Five personality traits (see Chapter 6) of more than 600 employees to determine the relationship between these variables and group performance (Barrick, Stewart, Neubert, & Mount, 1998). The authors concluded that selecting team members with higher levels of general mental ability, conscientiousness, agreeableness, and emotional stability appears to improve team performance—and that just one team member who is low on agreeableness, conscientiousness, or extraversion can result in increased stress and decreased performance among team members.

As with any selection situation, it is imperative that predictors be linked to criteria; indeed, the organization must assume responsibility for demonstrating this link when it chooses its predictors. A more recent study showed that conscientiousness, extraversion, and teamwork knowledge significantly predicted the contextual performance of team members (Morgeson, Reider, & Campion, 2005).

Other researchers have developed an instrument specifically geared toward identifying individuals likely to be successful in a team environment. Known as the Teamwork Test, the measure identifies KSAOs that more effectively predict teamwork than taskwork. The following KSAOs are tapped by this measure: conflict resolution, collaborative problem solving, communication, goal setting and performance management, and planning and task coordination (Stevens & Campion, 1999). The Teamwork Test is a situational judgment test in which respondents are provided with hypothetical teamwork situations and asked to select, from multiple solutions, which one they would likely use. Correct answers are determined on the basis of the research literature. The authors found that scores on the Teamwork Test were correlated with ratings of teamwork performance and that these ratings were predicted even after aptitudes and abilities measured by nine other different tests had been controlled for. The implication is that the Teamwork Test can be used for selection purposes in identifying individuals who are most likely to thrive in a team environment (Miller, 2001).

The latest step in this line of work is the development of the Team Role Test, which is intended to tap into one's knowledge about team roles, including in which situations certain roles are more important (Mumford, Van Iddekinge, Morgeson, & Campion, 2008). The researchers believe that an understanding and recognition of the various roles team members play are related to team effectiveness. The researchers present some data linking knowledge about task, social, and overall team roles to team effectiveness; furthermore, knowledge of team roles improved prediction of team effectiveness above and beyond cognitive ability and Big Five personality constructs (Mumford et al., 2008).

■ Summary

This chapter introduced the concepts of work groups and work teams and discussed the processes involved in the use of such groups in organizations. I began by defining work groups and reviewing group processes. Then I discussed social influence in groups in the context of norms, roles, cohesion, and social loafing, applying those elements to organizational functioning. I also presented Tuckman's model of group development and the popular punctuated equilibrium model.

Group decision making was another area emphasized in this chapter. Because groups are entrusted with important organizational decisions, I spent considerable time discussing a process that, when followed, is likely to result in effective decision making. This five-step process emphasizes the quality of the social interaction among group members—an issue I discussed in connection with some of the common mistakes made at certain points in the process. This topic led logically to ineffective decision making, with a particular emphasis on groupthink. Here I presented historical examples of groupthink and discussed its antecedents and symptoms in light of organizational situations.

In the last section, I focused on work teams, which have become incredibly popular in modern-day organizations. I discussed various types of work teams and gave examples of each, placing particular emphasis on self-managed work teams both because of their prevalence in organizations and because of their inherent complexities. I also provided a few examples of organizations currently using work teams, introduced the idea of shared mental models, and identified the determinants of work-team effectiveness. I concluded the chapter with a discussion of current trends such as the growth of virtual teams and recent focus on selection for teams.

■ Key Terms

brainstorming (p. 370)

cohesion (p. 363)

cross-functional teams (p. 378)

free riding (p. 368)

groupthink (p. 373)

mental model (p. 375)

mindguard (p. 375)

norms (p. 362)

process loss (p. 372)

role differentiation (p. 363)

self-managed work team (SMWT) (p. 379)

shared mental models (p. 376)

social loafing (p. 367)

sucker effect (p. 368)

taskwork (p. 380)

teamwork (p. 380)

work group (p. 361)

■ TAKING IT TO THE FIELD

Building effective teams can often be difficult. In many organizations, work groups tend to forget that they are part of a larger organization and become competitive with one another for resources and attention. One of your clients, Siran Belekdanian, has come to you for advice on how to build better teams at WeldCo. Please read her e-mail, and provide three suggestions for how she can improve the teamwork within her organization.

Hello—

Thank you for being willing to work with me on this project. Here at WeldCo, we have two main teams. First, we have salespeople, who sell updated welding equipment to plants. Second, we have service people, who provide training on the equipment and repair the equipment when it breaks down. Over the past year, relations between these two teams have been strained.

Our salespeople have recently been promising faster training and repairs than our service department can handle. On the one hand, the sales department has been claiming that it needs to promise these quick turnaround times to close sales. On the other hand, we have also been experiencing an increase in customer complaints because the service side has not been able to do what the salespeople promise. In fact, some of the service people are actively slowing down in order to make the salespeople look bad.

I'm not sure what to do next. I've tried to explain to both groups separately that they need each other to make the business run smoothly, but they continue to undermine each other. Any suggestions you have would be helpful.

SB

■ Critical Thinking Questions

1. Say you are a high-level manager in an organization. How would you go about assembling a team for a very important work project?

2. What does diversity mean in the context of work teams, and how does it impact team effectiveness?

3. How might work groups prevent groupthink?

4. What makes virtual teams so effective despite the potential complexities?

5. How has the globalization trend impacted work teams?

■ Application Questions

1. What is an example of a group you've been a part of that was highly cohesive? What made it that way? How could some of those qualities be instilled in a workplace team?

2. Consider a time when you experienced social loafing in a group (in a class or at work). What were some aspects of the situation that caused social loafing to occur? What could your instructor or boss have done to decrease social loafing?

3. Think about a group you are currently a member of. Where in Tucker's stages of development is this group? Give examples to support your opinion.

4. Although brainstorming can be useful, sometimes it prevents groups from thinking creatively about solving a problem. What are some reasons why this might happen, and what are some ways you could avoid those problems?

5. Consider a job you once had or a group project you worked on in a class. In order to work well with others, you likely had a shared mental model. Give some examples of what might have been part of this mental model you shared with other group members.

■ Suggested Readings

De Vries, M. F. R. K. (1999). High performance teams: Lessons from the Pygmies. *Organizational Dynamics, 27*(3), 66–77. This is an interesting, albeit unusual, application of work teams by an expert in the area.

Forsyth, D. (1999). *Group dynamics* (3rd ed.). Belmont, CA: Brooks/Cole. Far and away the best book on the psychology of groups, this is a very readable account and has good examples.

Ilgen, D. R., Hollenbeck, J. R., Johnson, M., & Jundt, D. (2005). Teams in organizations: From input-process-output models to IMOI models. *Annual Review of Psychology, 56,* 517–543. This review chapter portrays teams as complex, dynamic systems and focuses on the way teams evolve over time.

Kozlowski, S.W. J., & Ilgen, D. R. (2006). Enhancing the effectiveness of work groups and teams. *Psychological Science in the Public Interest, 7,* 77–124. In this monograph, two teams of experts make recommendations for improving work-team effectiveness.

Mannix, E., & Neale, M. A. (2005). What differences make a difference? The promise and reality of diverse teams in organizations. *Psychological Science in the Public Interest, 6,* 31–55. This article takes an honest, pragmatic look at team diversity within organizations.

Sundstrom, E., McIntyre, M., Halfhill, T., & Richards, H. (2000). Work groups: From the Hawthorne Studies to work teams of the 1990s and beyond. *Group Dynamics: Theory, Research, and Practice, 4*(1), 44–67. This excellent review and discussion of work teams is a good place to start for those interested in this area.

CHAPTER **13**

BOB ADELMAN/CORBIS

Leadership

LEARNING OBJECTIVES

This chapter should help you understand:

- What leadership is and how the effectiveness of leaders is evaluated
- The various types of power and how they are employed by leaders
- The major elements of the various leadership theories
- The historical development of leadership research and conceptualization
- How to distinguish between leader traits and behaviors
- What kinds of contingencies affect leadership processes
- The most recent theories about leadership, such as leader–member exchange theory, implicit leadership theory, and transformational leadership theory
- The differences between transformational and transactional leaders
- How both gender and culture affect leadership processes
- The role of leader and subordinate emotions in organizational effectiveness

Certainly, the use of the term *leadership* is not limited to academic circles. We are fascinated by leadership—in government, in the community, in the boardroom, on the football field, and on the shop floor. Leadership is an important dimension along which people are evaluated in all walks of life. Leadership is an especially hot topic during political elections. We heard a great deal about the leadership style and qualities of Barack Obama versus Mitt Romney during the U.S. presidential campaign of 2012. The leadership qualities of these two men were a central focus of campaign advertising and constantly debated on news shows.

▼ A Closer Look
What qualities are necessary to be a successful leader?

Defining leadership is no simple matter. Most business professionals would consider Jack Welch, Bill Gates, and the late Steve Jobs to be outstanding leaders, but their personalities and circumstances certainly differed considerably. Have you had the good fortune to spend time with a really terrific leader? What was this person like? If this person was your boss, was he or she able to motivate you to work hard and remain committed to the company? As this last question implies, leadership is intricately linked to other topics in organizational psychology such as work motivation and job attitudes.

Many of us have also known people who seemed to be terrible leaders. These individuals most likely had poor relationships with others, were not respected or trusted, and seemed unable to identify the best way to get work done. Although at times it might seem easy to classify people as good or bad leaders, we'll see in this chapter that the issue is more complex than that.

We will spend considerable time discussing leadership theories and the research that has been conducted about leadership—much of which provides a foundation for the application of leadership theories to organizations. Then, in Chapter 14, we will discuss organizational development techniques and discover how the leadership theories presented in this chapter are applied to organizations.

■ What Is Leadership?

Among the many different definitions of leadership, the one I prefer is this: **Leadership** is a social process through which an individual intentionally exerts influence over others to structure their behaviors and relationships. There are good leaders and bad leaders; merely being given the responsibility and status of a leader doesn't make a person a good leader. Rather, **effective leadership** is a function of the outcomes produced by those who are being led, usually operationalized as the successful long-term performance of the leader's work group or subordinates. The core of leadership, then, is influence over others, and this is typically linked to relationship building. To understand this influence, we need to examine the issue of power in organizations.

■ Theories

Power is defined as an individual's potential influence over the attitudes and behaviors of one or more other individuals (Yukl, 2002). It is a resource that leaders can use to exert influence over their followers or subordinates. Although power is often viewed as something inherently negative, organizations could not survive without power as the basis of influence (Steers, Porter, & Bigley, 1996). John French and Bertram Raven (1958) developed the most often cited and discussed typology of power in the literature. This typology identifies five major bases of power (see Table 13.1), each of which has the potential to play an important role in the leadership and dynamics of an organization.

leadership A social process through which an individual intentionally exerts influence over others to structure their behaviors and relationships.

effective leadership Usually operationalized as the successful long-term performance of the leader's work group or subordinates.

power An individual's potential influence over the attitudes and behavior of one or more other individuals.

Table 13.1 Bases of Power

Legitimate power	Conferred on a person by the organization
Reward power	Exists when an individual controls the reward of others
Coercive power	Exists when an individual controls the punishment of others
Expert power	Held by those who have specific expertise or proficiencies
Referent power	Gained when one is shown respect and admiration by others

Source: French & Raven (1958)

The first base, *legitimate power*, is the power bestowed on an individual by the organization. This is what we think of when we talk about authority. When we question whether a particular employee has the authority to make an important decision, we are asking whether the organization has provided this person with the legitimate power to make that decision. We can certainly think of individuals who, based on the nature of their job titles and responsibilities, have legitimate power. However, they do not necessarily use that power—or use it in effective ways. Some individuals think that all they need to be successful and respected leaders is the legitimate power provided by the company, but as we will soon see, a good deal more than this is required for successful leadership.

The second base, *reward power*, is simply the power that results from controlling the rewards or outcomes that others strive for. Parents have almost unlimited reward power over their kids because they control access to the candy, video games, and Build-a-Bear paraphernalia that children covet. In organizations, the person who makes decisions about employees' raises, promotions, and assignments is said to have reward power. The other side of this coin, however, is the third base: *coercive power*. People with coercive power have control over punishments, which they often use to get others to do what they want. The manager who consistently intimidates employees by arousing fear in them and insinuating that if they don't produce at a particular level, they will be written up, forced to work additional hours, or transferred to a less desirable position is someone who manages through coercion.

Expert power, the fourth base, is associated with an employee's special knowledge or proficiency, but it is not limited to those at the top of an organizational hierarchy. Consider computer technicians, for instance. They're not at the top of the organizational structure, but they have a great deal of expert power that is essential for the functioning of the organization. Without their knowledge, the organization could be crippled. Expert power at lower levels of the organization sometimes balances the legitimate power at upper levels (Steers et al., 1996).

The fifth base, *referent power*, is power gained through respect or admiration. Though strongly related to reputation and status, referent power can be obtained by anyone in the organization, regardless of hierarchical position. For example, an

▼ **A Closer Look**
Think of a time when a boss or leader has taken this approach with you. How did it make you feel? Why wasn't it successful?

employee who is not high up in the organization and thus has low legitimate reward and coercive power may nevertheless have a high level of referent power because she is a well-respected team player who always seems to say and do the right things and is considerate of others' needs and perspectives.

Power certainly plays a role in the classroom. A recent study of 555 undergraduates revealed that when professors operate and behave in accordance with what the authors call "prosocial bases of power"—reward, reference, and expert—students perceive that the professors understand them and so relate to them better (Finn, 2012). More negative perceptions emerge when students perceive that professors behave in accordance with "antisocial bases of power"—legitimate and coercive.

In the remaining sections of this chapter, I will trace the historical development of various leadership theories and summarize the empirical evidence for and against these theories. Before we get started, however, think about the successful leaders you've encountered and consider their similarities and differences. You may be able to identify some similarities, such as being conscientious and having good people skills (although I can think of successful leaders whom I didn't like very much and who didn't have good people skills), but I'm quite certain you can also identify many differences in style, approach, beliefs, values, vision, and behaviors among those effective leaders. In short, there isn't one "best" way to lead. As we proceed with our review of the leadership research, this fact will become clear to you. Indeed, the complexity of effective leadership is what makes studying, predicting, and understanding it both interesting and challenging.

Trait Theories

The first systematic study of leadership began in the 1930s with the development of **trait theories,** which focus on identifying the individual characteristics that make people good leaders. The central question posed by such research concerned what effective leaders had in common. Was it intelligence? Was it a domineering personality? Was it aggressiveness? This trait approach to leadership, sometimes called the *great man/great woman theory*, dominated leadership research into the 1950s. During this beginning phase, the research was largely atheoretical (House & Aditya, 1997), based mostly on commonsense notions of leadership and social interactions. Numerous individual characteristics were studied, including gender, dominance, intelligence, appearance, physical energy, need for power, and need for achievement. In 1948, a seminal review was published by R. M. Stogdill, who uncovered studies in which traits such as intelligence and dominance were significantly related to leader effectiveness. However, the overall results were not very supportive of these relationships, and there didn't appear to be much consistency in the findings. Scholars concluded that there were few, if any, universal traits that predicted leadership (Stogdill, 1948).

Interest in traits waned as a result of reviews like Stogdill's, but interest in their potential role in leadership has remerged in the last 30 years. One

trait theories Leadership theories that focus on identifying the individual characteristics that make people good leaders; sometimes called the *great man/great woman theory*.

TECHNICAL TIP

Recall from Chapter 6 that the Big Five model is a popular and validated classification scheme in which personality is described in terms of five broad dimensions: openness, conscientiousness, extraversion, agreeableness, and neuroticism (OCEAN).

review concluded that factors such as intelligence, dominance, and masculine orientation were consistent predictors not of effective leadership but of the type of person who tends to emerge as a leader in small groups (Lord, DeVader, & Alliger, 1986). That is, in groups without an assigned leader, men viewed as more intelligent and dominant than the others tend to take on the leadership role. In other studies, David Kenny and his colleagues demonstrated that behavioral flexibility—the extent to which an individual is willing and able to consider what behaviors and approaches might work best in a particular situation—is a very useful predictor of who emerges as a leader in small groups (Kenny & Zaccaro, 1983; Zaccaro, Foti, & Kenny, 1991).

One study found that individuals high on dominance, intelligence, and self-efficacy were more likely to emerge as leaders than those with other personality trait patterns (Smith & Foti, 1998). Stogdill himself concluded in 1974 that his earlier paper might have drawn too negative a conclusion regarding the role of traits in leadership. Thus, it appears that traits play a larger role in leadership processes than was believed in the 1950s.

Other recent research has focused on the Big Five traits. A meta-analysis of more than 70 studies found that the Big Five traits accounted for 53% of the variance in leader emergence and 39% in leader effectiveness. In particular, extraversion and conscientiousness appeared to be the most important and consistent predictors (Judge, Bono, Ilies, & Gerhardt, 2002). More recent research has begun teasing apart the effects of the Big Five on leadership outcomes. For instance, one study of military personnel in Singapore found that extraversion plays an important role in **leadership self-efficacy (LSE),** the perceived ability of an individual to successfully accomplish leadership tasks (Ng, Ang, & Chan, 2008). Individuals high on extraversion (i.e., being sociable and assertive) tend to rate highly on leadership self-efficacy scales, which often results in their being effective leaders. A recent laboratory study also found support for these links (Big Five → LSE → leader behaviors/effectiveness). The researchers argue that the Big Five characteristics appear to be more distal leadership traits (i.e., farther from proper leadership behavior in the variable chain) and that distal leadership, in turn, influences motivation constructs like LSE and goal orientation, which impact directly on effectiveness (Hendricks & Payne, 2007).

leadership self-efficacy (LSE)
The perceived capabilities of an individual to successfully accomplish leadership tasks.

Behavior Theories

In the 1950s, after researchers had concluded that no specific traits could consistently predict effective leadership, a new direction was taken. Now the emphasis was on leader *behaviors.* Indeed, the rationale for **behavior theories** was that if traits aren't particularly useful in helping us understand the leadership process and what makes a good leader, perhaps we should begin to look at what leaders actually *do.* Much of the research in this area was conducted at The Ohio State University, the University of Michigan, and the University of Iowa. The Iowa studies, led by Kurt Lewin, examined three types of leadership styles: authoritarian, democratic, and laissez-faire. They revealed that most subordinates prefer democratic leaders but that there isn't much of a relationship between leader style and subordinate behaviors. The conclusions of the Ohio State and Michigan studies were very similar; I focus here on the former

behavior theories
Leadership theories that focus on identifying what leaders actually do, in the hope that this approach will provide a better understanding of leadership processes.

because Ohio State was the location of the most extensive research program ever conducted on leader behaviors.

The Ohio State studies gathered self-reports of leader behaviors using a survey called the Leader Opinion Questionnaire (LOQ), as well as observations and ratings of leader behaviors using a questionnaire called the Leader Behavior Descriptive Questionnaire (LBDQ). The LBDQ items were rated on a five-point scale ranging from "Never" to "Always." After hundreds of different leader behaviors were identified and many dimensions examined, they were categorized in terms of two major dimensions (Fleishman & Harris, 1962). The first dimension, **initiating structure,** refers to behaviors through which leaders define the roles both they and their subordinates play in achieving the group's formal goals. Examples of initiating-structure behaviors include assigning specific tasks to subordinates, planning ahead for the next job to be done, pushing for higher production by setting difficult goals, defining procedures, and so on.

The second dimension, **consideration,** concerns the extent to which leaders act in a supportive way and show concern and respect for their subordinates. Examples of consideration behaviors include emphasizing participative decision making, forging two-way communication, and working to establish a favorable rapport with subordinates. Interestingly, the University of Michigan studies identified two very similar dimensions: *task-oriented behaviors* and *relationship-oriented behaviors.* The terms from the two sets of studies (*initiating structure/task-oriented* and *consideration/relationship-oriented*) are often used interchangeably.

The consideration and initiating-structure dimensions of the LBDQ are shown in Table 13.2, along with 10 behavior statements related to each. Consideration is clearly reflected in such statements as "Does little things to make it pleasant to be a member of the group." Indicative of initiating structure are statements like "Lets group members know what is expected of them." One thing to keep in mind is that leaders are not necessarily one or the other; for instance, a leader can be either high or low on both initiating structure and consideration. In fact, there tends to be a small positive correlation between the two dimensions.

Can you think of a boss you've worked with who was very directive in terms of deadlines and goals but also supportive in his or her interactions with employees? If so, then you have an example of a supervisor who is high on both facets of leadership behaviors. Of course, there are other leaders who have been known to lean fairly far in one direction or the other. For instance, Generals George Patton and Omar Bradley were both extremely successful and respected military leaders during World War II, but Patton was low on consideration and high on initiating structure, whereas Bradley was high on consideration and relatively low on initiating structure. In short, these were leaders in the same field at the same time who attained impressive goals in very different ways.

The most important contribution of the behavioral approach to leadership has been the classification of leader behaviors in terms of the two broad dimensions just discussed. Unfortunately, specific findings have been inconsistent. For instance, some studies have found a negative correlation between consideration behaviors and leader

initiating structure Behaviors through which leaders define their own and their subordinates' roles in achieving the group's formal goals.

consideration The extent to which leaders act in a supportive way and show concern and respect for their subordinates.

Table 13.2 Items from the Leadership Behavior Description Questionnaire (LBDQ)

My Leader/Boss:	Never				Always
	1	2	3	4	5

Consideration

1. Is friendly and approachable.
2. Does little things to make it pleasant to be a member of the group.
3. Puts suggestions made by the group into operation.
4. Treats all group members as his or her equals.
5. Gives advance notice of changes.
6. Keeps to him- or herself. (R)*
7. Looks out for the personal welfare of group members.
8. Is willing to make changes.
9. Refuses to explain his or her actions. (R)
10. Acts without consulting the group. (R)

Initiating Structure

1. Lets group members know what is expected of them.
2. Encourages the use of uniform procedures.
3. Tries out his or her ideas in the group.
4. Makes his or her attitudes clear to the group.
5. Decides what shall be done and how it will be done.
6. Assigns group members to particular tasks.
7. Makes sure that his or her part in the group is understood by group members.
8. Schedules the work to be done.
9. Maintains definite standards of performance.
10. Asks that group members follow standard rules and regulations.

---

*(R) signifies that the item is reverse scored so that the favorability of the item lines up with the rest.

Source: Stogdill, R. M. (1963). *Manual for the Leader Behavior Description Questionnaire–Form XII: An experimental revision.* Columbus, OH: Bureau of Business Research, The Ohio State University.

effectiveness, whereas others have found a positive correlation (for a review, see Bass, 1985). Most of this research was conducted in the 1960s and 1970s, but more recent studies have continued to examine leader behaviors.

Judge, Piccolo, and Ilies (2004) examined the relationships between both consideration and initiating structure and a set of leadership effectiveness indicators via a meta-analysis. In arguing that these leadership behaviors are important and should not be viewed as relevant only to the history of leadership, they reported correlations from .22 to .78 between these behaviors and constructs such as follower job satisfaction, follower motivation, leader performance, and leader effectiveness. A 2008 study has begun to expand our knowledge base in this area. Supervisors' ratings of almost 400 mid-level leaders' consideration behaviors more strongly affected performance ratings than did their ratings of initiating-structure behaviors (Zimmerman, Mount, & Goff, 2008). The authors reasoned that supervisors may weight consideration behaviors so heavily because they understand the role that interpersonal skills play in effective leadership.

A very intriguing approach to traits and behaviors has been presented recently. Researchers have proposed an integrated trait–behavioral model of leadership effectiveness (DeRue, Nahrgang, Wellman, & Humphrey, 2011). Their meta-analysis found that leader traits associated with task competence were related to task-oriented leader behaviors, which had an effect on performance-related leadership outcomes. On the other hand, interpersonal attributes of leaders were related to relationship-oriented behaviors, which had an effect on affect-based criteria like satisfaction with the leader. This approach is likely to get more research attention as leadership researchers continue working to better understand this important process.

As with trait theory, no one set of behaviors has emerged as being consistently predictive of effective leadership across a series of studies. This inconsistency may be due to the use of several different measures of leader behaviors (Schriesheim, House, & Kerr, 1976), the use of questionnaires that relied on participants' recall of behaviors, and a chief focus on lower-level managers (House & Aditya, 1997). It may also be due to the impact of situational variables on the leadership process; this is where the journey takes us next—to contingency theories.

Contingency Theories

Because researchers were unable to discover a specific set of traits or behaviors that predicted effective leadership, they began to consider the role of the situation. In the 1960s, contingency theories grew out of this new approach to the study of leadership. **Contingency theories** differ from both trait and behavioral theories by formally taking into account situational or contextual variables. The central question, in other words, is whether leadership is contingent on the context or situation in which it takes place. We now turn to a brief discussion of two of the best-known contingency theories: Fiedler's contingency theory and path–goal theory.

contingency theories
Leadership theories that differ from both trait and behavioral theories by formally taking into account situational or contextual variables.

Fiedler's Contingency Theory
In 1967, Fred Fiedler published his contingency theory of leader effectiveness, which maintains that effective leadership is a joint function of the characteristics of the leader and the features of the situation. Specifically, he argued that task-oriented leaders are best suited for some situations and that relationship-oriented leaders are best suited for others. This was the first theory to consider how leader characteristics (i.e., traits and behaviors) might interact with situational

variables to determine leader effectiveness. Given that leadership research to this point was dominated by trait and behavioral theories, it was a groundbreaking approach.

Fiedler's theory is described in terms of *situational favorability*, or the extent to which the leader perceives that she has control of the situation. Thus, the situation is deemed favorable (i.e., controllable by the leader) if the leader has a positive relationship with subordinates, if the subordinates' tasks are well defined, and if the leader has the power to make important decisions.

The degree of situational favorability matches up with *leader style* or orientation, which can be measured by the *least preferred coworker (LPC)* scale. On this scale, which contains a list of bipolar adjectives, the leader is asked to describe the single worst coworker that he or she has ever encountered. However, because the construct measured by this scale has never been very well defined, Fiedler's theory has come under criticism (e.g., Hosking & Schriesheim, 1978).

According to Fiedler, rather than measuring a leader's attitudes directly, the LPC scale requires that we infer the leader's investment in task accomplishment through his or her reactions to a coworker who gets in the way of accomplishments. For example, if a leader gave the LPC a very negative rating, we would infer that the rating reflected the leader's frustration or anger (Ayman, Chemers, & Fiedler, 1995). We would also conclude that the leader is task-oriented, meaning that the leader prefers to work toward goals by structuring and controlling tasks. Alternatively, if the leader rated the LPC in favorable terms, the leader would be considered person-oriented, meaning that the leader prefers to reach group goals by working closely with people on an interpersonal basis. Many researchers have criticized the definition of this construct, noting that it has changed considerably with the development of the theory and at times has seemed rather unstable. Fiedler maintains that task-oriented leaders perform best in situations of high and low control, whereas relationship-oriented leaders perform best in situations of moderate control. The empirical results have been mixed, with support for some of the relationships and no support for others (House & Aditya, 1997).

So in the final analysis, despite the many criticisms of Fiedler's theory, it was the first leadership approach to consider *both* situational and individual factors; it should thus be considered an important historical contribution to the development of the field.

In an interesting twist, a meta-analysis found support for an extension of Fiedler's contingency theory called cognitive resource theory, which focuses on intelligence as an important element of leadership. Fiedler (1995) argued, consistent with his contingency theory, that the effect of leader intelligence on leader success was contingent on other variables. In a meta-analysis, researchers found support for this contingency approach by showing that intelligence had a moderately positive effect on leadership success when leaders were under low stress but had no effect on leadership success when leaders were under high stress (Judge, Colbert, &

Ilies, 2004). This supports Fiedler's theory that in stressful situations, an individual uses intelligence to deal with the stress, making that individual unavailable for leadership; meanwhile, the stress distracts the individual from the tasks at hand.

Path–Goal Theory Given that leadership is the process of motivating subordinates, an effective leader is one who adopts whatever approach is most likely to accomplish this goal. With this in mind, we turn to the path–goal theory of leader effectiveness (House, 1971). This theory emerged from a historical context in which results regarding leader behaviors on work group performance and subordinate satisfaction were very inconsistent and in which a cognitive emphasis was inherent in the popular motivational theories of the day. In particular, the path–goal theory arose out of the motivational concepts related to the expectancy theory of Victor Vroom (1964; see also Chapter 9). As you may recall, expectancy theory maintains that individuals are motivated to exhibit particular behaviors if they expect positive outcomes from doing so and if they value those outcomes. According to path–goal theory, leaders will be effective to the extent that they provide subordinates with what they need to increase their motivation to perform.

The path–goal theory specifies a number of situational moderators that influence the relationship between leadership behaviors and their effectiveness. It also identifies four kinds of leader behaviors: *directive leader behaviors, achievement-oriented leader behaviors, supportive leader behaviors,* and *participative leader behaviors* (House, 1996). These categories are presented and defined in Table 13.3. It is interesting to note that directive leader behavior is analogous to initiating-structure behavior (task orientation), while supportive leader behavior is akin to consideration behavior (relationship orientation). Leader behaviors are predicted to have direct effects on subordinates' expectancies and values (as moderated by both subordinate and environmental characteristics), and subordinates' perceptions regarding these expectancies and values

Table 13.3 Path–Goal Theory: Leader Behaviors

Directive leader behaviors	Provide structure by clarifying subordinates' performance goals and clarifying standards used to evaluate subordinates.
Achievement-oriented leader behaviors	Stress personal accomplishments and encourage performance excellence.
Supportive leader behaviors	Focus on interpersonal relations and provide psychological and emotional support for subordinates.
Participative leader behaviors	Encourage subordinates to take an active role through mentoring, guidance, and coaching.

▲ **A Closer Look**
Have your
employment
experiences been
shaped by those
in leadership
positions?

leader–member
exchange (LMX)
theory
A theory about
work dyads that
focuses on the rela-
tionships between
subordinates and
leaders rather than
on leader behaviors
or traits.

affect their satisfaction, effort, and performance (as would be predicted by expectancy theory).

A meta-analysis of these studies found support for the basic propositions related to directive behaviors, task characteristics, and employee satisfaction; however, the results for predicting performance, as well as those involving supportive behaviors as predictors, were much less consistent (Schriesheim & Neider, 1996). Reviews and critical evaluations of the theory and its accompanying research indicate that the theory has not been well tested, owing to methodological problems such as poor measures of the constructs, lack of attention to intermediate variables (i.e., subordinate expectancies and perceptions of values), and lack of control regarding other relevant variables (House, 1996; Schriesheim & Neider, 1996). Recent work has lent support to the basic notion that leader behaviors affect subordinate satisfaction and performance and that this relationship is moderated by the situation or context (see Sarin & O'Connor, 2009; Sims, Faraj, & Yun, 2009).

Contemporary Theories

Newer leadership theories developed in the past 30 years have captured the attention of leadership researchers and practitioners alike. In this section, I will talk about three of these theories in particular: leader–member exchange theory, implicit leadership theory, and transformational leadership theory.

Leader–Member Exchange Theory
We have talked about leadership as being based on behaviors, traits, and interactions between the individual and the situation. Leadership researchers have also begun to view leadership as a reciprocal interaction between two parties (Lord, 2000). **Leader–member exchange (LMX) theory,** for instance, is a theory about work dyads that focuses on the relationships between subordinates and leaders rather than on leader behaviors or traits. A precursor to LMX, developed in the 1970s, was called *vertical dyad linkage (VDL) theory* (Dansereau, Graen, & Haga, 1975). A major premise of VDL theory that has carried over to LMX is the notion that leaders have different relationships with different subordinates. Whereas both trait- and behavior-based theories assume that leaders use the same style or orientation (called *average leadership style*) with all their subordinates, LMX suggests that their styles vary across subordinates. This results in subordinates being placed or classified in the in-group or the out-group. Subordinates in the in-group tend to have good relationships with their leaders based on mutual trust, shared responsibility, and support; those in the out-group do not experience particularly strong relationships with their supervisors and tend to be treated in a more task-oriented fashion (Yukl, 2002).

According to LMX theory, the quality of the leader–follower relationship is predictive of individual-, group-, and organizational-level outcomes (Gerstner & Day, 1997). According to a meta-analysis of about 80 LMX studies, the quality of LMX relationships was significantly related to such outcomes as subordinate performance ratings, job satisfaction, organizational commitment, role clarity, role conflict, and turnover intentions. (In the case of the latter two outcomes, the relationship was negative.)

More recent work has begun teasing out the effects of LMX on performance-related factors (Hofmann, Morgeson, & Gerras, 2003). For example, previous work has been replicated by another study that found positive LMX relationships to be related to favorable performance ratings (see Chapter 5) if the members of the dyad communicated frequently (Kacmar, Witt, Zivnuska, & Gully, 2003). A more recent study of 193 Israeli workers found that favorable LMX relationships predicted employee energy levels and the level of creative work (Atwater & Carmeli, 2009). Finally, in a survey of 181 nurses across seven hospitals of a large healthcare system, job satisfaction was found to mediate the relationship between LMX and turnover. An unfavorable relationship was associated with job dissatisfaction, which was related to high turnover levels (Han & Jekel, 2011).

Some new work has begun to focus on LMX in work teams. A recent study argued that the variability in LMX *within* a work group may have a negative effect on outcomes because team members perceive that the equality principle has been violated if team members receive different levels of respect, trust, and tangible resources (Hooper & Martin, 2008). In a sample of over 400 employees across various jobs, the authors found that perceptions of LMX variability related to more team conflict, which was related to lower levels of job satisfaction and employee well-being. Perhaps leaders need to be careful about developing relationships of different quality with team members. These studies suggest the potential importance and breadth of LMX effects.

Additional new work has focused on the idea of LMX differentiation within individual work teams. A study surveyed over 4,000 employees across 384 departments of a large supermarket chain in an attempt to better understand the role of LMX in affecting team turnover (Nishii & Mayer, 2009). Among the most interesting findings was that turnover was highest when the leader developed very strong LMX relationships with *only some* of the team members, which the authors referred to as high LMX differentiation; this certainly suggests that how managers treat and interact differentially with their team members has huge organizational implications.

A more recent study reports results that qualify those of Nishii and Mayer (2009). In a study of 125 small project teams composed of engineering students, the authors found support for their idea that LMX differentiation would have a positive effect on performance at later time periods (Naidoo, Scherbaum, Goldstein, & Graen, 2011). The researchers argued that LMX differentiation is a result of leaders knowing and understanding their team members; in other words, over time, as leaders recognize the strengths, abilities, and weaknesses of their team members, they learn to treat them differently (e.g., in assignment of tasks varying in difficulty/importance or in how they choose to motivate them), which results in improved performance over time.

Implicit Leadership Theory A very different approach to leadership has been developed by Robert Lord and his colleagues (Lord, Foti, & DeVader, 1984; Lord & Maher, 1991) at the University of Akron. This approach—known as **implicit leadership theory (ILT)**—emphasizes subordinates' perceptions of leader behaviors,

implicit leadership theory (ILT)
A leadership theory that views leadership as the outcome of a perceptual process involving both leaders and subordinates.

in contrast to the theories we've previously discussed, which maintain that leaders affect the performance of subordinates through their own behaviors, traits, charismatic qualities, and ability to structure situations and define roles (Lord, 2000). Specifically, ILT views leadership as the outcome of a perceptual process involving both leaders and subordinates. Lord and Maher (1991) actually define leadership in terms of whether one is perceived by others as a leader. In his more recent work, Lord defines leadership as a process through which the leader changes the way followers envision themselves (Lord & Brown, 2004).

The central idea here is that we all hold implicit beliefs about the personal qualities and behaviors of leaders. These beliefs develop over time and are influenced by experience and socialization. The word **prototype** is sometimes used to refer to one's mental representation of a leader. (My own prototype of a leader, for instance, is someone who is intelligent, has excellent communication skills, is committed to the work that needs to be done and to the people who do it, and knows how to motivate employees.) Lord and his colleagues (1984) have demonstrated in experimental studies that when people observe someone behaving in a way that is consistent with their prototype for an effective leader, they conclude that this person is an effective leader. The implication is that leadership effectiveness may be more about followers' perceptions than about leaders' actions. In an interesting study that connects LMX to ILT, it was shown that employees whose ILT did not match their manager's ILT reported being in a lower-quality LMX relationship (Epitropaki & Martin, 2005).

Other research (Phillips & Lord, 1981) has demonstrated that people develop global impressions of leader effectiveness based on the extent to which a particular leader matches their prototype. Even more important, however, is the finding that people use that global impression to describe the leader and to recall leader behaviors and traits— and that in doing so, they often make errors. An example is presented in Figure 13.1, which concerns my perceptions of my boss, Jared. My experience with Jared's behaviors is evaluated in light of my effective leader prototype (Box A); I have decided that Jared is an effective leader (Box C) because he matches up with salient parts (Box B) of that prototype (i.e., intelligent, excellent communication skills, committed). Now, suppose that I'm asked to rate Jared on whether he is a *self-starter* or on any other dimension of his behavior that I have not observed. I decide that because Jared is an effective leader, and because being a self-starter is part of my effective leader prototype, Jared himself must also be a self-starter (Box D) even though I haven't directly observed this.

The process I've just described is akin to the cart pulling the horse: Jared's behaviors are not driving my ratings of him; rather, my global impression of him as an effective leader colors my ratings of him on other, unobserved dimensions. The implications of this process are fairly serious: When subordinates are asked to rate their leaders on scales such as the LBDQ, we can't be sure whether they are providing valid ratings of their leaders' behaviors. Perhaps they are relying instead on their general impression of their leader as effective or ineffective based on their leadership prototype and how well the leader seems to match that prototype—or, worse, only a few dimensions of that prototype. Lord's work on ILT has been at the center

prototype
One's mental representation of something or someone, such as a leader.

FIGURE 13.1 Implicit Leadership Theory and Leadership Ratings

A

Effective Leader Prototype

1. Intelligent
2. Excellent communication skills
3. Committed
4. Self-starter

B

Jared's Behaviors/Traits

1. Intelligent
2. Excellent communication skills
3. Committed

Prototype Matching Process

C

Leader Evaluation
Jared is an effective leader.

D

Rating Behaviors or Using Global Impressions
Question: Is Jared a self-starter?
Reasoning: "Well, he's an effective leader. Therefore, he is a self-starter."

of leadership research over the past two decades and clearly raises many important issues for future research to consider. His recent work has demonstrated that leader characteristics transfer from old leaders to similar new leaders, but when the new leader is not similar to an old leader, people rely on the general leadership prototype (Ritter & Lord, 2007).

A slightly different wrinkle has been added to this by focusing not only on how subordinates view their leaders as compared to a prototype but also on the role played by subordinates' own views of themselves along a leader prototype scale. A series of studies looking at the perceptions of over 700 employees found that the more subordinates' perceptions of their leader matched their leader prototype, the more they respected the leader and the more effective they perceived him or her to be; these studies also found that this relationship between leader prototype matching and favorable evaluation of the leader was moderated by subordinates' perception of how much they themselves possessed these prototypical leadership qualities (van Quaquebeke, van Knippenberg, & Brodbeck, 2011). For instance, the relationship between leadership prototype matching and the evaluation of the leader's effectiveness was stronger when the subordinate viewed him- or herself as possessing prototypical leadership qualities. The researchers argue that these findings demonstrate how central and important the leadership prototype is to an individual's self-concept.

ILT has been applied to the issues of gender and race as well. Let's look at an example of each. In four studies, researchers examined whether being White was part of the U.S. business leader prototype and found convincing support that participants, regardless of race, tended to assume profiled leaders to be White (Rosette, Leonardelli, & Phillips, 2008). Furthermore, they also found that White leaders were evaluated more favorably than were African American leaders regardless of the

STEVE HIX/SOMOS IMAGES/CORBIS

▲ **A Closer Look**
What does ILT tell us about perceptions of men's versus women's abilities as leaders?

race of the participant. These results are consistent with ILT, where prototypical leaders are predicted to be evaluated more favorably.

In a laboratory investigation that examined the role of gender in leader perceptions (Hall, Workman, & Marchioro, 1998), several groups, each consisting of two men and two women, were assigned to work on either a masculine-typed or feminine-typed task. Each group member provided leader ratings of every other group member. Overall, men were rated higher on leadership scales than women; they were also more likely to emerge as leaders. Specifically, men emerged as leaders in about 70% of the groups. The relationship of gender to leadership ratings was also moderated by task type, such that the differences between males and females on leadership dimensions were greatest when the groups were working on a masculine-typed task. Because the issue of gender is so important in the workplace, we will discuss it in more detail later; it is worth noting here, however, that participants in a recent survey rated "an ideal U.S. president" as more similar to male than female candidates and higher in masculinity than femininity (Powell & Butterfield, 2011).

Transformational Leadership Theory

A major paradigm shift occurred in the leadership work of the mid-1970s, resulting in a class of theories referred to as the *new leadership theories* (House & Aditya, 1997). These theories have the following four characteristics in common: (1) They explain how leaders can take organizations to new heights; (2) they explain how certain leaders are able to achieve extraordinary levels of motivation, commitment, dedication, and so on; (3) they stress emotionally appealing behaviors such as empowering, developing a vision, and role modeling for their subordinates; and (4) they encourage increased follower self-esteem and satisfaction, as well as identification with the leader's values and vision (House & Aditya, 1997).

One of the best known of these leadership theories is **transformational leadership,** in which the interaction of leader and follower raises both to higher levels of motivation and morality than they would achieve individually (Bass, 1985). In effect, transformational leaders attempt to motivate subordinates to transcend their self-interest and achieve more than they think is possible. Both the leader and follower are thus *transformed*, or changed, in some noticeable and important way.

Transformational leadership is distinguished from **transactional leadership,** in which the relationship between leader and follower is based on exchanges and not much more (Bass, 1985; Bass & Steidlmeier, 1999). For instance, leaders who are more transactional than transformational tend to tell their subordinates what is expected of them and what they will get if they meet these expectations rather than emphasizing

transformational leadership
A form of leadership in which the interaction of leader and follower raises both to higher levels of motivation and morality than they would achieve individually.

transactional leadership
A form of leadership in which the relationship between leader and follower is based chiefly on exchanges, with an emphasis on contingent reinforcement.

how the subordinates can grow and develop within the organization. In short, transactional leaders operate on the basis of *contingent reinforcement*, rewarding subordinates for specific behaviors. In real life, all leaders are partly transformational and partly transactional; thus, for example, when I speak of a "transformational leader," I am referring to a leader who tends to be more transformational than transactional.

Transformational leadership can be described in terms of four main components (Bass & Steidlmeier, 1999). The first of these, *idealized influence*, refers to the charisma brought to a relationship by a leader who arouses in the follower a strong desire to identify with or emulate the leader. Leaders who provide the second component, *inspirational motivation*, give followers challenges and a reason to engage in shared goals. Their inspirational appeal focuses on the best in people, such as harmony, charity, and good works (Bass & Steidlmeier, 1999). The third component, *intellectual stimulation*, refers to the process through which transformational leaders increase follower awareness of problems from a new perspective. This approach helps followers to think critically and to approach problems with an open and flexible mind, thus encouraging creative problem solving. Finally, *individualized consideration* is what leaders share with followers when they treat each as an individual, providing support, encouragement, and growth experiences to all.

Overall, transformational leaders concentrate their efforts on long-term goals, develop and articulate a vision to share, inspire followers to enthusiastically pursue that vision, and coach followers to take greater responsibility for their own and others' development. They go the extra mile and do more than just *motivate* their followers; they *inspire* them.

Research has connected transformational leadership to important organizational outcomes like job satisfaction, organizational commitment, and work group performance (House & Aditya, 1997). A meta-analysis has demonstrated that the four main transformational behaviors—idealized influence, inspirational motivation, intellectual stimulation, and individualized consideration—are significantly correlated with leadership effectiveness (Lowe, Kroeck, & Sivasubramaniam, 1996). Transformational leadership results in a high level of subordinate motivation and commitment, in addition to well-above-average performance (House & Aditya, 1997). Of course, elements of transactional leadership are important, too, such as reinforcing subordinates based on their performance. Thus, transformational leaders are more successful if they exhibit some transactional behavior as well, but transactional leadership alone is typically not so successful (Bass, 1985). It has been shown that in military platoons under stressful situations, the best performance resulted from platoon leaders and sergeants who exhibited transactional contingent reward and transformational behaviors (Bass, Avolio, Jung, & Berson, 2003).

Research on transformational leadership continues at a blistering clip. Let's look at a few examples. First, because transformational leadership is believed to bring followers to a higher level of commitment to and identification with the leader and organization, it seems reasonable to expect that it will influence organizational citizenship behaviors (OCBs). Recall from Chapter 4 that OCBs are behaviors that seem to go above and beyond the call of duty—though not necessarily included in one's job description, they tend to be in the best interests of both the organization and one's coworkers. In one study of bankers in Korea, researchers found that transformational leadership worked through justice perceptions to affect OCBs directed at one's supervisor and coworkers (Cho & Dansereau, 2010). For instance, when a leader showed individualized consideration toward followers, those followers perceived the leader as being interpersonally just and proceeded to help the leader through OCBs. A very interesting study was conducted with Israeli kibbutz teachers, who tend to be more collectivistic in their perspective, or *allocentric*, and teachers from an urban location, who tend to be more individualistic, or *idocentric* (Nahum-Shani, & Somech, 2011). The researchers found the relationship between transformational leadership and OCBs to be positive and moderated by allocentrism, such that teachers expressing charisma were also rated as more altruistic by their school principals; this relationship was stronger when teachers were allocentric.

Second, a team of authors have suggested that transformational leadership can actually result in two conflicting outcomes: dependence on the leader or empowered self-direction (Kark, Shamir, & Chen, 2003). These scholars propose that transformational leadership can lead to such a strong personal identification with the leader that the followers become dependent on him or her. On the other hand, transformational leadership can also lead to social identification with coworkers and the organization, resulting in an increase in self-efficacy and self-esteem. In their study of Israeli mid-level managers, they found empirical support for these theoretical relationships. Future research seems necessary to uncover the contextual variables that are likely to result in transformational leadership leading to more empowerment than dependence and vice versa. Of course, links from dependence and empowerment to follower behaviors would be an interesting avenue for additional research as well.

In a very intriguing study of 152 CEOs and over 400 top management team members, researchers demonstrated that the transformational leadership of the CEOs directly impacted the behaviors of top management team members (e.g., risk-taking propensity, collaborative behavior, information exchange), which in turn had an effect on corporate entrepreneurship regarding product innovation and strategic activities (Ling, Simsek, Lubatkin, & Veiga, 2008). This study draws very clear implications for organizations and shows an effect of transformational leadership that goes beyond laboratory studies and theoretical posturing to produce real-world, bottom-line effects. Some studies have also begun examining transformational leadership in teams and have shown positive effects on team functioning.

Another recent study (Schaubroeck, Lam, & Cha, 2007) found this positive transformational leadership–team performance relationship to be strengthened when the team was high on collectivism (i.e., high on shared goals and cohesiveness) and power distance (i.e., having great respect for authority and viewing status differences as legitimate). Because this study's participants were financial services employees in either Hong Kong or the United States, however, the results likely have cultural implications; Western cultures like the United States tend to be low on collectivism and power distance, whereas Eastern cultures like Hong Kong tend to be high on both of these dimensions.

COURTESY OF JAMEN GRAVES

Jamen Graves
PhD, 1999, I/O Psychology, Alliant International (formerly California School of Professional Psychology)
Managing Principal, Korn/Ferry International

As you can see from this chapter, organizational researchers have been trying for a long time to answer the question: "What is leadership?" Similarly, organizations have invested considerable resources to define and operationalize leadership in a manner that fits their strategy and culture. After many years of consulting with organizations of all shapes and sizes, I have seen all types of leadership models. In fact, there are probably as many leadership models as there are organizations. While we could argue that some models are better than others, they have rarely clarified what leadership looks like at each critical level in the organization.

There are many benefits associated with building leadership models, such as giving clarity and priority to particular sets of personal, interpersonal, and organizational competencies that are seen as critical to driving business success. Yet a drawback of these models is that they are based on the assumption that leadership is similar at each level of the organization. Not surprisingly, leaders at each level struggle to put these models into practice. For example, I recall hearing a group of employees from a large financial company respond to the new leadership model by saying, "We get that strategic agility is important to our company, but what does this mean for us?"

Organizations are gradually shifting their models away from a one-size-fits-all approach to a level-specific one. Competencies are moving from broad definitions to specific behavioral indicators. I recently partnered with a large healthcare organization to help define leadership requirements at three different levels. Using the Lominger competency framework, we used three criteria to differentiate leadership expectations at the manager, director, and executive levels. The criteria were time, values, and skills. We found that as the company's leaders move from one level to the next, they spend their time on very different activities, specific values shift, and the skills required also change. For example, as leaders move up to higher levels, they must learn to spend more time developing others and empowering them as opposed to doing the work for them. They must also value success as a result of their team's accomplishments as opposed to viewing success in terms of their individual contributions.

These are not easy transitions to make, yet organizations that can help align and stratify leadership expectations by level are reaping great benefits. Not only can they maximize business performance, they can also attract leaders who are better suited to particular levels and improve how they engage, develop, and retain them.

Applying Your Knowledge

1. What theories discussed thus far in this chapter would help inform the concept of different leadership skills being required for different leadership levels?

2. How does the latest research on LMX on page 401 align with the leadership model described here?

3. How does this leadership model relate to what we know about situational factors in leadership outcomes?

■ New Directions in Leadership Research

Now that we have discussed the various leadership theories at length, I will take a closer look at the impact of gender issues on leadership—a topic with significant implications for the effectiveness of organizations. After that, we will consider the influence of culture on leadership and the role of emotions in leadership.

Gender and Leadership

Certainly, we are all aware of the changing nature of our workforce. Women and minorities are currently being employed at rates far greater than this country has ever seen before. Six out of every 10 women age 16 and over were labor-force participants in 2007; they made up 46% of the labor force, and that number is projected to increase (U.S. Department of Labor, 2008).

About 50% of all high-paying management, professional, and related occupations were held by women in 2007. Sixteen million jobs have been created in the United States over the past decade, and women have secured about half of them (U.S. Department of Labor, 2008).

glass ceiling
Refers to a situation in which qualified individuals are prevented from truly achieving all that they can because of some form of discrimination.

The **glass ceiling** refers to a situation in which qualified individuals are prevented from truly achieving all that they can because of some form of discrimination. The Glass Ceiling Commission was established in 1991 to study the barriers preventing women from rising to the top of the corporate ladder. Its report indicated that although women made up 43% of executive, administrative, and management workers at that time, they held only 3% to 5% of the top executive positions. Furthermore, surveys of Fortune 500 companies reveal that only 12 of the top 500 companies are headed by a female CEO ("Fortune 500," 2008). Other relevant data include the fact that 17% of the members of the 111th Congress were female (17 senators and 74 members of the House of Representatives) ("Women in Government Relations," 2008); women make up over 40% of college faculty but only 23% of college presidents (American Council on Education, 2002); and although about 42% of the associates in our nation's law firms are women, only 16% are partners (American Bar Association, 2004). These data are not limited to the United States. For instance, women in Ireland are not achieving leadership roles in organizations at the same rate as their male counterparts. A series of interviews of 30 female managers in Ireland identified two major individual barriers: (1) a woman's current career stage and (2) a family's current life-cycle stage (Cross, 2010). The women also noted that pregnancy leave often renders women forgotten: They are no longer visible to the organization and seem to get passed over or have their role minimized.

In 2008, Hillary Clinton ran a very strong campaign in the Democratic primaries, coming closer than any woman before to becoming a major political party's candidate for president of the United States. During this time, she noted that her campaign was "making cracks" in the glass ceiling. However, four years later, in the run-up to the 2012 presidential election, only one woman, Minnesota congresswoman Michele Bachmann, declared herself a candidate, and she did not make it very far in the primary process. Indeed, even as women continue to make progress in the workforce and in leadership positions, there is still a long way to go.

Alice Eagly has been a leader herself in bringing issues of gender to the forefront of leadership studies. In a series of meta-analyses, she and her colleagues identified the important variables involved in linking gender to leadership and summarized the big picture. For instance, they have looked at the role of gender in leadership style and found consistent (albeit small) differences between men and women, including the fact that women are more participative and interpersonally oriented than men (Eagly & Johnson, 1990). Their results also demonstrated that in situations that were congenial to a particular gender—such that the characteristics of the situation matched well with the gender roles (e.g., women in the role of head nurse and men in the role of construction manager)— both men and women leaders tended to be task-oriented. This last finding is consistent with Eagly's work on gender role theory. The authors concluded from their extensive review that women tend to lose authority or legitimate power if they employ feminine (participative and interpersonally oriented) styles of leadership in male-dominated roles (Eagly & Johnson, 1990).

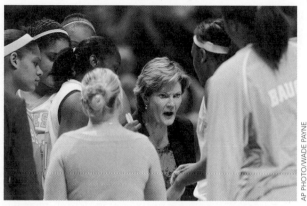

AP PHOTO/WADE PAYNE

▲ **A Closer Look**
Pat Summitt is the all-time winningest coach in NCAA basketball history for either men or women. In 38 years, she never had a losing season, and in 2012 she was awarded the Presidential Medal of Freedom. How do women like Pat Summitt impact the perception of women as leaders?

Another meta-analysis looking at the role of gender in leadership effectiveness (Eagly, Karau, & Makhijani, 1995) asked two very important questions: (1) Are leaders of one gender more effective than leaders of the other gender? (2) Do situations or contexts affect the likelihood that leaders of one gender or the other will be more effective? Again based on gender role theory, these researchers predicted that men would be more effective—or at least *perceived* to be more effective—than women in leadership roles that have been defined in masculine terms. In other words, they anticipated that gender congeniality would moderate the relationship between gender and leader effectiveness.

Some interesting results emerged. First, women and men did not differ overall in terms of their perceived effectiveness as leaders. Second, gender congeniality did moderate the gender/leader effectiveness relationship: Male leaders were perceived as more effective in contexts that were congenial to men, and female leaders were perceived as more effective in contexts that were congenial to women (Eagly et al., 1995). This last finding is especially interesting; it suggests that both men and women are unlikely to be perceived as effective leaders in situations that are not traditionally viewed as gender-congruent. Of course, considering that leadership tends to be defined in masculine terms, women are already at a disadvantage in many leadership situations: In order to behave in a way that is consistent with prototypical leadership (e.g., being aggressive and directive), they must behave in contrast to their gender roles (e.g., being nurturing, supportive, and participative). Thus, women are criticized for not being "leader-like" due to their feminine characteristics—but when they adjust and take on more masculine traits in order to be viewed as "leader-like," they are criticized for not being true to their femininity. This conflict is at the root of the stress and struggles faced by many women in leadership positions today.

Of course, the position of leader has traditionally been viewed by the general public as being a male role, so the fact that women have been hindered in obtaining and being successful in leadership positions has more to do with stereotypes about leadership than about women's actual ability to lead. A recent meta-analysis by Eagly and her colleagues summarized over 200 effects and concluded that stereotypes of leaders are "decidedly masculine" (Koenig, Eagly, Mitchell, & Ristikari, 2011). This is consistent with Lord's work on ILT, discussed earlier in the chapter. In fact, one recent study speaks directly to this issue. Following from Lord's work on leader categorization theory (or ILT), researchers asked whether gender stereotypes bias leadership perceptions during encoding (i.e., processing and storage of behaviors) rather than just at the point at which the target's behaviors are compared with his or her leadership prototype. In a series of studies, it was found that participants were less likely to encode task-based (or masculine) leadership traits when the leader was female rather than male (Scott & Brown, 2006). In other words, people store behaviors as being indicative of different traits, depending on the gender of the leader. Furthermore, task-based behaviors tend to be more typically linked with favorable leadership traits when exhibited by men than when exhibited by women.

Using gender role theory as a background, Eagly and her colleagues predicted that men would emerge as leaders in contexts or situations that were consistent with male gender roles and that women would emerge as leaders in contexts or situations that were consistent with female gender roles. An extensive meta-analysis of the existing literature supported their predictions: Men emerged more often as leaders in task-oriented situations, whereas women emerged more often as leaders in socially oriented situations (Eagly & Karau, 1991). A recent study found that women high on dominance (an empirically identified leader trait) were more likely to emerge as a leader in a laboratory setting with a male partner when provided with a female leader role model. However, even women high on dominance as a personality trait tended not to emerge as leaders when experiencing a male leader model (Carbonell & Castro, 2008).

Another line of research has used identical and fraternal twins to demonstrate that only about 30% of the variance in leadership occupancy (i.e., the extent to which individuals have held leadership positions) in both males and females could be accounted for by genetic factors; almost 70% was due to environmental factors (Arvey, Rotundo, Johnson, Zhang, & McGue, 2006; Arvey, Zhang, Avolio, & Kreuger, 2007). The researchers conclude that most of the variance in leadership ratings and leadership occupancy appears attributable to work, broader life events, and other yet undiscovered factors. This suggests that learning how to lead is a very reasonable goal for both males and females who aspire to be future leaders—perhaps leaders are not born but made! Obviously, the social context and our experiences with others impact our leadership behaviors and successes.

Some have argued over the years for the "feminine advantage" perspective on leadership effectiveness (Yukl, 2002). The notion is that because women are more adept at being inclusive, interpersonally sensitive, and nurturing than are men, they should be better leaders. Vecchio (2002) argues convincingly against this perspective by citing a good deal of research that did not find these differences between the genders. However, a meta-analysis of leadership behaviors across genders found that female leaders tended to exhibit higher levels of transformational leadership behaviors and transactional contingent reward behaviors than did male leaders, who tended to exhibit higher levels of the typically less effective transactional behaviors than did female leaders (Eagly, Johannesen-Schmidt, & van Engen, 2003). Although these differences were generally small, they were statistically significant; there were also small statistical differences between genders on leadership outcomes such as effectiveness, with females performing better than males. Obviously, Vecchio's analysis and Eagly and her colleagues' review lead to different conclusions, suggesting the need for additional research and better conceptual development (for a review, see Eagly, 2007).

Culture and Leadership

Although cultural issues were ignored by leadership researchers for many years, they have since become the focus of research (Dickson, Hanges, & Lord, 2000) due to the global economy and the increased diversification of organizations. Some scholars have referred to the interest in cross-cultural leadership as an "explosion" in the field (Dickson, Den Hartog, & Mitchelson, 2003). Indeed, Robert House and his colleagues have proposed a theory of cross-cultural leadership maintaining that expected, accepted, and effective leader behavior varies by culture (House & Aditya, 1997). According to these authors, what a particular culture values in its leaders is based on the implicit leadership theory endorsed by that culture. This idea is, of course, an extension of Lord's work on ILT (Lord, 2000; Lord et al., 1984; Lord & Maher, 1991).

An interesting study demonstrated that leadership prototypes develop through different processes in individualistic versus collectivistic cultures (Ensari & Murphy, 2003). Ideas along these lines constitute one focus of the ongoing Global Leadership and Organizational Behavior Effectiveness (GLOBE) research project, which involves 61 countries and more than 200 researchers led by House. These researchers argue that although some leader behaviors or traits are universally accepted and effective, there are many others for which acceptance and effectiveness are more culture specific (House & Aditya, 1997). GLOBE researchers argue that future research from the GLOBE project should show with increasing frequency the many leadership effects or processes that are moderated by culture (Dickson et al., 2003). Two books are noted in the list of suggested readings at the end of this chapter that report on results from the GLOBE research program.

It is likely that many other traits and behaviors vary across cultures. One study demonstrates just such expected differences (Gerstner & Day, 1994). When these researchers administered a survey measuring 59 leadership traits to a sample of international and American graduate students (the international sample consisted of students from China, France, Germany, Honduras, India, Japan, and Taiwan), they found that the traits seen as most characteristic of business leaders varied across cultures. This result suggests that leadership prototypes also vary across cultures. For instance, the five most prototypical traits identified by Japanese participants were *disciplined,*

ASIA IMAGES GROUP/ASIAPIX

▲ **A Closer Look**
How much overlap is there between what Western and Eastern cultures consider leadership traits?

intelligent, trustworthy, educated, and *responsible;* those identified by U.S. participants were *persistent, industrious, good verbal skills, goal-oriented,* and *determined.* In short, there are clear differences between these two cultures in terms of what they view as prototypical leadership.

Two other findings are interesting. First, no single trait emerged in the top-five category across all eight countries, indicating the considerable variability of leadership prototypes; however, *goal-oriented* was the trait seen as prototypical in the largest number of countries. Second, categorizing cultures as either Western or Eastern resulted in some consistency within these two subgroups. In cultures categorized as Western (i.e., France, Germany, Honduras, India, and the United States), *determined* was highly prototypical, while in those categorized as Eastern (i.e., Taiwan, China, and Japan), *intelligence* was highly prototypical.

More recent work looking at attitudes and perceptions across 21 countries found that self-ratings of leadership characteristics were more apt to relate to both peer and subordinate ratings in cultures characterized by high assertiveness (Atwater, Wang, Smither, & Fleenor, 2009). Other findings of this study also suggest that self-awareness is really important and may explain differences in leader effectiveness across cultures. Another important cultural variable, *power distance*—the extent to which an individual or culture sees power and authority as hierarchical or egalitarian—has been examined in terms of leadership. A recent study of employees in the United States and China found that transformational leadership was more positively linked to procedural justice when employees were lower on power distance (Kirkman, Chen, Farh, Chen, & Lowe, 2009). The effects of transformational leadership also impacted the frequency of OCBs through perceptions of justice and power distance.

The authors of this study concluded that there are reliable differences in leadership perceptions across cultures. The implication is that we need to understand these and other differences much more thoroughly if we are to comprehend the true nature of leadership processes. Indeed, a heightened awareness of such differences may help employees understand their coworkers better and may help organizations understand their employees better as the workplace continues to become more diverse and global in nature. One of the great scholars in the area of gender and leadership, Alice Eagly, argues that we have compartmentalized diversity constructs from the leadership literature (Eagly & Chin, 2010). By this she means that our leadership theories have developed with little regard for diversity issues and that when we do consider diversity issues, we do so separately from the leadership theory per se—there isn't much integration. She strongly encourages researchers to consider how their leadership theories can incorporate gender, race, ethnicity, culture, and sexual orientation. Furthermore, she proposes that researchers should draw on the research and theory that has addressed these diversity issues and build new leadership theories that truly consider these issues as mainstream and important—or alter existing ones to incorporate them.

Emotions and Leadership

Mood, emotions, and affect have become hot topics in I/O psychology in recent years. Accordingly, leadership researchers have begun to examine the role of emotions in the leadership process. For instance, research has begun drawing links between transformational leaders' emotional expressions and various outcomes. A recent study showed clearly that transformational leaders express more positive emotions than do less transformational leaders and that these positive emotions have a direct effect on followers' moods. Furthermore, both leaders' emotions and followers' moods had positive effects on leader effectiveness and the perceived attractiveness of the leader (Bono & Ilies, 2006).

A second area where emotions and leadership are being connected involves **emotional intelligence (EI),** or the ability to assess and manage one's own emotions as well as understand those of others. Emotional intelligence and cognitive ability are often identified as key variables in determining leader effectiveness. A recent study demonstrated that an element of EI, empathy (the ability to understand and identify with another's feelings), plays a central role in affecting leadership perceptions as well as both relational and task-based leadership behaviors (Kellett, Humphrey, & Sleeth, 2006). These results suggest that emotionally intelligent leaders create a bond with their followers because the followers feel valued and understood.

The link between EI and organizational outcomes has been investigated in a recent study of South Korean employees in which it was argued that EI worked through transformational leadership in affecting leader effectiveness (Hur, van den Berg & Wilderom, 2011). The researchers concluded that leaders high in EI are more effective leaders because they exhibit more transformational behaviors. Here, we see a very clear integration of the interplay of affective variables (EI) with leader behaviors from the theory of transformational leadership in an Eastern culture; this research is a great example of how a few of the major elements in this chapter can be combined in one research program.

In a recent review and analysis, the authors noted the likely importance of EI in leadership but also pointed out that the evaluation data on the effectiveness of training programs teaching emotional/social skills are weak and inconclusive (Riggio & Lee, 2007). More sophisticated research is necessary to provide more direction regarding how to best develop leaders' emotional skills.

In talking about emotional labor in Chapter 10, we made the point that some employees, such as those in customer service jobs, often have to work at suppressing their negative emotions and displaying only positive ones. A very interesting conceptual paper has recently posited a model of leader emotional labor that includes elements like affective events and individual difference as antecedents to leaders' emotional displays (Gardner, Fischer, & Hunt, 2009). Emotional displays then impact leader well-being through followers' perceptions of favorability, trust, and authenticity

emotional intelligence (EI) The ability, capacity, or skill to identify and manage one's own emotions and understand the emotions of others.

for the leader. Although no research has been published testing the model's propositions, I expect the research is on the way and should prove quite interesting in the area of leader emotion regulation and emotional labor.

■ Summary

This chapter provided an overview of leadership, with an emphasis on the theoretical and empirical work done in the field. I began by defining leadership and demonstrating how the concept of power and its different types relate to leadership processes. I then emphasized that leaders use different types of power in different situations and that some leaders rely on some types of power more than other types.

Next, I presented the major theories of leadership, with an eye toward tracing their historical development; my rationale here was to show that history provides clues about how our thinking on leadership has evolved and become more sophisticated. I then described trait theories as the first real systematic approach to leadership, explaining that because no traits consistently emerged as necessary to be a good leader, this approach was largely abandoned (albeit revived later) in favor of research on leadership behaviors. The latter has revealed that some effective leaders exhibit mostly consideration behaviors, whereas others exhibit mostly initiating-structure behaviors. Taking a different direction, I then considered research on situational and individual moderators, as well as contingencies. In particular, I presented Fiedler's theory as an important new approach that eventually came under criticism—with the result that leadership advocates began looking elsewhere for a theoretical orientation.

In a later section, I spent considerable time discussing three contemporary theories— LMX theory, ILT, and transformational leadership theory—that have great potential to help us understand leadership processes. I also noted that the perspective on leadership taken by both LMX and ILT is very different from that of more traditional theories. At the conclusion of the chapter, I described three cutting-edge issues in leadership that promise to be relevant in the 21st century—gender, culture, and emotions. These issues merit further study, as an understanding of their impact on leadership processes promises to enhance organizational practice.

■ Key Terms

behavior theories (p. 394)
consideration (p. 395)
contingency theories (p. 397)
effective leadership (p. 391)
emotional intelligence (EI) (p. 413)
glass ceiling (p. 408)
implicit leadership theory (ILT)
    (p. 401)
initiating structure (p. 395)

leader–member exchange (LMX) theory
    (p. 400)
leadership (p. 391)
leadership self-efficacy (LSE) (p. 394)
power (p. 391)
prototype (p. 402)
trait theories (p. 393)
transactional leadership (p. 404)
transformational leadership (p. 404)

■ TAKING IT TO THE FIELD

Leadership is a topic that has generated considerable interest. Unfortunately, many different pop psychology and management resources provide suggestions and recommendations that lack empirical support. As a result, people without a background in research may sometimes fall prey to bad advice. Kyle and Sophie Konig are the founders of KoniGames, a company that designs and manufactures children's games. Their company has recently experienced an uptick in turnover, and during some of the exit interviews, departing employees complained about the "lack of leadership" in the company. Kyle and Sophie have consulted Hollister Consulting on what to do about the problem and are now looking to you for a second opinion on the change strategy proposed by Hollister. Review and evaluate each of the three items Hollister put forth. Be sure to cite any flaws and propose alternate steps that Kyle and Sophie can take to remedy their situation.

Hi again—

KoniGames has gone through a lot of changes over the past year. We were previously a very small company (fewer than 100 employees), and we were able to get to know each and every one of our employees. Once our games took off, though, we had to expand rapidly, and we both feel like we've lost a connection with our employees. We contacted Hollister Consulting to get their suggestions, but we want to see what you think of what they said.

First, Hollister suggested that we increase our legitimate power by giving ourselves new titles. We've always referred to ourselves as "Founders," but Hollister indicated that we should designate ourselves as "CEOs" so that our employees know we are in charge and will respond more quickly when we tell them what to do.

Second, Hollister suggested that we choose our best employees as "favorites" and provide them with a lot of rewards. They said that LMX theory has been proven to show that when other employees see these favorites earning special privileges, it will motivate them to work harder to become favorites as well.

Third, Hollister suggested that we restructure the hierarchy so that Kyle is in charge and Sophie works under him. They indicated that this would be a better structure because men tend to be more effective as leaders.

What do you think? If these aren't good suggestions, what would you advise instead?

Kyle & Sophie

■ Critical Thinking Questions

1. The theories of transformational and transactional leadership suggest two very different ways to lead. Is one of these approaches universally more effective than the other, or do both approaches work equally well in certain situations? How could you use both? What would that theory look like?

2. Based on what you read in this chapter, how has the role of gender in leadership changed over the past few decades? How do you think gender will factor into

leadership in the future? How about race—what do you expect to see happen in that domain and why?

3. The trait theory of leadership suggests that certain individual characteristics make people more effective leaders. Based on this perspective, do you believe that leaders are "born" or "made"?

4. Leader–member exchange theory focuses on relationships that are formed between leaders and followers. Leadership research often focuses on the leader, but what sort of role do followers play in contributing to effective leadership?

5. The chapter talked a great deal about leadership perceptions. Why are leadership perceptions so important? Where do relationships fit into this puzzle?

■ Application Questions

1. Consider each of the bases of power. How might a college instructor demonstrate each of these? How do you react when instructors use these types of power?

2. One aspect of LMX theory that researchers are beginning to explore is the varying quality of relationships within a team. Research demonstrates that when leaders have very strong relationships with only a few team members, it leads to turnover. Have you ever experienced something like this? Were you one of the favorites or one of the "outsiders"? What effect did this have on you?

3. Imagine you have a friend who is interested in becoming more transformational in her leadership style. What behaviors would you suggest she increase in order to become more transformational?

4. Consider some examples of famous female leaders. What are some ways in which female leaders are treated differently from male leaders (by the media as well as by peers and followers)?

5. Consider implicit leadership theory. People's reliance on stereotypes and prototypes are not an issue only in the study of leadership. What is another example from I/O psychology of people relying on stereotypes to evaluate others?

■ Suggested Readings

Chhokar, J. S., Brodbeck, F. C., & House, R. J. (2007). *Culture and leadership across the world: The GLOBE book of in-depth studies of 25 societies.* Thousand Oaks, CA: SAGE. This book describes the culture of particular countries and the leadership behaviors that go hand in hand with the respective culture. This is a very interesting read that makes recommendations for how to lead in cultures that are not your own.

Eagly, A. H., & Chin, J. L. (2010). Diversity and leadership in a changing world. *American Psychologist, 65*(3), 216–224. This paper provides great insight into leadership and the role diversity plays. Eagly is a dynamic leader in this field and she draws on her career's work to present a foundation and a look to the future.

House, R. J., & Aditya, R. N. (1997). The social scientific study of leadership: Quo vadis? *Journal of Management, 23*(3), 409–473. A great review of leadership theories—and one that presents relevant research on each theory.

House, R. J., Hanges, P. J., Javidan, M., Dorfman, P. W., & Gupta, V. (2004). *Culture, leadership, and organizations.* Thousand Oaks, CA: SAGE. This book summarizes surveys of over 17,000 middle managers in three industries across 62 cultures. A fascinating study is described in this book by the actual researchers who have been intricately involved in this huge and important project.

Lord, R. G., & Brown, D. J. (2004). *Leadership process and follower identity.* Mahwah, NJ: Erlbaum. Lord's latest scholarly take on the leadership field is both fascinating and very readable.

Steers, R. M., Porter, L. M., & Bigley, G. A. (1996). *Motivation and leadership at work* (6th ed.). New York: McGraw-Hill. This easy read covers all the major theories in the areas of both motivation and leadership.

STEWART COHEN/GETTY IMAGES

CHAPTER **14**

Organizational Theory and Development

What do you think about the company you work for? Is it a good company? Is it a company for which you expect to work for a long time, or is it just serving your needs right now? If your company is a good one to work for, what is it that makes it good? Is it financially successful? Does it treat its employees with respect and dignity? Do employees have input into the company's direction? I think these are all good questions, and the answers say a great deal about the organization that employs you.

Over the course of the past decade, Apple has been at or near the top of *Fortune* magazine's list of 100 Best Companies to Work For and in 2011 topped the list of the most admired companies in the world for the fourth straight year ("World's Most Admired Companies," 2011). Wegman's Food Markets, a leader in grocery stores, has also been consistently rated as one of the best 100 companies to work for ("100 Best Companies to Work For," 2012). What do these companies have in common that allows them to be so successful—not only economically and competitively but also from the perspective of employees and applicants? In addition to providing employee-centered benefits such as medical benefits, fitness centers, onsite stores, profit sharing, and elder-care assistance (as we have discussed in earlier chapters), companies like these emphasize the culture or environment in which their employees work.

One theme throughout this text has been that, given the changes confronting the world of work (e.g., downsizing, empowerment, global competition, diversity), organizations need to be forward-looking. Indeed, to remain competitive economically, attractive to applicants, and valued by employees, organizations today must be willing and able to alter their environment—a move that sometimes necessitates a complete change of direction. As a reflection of the need to change, this chapter discusses organizational theories that are used to categorize, analyze, and improve organizations, with a focus on how organizations behave and what techniques they can use to operate more effectively and efficiently to compete in this ever-changing and increasingly competitive business environment.

■ Organizational Theory

Organizational theory can be defined as a set of propositions that explains or predicts how groups and individuals behave in varying organizational structures and circumstances (Shafritz, Ott, & Jang, 2011). It is not a stretch to say that much of how the world behaves is relevant to the study of organizational theory. From our various community associations to our local churches, from government agencies to local and national charities to the workplace, organizational theory can help explain and predict behaviors that take place in many aspects of our lives. In order to explain the structure and functioning of organizations, I discuss organizational theory specifically in the context of the last category, the workplace. *Classical organizational theory*—one of three major organizational approaches—is important in this context.

organizational theory
A set of propositions that explains or predicts how groups and individuals behave in varying organizational structures and circumstances.

Classical Organizational Theory

Some scholars have argued that organizational theory has its roots in ancient or medieval times, but the formal study of organizational theory appears to have begun when factories became popular in Great Britain in the 1700s (Shafritz & Ott, 1996). Classical organizational theory, the first type of organizational theory to develop, has four basic tenets (Shafritz & Ott, 1996):

- Organizations exist for economic reasons and to accomplish productivity goals.
- Scientific analysis will identify the one best way to organize for production.
- Specialization and the division of labor maximize production.
- Both people and organizations act in accordance with rational economic principles.

With the building of large, complex factories came a multitude of new and sophisticated problems managers had to handle. To be successful in this new economy, industrial and mechanical engineers needed to organize production systems to keep the machines busy and work flowing. Toward this end, workers were viewed as merely part of the mix—as interchangeable cogs in an organization-wide machine. In fact, a common argument was that organizations should work like machines, with people and technology as their components. The four preceding tenets helped maintain this focus.

Two particular developments occurred within classical organizational theory: scientific management and bureaucracy. We will consider each in turn.

Scientific Management
In the late 1800s and early 1900s, Frederick Taylor provided a framework that he believed would be useful in structuring organizations. From the perspective of this framework, which he called *Scientific Management,* the

FRIEDRICH STARK/ALAMY

▲ A Closer Look
How did
Frederick Taylor
improve the effi-
ciency of assem-
bly lines in U.S.
factories of the
early 1900s?

organization is a machine—a pragmatic machine whose focus is simply to run more effectively. The Scientific Management school conducted time and motion studies and analyzed temperature, illumination, and other conditions of work, all the while looking at the effects of these conditions on productivity and efficiency. *Taylorism,* as this approach was sometimes called, had as its premise the notion that there is one best way to get the job done. Accordingly, its tactics were quite simple: Conduct studies that gather data indicating what the fastest and most efficient method is, then implement that method. In short, Taylorism maintained that factory workers would be much more productive if their work was designed scientifically. In the early 1900s, this notion became a movement; sweeping through our nation's factories, it had a profound—almost revolutionary—effect on the business field (Shafritz & Ott, 1996).

Scientific Management can be summarized in terms of four principles (Taylor, 1916/1996). First, management gathers data from the workers, who are in the best position to understand the job duties and tasks. These data are analyzed and reduced to laws and rules, which are applied to workers' jobs in the form of detailed procedures and how-to explanations. Second, workers are selected carefully—or, as Taylor put it, "scientifically"—and then trained so that they become more efficient than ever before. Third, scientific selection, data collection, and training are combined to enhance efficiency. Taylor argued that these processes must be brought together because science and workers are not a "natural combination." Finally, the work itself is redistributed, with management taking over tasks previously left to subordinates (e.g., factory workers). Taylor emphasized that cooperation and genuine sharing of the labor were important if the overall process was to work (see Wagner-Tsukamoto, 2007).

In one of his last addresses before he died in 1915, Taylor gave an example of how Scientific Management, when applied to the "science of shoveling," had worked at Bethlehem Steel (Taylor, 1916/1996). Taylor noticed that there was great variability in the loads that men placed on their shovels; he proceeded to scientifically study this process by paying a couple of employees to shovel for a specified period of time with varying loads. What he found was that efficiency—that is, amount shoveled in a specified amount of time—varied as a function of the size of the shovel load (see Figure 14.1). The employees started with a 38.5-pound load, using increasingly smaller loads as testing continued. As the loads got smaller, efficiency improved, due largely to the employees' greater strength and energy. However, at about 20 pounds, efficiency began to decrease. The optimum shovel load turned out to be about 20.5 pounds—the weight at which the most ore or coal could be moved in a fixed amount of time. Taylor then developed shovels with a maximum capacity of 21 pounds and taught

FIGURE 14.1 An Example of Taylorism

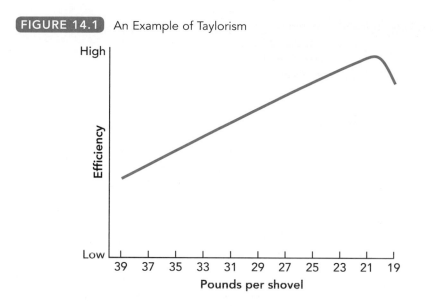

employees how to use them. The use of these new shovels resulted in an almost immediate increase in efficiency: Each shoveler's daily yield of coal went from 16 tons to 59 tons!

Bureaucracy Max Weber was a German sociologist who studied organizations in the late 1800s and early 1900s. Specifically, he analyzed historically large and efficient organizations such as the Egyptian empire, the Prussian army, and the Roman Catholic Church (Wagner & Hollenbeck, 1998). Weber used these careful analyses to develop the notion of *bureaucracy*, which, in his view, described the structure, organization, and operation of many efficient organizations. Let's consider four major features of a bureaucratic organization.

First, each job in a bureaucratic organization is a specialized position with its own set of responsibilities and duties. Weber called this idea **division of labor**—a rather simple approach in which employees are narrowly trained to do only the particular tasks and duties assigned to their jobs. Dividing up tasks in this manner allows the organization to take advantage of individuals' particular strengths, thus avoiding the problems that result from asking people to perform tasks requiring skills they don't have. Of course, one potential difficulty in bureaucracies involves the coordination of various tasks handled by various employees. In other words, it is good that each employee has his or her particular task to do, but it can be difficult to coordinate the many tasks done by all employees while at the same time ensuring a particular outcome or end product for the organization.

Second, bureaucracies tend to be top-down pyramidal organizations, like the one shown in the top panel of Figure 14.2. At every level of the organization (except for the very top), employees report to a person one level up in the chain of command.

division of labor
An approach whereby each job in a bureaucratic organization is a specialized position with its own set of responsibilities and duties.

FIGURE 14.2 Contrasting Organizational Structures

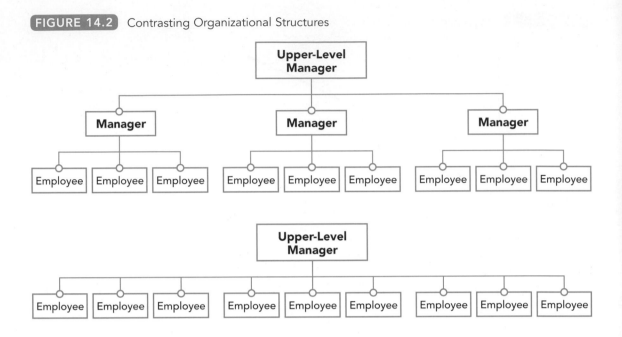

According to Weber, this hierarchical system of supervision is necessary if the division of labor is to be beneficial.

Third, bureaucracies rely on the principle of **delegation of authority**, an approach whereby supervisors, rather than trying to do everything themselves, assign particular tasks to separate employees and hold them responsible for completing these tasks. We have all experienced managers who are incapable of delegating; these managers—often called **micro-managers**—try to take charge of everything that goes on in the organization rather than holding employees responsible for individual tasks.

Finally, bureaucracies are characterized by a **span of control**. This feature, which is related to the chain-of-command idea, refers to the number of subordinates who report to a given supervisor. As you might imagine, the goal for organizations is to find just the right span of control. If the span of control is too large, supervisors are unable to effectively manage the many subordinates; if it is too small, there is an over-abundance of supervisors managing too few employees. Historically, the optimal span of control has varied considerably across companies, but the trend in the late 20th and early 21st centuries has been toward larger spans of control as a result of smaller numbers of middle-level managers (see Chapter 1). A comparison of the top and bottom panels in Figure 14.2 shows what happens to the span of control when layoffs or organizational restructuring results in the reduction of middle-level management, as happened dramatically in the United States during the 1990s and has happened again with the recent recession.

delegation of authority
An approach whereby supervisors assign particular tasks to separate employees and hold them responsible for completing these tasks.

micro-managers
Managers who, instead of delegating individual tasks to employees, try to take charge of all tasks.

span of control
The number of subordinates who report to a given supervisor.

In a classic text on the psychology of organizations, Daniel Katz and Robert Kahn (1978) emphasize two additional issues that are important to Weberian bureaucracy: *standardization of tasks* and *centralized decision making*. Task standardization is analogous to Taylor's notion of the "one best way" to get a job done, in that it pertains to the training of employees toward that end. Related to the notion of a chain of command is the idea that decision making should be centralized. I noted earlier that it can be difficult to coordinate the many tasks done by individual employees while at the same time moving the work of the organization along. This becomes easier in a bureaucratic system, in which major decisions are made by one or more individuals who are centralized under one command, as in the military.

It is no secret that bureaucracies today are viewed with skepticism and perhaps even disdain. The U.S. government and even universities are often described as excessively bureaucratic. Here, too, however, we need to consider the historical period in question—specifically, the context in which Weber developed his model of bureaucracy and Taylor developed the concept of Scientific Management. At this point in the late 19th and early 20th centuries, there were no theories of organizations and no reliable format or framework to follow in developing an organization or improving organizational functioning. The industrial revolution had begun in the 18th century, and large factories came into their own throughout the 19th century. During these early years, there was little or no sense of how industrial organizations should be run, and disorder and chaos were prevalent. Indeed, Scientific Management and bureaucracies were developed to provide these directionless organizations with formal, orderly, and efficient functioning. Both of these approaches proved to be very helpful at the time.

In more modern times, however, theorists have begun to argue that bureaucratic structures are ineffective for organizations operating in rapidly changing environments, such as the high-tech industry. For instance, in 2007 Andrew Speaker was allowed to fly to Europe for his wedding and honeymoon despite the fact that he had drug-resistant tuberculosis. His name was left off the no-fly list due to legal concerns, bad judgment, poor communication, bureaucratic turf fights, and technological problems (Hsu, 2007).

Weber himself warned that work in a bureaucracy can be so simplified and unchallenging that workers might become dissatisfied and unmotivated, resulting in lower productivity overall (Wagner & Hollenbeck, 1998). Some recent work has demonstrated the complexities involved in changing a bureaucracy into a different type of organization (Hopfl, 2006; Josserand, Teo, & Clegg, 2006). Arguably, it was these basic criticisms of both bureaucracy and Scientific Management that led to the development of alternative theories of organizations.

▼ **A Closer Look**
The military uses a central decision making body reflective of a bureaucratic system. What are the benefits and drawbacks to bureaucratic systems?

DoD PHOTO BY MASS COMMUNICATION SPECIALIST
1ST CLASS CHAD J. MCNEELY

Humanistic Theory

The human relations movement resulted, in part, from a reaction to the rigidity of classical organizational theory. Factors that were not even remotely associated with the classical approach to organizations—such as employees' motives, goals, and aspirations—were emphasized by those in the human relations movement (Katz & Kahn, 1978). The relationship between supervisor and subordinate has been especially important in the humanistic theory of organizations, which explains organizational success in terms of employee motivation and the interpersonal relationships that emerge within the organization.

Perhaps the best example of humanistic theory is D. M. McGregor's (1960) work on Theory X and Theory Y. McGregor argued that managers' beliefs and assumptions about their employees determine how they behave toward those employees. Managers' behaviors, of course, affect employees' attitudes and behaviors, which in turn affect managers' attitudes, beliefs, and behaviors (see Chapters 10 and 13 for more details). This cycle is illustrated in Figure 14.3, which clearly shows the importance of the interaction between employees and management. This interaction often involves a *self-fulfilling prophecy* in which employees, over time, learn to act and believe in ways consistent with how managers think they act and believe—even if this wasn't the case initially.

According to McGregor, employees were traditionally viewed as lazy, interested only in what's best for themselves, inherently uninterested in work, lacking in ambition, and not very intelligent. Management's job, therefore, was to control and direct employees in order to make economic profits. Without a firm hand, it was thought, employees would be passive and unresponsive to the organization's needs. This perspective is what McGregor refers to as *Theory X*; he argues that it was the most prevalent set of beliefs about employees from the birth of industry until the mid-1900s.

FIGURE 14.3 Self-Fulfilling Theory X Cycle

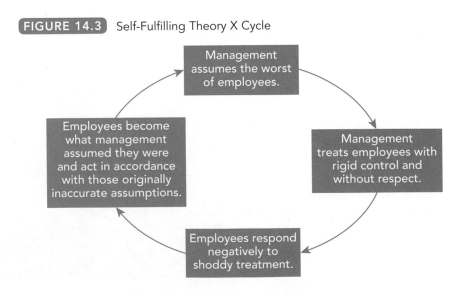

In order for organizations to develop and become truly effective, a different approach was needed—and, according to McGregor, this had to start with management's view of employees. McGregor did not dispute the notion that employees lacked ambition and were somewhat lazy, but he argued that they had developed these behaviors because of the way they were treated by managers, whose behaviors in turn stemmed from their preconceived notions about employees. So, again, we see the vicious cycle depicted in Figure 14.3. McGregor proposed *Theory Y* as a new perspective necessary for improving both employees and organizations.

Table 14.1 presents the assumptions and responsibilities of management under both Theory X and Theory Y. The differences are clear: Compared with Theory X, Theory Y takes a much more humanistic and developmental orientation, emphasizing not only the inherent goodness, capacity, and potential of employees but also their readiness to develop those inherent characteristics. Theory Y also emphasizes management's responsibility for nurturing those qualities and providing employees with opportunities to develop their inherently positive characteristics in the workplace (McGregor, 1957).

Table 14.1 Theory X and Theory Y

Theory X	Theory Y
1. Management is responsible for the economic well-being of the organization.	1 Management is responsible for the economic well-being of the organization.
2. Management of employees requires directing, controlling, motivating, and modifying their behavior to fit the needs of the organization.	2. Employees have become passive and resistant only as a result of their experience in organizations.
3. Without active intervention by management, employees would be passive and resistant to organizational needs.	3. Motivation, potential for development, capacity for assuming responsibility, and readiness to work toward organizational goals are inherent in employees.
4. The average employee is lazy, works as little as possible, lacks ambition, and dislikes responsibility.	4. It is management's job to allow employees to recognize and develop the characteristics listed above.
5. The average employee is self-centered, indifferent to organizational needs, and, by nature, resistant to change.	5. The chief job of management is to arrange organizational conditions so that employees can achieve their own goals by directing their own efforts.
6. The average employee is gullible and not very bright.	

Throughout this text, we have talked about many "new" concepts in management, including empowerment, participation, self-managed work teams, transformational leadership, self-assessment, and organizational citizenship behavior. If you think back to our discussion of these and other developments in I/O psychology, you can see that they are all consistent with the human relations movement—or what McGregor called the *Theory Y approach* to organizational management. Most of McGregor's work was done in the late 1950s and early 1960s, but it has taken on great importance since it first came on the scene, shaping to a considerable degree the approach taken by many successful organizations worldwide.

Recent theoretical work in this area emphasizes learning and ethics (Rosanas, 2008). The learning that happens between people in organizations is central to the relationships that form and the effectiveness that follows. Furthermore, it is argued that decisions made in organizations ought to be evaluated along a series of dimensions (e.g., effectiveness, distinctive competence, and identification with the organization) in which ethics plays a central role. Thinking along these lines is consistent with the traditional humanistic approach—and also extends it.

Open-System Theory

It is important to recognize that organizations are not always well defined by the purposes for which they were developed. On the contrary, organizations develop and change over time as a result of both internal and external forces. This is the basic premise of Katz and Kahn's (1978) *open-system theory* of organizations (see Figure 14.4). The three key elements of open-system theory are inputs, throughputs, and outputs. *Inputs* are transformed during the *throughputs* stage into *outputs*, which in turn are brought back into the process as additional inputs—and thus the process continues.

For example, a car manufacturer that uses production processes to transform raw materials into automobiles is, in effect, using throughputs to transform inputs into outputs. The outputs (automobiles) are then sold for money, which is reinvested as inputs into the system—and transformation or production continues. Katz and Kahn (1978) point out that organizations thrive only as long as there is a continuous flow of energy

FIGURE 14.4 The Cycle of Open-System Theory

Feedback Cycle

from the external environment into the system and a continuous export of products out of the system. This simple principle is at the heart of several disciplines, including economics, psychology, and biology. And, indeed, Katz and Kahn developed their theory based on the principles of biology that define all living things as open systems.

Plants and animals, for instance, both give to and take from the environment in which they exist—and well-run organizations operate in a very similar way. In our car manufacturer scenario, for example, the organization would be headed toward eventual death if the automobiles stopped bringing in money and production was negatively affected. In fact, this is exactly the position that the big three American car manufacturers found themselves in a couple of years ago. The declining economy and rising oil prices reduced profits and led to budget cuts and layoffs at all three. Eventually, General Motors and Chrysler filed for bankruptcy in 2009. This was followed by a government bailout to try to revive the struggling automotive industry, which seemed to be on more solid footing in 2012 than it had been a few years earlier.

Table 14.2 presents the 10 characteristics of open systems as presented by Katz and Kahn (1978). We've already discussed inputs, throughputs, outputs, and the cyclic

Table 14.2 Characteristics of Open Systems

Importation of energy	Energy is brought in from the external environment for use by the system.
The throughput	That energy is transformed.
The output	A product or service is exported.
Systems as cycles	The pattern of importation of energy and exportation of products and services continues.
Negative entropy	The tendency of all systems to move eventually toward death is reversed.
Information input and negative feedback	Information input and negative feedback allow the system to correct or adjust its course.
The steady state	Surviving open systems are characterized by a balance in energy exchange.
Differentiation	Open systems move toward more specialized functions.
Integration and coordination	Bringing the system together as a unified process is necessary for the system to continue.
Equifinality	There are many ways within the system to get to the same conclusion or endpoint.

nature of the process, but there are other important characteristics of open systems, too—such as *negative entropy*. Entropy is a principle in many branches of science positing that all forms of organization move toward disorganization or death (Katz & Kahn, 1978), whereas the principle of negative entropy suggests that organizations must avoid this movement toward death by continuing to import energy from outside the system. Thus, for example, our car manufacturer must continue to transform raw materials (inputs) into cars (outputs)—for if this cycle is broken, entropy will follow and the company will crumble. To avoid entropy, companies store up resources during good times—resources they can use to maintain the cycle during bad times. This often requires organizations to adapt to the changing environment and consider other options (e.g., government bailout, restructuring through bankruptcy, etc.) outside of their traditional supply-and-demand structure.

Information input and *negative feedback* are also important parts of the open-system cycle. Recall our discussion of control theory in Chapter 9—how the negative feedback loop is instrumental in determining individuals' motivation to exhibit particular behaviors. In an organizational context, the negative feedback loop provides information about where and how the organization is getting off-course. For instance, if outputs are not bringing in sufficient resources to enable continual production of those outputs, changes need to be made at the input or throughput stage.

The last characteristic I'll mention here is *equifinality*, the notion that a system can reach the same end state in different ways. In other words, there isn't just one way to achieve a particular outcome. Note that this is inconsistent with the basic premise of Scientific Management that there is "one best way" to do everything. The idea of equifinality reflects the human element in organizations, providing more flexibility and allowing for more creativity in their development and operations. Given this human element, the only stable aspect of organizations and the environment they interact with is that they change—a lot and often! Thus, being limited to "one best way" tends not to result in effective organizations.

■ Organizational Development

organizational development (OD)
A planned, organization-wide effort to increase organizational effectiveness through behavioral science knowledge and technology.

Organizational development is not an easy topic to explain, but let's start with this definition: **Organizational development (OD)** is a planned, organization-wide effort to increase organizational effectiveness through behavioral science knowledge and technology (Beckhard, 1969). Many argue that OD is really about promoting positive humanistic changes in organizations; that is, it's as much about helping the people in an organization as it is about helping make the organization more productive (Church, Waclawski, & Siegal, 1999). But some newer thinking in this area is starting to broaden OD interventions (Marshak & Grant, 2008) to include other less traditional approaches, which we will discuss later in the chapter. OD programs share some important characteristics among themselves. In particular, they tend to do the following:

- Involve the total organization
- Be supported (and initiated) by top management

- Entail a diagnosis of the organization, as well as an implementation plan
- Be long-term processes
- Focus on changing attitudes, behaviors, and performance of groups/teams
- Emphasize the importance of goals, objectives, and planning

These characteristics explain what OD is; what OD *isn't* is a short-term patch to hide an organizational problem. In fact, when OD fails, it is often because the characteristics just listed have been ignored in favor of superficial changes that have very little impact on the organization's effectiveness and result in greater stress and lower morale at the company. If anything, bad OD programs take organizations back a few steps rather than moving them forward. New CEOs are frequently expected by their boards to immediately initiate successful organizational change efforts, but these efforts are rarely successful because changing organizations is such a complex endeavor (Greiner, Cummings, & Bhambri, 2003), especially for new leaders. For instance, Andrea Jung was made CEO of Avon Products in 1999, but her tenure didn't end well; she was removed from the CEO position in 2011. Her first few years were very successful, but in 2005 stock prices were tumbling and there was a strong push to restructure and to make some serious organizational changes. Under her leadership, Avon attempted to make those changes; however, after about five more years, it became clear that the change efforts weren't working, and the organization decided to try some new leadership (Lublin & Karp, 2011).

Why Organizations Need Organizational Development

Organizations embark upon OD interventions for many reasons, but much of the time it is because of changes in an organization's operating environment. Like everything else we've covered in this book, organizational practices and programs operate not in a vacuum but, rather, in a context that affects those practices and programs. Whether social, technical, economic, or political in nature, sometimes environmental changes necessitate development of the organization to make it more effective. The key to meeting these challenges is utilizing the knowledge, expertise, and commitment of individuals to enhance organizational effectiveness (Wirtenberg, Lipsky, Abrams, Conway, & Slepian, 2007)—this is where OD comes into the picture. Can you think of any creatures—or technologies, for that matter—durable enough to survive without adapting to new environments? Certainly, humans and computers have evolved. In order for organizations to survive, they, too, must be adaptable enough to change over time.

In a thought-provoking and very readable analysis of management in the 21st century, Michael Hitt (2000) discusses changes over the previous 15 to 20 years, changes to come in the next 20 to 30 years, and the accompanying challenges that organizations now face. In fact, this section of the chapter is partly based on this fascinating article. We often hear about how much things have changed in recent years. Here is an incredible example: In 1990, use of the Internet was limited to scientific exchanges and some government correspondence—and that's all. A decade later, almost 1 billion people were communicating and conducting business on the Internet. When I started my job at the University of Akron in 1989, I had some access to an archaic e-mail system from a computer lab in our department but no access at all from my office, and I had very little idea what the Internet was. Now, my 13-year-old uses the mouse like he was born with it in his hand, my 16-year-old uses the Internet routinely for school projects, and my 19-year-old serves as my IT consultant!

Hitt (2000) argues that the competitive landscape of the 21st century will be characterized by substantial and sporadic changes. He focuses on two major changes in this landscape that successful companies will need to navigate through organizational development. The first one concerns the technological revolution and the knowledge explosion that accompanies it; according to one estimate, due to incredible advances in medicine, communications, and technology, we double our knowledge every 50 years.

The second change concerns globalization, which has become the norm for successful organizations as additional countries become more active in the world economy, as different economies and markets develop, and as new economic rules and alliances emerge. One rapid change that we've explored has to do with the increasing diversity of the workforce—in terms of age, gender, race, ethnicity, and mental and physical disability. Because today's workforce is so different from that of previous generations, organizations need to make adjustments in the way they operate. In fact, the most competitive firms are likely to be those that use this incredible diversity to increase knowledge, creativity, and overall effectiveness. Organizations have to find ways to turn this diversity into a 21st-century advantage. (Recall Chapter 11, in which we examined family-friendly policies in the context of diversity.)

We have talked historically about the "Fortune 500"; we are beginning now to focus more on the "Global 500"—companies that are active across the globe, not just in the United States. Companies that aren't ready to make the changes necessitated by the technological revolution and globalization can quickly lose their competitive advantage. For instance, IBM and Apple were the undeniable leaders in the business and home computer industries in the 1980s and 1990s. However, by the early 2000s IBM was losing money on its PCs even though it had introduced personal computers years before. IBM was forced to sell its computer division to Lenovo in 2004. The Gap has seen huge sales declines in recent years; some of the reasons include poor retail plans and designs as well as stores that are too large given the e-commerce boom (Gorenstein, 2011).

One result of the technological revolution is the incredible speed with which products become obsolete. Technology changes so quickly that last year's cutting-edge product, which seemed to secure the future of one company, is completely replaced by this year's cutting-edge product, which may be developed and manufactured by a different company. If the first company is not prepared to keep pace, it can be left behind (as happened to Borders and Tower Records) and lose its competitive advantage to other companies (Amazon and Apple) that are more prepared and willing to change with the environment. The rise and fall of the dot-coms (i.e., Internet companies such as E-Toys.com, Pets.com, and CDWorld.com) exemplify this rapid change. When they were launched, these companies seemed to be market leaders with a long future; less than one year later, most of them had ceased to exist.

As for how to deal with these many fast-paced changes in the workplace, Hitt (2000) makes a few interesting suggestions. First, managers need to adopt new forms of managerial thinking that are global in orientation and allow for strategic flexibility, as well as new organizational structures. Similarly, managers have to be able to operate and thrive in environments characterized by ambiguity and uncertainty because the changes occurring in these environments are neither predictable nor amenable to deliberate step-by-step procedures. Second, organizations must have highly developed human capital. Indeed, well-trained and highly skilled employees are essential if companies are to maintain a competitive edge. Achieving this goal, of course, requires careful and thorough recruitment, selection, placement, training, and development of employees.

Finally, an emphasis on continuous learning and knowledge dissemination throughout the organization is what will set successful companies apart from those that don't survive. It's not enough for only a few employees to continue to learn; new knowledge needs to be shared throughout all levels of the organization. (We'll revisit this point later in the chapter.) In addition, Greiner and his colleagues (2003) emphasize the match among a CEO's orientation, organizational flexibility, characteristics of the team members, and the organization's change history as important to successful organizational development.

Some companies on the cutting edge actually try to stockpile employees with a vast array of knowledge and skills because they recognize that, as things change, what these individuals have to offer will become especially valuable. The ability to "think outside the box" is also important; in other words, employees and managers must be capable of coming up with creative and novel ideas. Sometimes the old ways and old approaches don't work anymore; to stay ahead, companies need to be flexible and innovative.

Let's talk a bit about innovation, which we can define as the process of developing new ideas, methods, or products. An interesting example of innovation comes from the largest consumer products company in the world, Procter and Gamble (P&G). In what it calls the biggest innovation in laundry in 25 years, P&G developed Tide Pods, which are palm-size detergent tablets to be tossed into the washing machine with no fuss or mess (Anderson, 2012). Only about 15% to 20% of all new products are successful, but P&G's rate is about 50%. Innovations like the Tide Pod can take years to refine and can cost as much as the entire first year's sales. Indeed, innovation is both important and risky; of course, you can argue that not innovating may be the riskier alternative (see Borders, Tower Records, etc.).

As a world leader in innovation, P&G spends billions of dollars on product testing. It has 25 facilities worldwide where employees watch consumers use its products (Anderson, 2012). About 50 P&G researchers work at the Beckett Ridge Innovation Center outside Cincinnati, where they watch and videotape 20,000 people per year wash dishes, wash clothes, change diapers, and so on. The 3,000-square-foot grocery store and 2,000-square-foot mock house are instrumental in the testing process and so important for innovation. Once the testing of Tide Pods was complete and the product tweaked, P&G spent $150 million on the marketing campaign before rolling it out to stores in February 2012. P&G forecasts $300 million in sales in the first year. Of course, those sales alone won't cover the cost of the innovation, but if the product is successful for a few years, then the sales will more than offset the costs. Innovation

is incredibly important for companies that want to
remain leaders or major players in their industries.

A recent empirical study examined the roles of
transformational leadership and climate for excellence in affecting team innovation (Eisenbeiss, van
Knippenberg, & Boerner, 2008). The authors studied
33 research and development teams and found that
transformational leadership was positively related
to the extent to which team members perceived that there was support for innovation.
When team members felt supported, they were more likely to be innovative as long as
the team was focused on performance and the normative climate was one of excellence.
This study suggests that team innovation is related to team-level beliefs and perceptions
and leadership behaviors, but the relationships are complex ones.

Hitt (2000) concludes by saying that "[m]anagement in the new millennium
must build an organization that is constantly being transformed. It must develop and
respond continuously to new technologies, new markets, new businesses, and new
people in the form of employees and customers" (p. 15). Organizational development
and change are the means by which we can accomplish this.

Some recent work has articulated variables and processes necessary for such successful change. A study of employees from two companies—one in the automotive parts
industry and the other in financial services—found that the effectiveness of managerial influence tactics was affected by leader–member exchange (LMX) (see Chapter
13 for a more detailed discussion of LMX; Furst & Cable, 2008). In particular, when
employees experience high LMX, they tend not to be resistant to change tactics by
the supervisor. Researchers also found that employees interpret change tactics on the
part of others based on the attributions they make for the others' behaviors. In other
words, employees in a positive relationship with their manager may attribute sanctions
to situational factors rather than to the manager and, thus, exhibit low resistance to
the change effort.

In-depth interviews of employees at all levels of a hospital found that participants
emphasized three categories of variables as important to their subjective experience
of change: emotional/attitudinal issues, process issues, and outcome issues (Jones
et al., 2008). Participants emphasized the importance of positive attitudes toward
change but warned of communication problems and conflict while noting the
importance of planning and recognizing both positive and negative outcomes. Other
researchers demonstrate the importance of coping in the change process. They argue
that knowing how employees appraise organizational change efforts (e.g., attitudes
and cognitive evaluations) is not enough; knowing about the coping strategies used
and emotional reactions is also important (Fugate, Kinicki, & Prussia, 2008).

change agent
The individual who
initiates the change
process in an orga-
nization; also called
the *interventionist.*

Models of Organizational Change

Organizational development interventions are focused on making changes in organizations. To understand how organizations change, we must understand three basic
elements of the process. First, the **change agent** (sometimes called the *interventionist*)

is the individual who initiates the change process. This person is usually external to the organization, such as an organizational consultant; less often it is someone internal to the organization. On the whole, however, this person is significantly involved in diagnosing and classifying the organization's problems so as to define what changes need to be made.

As the recipient of the *change effort*, the **client** is also central to the process. This effort is most likely to have an effect if the client is receptive to it; thus, the client needs to be kept abreast of whatever ideas are being considered by the change agent. The client may be a particular individual, a work team, or perhaps the entire organization.

A key concept for organizational change that involves both the change agent and the client is called **resistance to change**, which has traditionally been defined as the state in which clients create or choose unreasonable obstacles or barriers, intent on preventing or sinking the change (Ford, Ford, & D'Amelio, 2008). The argument has always been that clients or the recipients of the change effort have to be open and willing to change or the change effort will fail—resistance to change will lead to an unsuccessful change effort.

Rather than placing all the blame on the recipients, some recent scholars take a different view, arguing that the change agent may also contribute to resistance to change through his or her attitudes, behaviors, or inaction (Ford et al., 2008). The authors also suggest that resistance to change might be a self-serving perception of change agents who are looking to blame others for ineffective change efforts; they further propose that resistance to change could be a positive thing (as healthy dissent is in other situations) that leads to altered change efforts and eventual success. They argue for a revision in how we think of resistance to change and a broader, more flexible understanding of what is involved in resistance to organizational change with the goal of improving the effectiveness of change efforts.

Finally, the **intervention** is the program or initiative suggested or implemented by the change agent. An intervention consists of sequenced activities intended to help an organization increase its effectiveness (Cummings & Worley, 2005). As such, it intentionally disrupts the status quo in its attempt to change the organization. Some recent work has taken a slightly different approach and shown that career management is important during organizational change efforts (Lips-Wiersma & Hall, 2007). Furthermore, the researchers argue from their data that individuals take more responsibility for their career development during times of organizational change. They refer to the interdependence of the employee and the organization as an "organizational dance" in which there is reciprocal influence on the career development process.

There are two well-established models of organizational change, both of which stem from the early work of Kurt Lewin. Let's consider each in turn.

client
The recipient of an organizational change effort in an organization.

resistance to change
The characteristic of some individuals who so prefer to keep things the way they are that they intentionally or otherwise work to make change more difficult and less successful.

intervention
The program or initiative that is suggested or implemented by the change agent in an organizational change effort.

▼ **A Closer Look**
We often think of resistance to change as an obstacle to overcome, but can such resistance actually be a positive and productive stance to take?

MEDIAPHOTOS/ISTOCKPHOTO

▲ **A Closer Look**
Kurt Lewin was one of the leaders of early applied psychology involving organizational leadership and change. How has Lewin's work impacted organizational change theories and interventions?

Lewin's Change Model Lewin is considered a pioneer of I/O psychology because of his interests in organizational change, as well as his work on group processes and leadership. He characterized change as a matter of modifying those forces that are acting to keep things stable (Lewin, 1951). Any behavioral situation, according to Lewin, is characterized both by forces operating to maintain stability or equilibrium and by forces pushing for change. Stability results when the former win out over the latter. Lewin suggested that for planned change to occur in organizations with the least amount of tension and resistance, it is best to try to modify the forces that are maintaining the status quo rather than dramatically increasing the forces for change.

The three steps in his change process are depicted in the top panel of Figure 14.5. In the first of these steps, known as *unfreezing*, the forces maintaining the status quo are broken down, and the system is opened up for change. This step is often accomplished by demonstrating that the behaviors and outcomes prevalent in the organization are not consistent with the organization's goals and objectives. Once the organization has been opened up for change, the second step of the process, *moving*, begins. At this point, real organizational change begins to happen, as reflected in the new attitudes, values, and behaviors that result from the intervention. During the final step, called *refreezing*, the changes that were implemented become stabilized, and the organization reaches a new level of equilibrium.

FIGURE 14.5 Change Models

Organizational policies, norms, and structures are used to support these changes, resulting in a new sense of stability. This basic three-step model, though still perceived as a major factor in organizational change processes, has been developed and enhanced by other theorists, resulting in more steps but holding to the basic premises of Lewin's early work.

Action Research Model
In the 1940s, Lewin developed a second model of organizational change—the *action research model*. In this case, he was motivated by what he viewed as social problems that needed to be addressed from both a methodological and social perspective. Toward this end, he called for social scientists to take a more active role by combining theory building with research on real-world practical problems. Lewin died before he was able to fully develop and expand his ideas for action research, but others have followed his lead.

The major characteristic of the action research model is its cyclical nature. Initial research about the organization is the foundation on which subsequent action is built. The results of this action, in turn, provide information that can be used to guide further action—and the cyclical process continues. The various steps in the action research model are presented in the bottom panel of Figure 14.5. Here, we can clearly see a research orientation with multiple data-gathering and problem-diagnosis stages. Lewin's idea was that research informs practice—a central theme of his model. He conceived of a process whereby I/O psychologists could attain a deeper understanding of an organizational phenomenon through cycles of fact finding and taking action (Dickens & Watkins, 1999).

A recent study at the Danish Lego Company applied action research to organizational change and **sensemaking**, which is what employees do to gain a better understanding of their workplace (Luscher & Lewis, 2008). This study uncovered and demonstrated a process that makes use of paradoxes to enhance openness to organizational change among managers. This process may prove helpful to managers in understanding organizational change and how to push through the various constraints to successful change interventions.

sensemaking
The process whereby employees exert effort to interpret and understand work-related events.

Organizational Development Interventions
Effective interventions can be described as those that (1) fit the needs of the organization, (2) are based on causal knowledge of intended outcomes, and (3) transfer change-management competence to organization members (Cummings & Worley, 2005). The first criterion suggests that not all interventions are right for all organizations. Indeed, an intervention is more likely to succeed if it fits with what organization members believe and perceive to be appropriate—and if they are committed to being a part of it and its eventual success.

The second criterion implies that because interventions usually have goal- or objective-based outcomes, the interventions themselves must be based on the knowledge that these outcomes will reasonably result from them. Of course, we don't always know with certainty that a particular intervention will work—especially given the complexity of human behavior in both our personal lives and our work lives.

As for the last criterion, which implies that organizational members should be better able to carry out planned change activities on their own following an intervention (Cummings & Worley, 2005), OD interventions are developed and implemented in such a way that they eventually become part of the organization's routine and thus become less driven by the OD consultant. In fact, one sign that an OD intervention has succeeded is that the OD consultant becomes more and more expendable with the passage of time. (This point needs qualifying, of course, because in situations in which new opportunities for change have developed, the further expertise of OD consultants is necessary.)

There are many different OD interventions available, and numerous experts have proposed categorical schemes for how to organize them. However, I will focus on seven of the most popular interventions here.

Survey Feedback One widely used intervention strategy involves the systematic collection of data via organizational surveys. These data are then summarized, analyzed, fed back to people employed by the organization, and used as a basis for planning, with the outcome being a framework for organizational changes. The steps involved in survey feedback are rather simple:

- Top management supports and actively participates in the survey process.
- An anonymous survey is administered to organization members, tapping their attitudes, perceptions, and beliefs.
- Survey results are compiled by department, plant, or demographic segment.
- The consultant provides feedback to organizational members in the form of a data compilation and summary.
- Managers, task forces, and other employees meet with the consultant to identify potential changes for implementation.

I myself have been involved in many survey feedback programs while doing work for various organizations. For instance, I did some survey work for a provider of clinical and behavioral services—a mental health clinic. I met with the chair of the task force that was charged with gathering information from employees in order to evaluate the company's strengths and weaknesses. After a couple of meetings with this individual and other task force members, I developed a 140-item survey that measured employees' level of job satisfaction, level of trust in management, level of stress and tension, attitudes toward the team emphasis, beliefs about organizational citizenship behaviors (OCBs), and so on. Demographic data such as gender, age, experience, and education were also gathered.

After surveying about 200 employees, I compiled the data and presented the task force with a detailed written report of my findings; in addition, I made an onsite oral presentation to the task force members. All employees had access to the complete report, as well as to a memo that I had written directly to the employees summarizing the data. Finally, I made a series of recommendations

TECHNICAL TIP

In Chapter 2, we talked a good bit about different methods for collecting data, such as self-administered questionnaires. Typically, these questionnaires or surveys are administered to a subset of employees (a sample) and valuable data about attitudes, opinions, desires, or beliefs are obtained.

based on the data that I thought would enhance the effectiveness, morale, and productivity of this particular organization. Some of my recommendations were implemented, and I was hired two years later to develop and conduct a follow-up survey. This survey revealed that, although some employees still had concerns, the organization overall had experienced sizable improvements in the targeted areas as a result of this OD intervention.

Team Building   As you may recall, we discussed the organizational role played by teams in Chapter 12. Here, we're concerned specifically with **team building,** a technique used by organizations to develop teams or to enhance the effectiveness of existing teams. Most of the experts in this area assume that in order for work groups or teams to be successful, the members must collaborate and be interdependent. One of the best parallel examples of team building is the process through which sports teams develop. Whether they're involved in Little League, high school, college, or professional sports, team members must learn how to pool their individual abilities, coordinate their individual efforts, strive for agreed-upon goals, and establish a uniform set of work patterns and structures to maximize team performance (Forsyth, 1999). Specifically, team-building interventions focus on the following objectives:

- Clarifying role expectations and responsibilities among team members
- Improving supervisor–subordinate relations
- Improving problem solving, decision making, and planning by team members
- Reducing conflict among team members
- Developing a vision, mission, or set of goals
- Building cohesion and unity within the team

Team building is an extremely popular OD intervention and has been used in a variety of industries, such as hotel management, manufacturing, urban transit, health, and sports (Salas, Rozell, Mullen, & Driskell, 1999). Despite widespread practitioner enthusiasm for the effectiveness of team building, there has been little in the way of well-controlled research. Nevertheless, one meta-analysis that reviewed the studies that do exist found strong support for the impact of team building on team performance (Svyantek, Goodman, Benz, & Gard, 1999). This review also took an applied perspective and examined the role played by different organizational characteristics in affecting the relationship between team building and team performance. The results indicated that team building had a stronger impact on team performance when (1) it was initiated to correct existing problems; (2) it was combined with other OD interventions; (3) the intervention was strongly supported by members of the organization, including the immediate team supervisor; (4) it was implemented in a participative management climate; and (5) performance was measured at the group level.

team building
A technique used by organizations to develop teams or to enhance the effectiveness of existing teams.

▼ **A Closer Look**
How is team building in sports similar to team building in other organizations?

AP PHOTO/GAIL BURTON

Outdoor experiential training (OET) is a newer approach to team building that makes use of the outdoors and entails various physical and mental exercises, as well as group activities. One review uncovered some support for its effectiveness and even suggested that this approach has a positive effect on the organization's return on investment, or ROI (Williams, Graham, & Baker, 2003).

Total Quality Management

total quality management (TQM) An initiative that focuses on employee involvement in the control of quality in organizations; also called *continuous improvement* or *quality management*.

Total quality management (TQM)—also called *continuous improvement* or *quality management*—focuses on employee involvement in the control of quality in organizations. Many organizations have implemented a quality initiative in which all of the organization's activities concentrate on the quality of products made or services provided. This emphasis on quality was spearheaded by the work of W. Edwards Deming and Joseph M. Juran, who presented their ideas to U.S. companies during World War II. However, their ideas were much better received by the Japanese than by Americans (Cummings & Worley, 2005). As Japanese companies became increasingly formidable in their competition with American companies (especially in the automobile industry), American executives began to take notice and, eventually, Deming's ideas were also well received in the United States.

In fact, they are now so popular that the U.S. government gives an award to companies that best meet the ideals of the TQM movement—namely, the Malcolm Baldrige National Quality Award. The criteria used for the Baldrige Award are (1) the extent to which quality values are communicated throughout the organization, (2) the organization's ability to meet customer needs, (3) the extent and caliber of the approaches used to monitor the quality of goods and services produced, (4) the effective use of data supporting the TQM system, and (5) the extent to which the full potential of employees has been utilized (Tata, Prasad, & Thorn, 1999). TQM has become a vast enterprise, including consulting firms that specialize in quality work; nationwide training programs on the basic principles of TQM; and numerous national associations, including the American Society for Quality and the Association for Quality and Participation.

TQM interventions are typically conducted in a series of stages. They begin, like many of the other programs discussed throughout this book, with the support of top management. This means that senior management must receive training on what TQM is, how it operates, and what their responsibilities are. During the second stage, employees are trained in quality methods such as *statistical process control*—a technique proposed by Deming that focuses on identifying problems reflective of a low-quality product or service.

An empirical investigation found that individual differences among those involved in the TQM effort predicted its success. In particular, employees' trust in colleagues, commitment to the organization, and higher-order-need strength were more strongly related to the effectiveness of TQM than were situational variables. Given that participants' individual differences important to the TQM process have received very little research attention, these findings suggest that we need a stronger conceptual understanding of how these and other variables operate in this context (Coyle-Shapiro & Morrow, 2003). In an attempt to advance what we know about this process, one study of six semiconductor plants in Malaysia demonstrated that TQM practices resulted in employees' feelings of empowerment and high levels of job involvement (Boon, Arumugam, Safa, & Bakar, 2007).

The third, or active, stage involves the actual implementation of TQM processes and procedures. At this time, employees identify not only areas in which their department or division excels but also deviations from quality standards (i.e., error). The potential causes of these deviations, or *output variations,* are examined, corrected, and brought within the range of acceptable quality.

The fourth stage in the process is a self-comparison analysis whereby the organization compares its effectiveness to that of competitors that set the benchmarks for the industry. For instance, an organization attempting to improve its customer service is likely to compare its performance to Disney's benchmarks because Disney is widely recognized as a world leader in customer service (Cummings & Worley, 2005). Then, during the final stage of the process, rewards are linked to the achievement of the TQM intervention's goals. This, of course, is the main point of the whole process. Because the focus is on developing or employing a work process that produces high-quality goods and services that are as good as or better than those produced by the competition, the rewards are linked to processes that achieve those results. In the airline industry, for example, these processes would include being on time most often, having the lowest rate of lost luggage, having the fewest customer complaints, and having the smallest percentage of canceled flights.

One criticism of TQM is that it is so rational and technical in its approach that it ignores the importance of social-political conditions and the consequences of change (Knights & McCabe, 2002). A recent review was critical of the level of rigor of the research projects designed to evaluate the effectiveness of TQM initiatives (Wayhan & Balderson, 2007). However, the authors noted that more recent studies have been more sophisticated and rigorous and that they have demonstrated a link between TQM initiatives and the firm's financial performance. A recent study of 223 CEOs of Taiwanese high-tech companies found that TQM was related to organizational learning and that both TQM and learning had positive effects on innovation performance (Hung, Lien, Wu, & Kuo, 2011).

▲ **A Closer Look**
Because Disney is so highly regarded for its customer service, it is often used as a benchmark by other companies looking to improve their customer service. What part of the TQM process does benchmarking reflect and why is it important?

Gainsharing

Gainsharing is an OD intervention that involves paying employees a bonus based on improvements in productivity. This approach to increasing employee participation and benefits while also improving organizational productivity was first documented in 1935 by the Nunn-Bush Shoe Company of Milwaukee. One of the most frequently used varieties of gainsharing—the Scanlon Plan—was developed a few years later by Joseph Scanlon of the Empire Steel and Tin Plate Company of Cleveland (Gowen, 1991). The use of gainsharing continued to grow quickly after that; in fact, many contemporary organizations, such as General Electric, DuPont, Motorola, and General Motors, have instituted some form of gainsharing. In 1990, about 47% of American companies used some form of variable pay program; that number increased to almost 90% in 2008 (Berger & Berger, 2008).

gainsharing
An OD intervention that involves paying employees a bonus based on improvements in productivity.

Gainsharing plans have as their basic premise a link between pay and performance—the assumption being that this link will lead to increased employee involvement and job satisfaction, as well as improved productivity and self-management. Although there are a few different types of gainsharing plans, and even these are sometimes altered to be organization-specific, most such plans have the following components in common. The first is a *suggestion system* that encourages employees to think about ways to improve productivity and then share those ideas. The second is an election of *department teams* composed of nonmanagement employees who are charged with overseeing the formal procedures used in considering, evaluating, and implementing the employees' suggestions. The third is a *review board* composed of both management and nonmanagement employees whose purpose is to improve communication between the two groups and allow management to answer questions posed by nonmanagement. By means of this review board, the two groups can educate each other about how the "other half " lives and what issues are important to them. Finally, all gainsharing plans are based on a formula that generates a *bonus pool* of dollars that are then distributed among employees.

In essence, gainsharing revolves around two factors that we've discussed at length throughout this text: participation and justice. Gainsharing programs create a sense of justice, or fairness, by distributing "gains" equally between the employer and employees. One study found that both distributive justice and procedural justice were correlated with gainsharing satisfaction across two different gainsharing organizations. Gainsharing is successful when employees have favorable reactions to it because these reactions lead to organizational commitment and trust in management, which results in greater effort and performance (Coyle-Shapiro, Morrow, Richardson, & Dunn, 2002). Indeed, the role of trust in organizational change was highlighted in one article that placed it at the center of organizational change processes (Morgan & Zeffane, 2003).

Finally, one study found that individuals opted for pay alternatives that, although more risky, had a greater potential payoff—one tied to individual rather than group performance (Kuhn & Yockey, 2003). Another study argues that the value of employee suggestions declines quickly over time and that, therefore, maintaining a stream of new suggestions is important (Arthur & Huntley, 2005).

Technostructural Interventions

OD interventions that focus on the technology and structure of organizations have increased in popularity as organizations have become more and more focused on effectiveness, efficiency, and productivity. One basic technostructural intervention has to do with the structural design of organizations, which determines how the work of an organization progresses throughout the various layers of the organization. Some OD practitioners alter this structural design to meet particular needs or goals of an organization and its employees. The most basic version—the *functional* organizational design—is structured according to the various functions of the employees.

Figure 14.6 provides an example of this design. Notice that the president/CEO has a number of employees (all vice presidents) immediately below him or her and that

FIGURE 14.6 Functional Organizational Design

each of these, in turn, is responsible for a particular function within the organization. For instance, someone is in charge of the manufacturing process, and someone else is in charge of marketing. The responsibilities for these different functions are independently held by various employees. Although this structure prevents duplication of labor by locating employees who are doing the same or similar jobs in the same department, it can also result in departments that become very limited or narrow in their views and approaches because they don't interact as much with employees in other departments.

Other organizations are structured by *product* rather than by function, as shown in Figure 14.7, which depicts an organization that produces three different products. For each product there is a separate director of manufacturing, a separate director of marketing, and so on. It's as if there are separate divisions or subcompanies for each product, enabling all of the jobs associated with a particular product to be housed within one division. This design allows the managers of a particular division to focus exclusively on that division; it also creates the potential for greater commitment and cohesion within the division. However, there is also a greater potential for duplication of effort and costs. For example, similar research and development (R&D) equipment for each division is probably necessary, along with perhaps more R&D personnel than would be required by a functional design. Another drawback is that potential communication across product lines can be problematic, resulting in coordination difficulties and conflict across these lines.

A more recent organizational design sometimes employed by OD practitioners is called the *matrix structure*. This design combines the function and product structures

FIGURE 14.7 Product-Based Organizational Design

we've just talked about. Figure 14.8 presents an example of a matrix organizational design; as you can see, the manufacturing employees for product A work for both the VP of manufacturing and the product A coordinator. In effect, the employees have two bosses; but this also means that the bosses—in this case, the VP of manufacturing and the product A coordinator—have to work together as supervisors because neither has ultimate authority. Reading across Figure 14.8 demonstrates product-based authority; reading down demonstrates functional-based authority. Certainly, this structure is more complex than either of the other two structures that combine to form this matrix. One advantage of this approach is that it encourages communication and cooperation between managers, thereby maintaining consistency across product lines and across functional departments. However, given its complexity, a matrix structure can be very difficult to introduce, especially in the absence of a preexisting supportive culture.

The last technostructural intervention we will consider is **reengineering**, also known as *business process redesign,* which involves the fundamental rethinking and redesign of business processes to improve critical performance as measured by cost, quality, service, and speed (Hammer & Champy, 1993). There are four elements of reengineering. First is the *fundamental* element, an examination of what the company does and why. Second is the *radical* element, a willingness to make crucial and far-reaching organizational changes rather than merely superficial changes. Third is the *dramatic* element, which focuses on

reengineering
The fundamental rethinking and redesign of business processes to improve critical performance as measured by cost, quality, service, and speed; also called *business process redesign.*

FIGURE 14.8 Matrix Organizational Design

making striking performance improvements rather than slight performance improvements. The last element is the idea that the reengineering intervention is centered on the *processes* of the organization, not just the tasks, jobs, or structures (Beugré, 1998). A recent study found that the communication aspects of the redesign process were especially important for the success of a reengineering effort (Kock, Danesh, & Komiak, 2008).

Reengineering generally implies a revolutionary change in the operation of the organization. The organization alters its overall structure, as well as the way in which its work is structured. Most of the reengineering currently taking place in organizations revolves around **information technology (IT)**, which is typically defined as "the new science of collecting, storing, processing, and transmitting information" (McDonagh & Coghlan, 1999, p. 41). Any drastic change in the way an organization functions that is related to information gathering, storing, processing, or transmitting would qualify as an IT intervention. This type of reengineering occurs, for example, when a company computerizes all of its files and records or switches from a manual inventory and bookkeeping procedure to a computer-based one, as is being suggested for the U.S. healthcare industry, which now relies largely on paper-based record keeping. These kinds of changes certainly alter the company's or industry's entire structure and way of doing business.

information technology (IT)
The science of collecting, storing, processing, and transmitting information.

Positive Organizational Development In recent years, the field of psychology has been reenergized by a new emphasis called **positive psychology**, which focuses on the strengths and virtues of individuals rather than on their weaknesses and impairments. The assumption of positive psychology is that individuals want to

positive psychology
The scientific study of the strengths and virtues of individuals and institutions.

be productive and lead meaningful and enriching lives. Researchers at universities like the University of Pennsylvania and the University of Michigan have been leading the way in studying positive experiences regarding the domains of love, work, and play (Positive Psychology Center, 2007).

As an offshoot of research and theorizing, positive psychology has spawned positive organizational behaviors and positive organizational scholarship (Luthans & Youssef, 2007). The notion is rather simple: Organizations can benefit from scholarship focused on positive organizational practices and behaviors. Furthermore, tools can be used by and techniques can be taught to organizational members that will allow them to be effective positive organizational change agents. This approach has become so popular in recent years that a special issue of the *Journal of Organizational Behavior* was dedicated to positive organizational behavior/scholarship in 2008. Positive organizational scholarship focuses on emotional intelligence, creativity, wisdom, work engagement, humor, self-efficacy, optimism, hope, and resilience and how these can help individuals meet organizational demands and foster performance (Bakker & Schaufeli, 2008).

Stemming from the positive psychology movement is a newer OD technique called **appreciative inquiry (AI)**, which engages employees by focusing on positive messages, the best of what the employees have to offer, and the affirmation of past and present strengths and successes. Developed by researchers at Case Western University, it uses the art of asking questions to search for the best in people, organizations, and the world around them (Egan & Lancaster, 2005). Organizations, such as Verizon, Avon, the U.S. Navy, and John Deere, have been identified as employing AI in their OD efforts (Egan & Lancaster, 2005).

appreciative inquiry (AI)
The art and practice of using questions to help an organization enhance its positive potential.

The process is defined by four stages. First, questioning is used in *discovery* to determine the strengths of the organization and its people. Second, in the *dream* stage, the information gathered at discovery is analyzed and elaborated upon to arrive at a vision statement or focused intent. Third, this information is used to *design* innovative ways to identify where the organization should be going. Finally, the design of the future company is sustained or maintained in the *destiny* stage. The distinctive characteristic of this approach is its unyielding emphasis on positive elements, traits, experiences, and possibilities. AI is not about fixing the problems; it's about building from strengths.

Let's talk briefly about AI at American Express as an illustration of the process (for a more detailed discussion, see Giglio, Michalcova, & Yates, 2007). The CEO believed that the core values of American Express had carried the company through hard times and that reengineering employees around a "refreshed" set of core organizational values would lead them successfully into the future. American Express used the four stages I just described to change the organization. For instance, in the discovery stage, it began the process of reengaging key leaders and employees by asking participants to recall moments of peak performance, to recount when they were most proud of working for American Express, and to describe what they expected the ideal future to look like for the company.

The leaders of this intervention argue that AI promoted a sense of ownership and rallied people around a common set of core values (Giglio et al., 2007). They were amazed that leadership groups around the world identified the same core values, cultural variables, and relevant solutions—culture did not seem to be a barrier to coming together

COURTESY OF LAURA HEFT

Laura Heft
PhD, 1999, I/O Psychology, University of Missouri, St. Louis
Director of Organization Effectiveness
Edward Jones

One of the keys to implementing a solution that delivers sustainable results is to take a "systems" approach to the intervention. The work of organization development includes attacking a problem holistically by designing an intervention (or series of interventions) aimed at addressing the multiple factors that influence the organization's ability to perform (e.g., work process, culture, talent, structure). An example is provided below.

In an important area of our business, sluggish results, changing market conditions, and opportunities to leverage new social media technologies required a change in our strategy. The process began with the establishment of a senior-level task force to diagnose and analyze the root cause. After the problem and the contributing factors were deeply understood, a new leader was brought in to develop a vision for the future and put it into action.

The change was substantial and required a complete reengineering of the area. In order to implement the new strategy, changes were needed in how the work was done (new processes and job redesign), where the work was done (move from centralized to decentralized, geographically dispersed work), and by whom (new skills sets and expertise were required to do the work).

The existing employees in the area were evaluated and then assigned to new roles or redeployed to other jobs in the firm. As the change was being implemented, the impact on employees was monitored through the administration of an employee survey, which was subsequently repeated at relevant intervals. The senior leader took responsibility for the results of the survey

and developed action plans to respond to issues that emerged.

Another part of the change intervention included team development meetings with the senior leadership team. These meetings were designed to help the team come together to identify new objectives for the work, clarify roles, and develop guidelines on how the team was going to communicate and work together (i.e., establishing a new culture). Within six months, this new area was beginning to see results.

Frequently, large-scale organizational changes are not proactively managed and, as a result, are not successful. Leaders are often reluctant to tackle the complexity and scope of the entire integrated system and instead opt for addressing only part of the solution. The early success of this intervention is most likely attributable to the "systems" approach taken to align the work, talent, goals, and culture in an integrated way to execute on the strategy.

Applying Your Knowledge

1. How does the "systems" approach implemented by Edward Jones align with open-system theory, discussed earlier in the chapter? Use Figure 14.4 to diagram the change implemented at Edward Jones to solve this problem.

2. What role did leadership play in implementing change? Do you think it's possible to implement large-scale change without strong centralized leadership?

3. How did this change plan try to account for resistance to change? How important do you think accounting for such resistance is to implementing a successful change strategy? Why?

around the future of American Express. Finally, they argue that the AI approach—focusing on stories of success, integrity, and responsibility—led to growth in these values and, therefore, to a strengthening of the corporate culture (Giglio et al., 2007).

I expect that AI will continue to grow as a popular and effective OD technique—in fact, some have suggested it as the ideal technique for the current state of the world.

organizational transformation
A term that refers to any intervention primarily directed toward creating a new vision for an organization and changing its beliefs, purpose, and mission.

Organizational Transformation To this point, we have discussed organizational development in a somewhat traditional way. Now, however, we turn to the work of Jerry Porras, a leader in the OD field, who draws a distinction between OD and what he says is at the cutting edge of OD—namely, **organizational transformation** (Porras & Silvers, 1991).

Organizational transformation refers to any intervention primarily directed toward creating a new vision for an organization and changing its beliefs, purpose, and mission. OD, by contrast, focuses more on work-setting variables that are mismatched with the organization's desires (although some would say that organizational transformation is OD at a deeper level). Porras himself suggests that organizational transformation is an approach that will continue to grow in popularity as more upper-level executives recognize the need for and potential benefit of profound shifts in the vision and direction of their organizations (Porras & Silvers, 1991). Such shifts are indeed becoming commonplace in today's organizations as they find themselves in the center of a changing world that is becoming more knowledge-intensive, fast-paced, global, and dynamic (Karakas, 2009).

Organizational transformation usually results from a serious jolt to a company that prompts the CEO and other senior executives to change their business strategy and, with that, their mission and vision for the company. At the forefront of many attempts at organizational transformation is **culture change**, the alteration of a pattern of beliefs, values, norms, and expectations shared by organizational members. The culture of an organization evolves historically, stemming directly from the leaders, and often founders, of a company. Several companies are famous for their organizational cultures; examples include Disney, Nordstrom, IBM, and Apple. In some cases, the culture is so much a part of the company that it can't be changed.

culture change
The alteration of a pattern of beliefs, values, norms, and expectations shared by organizational members.

In fact, there are experts who believe that culture change, in general, is too difficult and never very likely to be successful . . . Others, however, recognize its difficulty but embrace its potential and believe in its usefulness. Although an organization's culture can be instrumental in a company's success (as is true of the companies just mentioned), it can also be detrimental, leading companies to attempt to change the ineffective culture. Finally, because of the complexities involved, culture change itself can lead to many unintended consequences, such as behavioral compliance and cultural erosion (Harris & Ogbonna, 2002). Recently, large investment banks have served as a good example of this idea: They made some changes that were quite risky (various types of mortgages to "unqualified" people) and resulted, in part, in the market crash of 2008 and serious consequences for customers and the organizations themselves.

T. G. Cummings and C. G. Worley (2005) present an excellent list of the determinants of successful culture change. First, the organization and change agent must develop a clear vision of the new strategy, as well as of the shared values, attitudes, and action steps needed to make it a reality. Second, as with any organizational intervention, culture change is likely to succeed only with support from top management; in fact, this is especially the case with culture change. Third, senior executives not only have to support the culture-change efforts but also must live by them. Instead of just paying lip service to the changes in attitudes and behaviors, these executives need to implement them, believe in them, and demonstrate their complete alignment with them in their day-to-day activities. Fourth, the supportive systems of the organization must be intricately involved in the financial and control systems, and management systems must provide the support and resources necessary to give the culture change an opportunity for success.

The fifth determinant of culture change has to do with issues of selection. Because it is important that new hires be socialized into the new culture rather than into the culture that is being left behind, consideration should be given to hiring employees (especially at higher levels) based on their match to or consistency with the new shared values, beliefs, and behaviors. Furthermore, employees who don't fit with the new culture should be let go. Senior employees who prefer the old culture and don't see the need or opportunity for change are often leaders in the resistance against change—a situation that is very detrimental to the change process. Karakas (2009) says it very well: "Too many of the problems in societies today stem from management that is ill prepared to deal with the chaos and complexity of today's world. We suffer from the lack of new managers equipped with new roles, qualifications, capacities, and skills" (p. 17). Some argue that the Prudhoe Bay oil spill in 2006 was exacerbated because BP was not prepared to deal with such a potentially catastrophic accident. Organizational change and transformation are key to preparing managers, organizations, and employees to be better equipped.

A second approach to organizational transformation that has taken companies by storm is **knowledge management**—a method in which organizations enhance their operations through attempts to generate, transform, disseminate, and use knowledge (Geisler, 2007) Although there is widespread belief in the effectiveness of knowledge management and its close cousin, the development of *learning organizations*, these concepts are still so new as to be lacking empirical support. Nevertheless, experts agree that learning organizations tend to be characterized by (1) an organizational structure that facilitates learning, (2) a sophisticated information system that allows companies to manage knowledge for a competitive advantage, (3) a human resources system that promotes and rewards employees for continuous learning and knowledge management, (4) a strong organizational culture that fosters openness and creativity, and (5) supportive leaders who are active participants in learning and knowledge management (Cummings & Worley, 2005).

As Lew Platt, former CEO of Hewlett-Packard (HP), put it: "Successful companies of the 21st century will be those who do the best jobs of capturing, storing, and leveraging what their employees know" (quoted in Martiny, 1998, p. 71). In 1996, Hewlett-Packard embarked on a knowledge-management initiative that was designed to deliver more value to customers, bring more intellectual capital to solutions, and create an enthusiastic environment about knowledge sharing. The HP credo for this initiative was to make "the knowledge of the few, the knowledge of the many" (Martiny, 1998, p. 72). Knowledge management has been successfully integrated into the business strategy of HP and many other organizations as well. Its importance at General Electric, for example, is attested to by the fact that knowledge management was one of three business processes for which former CEO Jack Welsh took personal responsibility (Stewart, 2000).

knowledge management
A method in which organizations enhance their operations through attempts to develop, disseminate, and use knowledge.

DILBERT © SCOTT ADAMS/DIST. BY UNITED FEATURE SYNDICATE, INC.

▶ **A Closer Look**
Labeling their employees "knowledge assets" is not a characteristic of a learning organization. What are the five characteristics of learning organizations?

Knowledge management has become such an integral part of organizations that many companies have created a new position—that of "chief knowledge officer," who is responsible for spearheading knowledge and learning initiatives. At Caterpillar, Inc., the Fortune 100 company that makes heavy construction equipment, the management of knowledge has become so important that the company has introduced the Knowledge Network, an intranet-based system designed to provide the structure for knowledge management throughout the corporation. The network is supported by knowledge experts at Caterpillar's corporate university (Ardichvili, Page, & Wentling, 2003). Employees are motivated to contribute to the electronic sharing of information out of a moral obligation, community interest, a belief in giving back to the organizational community, and a desire to develop one's expertise at work (Ardichvili et al., 2003).

According to John Peetz, the former chief knowledge officer at Ernst & Young, knowledge management was one of four core work processes at that company: sell work, do work, manage people, and manage knowledge. Among his job duties was evangelizing about the importance of sharing knowledge, as well as managing and backing projects that found, published, and distributed knowledge throughout the firm (Stewart, 1998). Although it appears clear to organizations that managing and sharing knowledge are important to maintaining a competitive edge, one successful and respected management guru, Jeffrey Pfeffer, suggests that organizations need to go one step beyond knowledge management. Pfeffer argues that knowing what to do is not enough; organizations must also put that knowledge to good use. In short, truly successful and cutting-edge organizations must work to bridge the knowing–doing gap (Pfeffer & Sutton, 1999).

Recently, knowledge management has been linked to innovation, which is of paramount importance to all organizations (du Plessis, 2007). Knowledge management provides the tools and processes to ensure that knowledge is both available and accessible for use in the creation of new knowledge. Others argue that tacit knowledge—know-how acquired through experience that is hard to communicate to others—is intricately linked to innovation and leads to competitive advantage (Seidler-de Alwis & Hartmann, 2008).

Learning companies that have a handle on knowledge can respond faster and more effectively to the chaos and dynamics of current organizations, markets, and industries. It is widely believed that organizational culture plays an important role in the learning and innovation process. However, despite the belief that culture, learning, and innovation are related, there is little empirical literature on these linkages. One of these few empirical studies interviewed 451 CEOs of Spanish organizations and found a positive effect of organizational culture on organizational learning; organizational learning, in turn, had a positive effect on technical innovation (Sanz-Valle, Naranjo-Valencia, Jimenez-Jimenez, & Perez-Caballero, 2011). Specifically, the authors found that organizational learning mediated the relationship between organizational culture and technical innovation. This research provides a great first step in trying to empirically determine how culture, learning, and knowledge impact organizational innovation, but more research is needed.

■ Summary

This chapter presents information about two related organizational topics: organizational theory and organizational development. These were defined and discussed in terms of their importance to the effectiveness of organizations. I then presented three organizational theories: classical organizational theory, with its emphasis on Scientific Management and bureaucracy, and the more recent approaches known as humanistic theory and open-system theory.

Before discussing various techniques of organizational development, I spent considerable time highlighting reasons why companies, if they are to be successful, must pursue OD. I also presented examples of companies that have succeeded in part because of OD, as well as examples of companies that did not succeed owing to a lack of flexibility and willingness to change. In this context, I provided a detailed discussion of Lewin's general change model and the more well-developed action research model.

Next, I considered some of the most frequently used OD interventions, such as survey feedback, team building, total quality management, and gainsharing; empirical support was cited, along with a description of their potential benefits and disadvantages. I also introduced more recently conceived OD interventions such as reengineering, information technology, and appreciative inquiry. Finally, I discussed organizational transformation in the context of interventions that profoundly change the nature of the organization. Here, I discussed the role of culture change and knowledge management specifically as determinants of organizational innovation.

■ Key Terms

appreciative inquiry (AI) (p. 446)
change agent (p. 434)
client (p. 435)
culture change (p. 448)
delegation of authority (p. 424)
division of labor (p. 423)
gainsharing (p. 441)
information technology (IT) (p. 445)
intervention (p. 435)

knowledge management (p. 449)
micro-managers (p. 424)
organizational development (OD) (p. 430)
organizational theory (p. 421)
organizational transformation (p. 448)
positive psychology (p. 445)
reengineering (p. 444)
resistance to change (p. 435)

sensemaking (p. 437)
span of control (p. 424)

team building (p. 439)
total quality management (TQM)
(p. 440)

■ TAKING IT TO THE FIELD

Organizational development is an area that seems straightforward at first; however, each intervention requires a number of steps that can become quite complex, especially for large organizations. The CEO of Arianda Consulting, Gavin McBride, has asked for your help in implementing an intervention in his own I/O firm. Read through the information he has provided, and answer his questions.

Hello—

Thanks for being willing to help Arianda Consulting with our internal organizational development project. I think we really need to make some changes to serve our customers better.

We are currently planning to get some survey feedback from our employees. I've been hearing some buzz about the following issues at Arianda:

- We have several offices (in Minneapolis, Cincinnati, Philadelphia, and Boston), and I have been hearing that some employees feel that some locations are treated better and have more supportive management than others.
- We've recently hired several high-level managers away from other consulting companies. It sounds like some employees are bothered by this, and I'm not sure why. I've also noticed a small increase in turnover rates over the past few years.
- In one of our locations (Philadelphia), we've been receiving more customer complaints about the quality of our products and services. I think there may be something going on at that location.

I'd like you to tell me the following:

1. What steps would you take in implementing this survey?
2. Provide five example items you would plan to ask my employees.
3. What do you need from me to help you accomplish this task?

Best,
Gavin

■ Critical Thinking Questions

1. The similar-sounding concepts of organizational change, organizational development, and organizational transformation are all discussed in the chapter. How do these three concepts differ? How are they similar?

2. Frederick Taylor's concept of Scientific Management was one of the earliest theories in the history of I/O psychology. Since then, how have organizational

theories developed from the foundation laid by Scientific Management? To what extent do later theories draw on or diverge from the concepts of Scientific Management?

3. Among other things, this chapter presents two common types of organizational structures: matrix and hierarchical. How are these two types of organizational structures different? What are the advantages and disadvantages of each? If you were designing an organization, which would you select and why?

4. Total quality management (TQM) is one type of organizational development intervention discussed in the chapter. It is widely used and believed to be highly effective. What makes TQM so effective? How do the components of TQM influence or enhance organizations?

5. One approach to organizational change—appreciative inquiry—is becoming increasingly popular in a wide variety of organizations. This approach incorporates the input and perspectives of not only managers and organizational leaders but also employees throughout the organization. Drawing on concepts you have learned throughout the book, what do you think some outcomes of this employee participation might be? In other words, when given the chance to provide their input in organizational change initiatives, how might individual employees benefit?

■ Application Questions

1. Think of a time when you had to deal with a bureaucracy. What did you need to do? Did you see any reason for that bureaucracy's existence?

2. Have you ever been in an organization that was undergoing an organizational development intervention? What happened? How did employees react?

3. Consider an organization where you have worked. Do you think this organization was a "learning organization"? Why or why not?

4. Consider positive organizational development. Do you believe people should spend more time focusing on using their strengths or addressing their weaknesses? Why?

5. Imagine you work for a company that uses gainsharing. Do you think you would like it? Why or why not?

■ Suggested Readings

Bakker, A. B., & Schaufeli, W. B. (2008). Positive organizational behavior: Engaged employees in flourishing organizations. *Journal of Organizational Behavior, 29*, 147–154. This article is the introduction to the journal's special issue on positive organizational behavior. This whole issue is fascinating stuff.

Cummings, T. G., & Worley, C. G. (2005). *Organization development and change* (8th ed.). Cincinnati, OH: South-Western College Publishing. This book is an extremely readable overview of organizational change and OD.

Easterby-Smith, M., & Lyles, M. A. (2011). *Handbook of organizational learning and knowledge management* (2nd ed.). West Sussex, UK: Wiley. A thorough discussion of the recent work focused on learning and knowledge management in organizations. This compilation is current and very informative.

Hitt, M. A. (2000). The new frontier: Transformation of management for the new millennium. *Organizational Dynamics, 28*(3), 7–17. This stimulating review of issues confronting organizations includes suggestions from an expert about how to approach such issues in the 21st century.

Katz, D., & Kahn, R. L. (1978). *The social psychology of organizations* (2nd ed.). New York: Wiley. Though not an easy read, this classic text is still recognized as the authority on organizational topics such as change, development, power, structure, and groups.

Luthans, F., & Youssef, C. M. (2007). Emerging positive organizational behavior. *Journal of Management, 33*, 321–349. This is a terrific introduction and review of the whole positive organizational behavior movement.

Glossary

actual criterion Our best real-world representative of the ultimate criterion, which we develop to reflect or overlap with the ultimate criterion as much as possible.

adverse impact The most accepted operationalization of discrimination, defined in the EEOC Guidelines as the "80% rule of thumb." A selection battery exhibits adverse impact (i.e., discriminates) against a group if the selection rate for that group is less than 80% of the selection rate for the group with the highest selection rate.

affective commitment Emotional attachment to an organization, characterized by a strong belief in and acceptance of the organization's goals and values, a willingness to exert effort on behalf of the organization, and a strong desire to remain a part of the organization.

affective disposition The tendency to respond to classes of environmental stimuli in predetermined, affect-based ways.

affirmative action (AA) A practice employed in many organizations to increase the number of minorities or protected class members in targeted jobs.

appreciative inquiry (AI) The art and practice of using questions to help an organization enhance its positive potential.

archival research Research relying on secondary data sets that were collected either for general or specific purposes identified by an individual or organization.

Army Alpha and Army Beta Mental ability tests developed by I/O psychologists during World War I that were used to select and classify army personnel.

assessment center (AC) An approach or method in which multiple raters (*assessors*) evaluate applicants or incumbents (*assessees*) on a standardized set of predictors (*exercises*).

attitude The degree of positive or negative feeling a person has toward a particular person, place, or thing.

attribute A dimension along which individuals can be measured and along which they vary.

base rate The percentage of current employees who are successful on the job.

behavior description interview An interviewing technique that relies on candidates sharing examples of past behaviors related to tasks required for the new job.

behavior theories Leadership theories that focus on identifying what leaders actually do, in the hope that this approach will provide a better understanding of leadership processes.

behavioral criteria In Kirkpatrick's taxonomy, criteria that refer to changes that take place back on the job; along with results criteria, also called *external criteria*.

biodata Personal history information obtained through a biographical information blank (BIB) that asks respondents about their attitudes, hobbies, experiences, and so on.

biographical information In the context of selection, any information that is descriptive of an individual's personal history.

bona fide occupational qualification (BFOQ) A characteristic such as one's gender, religion, or national origin that is required or necessary to effectively do the job.

brainstorming A technique in which all members of a group generate potential solutions without fear of having their suggestions criticized by other members.

burnout A condition that occurs when employees become so stressed that they experience emotional exhaustion, depersonalization, and a sense of reduced personal accomplishment.

case studies Examinations of a single individual, group, company, or society.

causal inference A conclusion, drawn from research data, about the likelihood of a causal relationship between two variables.

central tendency The tendency to use only the midpoint of the scale in rating one's employees.

change agent The individual who initiates the change process in an organization; also called *the interventionist*.

chronic stress Consistent, debilitating stress arising from lifelong experiences that can result in suicide and violence.

clerical ability A specific cognitive ability, relevant for jobs such as secretary, administrative assistant, and bookkeeper, involving a focus on both perceptual speed and accuracy in processing verbal and numerical data.

client The recipient of an organizational change effort in an organization.

coaching One-on-one collaborative relationship in which an individual provides performance-related guidance to an employee.

coefficient of determination The percentage of variance in a criterion that is accounted for by a predictor.

cohesion The strength of members' motivation to maintain membership in a group and of the links or bonds that have developed among the members.

Common-Metric Questionnaire (CMQ) A newly developed worker-oriented job analysis instrument that attempts to improve the generalizability of worker-oriented approaches through the use of items focused on slightly less general work behaviors.

comparable worth A doctrine maintaining that jobs of equal (or comparable) worth to the organization should be compensated equally.

compensable factors Dimensions or factors that are used to rate jobs, indicating that employees are compensated based on these factors. Examples include effort, skill, responsibility, and working conditions.

competencies The skills, behaviors, and capabilities that allow employees to perform specific functions.

composite criterion A weighted combination of multiple criteria that results in a single index of performance.

computer adaptive testing The process through which computer technology is used to identify easier and harder questions for applicants that eventually estimate their true ability level.

concurrent validity The extent to which a test predicts a criterion that is measured at the same time that the test is conducted.

consideration The extent to which leaders act in a supportive way and show concern and respect for their subordinates.

construct An abstract quality, such as intelligence or motivation, that is not observable and is difficult to measure.

construct validity The extent to which a test measures the underlying construct that it was intended to measure.

content validity The degree to which a test or predictor covers a representative sample of the quality being assessed.

context The social-psychological climate in which performance appraisal takes place.

contextual performance Activities performed by employees that help to maintain the broader organizational, social, and psychological environment in which the technical core operates.

contingency theories Leadership theories that differ from both trait and behavioral theories by formally taking into account situational or contextual variables.

continuance commitment Attachment to an organization as a function of what the employee has invested in it; also called *sunk-costs commitment.*

continuous learning Directed and long-term effort to learn; stems from an intense desire to acquire knowledge and improve results and from participation in activities that facilitate learning.

convergent validity The degree to which a measure of the construct in which we are interested is related to measures of other, similar constructs.

coping Efforts that help people manage or reduce stress.

correlation coefficient (r) A statistic that measures the strength and direction of the relationship between two variables.

counterproductive work behaviors (CWBs) Any behaviors that bring, or are intended to bring, harm to an organization, its employees, or its stakeholders.

criteria Evaluative standards that can be used as yardsticks for measuring an employee's success or failure.

criterion contamination A condition in which things measured by the actual criterion are not part of the ultimate criterion.

criterion deficiency A condition in which dimensions in the ultimate measure are not part of or are not captured by the actual measure.

critical incidents Examples of job performance used in behaviorally anchored rating scales or job-analytic approaches.

cross-functional teams Work teams that are composed of members from diverse departments of the organization, each with its own function; also called *project teams.*

culture change The alteration of a pattern of beliefs, values, norms, and expectations shared by organizational members.

cybervetting The use of social media as part of background investigations used to make employee selection decisions.

deduction An approach to science in which we start with theory and propositions and then collect data to test those propositions—working from theory to data.

delegation of authority An approach whereby supervisors assign particular tasks to separate employees and hold them responsible for completing these tasks.

dependent variable The variable of interest, or what we design experiments to assess.

***Dictionary of Occupational Titles* (DOT)** A tool developed by the Department of Labor in the 1930s that has been used to classify occupations and jobs, consisting of narrative descriptions of tasks, duties, and working conditions of about 12,000 jobs.

disparate impact cases Cases involving employment procedures that apparently unintentionally discriminate against or unfairly affect a minority group.

disparate treatment cases Cases involving discrimination that results from intentional differential treatment or behavior.

dissertation A unique piece of scholarly research that is usually the last hurdle before obtaining a PhD.

distance learning (DL) The delivery of material to all participants at the same time even though participants are separated by geographical distance.

distributed practice Training in which the practice is divided into segments, usually with rest periods in between.

distributional errors Rating errors, such as severity, central tendency, and leniency, that result from a mismatch between actual rating distributions and expected rating distributions.

divergent validity The degree to which a measure of the construct in which we are interested is related to measures of other, dissimilar constructs.

division of labor An approach whereby each job in a bureaucratic organization is a specialized position with its own set of responsibilities and duties.

dual-earner couple A couple in which both members are employed and maintain a family life.

dynamic criteria Measures reflecting performance levels that change over time.

effective leadership Usually operationalized as the successful long-term performance of the leader's work group or subordinates.

element In job analysis, the smallest unit of work activity.

emotion regulation The ways in which individuals monitor their emotions and the expression of those emotions.

emotion-focused coping A coping style that involves cognitive, or thought-related, strategies that minimize the emotional effects of stress-inducing events.

emotional intelligence (EI) The ability, capacity, or skill to identify and manage one's own emotions and understand the emotions of others.

emotional labor The effort, planning, and control required by employees to express organizationally desired emotions during interpersonal interactions.

employment at-will A common law doctrine stating that employers and employees have the right to initiate and terminate the employment relationship at any time, for any reason or for no reason at all.

episodic stress Stress resulting from life experiences and situations that varies with those experiences.

equity sensitivity An individual difference indicating the extent to which people are affected by overreward or underreward situations.

essential functions Tasks that are significant and meaningful aspects of the job.

expatriate An employee who is temporarily working and residing in a foreign country.

expectancy An individual's belief about the likelihood of achieving a desired performance level when exerting a certain amount of effort.

experience sampling methodology (ESM) A technique that allows researchers to obtain repeated real-time reports of phenomena such as moods and emotions through the use of technology such as personal digital assistants (PDAs).

experimental methods Research procedures that are distinguished by random assignment of participants to conditions and the manipulation of independent variables.

external validity The extent to which the results obtained in an experiment generalize to other people, settings, and times.

extraneous variable Anything other than the independent variable that can contaminate our results or be thought of as an alternative to our causal explanation; also called a *confounding variable*.

feedback environment (FE) The contextual aspects of the day-to-day supervisor–subordinate and coworker–coworker feedback process.

feedback orientation (FO) An individual's overall receptivity to feedback.

Frame of Reference (FOR) Training A type of training designed to enhance raters' observational and categorization skills so that all raters share a common frame of reference and improve rater accuracy.

free riding A situation that occurs when employees do less than their share of the work but still share equally in the rewards.

Functional Job Analysis (FJA) A highly structured job-oriented approach developed by Sidney Fine in which data are obtained about what tasks a worker does and how those tasks are performed.

gainsharing An OD intervention that involves paying employees a bonus based on improvements in productivity.

glass ceiling Refers to a situation in which qualified individuals are prevented from truly achieving all that they can because of some form of discrimination.

group tests Tests in which many applicants can be tested at one time.

groupthink A mode of thinking that individuals engage in when the desire to agree becomes so dominant in a cohesive group that it tends to override the realistic appraisal of alternative courses of action.

growth need strength The extent to which individuals value higher-order needs or desire to fulfill them.

halo The rating error that results from either (1) a rater's tendency to use his or her global evaluation of a ratee in making dimension-specific ratings for that ratee or (2) a rater's unwillingness to discriminate between independent dimensions of a ratee's performance.

human capital The education, training, and experiences of individual employees that provide value to organizations.

hypothesis A tentative statement about the relationship between two or more variables.

implicit leadership theory (ILT) A leadership theory that views leadership as the outcome of a perceptual process involving both leaders and subordinates.

in-basket An individual exercise in which assessees are asked to act as a manager in a particular company with certain issues or ideas that need to be considered and responded to.

incumbents In job analysis, employees who are currently occupying the job of interest.

independent variable A variable that is systematically manipulated by the experimenter or, at the least, measured by the experimenter as an antecedent to other variables.

individual tests Tests that are administered to one person at a time.

induction An approach to science that consists of working from data to theory.

industrial/organizational (I/O) psychology The application of psychological principles and theories to the workplace.

information technology (IT) The science of collecting, storing, processing, and transmitting information.

informed consent Participants signifying (usually in writing) their willingness and desire to participate in a particular research study after being provided with important and relevant information about the risks, procedures, and benefits of such participation.

initiating structure Behaviors through which leaders define their own and their subordinates' roles in achieving the group's formal goals.

instructional design A set of events that facilitate training through their impact on trainees.

instrumentality The perceived relationship between the performance of a particular behavior and the likelihood that a certain outcome will result from that behavior.

integrity tests Tests used in an attempt to predict whether an employee will engage in counterproductive or dishonest work-related behaviors such as cheating, stealing, or sabotage; also called *honesty tests*.

internal consistency An indication of the extent to which individual test items seem to be measuring the same thing.

internal validity The extent to which we can draw causal inferences about our variables.

interrater reliability The extent to which multiple raters or judges agree on ratings made about a particular person, thing, or behavior.

intervention The program or initiative that is suggested or implemented by the change agent in an organizational change effort.

interviews Procedures designed to predict future performance based on an applicant's oral responses to a series of oral questions.

job A collection of positions similar enough to one another to share a common job title.

job analysis The process of defining a job in terms of its component tasks or duties and the knowledge or skills required to perform them.

job crafting The process through which employees are allowed to customize, modify, and craft their own job with respect to tasks, responsibilities, and processes.

job description As an outcome of job analysis, a written statement of what jobholders actually do, how they do it, and why they do it.

Job Element Method (JEM) A worker-oriented approach to job analysis that was designed to identify the characteristics of superior workers in a particular job.

job enrichment The process of increasing the motivating potential of jobs, often by strengthening the key motivating characteristics identified by job characteristics theory.

job evaluation As an outcome of job analysis, a technique that attempts to determine the value or worth of particular jobs to organizations so that salaries can be set accordingly.

job involvement The extent to which employees are cognitively engaged in their jobs.

job satisfaction A pleasurable, positive emotional state resulting from the cognitive appraisal of one's job or job experiences.

job specifications An outcome of job analysis delineating the KSAOs deemed necessary to perform a job; often called job specs.

job-oriented Referring to approaches to job analysis that focus on describing the various tasks that are performed on the job.

knowledge management A method in which organizations enhance their operations through attempts to develop, disseminate, and use knowledge.

KSAOs The knowledge, skills, abilities, and other characteristics that are required for successful job performance.

leader–member exchange (LMX) theory A theory about work dyads that focuses on the relationships between subordinates and leaders rather than on leader behaviors or traits.

leaderless group discussion (LGD) A group exercise designed to tap managerial attributes that requires the interaction of a small group of individuals.

leadership A social process through which an individual intentionally exerts influence over others to structure their behaviors and relationships.

leadership self-efficacy (LSE) The perceived capabilities of an individual to successfully accomplish leadership tasks.

learning The relatively permanent change in behavior that occurs as a result of experience or practice.

learning criteria In Kirkpatrick's taxonomy, criteria that reflect how much of the material is actually learned in the training program; along with reaction criteria, also called *internal criteria*.

leniency The rating error that results when (1) the mean of one's ratings across ratees is higher than the mean of all ratees across all raters or (2) the mean of one's ratings is higher than the midpoint of the scale.

manipulation The systematic control, variation, or application of independent variables to different groups of participants.

massed practice Training in which all the practice takes place at one time, without breaks.

mean The arithmetic average of a group of scores, typically the most useful measure of central tendency.

measurement The assignment of numbers to objects or events using rules in such a way as to represent specified attributes of the objects.

mechanical ability A specific cognitive ability involving a focus on mechanical relations, recognition of tools used for various purposes, and sometimes actual mechanical skills.

median The score in the middle of the distribution.

mental model An organized knowledge structure that helps an individual make sense of the world around him or her.

meta-analysis A methodology that is used to conduct quantitative literature reviews.

micro-managers Managers who, instead of delegating individual tasks to employees, try to take charge of all tasks.

mindguard A member of a cohesive group whose job it is to protect the group from outside information that is inconsistent with the group's views.

mode The most frequent single score in a distribution.

multiple cutoff approach A noncompensatory model of employee selection in which "passing scores," or cut-offs, are set on each predictor.

multiple hurdle approach A rendition of the multiple cutoff approach in which the predictors are administered in a predetermined order and applicants are measured on the next predictor only if they scored above the cutoff on the previous predictor.

multiple regression A statistical technique that, when used in the selection context, allows us to estimate how well a series of predictors forecasts a performance criterion.

need A force that organizes perceptions, beliefs, cognitions, and actions, giving rise to behaviors that reduce the force and bring about a steady state.

normal distribution A mathematically based distribution depicted as a bell-shaped curve, in which most of the observations cluster around the mean and there are few extreme observations.

normative commitment Attachment to an organization that reflects one's obligation to continue employment with the organization; also called *moral commitment*.

norms Shared expectations about appropriate ways of responding in a group.

objective criteria Performance measures that are based on counting rather than on subjective judgments or evaluations; sometimes called hard or *nonjudgmental* criteria.

organization-based self-esteem (OBSE) A measure of how valuable employees view themselves as organization members.

organization-motivated aggression Attempts by someone inside or outside the organization to cause injury or to be destructive as a result of some organizational factor.

organization-motivated violence The negative effects on people or property that result from organization-motivated aggression.

organizational-behavior management (OBM) The application of the principles of behavioral psychology to the study and control of individual and group behavior within organizational settings.

organizational commitment (OC) The relative strength of an individual's identification with and involvement in a particular organization.

organizational development (OD) A planned, organization-wide effort to increase organizational effectiveness through behavioral science knowledge and technology.

organizational justice The role of fairness in the workplace.

organizational justice The study of people's perceptions of fairness in organizational contexts.

organizational psychology The systematic study of dispositional and situational variables that influence the behaviors and experiences of individuals and groups at work.

organizational socialization The process by which an individual acquires the attitudes, behavior, and knowledge needed to participate as an organizational member.

organizational theory A set of propositions that explains or predicts how groups and individuals behave in varying organizational structures and circumstances.

organizational transformation A term that refers to any intervention primarily directed toward creating a new vision for an organization and changing its beliefs, purpose, and mission.

overlearning The process of giving trainees continued practice even after they have appeared to master the behavior, resulting in high levels of learning.

paper-and-pencil tests Frequently used tests in which individuals respond to questions in a test booklet or mark answers on computer sheets to be scanned.

parallel forms reliability The extent to which two independent forms of a test are equivalent measures of the same construct; sometimes called *equivalent forms reliability* or *a coefficient of equivalence*.

parental leave A program offered by organizations that enables employees to combine work and family responsibilities related to child rearing.

perceived behavioral control An individual's belief about how easy or difficult performance of a behavior is likely to be.

perceived organizational support (POS) Employees' global beliefs concerning the extent to which the organization values and cares about them.

performance Actual on-the-job behaviors that are relevant to the organization's goals.

performance appraisal Systematic review and evaluation of job performance.

performance management A system of individual performance improvement that typically includes (1) objective goal setting, (2) continuous coaching and feedback, (3) performance appraisal, and (4) development planning.

performance tests Tests that require the manipulation of an object or a piece of equipment.

person–environment (PE) fit The agreement or match between an individual's KSAOs and values and the demands of a job and characteristics of an organization.

personality tests Tests in which numbers are systematically assigned to individuals' characteristics.

physical fidelity The extent to which the operation of equipment in training mimics that in the real world.

point system The most common approach to job evaluation, which involves estimating the value of jobs based on points assigned to various predetermined dimensions.

position An individual's place in the organization defined by the tasks performed.

Position Analysis Questionnaire (PAQ) A widely used job analysis instrument that focuses on general work behaviors.

positive psychology The scientific study of the strengths and virtues of individuals and institutions.

power An individual's potential influence over the attitudes and behavior of one or more other individuals.

power test A test with no fixed time limits and relatively difficult items.

predictive validity The extent to which test scores obtained at one point in time predict criteria obtained in the future.

problem-focused coping A coping style that involves behaviors or actions targeted toward solving or handling the stress-inducing problem itself.

process loss Any nonmotivational element of a group situation that detracts from the group's performance.

prototype One's mental representation of something or someone, such as a leader.

psychological fidelity The extent to which the essential behavioral processes needed for success on the job are also necessary for success in the training simulation.

psychomotor tests Tests that measure both the speed and the accuracy of motor and sensory coordination.

quasi-experiment A research design that resembles an experimental design but does not include random assignment.

random assignment The procedure by which research participants, once selected, are assigned to conditions such that each one has an equally likely chance of being assigned to each condition.

range The simplest measure of dispersion, reflecting the spread of scores from the lowest to the highest.

Rater Error Training (RET) A type of training originally developed to reduce rater errors by focusing on describing errors like halo to raters and showing them how to avoid making such errors.

reaction criteria In Kirkpatrick's taxonomy, trainees' attitudinal reactions to the training program; along with learning criteria, also called *internal criteria*.

readiness Possessing the background characteristics and necessary level of interest that make learning possible.

realistic job preview (RJP) During an employment interview, the presentation of an accurate glimpse of what the job would be like.

reasonable accommodations Changes or exceptions made by an employer that allow qualified disabled individuals to successfully do a job.

recruitment The process of encouraging potentially qualified applicants to seek employment with a particular company.

reengineering The fundamental rethinking and redesign of business processes to improve critical performance as measured by cost, quality, service, and speed; also called *business process redesign*.

reliability The consistency or stability of a measure.

resistance to change The characteristic of some individuals who so prefer to keep things the way they are that they intentionally or otherwise work to make change more difficult and less successful.

results criteria In Kirkpatrick's taxonomy, the ultimate value of the training program to the company; along with behavioral criteria, also called *external criteria*.

role A set of behaviors expected of a person who occupies a particular position in a group.

role ambiguity A situation that results when role expectations are unclear and employees are thus not sure what is expected of them.

role conflict A situation that results when role expectations are inconsistent, as when a supervisor sends employees mixed messages about their roles.

role differentiation The process by which a group or organization establishes distinct roles for various members of the group or organization.

science A process or method for generating a body of knowledge.

scientist/practitioner model An approach used to train I/O psychologists maintaining that because I/O psychologists are both generators and consumers of knowledge, training must be focused on both theory and application.

selection battery A set of predictors, or tests, that are used to make employee hiring decisions.

selection ratio The number of job openings divided by the number of applicants.

self-efficacy expectations Individuals' perceptions of their ability to successfully complete a task or attain a goal.

self-managed work team (SMWT) A work team that is responsible for monitoring and controlling the overall process or product, as well as for doling out specific tasks to team members.

self-regulation The manner in which individuals monitor their own behaviors and make adjustments to those behaviors in the pursuit of goals.

sensemaking The process whereby employees exert effort to interpret and understand work-related events.

severity The tendency to use only the low end of the scale or to give consistently lower ratings to one's employees than other raters do.

sexual harassment Behaviors such as unwelcome sexual advances, requests for sexual favors, and other conduct of a sexual nature, submission to or rejection of which affects one's job or creates an offensive work environment.

shared mental models Organized structures combining the knowledge, beliefs, and understandings of two or more individuals that help coordinate their efforts.

situational interview An interviewing technique that relies on candidates sharing responses or intentions about job-related dilemmas or situations proposed to them with respect to the new job.

situational judgment tests (SJTs) Paper-and-pencil test or video vignette that provides hypothetical scenarios for candidates to respond to by choosing the best alternative.

situational specificity The belief that test validities are specific to particular situations.

social loafing The reduction in individual effort that occurs when people work in groups instead of alone.

span of control The number of subordinates who report to a given supervisor.

spatial ability A specific cognitive ability involving a focus on geometric relations, such as visualizing objects and rotating them spatially to form a particular pattern.

speed test A test containing relatively easy items with a short time limit in which individuals must complete as many items as they can.

standard deviation A measure of dispersion that is calculated as the square root of the variance.

statistic An efficient device for summarizing in a single number the values, characteristics, or scores describing a series of cases.

strains Undesirable personal outcomes resulting from the combined stressful experiences of various life domains.

strategic job analysis An approach to job analysis that considers the status of jobs as they currently exist but also factors in how jobs are likely to change in the future as a result of anticipated organizational or industry changes.

stress Any force that pushes a psychological or physical function beyond its range of stability, producing a strain within the individual.

subject matter experts (SMEs) Individuals who participate in job analyses as a result of their job-related expertise.

subjective criteria Performance measures that are based on the judgments or evaluations of others rather than on objective measures such as counting; sometimes called *soft* or *judgmental criteria*.

subjective norm An individual's perception of the social pressures to perform or not perform a particular behavior.

sucker effect An outcome that occurs when group members become concerned that their coworkers are holding back, at which point they reduce their own efforts to the level they believe is being exhibited by their coworkers.

surveys A data collection technique that involves selecting a sample of respondents and administering some type of questionnaire.

synthetic validity Validity that is inferred based on the links between job components and KSAs.

task A work activity that is performed to achieve a specific objective.

Task Inventory Approach A job-oriented approach to job analysis in which task statements are generated by experts who are familiar with the job in question.

task performance The work-related activities performed by employees that contribute to the technical core of the organization.

taskwork Activities, behaviors, or actions that involve the task-oriented aspects of work.

team building A technique used by organizations to develop teams or to enhance the effectiveness of existing teams.

teamwork Activities, behaviors, or actions that involve the process-oriented aspects of work.

telework Working arrangements in which employees enjoy flexibility in work hours and/or location.

test A systematic procedure for observing behavior and describing it with the aid of numerical scales or fixed categories.

test–retest reliability The stability of a test over time; often called a *coefficient of stability*.

theory A set of interrelated constructs (concepts), definitions, and propositions that present a systematic view of a phenomenon by specifying relations among variables, with the purpose of explaining and predicting the phenomenon.

360-degree feedback A method of performance appraisal in which multiple raters at various levels of the organization evaluate a target employee and the employee is provided with feedback from these multiple sources.

total quality management (TQM) An initiative that focuses on employee involvement in the control of quality in organizations; also called *continuous improvement* or quality management.

training The formal procedures that a company utilizes to facilitate learning so that the resultant behavior contributes to the attainment of the company's goals and objectives.

trait theories Leadership theories that focus on identifying the individual characteristics that make people good leaders; sometimes called the *great man/great woman theory*.

transactional leadership A form of leadership in which the relationship between leader and follower is based chiefly on exchanges, with an emphasis on contingent reinforcement.

transfer of training The extent to which the material, skills, or procedures learned in training are taken back to the job and used by the employee in some regular fashion.

transformational leadership A form of leadership in which the interaction of leader and follower raises both to higher levels of motivation and morality than they would achieve individually.

true halo Halo that results from accurate intercorrelations among performance dimensions rather than from rating error.

ultimate criterion A theoretical construct encompassing all performance aspects that define success on the job.

undue hardship An accommodation for the disabled that would result in significant difficulty or expense given the employer's size and financial resources.

unobtrusive naturalistic observation An observational technique whereby the researcher unobtrusively and objectively observes individuals but does not try to blend in with them.

upward appraisal ratings Ratings provided by individuals whose status, in an organizational-hierarchy sense, is below that of the ratees.

utility The degree to which a selection battery is useful and cost efficient.

valence (value) The expected level of satisfaction to be derived from some outcome.

validity coefficient (r) A correlation that serves as an index of the relationship between a predictor and a criterion, used by selection researchers and practitioners as evidence that a particular test is a valid predictor of a performance criterion.

validity generalization (VG) A statistical approach used to demonstrate that test validities do not vary across situations.

validity shrinkage A statistical phenomenon reflecting the likelihood that a given selection battery will demonstrate lower validity when employed with a different sample.

variance A useful measure of dispersion reflecting the sum of the squared differences between each score and the mean of the group divided by the number of total scores.

work centrality The degree of importance that work holds in one's life.

work group An interdependent collection of individuals who share responsibility for specific outcomes for their organizations.

work motivation A force that drives people to behave in a way that energizes, directs, and sustains their work behavior.

work sample tests Tests that attempt to duplicate performance criteria measures and use them as predictors, thus forming miniature replicas of the job.

work–family conflict (WFC) A model of work–family relations in which work and family demands are incompatible.

work–family enrichment A model of work–family relations in which positive attitudes and behaviors are believed to carry over from one domain to the other.

workaholic An individual whose high drive to work and high work involvement become so intense that they result in work–life imbalance issues.

worker-oriented Referring to approaches to job analysis that examine broad human behaviors involved in work activities.

References

100 Best Companies to Work For. (2008). *Fortune.* Retrieved August 21, 2008, from http://money.cnn.com /magazines/fortune/bestcompanies/2008/index.html

100 Best Companies to Work For. (2011). *Fortune.* Retrieved January 2, 2012, from http://money.cnn .com/magazines/fortune/bestcompanies/2011/full_list/

100 Best Companies to Work For. (2012). Retrieved July 19, 2012, from http://money.cnn.com /magazines/fortune/best companies/2012/snapshots/4 .html

2011 Turnover Rates by Industry. (2011, October 26). Retrieved July 5, 2012, from http://www .compensationforce.com/2011/10/2011-turnover-rates- by-industry.html

AARP. (2008). *Caregiving benefits: 2008 AARP best employers for workers over 50.* Retrieved April 19, 2009, from http://www.aarp.org/money/work/best_employers /articles/caregiving_benefits_2008_best_employers .html

Aberson, C. L. (2003). Support for race-based affir- mative action: Self-interest and procedural justice. *Journal of Applied Social Psychology, 33*(6), 1212–1225.

Adams, J. S. (1965). Inequity in social exchange. In L. Berkowitz (Ed.), *Advances in experimental psychology* (Vol. 2, pp. 267–299). New York: Academic Press.

Aguinis, H., & Kraiger, K. (2009). Benefits of train- ing and development for individuals and teams, organi- zations, and society. *Annual Review of Psychology, 60*(1), 451–474.

Ajzen, I., & Fishbein, M. (1980). *Understanding attitudes and predicting social behavior.* Englewood Cliffs, NJ: Prentice-Hall.

Ajzen, I., & Fishbein, M. (2005). The influence of attitudes on behavior. In D. Albarracín, B. T. Johnson, & M. P. Zanna (Eds.), *The handbook of attitudes* (pp. 173–221). Mahwah, NJ: Erlbaum.

Ajzen, I., & Madden, T. J. (1986). Prediction of goal-directed behavior: The role of intention, perceived control, and prior behavior. *Journal of Experimental Social Psychology, 22,* 453–474.

Allen, D. G., Shore, L. M., & Griffeth, R. W. (2003). The role of perceived organizational support and supportive human resource practices in the turnover process. *Journal of Management, 29*(1), 99–118.

Allen, N. J., & Meyer, J. P. (1996). Affective, continuance, and normative commitment to the orga- nization: An examination of construct validity. *Journal of Vocational Behavior, 49,* 252–276.

Allen, R. S., & White, C. S. (2002). Equity sensitivity theory: A test of responses to two types of under-reward situations. *Journal of Managerial Issues, 14*(4), 435–451.

Allen, T. D., Facteau, J. D., & Facteau, C. L. (2004). Structured interviewing for OCB: Construct validity, faking, and the effects of question type. *Human Performance, 17*(1), 1–24.

Alliger, G. M., & Dwight, S. A. (2000). A meta- analytic investigation of the susceptibility of integrity tests to faking and coaching. *Educational and Psychological Measurement, 60*(1), 59–72.

Alliger, G. M., & Janak, E. A. (1989). Kirkpatrick's levels of training criteria: Thirty years later. *Personnel Psychology, 42,* 331–342.

Alliger, G. M., Tannenbaum, S. I., Bennett, W., Jr., Traver, H., & Shotland, A. (1997). A meta-analysis of the relations among training criteria. *Personnel Psychology, 50,* 341–358.

Allworth, E., & Hesketh, B. (2000). Job require- ments biodata as a predictor of performance in customer service roles. *International Journal of Selection and Assessment, 83*(3), 137–147.

Aluja, A., Rossier, J., & Zuckerman, M. (2007). Equivalence of paper and pencil vs. Internet forms of the ZKPQ-50-CC in Spanish and French samples. *Personality and Individual Differences, 43,* 2022–2032.

Ambient Insight. (2011). Ambient Insight compre- hensive report. Retrieved from http:// www.ambientinsight.com/Resources/Documents /Ambient-Insight-2009-2014-US-Mobile-Learning -Market-Executive-Overview.pdf

Ambrose, M. L., & Kulik, C. T. (1999). Old friends, new faces: Motivation research in the 1990s. *Journal of Management, 2*(3), 231–292.

America in 2050: Even older and more diverse. (2012). MSNBC. Retrieved March 13, 2012, from http://www.msnbc.msn.com/id/26186087/ns/us _news-life/t/america-even-older-more-diverse/

American Bar Association. (2004). *Commission on women in the profession* [Brochure]. Retrieved April 14, 2009, from http://www.abanet.org/women /glance2003.pdf

American Council on Education. (2002, December 9). Rate of increase for women and minorities as college presidents slows according to a new report on the college presidency from the American Council on Education. Retrieved April 21, 2009, from http://www.acenet.edu/AM/Template .cfm?Section=Search&template=/CM/HTMLDisplay .cfm&ContentID=17678

American Psychological Association. (2001). *Publication manual of the American Psychological Association* (5th ed.). Washington, DC: Author.

American Psychological Association. (2002). *Ethical principles of psychologists and code of conduct.* Retrieved January 2, 2007, from http://www.apa.org /ethics/code2002.html

American Psychological Association. (2009). *Publication manual of the American Psychological Association* (6th ed.). Washington, DC: Author.

American Society for Training and Development. (2007). *ASTD releases new data on workplace learning investments and practices.* Retrieved April 19, 2009, from http://www.klagroup.com/PDFs /ASTD2006StateoftheIndustryReportpressrelease _013107.pdf

American Society for Training and Development. (2011). *State of the industry: ASTD's annual review of trends in workplace learning and performance.* Alexandria, VA: Author.

Anderson, L. (2000, October 23). Business education survey: Corporate universities. *Financial Times.*

Anderson, M. (2012, March 4). From idea to store shelf: A new product is born. *Yahoo! News.* Retrieved from http://news.yahoo.com/idea-store-sehlf-product -born-174428924.html

Antecol, H., & Cobb-Clark, D. (2003). Does sexual harassment training change attitudes? A view from the federal level. *Social Science Quarterly, 84,* 826–842.

Ardichvili, A., Page, V., & Wentling, T. (2003). Motivation and barriers to participation in virtual knowledge-sharing communities of practice. *Journal of Knowledge Management, 7*(1), 64–77.

Arthur, J. B., & Huntley, C. L. (2005). Ramping up the organizational learning curve: Assessing the impact of deliberate learning on organizational performance under gain-sharing. *Academy of Management Journal, 48,* 1159–1170.

Arthur, W., Jr., Bennett, W., Jr., Edens, P. S., & Bell, S. T. (2003a). Effectiveness of training in organizations: A meta-analysis of design and evaluation features. *Journal of Applied Psychology, 88*(2), 234–245.

Arthur, W., Jr., Day, E. A., McNelly, T. L., & Edens, P. S. (2003b). A meta-analysis of the criterion-related validity of assessment center dimensions. *Personnel Psychology, 56*(1), 125–154.

Arthur, W., Jr., Glaze, R. M., Villado, A. J., & Taylor, J. E. (2010). The magnitude and extent of cheating and response distortion effects on unproctored Internet-based tests of cognitive ability and personality. *International Journal of Selection and Assessment, 18*(1), 1–16.

Arthur, W., Jr., Woehr, D. J., & Maldegen, R. (2000). Convergent and discriminate validity of assessment center dimensions: A conceptual and empirical reexamination of the assessment center construct-related validity paradox. *Journal of Management, 26*(4), 813–835.

Arvey, R. D., & Begalla, M. E. (1975). Analyzing the homemaker job using the Position Analysis Questionnaire (PAQ). *Journal of Applied Psychology, 60,* 513–517.

Arvey, R. D., Bouchard, T. J. J., Segal, N. L., & Abraham, L. M. (1989). Job satisfaction: Environmental and genetic components. *Journal of Applied Psychology, 74*(2), 187–192.

Arvey, R. D., Rotundo, M., Johnson, W., Zhang, Z., & McGue, M. (2006). The determinants of leadership role occupancy: Genetic and personality factors. *Leadership Quarterly, 17,* 1–20.

Arvey, R. D., Zhang, Z., Avolio, B. J., & Kreuger, R. F. (2007). Developmental and genetic determinants of leadership role occupancy among women. *Journal of Applied Psychology, 92,* 693–706.

Aryee, S., & Luk, V. (1996). Work and nonwork influences on the career satisfaction of dual-earner couples. *Journal of Vocational Behavior, 49,* 38–52.

Ash, R. A., & Edgell, S. L. (1975). A note on the readability of the Position Analysis Questionnaire (PAQ). *Journal of Applied Psychology, 60,* 765–766.

Ashmos, D. P., & Nathan, M. L. (2002). Team sense-making: A mental model for navigating uncharted territories. *Journal of Managerial Issues, 14*(2), 198–217.

Atwater, L. E., & Carmeli, A. (2009). Leader–member exchange, feelings of energy, and involvement in creative work. *The Leadership Quarterly, 20,* 264–275.

Atwater, L. E., Daldman, D. A., Atwater, D., & Cartier, P. (2000). An upward feedback field experiment: Supervisors' cynicism, reactions, and commitment to subordinates. *Personnel Psychology, 53,* 275–297.

Atwater, L. E., Wang, M., Smither, J. W., & Fleenor, J. W. (2009). Are cultural characteristics associated with the relationship between self and others' ratings of leadership? *Journal of Applied Psychology, 94*(4), 876–886.

Austin, J. T., & Davies, S. A. (2000). History of industrial-organizational psychology. In A. E. Kazdin (Ed.), *Encyclopedia of psychology* (Vol. 4, pp. 252–255). Oxford, UK: Oxford University Press

Austin, J. T., & Villanova, P. D. (1992). The criterion problem: 1917–1992. *Journal of Applied Psychology, 77,* 836–874.

Austin, J. T., Villanova, P. D., & Hindman, H G. (1995). Legal requirements and technical guidelines involved in implementing performance appraisal systems. In G. R. Ferris & M. R. Buckley (Eds.), *Human resource management: Perspectives, context, functions, and outcomes* (pp. 271–288). Boston: Allyn & Bacon.

Avery, D. R., & McKay, P. F. (2006). Target practice: An organizational impression management approach to attracting minority and female job applicants. *Personnel Psychology, 59,* 157–187.

Avolio, B. J., Waldman, D. A., & McDaniel, M. A. (1990). Age and work performance in nonmanagerial jobs: The effects of experience and occupational type. *Academy of Management Journal, 33*(2), 407–422.

Awoniyi, E. A., Griego, O. V., & Morgan, G. A. (2002). Person–environment fit and transfer of training. *International Journal of Training and Development, 6*(1), 25–35.

Ayman, R., Chemers, M. M., & Fiedler, F. (1995). The contingency model of leadership effectiveness: Its level of analysis. *Leadership Quarterly, 6*(2), 147–167.

Aziz, A., & Zickar, M. J. (2006). A cluster analysis investigation of workaholism as a syndrome. *Journal of Occupational Health Psychology, 11,* 52–62.

Babbie, E. (1998). *The practice of social research.* Belmont, CA: Wadsworth.

Bachrach, D. G., Powell, B. C., Collins, B. J., & Richey, R. G. (2006). Effects of task interdependence on the relationship between helping behavior and group performance. *Journal of Applied Psychology, 91*(6), 1396–1405.

Bakker, A. B., Demerouti, E., & Dollard, M. F. (2008). How job demands affect partners' experience of exhaustion: Integrating work–family conflict and crossover theory. *Journal of Applied Psychology, 93,* 901–911.

Bakker, A. B., & Schaufeli, W. B. (2008). Positive organizational behavior: Engaged employees in flourishing organizations. *Journal of Organizational Behavior, 29,* 147–154.

Baldwin, T. P., & Ford, J. K. (1988). Transfer of training: A review and directions for future research. *Personnel Psychology, 41,* 63–105.

Baltes, B. B., & Heydens-Gahir, H. A. (2003). Reduction of work–family conflict through the use of selection, optimization, and compensation behaviors. *Journal of Applied Psychology, 88*(6), 1005–1018.

Bandura, A. (1986). *Social foundations of thought and action.* Englewood Cliffs, NJ: Prentice-Hall

Bandura, A., & Locke, E. A. (2003). Negative self-efficacy and goal effects revisited. *Journal of Applied Psychology, 88*(1), 87–99.

Bardsley, J. J., & Rhodes, S. R. (1996). Using the Steers–Rhodes (1984) framework to identify correlates of employee lateness. *Journal of Business and Psychology, 10*(3), 351–365.

Barger, P., & Grandey, A. (2006). "Service with a smile" and encounter satisfaction: Emotional contagion and appraisal mechanisms. *Academy of Management Journal, 49,* 1229–1238.

Barrett, G. V., Caldwell, M. S., & Alexander, R. A. (1985). The concept of dynamic criteria: A critical reanalysis. *Personnel Psychology, 38*(1), 93–97.

Barrett, G. V., & Kernan, M. C. (1988). Performance appraisal and terminations: A review of court decisions since Brito v. Zia with implications for personnel practices. *Personnel Psychology, 40*(3), 489–503.

Barrick, M. R., Mount, M. K., & Judge, T. A. (2001). Personality and performance at the beginning of the new millennium: What do we know and where do we go next? *International Journal of Selection & Assessment, 9*(1/2), 9–30.

Barrick, M. R., Stewart, G. L., Neubert, M. J., & Mount, M. K. (1998). Relating member ability and personality to work-team processes and team effectiveness. *Journal of Applied Psychology, 83*(3), 377–391.

Bass, B. M. (1985). *Leadership and performance beyond expectations.* New York: Free Press.

Bass, B. M. (1997). Does the transactional–transformational leadership paradigm transcend organizational and national boundaries? *American Psychologist, 52*(2), 130–139.

Bass, B. M., Avolio, B. J., Jung, D. I., & Berson, Y. (2003). Predicting unit performance by assessing transformational and transactional leadership. *Journal of Applied Psychology, 88*(2), 207–218.

Bass, B. M., & Steidlmeier, P. (1999). Ethics, character, and authentic transformational leadership behavior. *Leadership Quarterly, 10*(2), 181–217.

Bauer, T. N., Morrison, E. W., & Callister, R. R. (1998). Organizational socialization: A review and directions for future research. In G. R. Ferris (Ed.), *Research in personnel and human resources management* (Vol. 16, pp. 149–214). Stamford, CT: JAI Press.

Baumohl, B. (1993, March 15). When downsizing becomes "dumbsizing." *Time, 141,* 55.

Beal, D. J., Trougakos, J. P., Weiss, H. M., & Green, S. G. (2006). Episodic processes in emotional labor: Perceptions of affective delivery and regulation strategies. *Journal of Applied Psychology, 91*(5), 1053–1065.

Beal, D. J., & Weiss, H. M. (2003). Methods of ecological momentary assessment in organizational research. *Organizational Research Methods, 6*(4), 430–464.

Beaty, J. C., Nye, C. D., Borneman, M. J., Kantrowitz, T. M., Drasgow, F., & Grauer, E. (2011). Proctored versus unproctored Internet tests: Are unproctored noncognitive tests as predictive of job performance? *International Journal of Selection and Assessment, 19*(1), 1–10.

Beck, B. (1998, July 16). Women and work: At the double. *The Economist, 348*(8077), S12–S16.

Beckhard, R. (1969). *Organization development: Strategies and models.* Reading, MA: Addison-Wesley.

Bell, B. S., & Kozlowski, S. W. J. (2002). Adaptive guidance: Enhancing self-regulation, knowledge, and performance in technology-based training. *Personnel Psychology, 55*(2), 267–306.

Bell, S. T. (2007). Deep-level composition variables as predictors of team performance: A meta-analysis. *Journal of Applied Psychology, 92,* 595–615.

Bennis, W., & Biederman, P. W. (1997). *Organizing genius: The secrets of creative collaboration.* Reading, MA: Addison-Wesley.

Berdahl, J. L., & Aquino, K. (2009). Sexual behavior at work: Fun or folly? *Journal of Applied Psychology, 94,* 34–47.

Berger, L. A., & Berger, D. R. (2008). *The compensation handbook: A state-of-the-art guide to compensation and strategy design* (5th ed.). New York: McGraw-Hill.

Berkley, R. A., & Watt, A. H. (2006). Impact of same-sex harassment and gender-role. *Employee Responsibilities and Rights Journal, 18,* 3–19.

Bernardin, H. J. (1978). Effects of rater training on leniency and halo errors in student ratings of instructors. *Journal of Applied Psychology, 63*(3), 301–308.

Bernardin, H. J., & Beatty, R. W. (1984). *Performance appraisal: Assessing human behavior at work.* Boston: Kent.

Bernardin, H. J., & Buckley, M. R. (1981). Strategies in rater training. *Academy of Management Review, 6,* 205–212.

Bernardin, H. J., Cooke, D. K., & Villanova, P. D. (2000). Conscientiousness and agreeableness as predictors of rating leniency. *Journal of Applied Psychology, 85*(2), 232–236.

Bernardin, H. J., Orban, J., & Carlyle, J. (1981). Performance ratings as a function of trust in appraisal and rater individual differences. Paper presented at the 41st annual meeting of the Academy of Management, San Diego, CA.

Bernardin, H. J., & Pence, E. C. (1980). Effects of rater training: Creating new response sets and decreasing accuracy. *Journal of Applied Psychology, 65,* 60–66.

Bernardin, H. J., & Villanova, P. (2005). Research streams in rater self-efficacy. *Group & Organization Management, 30*(1), 61–88.

Berry, C. M., Sackett, P. R., & Wiemann, S. (2007). A review of recent developments in integrity test research. *Personnel Psychology, 60*(2), 271–301.

Berry, G. R. (2011). Enhancing effectiveness on virtual teams: Understanding why traditional team skills are insufficient. *Journal of Business Communication, 48*(2), 186–206.

Bersin, J. (2005). *The four stages of e-learning: A maturity model for online corporate training.* Oakland, CA: Bersin & Associates.

Bertua, C., Anderson, N., & Salgado, J. F. (2005). The predictive validity of cognitive ability tests: A UK meta-analysis. *Journal of Occupational and Organizational Psychology, 78*(3), 387–409.

Bettenhausen, K. L., & Fedor, D. B. (1997). Peer and upward appraisals: A comparison of their benefits and problems. *Group and Organization Management, 22*(2), 236–263.

Beugré, C. D. (1998). Implementing business process reengineering: The role of organizational justice. *Journal of Applied Behavioral Science, 34*(3), 347–360.

Bhagat, R. S., Allie, S. M., & Ford, D. L., Jr. (1995). Coping with stressful life events: An empirical analysis. In R. Crandall & P. L. Perrewé (Eds.), *Occupational stress: A handbook* (pp. 93–112). Washington, DC: Taylor & Francis.

Biles, P. D. (1999). *OSHA workplace violence prevention guidelines.* Paper presented at the Work, Stress, and Health '99: Organization of Work in a Global Economy conference. Abstract retrieved April 9, 2009, from the American Psychological Association, Public Interest Directorate website: http://www.apa.org/pi/wpo /niosh/abstract12.html

Bisio, J. (1999). The age boom. *Risk Management, 46*(2), 22–27.

Blackmore, E. R., Stansfield, S. A., Weller, I., Munce, S., Zagorski, B. M., & Stewart, D. E. (2007). Major depressive episodes and work stress: Results from a national population survey. *American Journal of Public Health, 97,* 2088–2093.

Blake, R. (2006, July 24). Employee retention: What employee turnover really costs your company. Retrieved April 21, 2009, from http://archive.managernewz .com/2006/0724.html

Blakely, G. L., Blakely, E. H., & Moorman, R. H. (1998). The effects of training on perceptions of sexual harassment allegations. *Journal of Applied Social Psychology, 28*(1), 71–83.

Blau, G. (1994). Developing and testing a taxonomy of lateness behavior. *Journal of Applied Psychology, 79*(6), 959–970.

Blau, G. (1999). Testing the longitudinal impact of work variables and performance appraisal satisfaction on subsequent overall job satisfaction. *Human Relations, 52*(8), 1099–1113.

Bliese, P. D., & Britt, T. W. (2001). Social support, group consensus, and stressor–strain relationships: Social context matters. *Journal of Organizational Behavior, 22,* 425–436.

Bloom, A. J., Yorges, S. L., & Ruhl, A. J. (2000). Enhancing student motivation: Extensions from job enrichment theory and practice. *Teaching of Psychology, 27*(2), 135–137.

Blum, M. L., & Naylor, J. C. (1968). *Industrial psychology.* New York: Harper & Row.

Blume, B. D., Ford, J. K., Baldwin, T. T., & Huang, J. L. (2010). Transfer of training: A meta-analytic review. *Journal of Management, 36*(4), 1065–1105.

Bolino, M. C., & Turnley, W. H. (2005). The personal costs of citizenship behavior: The relationship between individual initiative and role overload, job stress, and work–family conflict. *Journal of Applied Psychology, 90*(4), 740–748.

Bolino, M. C., Turnley, W. H., & Bloodgood, J. M. (2002). Citizenship behavior and the creation of social capital in organizations. *Academy of Management Review, 27*(4), 505–522.

Bolino, M. C., Turnley, W. H., & Niehoff, B. P. (2004). The other side of the story: Reexamining prevailing assumptions about organizational citizenship behavior. *Human Resource Management Review, 14*(2), 229–246.

Boller, S. (2012). "Make it social: How we use Twitter as a learning tool." Bottom-Line Performance. Retrieved August 15, 2012, from http://www .bottomlineperformance.com/make-it-social-how-we -use-twitter-as-a-learning-tool/

Bond, J. T. (with Thompson, C., Galinsky, E., & Prottas, D.). (2002). *Highlights of the National Study of the Changing Workforce executive summary.* Retrieved April 8, 2009, from the Families and Work Institute website: http://www.familiesandwork.org/summary /nscw2002.pdf

Bond, J. T., & Galinsky, E. (2006, November). *What workplace flexibility is available to entry-level, hourly employees?* Retrieved April 8, 2009, from the Families and Work Institute website: http://familiesandwork .org/site/research/reports/brief3.pdf

Bono, J. E., & Colbert, A. E. (2005). Understanding responses to multi-source feedback: The role of core self-evaluations. *Personnel Psychology, 58*(1), 171–203.

Bono, J. E., & Ilies, R. (2006). Charisma, positive emotions and mood contagion. *Leadership Quarterly, 17,* 317–334.

Bono, J. E., Folds, H. J., Vinson, G., & Muros, J. P. (2007). Workplace emotions: The role of supervision and leadership. *Journal of Applied Psychology, 92*(5), 1357–1367.

Boon, O. K., Arumugam, V., Safa, M. S., & Bakar, N. A. (2007). HRM and TQM: Association with job involvement. *Personnel Review, 36,* 939–962.

Borman, W. C. (2004). The concept of organizational citizenship. *Current Directions in Psychological Science, 13,* 238–241.

Borman, W. C., Buck, D. E., Hanson, M. A., Motowidlo, S. J., Stark, S., & Drasgow, F. (2001). An examination of the comparative reliability, validity, and accuracy of performance ratings made using computerized adaptive rating scales. *Journal of Applied Psychology, 86*(5), 965–973.

Borman, W. C., Hanson, M. A., & Hedge, J. W. (1997). Personnel selection. *Annual Review of Psychology, 48,* 299–337.

Borman, W. C., & Motowidlo, S. J. (1997). Task performance and contextual performance: The meaning for personnel selection research. *Human Performance, 10*(2), 99–109.

Boudreau, J. W., & Ramstad, P. M. (2003). Strategic industrial and organizational psychology and the role of utility analysis models. In W. C. Borman, D. R. Ilgen, and R. Klimoski (Eds.), *Handbook of psychology: Vol. 12. Industrial and organizational psychology* (pp. 193–221). New York: Wiley.

Bowling Green State University, Department of Psychology. (2009). *Job descriptive index.* Reprinted with permission of Bowling Green State University, Department of Psychology, Bowling Green, OH, 43403.

Boye, M. W., & Jones, J. W. (1997). Organizational culture and employee counterproductivity. In R. A. Giacalone & J. Greenberg (Eds.), *Antisocial behavior in organizations* (pp. 172–184). Thousand Oaks, CA: SAGE.

Brannick, M. T., Levine, E. L., & Morgeson, F. P. (2007). *Job and work analysis: Methods, research,* and applications for human resource management (2nd ed.). Los Angeles: SAGE.

Bray, D. W., Campbell, R. J., & Grant, D. L. (1974). *Formative years in business: A long-term AT&T study of managerial lives.* New York: Wiley.

Breaugh, J. A., Greising, L. A., Taggart, J. W., & Chen, H. (2003). The relationship of recruiting sources and pre-hire outcomes: Examination of field ratios and applicant quality. *Journal of Applied Social Psychology, 33*(11), 2267–2287.

Brennan v. Prince William Hospital Corp., 503 F.2d 282 (4th Cir. 1972).

Briel, J. B., O'Neill, K., & Scheuneman, J. D. (Eds.). (1993). *GRE technical manual.* Princeton, NJ: Educational Testing Service.

Brockner, J. (1988). *Self-esteem at work.* Lexington, MA: Lexington Books.

Brockner, J., Wiesenfeld, B. M., & Martin, C. L. (1995). Decision frame, procedural justice, and survivors' reactions to job layoffs. *Organizational Behavior and Human Decision Processes, 63,* 59–68.

Brodbeck, F. C., Kerschreiter, R., Mojzisch, A., Frey, D., & Schulz-Hardt, S. (2002). The dissemination of critical, unshared information in decision-making groups: The effects of prediscussion dissent. *European Journal of Social Psychology, 32,* 35–56.

Brody, H. M., & Grodan, A. (2010). The effect of the fair pay act on disparate-impact cases. *Employment Relations Today.* doi: 10.1002/ert.20276

Brown, J. (2002). Training needs assessment: A must for developing an effective training program. *Public Personnel Management, 31*(4), 569–578.

Brown, J., & Metcalf, D. (2008). *Mobile learning update.* Retrieved January 7, 2008, from http://www.usdla.org/MobileLearningUpdate.pdf

Brown, M., & Benson, J. (2003). Rated to exhaustion? Reactions to performance appraisal processes. *Industrial Relations Journal, 34,* 67–81.

Bruck, C. S., Allen, T. D., & Spector, P. E. (2002). The relation between work–family conflict and job satisfaction: A finer-grained analysis. *Journal of Vocational Behavior, 60*(3), 336–353.

Brunelli, M. (1999, November 4). How Harley-Davidson uses cross-functional teams. *Purchasing, 127,* 144.

Bruppacher, H. R., Alam, S. K., LeBlanc, V. A., Latter, D., Laik, V. N., Savoldelli, G. L., Mazer, C. D., Kurrek, M. M., & Joo, H. S. (2010). Simulation-based training improves physicians' performance in patient care in high-stakes clinical setting of cardiac surgery. *Anesthesiology, 112*(4), 985–992.

Brutus, S. (2010). Words versus numbers: A theoretical exploration of giving and receiving narrative comments in performance appraisal. *Human Resource Management Review, 20*(2), 144–157.

Bucklin, B. R., Alvero, A. M., Dickinson, A. M., Austin, J., & Jackson, A. K. (2000). Industrial-organizational psychology and organizational behavior management: An objective comparison. *Journal of Organizational Behavior Management, 20*(2), 27–75.

Burgess, J. R. D., & Russell, J. E. A. (2003). The effectiveness of distance learning initiatives in organizations. *Journal of Vocational Behavior, 63*(2), 289–303.

Burke, R. J. (2000). Workaholism in organizations. Psychological and physical well-being consequences. *Stress Medicine, 16*, 11–16.

Burnett, J. R., & Motowidlo, S. J. (1998). Relations between different sources of information in the structured selection interview. *Personnel Psychology, 51*, 964–983.

Cable, D. M., & Turban, D. B. (2003). The value of organizational reputation in the recruitment context: A brand-equity perspective. *Journal of Applied Social Psychology, 33*(11), 2244–2266.

Cadsby, C. B., Song, F., & Tapon, F. (2007). Sorting and incentive effects of pay for performance: An experimental investigation. *Academy of Management Journal, 50*, 387–405.

Camara, W. J., & Kimmel, E. W. (2005). *Choosing students: Higher education admissions tools for the 21st century.* Mahwah, NJ: Erlbaum.

Campbell Interest and Skill Survey (CISS). (n.d.). Retrieved October 10, 2006, from http://www .pearsonassessments.com/tests/ciss.htm

Campbell, J. P. (1990). Modeling the performance prediction problem in industrial and organizational psychology. In M. Dunnette & L. M. Hough (Eds.), *Handbook of industrial and organizational psychology* (2nd ed., Vol. 1, pp. 687–732). Palo Alto, CA: Consulting Psychologists Press.

Campbell, J. P., Gasser, M. B., & Oswald, F. L. (1996). The substantive nature of job performance variability. In K. R. Murphy (Ed.), *Individual differences and behavior in organizations* (pp. 258–299). San Francisco: Jossey-Bass.

Campbell, J. P., McCloy, R. A., Oppler, S. H., & Sager, C. E. (1993). A theory of performance. In N. Schmitt & W. C. Borman (Eds.), *Personnel selection in organizations* (pp. 35–70). San Francisco: Jossey-Bass.

Campbell, J. P., McHenry, J. J., & Wise, L. L. (1990). Modeling performance in a population of jobs. *Personnel Psychology, 43*, 313–333.

Carbonell, J. L., & Castro, Y. (2008). The impact of a leader model on high dominant women's self-selection for leadership. *Sex Roles, 58*, 776–783.

Carless, S., & De Paola, C. (2000). The measurement of cohesion in work teams. *Small Groups Research, 31*(1), 71–88.

Carlson, D. S., Grzywacz, J. G., Ferguson, M., Hunter, E. M., Clinch, C. R., & Arcury, T. A. (2011). Health and turnover of working mothers after childbirth via the work–family interface: An analysis across time. *Journal of Applied Psychology, 96*(5), 1045–1054.

Carlson, D. S., & Perrewé, P. L. (1999). The role of social support in the stressor–strain relationship: An examination of work–family conflict. *Journal of Management, 25*(4), 513–540.

Carmeli, A., & Josman, Z. E. (2006). The relationship among emotional intelligence, task performance, and organizational citizenship behaviors. *Human Performance, 19*(4), 403–419.

Carpal tunnel syndrome reaching epidemic proportions. (2005, January 18). Retrieved April 21, 2009, from *Medical News Today* website: http://www .medicalnewstoday.com/articles/19014.php

Cartwright, S., & Cooper, C. L. (1997). *Managing workplace stress.* Thousand Oaks, CA: SAGE.

Carver, C. S., & Scheier, M. F. (1998). *On the self-regulation of behavior.* Cambridge, UK: Cambridge University Press.

Cascio, W. F. (1995). Whither industrial and organizational psychology in a changing world of work? *American Psychologist, 50*(11), 928–939.

Cascio, W. F. (1998). *Applied psychology in human resource management* (5th ed.). Upper Saddle River, NJ: Prentice-Hall.

Cascio, W. F. (2003). *Managing human resources: Productivity, quality of work life, profits* (6th ed.). New York: McGraw-Hill.

Cascio, W. F., & Aguinis, H. (2004). *Applied psychology in human resource management* (6th ed.). Upper Saddle River, NJ: Prentice-Hall.

Cascio, W. F., & Aguinis, H. (2008). Research in industrial and organizational psychology from 1963 to 2007: Changes, choices, and trends. *Journal of Applied Psychology, 93*(5), 1062–1081.

Catanzaro, D. (1997). Course enrichment and the job characteristics model. *Teaching of Psychology, 24*(2) 85–87.

Cavanaugh, M. A., Boswell, W. R., Roehling, M. V., & Boudreau, J. W. (2000). An empirical examination of self-reported work stress among U.S. managers. *Journal of Applied Psychology, 85*(11), 65–74.

Cawley, B. D., Keeping, L. M., & Levy, P. E. (1998). Participation in the performance appraisal process and employee reactions: A meta-analytic review of field investigations. *Journal of Applied Psychology, 83*(4), 615–633.

CCH. (2002, October 16). Absenteeism costs companies more than ever. Retrieved April 21, 2009, from http://www.cch.com/press/news/2002/20021016h.asp

Centers for Disease Control. (2009, February 19). *Heart disease and stroke prevention: Addressing the nation's leading killers.* Retrieved April 8, 2009, from http://www.cdc.gov/nccdphp/publications/AAG/dhdsp.htm

Chamorro-Premuzic, T., & Furnham, A. (2008). Personality, intelligence and approaches to learning as predictors or academic performance. *Personality and Individual Differences, 44,* 1596–1603.

Chan, D., & Schmitt, N. (2002). Situational judgment and job performance. *Human Performance, 15*(3), 233–254.

Chang, A., Bordia, P., & Duck, J. (2003). Punctuated equilibrium and linear progression: Toward a new understanding of group development. *Academy of Management Journal, 46*(1), 106–117.

Chavez, C. I., & Weisinger, J. Y. (2008). Beyond diversity training: A social infusion for cultural inclusion. *Human Resource Management, 47*(2), 331–350.

Chemers, M. M. (2000). Leadership research and theory: A functional integration. *Group Dynamics, 4*(1), 27–43.

Chen, G., Goddard, T. G., & Casper, W. J. (2004). Examination of the relationships among general and work-specific self-evaluations, work-related control beliefs, and job attitudes. *Applied Psychology: An International Review, 53*(3), 349–370.

Chen, G., Ployhart, R. E., Thomas, H. C., Anderson, N., & Bliese, P. D. (2011). The power of momentum: A new model of dynamic relationships between job satisfaction and turnover intentions. *The Academy of Management Journal, 54,* 159–181.

Cheng, Y., & Stockdale, M. S. (2003). The validity of the three-component model of organizational commitment in a Chinese context. *Journal of Vocational Behavior, 62*(3), 465–489.

Chiaburu, D. S., Oh, I., Berry, C. M., Li, N., & Gardner, R. G. (2011). The five-factor model of personality traits and organizational citizenship behaviors: A meta-analysis. *Journal of Applied Psychology.*

Cho, J., & Dansereau, F. (2010). Are transformational leaders fair? A multi-level study of transformational leadership, justice perceptions, and organizational citizenship behaviors. *The Leadership Quarterly, 21,* 409–421.

Choi, J. N., & Sy, T. (2010). Group-level organizational citizenship behavior: Effects of demographic faultlines and conflict in small work groups. *Journal of Organizational Behavior, 31,* 1032–1054.

Choi, S., & Rainey, H. G. (2010). Managing diversity in U.S. federal agencies: Effects of diversity and diversity management on employee perceptions of organizational performance. *Public Administration Review, 70*(1), 109–121.

Christensen, L. B. (1994). *Experimental methodology.* Boston: Allyn & Bacon.

Christian, M. S., Edwards, B. D., & Bradley, J. C. (2010). Situational judgment tests: Constructs assessed and a meta-analysis of their criterion-related validities. *Personnel Psychology, 63,* 83–117.

Church, A. H., & Bracken, D. W. (1997). Advancing the state of the art of 360-degree feedback: Guest editors' comments on the research and practice of multirater assessment methods. *Group and Organization Management, 22*(2), 149–161.

Church, A. H., Waclawski, J., & Siegal, W. (1999). Will the real O.D. practitioner please stand up? A call for change in the field. *Organization Development Journal, 17*(2), 49–59.

Claes, R. & Heymans, M. (2008). HR professionals' views on work motivation and retention of older workers: A focus group study. *Career Development International, 13(2)*, 95–111.

Clarke, N. (2002). Job/work environment factors influencing training transfer within a human service agency: Some indicative support for Baldwin and Ford's transfer climate construct. *International Journal of Training and Development, 6(3)*, 146–162.

Cleverly v. Western Electric, 594 F.2d 638 (8th Cir. 1979).

Cober, R. T., Brown, D. J., Blumental, A. J., Doverspike, D., & Levy, P. E. (2000). The quest for the qualified job surfer: It's time the public sector catches the wage. *Public Personnel Management, 29(4)*, 479–496.

Cober, R. T., Brown, D. J., Keeping, L. M., & Levy, P. E. (2004). Recruitment on the net: How do organizational web site characteristics influence applicant attraction? *Journal of Management, 30(5)*, 623–646.

Cober, R. T., Brown, D. J., Levy, P. E., Cober, A. B., & Keeping, L. M. (2003). Organizational web sites: Web site content and style as determinants of organizational attraction. *International Journal of Selection and Assessment, 11(2/3)*, 158–169.

Cohen, A. (1997). Facing pressure. *Sales and Marketing Management, 149*, 30–38.

Cohen, S. G. (1994). Designing effective self-managing work teams. In M. M. Beyerlein & D. A. Johnson (Eds.), *Advances in interdisciplinary studies of work teams* (Vol. 1, pp. 67–102). Greenwich, CT: JAI Press.

Cohen, S. G., & Bailey, D. (1997). What makes teams work: Group effectiveness research from the shop floor to the executive suite. *Journal of Management, 23*, 239–290.

Cole, M. S., Bedeian, A. G., & Feild, H. S. (2006). The measurement equivalence of web-based and paper-and-pencil measures of transformational leadership. *Organizational Research Methods, 9(3)*, 339–368.

College Board. (2008). *SAT scores stable as record numbers take test.* Retrieved April 22, 2009, from http://www.collegeboard.com/press/releases/197846.html

Collins, C. J., & Stevens, C. K. (2002). The relationship between early recruitment-related activities and the application decisions of new labor-market entrants: A brand equity approach to recruitment. *Journal of Applied Psychology, 87(6)*, 1121–1133.

Collins, J. M., & Schmidt, F. L. (1993). Personality, integrity, and white collar crime: A construct validity study. *Personnel Psychology, 46*, 295–311.

Conte, J. M., Dean, M. A., Ringenbach, K. L., Moran, S. K., & Landy, F. J. (2005). The relationship between work attitudes and job analysis ratings: Do rating scale type and task discretion matter? *Human Performance, 18(1)*, 1–21.

Cook, T. D., & Campbell, D. T. (1979). *Quasi-experimentation: Design and analysis issues for field settings.* Boston: Houghton Mifflin.

Cordes, C. L., & Dougherty, T. W. (1993). A review and an integration of research on job burnout. *Academy of Management Review, 18(4)*, 621–656.

Cortina, J. M., Goldstein, N. B., Payne, S. C., Davison, H. K., & Gilliland, S. W. (2000). The incremental validity of interview scores over and above cognitive ability and conscientiousness scores. *Personnel Psychology, 53(2)*, 325–353.

Cota, A. A., Evans, C. R., Dion, K. L., Kilik, L., & Longman, R. S. (1995). The structure of group cohesion. *Personality and Social Psychology Bulletin, 21(6)*, 572–580.

Cote, S., & Morgan, L. M. (2002). A longitudinal analysis of the association between emotion regulation, job satisfaction, and intentions to quit. *Journal of Organizational Behavior, 23(8)*, 947–962.

Coyle-Shapiro, J. A.-M., & Morrow, P. C. (2003). The role of individual differences in employee adoption of TQM orientation. *Journal of Vocational Behavior, 62(2)*, 320–340.

Coyle-Shapiro, J. A.-M., Morrow, P. C., Richardson, R., & Dunn, S. (2002). Using profit sharing to enhance employee attitudes: A longitudinal examination of the effects on trust and commitment. *Human Resource Management, 41(4)*, 423–439.

Cronbach, L. J. (1990). *Essentials of psychological testing* (5th ed.). New York: Harper & Row.

Cropanzano, R., Slaughter, J. E., & Bachiochi, P. D. (2005). Organizational justice and black applicants' reactions to affirmative action. *Journal of Applied Psychology, 90(6)*, 1168–1184.

Cross, C. (2010). Barriers to the executive suite: Evidence from Ireland. *Leadership and Organization Development Journal, 31(2)*, 104–119.

Crute, S. (2007, November & December). *Caring for the caregiver.* Retrieved April 19, 2009, from http://www.aarpmagazine.org/family/caregiving/caring_for_the_caregiver.html

Cucina, J. M., Vasilopoulos, N. L., & Sehgal, K. G. (2005). Personality-based job analysis and the self-serving bias. *Journal of Business and Psychology, 20*(2), 275–290.

Cummings, T. G., & Worley, C. G. (2005). *Organization development and change* (8th ed.). Cincinnati, OH: South-Western.

Curtis, A. B., Darvey, R. D., & Ravden, D. (2005). Sources of political distortions in performance appraisals: Appraisal purpose and rater accountability. *Group and Organizational Management, 30*(1), 42–60.

Dahling, J., O'Malley, A., & Chau, S. (in press). Why do employees seek feedback? Measuring the motives that shape feedback-seeking behavior, *Educational and Psychological Measurement.*

Dalal, R. S. (2005). A meta-analysis of the relationship between organizational citizenship behavior and counterproductive work behavior. *Journal of Applied Psychology, 90*(6), 1241–1255.

Dansereau, F., Graen, G. B., & Haga, W. (1975). A vertical dyad linkage approach to leadership in formal organizations. *Organizational Behavior and Human Performance, 13,* 46–78.

Day, D. V., Sin, H., & Chen, T. T. (2004). Assessing the burdens of leadership: Effects of formal leadership roles on individual performance over time. *Personnel Psychology, 57*(3), 573–605.

De Vries, M. F. R. K. (1999). High performance teams: Lessons from the Pygmies. *Organizational Dynamics, 27(3),* 66–77.

Deadrick, D. L., Bennett, N., & Russell, C. J. (1997). Using hierarchical linear modeling to examine dynamic performance criteria over time. *Journal of Management, 23*(6), 745–757.

Deadrick, D. L., & Madigan, R. M. (1990). Dynamic criteria revisited: A longitudinal study of performance stability and predictive validity. *Personnel Psychology, 43,* 717–744.

Deci, E. L. (1975). *Intrinsic motivation.* New York: Plenum Press.

Demerouti, E., Bakker, A. B., Nachreiner, F., & Schaufeli, W. B. (2001). The job demands–resources model of burnout. *Journal of Applied Psychology, 86*(3), 499–512.

den Hartog, D. N., Boselie, R., & Paauwe, J. (2004). Performance management: A model and research agenda. *Applied Psychology: An International Review, 53*(4), 556–569.

DeNisi, A. S., Cafferty, T., & Meglino, B. (1984). A cognitive view of the performance appraisal process: A model and research propositions. *Organizational Behavior and Human Decision Processes, 33,* 360–396.

DeNisi, A. S., & Kluger, A. N. (2000). Feedback effectiveness: Can 360-degree appraisals be improved? *Academy of Management Executive, 14*(1), 129–139.

DeNisi, A. S., & Pritchard, R. D. (2006). Performance appraisal, performance management, and improving individual performance: A motivational framework. *Management and Organizational Review, 2,* 253–277.

DeRue, D. S., Nahrgang, J. D., Wellman, N., & Humphrey S. E. (2011). Trait and behavioral theories of leadership: An integration and meta-analytic test of their relative validity. *Personnel Psychology, 64,* 7–52.

DeShon, R. P., & Gillespie, J. Z. (2005). A motivated action account theory of goal orientation. *Journal of Applied Psychology, 90,* 1096–1127.

Diaz v. Pan American World Airways, Inc., 442. F.2d 385 (5th cir. 1971).

Dickens, L., & Watkins, K. (1999). Action research: Rethinking Lewin. *Management Learning, 300*(2), 127–140.

Dickson, M. W., Den Hartog, D. N., & Mitchelson, J. K. (2003). Research on leadership in a cross-cultural context: Making progress, and raising new questions. *Leadership Quarterly, 14,* 729–768.

Dickson, M. W., Hanges, P. J., & Lord, R. G. (2000). Trends, developments and gaps in cross-cultural research on leadership. In W. Mobley (Ed.), *Advances in global leadership* (Vol. 2, pp. 2–22). Stamford, CT: JAI Press.

Diefendorff, J. M., & Gosserand, R. H. (2003). Understanding the emotional labor process: A control theory perspective. *Journal of Organizational Behavior, 24*(8), 945–959.

Diefendorff, J. M., & Lord, R. G. (2003). The volitional and strategic effects of planning on task performance and goal commitment. *Human Performance, 16*(4), 365–387.

Dimotakis, N., Scott, B. A., & Koopman, J. (2010). An experience sampling investigation of workplace interactions, affective states, and employee well-being. *Journal of Organizational Behavior, 32*(4), 572–588.

Dobbins, G. H., Cardy, R. K., & Platz-Vieno, S. J. (1990). A contingency approach to appraisal satisfaction: An initial investigation of the joint effects of organizational variables and appraisal characteristics. *Journal of Management, 16,* 619–632.

Dobbins, G. H., Lane, I. M., & Steiner, D. D. (1988). A note on the role of laboratory methodologies in applied behavioural research: Don't throw out the baby with the bath water. *Journal of Organizational Behavior, 9,* 281–286.

Dodd, Stevens introduce landmark bill to provide paid leave for workers. (2007, June 21). Retrieved April 20, 2009, from http://dodd.senate.gov/?q=node/3953

Donnelly, D. P., & Quirin, J. J. (2006). An extension of Lee and Mitchell's unfolding model of voluntary turnover. *Journal of Organizational Behavior, 27,* 59–77.

Donovan, J. J., & Radosevich, D. J. (1999). A meta-analytic review of the distribution of practice effect: Now you see it, now you don't. *Journal of Applied Psychology, 84*(5), 795–805.

Donovan, M. A., Drasgow, F., & Munson, L. J. (1998). The Perceptions of Fair Interpersonal Treatment scale: Development and validation of a measure of interpersonal treatment in the workplace. *Journal of Applied Psychology, 83*(5), 683–692.

Dooney, J. (2005). *Cost of turnover.* Retrieved April 26, 2009, from Society for Human Resource Management website: http://moss07.shrm.org/Research/Articles/Articles/Pages/ROI_20Series__20Cost_20of_20Turnover.aspx

Douglas, S. C., Kiewitz, C., Martinko, M. J., Harvey, P., Kim, Y., & Chun, J. U. (2008). Cognitions, emotions, and evaluations: An elaboration likelihood model for workplace aggression. *Academy of Management Review, 33,* 425–451.

Doverspike, D., Cober, A. B., & Arthur, W., Jr. (2004). Multi-aptitude test batteries. In J. C. Thomas (Ed.), *Comprehensive handbook of psychological assessment* (Vol. 4, pp. 21–34). Hoboken, NJ: Wiley.

Doverspike, D., & O'Malley, A. (2006, February). When generations collide. *International Public Management Association for Human Resources News, 1,* 5–6.

Drug testing in the workplace. (n.d.). Retrieved April 18, 2009, from http://www.globalchange.com/drugtest.htm

du Plessis, M. (2007). The role of knowledge management in innovation. *Journal of Knowledge Management, 11,* 20–29.

Duarte, N. T., Goodson, J. R., & Klich, N. R. (1993). How do I like thee? Let me appraise the ways. *Journal of Organizational Behavior, 14*(3), 239–249.

Duncan, T. S. (1995). Death in the office—Workplace homicides. *Law Enforcement Bulletin, 64*(4), 20–25.

Dunford, B. B., & Devine, D. J. (1998). Employment at-will and employee discharge: A justice perspective on legal action following termination. *Personnel Psychology, 51,* 903–934.

Dunham, R. B., & Herman, J. B. (1975). Development of a female Faces Scale for measuring job satisfaction. *Journal of Applied Psychology, 60*(5), 629–631.

Dunlop, P. D., & Lee, K. (2004). Workplace deviance, organizational citizenship behavior, and business unit performance: The bad apples do spoil the whole barrel. *Journal of Organizational Behavior, 25*(1), 67–80.

Dunnette, M. D. (1962). Personnel management. *Annual Review of Psychology, 13,* 285–314.

Dupré, K. E., & Barling, J. (2006). Predicting and preventing supervisory workplace aggression. *Journal of Occupational Health Psychology, 11,* 13–26.

Eagly, A. H. (2007). Female leadership advantage and disadvantage: Resolving the contradictions. *Psychology of Women Quarterly, 31,* 1–12.

Eagly, A. H., & Chin, J. (2010). Diversity and leadership in a changing world. *American Psychologist, 65,* 216–224.

Eagly, A. H., Johannesen-Schmidt, M. C., & van Engen, M. L. (2003). Transformational, transactional, and laissez-faire leadership styles: A meta-analysis comparing women and men. *Psychological Bulletin, 129*(4), 569–591.

Eagly, A. H., & Johnson, B. T. (1990). Gender and leadership style: A meta-analysis. *Psychological Bulletin, 108*(2), 233–256.

Eagly, A. H., & Karau, S. J. (1991). Gender and the emergence of leaders. *Journal of Personality and Social Psychology, 60*(5), 685–710.

Eagly, A. H., Karau, S. J., & Makhijani, M. G. (1995). Gender and the effectiveness of leaders: A meta-analysis. *Psychological Bulletin, 117*(1), 125–145.

Eatough, E. M., Chang, C., Miloslavic, S. A., & Johnson, R. E. (2011). The relationship of role stressors with organizational citizenship behavior: A meta-analysis. *Journal of Applied Psychology, 96*(3), 619–632.

Educational Testing Service. (2007). *Adaptive tests.* Retrieved March 19, 2008, from http://www.ets.org

Edwards, J. C., Rust, K. G., McKinley, W., & Moon, G. (2003). Business ideologies and perceived breach of contract during downsizing: The role of the ideology of employee self-reliance. *Journal of Organizational Behavior, 24*(1), 1–23.

EEOC v. Atlas Paper Box Co., 868 F.2d 1487 (6th Cir. 1989).

EEOC v. Univ. of Texas Health Science Center at San Antonio, 710 F.2d 1091 (5th Cir. 1983).

Egan, T. M., & Lancaster, C. M. (2005). Comparing appreciative inquiry to action research: OD practitioner perspectives. *Organization Development Journal, 23*, 29–49.

Eisenbeiss, S. A., van Knippenberg, D., & Boerner, S. (2008). Transformational leadership and team innovation: Integrating team climate principles. *Journal of Applied Psychology, 93*(6), 1438–1446.

El-Tannir, A. A. (2002). The corporate university model for continuous learning, training and development. *Education and Training, 44*(2), 76–81.

Elicker, J. D., Foust, M. S., O'Malley, A. L., & Levy, P. E. (2008). Employee lateness behavior: The role of lateness climate and individual lateness attitude. *Human Performance, 21*(4), 427–441.

Elicker, J. D., Levy, P. E., & Hall, R. J. (2006). The role of leader–member exchange in the performance appraisal process. *Journal of Management, 32*(4), 531–551.

Engle, E. M., & Lord, R. G. (1997). Implicit theories, self-schemas, and leader–member exchange. *Academy of Management Journal, 40*(4), 988–1010.

Ensari, N., & Murphy, S. E. (2003). Cross-cultural variations in leadership perceptions and attribution of charisma to the leader. *Organizational Behavior and Human Decision Processes, 92*(1–2), 52–66.

Epitropaki, O., & Martin, R. (2005). From ideal to real: A longitudinal study of the role of implicit leadership theories on leader–member exchanges and employee outcomes. *Journal of Applied Psychology, 90*(4), 659–676.

Equal Employment Opportunity Commission. (2002a, December 2). *EEOC updates guidance on national origin discrimination.* Retrieved March 30, 2009, from http://www.eeoc.gov/press/12-2-02.html

Equal Employment Opportunity Commission. (2002b, May 14). *Questions and answers about the workplace rights of Muslims, Arabs, South Asians, and Sikhs under the equal employment opportunity laws.* Retrieved April 20, 2009, from http://www.eeoc.gov/facts/backlashemployee.html

Equal Employment Opportunity Commission. (2004, September 2). *Discriminatory practices.* Retrieved April 20, 2009, from http://www.eeoc.gov/abouteeo/overview_practices.html

Equal Employment Opportunity Commission. (2005, March 21). *The ADA: Your employment rights as an individual with a disability.* Retrieved April 20, 2009, from http://www.eeoc.gov/facts/ada18.html

Equal Employment Opportunity Commission. (2007, February 2). *Sexual harassment.* Retrieved March 30, 2009, from http://www.eeoc.gov/types/harassment.html

Equal Employment Opportunity Commission. (2009a, March 11). *Age discrimination.* Retrieved March 30, 2009, from http://www.eeoc.gov/types/age.html

Equal Employment Opportunity Commission. (2009b, March 11). *National origin discrimination.* Retrieved March 30, 2009, from http://www.eeoc.gov/origin/index.html

Equal Employment Opportunity Commission. (2009c, March 11). *National origin-based charges FY 1997–FY 2007.* Retrieved March 30, 2009, from http://www.eeoc.gov/stats/origin.html

Equal Employment Opportunity Commission. (2009d, March 11). *Pregnancy discrimination.* Retrieved March 30, 2009, from http://www.eeoc.gov/types/pregnancy.html

Equal Employment Opportunity Commission. (2009e, March 11). *Religious discrimination.* Retrieved March 30, 2009, from http://www.eeoc.gov/types /religion.html

Erickson, R. J., Nichols, L., & Ritter, C. (2000). Family influences on absenteeism: Testing an expanded process model. *Journal of Vocational Behavior, 57,* 246–272.

Ethridge v. Alabama, 847 F.Supp. 903, 906-07 (M.D. Ala.1993).

Ethridge v. State of Alabama, 847 F.Supp. 903, 906-07 (M.D. Ala.1993).

Evans, C. R., & Dion, K. L. (1991). Group cohesion and performance: A meta-analysis. *Small Group Research, 22*(2), 175–186.

Evans, D. C. (2003). A comparison of the other-directed stigmatization produced by legal and illegal forms of affirmative action. *Journal of Applied Psychology, 88*(1), 121–130.

Families and Work Institute. (2007). *When work works: Making work "work."* Retrieved December 9, 2008, from http://familiesandwork.org/site/research /reports/3wbooklet.pdf

Farr, J. L., & Tippins, N. T. (2010). *Handbook of employee eelection.* New York: Taylor & Francis.

Feder, J., & Levine, L. (2010). *Pay equity legislation.* Washington, DC: Congressional Research Service. Retrieved July 11, 2012, from http://digitalcommons .ilr.cornell.edu/key_workplace/763

Ferris, G. R., Munyon, T. P., Basik, K., & Buckley, M. R. (2008). The performance evaluation context: Social, emotional, cognitive, political, and relationship components. *Human Resource Management Review, 18,* 146–163.

Fiedler, F. E. (1967). *A theory of leadership effectiveness.* New York: McGraw-Hill.

Fiedler, F. E. (1995). Cognitive resources and leadership performance. *Applied Psychology: An International Review, 44*(1), 5–28.

Findley, H. M., Giles, W. F., & Mossholder, K. W. (2000). Performance appraisal process and system facets: Relationships with contextual performance. *Journal of Applied Psychology, 85*(4), 634–640.

Fine, S. A. (1988). Functional job analysis. In S. Gael (Ed.), *The job analysis handbook for business, industry, and government* (Vol. 2, pp. 1019–1035). New York: Wiley.

Finn, A. N. (2012). Teacher use of prosocial and antisocial power bases and students' perceived instructor understanding and misunderstanding in the college classroom. *Communication Education, 61*(1), 67–79.

Fishbein, M., & Ajzen, I. (1975). *Belief, attitude, intention and behavior: An introduction to theory and research.* Reading, MA: Addison-Wesley.

Fisher v. University of Texas at Austin, 631 F.3d 213 (5th Cir. 2011).

Fisher, C. D. (2000). Mood and emotions while working: Missing pieces of job satisfaction? *Journal of Organizational Behavior, 21,* 185–202.

Fisher, C. D. (2003). Why do lay people believe that satisfaction and performance are correlated? Possible sources of a commonsense theory. *Journal of Organizational Behavior, 24,* 753–777.

Fitzpatrick, L. (2010). Why do women still earn less than men? Retrieved December 29, 2010, from http:// www.time.com/time/printout/0,8816,1983,185,00.html

Fleishman, E. A., & Harris, E. F. (1962). Patterns of leadership behavior related to employee grievances and turnover. *Personnel Psychology, 15,* 43–56.

Fletcher, C., & Anderson, N. (1998). A superficial assessment. *People Management, 4*(10), 44–46.

Fletcher, C., & Baldry, C. (1999). Multi-source feedback systems: A research perspective. *International Review of Industrial and Organizational Psychology, 14,* 149–193.

Folger, R., Konovsky, M., & Cropanzano, R. (1992). A due process metaphor for performance appraisal. In B. Staw and L. Cummings (Eds.), *Research in organizational behavior* (Vol. 14, pp. 129–177). Greenwich, CT: JAI Press.

Ford, J. D., Ford, L. W., & D'Amelio, A. (2008). Resistance to change: The rest of the story. *Academy of Management Review, 33,* 362–377.

Ford, M. T., Heinen, B. A., & Langkamer, K. L. (2007). Work and family satisfaction and conflict: A meta-analysis of cross-domain relations. *Journal of Applied Psychology, 92,* 57–80.

Forsyth, D. (1999). *Group dynamics* (3rd ed.). Belmont, CA: Brooks/Cole.

Fortune 500. (2008). Retrieved April 21, 2009, from http://money.cnn.com/magazines/fortune/fortune500 /2008/

Foust, M. S., Elicker, J. D., & Levy, P. E. (2006). Development and validation of a measure of an individual's lateness attitude. *Journal of Vocational Behavior, 69,* 119–133.

Franklin, Gringer & Cohen, P. C. (n.d.). *Key provisions of the Family and Medical Leave Act of 1993.* Retrieved March 30, 2009, from http://www.franklingringer.com/articles/labor_employment_law_articles/key_provisions.html

French, J., & Raven, B. H. (1958). The bases of social power. In D. Cartwright (Ed.), *Studies of social power* (pp. 607–623). Ann Arbor, MI: Institute for Social Research.

Frone, M. R., Yardley, J. K., & Markel, K. S. (1997). Developing and testing an integrative model of the work–family interface. *Journal of Vocational Behavior, 50,* 145–167.

Fugate, M., Kinicki, A. J., & Prussia, G. E. (2008). Employee coping with organizational change: An examination of alternative theoretical perspectives and models. *Personnel Psychology, 61,* 1–36.

Fugate, M., Kinicki, A. J., & Scheck, C. L. (2002). Coping with an organizational merger over four stages. *Personnel Psychology, 55*(4), 905–928.

Fullagar, C. J., & Egleston, D. O. (2008). Norming and performing: Using microworlds to understand the relationship between team cohesiveness and performance. *Journal of Applied Social Psychology, 38,* 2574–2593.

Funderburg, S. A., & Levy, P. E. (1997). The influence of individual and contextual variables on 360-degree feedback system attitudes. *Group and Organization Management, 22*(2), 210–235.

Furst, S. A., & Cable, D. M. (2008). Employee resistance to organizational change: Managerial influence tactics and leader–member exchange. *Journal of Applied Psychology, 93,* 453–462.

Gagné, M., & Deci, E. L. (2005). Self-determination theory and work motivation. *Journal of Organizational Behavior, 26,* 331–362.

Gagné, R. M., Briggs, L. J., & Wager, W. W. (1992). *Principles of instructional design* (4th ed.). Fort Worth, TX: Harcourt Brace Jovanovich.

Gajendran, R. S., & Harrison, D. A. (2007). The good, the bad, and the unknown about telecommuting: Meta-analysis of psychological mediators and individual consequences. *Journal of Applied Psychology, 92*(6), 1524–1541.

Galinsky, E., Bond, J. T., Kim, S. S., Backon, L., Brownfield, E., & Sakai, K. (2004). *Overwork in America: When the way we work becomes too much.* Retrieved December 11, 2008, from http://www.familiesandwork.org/summary/overwork2005.pdf

Gammon, A.R., Griffith, R.L., & Kung, M. (2011). *How do real applicants who are fakers compare to nonfakers?* Paper presented at the annual meeting of the Society for Industrial and Organizational Psychology, Chicago.

Ganzach, Y., Kluger, A. N., & Klayman, N. (2000). Making decisions from an interview: Expert measurement and mechanical combination. *Personnel Psychology, 53,* 1–20.

Gardner, D. & Diedrick, D. L. (2009). Underprediction of performance for U.S. minorities using cognitive abilities measures. *Equal Opportunities International, 27*(50), 455–464.

Gardner, S. E., & Daniel, C. (1998). Implementing comparable worth/pay equity: Experiences of cutting-edge states. *Public Personnel Management, 27*(4), 475–489.

Gardner, W. L., Fischer, D., & Hunt, J. G. (2009). Emotional labor and leadership: A threat to authenticity? *The Leadership Quarterly, 20,* 466–482.

Garofano, C. M., & Salas, E. (2005). What influences continuous employee development decisions? *Human Resource Management Review, 15*(4), 281–304.

Gatewood, R. D., & Feild, H. S. (2001). *Human resource selection* (5th ed.). Fort Worth, TX: Harcourt College.

Gatewood, R. D., Feild, H. S., & Barrick, M. (2007). *Human resource selection* (6th ed.). Fort Worth, TX: Harcourt College.

Gaugler, B. B., Rosenthal, D. B., Thornton, G. C., III, & Bentson, C. (1987). Meta-analysis of assessment center validity. *Journal of Applied Psychology, 72*(3), 493–511.

Geisinger, K. F., Spies, R. A., Carlson, J. F., & Plake, B. S. (Eds.). (2007). *Mental measurements yearbook* (17th ed.). Lincoln, NE: Buros Institute of Mental Measurements.

Geisler, E. (2007). A typology of knowledge management: Strategic groups and role behavior in organizations. *Journal of Knowledge Management, 11,* 84–96.

Gellatly, I. R. (1995). How important are dispositional factors as determinants of job satisfaction? Implications for job design and other personnel programs. *Journal of Applied Psychology, 72*(3), 366–373.

Gerhart, B. (1987). How important are dispositional factors as determinants of job satisfaction? Implications for job design and other personnel programs. *Journal of Applied Psychology, 72*(3), 366–373.

Gersick, C. J. G. (1989). Making time: Predictable transitions in task groups. *Academy of Management Journal, 32,* 274–309.

Gerstner, C. R., & Day, D. V. (1994). Cross-cultural comparison of leadership prototypes. *Leadership Quarterly, 5*(2), 121–134.

Gerstner, C. R., & Day, D. V. (1997). Meta-analytic review of leader–member exchange theory: Correlates and construct issues. *Journal of Applied Psychology, 82*(6), 827–844.

Ghorpade, J. (2000). Managing five paradoxes of 360-degree feedback. *Academy of Management Executive, 14*(1), 140–150.

Giacalone, R. A., & Greenberg, G. (1997). *Antisocial behavior in organizations.* Thousand Oaks, CA: SAGE.

Giangreco, A., Carugati A., & Sebastiano, A. (2010). Are we doing the right thing? Food for thought on training evaluation and its context. *Personnel Review, 39*(2), 162–177.

Giglio, G., Michalcova, S., & Yates, C. (2007). Instilling a culture of winning at American Express. *Organizational Development Journal, 25,* 33–37.

Gillespie, I., Rose, D. S., & Robinson, G. N. (2006). *Narrative comments in 360 degree feedback: Who says what?* Paper presented at the 21st Annual Conference of the Society for Industrial and Organizational Psychology, Dallas, TX.

Gilmer, B. V. H. (1981). The early development of industrial-organizational psychology. In J. A. Sgro (Ed.), *Virginia Tech Symposium on Applied Behavioral Science* (Vol. 1, pp. 3–16). Lexington, MA: Lexington Books.

Goffin, R. D., Jelley, R. B., & Wagner, S. H. (2003). Is halo helpful? Effects of inducing halo on performance rating accuracy. *Social Behavior and Personality, 31*(6), 625–636.

Goldberg, C. B., & Waldman, D. A. (2000). Modeling employee absenteeism: Testing alternative measures and mediated effects based on job satisfaction. *Journal of Organizational Behavior, 21,* 665–676.

Golden, T. D. (2006). Avoiding depletion in virtual work: Telework and the intervening impact of work exhaustion on commitment and turnover intentions. *Journal of Vocational Behavior, 69,* 176–187.

Golden, T. D., Barnes-Farrell, J. L., & Mascharka, P. B. (2009). Implications of virtual management for subordinate performance appraisals: A pair of simulation studies. *Journal of Applied Social Psychology, 39*(7), 1589–1608.

Golden, T. D., Veiga, J. F., & Simsek, Z. (2006). Telecommuting's differential impact on work–family conflict: Is there no place like home? *Journal of Applied Psychology, 91*(6), 1340–1350.

Goldman, B. M., Gutek, B. A., Stein, J. H., & Lewis, K. (2006). Employment discrimination in organizations: Antecedents and consequences. *Journal of Management, 32,* 786–830.

Goldstein, H. W., Zedeck, S., & Goldstein, I. L. (2002). Is this your final answer? *Human Performance, 15*(1–2), 123–142.

Goldstein, I. L., & Ford, J. K. (2002). *Training in organizations: Needs assessment, development, and evaluation* (4th ed.). Belmont, CA: Wadsworth.

Gollwitzer, P. M., & Sheeran, P. (2006). Implementation intentions and goal achievement: A meta-analysis of effects and processes. *Advances in Experimental Social Psychology, 38,* 69–120.

Gonzalez, G. (2004). Elder care resources offer comfort to workers. *Business Insurance, 38*(13), 11–12.

Goodman, P. S., & Dabbish, L. A. (2011). Methodological issues in measuring group learning. *Small Group Research, 42*(4), 379–404.

Goodstein, J. (1995). Employer involvement in eldercare: An organizational adaptation perspective. *Academy of Management Journal, 38*(6), 1657–1671.

Goren, H., Kurzban, R., & Rapoport, A. (2003). Social loafing vs. social enhancement: Public goods provisioning in real-time with irrevocable commitments. *Organizational Behavior and Human Decision Processes, 90*(2), 277–290.

Gorenstein, P. (2011, October 14). The Gap slashes stores: What went wrong and how they can fix it. *The Daily Ticker.*

Gould, K. E. (2005). The corporate university: A model for sustaining an expert workforce in the human services. *Behavior Modification, 29*(3), 508–520.

Gowan, M. A., Riordan, C. M., & Gatewood, R. D. (1999). Test of a model of coping with involuntary job loss following a company closing. *Journal of Applied Psychology, 84*(1), 75–86.

Gowen, C. R., III. (1991). Gain-sharing programs: An overview of history and research. *Journal of Organizational Behavior Management, 11*(2), 77–99.

Grandey, A. A., & Brauburger, A. L. (2002). The emotion regulation behind the customer service smile. In R. G. Lord, R. J. Klimoski, & R. Kanfer (Eds.), *Emotions in the workplace: Understanding the structure and role of emotions in organizational behavior* (pp. 260–294). San Francisco: Jossey-Bass.

Grandey, A. A., Fisk, G. M., Mattila, A. S., Jansen, K. J., & Sideman, L. A. (2005). Is "service with a smile" enough? Authenticity of positive displays during service encounters. *Organizational Behavior and Human Decision Processes, 96*, 38–55.

Grant, A. M., Fried, Y., Parker, S. K., & Frese, M. (2010). Putting job design in context: Introduction to the special issue. *Journal of Organizational Behavior, 31*, 145–157.

Grant, S., & Barling, J. (1994). Linking unemployment experiences, depressive symptoms, and marital functioning: A mediational model. In G. P. Keita & J. J. Hurrell, Jr. (Eds.), *Job stress in a changing workforce: Investigating gender, diversity, and family issues* (pp. 311–327). Washington, DC: American Psychological Association

Gratz v. Bollinger, 539 U.S. 244 (2003).

Green, C., & Heywood, J. S. (2008). Does performance pay increase job satisfaction? *Economica, 75*(300), 710–728.

Green, S. G., Anderson, S. E., & Shivers, S. L. (1996). Demographic and organizational influences on leader–member exchange and related work attitudes. *Organizational Behavior and Human Decision Processes, 66*(2), 203–214.

Greenhaus, J. H., & Powell, G. N. (2006). When work and family are allies: A theory of work–family enrichment. *Academy of Management Review, 31*(1), 72–92.

Greenwald, J. (2001, June 18). Rank and fire. *Time, 157,* 38–40.

Gregg, L. (1998). Humanity in the workplace: When work/family becomes an HR issue. *Credit Union Executive, 38,* 32–34.

Greiner, L., Cummings, T., & Bhambri, A. (2003). When new CEOs succeed and fail: 4-H theory of strategic transformation. *Organizational Dynamics, 32*(1), 1–16.

Griffeth, R. W., Hom, P. W., & Gaertner, S. (2000). A meta-analysis of antecedents and correlates of employee turnover: Update, moderator tests, and research implications for the next millennium. *Journal of Management, 26*(3), 463–488.

Griffith, R. L., & Converse, P. D. (2011). The rules of evidence and the prevalence of applicant faking. In M. Ziegler, C. McCann, & R. Roberts (Eds.), *New perspectives on faking in personality assessments.* Oxford, UK: Oxford University Press.

Griggs v. Duke Power, 401 U.S. 424 (1971).

Grindle, A. C., Dickinson, A. M., & Boettcher, W. (2000). Behavioral safety research in manufacturing settings: A review of the literature. *Journal of Organizational Behavior Management, 20*(1), 29–68.

Gross, J. (1998). Antecedent- and response-focused emotion regulation: Divergent consequences for experience, expression, and physiology. *Journal of Personality and Social Psychology, 74*(1), 224–237.

Grunberg, L., Anderson-Connolly, R., & Greenberg, E. S. (2000). Surviving layoffs: The effects of organizational commitment and job performance. *Work and Occupations, 27*(1), 7–31.

Grutter v. Bollinger, 539 U.S. 306 (2003).

Grzywacz, J. G., Almeida, D. M., & McDonald, D. (2002). Work–family spillover and daily reports of work and family stress in the adult labor-force. *Family Relations, 51,* 28–36.

Grzywacz, J. G., Arcury, T. A., Marin, A., Carrillo, L., Burke, B., Coates, M. L., et al. (2007). Work–family conflict: Experiences and health implications among immigrant Latinos. *Journal of Applied Psychology, 92,* 1119–1130.

Gully, S. M., Payne, S. C., Koles, K. L. K., & Whiteman, J.-A. K. (2002). The impact of error training and individual differences on training outcomes: An attribute–treatment interaction perspective. *Journal of Applied Psychology, 87*(1), 143–155.

Gutek, B. A., & Koss, M. P. (1993). Changed women and changed organizations: Consequences of and coping with sexual harassment. *Journal of Vocational Behavior, 42*, 28–48.

Gutman, A. (2000). *EEO law and personnel practices* (2nd ed.). Thousand Oaks, CA: SAGE.

Gutman, A. (2003). The Grutter, Gratz, & Costa rulings. *Industrial-Organizational Psychologist, 41*(2), 117–127.

Gutman, A. & Dunleavy, E. (2007). The Supreme Court ruling in Parents v. Seattle School District: Sending Grutter and Gratz back to school. *The Industrial-Organizational Psychologist, 45*(2), 41–49.

Hackett, R. D., Bycio, P., & Hausdorf, P. A. (1994). Further assessments of Meyer and Allen's (1991) three-component model of organizational commitment. *Journal of Applied Psychology, 79*, 15–23.

Hackett, R. D., & Guion, R. M. (1985). A reevaluation of the absenteeism–job satisfaction relationship. *Organizational Behavior and Human Decision Processes, 35*, 340–381.

Hackman, J. R., & Oldham, G. R. (1976). The job characteristics model. *Organizational Behavior and Human Decision Processes, 16*, 256.

Hackman, J. R., & Oldham, G. R. (1980). *Work redesign.* Upper Saddle River, NJ: Pearson.

Hall, R. J., Workman, J. W., & Marchioro, C. A. (1998). Sex, task, and behavioral flexibility effects on leadership perceptions. *Organizational Behavior and Human Decision Processes, 74*(1), 1–32.

Hallett, M. B., & Gilbert, L. A. (1997). Variables differentiating university women considering role-sharing and conventional dual-career marriages. *Journal of Vocational Behavior, 50*, 308–322.

Hammer, L. B., Cullen, J. C., Neal, M. B., Sinclair, R. R., & Shafiro, M. V. (2005). The longitudinal effects of work–family conflict and positive spill-over on depressive symptoms among dual-earner couples. *Journal of Occupational Health Psychology, 10*(2), 138–154.

Hammer, M., & Champy, J. (1993). *Reengineering the corporation: A manifesto for business revolution.* New York: HarperCollins.

Han, G., & Jekel, M. (2011). The mediating role of job satisfaction between leader–member exchange and turn-over intentions. *Journal of Nursing Management, 19*, 41–49.

Hanover, J. M. B., & Cellar, D. F. (1998). Environmental factors and the effectiveness of work-force diversity training. *Human Resource Development Quarterly, 9*(2), 105–124.

Hanson, G. C., Hammer, L. B., & Colton, C. L. (2004). Development and validation of a multidimensional scale of work–family enrichment. Unpublished manuscript, Portland State University, OR.

Harris, L. C., & Ogbonna, E. (2002). The unintended consequences of culture interventions: A study of unexpected outcomes. *British Journal of Management, 13*(1), 31–49.

Harrison, D. A., Kravitz, D. A., Mayer, D. M., Leslie, L. M., & Lev-Arey, D. (2006). Understanding attitudes toward affirmative action programs in employment: Summary and meta-analysis of 35 years of research. *Journal of Applied Psychology, 91*(3), 1013–1036.

Harrison, D. A., Newman, D. A., & Roth, P. L. (2006). How important are job attitudes? Meta-analytic comparisons of integrative behavioral outcomes and time sequences. *Academy of Management Journal, 40*, 305–325.

Harvey, R. J. (1991). Job analysis. In M. D. Dunnette & L. M. Hough (Eds.), *Handbook of industrial and organizational psychology* (2nd ed., Vol. 2, pp. 71–163). Palo Alto, CA: Consulting Psychologists Press.

Harvey, R. J. (1993). *Research monograph: Development of the Common-Metric Questionnaire (CMQ).* Retrieved April 22, 2009, from Personnel Systems & Technologies Corporation website: http://www.pstc.com/documents/monograph.pdf

Harvey, R. J. (2010). Motor oil or snake oil: Synthetic validity is a tool not a panacea. *Industrial and Organizational Psychology, 3*(3), 351–355.

Hatala, J. P., & Fleming, P. R. (2007). Making transfer climate visible: Utilizing social network analysis to facilitate the transfer of training. *Human Resource Development Review, 6*(1), 33–63.

Hattrup, K., O'Connell, M. S., & Wingate, P. H. (1998). Prediction of multidimensional criteria: Distinguishing task and contextual performance. *Human Performance, 11*(4), 305–319.

Hauenstein, N. M. A. (1998). Training raters to increase the accuracy of appraisals and the usefulness of feedback. In J. W. Smither (Ed.), *Performance appraisal: State of the art in practice* (pp. 404–442). San Francisco: Jossey-Bass.

Hedge, J. W., & Borman, W. C. (1995). Changing conceptions and practices in performance appraisal. In A. Howard (Ed.), *The changing nature of work* (pp. 451–482). San Francisco: Jossey-Bass.

Hedge, J. W., & Teachout, M. S. (2000). Exploring the concept of acceptability as a criterion for evaluating performance measures. *Group and Organizational Management, 25*(1), 22–44.

Heller, M. (2005). Court ruling that employer's integrity test violated ADA could open door to litigation. *Workforce Management, 84*(9), 74–77.

Hemel, Daniel J. (2007). '07 men make more. Retrieved April 18, 2009, from http://www.thecrimson.com/article.aspx?ref=519172

Hendricks, J. W., & Payne, S. C. (2007). Beyond the Big Five: Leader goal orientation as a predictor of leadership effectiveness. *Human Performance, 20,* 317–343.

Hennessy, D. A. (2008). The impact of commuter stress on workplace aggression. *Journal of Applied Social Psychology, 38*(9), 2315–2335.

Henningsen, D. D, Henningsen, M. L. M., Eden, J., & Cruz, M. G. (2006). Examining the symptoms of groupthink and retrospective sensemaking. *Small Group Research, 37,* 36–64.

Hermelin, E., Lievens, F., & Robertson, I. T. (2007). The validity of assessment centres for the prediction of supervisory performance ratings. *International Journal of Selection and Assessment, 15*(4), 405–411.

Herold, D. M., Davis, W., Fedor, D. B., & Parsons, C. K. (2002). Dispositional influences on transfer of learning in multistage training programs. *Personnel Psychology, 55*(4), 851–869.

Hertel, G., Geister, S., & Konradt, U. (2005). Managing virtual teams: A review of current empirical research. *Human Resource Management Review, 15,* 69–95.

Herzberg, F., Mausner, B., & Snyderman, B. (1959). *The motivation to work.* New York: Wiley.

Heslin, P. A. & VandeWalle, D. (2011). Performance appraisal procedural justice: The role of a manager's implicit person theory. *Journal of Management, 37*(6), 1694–1718.

Heslin, P. A., Vandewalle, D., & Latham, G. P. (2006). Keen to help? Managers' implicit person theories and their subsequent employee coaching. *Personnel Psychology, 59,* 871–902.

Highhouse, S. (1999). The brief history of personnel counseling in industrial-organizational psychology. *Journal of Vocational Behavior, 55*(3), 318–336.

Highhouse, S., Hoffman, J. R., Greve, E. M., & Collins, A. E. (2002). Persuasive impact of organizational value statements in a recruitment context. *Journal of Applied Social Psychology, 32,* 1737–1755.

Hirschfeld, R. R., & Feild, H. S. (2000). Work centrality and work alienation: Distinct aspects of a general commitment to work. *Journal of Organizational Behavior, 21,* 789–800.

Hislop, D. (2003). Linking human resource management and knowledge management via commitment: A review and research agenda. *Employee Relations, 25*(2), 182–202.

Hitt, M. A. (2000). The new frontier: Transformation of management for the new millennium. *Organizational Dynamics, 28*(3), 7–17.

Hochwarter, W. A., Kacmar, C., Perrewé, P. L., & Johnson, D. (2003, December). Perceived organizational support as a mediator of the relationship between politics, perceptions, and work outcomes. *Journal of Vocational Behavior, 63*(3), 438–456.

Hochwarter, W. A., Witt, L. A., & Kacmar, K. M. (2000). Perceptions of organizational politics as a moderator of the relationship between conscientiousness and job performance. *Journal of Applied Psychology, 85*(3), 472–478.

Hodgkinson, G. P., & Healey, M. P. (2008). Cognition in organizations. *Annual Review of Psychology, 59,* 387–417.

Hoffman, B. J., Blair, C. A., Meriac, J. P., & Woehr, D. J. (2007). Expanding the criterion domain? A quantitative review of the OCB literature. *Journal of Applied Psychology, 92*(2), 555–566.

Hoffman, B. J., Lance, C. E., Bynum, B., & Gentry, W. A. (2010). Rater source effects are alive and well after all. *Personnel Psychology, 63,* 119–151.

Hofmann, D. A., Jacobs, R., & Baratta, J. E. (1993). Dynamic criteria and the measurement of change. *Journal of Applied Psychology, 78,* 194–204.

Hofmann, D. A., Jacobs, R., & Gerras, S. J. (1992). Mapping individual performance over time. *Journal of Applied Psychology, 77*(2), 185–195.

Hofmann, D. A., Morgeson, F. P., & Gerras, S. J. (2003). Climate as a moderator of the relationship between leader–member exchange and content specific citizenship: Safety climate as an exemplar. *Journal of Applied Psychology, 88*(1), 170–178.

Hogan, J., Barrett, P., & Hogan, R. (2007). Personality measurement, faking, and employment selection. *Journal of Applied Psychology, 92*(5), 1270–1285.

Hogan, R., & Hogan, J. (1995). *Hogan Personality Inventory manual* (2nd ed.). Tulsa, OK: Hogan Assessment Systems.

Hogan, R., Hogan, J., & Roberts, B. W. (1996). Personality measurement and employment decisions: Questions and answers. *American Psychologist, 51*(5), 469–477.

Holman, D. J., Axtell, C. M., Sprigg, C. A., Totterdell, P., & Wall, T. D. (2010). The mediating role of job characteristics in job redesign interventions: A serendipitous quasi-experiment. *Journal of Organizational Behavior, 31*, 84–105.

Holtom, B. C., Lee, T. W., & Tidd, S. T. (2002). The relationship between work status congruence and work-related attitudes and behaviors. *Journal of Applied Psychology, 87*(5), 903–915.

Holton, E. F., Coco, M. L., Lowe, J. L., & Dutsch, J. V. (2006). Blended delivery strategies for competency-based training. *Advances in Developing Human Resources, 8*(2), 210–228.

Hom, P. W., & Griffeth, R. W. (1991). Structural equations modeling test of a turnover theory: Cross-sectional and longitudinal analyses. *Journal of Applied Psychology, 76*(3), 350–366.

Hong, Y., Wyer, R. S., & Fong, C. P. S. (2008). Chinese working in groups: Effort dispensability versus normative influence. *Asian Journal of Social Psychology, 11*(3), 187–195.

Hooper, D. T., & Martin, R. (2008). Beyond personal leader–member exchange (LMX) quality: The effects of perceived LMX variability on employee reactions. *Leadership Quarterly, 19*, 20–30.

Hopfl, H. M. (2006). Post-bureaucracy and Weber's "modern" bureaucrat. *Journal of Organizational Change Management, 19*, 8–21.

Hornung, S., Rousseau, D. M., Glaser, J., Angerer, P., & Weigl, M. (2010). Beyond top-down and bottom–up work redesign: Customizing job content through idiosyncratic deals. *Journal of Organizational Behavior, 31*, 187–215.

Horwitz, S. K., & Horwitz, I. B. (2007). The effects of team diversity on team outcomes: A meta-analytic review of team demography. *Journal of Management, 33*, 987–1015.

Hosking, D. M., & Schriesheim, C. A. (1978). Improving leadership effectiveness: The leader match concept—A book review. *Administrative Science Quarterly, 23*, 496–505.

Hough, L. (1998). Personality at work: Issues and evidence. In M. Hakel (Ed.), *Beyond multiple choice: Evaluating alternatives to traditional testing for selection* (pp. 131–159). Hillsdale, NJ: Erlbaum.

House, R. J. (1971). A path-goal theory of leader effectiveness. *Administrative Science Quarterly, 16*, 321–338.

House, R. J. (1996). Path-goal theory of leadership: Lessons, legacy, and a reformulated theory. *Leadership Quarterly, 7*(3), 323–352.

House, R. J., & Aditya, R. N. (1997). The social scientific study of leadership: Quo vadis? *Journal of Management, 23*(3), 409–473.

House, R. J., Hanges, P. J., Ruiz-Quintanilla, S. A., Dorfman, P. W., Javidan, M., Dickson, M. W., et al. (1999). Cultural influences on leadership and organizations: Project GLOBE. In W. Mobley (Ed.), *Advances in global leadership* (Vol. 1, pp. 171–233). Stamford, CT: JAI Press.

House, R. J., Wright, N., & Aditya, R. N. (1997). Cross-cultural research on organizational leadership: A critical analysis and a proposed theory. In P. C. Earley & M. Erez (Eds.), *New perspectives on international industrial/organizational psychology* (pp. 535–625). San Francisco: Jossey-Bass.

Howard, J. L., & Frink, D. D. (1996). The effects of organizational restructure on employee satisfaction. *Group and Organization Management, 21*(3), 278–303.

Howard, L. (1999). Validity evidence for measures of procedural/distributive justice and pay/benefit satisfaction. *Journal of Business and Psychology, 14*(1), 135–147.

Hoyt, W. T. (2000). Rater bias in psychological research: When is it a problem and what can we do about it? *Psychological Methods, 5*(1), 64–86.

Hsu, C. (2004, September 20). The testing of America. *U.S. News & World Report, 137*(9), 68–69.

Hsu, S. S. (2007, June 5). Bureaucratic failings are cited in TB case. *Washington Post.*

Humphrey, S. E., Hollenbeck, J. R., Meyer, C. J., & Ilgen, D. R. (2011). Personality configurations in self-managed teams: A natural experiment on the effects of maximizing and minimizing variance in traits. *Journal of Applied Social Psychology, 41*(7), 1701–1732.

Humphrey, S. E., Morgeson, F. P., & Mannor, M. J. (2009). Developing a theory of the strategic core of teams: A role composition model of team performance. *Journal of Applied Psychology, 94*, 48–61.

Humphrey, S. E., Nahrgang, J. D., & Morgeson, F. P. (2007). Integrating motivational, social, and contextual work design features: A meta-analytic summary and theoretical extension of the work design literature. *Journal of Applied Psychology, 92*, 1332–1356.

Hung, R. Y. Y., Lien, B. Y., Wu, C., & Kuo, Y. (2011). The impact of TQM and organizational learning on innovation performance in the high-tech industry. *International Business Review, 20*(2), 213–225.

Hunter, J. E., & Hunter, R. F. (1984). Validity and utility of alternative predictors of job performance. *Psychological Bulletin, 96*(1), 72–98.

Hunter, J. E., & Schmidt, F. L. (1990). *Methods of meta-analysis: Correcting error and bias in research findings.* Thousand Oaks, CA: SAGE.

Hur, Y., van den Berg, P. T., & Wilderom, C. P. M. (2011). Transformational leadership as a mediator between emotional intelligence and team outcomes. *The Leadership Quarterly, 22*(4), 591–603.

Hurtz, G. M., & Donovan, J. J. (2000). Personality and job performance: The Big Five revisited. *Journal of Applied Psychology, 85*(6), 869–879.

Hutchison, S., Valentino, K. E., & Kirkner, S. L. (1998). What works for the gander does not work as well for the goose: The effects of leader behavior. *Journal of Applied Social Psychology, 28*(2), 171–182.

Iaffaldano, M. T., & Muchinsky, P. M. (1985). Job satisfaction and job performance: A meta-analysis. *Psychological Bulletin, 97*(2), 251–273.

Ilgen, D. R., Barnes-Farrell, J. L., & McKellin, D. B. (1993). Performance appraisal process research in the 1980s: What has it contributed to appraisals in use? *Organizational Behavior and Human Decision Processes, 54*, 321–368.

Ilgen, D. R., Fisher, C. D., & Taylor, M. S. (1979). Consequences of individual feedback on behavior in organizations. *Journal of Applied Psychology, 64*, 349–371.

Ilies, R., & Judge, T. A. (2003). On the heritability of job satisfaction: The mediating role of personality. *Journal of Applied Psychology, 88*(4), 750–759.

Institute for Women's Policy Research. (2003). *The gender wage gap: Progress of the 1980s fails to carry through.* Retrieved March 5, 2009, from http://www.iwpr.org/pdf/C353.pdf

Jackson, S. E., & Schuler, R. S. (2000). *Managing human resources: A partnership perspective* (7th ed.). Cincinnati, OH: South-Western.

Janis, I. L. (1972). *Victims of groupthink.* Boston: Houghton Mifflin.

Janis, I. L. (1982). *Groupthink.* Boston: Houghton Mifflin.

Janis, I. L., & Mann, L. (1977). *Decision making: A psychological analysis of conflict, choice, and commitment.* New York: Free Press.

Jawahar, I. M., Stone, T. H., & Kisamore, J. L. (2007). Role conflict and burnout: The direct and moderating effects of political skill and perceived organizational support on burnout dimensions. *International Journal of Stress Management, 14*, 142–159.

Jeanneret, P. R., & Strong, M. H. (2003). Linking O*NET job analysis information to job requirement predictors: An O*NET application. *Personnel Psychology, 56*, 465–492.

Jex, S. M., Bliese, P. D., Buzzell, S., & Primeau, J. (2001). The impact of self-efficacy on stressor–strain relations: Coping style as an explanatory mechanism. *Journal of Applied Psychology, 86*(3), 401–409.

Johnson, C. (1999). Teams at work. *HR Magazine, 44*(5), 30–36.

Johnson, J. W., Steel, P., Scherbaum, C. A., Hoffman, C. C., Jeanneret, P. R., & Foster, J. (2010). Validation is like motor oil: Synthetic is better. *Industrial and Organizational Psychology, 3*(3), 305–328.

Johnson, R. J., Chang, C. H., & Lord, R. G. (2006). Moving from cognition to action. *Psychological Bulletin, 132*, 381–415.

Johnson, S. K., Bettenhausen, K., & Gibbons, E. (2009). Realities of working in virtual teams: Affective and attitudinal outcomes of computer-mediated communication. *Small Group Research, 40*(6), 623–649.

Jones, L., Watson, B., Hobman, E., Bordia, P., Gallois, C., & Callan, V. J. (2008). Employee perceptions of organizational change: Impact of hierarchical level. *Leadership & Organization Development Journal, 29,* 294–316.

Joni, S.-N. (2004). *The third opinion: How successful leaders use outside insight to create superior results.* New York: Portfolio/Penguin.

Josserand, E., Teo, S., & Clegg, S. (2006). From bureaucratic to post-bureaucratic: The difficulties of transition. *Journal of Organizational Change Management, 19,* 54–64.

Judge, T. A., Bono, J. E., Erez, A., & Locke, E. A. (2005). Core self-evaluations and job and life satisfaction: The role of self-concordance and goal attainment. *Journal of Applied Psychology, 90,* 257–268.

Judge, T. A., Bono, J. E., Ilies, R., & Gerhardt, M. W. (2002). Personality and leadership: A qualitative and quantitative review. *Journal of Applied Psychology, 87*(4), 765–780.

Judge, T. A., Bono, J. E., & Locke, E. A. (2000). Personality and job satisfaction: The mediating role of job characteristics. *Journal of Applied Psychology, 85*(2), 237–249.

Judge, T. A., Colbert, A. E., & Ilies, R. (2004). Intelligence and leadership: A quantitative review and test of theoretical propositions. *Journal of Applied Psychology, 89*(3), 542–552.

Judge, T. A., & Hulin, C. L. (1993). Job satisfaction as a reflection of disposition: A multiple-source causal analysis. *Organizational Behavior and Human Decision Processes, 56,* 388–421.

Judge, T. A., Locke, E. A., Durham, C. C., & Kluger, A. N. (1998). Disposition effects on job and life satisfaction: The role of core evaluations. *Journal of Applied Psychology, 83*(1), 17–34.

Judge, T. A., Piccolo, R. E., & Ilies, R. (2004). The forgotten ones? The validity of consideration and initiating structure in leadership research. *Journal of Applied Psychology, 89*(1), 36–51.

Judge, T. A., Piccolo, R. F., Podsakoff, N. P, Shaw, J. C., & Rich, B. L. (2010). The relationship between pay and job satisfaction: A meta-analysis. *Journal of Vocational Behavior, 77,* 157–167.

Judge, T. A., Scott, B. A., & Ilies, R. (2006). Hostility, job attitudes, and workplace deviance. *Journal of Applied Psychology, 91,* 126–138.

Judge, T. A., Thoresen, C. J., Bono, J. E., & Patton, G. K. (2001). The job satisfaction–job performance relationship: A qualitative and quantitative review. *Journal of Applied Psychology, 127,* 376–407.

Jung, D. I., & Sosik, J. J. (1999). Effects of group characteristics on work group performance: A longitudinal investigation. *Group Dynamics: Theory, Research, and Practice, 3*(4), 279–290.

Kacmar, K. M., Witt, L. A., Zivnuska, S., & Gully, S. M. (2003). The interactive effect of leader–member exchange and communication frequency on performance ratings. *Journal of Applied Psychology, 88*(4), 764–772.

Kanfer, R. (1990). Motivation theory and industrial and organizational psychology. In M. Dunnette & L. Hough (Eds.), *Handbook of industrial and organizational psychology* (2nd ed., Vol. 1., pp. 75–170). Palo Alto, CA: Consulting Psychologists Press.

Kanter, R. M. (1999). Change in everyone's job: Managing the extended enterprise in a globally connected world. *Organizational Dynamics, 28*(1), 7–23.

Karakas, F. (2009). New paradigms in organization development: Positivity, spirituality, and complexity. *Organization Development Journal, 27*(1), 11–26.

Karasek, R. (1990). Lower health risk with increased job control among white-collar workers. *Journal of Organizational Behaviour, 11,* 171–185.

Karau, S. J., & Hart, J. W. (1998). Group cohesiveness and social loafing: Effects of a social interaction manipulation on individual motivation within groups. *Group Dynamics: Theory, Research, and Practice, 2*(3), 185–191.

Karau, S. J., & Williams, K. D. (1993). Social loafing: A meta-analytic review and theoretical integration. *Journal of Personality and Social Psychology, 26,* 377–384.

Karau, S. J., & Williams, K. D. (1997). The effects of group cohesiveness on social loafing and social compensation. *Group Dynamics: Theory, Research, and Practice, 1,* 156–168.

Kark, R., Shamir, B., & Chen, G. (2003). The two faces of transformational leadership: Empowerment and dependency. *Journal of Applied Psychology, 88*(2), 246–255.

Kate, N. T. (1998). Two careers, one marriage. *American Demographics, 20*(4), 28.

Kath, L. M., Swody, C. A., Magley, V. J., Bunk, J. A., & Gallus, J. A. (2009). Cross-level, three-way interactions among work-group climate, gender, and frequency of harassment on morale and withdrawal outcomes of sexual harassment. *Journal of Occupational and Organizational Psychology, 82*, 159–182.

Katz, D., & Kahn, R. L. (1978). *The social psychology of organizations* (2nd ed.). New York: Wiley.

Katzell, R. A., & Austin, J. T. (1992). From then to now: The development of industrial-organizational psychology in the United States. *Journal of Applied Psychology, 77*(6), 803–835.

Kauffeld, S., & Lehmann-Willenbrock, N. (2009). Sales training: Effects of spaced practice on training transfer. *Journal of European Industrial Training, 34*(1), 23–37.

Kaufman, A. S. (1994). *Intelligent testing with the WISC-III.* New York: Wiley.

Kaufman, A. S., & Lichtenberger, E. (1999). *Essentials of WAIS-III assessment.* New York: Wiley.

Keeping, L. M., & Levy, P. E. (2000). Performance appraisal reactions: Measurement, modeling, and method bias. *Journal of Applied Psychology, 85*(5), 708–723.

Kelleher, E. (2007). *In dual-earner couples, family roles are changing in U.S.* Retrieved December 8, 2008, from http://www.America.gov/st/washfile-english/2007/March/20070321162913berehellek0.6708338.html

Kellett, J. B., Humphrey, R. H., & Sleeth, R. G. (2006). Empathy and the emergence of task and relations leaders. *Leadership Quarterly, 17*, 146–162.

Kenny, D. A., & Zaccaro, S. J. (1983). An estimate of the variance due to traits in leadership. *Journal of Applied Psychology, 68*(4), 678–685.

Kerlinger, F. N. (1986). *Foundations of behavioral research* (3rd ed.). Fort Worth, TX: Holt, Rinehart and Winston.

Kerr, N. L., & Tindale, R. S. (2004). Group performance and decision making. *Annual Review of Psychology, 55*, 623–655.

Kickul, J., Lester, S. W., & Finkl, J. (2002). Promise breaking during radical organizational change:

Do justice interventions make a difference? *Journal of Organizational Behavior, 23*, 469–488.

Kim, S. (1998). Toward understanding family leave policy in public organizations: Family leave use and conceptual framework for the family leave implementation process. *Public Productivity and Management Review, 22*(1), 71–87.

Kinicki, A. J., McKee-Ryan, F. M., Schriesheim, C. A., & Carson, K. P. (2002). Assessing the construct validity of the Job Descriptive Index: A review and meta-analysis. *Journal of Applied Psychology, 87*(1), 14–32.

Kirkman, B. L., Chen, G., Farh, J., Chen, Z. X., & Lowe, K. B. (2009). Individual power distance orientation and follower reactions to transformational leaders: A cross-level, cross-cultural examination. *Academy of Management Journal, 52*(4), 744–764.

Kirkman, B. L., & Mathieu, J. E. (2005). The dimensions and antecedents of team virtuality. *Journal of Management, 31*, 700–718.

Kirkman, B. L., & Rosen, B. (1999). Beyond self-management: Antecedents and consequences of team empowerment. *Academy of Management Journal, 42*(1), 58–74.

Kirkpatrick, D. L. (1976). Evaluation of training. In R. L. Craig (Ed.), *Training and development handbook* (pp. 18–27). New York: McGraw-Hill.

Kish-Gephart, J. J., Harrison, D. A., & Treviño, L. K. (2010). Bad apples, bad cases, and bad barrels: Meta-analytic evidence about sources of unethical decisions at work. *Journal of Applied Psychology, 95*(1), 1–31.

Klein, H. J., Molloy, J. C., & Cooper, J. T. (2009). Conceptual foundations: Construct definitions and theoretical representations of workplace commitments. In H. J. Klein, T. E. Becker, & J. P. Meyer (Eds.), *Commitment in organizations: Accumulated wisdom and new directions.* New York: Routledge/Taylor & Francis.

Klein, H. J., & Weaver, N. A. (2000). The effectiveness of an organizational-level orientation training program in the socialization of new hires. *Personnel Psychology, 53*, 47–66.

Kluger, A. N., & DeNisi, A. (1996). The effects of feedback interventions on performance: A historical review, a meta-analysis, and a preliminary Feedback Intervention Theory. *Psychological Bulletin, 119*, 254–284.

Kluger, A. N., & Nir, D. (2010). The Feedforward Interview. *Human Resource Management Review, 20*(3), 235–246.

Knights, D., & McCabe, D. (2002). A road less travelled: Beyond managerialist, critical and processural approaches to total quality management. *Journal of Organizational Change Management, 15*(3), 235–254.

Kock, N., Danesh, A., & Komiak, P. (2008). A discussion and test of a communication flow optimization approach for business process redesign. *Knowledge and Process Management, 15,* 72–85.

Koenig, A. M., Eagly, A. H., Mitchell, A. A., & Ristikari, T. (2011). Are leader stereotypes masculine? A meta-analysis of three research paradigms. *Psychological Bulletin, 137*(4), 616–642.

Koltko-Rivera, M. E. (2006). Rediscovering the later version of Maslow's hierarchy of needs: Self-transcendence and opportunities for theory, research, and unification. *Review of General Psychology, 10,* 302–317.

Komar, S., Brown, D. J., Komar, J., & Robie, C. (2008). Faking and the validity of conscientiousness: A Monte Carlo investigation. *Journal of Applied Psychology, 93,* 140–154.

Konovsky, M. A., & Cropanzano, R. (1991). Perceived fairness of employee drug testing as a predictor of employee attitudes and job performance. *Journal of Applied Psychology, 76,* 698–707.

Koppes, L. L. (1997). American female pioneers of industrial and organizational psychology during the early years. *Journal of Applied Psychology, 82*(4), 500–515.

Koppes, L. L. (Ed.). (2007). *Historical perspectives in industrial and organizational psychology.* Mahwah, NJ: Erlbaum.

Koppes, L. L., & Pickren, W. (2007). Industrial and organizational psychology: An evolving science and practice. In L. L. Koppes (Ed.), *Historical perspectives in industrial and organizational psychology* (pp. 3–36). Mahwah, NJ: Erlbaum.

Koslowsky, M., Sagie, A., Krausz, M., & Singer, A. D. (1997). Correlates of employee lateness: Some theoretical considerations. *Journal of Applied Psychology, 82*(1), 79–88.

Kossek, E. E., & Nichol, V. (1992). The effects of on-site child care on employee attitudes and performance. *Personnel Psychology, 45,* 485–509.

Kossek, E. E., & Ozeki, C. (1998). Work–family conflict, policies, and the job-life satisfaction relationship: A review and directions for organizational behavior–human resources research. *Journal of Applied Psychology, 83*(2), 139–149.

Kotsou, I., Nelis, D., Gregoire, J., & Mikolajczak, M. (2011). Emotional plasticity. *Journal of Applied Psychology, 96*(4), 827–839.

Kraiger, K., Ford, J. K., & Salas, E. (1993). Application of cognitive, skill-based, and affective theories of learning outcomes to new methods of training evaluating. *Journal of Applied Psychology, 78*(2), 311–328.

Kreiner, G. E., Hollensbe, E. C., & Sheep, M. L. (2009). Balancing borders and bridges: Negotiating the work–home interface via boundary work tactics. *Academy of Management Journal, 52*(4), 704–730.

Kristof-Brown, A. L., Zimmerman, R. D., & Johnson, E. (2005). Consequences of individuals' fit at work: A meta-analysis of person–job, person–organization, person–group, and person–supervisor fit. *Personnel Psychology, 58,* 281–342.

Kuhn, K. M., & Yockey, M. D. (2003). Variable pay as a risky choice: Determinants of the relative attractiveness of incentive plans. *Organizational Behavior and Human Decision Processes, 90*(2), 323–341.

Kulik, C. T., Pepper, M. B., Roberson, L., & Parker, S. K. (2007). The rich get richer: Predicting participation in voluntary diversity training. *Journal of Organizational Behavior, 28*(6), 753–769.

Kulik, C. T., & Roberson, L. (2008). Diversity initiative effectiveness: What organizations can (and cannot) expect from diversity recruitment, diversity training, and formal mentoring programs. In A. P. Brief (Ed.), *Diversity at work* (pp. 265–317). Cambridge, UK: Cambridge University Press.

Kuncel, N. R., Hezlett, S. A., & Ones, D. S. (2001). A comprehensive meta-analysis of the predictive validity of the Graduate Record Examinations: Implications for graduate student selection and performance. *Psychological Bulletin, 127*(1), 162–181.

Kuncel, N. R., Hezlett, S. A., & Ones, D. S. (2004). Academic performance, career potential, creativity, and job performance: Can one construct predict them all? *Journal of Personality and Social Psychology, 86*(1), 148–161.

Kuncel, N. R., Ones, D. S., & Sackett, P. R. (2010). Individual differences as predictors of work, educational and broad life outcomes. *Personality and Individual Differences, 49,* 331–336.

Kunin, T. (1955). The construction of a new type of attitude measure. *Personnel Psychology, 8,* 65–77.

Kunin, T. (1998). The construction of a new type of attitude measure. *Personnel Psychology, 51,* 823–824.

Kurtzberg, T. R., Naquin, C. E., & Belkin, L. Y. (2005). Electronic performance appraisals: The effects of e-mail communication on peer ratings in actual and simulated environments. *Organizational Behavior and Human Decision Processes, 98*(2), 216–226.

Landy, F. J., & Farr, J. L. (1980). Performance rating. *Psychological Bulletin, 87,* 72–107.

Lang, J. W. B., Kersting, M., Hülsheger, U. R., & Lang, J. (2010). General mental ability, narrower cognitive abilities, and job performance: The perspective of the nested-factors model of cognitive abilities. *Personnel Psychology, 63,* 595–640.

Langfred, C. W. (2000). Work group design and autonomy: A field study of the interaction between task interdependence and group autonomy. *Small Group Research, 31*(1), 54–70.

Langfred, C. W. (2007). The downside of self-management: A longitudinal study of the effects of conflict on trust, autonomy, and task interdependence in self-managing teams. *Academy of Management Journal, 50,* 885–900.

Lapierre, L. M., & Allen, T. D. (2006). Work-supportive family, family-supportive supervision, use of organizational benefits, and problem-focused coping: Implications for work–family conflict and employee well-being. *Journal of Occupational Health Psychology, 11,* 169–181.

Larson, J. R., Jr., Christensen, C., Franz, T. M., & Abbott, A. S. (1998a). Diagnosing groups: The pooling, management, and impact of shared and unshared case information in team-based medical decision making. *Journal of Personality and Social Psychology, 75,* 93–108.

Larson, J. R., Jr., Foster-Fishman, P. G., & Franz, T. M. (1998b). Leadership style and the discussion of shared and unshared information in decision-making groups. *Personality and Social Psychology Bulletin, 24*(5), 482–495.

Latham, G. P. (1988). Human resource training and development. *Annual Review of Psychology, 39,* 545–582.

Latham, G. P., & Saari, L. M. (1979). The application of social learning theory to training supervisors through behavior modeling. *Journal of Applied Psychology, 64,* 239–246.

Lau, V. C. S., Au, W. T., & Ho, J. M. C. (2003). A qualitative and quantitative review of antecedents of counterproductive behavior in organizations. *Journal of Business and Psychology, 18*(1), 73–99.

Lauby, S. (2010). How job seekers may use social media in the future. Retrieved July 23, 2011, from http://mashable.com/2010/10/11/job-seekers-social-media-future/

Lawler, E. E. (2001). *Organizing for high performance.* San Francisco: Jossey-Bass.

Lawler, E. E., Mohrman, S. A., & Ledford, G. E. (1992). *Employee involvement and total quality management: Practices and results in Fortune 1000 companies.* San Francisco: Jossey-Bass.

Lawler, E. E., & Porter, L. W. (1967). The effects of performance on job satisfaction. *Industrial Relations, 7,* 20–28.

Lawson, R. B., & Shen, Z. (1998). *Organizational psychology: Foundations and applications.* New York: Oxford University Press.

LeBlanc, M. M., & Barling, J. (2004). Workplace aggression. *Current Directions in Psychological Science, 13*(1), 9–12.

LeBlanc, M. M., & Kelloway, E. K. (2002). Predictors and outcomes of workplace violence and aggression. *Journal of Applied Psychology, 87*(3), 444–453.

Ledbetter v. Goodyear Tire & Rubber Co., 550 U.S. 618 (2007).

Lee, B. A. (2003). A decade of the Americans with Disabilities Act: Judicial outcomes and unresolved problems. *Industrial Relations: A Journal of Economy & Society, 42*(1), 11–30.

Lee, T. H., Gerhart, B., Weller, I., & Trevor, C. O. (2008). Understanding voluntary turnover: Path-specific job satisfaction effects and the importance of unsolicited job offers. *Academy of Management Journal, 51,* 651–671.

Lee, T. W., Mitchell, T. R., Holtom, B. C., McDaniel, L. S., & Hill, J. W. (1999). The unfolding model of voluntary turnover: A replication and extension. *Academy of Management Journal, 42*(4), 450–462.

LePine, J. A., Piccolo, R. F., Jackson, C. L., Mathieu, J. E., & Saul, J. R. (2008). A meta-analysis of teamwork processes: Tests of a multidimensional model and relationships with team effectiveness criteria. *Personnel Psychology, 61,* 273–307.

Leung, D. Y. P., & Kember, D. (2005). Comparability of data gathered from evaluation questionnaires on paper and through the Internet. *Research in Higher Education, 46*(5), 571–591.

Levy, P. E., & Steelman, L. A. (1994). Determinants of feedback seeking: Costs, environment, and the performance appraisal process. Paper presented at the 9th annual meeting of the Society for Industrial and Organizational Psychology, Nashville, TN.

Levy, P. E., & Steelman, L. A. (1997). Performance appraisal for team based organizations: A prototypical multiple rater system. In M. Beyerlein, D. Johnson, & S. Beyerlein (Eds.), *Advances in interdisciplinary studies of work teams: Vol. 4. Team implementations issues* (pp. 141–165). Greenwich, CT: JAI Press.

Levy, P. E., & Williams, J. R. (1998). The role of perceived system knowledge in predicting appraisal reactions, job satisfaction, and organizational commitment. *Journal of Organizational Behavior, 19,* 53–65.

Levy, P. E., & Williams, J. R. (2004). The social context of performance appraisal: A review and framework for the future. *Journal of Management, 30*(6), 881–905.

Lewin, K. (1951). *Field theory in social science.* New York: Harper.

Lewin, K., Dembo, T., Festinger, L., & Sears, P. (1944). Level of aspiration. In J. M. Hunt (Ed.), *Personality and the behavior disorders* (Vol. 1, pp. 333–378). New York: Ronald.

Li, N., Liang, J., & Crant, J. M. (2010). The role of proactive personality in job satisfaction and organizational citizenship behavior: A relational perspective. *Journal of Applied Psychology, 95,* 395–404.

Liao, H., & Rupp, D. (2005). The impact of justice climate and justice orientation on work outcomes: A cross-level multifoci framework. *Journal of Applied Psychology, 90,* 242–256.

Lievens, F., & Anseel, F. (2004). Confirmatory factor analysis and invariance of an organizational citizenship behaviour measure across samples in a Dutch-speaking context. *Journal of Occupational and Organizational Psychology, 77*(3), 299–306.

Lievens, F., Buyse, T., & Sackett, P. R. (2005). The operational validity of a video-based situational judgment test for medical college admissions: Illustrating the importance of matching predictor and criterion construct domains. *Journal of Applied Psychology, 90*(3), 442–452.

Lievens, F., & Highhouse, S. (2003). The relation of instrumental and symbolic attributes to a company's attractiveness as an employer. *Personnel Psychology, 56*(1), 75–102.

Lievens, F., Ones, D. S., & Dilchert, S. (2009). Personality scale validities increase throughout medical school. *Journal of Applied Psychology, 94*(6), 1514–1535.

Lievens, F., Sanchez, J. I., Bartram, D., & Brown, A. (2010). Lack of consensus among competency ratings of the same occupation: Noise or substance? *Journal of Applied Psychology, 95*(3), 562–571.

Lievens, F., Sanchez, J. I., & De Corte, W. (2004). Easing the inferential leap in competency modeling: The effects of task-related information and subject matter experts. *Personnel Psychology, 57*(4), 881–904.

Liljenstrand, A. M., & Nebeker, D. M., (2008). Coaching services: A look at coaches, clients, and practices. *Consulting Psychology Journal: Practice and Research, 60*(1), 57–77.

Linderbaum, B. G., & Levy, P. E. (2007). *The development and validation of the Feedback Orientation Scale.* Paper presented at the 22nd annual meeting of the Society for Industrial and Organizational Psychology, New York.

Linderbaum, D. G., & Levy, P. E. (2010). The development and validation of the feedback orientation scale. *Journal of Management, 36*(6), 1372–1405.

Ling, Y., Simsek, Z., Lubatkin, M. H., & Veiga, J. F. (2008). Transformational leadership's role in promoting corporate entrepreneurship: Examining the CEO–TMT interface. *Academy of Management Journal, 51*(3), 557–576.

Lips-Wiersma, M., & Hall, D. T. (2007). Organizational career development is not dead: A case study on managing the new career during organizational change. *Journal of Organizational Behavior, 28,* 771–792.

Locke, E. A. (1976). The nature and causes of job satisfaction. In M. D. Dunnette (Ed.), *Handbook of industrial and organizational psychology* (pp. 1297–1349). Chicago: Rand McNally.

Locke, E. A. (1990). *A theory of goal setting and task performance.* Englewood Cliffs, NJ: Prentice-Hall.

Locke, E. A., & Latham, G. P. (2002). Building a practically useful theory of goal setting and task motivation: A 35-year odyssey. *American Psychologist, 57*(9), 705–717.

Locke, E. A., & Latham, G. P. (2006). New directions in goal-setting theory. *Current Directions in Psychological Science, 15,* 265–268.

Lofquist, L. H., & Dawis, R. V. (1969). *Adjustment to work: A psychological view of man's problems in a word-oriented society.* New York: Appleton-Century-Crofts.

Loher, B. T., Noe, R. A., Moeler, N. L., & Fitzgerald, M. P. (1985). A meta-analysis of the relation of job characteristics to job satisfaction. *Journal of Applied Psychology, 70*(2), 280–289.

Loi, R., Hang-yue, N., & Foley, S. (2006). Linking employees' justice perceptions to organizational commitment and intention to leave: The mediating role of perceived organizational support. *Journal of Occupational and Organizational Psychology, 79,* 101–120.

London, M., & Smither, J. W. (1999). Empowered self-development and continuous learning. *Human Resource Management, 38*(1), 3–15.

London, M., & Smither, J. W. (2002). Feedback orientation, feedback culture, and the longitudinal performance management process. *Human Resource Management Review, 12(*1), 81.

Longenecker, C. O., Sims, H. P., Jr., & Gioia, D. A. (1987). Behind the mask: The politics of employee appraisal. *Academy of Management Executive, 1,* 183–193.

Lopez, E. M., & Greenhaus, J. H. (1978). Self-esteem, race, and job satisfaction. *Journal of Vocational Behavior, 13,* 75–83.

Lord, R. G. (2000). Leadership. In A. E. Kazdin (Ed.), *Encyclopedia of psychology* (Vol. 3, pp. 775–786). Washington, DC: American Psychological Association.

Lord, R. G., & Brown, D. J. (2004). *Leadership processes and follower self-identity.* Mahwah, NJ: Erlbaum.

Lord, R. G., DeVader, C. L., & Alliger, G. M. (1986). A meta-analysis of the relation between personality traits and leadership perceptions: An application of validity generalization procedures. *Journal of Applied Psychology, 71*(3), 402–410.

Lord, R. G., Foti, R. J., & DeVader, C. L. (1984). A test of leadership categorization theory: Internal structure, information processing, and leadership perceptions. *Organizational Behavior and Human Performance, 34,* 343–378.

Lord, R. G., & Maher, K. J. (1991). *Leadership and information processing: Linking perception and performance.* Boston: Unwin Hyman.

Lowe, G. S. (1987). *Women in the administrative revolution: The feminization of clerical work.* Oxford, UK: Polity Press.

Lowe, K. B., Kroeck, K. G., & Sivasubramaniam, N. (1996). Effectiveness correlates of transformational and transactional leadership: A meta-analytic review of the MLQ. *Leadership Quarterly, 7,* 385–425.

Lowery, C. M., Beadles, N. A. I., & Krilowicz, T. J. (2002). Note on the relationships among job satisfaction, organizational commitment, and organizational citizenship behavior. *Psychological Reports, 91*(2), 607–617.

Lowman, R. L., Kantor, J., & Perloff, R. (2007). A history of I-O psychology educational programs in the United States. In L. L. Koppes (Ed.), *Historical perspectives in industrial and organizational psychology* (pp. 111–138). Mahwah, NJ: Erlbaum.

Lublin, J., & Karp, H. (2011, December 14). Avon replacing Andrea Jung as CEO. *Wall Street Journal.*

Ludwig, T. D., & Geller, E. S. (1997). Assigned versus participative goal setting and response generalization: Managing injury control among professional pizza deliverers. *Journal of Applied Psychology, 82*(2), 253–261.

Ludwig, T. D., & Geller, E. S. (2000). Intervening to improve the safety of delivery drivers: A systematic behavioral approach. *Journal of Organizational Behavior Management, 19*(4), 1–124.

Luscher, L. S., & Lewis, M. W. (2008). Organizational change and managerial sense-making: Working through paradox. *Academy of Management Journal, 51,* 221–240.

Luthans, F., & Youssef, C. M. (2007). Emerging positive organizational behavior. *Journal of Management, 33,* 321–349.

MacGregor, R. (1999). *Work and family policies: A "win–win" formula for business and society.* Minneapolis, MN: Minnesota Center for Corporate Responsibility.

Machan, D. (1999). A dyed-in-the-wool skeptic. *Forbes, 163*(1), 96–98.

Mael, F. A. (1991). A conceptual rationale for the domain and attributes of biodata items. *Personnel Psychology, 44,* 763–792.

Makiney, J. D., & Levy, P. E. (1998). The influence of self ratings versus peer ratings on supervisors' performance judgments. *Organizational Behavior and Human Decision Processes, 74*, 212–228.

Malos, S. B. (1998). Current legal issues in performance appraisal. In J. W. Smither (Ed.), *Performance appraisal: State of the art in practice* (pp. 49–94). San Francisco: Jossey-Bass.

Marini, M. M. & Fan, P.-L. (1997). The gender gap in earnings at career entry. *American Sociological Review, 62*, 588–604.

Marique, G., & Stinglhamber, F. (2011). Identification to proximal targets and affective organizational commitment: The mediating role of organizational identification. *Journal of Personnel Psychology, 10*(3), 107–117.

Marriott International. (n.d.). *Corporate diversity.* Retrieved April 1, 2009, from http://www.marriott .com/corporateinfo/culture/Diversity.mi

Marshak, R. J., & Grant, D. (2008). Organizational discourse and new organization development practices. *British Journal of Management, 19*(Suppl. 1), S7–S19.

Martin v. PGA Tour, Inc., 994 F. Supp. 12452 (D.Or 1998).

Martinko, M. J., & Zellars, K. L. (1998). Toward a theory of workplace violence and aggression: A cognitive appraisal perspective. In R. W. Griffin, A. O'Leary-Kelly, & J. M. Collins (Eds.), *Dysfunctional behavior in organizations: Violent and deviant behavior* (pp. 1–42). Stamford, CT: JAI Press.

Martins, L. L., Eddleston, K. A., & Veiga, J. F. J. (2002). Moderators of the relationship between work–family conflict and career satisfaction. *Academy of Management Journal, 45*(2), 399–409.

Martins, L. L., & Shalley, C. E. (2011). Creativity in virtual work: Effects of demographic differences. *Small Group Research, 42*(5), 536–561.

Martiny, M. (1998). Knowledge management at HP consulting. *Organizational Dynamics, 27*(2), 71–77.

Maslach, C. (2003). Job burnout: New directions in research and intervention. *Current Directions in Psychological Science, 12*(5), 189–192.

Masterson, S. S., Lewis, K., Goldman, B. M., & Taylor, M. S. (2000). Integrating justice and social exchange: The differing effects of fair procedures and treatment on work relations. *Academy of Management Journal, 43*(4), 738–748.

Mathieu, J. E., Heffner, T. S., Goodwin, G. F., Salas, E., & Cannon-Bowers, J. A. (2000). The influence of shared mental models on team process and performance. *Journal of Applied Psychology, 85*(2), 273–283.

Mathieu, J. E. & Rapp, T. L. (2009). Laying the foundation for successful team performance trajectories: The roles of team charters and performance strategies. *Journal of Applied Psychology, 94*(1), 90–103.

Mathieu, J. E., & Zajac, D. M. (1990). A review and meta-analysis of the antecedents, correlates, and consequences of organizational commitment. *Journal of Applied Psychology, 108*(2), 171–194.

Mathiowetz, V., Rogers, S. L., Dowe-Keval, M., Donahoe, L., & Rennels, C. (1986). The Purdue Pegboard: Norms for 14- to 19-year-olds. *American Journal of Occupational Therapy, 3*, 174–179.

Mauno, S., & Kinnunen, U. (1999). The effects of job stressors on marital satisfaction in Finnish dual-earner couples. *Journal of Organizational Behavior, 20*, 879–895.

Maurer, T. J., Mitchell, D. R. D., & Barbeite, F. G. (2002). Predictors of attitudes toward a 360-degree feedback system and involvement in post-feedback management development activity. *Journal of Occupational and Organizational Psychology, 75*(1), 87–107.

Mayer, R. C., & Davis, J. H. (1999). The effect of the performance appraisal system on trust for management: A field quasi-experiment. *Journal of Applied Psychology, 84*(1), 123–136.

Maysent, M., & Spera, S. (1995). Coping with job loss and career stress: Effectiveness of stress management training with outplaced employees. In L. R. Murphy, J. J. Hurrell, Jr., S. L. Sauter, & G. P. Keita (Eds.), *Job stress interventions* (pp. 159–170). Washington, DC: American Psychological Association.

McCann, M. A. (2006). *The Wonderlic test for the NFL draft: Linking stereotype threat and the law.* Retrieved March 24, 2008, from http://ssrn.com/abstract=934307

McCormick, E. J. (1976). Job and task analysis. In M. D. Dunnette (Ed.), *Handbook of industrial and organizational psychology* (pp. 651–696). Chicago: Rand McNally.

McCormick, E. J. (1979). *Job analysis: Methods and applications.* New York: AMACOM.

McCormick, E. J., Jeanneret, P. R., & Mecham, R. C. (1972). A study of characteristics and job dimensions as based on the Position Analysis Questionnaire (PAQ). *Journal of Applied Psychology, 56,* 347–368.

McCrae, R. R., & Terracciano, A. (2005). Universal features of personality traits from the observer's perspective: Data from 50 cultures. *Journal of Personality and Social Psychology, 88*(3), 547–561.

McDaniel, M. A., Hartman, N. S., Whetzel, D. L., & Grubb, W. L., III. (2007). Situational judgment test, response instructions, and validity: A meta-analysis. *Personnel Psychology, 60*(1), 63–91.

McDaniel, M. A., Morgeson, F. P., Finnegan, E. B., Campion, M. A., & Braverman, E. P. (2001). Use of situational judgment tests to predict job performance: A clarification of the literature. *Journal of Applied Psychology, 86*(4), 730–740.

McDaniel, M. A., Schmidt, F. L., & Hunter, J. E. (1988). Job experience correlates of job performance. *Journal of Applied Psychology, 73*(22), 327–330.

McDaniel, M. A., Whetzel, D. L., Schmidt, F. L., & Maurer, S. D. (1994). The validity of employment interviews: A comprehensive review and meta-analysis. *Journal of Applied Psychology, 79*(4), 599–616.

McDonagh, J., & Coghlan, D. (1999). Can O.D. help solve the IT dilemma? O.D. in IT-related change. *Organization Development Journal, 17*(4), 41–48.

McEntire, L. E., Dailey, L. R., Osburn, H. K., & Mumford, M. D. (2006). Innovations in job analysis: Development and application of metrics to analyze job data. *Human Resource Management Review, 16*(3), 310–323.

McGehee, W., & Thayer, P. W. (1961). *Training in business and industry.* New York: Wiley.

McGregor, D. M. (1957). The human side of enterprise. *Management Review, 46,* 22–28.

McGregor, D. M. (1960). *The human side of enterprise.* New York: McGraw-Hill.

McHenry, J. J., Hough, L. M., Toquam, J. L., Hanson, M. A., & Ashworth, S. (1990). Project A validity results: The relationship between predictor and criterion domains. *Personnel Psychology, 43,* 336–354.

McIntyre, R. M., & Salas, E. (1995). Measuring and managing for team performance: Emerging principles from complex team environments. In R. A. Guzzo & E. Salas (Eds.), *Team effectiveness and decision making in organizations* (pp. 9–45). San Francisco: Jossey-Bass.

McKay, P. F., & Avery, D. R. (2006). What has race got to do with it? Unraveling the role of racioethnicity in job seekers' reactions to site visits. *Personnel Psychology, 59,* 395–429.

McKinley, W., Zhao, J., & Rust, K. G. (2000). A sociocognitive interpretation of organizational downsizing. *Academy of Management Reviews, 25*(1), 227–243.

Meade, A. W., Michels, L. C., & Lautenschlager, G. J. (2007). Are Internet and paper-and-pencil personality tests truly comparable? *Organizational Research Methods, 10*(2), 322–345.

Meisler, A. (2003). Dead man's curve. *Workforce Management, 82*(7), 44–49.

Melchers, K. G., & Annen, H. (2010). Officer selection for the Swiss armed forces: An evaluation of validity and fairness issues. *Swiss Journal of Psychology, 69*(2), 105–115.

Melchior, M., Caspi, A., Milne, B. J., Danese, A., Poulton, R., & Moffitt, T. E. (2007). Work stress precipitates depression and anxiety in young working men and women. *Psychological Medicine, 37,* 1119–1129.

Melzer, H., Bebbington, P., Brugha, T., Jenkins, R., McManus, S., & Stansfeld, S. (2010). Job insecurity, socio-economic circumstances, and depression. *Psychological Medicine, 40,* 1401–1407.

Meriac, J. P., Hoffman, B. J., Woehr, D. J., & Fleisher, S. (2008). Further evidence for the validity of assessment center dimensions: A meta-analysis of the incremental criterion-related validity of dimension ratings. *Journal of Applied Psychology, 93*(5), 1042–1052.

Meritor Savings Bank v. Vinson, 477 U.S. 57 (1986).

Mero, N. P., Guidice, R. M., & Anna, A. L. (2006). The interacting effects of accountability and individual differences on rater response to a performance-rating task. *Journal of Applied Social Psychology, 36*(4), 795–819.

Mero, N. P., Guidice, R. M., & Brownlee, A. L. (2007). Accountability in a performance appraisal context: The effect of audience and form of accounting on rater response and behavior. *Journal of Management, 33*(2), 223–252.

Mero, N. P., & Motowidlo, S. J. (1995). Effects of rater accountability on the accuracy and the favorability of performance ratings. *Journal of Applied Psychology, 80,* 517–524.

Mesmer-Magnus, J. R., & DeChurch, L. A. (2009). Information sharing and team performance: A meta analysis. *Journal of Applied Psychology, 94*(2), 535–546.

Mesmer-Magnus, J. R., & Viswesvaran, C. (2010). The role of pre-training interventions in learning: A meta-analysis and integrative review. *Human Resource Management Review, 20,* 261–282.

MetLife Mature Market Institute. (2006, July). *The MetLife caregiving cost study: Productivity losses to U.S. business.* Retrieved April 8, 2009, from http://www.metlife.com/assets/cao/mmi/publications/studies/MMIStudies-Caregiver-Cost-Study.pdf

Meyer, A. (1992). Getting to the heart of sexual harassment. *HR Magazine, 37,* 82–84.

Meyer, H. H. (1991). A solution for the performance appraisal feedback enigma. *Academy of Management Executive, 5,* 68–76.

Meyer, J. P., & Allen, N. J. (1997). *Commitment in the workplace: Theory, research, and application.* Thousand Oaks, CA: SAGE.

Meyer, J. P., Stanley, D. J., Herscovitch, L., & Topolnytsky, L. (2002). Affective, continuance, and normative commitment to the organization: A meta-analysis of antecedents, correlates, and consequences. *Journal of Vocational Behavior, 61*(1), 20–52.

Milkovich, G. T., & Newman, J. M. (1984). *Compensation.* Plano, TX: Business Publications.

Miller, D. L. (2001). Reexamining teamwork KSAs and team performance. *Small Group Research, 32*(6), 745–766.

Mitchell, T. R., Holtom, B. C., Lee, T. W., Sablynski, C. J., & Erez, M. (2001). Why people stay: Using job embeddedness to predict voluntary turnover. *Academy of Management Journal, 44*(6), 1102–1121.

Mohammed, S., Mathieu, J. E., & Bartlett, A. L. B. (2002). Technical-administrative task performance, leadership task performance, and contextual performance: Considering the influence of team- and task-related composition variables. *Journal of Organizational Behavior, 23*(7), 795–814.

Mohsen, A., & Nguyen, T. T. (1999). Succeeding with self-managed work teams. *Industrial Management, 41*(4), 24–28.

Mol, S. T., Born, M. P., & van der Molen, H. T. (2005). Developing criteria for expatriate effectiveness: Time to jump off the adjustment bandwagon.

International Journal of Intercultural Relations, 29(3), 339–353.

Moravec, M., Juliff, R., & Hesler, K. (1995). Partnerships help a company manage performance. *Personnel Journal, 74*(1), 104–107.

Morgan, D. E., & Zeffane, R. (2003). Employee involvement, organizational change and trust in management. *International Journal of Human Resource Management, 14*(1), 55–75.

Morgan, R. B., & Casper, W. J. (2000). Examining the factor structure of participant reactions to training: A multidimensional approach. *Human Resource Development Quarterly, 11*(3), 301–317.

Morgeson, F. P., Campion, M. A., Dipboye, R. L., Hollenbeck, J. R., Murphy, K., & Schmitt, N. (2007). Reconsidering the use of personality tests in personnel selection contexts. *Personnel Psychology, 60*(3), 683–729.

Morgeson, F. P., Delaney-Klinger, K., Mayfield, M. S., Ferrara, P., & Campion, M. (2004). Self-presentation processes in job analysis: A field experiment investigating inflation in abilities, tasks, and competencies. *Journal of Applied Psychology, 89*(4), 674–686.

Morgeson, F. P., & Humphrey, S. E. (2006). The Work Design Questionnaire (WDQ): Developing and validating a comprehensive measure for assessing job design and the nature of work. *Journal of Applied Psychology, 91*(6), 1321–1339.

Morgeson, F. P., Reider, M. H., & Campion, M. A. (2005). Selecting individuals in team settings: The importance of social skills, personality characteristics, and teamwork knowledge. *Personnel Psychology, 58,* 583–611.

Morris, J. A., & Feldman, D. C. (1996). The dimensions, antecedents, and consequences of emotional labor. *Academy of Management Review, 21*(4), 986–1010.

Motowidlo, S. J., Borman, W. C., & Schmit, M. J. (1997). A theory of individual differences in task and contextual performance. *Human Performance, 10*(2), 71–83.

Mount, M. K., Oh, I., & Burns, M. (2008). Incremental validity of perceptual speed and accuracy over general mental ability. *Personnel Psychology, 61,* 113–139.

Mount, M. K., Witt, L. A., & Barrick, M. R. (2000). Incremental validity of empirically keyed bio-data scales from GMA and the Five Factor personality constructs. *Personnel Psychology, 53*(2), 299–323.

Mowday, R. T. (1991). Equity theory predictions of behavior in organizations. In R. M. Steers and L. W. Porter (Eds.), *Motivation and work behavior* (5th ed., pp. 111–130). New York: McGraw-Hill.

Mowday, R. T., Steers, R. M., & Porter, L. W. (1979). The measurement of organizational commitment. *Journal of Vocational Behavior, 14,* 224–247.

Mueller-Hanson, R., Heggestad, E. D., & Thornton, G. C., III. (2003). Faking and selection: Considering the use of personality from select-in and select-out perspectives. *Journal of Applied Psychology, 88*(2), 348–355.

Mullen, B., & Copper, C. (1994). The relation between group cohesiveness and performance: An integration. *Psychological Bulletin, 115,* 210–227.

Mulrine, A. (2008, May 15). The army trains a skeptics corps to battle groupthink. Retrieved April 19, 2009, from *U.S. News & World Report* website: http://www.usnews.com/articles/news/world/2008/05/15/thearmy-trains-a-skeptics-corps-to-battle-groupthink.html

Mumford, T. V., Van Iddekinge, C. H., Morgeson, F. P., & Campion, M. A. (2008). The team role test: Development and validation of a team role knowledge situational judgment test. *Journal of Applied Psychology, 93,* 250–267.

Munsterberg, H. (1913). *Psychology and industrial efficiency.* Boston: Houghton Mifflin.

Murphy, K. R. (2002). Can conflicting perspectives on the role of g in personnel selection be resolved? *Human Performance, 15*(1–2), 173–186.

Murphy, K. R. (2003). *Validity generalization: A critical review.* Mahwah, NJ: Erlbaum.

Murphy, K. R., & Cleveland, J. N. (1995). *Understanding performance appraisal: Social, organizational and goal-based perspectives.* Thousand Oaks, CA: SAGE.

Murphy, K. R., & Jako, B. (1989). Under what conditions are observed intercorrelations greater than or smaller than true intercorrelations? *Journal of Applied Psychology, 74,* 827–830.

Murphy, K. R., & Reynolds, D. H. (1988). Does true halo affect observed halo? *Journal of Applied Psychology, 73,* 235–238.

Murphy, S. E., & Ensher, E. A. (1999). The effects of leader and subordinate characteristics in the development of leader–member exchange quality. *Journal of Applied Social Psychology, 29*(7), 1371–1394.

Murrell, A. J., Frieze, I. H., & Olson, J. E. (1996). Mobility strategies and career outcomes: A longitudinal study of MBAs. *Journal of Vocational Behavior, 49,* 324–335.

Nahum-Shani, I., & Somech, A. (2011). Leadership, OCB and individual differences: Idiocentrism and allocentrism as moderators of the relationship between transformational and transactional leadership and OCB. *The Leadership Quarterly, 22,* 353–366.

Naidoo, L. J., Scherbaum, C. A., Goldstein, H. W., & Graen, G. B. (2011). A longitudinal examination of the effects of LMX, ability, and differentiation on team performance. *Journal of Business and Psychology, 26,* 347–357.

National Coalition to Protect Family Leave (NCPFL). (n.d.). *Improvements to the FMLA regulations are urgently needed—Protect FMLA by clarifying "medical leave" provisions.* Retrieved March 30, 2009, from http://www.protectfamilyleave.org/about/issue.cfm

National Gay and Lesbian Task Force. (2008, July). *State nondiscrimination laws in the U.S.* [Map]. Retrieved March 30, 2009, from http://www.thetaskforce.org/downloads/reports/issue_maps/non_discrimination_7_08_color.pdf

National Gay and Lesbian Task Force. (2012, January). State nondiscrimination laws in the U.S. [Map]. Retrieved June 11, 2012, from http://www.thetaskforce.org/downloads/reports/issue_maps/non_discrimination_1_12_color.pdf

Neuman, G. A., & Wright, J. (1999). Team effectiveness: Beyond skills and cognitive ability. *Journal of Applied Psychology, 84*(3), 376–389.

Neuman, J. H., & Baron, R. A. (1998). Workplace violence and workplace aggression: Evidence concerning specific forms, potential causes, and preferred targets. *Journal of Management, 24*(3), 391–419.

Newton, T., & Keenan, T. (1991). Further analyses of the dispositional argument in organizational behavior. *Journal of Applied Psychology, 76*(6), 781–787.

Ng, K., Ang, S., & Chan, K. (2008). Personality and leader effectiveness: A moderated mediation model of leadership self-efficacy, job demands, and job autonomy. *Journal of Applied Psychology, 93,* 733–743.

Ng, T. W. H., Eby, L. T., Sorensen, K. L., & Feldman, D. C. (2005). Predictors of objective and subjective career success: A meta-analysis. *Personnel Psychology, 58,* 367–408.

Ng, T. W. H., Feldman, D. C., & Lam. S. S. K. (2010). Psychological contract breaches, organizational commitment, and innovation-related behaviors: A latent growth curve modeling approach. *Journal of Applied Psychology, 95*(4), 744–751.

Ng, T. W. H., Sorensen, K. L., & Feldman, D. C. (2007). Dimensions, antecedents, and consequences of workaholism: A conceptual integration and extension. *Journal of Organizational Behavior, 28,* 111–136.

Ng, T. W. H., Sorenson, K. L., & Yim, F. H. (2009). Does the job satisfaction–job performance relationship vary across cultures? *Journal of Cross-Cultural Psychology, 40,* 761–796.

Nielsen, T. M., Hrivnak, G. A., & Shaw, M. (2009). Organizational citizenship behavior and performance: A meta-analysis of group-level research. *Small Group Research, 40*(5), 555–577.

Nijstad, B. A., Stroebe, W., & Lodewijkx, H. F. M. (2003). Production blocking and idea generation: Does blocking interfere with cognitive processes? *Journal of Experimental Social Psychology, 39*(6), 531–548.

Nishii, L. H., & Mayer, D. M. (2009). Do inclusive leaders help reduce turnover in diverse groups? The moderating role of leader-member exchange in the diversity to turnover relationship. *Journal of Applied Psychology, 94,* 1412–1426.

Noonan, L. E., & Sulsky, L. M. (2001). Impact of frame-of-reference and behavioral observational training on alternative training effectiveness criteria in a Canadian military sample. *Human Performance, 14*(1), 3–26.

Norris-Watts, C., & Levy, P. E. (2004). The mediating role of affective commitment in the relation of the feedback environment to work outcomes. *Journal of Vocational Behavior, 65*(3), 351–365.

Northwestern National Life Employee Benefits Division. (1993). *Fear and violence in the workplace: A survey documenting the experience of American workers.* Minneapolis, MN: Northwestern National Life Insurance.

O'Boyle, E. H., Forsyth, D. R., & O'Boyle, A. S. (2011). Bad apples or bad barrels: An examination of group- and organizational-level effects in the study of counterproductive work behavior. *Group and Organization Management, 36*(1), 39–69.

O'Driscoll, M. P., Poelmans, S., Spector, P. E., Kalliath, T., Allen, T. D., Cooper, C. L., et al. (2003) Family-responsive interventions, perceived organizational and supervisor support, work–family conflict, and psychological strain. *International Journal of Stress Management, 10*(4), 326–344.

O'Leary-Kelly, A. M., Griffin, R. W., & Glew, D. J. (1996). Organization-motivated aggression: A research framework. *Academy of Management Review, 21*(1), 225–253.

O'Neill, B. S., & Mone, M. A. (1998). Investigating equity sensitivity as a moderator of relations between self-efficacy and workplace attitudes. *Journal of Applied Psychology, 83*(5), 805–816.

Occupational Information Network. (2009, January 13). *O*NET—Beyond information—Intelligence.* Retrieved March 5, 2009, from http://www.doleta.gov/programs/onet/

Oldham, G. R., & Hackman, J. R. (2010). Not what it was and not what it will be: The future of job design research. *Journal of Organizational Behavior, 31,* 463–479.

Ones, D. S., Dilchert, S., Viswesvaran, C., & Judge, T. A. (2007). In support of personality assessment in organization settings. *Personnel Psychology, 60*(4), 995–1027.

Ones, D. S., Viswesvaran, C., & Schmidt, F. L. (1993). Comprehensive meta-analysis of integrity test validities: Findings and implications for personnel selection and theories of job performance. *Journal of Applied Psychology, 78*(4), 679–703.

Orvis, K. A., Fisher, S. L., & Wasserman, M. E. (2009). Power to the people: Using learner control to improve trainee reactions and learning in web-based instruction environments. *Journal of Applied Psychology, 94*(4), 960–971.

Ostroff, C., & Atwater, L. E. (2003). Does whom you work with matter? Effects of referent group gender and age composition on managers' compensation. *Journal of Applied Psychology, 88*(4), 725–740.

Oyez Project. (n.d.). *PGA Tour v. Martin.* Retrieved April 20, 2009, from http://oyez.org/cases/2000-2009/2000/2000_00_24

Parents v. Seattle School District, 127 S. Ct. 2738 (2007).

Park, J., & Wentling, T. (2007). Factors associated with transfer of training in workplace e-learning. *Journal of Workplace Learning, 19*(5), 311–329.

Park, W. (2000). A comprehensive empirical investigation of the relationships among variables in the groupthink model. *Journal of Organizational Behavior, 21,* 873–887.

Patel, H., Pettitt, M., & Wilson, J. R. (2012). Factors of collaborative working: A framework for a collaboration model. *Applied Ergonomics, 43,* 1–26.

Paullay, I. M., Alliger, G. M., & Stone-Romero, E. F. (1994). Construct validation of two instruments designed to measure job involvement and work centrality. *Journal of Applied Psychology, 7*(92), 224–228.

Paulsen, N., Callan, V. J., Grice, T. A., Rooney, D., Gallois, C., Jones, E., et al. (2005). Job uncertainty and personal control during downsizing: A comparison of survivors and victims. *Human Relations, 58,* 463–496.

Payne, R. L. (2000). Eupsychian management and the millennium. *Journal of Managerial Psychology, 15*(3), 219–226.

Pedhazur, E. J., & Schmelkin, L. P. (1991). *Measurement, design, and analysis: An integrated approach* (2nd ed.). Hillsdale, NJ: Erlbaum.

Penttila, C. (2000). Testy, testy (weighing the value of employee drug testing). *Entrepreneur, 28*(6), 130.

Perretti, F., & Negro, G. (2007). Mixing genres and matching people: A study in innovation and team composition in Hollywood. *Journal of Organizational Behavior, 28,* 563–586.

Perry-Jenkins, M., Repetti, R. L., & Crouter, A. C. (2000). Work and family in the 1990s. *Journal of Marriage and the Family, 62,* 981–998.

Peterson, M. H., Griffith, R. L, & Converse, P. D. (2009). Examining the role of applicant faking in hiring decisions: Percentage of fakers hired and hiring discrepancies in single- and multiple-predictor selection. *Journal of Business and Psychology, 24,* 373–386.

Peterson, M. H., Griffith, R. L., Isaacson, J. A., O'Connell, M. S., & Mangos, P. M. (2011). Applicant faking, social desirability, and the prediction of counterproductive work behaviors. *Human Performance, 24,* 270–290.

Petit v. City of Chicago, 352 F.3d 1111 (7th Cir. 2003).

Petty, M. M., McGee, G. W., & Cavender, J. W. (1984). A meta-analysis of the relationships between individual job satisfaction and individual performance. *Academy of Management Review, 9*(4), 712–721.

Pfeffer, J. (1998). Seven practices of successful organizations. *California Management Review, 40*(2), 96–124.

Pfeffer, J., & Sutton, R. I. (1999). Knowing "what" to do is not enough: Turning knowledge into action. *California Management Review, 42*(1), 83–108.

Phillips, D. (1991, January 1). Pilots' training overcomes rare but deadly hazard. *The Washington Post,* p. A3.

Phillips, J. S., & Lord, R. G. (1981). Causal attributions and perceptions of leadership. *Organizational Behavior and Human Performance, 28,* 143–163.

Piedmont, R. L. (1998). *The revised NEO Personality Inventory: Clinical and research applications.* New York: Plenum Press.

Pierce, J. L., Gardner, D. G., Cummings, L. L., & Dunham, R. B. (1989). Organization-based self-esteem: Construct definition, measurement, and validation. *Academy of Management Journal, 32*(3), 622–648.

Pillai, R., Schriesheim, C. A., & Williams, E. S. (1999). Fairness perceptions and trust as mediators for transformational and transactional leadership: A two-sample study. *Journal of Management, 25*(6), 897–933.

Pinder, C. C. (1984). *Work motivation: Theories, issues and applications.* Dallas, TX: Scott, Foresman.

Pinder, C. C. (1998). *Work motivation in organizational behavior.* Upper Saddle River, NJ: Prentice-Hall.

Pinder, C. C. (2008). *Work motivation in organizational behavior.* Upper Saddle River, NJ: Psychology Press.

Ployhart, R. E. (2006). Staffing in the 21st century: New challenges and strategic opportunities. *Journal of Management, 32,* 868–897.

Podsakoff, N. P., Whiting, S. W., Podsakoff, P. M., & Blume, B. D. (2009). Individual- and organizational- level consequences of organizational citizenship behaviors: A meta-analysis. *Journal of Applied Psychology, 94*(1), 122–141.

Popovich, P. M., Scherbaum, C. A., Scherbaum, K. L., & Polinko, N. (2003). The assessment of attitudes toward individuals with disabilities in the workplace. *Journal of Psychology, 137*(2), 163–177.

Popper, K. (1959). *The logic of scientific discovery.* New York: Basic Books.

Porras, J. I., & Silvers, R. C. (1991). Organization development and transformation. *Annual Review of Psychology, 42,* 51–78.

Porter, C. O. L. H., Hollenbeck, J. R., Ilgen, D. R., Ellis, A. P. J., West, B. J., & Moon, H. (2003). Backing up behaviors in teams: The role of personality and legitimacy of need. *Journal of Applied Psychology, 88*(3), 391–403.

Positive Psychology Center (2007). *Positive psychology center.* Retrieved April 17, 2009, from http://www.ppc.sas.upenn.edu/

Posthuma, R. A. (2002). Employee selection procedures and the business necessity defense. *Applied HRM Research, 7*(1–2), 53–63.

Potosky, D., & Bobko, P. (2004). Selection testing via the Internet: Practical considerations and exploratory empirical findings. *Personnel Psychology, 57*(4), 1003–1034.

Powell, G.N., & Butterfield, D.A. (2011). Sex, gender, and the US presidency: Ready for a female president? *Gender in Management: An International Journal, 28*(6), 394–407.

Powers, D. E. (2004). Validity of Graduate Record Examinations (GRE) general test scores for admissions to colleges of veterinary medicine. *Journal of Applied Psychology, 89*(2), 208–219.

Preston, J. (2011). Social media history becomes a new job hurdle. Retrieved July 24, 2011, from http://www.nytimes.com/2011/07/21/technology/social-media-history-becomes-a-new-job-hurdle.html?

Primoff, E. S., & Eyde, L. D. (1988). Job element analysis. In S. Gael (Ed.), *The job analysis handbook for business, industry, and government* (Vol. 2, pp. 807–824). New York: Wiley.

Prince, C., & Stewart, J. (2002). Corporate universities: An analytical framework. *Journal of Management Development, 21*(10), 794–811.

Prince, J. B. (2003). Career opportunity and organizational attachment in a blue-collar unionized environment. *Journal of Vocational Behavior, 63,* 136–150.

Probst, T. M. (2000). Wedded to the job: Moderating effects of job involvement on the consequences of job insecurity. *Journal of Occupational Health Psychology, 5*(1), 63–73.

Procter & Gamble. (n.d.). *Diversity facts.* Retrieved April 1, 2009, from http://www.pg.com/company/who_we_are/diversity/global/diversity_facts.shtml

Psychological Corporation. (1979). *Revised manual for the Minnesota Clerical Test.* San Antonio, TX: Author.

Psychological Corporation. (1980). *The Bennett Mechanical Comprehension Test manual.* San Antonio, TX: Author.

Pulakos, E. D. (1984). A comparison of rater training programs: Error training and accuracy training. *Journal of Applied Psychology, 69,* 581–588.

Pulakos, E. D. (1986). The development of training programs to increase accuracy. *Organizational Behavior and Human Decision Processes, 38,* 76–91.

Qiao, J. X. (2008). Corporate universities in China: Processes, issues, and challenges. *Journal of Workplace Learning, 21*(2), 166–174.

Rademakers, M. (2005). Corporate universities: Driving force of knowledge innovation. *The Journal of Workplace Learning, 17*(1/2), 130–136.

Ree, J. M., Earles, J. A., & Teachout, M. S. (1994). Predicting job performance: Not much more than g. *Journal of Applied Psychology, 79*(4), 518–524.

Rees, C. J., & Metcalfe, B. (2003). The faking of personality questionnaire results: Who's kidding whom? *Journal of Managerial Psychology, 18*(2), 156–165.

Rego, A., & Cunha, M. P. (2010). Organisational justice and citizenship behaviors: A study in the Portuguese cultural context. *Applied Psychology: An International Review, 59*(3), 404–430.

Reilly, R. R., & McGourty, J. (1998). Performance appraisal in team settings. In J. W. Smither (Ed.), *Performance appraisal: State of the art in practice* (pp. 244–277). San Francisco: Jossey-Bass.

Reiter-Palmon, R., Brown, M., Sandall, D. L., Buboltz, C., & Nimps, T. (2006). Development of an O*NET web-based job analysis and its implementation in the U.S. Navy: Lessons learned. *Human Resource Management Review, 16,* 294–309.

Renko, M., Kroeck, K. G., & Bullough, A. (2011). Expectancy theory and nascent entrepreneurship. *Small Business Economics.* doi: 10.1007/s11187-011-9354-3

Rennie, J. (2007, January 22). *Stressed with work? Blame office politics*. Retrieved April 21, 2009, from http://www.eveningtimes.co.uk/news/display.Var.1137551.0.stressed_with_work_blame_office_politics.php

Rhoades, L., & Eisenberger, R. (2002). Perceived organizational support: A review of the literature. *Journal of Applied Psychology, 87*(4), 698–714.

Riggio, R. E., & Lee, J. (2007). Emotional and interpersonal competencies and leader development. *Human Resource Management Review, 17*, 418–426.

Riketta, M. (2002). Attitudinal organizational commitment and job performance: A meta-analysis. *Journal of Organizational Behavior, 23*(3), 257–266.

Ritter, B. A., & Lord, R. G. (2007). The impact of previous leaders on the evaluation of new leaders: An alternative to prototype matching. *Journal of Applied Psychology, 92*, 1683–1695.

Roberson, L., Kulik, C. T., & Pepper, M. B. (2003). Using needs assessment to resolve controversies in diversity training design. *Group and Organization Management, 28*(1), 148–174.

Roberson, L., Kulik, C. T., & Pepper, M. B. (2009). Individual and environmental factors influencing the use of transfer strategies after diversity training. *Group & Organization Management, 34*(1), 67–89.

Roch, S. G., & O'Sullivan, B. J. (2003). Frame of reference rater training issues: Recall, time and behavior observation training. *International Journal of Training and Development, 7*(2), 93–107.

Rode, J. C., Mooney, C. H., Arthaud-Day, M. L., Near, J. P., Baldwin, T. T., Rubin, R. S., et al. (2007). Emotional intelligence and individual performance: Evidence of direct and moderated effects. *Journal of Organizational Behavior, 28*(4), 399–421.

Rodgers, R., & Hunter, J. E. (1991). Impact of management by objectives on organizational productivity. *Journal of Applied Psychology, 76*(2), 322–336.

Roehling, M. V., & Wright, P. (2004). Organizationally sensible v. legal-centric responses to the eroding employment at-will doctrine. *Employee Responsibilities and Rights Journal, 16*(2), 89–103.

Roethlisberger, F. J., & Dickson, W. J. (1939). *Management and the worker.* Cambridge, MA: Harvard University Press.

Rogelberg, S. G., & Gill, P. M. (2004). The growth of industrial and organizational psychology: Quick facts. *The Industrial-Organizational Psychologist, 42*(1), 25–27.

Rooney v. Koch Air, LLC., 410 F.3d 376 (U.S. App. 2005).

Roppolo, L. P., Heymann, R., Pepe, P., Wagner, J., Commons, B., Miller, R., Allen, E., Horne, L., Wainscott, M. P., & Idris, A. H. (2011). A randomized controlled trial comparing traditional training in cardiopulmonary resuscitation (CPR) to self-directed CPR learning in first year medical students: The two-person CPR study. *Resuscitation, 82*(3), 319–325.

Rosanas, J. M. (2008). Beyond economic criteria: A humanistic approach to organizational survival. *Journal of Business Ethics, 78*, 447–462.

Rose, A., Timm, H., Pogson, C., Gonzalez, J., Appel, E., & Kolb, N. (2010). *Developing a cybervetting strategy for law enforcement: A special report.* Defense Personnel Security Research Center (PERSEREC). Washington, DC: U. S. Department of Defense.

Rosen, C. C., Chang, C. H., Johnson, R. E., & Levy, P. E. (2009). Perceptions of the organizational context and psychological contract breach: Assessing competing perspectives. *Organizational Behavior and Human Decision Processes, 108*, 202–217.

Rosen, C. C., Levy, P. E., & Hall, R. J. (2006). Placing perceptions of politics in the context of feedback environment, employee attitudes, and job performance. *Journal of Applied Psychology, 91*(1), 211–220.

Rosenthal, R. (1991). *Meta-analytic procedures for social research* (rev. ed.). Thousand Oaks, CA: SAGE.

Rosette, A. S., Leonardelli, G. J., & Phillips, K. W. (2008). The White standard: Racial bias in leader categorization. *Journal of Applied Psychology, 93*, 758–777.

Roth, P. L., Bobko, P., & Mabon, H. (2002). Utility analysis: A review and analysis at the turn of the century. In N. Anderson, D. S. Ones, C. Viswesvaran, & H. K. Sinangil (Eds.), *Handbook of industrial, work and organizational psychology: Vol. 1. Personnel psychology* (pp. 383–384). Thousand Oaks, CA: SAGE.

Roth, P. L., Bobko, P., & McFarland, L. A. (2005). A meta-analysis of work sample test validity: Updating and integrating some classic literature. *Personnel Psychology, 58*(4), 1009–1037.

Roth, P. L., Bobko, P., & Switzer, F. S., III. (2006). Modeling the behavior of the 4/5ths rule for determining adverse impact: Reasons for caution. *Journal of Applied Psychology, 91*(3), 507–522.

Rothausen, T. J., Gonzalez, J. A., Clarke, N. E., & O'Dell, L. L. (1998). Family-friendly backlash—Fact or fiction? The case of organizations' on-site child-care centers. *Personnel Psychology, 51,* 685–706.

Rotundo, M., & Sackett, P. R. (2002). The relative importance of task, citizenship, and counterproductive performance to global ratings of job performance: A policy-capturing approach. *Journal of Applied Psychology, 87*(1), 66–80.

Rounds. J., Armstrong, P. I., Liao, H. Y., Lewis, P., & Rivkin, D. (2008). *Second generation occupational interest profiles for the O*NET system: Summary.* Raleigh, NC: National Center for O*NET Development. Retrieved July 11, 2012, from http://www.onetcenter.org/dl_files/SecondOIP_Summary.pdf

Rousseau, D. M. (2001). Idiosyncratic deals: Flexibility vs. fairness? *Organizational Dynamics, 29,* 260–271.

Rudisill, J. R., & Edwards, J. M. (2002). Coping with job transitions. *Consulting Psychology Journal: Practice and Research, 54*(1), 55–64.

Rutkowski, K. A., & Steelman, L. A. (2005). Testing a path model for antecedents of accountability. *Journal of Management Development, 24*(5), 473–486.

Ryan, R. M., & Deci, E. L. (2000). Self-determination theory and the facilitation of intrinsic motivation, social development, and well-being. *American Psychologist, 55*(1), 68–78.

Rynes, S. L., & Cable, D. M. (2003). Recruitment research in the twenty-first century. In W. C. Borman, D. R. Ilgen, & R. Klimoski (Eds.), *Handbook of psychology: Vol. 12. Industrial and organizational psychology* (pp. 55–76). New York: Wiley.

Rynes, S. L., Gerhart, B., & Parks, L. (2005). Personnel psychology: Performance evaluation and pay for performance. *Annual Review of Psychology, 56,* 571–600.

Rynes, S. L., & Rosen, B. (1995). A field survey of factors affecting the adoption and perceived success of diversity training. *Personnel Psychology, 48,* 247–270.

Saal, F. E., Downey, R. G., & Lahey, M. A. (1980). Rating the ratings: Assessing the quality of rating data. *Psychological Bulletin, 88,* 413–428.

Sablynski, C. J., Lee, T. W., Mitchell, T. R., Burton, J. P., & Holtom, B. C. (2002). Turnover: An integration of Lee and Mitchell's unfolding model and job embeddedness construct with Hulin's withdrawal construct. In J. M. Brett & F. Drasgow (Eds.), *The psychology of work: Theoretically based empirical research* (pp. 189–203). Mahwah, NJ: Erlbaum.

Sachau, D. A. (2007). Resurrecting the motivation-hygiene theory: Herzberg and the positive psychology movement. *Human Resource Development Review, 6,* 377–393.

Sackett, P. R. (1994). *The content and process of the research enterprise within industrial and organizational psychology.* Presidential address presented at the 9th Annual Conference of the Society for Industrial and Organizational Psychology, Nashville, TN.

Sackett, P. R., & Laczo, R. M. (2003). Job and work analysis. In W. C. Borman, D. R. Ilgen, & R. J. Klimoski (Eds.), *Handbook of psychology: Industrial and organizational psychology* (Vol. 12, pp. 21–37). New York: Wiley.

Sackett, P. R., & Wanek, J. E. (1996). New developments in the use of measures of honesty, integrity, conscientiousness, dependability, trustworthiness, and reliability for personnel selection. *Personnel Psychology, 49,* 787–829.

Sagie, A. (1998). Employee absenteeism, organizational commitment, and job satisfaction: Another look. *Journal of Vocational Behavior, 52,* 156–171.

Sahibzada, K., Hammer, L. B., Neal, M. B., & Kuang, D. C. (2005). The moderating effects of work–family role combinations and work–family organizational culture on the relationship between family-friendly workplace supports and job satisfaction. *Journal of Family Issues, 26*(6), 820–839.

Salam, S., Cox, J. F., & Sims, H. P., Jr., (1997). In the eye of the beholder: How leadership relates to 360-degree feedback system attitudes. *Group and Organization Management, 22*(2), 185–209.

Salas, E., Rozell, D., Mullen, B., & Driskell, J. E. (1999). The effect of team building on performance: An integration. *Small Group Research, 30*(3), 309–329.

Salgado, J. F. (2002). The Big Five personality dimensions and counterproductive behaviors. *International Journal of Selection and Assessment, 10*(1–2), 117–125.

Salgado, J. F., & Anderson, N. (2003). Validity generalization of GMA tests across countries in the European community. *European Journal of Work and Organizational Psychology, 12*(1), 1–17.

Salgado, J. F., Anderson, N., Moscoso, S., Bertua, C., de Fruyt, F., & Rolland, J. P. (2003). A meta-analytic study of general mental ability validity for different occupations in the European community. *Journal of Applied Psychology, 88*(6), 1068–1081.

Sanchez, J. I., & Levine, E. L. (2009). What is (or should be) the difference between competency modeling and traditional job analysis? *Human Resource Management Review, 19*, 53–63.

Sanchez, R. J., Truxillo, D. M., & Bauer, T. N. (2000). Development and examination of an expectancy-based measure of test-taking motivation. *Journal of Applied Psychology, 85*(5), 739–750.

Sanz-Valle, R., Naranjo-Valencia, J. C., Jimenez-Jimenez, D., & Perez-Caballero, L. (2011). Linking organizational learning with technical innovation and organizational culture. *Journal of Knowledge Management, 15*(6), 997–1015.

Sarin, S., & O'Connor, G. C. (2009). First among equals: The effect of team leader characteristics on the internal dynamics of cross-functional product development teams. *Journal of Product Innovation Management, 26*(2), 188–205.

Schappe, S. P. (1998). Understanding employee job satisfaction: The importance of procedural and distributive justice. *Journal of Business and Psychology, 12*(4), 493–503.

Schaubroeck, J., Lam, S. S. K., & Cha, S. E. (2007). Embracing transformational leadership: Team values and the impact of leader behavior on team performance. *Journal of Applied Psychology, 92*, 1020–1030.

Scheer, L. K., Kumar, N., & Steenkamp, J.-B. E. M. (2003). Reactions to perceived inequity in U.S. and Dutch interorganizational relationships. *Academy of Management Journal, 46*(3), 303–316.

Schein, E. H. (1980). *Organizational psychology* (3rd ed.). Englewood Cliffs, NJ: Prentice-Hall.

Schellenberg, K., & Miller, G. A. (1998). Turbulence and bureaucracy. *Journal of Applied Behavioral Science, 34*(2), 202–221.

Schilling, M. S., Oeser, N., & Schaub, C. (2007). How effective are decision analyses? Assessing decision process and group alignment effects. *Decision Analysis, 4*(4), 227–242.

Schippmann, J. S., Ash, R. A., Battista, M., Carr, L., Eyde, L. D., Hesketh, B., et al. (2000). The practice of competency modeling. *Personnel Psychology, 53*, 703–740.

Schleicher, D. J., Day, D. V., Mayes, B. T., & Riggio, R. E. (2002). A new frame for frame-of-reference training: Enhancing the construct validity of assessment centers. *Journal of Applied Psychology, 87*(4), 735–746.

Schmidt, F. L., & Hunter, J. E. (1998). The validity and utility of selection methods in personnel psychology: Practical and theoretical implications of 85 years of research findings. *Psychological Bulletin, 124*(2), 262–274.

Schmidt, F. L., & Kaplan, L. B. (1971). Composite vs. multiple criteria: A review and resolution of the controversy. *Personnel Psychology, 24*, 419–434.

Schmidt, F. L., & Oh, I. (2010) Can synthetic validity methods achieve discriminant validity? *Industrial and Organizational Psychology, 3*(3), 344–350.

Schmidt, S. R. (1999). Long-run trends in workers' beliefs about their own job security: Evidence from the General Social Survey. *Journal of Labor Economics, 17*(Suppl. 4), S127–S141.

Schmitt, N., Gooding, R. Z., Noe, R. A., & Kirsch, M. (1984). Meta-analyses of validity studies published between 1964 and 1982 and the investigation of study characteristics. *Personnel Psychology, 37*, 407–422.

Schneider, B., Hanges, P. J., Goldstein, H. W., & Braverman, E. P. (1994). Do customer service perceptions generalize? The case of student and chair ratings of faculty effectiveness. *Journal of Applied Psychology, 79*(5), 685–690.

Schneider, R. J., Goff, M., Anderson, S., & Borman, W. C. (2003). Computerized adaptive rating scales for measuring managerial performance. *International Journal of Selection and Assessment, 11*(2/3), 237–246.

Schriesheim, C. A., House, R. J., & Kerr, C. (1976). Leader initiating structure: A reconciliation of discrepant research results and some empirical tests. *Organizational Behavior and Human Performance, 15*(2), 297–321.

Schriesheim, C. A., & Neider, L. L. (1996). Path-goal leadership theory: The long and winding road. *Leadership Quarterly, 7*(3), 317–321.

Schroeders, U., & Wilhelm, U. (2010). Testing reasoning ability with handheld computers, notebooks and paper and pencil. *European Journal of Psychological Assessment, 26*(4), 284–292.

Schuerger, J. M. (1995). Career assessment and the Sixteen Personality Factor Questionnaire. *Journal of Career Assessment, 3*(2), 157–175.

Schwartz, J. (1990, November 5). How safe is your job? *Newsweek, 5,* 44–47.

Scott, K. A. & Brown, D. J. (2006). Female first, leader second? Gender bias in the encoding of leadership behavior. *Organizational Behavior and Human Decision Processes, 101,* 130–242.

Scott, K. D., & Taylor, G. S. (1985). An examination of conflicting findings on the relationship between job satisfaction and absenteeism: A meta-analysis. *Academy of Management Journal, 28*(3), 599–612.

Scott, W. D. (1903). *The theory of advertising.* Boston: Small, Maynard.

Searle, B. J. (2008). Does personal initiative training work as a stress management intervention? *Journal of Occupational Health Psychology, 13,* 259–270.

Seaward, M. R. (1999). The sandwich generation copes with elder care. *Benefits Quarterly, 15*(2), 41–48.

Seidler-de Alwis, R., & Hartmann, E. (2008). The use of tacit knowledge within innovative companies: Knowledge management in innovative enterprises. *Journal of Knowledge Management, 12,* 133–147.

Seijts, G. H., & Kyei-Poku, I. (2010). The role of situational interviews in fostering positive reactions to selection decisions. *Applied Psychology: An International Review, 59*(30), 431–453.

Semadar, A., Robins, G., & Ferris, G. R. (2006). Comparing the validity of multiple social effectiveness constructs in the prediction of managerial job performance. *Journal of Organizational Behavior, 27*(4), 443–461.

Senécal, J., Loughead, T. M., & Bloom, G. A. (2008). A season-long team-building intervention program: Examining the effect of team goal setting on cohesion. *Journal of Sport & Exercise Psychology, 30*(2), 186–199.

Senge, P. M. (2006). *The leader's new work: Building learning organizations.* San Francisco: Jossey-Bass.

Shafritz, J. M., & Ott, J. S. (1996a). Classical organization theory. In J. M. Shafritz & J. S. Ott (Eds.), *Classics of organization theory* (4th ed., pp. 29–37). Belmont, CA: Wadsworth.

Shafritz, J. M., & Ott, J. S. (1996b). Introduction. In J. M. Shafritz & J. S. Ott (Eds.), *Classics of organization theory* (4th ed., pp. 1–28). Belmont, CA: Wadsworth.

Shafritz, J. M., Ott, J. S., & Jang, Y. S. (2011). *Classics of Organizational Theory* (Vol. 7). Belmont, CA: Wadsworth.

Shanock, L. R., & Eisenberger, R. (2006). When supervisors feel supported: Relationships with subordinates' perceived supervisor support, perceived organizational support, and performance. *Journal of Applied Psychology, 91,* 689–695.

Shore, L. M., Tetrick, L. E., Shore, T. H., & Barksdale, K. (2000). Construct validity of measures of Becker's side bet theory. *Journal of Vocational Behavior, 57,* 428–444.

Silverman, S. B. (1991). Individual development through performance appraisal. In K. N. Wexley (Ed.), *Developing human resources* (Vol. 5, pp. 120–151) Washington, DC: Bureau of National Affairs.

Simons, T., & Roberson, Q. (2003). Why managers should care about fairness: The effects of aggregate justice perceptions on organizational outcomes. *Journal of Applied Psychology, 88*(3), 432–443.

Sims, H. P., Jr., Faraj, S., & Yun, S. (2009). When should a leader be directive or empowering? How to develop your own situational theory of leadership. *Business Horizons, 52*(2), 149–158.

Singh, P. (2008). Job analysis for a changing workplace. *Human Resource Management Review, 18,* 87–99.

Singleton, J. L. (2001). Elder caregiving: The impact on paid job performance. *Dissertation Abstracts International, 62*(4), 1600A. (UMI No. AAI3014333)

Slaughter, J. E., Sinar, E. F., & Bachiochi, P. D. (2002). Black applications' reactions to affirmative action plans: Effects of plan content and previous experience with discrimination. *Journal of Applied Psychology, 87*(2), 333–344.

Smith, A. (2012). EEOC hearing highlights pregnancy and caregiver discrimination. Retrieved March 13, 2012, from http://www.shrm.org/LegalIssues/FederalResources/Pages/EEOCHearingPDA.aspx

Smith, J. A., & Foti, R. J. (1998). A pattern approach to the study of leader emergence. *Leadership Quarterly, 9*(2), 147–160.

Smith, P. C., & Kendall, L. M. (1963). Retranslation of expectations: An approach to the construction of unambiguous anchors for rating scales. *Journal of Applied Psychology, 47,* 149–155.

Smith, P. C., Kendall, L. M., & Hulin, C. L. (1969). *Measurement of satisfaction in work and retirement.* Chicago: Rand McNally.

Smither, J. W., London, M., Flautt, R., Vargas, Y., & Kucine, I. (2003). Can working with an executive coach improve multisource feedback ratings over time? A quasi-experimental field study. *Personnel Psychology, 56*(1), 23–44.

Snell, A. F., Sydell, E. J., & Lueke, S. B. (1999). Towards a theory of applicant faking: Integrating studies of deception. *Human Resource Management Review, 9*(2), 219–242.

Society for Industrial and Organizational Psychology. (n.d.). *Graduate training programs in industrial-organizational psychology and related fields.* Retrieved October 6, 2006, from http://www.siop.org/GTP/

Society for Industrial and Organizational Psychology. (1999). *Guidelines for education and training at the doctoral level in industrial-organizational psychology.* Retrieved October 11, 2006, from http://www.siop.org/PhDGuidelines98.Aspx

Society for Industrial and Organizational Psychology. (2006a). *Building better organizations.* Retrieved March 2, 2009, from http://www.siop.org/visibilitybrochure/siopbrochure.aspx

Society for Industrial and Organizational Psychology. (2006b). Personal communication, Larry Nader, March 20, 2009.

Society for Industrial and Organizational Psychology. (2010). Personal communication, Larry Nader, December 2, 2010.

Somech, A., & Drach-Zahavy, A. (2007). Strategies for coping with work–family conflict: The distinctive relationships of gender role ideology. *Journal of Occupational Health Psychology, 12,* 1–19.

Song, L. J., Huang, G., Peng, K. Z., Law, K. S., Wong, C., & Chen, Z. (2010). The differential effects of general mental ability and emotional intelligence on academic performance and social interactions. *Intelligence, 38*(1), 137–143.

Sonnentag, S., Binnewies, C., & Mojza, E. J. (2010). Staying well and engaged when demands are high: The role of psychological detachment. *Journal of Applied Psychology, 95*(5), 965–976.

Soroka v. Dayton Hudson, Cal. H143579-3 (1989).

Spector, P. E. (1997). The role of frustration in antisocial behavior at work. In R. A. Giacalone & J. Greenberg (Eds.), *Antisocial behavior in organizations* (pp. 1–17). Thousand Oaks, CA: SAGE.

Spector, P. E., Bauer, J. A., & Fox, S. (2010). Measurement artifacts in the assessment of counterproductive work behavior and organizational citizenship behavior: Do we know what we think we know? *Journal of Applied Psychology, 95*(4), 781–790.

Spector, P. E., & Fox, S. (2010). Counterproductive work behaviors and organizational citizenship behavior: Are they opposite forms of active behavior? *Applied Psychology: An International Review, 59*(1), 21–39.

Spector, P. E., Fox, S., Penney, L. M, Bruursema, K., Goh, A., & Kessler, S. (2006). The dimensionality of counterproductivity: Are all counterproductive behaviors created equal? *Journal of Vocational Behavior, 68*(3), 446–460.

Spector, P. E., & Jex, S. M. (1991). Relations of job characteristics from multiple data sources with employee affect, absence, turnover intentions, and health. *Journal of Applied Psychology, 76,* 46–53.

Spence, J. T., & Robbins, A. S. (1992). Workaholism: Definition, measurement, and preliminary results. *Journal of Personality Assessment, 58,* 160–178.

Spies, R. A., Carlson, J. F. & Geisinger, J. F. (2010). *The Eighteenth Mental Measurements Yearbook.* Lincoln, NE: Buros Institute of Mental Measurements.

Spink, K. S., Wilson, K. S., & Odnokon, P. (2010). Examining the relationship between cohesion and return to team in elite athletes. *Psychology of Sport and Exercise, 11,* 6–11.

Spool, M. D. (1978). Training programs for observers of behavior: A review. *Personnel Psychology, 31*(4), 853–888.

Srivastava, A., Locke, E. A., Judge, T. A., & Adams, J. W. (2010). Core self-evaluations as causes of satisfaction: The mediating role of seeking task complexity. *Journal of Vocational Behavior, 77,* 255–265.

Stajkovic, A. D., & Luthans, F. (1997). A meta-analysis of the effects of organizational behavior modification on task performance. *Academy of Management Journal, 40*(5), 1122–1149.

Stanton, J. M., & Coovert, M. D. (2004). Guest editors' note: Turbulent waters: The intersection of information technology and human resources. *Human Resource Management Journal, 43*(2–3), 121–125.

Stanton, J. M., & Rogelberg, S. G. (2001). Using Internet/intranet web pages to collect organizational research data. *Organizational Research Methods, 4*(3), 200–217.

Stanton, J. M., Sinar, E. F., Balzer, W. K., Julian, A. L., Thoresen, P., Aziz, S., et al. (2002). Development of a compact measure of job satisfaction: The abridged Job Descriptive Index. *Educational and Psychological Measurement, 62*(1), 173–191.

Staw, B. M., & Cohen-Charash, Y. (2005). The dispositional approach to job satisfaction: More than a mirage, but not yet an oasis. *Journal of Organizational Behavior, 26*, 59–78.

Staw, B. M., & Ross, J. (1985). Stability in the midst of change: A dispositional approach to job attitudes. *Journal of Applied Psychology, 7*(3), 469–480.

Steel, R. P., & Rentsch, J. R. (1997). The dispositional model of job attitudes revisited: Findings of a 10-year study. *Journal of Applied Psychology, 82*(6), 873–879.

Steel, R. P., Rentsch, J. R., & Van Scotter, J. R. (2007). Timeframes and absence frameworks: A test of Steers and Rhodes' (1978) model of attendance. *Journal of Management, 33*, 180–195.

Steele-Johnson, D., Beauregard, R. S., Hoover, P. B., & Schmidt, A. M. (2000). Goal orientation and task demand effects on motivation, affect, and performance. *Journal of Applied Psychology, 85*(5), 724–738.

Steele-Johnson, D., Osburn, H. G., & Pieper, K. F. (2000). A review and extension of current models of dynamic criteria. *International Journal of Selection and Assessment, 8*(3), 110–136.

Steelman, L. A., Levy, P. E., & Snell, A. F. (2004). The feedback environment scale (FES): Construct definition, measurement, and validation. *Education and Psychological Measurement, 64*(1), 165–184.

Steers, R. M., Mowday, R. T., & Shapiro, D. L. (2004). Introduction to special topic forum: The future of work motivation theory. *Academy of Management Review, 29*(3), 379–387.

Steers, R. M., Porter, L. M., & Bigley, G. A. (1996). *Motivation and leadership at work* (6th ed.). New York: McGraw-Hill.

Steers, R. M., & Rhodes, S. R. (1978). Major influences on employee attendance: A process model. *Journal of Applied Psychology, 63*(4), 391–407.

Steiner, I. D. (1972). *Group processes and productivity.* New York: Academic Press.

Sterns, H. L., Doverspike, D., & Lax, G. (2005). The age discrimination in employment act. In F. Landy (Ed.), *Employment discrimination litigation: Behavioral, quantitative, and legal perspectives* (pp. 256–293). San Francisco: Jossey-Bass.

Stevens, M. J., & Campion, M. A. (1999). Staffing work teams: Development and validation of a selection test for teamwork settings. *Journal of Management, 25*(2), 207–228.

Stevens, S. (1968, August 30). Measurement, statistics, and the schemapiric view. *Science, 161*, 849–856.

Stewart, G. L. (2006). A meta-analytic investigation of relationships between team design features and team performance. *Journal of Management, 32*, 29–55.

Stewart, G. L., Fulmer, I. S., & Barrick, M. R. (2005). An exploration of member roles as a multilevel linking mechanism for individual traits and team outcomes. *Personnel Psychology, 58*, 343–365.

Stewart, T. A. (1998, January 12). The leading edge: Is this job really necessary? *Fortune, 137*(1), 154–157.

Stewart, T. A. (2000, October 2). The house that knowledge built. *Fortune, 142*(7), 278–279.

Stogdill, R. M. (1948). Personal factors associated with leadership: A survey of the literature. *Journal of Psychology, 25*, 35–71.

Stogdill, R. M. (1963). *Manual for the Leader Behavior Description Questionnaire–Form XII: An experimental revision.* Columbus, OH: Bureau of Business Research, Ohio State University.

Stogdill, R. M. (1974). *Handbook of leadership: A survey of theory and research.* New York: Free Press.

Stokes, G. S., & Cooper, L. A. (1994). Selection using biodata: Old notions revisited. In G. S. Stokes, M. M. Mumford, & W. A. Owens (Eds.), *Biodata handbook: Theory, research, and use of biographical information in selection and performance prediction* (pp. 311–350). Palo Alto, CA: Consulting Psychologists Press.

Stone, D. L., & Lukaszewski, K. M. (2009). An expanded model of the factors affecting the acceptance and effectiveness of electronic human resource management systems. *Human Resource Management Review, 19*(2), 134–143.

Strong, E. K. (1927). Vocational interest test. *Educational Record, 8,* 107–121.

Student Loan Girl. (2008). *Number of students taking ACT goes up, scores go down.* Retrieved April 18, 2009, from the NextStudent website: http://www.nextstudent.com/student-loan-blog/blogs/sample_weblog/archive/2008/08/14/1017.aspx

Sulsky, L. M., & Day, D. V. (1994). Effects of frame-of-reference training and cognitive categorization: An empirical investigation of rater memory issues. *Journal of Applied Psychology, 79,* 535–543.

Sulzer-Azaroff, B., Loafman, B., Merante, R. J., & Hlavacek, A. C. (1990). Improving occupational safety in a large industrial plant: A systematic replication. *Journal of Organizational Behavior Management, 11*(1), 99–120.

Sundstrom, E., DeMeuse, K. P., & Futrell, D. (1990). Work teams: Applications and effectiveness. *American Psychologist, 45,* 120–133.

Sundstrom, E., McIntyre, M., Halfhill, T., & Richards, H. (2000). Work groups: From the Hawthorne Studies to work teams of the 1990s and beyond. *Group Dynamics: Theory, Research, and Practice, 4*(1), 44–67.

Sutton, J. (2004, April). *BellSouth business technical training transformation.* Retrieved April 19, 2009, from http://www.geewizwow.com/articles/BellSouth-Bus%20Tech-Training-Transforamtion-Final-Version-4-2004-b.pdf

Svyantek, D. J., Goodman, S. A., Benz, L. L., Gard, J. A. (1999). The relationship between organizational characteristics and team building success. *Journal of Business and Psychology, 14*(2), 265–283.

Sweeney, P. D., & McFarlin, D. B. (1993). Workers' evaluations of the "ends" and the "means": An examination of four models of distributive and procedural justice. *Organizational Behavior and Human Decision Processes, 55,* 23–40.

Tang, T. L., & Ibrahim, A. H. S. (1998). Antecedents of organizational citizenship behavior revisited: Public personnel in the United States and in the Middle East. *Public Personnel Management, 27*(4), 529–550.

Tangri, Ravi. (n.d.). *What stress costs.* Retrieved December 8, 2008, from http://www.cocreatingfutures.com/content.php?page_ID=690

Tata, J. (2002). The influence of managerial accounts on employees' reactions to negative feedback. *Group and Organization Management, 27*(4), 480–503.

Tata, J., Prasad, S., & Thorn, R. (1999). The influence of organizational structure on the effectiveness of TQM programs. *Journal of Managerial Issues, 11*(4), 440–453.

Taylor, F. M. (1996). The principles of scientific management. In J. M. Shafritz & J. S. Ott (Eds.), *Classics of organization theory* (4th ed., pp. 66–79). Belmont, CA: Wadsworth. (Reprinted from *Bulletin of the Taylor Society,* 1916).

Taylor, H. C., & Russell, T. (1939). The relationship of validity coefficients to the practical effectiveness of tests in selection: Discussion and tables. *Journal of Applied Psychology, 23,* 565–578.

Tepper, B. J., Lockhart, D., & Hoobler, J. (2001). Justice, citizenship, and role definition effects. *Journal of Applied Psychology, 86*(4), 789–796.

Tetrick, L. E., Miles, R. L., Marcil, L., & Van Dosen, C. M. (1994). Child-care difficulties and the impact on concentration, stress, and productivity among single and nonsingle mothers and fathers. In G. P. Keita & J. J. Hurrell, Jr. (Eds.), *Job stress in a changing workforce: Investigating gender, diversity, and family issues* (pp. 229–239). Washington, DC: American Psychological Association.

Tett, R. P., Jackson, D. N., Rothstein, M., & Reddon, J. R. (1999). Meta-analysis of bidirectional relationships in personality–job performance research. *Human Performance, 12*(1), 1–29.

Texas Instruments. (n.d.). *Diversity and inclusion.* Retrieved April 1, 2009, from http://www.Ti.com/corp/docs/csr/empwellbeing/diversity/

Theorell, T., & Karasek, R. A. (1996). Current issues relating to psychosocial job strain and cardiovascular disease research. *Journal of Occupational Health Psychology, 1*(1), 9–26.

Thorndike, R. L. (1949). *Personnel selection.* New York: Wiley.

Thurston, P.W., & McNall, L. (2010). Justice perceptions of performance appraisal practices. *Journal of Managerial Psychology, 25*(3), 201–228.

Timmermann, S. (1999). From childcare to eldercare: Our turn to care for mom and dad. *Journal of Financial Service Professionals, 53*(5), 28–31.

Tippins, N. T., Beaty, J., Gibson, W. M., Pearlman, K., Segall, D. O., & Shepherd, W. (2006). Unproctored Internet testing in employment settings. *Personnel Psychology, 59,* 189–225.

Tobin, T. J. (2001). Organizational determinants of violence in the workplace. *Aggression and Violent Behavior, 6,* 91–102.

Toffler, A. (1980). *The third wave.* New York: Morrow.

Tolman, E. C. (1932). *Purposive behavior in animals and men.* New York: Century.

Toossi, M. (2007, November). Labor force projections to 2016: More workers in their golden years. *Monthly Labor Review, 130,* 33–52.

Training magazine ranks 2012 top 125 organizations. (2012). Retrieved from http://www.trainingmag.com/article/training-magazine-ranks-2012-top-125-organizations

Tuckman, B. W. (1965). Developmental sequences in small groups. *Psychological Bulletin, 63,* 384–399.

Tuckman, B. W., & Jensen, M. A. C. (1977). Stages of small group development revisited. *Group and Organizational Studies, 2,* 419–427.

U.S. Bureau of Labor Statistics. (n.d.). *Mass layoff statistics.* Retrieved October 6, 2006, from http://www.bls.gov/data/home.htm

U.S. Bureau of Labor Statistics. (2007). *Injuries, illnesses, and fatalities: Fatal cases added on the revised 2005 file.* Retrieved August 21, 2008, from http://data.bls.gov/cgi-bin/print.pl/iif/oshwc/cfoi/cfoi_revised05.htm

U.S. Bureau of Labor Statistics. (2008a). *Economic news release: Mass layoffs summary.* Retrieved December 9, 2008, from http://www.bls.gov/news.release/mslo.nr0.htm

U.S. Bureau of Labor Statistics. (2008b, August 20). *Fatal occupational injuries by event or exposure, 2006–2007* [Table]. Retrieved April 25, 2009, from http://www.bls.gov/news.release/cfoi.T01.htm

U.S. Bureau of Labor Statistics. (2008c). *Table R31* [Electronic version]. Retrieved December 7, 2008, from www.bls.gov/iif/oshwc/osh/case/ostb1823.pdf

U.S. Bureau of Labor Statistics. (2010). *Occupational outlook handbook.* Retrieved November 27, 2010, from http://www.bls.gov/oco/ocos056.htm

U.S. Department of Labor. (n.d.). *Federal vs. state family and medical leave laws.* Retrieved March 30, 2009, from http://www.dol.gov/esa/programs/whd/state/fmla/index.htm

U.S. Department of Labor. (2005, October 7). *Obligation to solicit race and gender data for agency enforcement purposes.* [Electronic version]. *Federal Register, 70,* 58946–58963.

U.S. Department of Labor. (2008). *Employment status of women and men in 2008.* Retrieved April 21, 2009, from http://www.dol.gov/wb/factsheets/Qf-ESWM08.htm

U.S. Department of Labor. (2009). *The Family and Medical Leave Act of 1993.* Retrieved May 1, 2009, from http://www.dol.gov/esa/whd/regs/statutes/fmla.htm#SEC_2_FINDINGS_AND_PURPOSES

Uggerslev, K. L., & Sulsky, L. M. (2008). Using frame-of-reference training to understand the implications of rater idiosyncrasy for rating accuracy. *Journal of Applied Psychology, 93,* 711–719.

Van Aken v. Young (451 F. Supp. 448, 454, E.D. Mich. 1982, aff'd 750 F.2d. 43, 6th Cir. 1984).

van Dierendonck, D., Schaufeli, W. B., & Buunk, B. P. (2001). Burnout and inequity among human service professionals: A longitudinal study. *Journal of Occupational Health Psychology, 6*(1), 43–52.

Van Eerde, W., & Thierry, H. (1996). Vroom's expectancy models and work-related criteria. *Journal of Applied Psychology, 81*(5), 575–586.

Van Ginkel, W. P., Tindale, R. S., & van Knippenberg, D. (2009). Team reflexivity, development of shared task representations, and the use of distributed information in group decision making. *Group Dynamics: Theory, Research, and Practice, 13*(4), 265–280.

Van Ginkel, W. P., & van Knippenberg, D. (2009). Knowledge about distribution of information and group decision making: When and why does it work? *Organizational Behavior and Human Decision Processes, 108*(2), 218–229.

Van Iddekinge, C. H., Roth, P. L., Raymark, P. H., Odle-Dusseau, H. N. (2012). The criterion-related validity of integrity tests: An updated meta-analysis. *Journal of Applied Psychology, 97,* 499–530.

van Quaquebeke, N., van Knippenberg, D., & Brodbeck, F. C. (2011). More than meets the eye: The role of subordinates' self-perceptions in leader categorization processes. *The Leadership Quarterly, 22,* 367–382.

Van Rooy, D. L., & Viswesvaran, C. (2004). Emotional intelligence: A meta-analytic investigation of predictive validity and nomological net. *Journal of Vocational Behavior, 65*(1), 71–95.

Van Yperen, N. W., & Janssen, O. (2002). Fatigued and dissatisfied or fatigued but satisfied? Goal orientations and responses to high job demands. *Academy of Management Journal, 45*(6), 1161–1171.

Vancouver, J. B., More, K. M., & Yoder, R. J. (2008). Self-efficacy and resource allocation: Support for a nonmonotonic, discontinuous model. *Journal of Applied Psychology, 93,* 35–47.

Vandenberghe, C., Bentein, K., & Stinglhamber, F. (2004). Affective commitment to the organization, supervisor, and work group: Antecedents and outcomes. *Journal of Vocational Behavior, 64,* 47–71.

Vecchio, R. P. (2002). Leadership and gender advantage. *Leadership Quarterly, 13*(6), 643–671.

Veiga, J. F., Golden, T. D., & Dechant, K. (2004). Why managers bend the rules. *Academy of Management Executive, 18*(2), 84–90.

Velada, R., Caetano, A., Michel, J. W., Lyons, B. D., & Kavanaugh, M. J. (2007). The effects of training design, individual characteristics, and work environment on transfer of training. *International Journal of Training and Development, 11*(4), 282–294.

Villanova, P. D., Bernardin, H. J., Dahmus, S. A., & Sims, R. L. (1993). Rater leniency and performance appraisal discomfort. *Educational and Psychological Measurement, 53*(3), 789–799.

Vinchur, A. J., & Koppes, L. L. (2007). Early contributors to the science and practice of industrial psychology. In L. L. Koppes (Ed.), *Historical perspectives in industrial and organizational psychology* (pp. 37–60). Mahwah, NJ: Erlbaum.

Vinchur, A. J., Shippmann, J. S., Switzer, F. S., III, & Roth, P. L. (1998). A meta-analytic review of predictors of job performance for salespeople. *Journal of Applied Psychology, 83*(4), 586–597.

Viswesvaran, C. (2003). Introduction to special issue: Role of technology in shaping the future of staffing and assessment. *International Journal of Selection and Assessment, 11*(2–3), 107–112.

Vogl, A. J., & Budman, M. (1997). Can we have it all? *Across the Board, 34*(8), 16–23.

Von Bergen, C. W., Soper, B., & Foster, T. (2002). Unintended negative effects of diversity management. *Public Personnel Management, 31*(2), 239–251.

Voydanoff, P. (2005). Consequences of boundary-spanning demands and resources for work-to-family conflict and perceived stress. *Journal of Occupational Health Psychology, 10,* 491–503.

Vroom, V. (1964). *Work and motivation.* New York: Wiley.

Wagner, J. A., & Hollenbeck, J. R. (1998). *Organizational behavior: Securing competitive advantage.* Upper Saddle River, NJ: Prentice-Hall.

Wagner-Tsukamoto, S. (2007). An institutional economic reconstruction of scientific management: On the lost theoretical logic of Taylorism. *Academy of Management Review, 32,* 105–117.

Walczyk, J. J., Mahoney, K. T., Doverspike, D., & Griffith-Ross, D. A. (2009). Cognitive lie detection: Response time and consistency of answers as cues to deception. *Journal of Business and Psychology, 24,* 33–49.

Wang, G. G., & Wilcox, D. (2006). Training evaluation: Knowing more than is practiced. *Advances in Developing Human Resources, 8*(4), 528–539.

Wang, M., Liu, S., Zhan, Y., & Shi, J. (2010). Daily work–family conflict and alcohol use: Testing the cross-level moderation effects of peer drinking norms and social support. *Journal of Applied Psychology, 95*(2), 377–386.

Warr, P. (1999). Well-being and the workplace. In D. Kahneman, E. Diener, & N. Schwartz (Eds.), *Well-being: The foundations of hedonic psychology* (pp. 392–412). New York: Russell Sage Foundation.

Warr, P. (2007a). Searching for happiness at work. *The Psychologist, 20*(12), 726–729.

Warr, P. (2007b). *Work, happiness, and unhappiness.* Mahwah, NJ: Erlbaum.

Wayhan, V. B., & Balderson, E. L. (2007). TQM and financial performance: What has empirical research discovered? *Total Quality Management, 18,* 403–412.

Wayne, S. J., & Liden, R. C. (1995). Effects of impression management on performance ratings: A longitudinal study. *Academy of Management Journal, 38*(1), 232–260.

Weber, J. (2004, June 15). *More jobs—And more layoffs.* Retrieved April 8, 2009, from the *Business Week Online* website: http://www.businessweek.com/bwdaily/dnflash/jun2004/nf20040615_5695_db035.htm.

Wegge, J., & Haslam, S. A. (2005). Improving work motivation and performance in brainstorming groups: The effects of three group goal-setting strategies. *European Journal of Work and Organizational Psychology, 14*(4), 400–430.

Weick, K. E. (1995). *Sense-making in organizations.* Thousand Oaks, CA: SAGE.

Welsh, E. T., Wanberg, C. R., Brown, K. G., & Simmering, M. J. (2003). E-learning: Emerging uses, empirical results and future directions. *International Journal of Training and Development, 7*(4), 245–258.

Werner, J. M., & Bolino, M. C. (1997). Explaining U.S. courts of appeal decisions involving performance appraisal: Accuracy, fairness, and validation. *Personnel Psychology, 50,* 1–24.

Wesolowski, M. A., & Mossholder, K. W. (1997). Relational demography in supervisor–subordinate dyads: Impact on subordinate job satisfaction, burnout, and perceived procedural justice. *Journal of Organizational Behavior, 18,* 351–362.

Wexley, K. N., & Klimoski, R. (1984). Performance appraisal: An update. In K. Rowland & G. Ferris (Eds.), *Research in personnel and human resources* (Vol. 2, pp. 35–79). Greenwich, CT: JAI Press.

Wexley, K. N., & Latham, G. P. (1991). *Developing and training human resources in organizations.* New York: HarperCollins.

Wexley, K. N., & Latham, G. P. (2002). *Developing and training human resources in organizations* (3rd ed.). Upper Saddle River, NJ: Prentice-Hall.

Wexley, K. N., & Silverman, S. B. (1993). *Working scared: Achieving success in trying times.* San Francisco: Jossey-Bass.

Wheelan, S. A., Murphy, D., Tsumura, E., & Kline, S. F. (1998). Member perceptions of internal group dynamics and productivity. *Small Group Research, 29*(3), 371–393.

Whetten, D. A., & Cameron, K. S. (2002). *Developing management skills* (5th ed.). Upper Saddle River, NJ: Pearson Education.

Whisenant, W. (2003). How women have faired as interscholastic athletic administrators since the passage of Title IX. *Sex Roles, 49,* 179–184.

Whisenant, W. (2005). In Texas it's football: How women are denied access to the AD's office. *International Journal of Sport Management, 6,* 1–8.

Whitaker, B. G. (2007). Internet-based attitude assessment: Does gender affect measurement equivalence? *Computers in Human Behavior, 23,* 1183–1194.

Whitaker, B. G., Dahling, J. J., & Levy, P. E. (2007). The development of a feedback environment and role clarity model of job performance. *Journal of Management, 33*(4), 570–591.

Whitney, D. J., Diaz, J., Mineghino, M. E., & Powers, K. (1999). Perceptions of overt and personality-based integrity tests. *International Journal of Selection & Assessment, 7*(1), 35–45.

Wiesenfeld, B. M., Brockner, J., & Martin, C. (1999). A self-affirmation analysis of survivors' reactions to unfair organizational downsizings. *Journal of Experimental Social Psychology, 35,* 441–460.

Wiesenfeld, B. M., Brockner, J., & Thibault, V. (2000). Procedural fairness, managers' self-esteem, and managerial behaviors following a layoff. *Organizational Behavior and Human Decision Processes, 83*(1), 1–32.

Wilder, D. A., Austin, J., & Casella, S. (2009). Applying behavior analysis in organizations: Organizational behavior management. *Psychological Services, 6*(3), 202–211.

Williams, J. R. & Levy, P. E. (1992). The effects of perceived system knowledge on the agreement between self-ratings and supervisor ratings. *Personnel Psychology, 45,* 835–847.

Williams, J. R., & Levy, P. E. (1995). A forgotten dimension: The role of organizational psychology in the performance appraisal process. Paper presented at the 10th annual meeting of the Society for Industrial and Organizational Psychology, Orlando, FL.

Williams, M. L., McDaniel, M. A., & Nguyen, N. T. (2006). A meta-analysis of the antecedents and consequences of pay level satisfaction. *Journal of Applied Psychology, 91,* 392–413.

Williams, S. D., Graham, T. S., & Baker, B. (2003). Evaluating outdoor experiential training for leadership and team building. *Journal of Management Development, 22*(1), 45–59.

Williamson, I. O., Lepak, D. P., & King, J. (2003). The effect of company recruitment web site orientation on individuals' perceptions of organizational attractiveness. *Journal of Vocational Behavior, 63*(2), 242–263.

Wilson, C. (2004, July). *How to heal work force cuts.* Credit Union Executive Newsletter, 7.

Wirtenberg, J., Lipsky, D., Abrams, L., Conway, M., & Slepian, J. (2007). The future of organization development: Enabling sustainable business performance through people. *Organization Development Journal, 25,* 11–22.

Woehr, D. J., & Arthur, W., Jr. (2003). The construct-related validity of assessment center ratings: A review and meta-analysis of the role of methodological factors. *Journal of Management, 29*(2), 231–258.

Wolf, A., & Jenkins, A. (2006). Explaining greater test use for selection: The role of HR professionals in a world of expanding regulation. *Human Resource Management Journal, 16*(2), 193–213.

Women in Government Relations: Advancing and empowering women. (2008, November). *Record-breaking number of women will serve in the 111th Congress.* Retrieved April 14, 2009, from http://www.wgr.org/news_events/index.cfm?fa=whatarticle&id=244

Wonderlic, E. F. (1984). *Wonderlic Personnel Test manual.* Northfield, IL: Wonderlic & Associates.

Wong, K. F. E., & Kwong, J.Y.Y. (2007). Effects of rater goals on rating patterns: Evidence from an experimental field study. *Journal of Applied Psychology, 92*(2), 577–585.

Work Options Group. (2006). *Employers expand eldercare benefits.* Retrieved December 10, 2008, from http://www.workoptionsgroup.com/wsj_article.html

World's Most Admired Companies. (2011). Retrieved July 19, 2012, from http://money.cnn.com/magazines/fortune/mostadmired/2011/index.html

WorldatWork. (2009). *Telework trendlines for 2009.* Retrieved November 28, 2010, from www.workingfromanywhere.org/news/Trendlines_2009.pdf

Wright, T. A., & Bonett, D. G. (2007). Job satisfaction and psychological well-being as nonadditive predictors of workplace turnover. *Journal of Management, 33*(2), 141–160.

Yu, J. H., Albaum, G., & Swenson, M. (2003). Is a central tendency error inherent in the use of semantic differential scales in different cultures? *International Journal of Market Research, 45*(2), 213–228.

Yuan, Y. C., Fulk, J., Monge, P. R., & Contractor, N. (2010). Expertise directory development, shared task interdependence, and strength of communication network ties as multilevel predictors of transactive memory work groups. *Communication Research, 37*(1), 20–47.

Yukl, G. A. (2002). *Leadership in organizations* (5th ed.). Upper Saddle River, NJ: Prentice-Hall.

Yun, G. J., Donahue, L. M., Dudley, N. M., & McFarland, L. A. (2005). Rater personality, rating format, and social context: Implications for performance appraisal ratings. *International Journal of Selection and Assessment, 13*(2), 97–107.

Zaccaro, S. J. (1984). Social loafing: The role of task attractiveness. *Personality and Social Psychology Bulletin, 10*(1), 99–106.

Zaccaro, S. J., & Bader, P. (2003). E-leadership and the challenges of leading e-teams: Minimizing the bad and maximizing the good. *Organizational Dynamics, 31*(4), 377–387.

Zaccaro, S. J., Foti, R. J., & Kenny, D. A. (1991). Self-monitoring and trait-based variance in leadership: An investigation of leader flexibility across multiple group situations. *Journal of Applied Psychology, 76*(2), 308–315.

Zaitzow, B. H., & Fields, C. B. (1996). Using archival data sets. In F. T. L. Leong & J. T. Austin (Eds.), *The psychology research handbook* (pp. 251–261). Thousand Oaks, CA: SAGE.

Zammuto, R. F., Griffith, T. L., Majchrzak, A., Dougherty, D. J., & Faraj, S. (2007). Information technology and the changing fabric of organization. *Organization Science, 18*(5), 749–762.

Zapata-Phelan, C. P., Colquitt, J. A., Scott, B. A., & Livingston, B. (2009). Procedural justice, interactional justice, and task performance: The mediating role of intrinsic motivation. *Organizational Behavior and Human Decision Processes, 108*, 93–105.

Zapf, D. (2002). Emotion work and psychological well-being: A review of the literature and some conceptual considerations. *Human Resource Management Review, 12*(2), 237–268.

Zellars, K. L., & Perrewé, P. L. (2001). Affective personality and the content of emotional social support: Coping in organizations. *Journal of Applied Psychology, 86*(3), 459–467.

Zhao, H., Seibert, S. E., & Lumpkin, G. T. (2010). The relationship of personality to entrepreneurial intentions and performance: A meta-analytic review. *Journal of Management, 36*(2), 381–404.

Zimmerman, R. D., Mount, M., & Goff, M. (2008). Multisource feedback and leaders' goal performance: Moderating effects of rating purpose, rater perspective, and performance dimension. *International Journal of Selection and Assessment, 16*(2), 121–133.

Name Index

Subject Index

Note: Page numbers followed by f indicate figures; those followed by t indicate tables.

Instructor's Resource Manual
to accompany

INDUSTRIAL/ORGANIZATIONAL PSYCHOLOGY
Understanding the Workplace

FOURTH EDITION

Paul E. Levy
THE UNIVERSITY OF AKRON

Kristie Campana
MINNESOTA STATE UNIVERSITY—MANKATO

Worth Publishers

CHAPTER 1

I/O Psychology: Then and Now

LEARNING OBJECTIVES

This chapter should help students understand:

- How I/O psychologists are trained

- The work of I/O psychologists and how it benefits organizations and employees alike

- The diverse historical trends associated with the development and growth of I/O psychology

- The very important role currently being played by I/O psychology in the changing workplace, as well as the field's great potential to contribute to organizational functioning in the 21st century

CHAPTER SUMMARY

I/O psychology, the application of psychology to the workplace, encompasses such diverse areas as performance appraisal, employment testing, organizational development, and motivation. I/O psychologists receive extensive training in a wide range of areas, but their central approach is based on the scientist/practitioner model, which emphasizes both theory and practice. Most obtain an advanced degree such as a PhD. The training is quite intensive and includes a great deal of coursework, practical experience, and research experience. The culmination of the training is usually the completion of a dissertation. Some students choose to earn a master's degree instead, which typically takes about two years. The demand for I/O psychologists with either an MA or a PhD is rapidly growing.

About 40% of I/O psychologists work in academic settings such as psychology departments and business schools, where they teach undergraduate and graduate students and conduct research for the purposes of creating and applying knowledge. The majority of I/O psychologists, however, work outside of academia in the public or private sector, applying what they've learned in graduate school to their particular organization. Many of these I/O psychologists also work for consulting firms that provide services to organizations on a project-by-project basis. Other I/O psychologists work directly for both private and public organizations.

I/O psychology has a rich, albeit relatively short, history. Although its beginnings date to around the turn of the 20th century, its growth as a field emerged with World War I, when I/O psychologists were employed by the government to train, test, and measure the performance of soldiers. Other historical hallmarks include World War II, the civil rights movement of the 1960s, and the emergence of the global economy in the past

20 to 25 years. I/O psychology is positioned to play an ever-increasing role in the constantly changing world of work in the 21st century. In the remainder of this book, we will discuss the various topics and areas in which I/O psychology has, and will continue to have, an impact.

■ Teaching the Chapter

Similar to the instruction of any course, the first few class periods are critical for establishing student expectations regarding the quality of course instruction and the level of participation expected, as well as the instructor's ability to convey important concepts in a clear, organized, and entertaining way. With this first chapter, it is very important to lay the foundation on which to build students' knowledge of I/O psychology and to foster a positive classroom environment in which exploration and inquiry are promoted.

Therefore, it is recommended that you supplement the administrative tasks on the first day of class with the ice breaker exercise suggested below (or a similar exercise of your own choosing). The formal terminology of numerous I/O topics will likely be new to your students; however, many of them will have had some work experience with most of the topics addressed in this book. Helping them apply their experiences to bring I/O psychology to life is an important first step in making this class an enlightening, relevant, and worthwhile learning experience.

This chapter outlines many of the important milestones during the last 100 years that have contributed to the growth of I/O psychology. In addition, it offers a preliminary introduction to some of the important topics covered later in the book. Topics such as performance appraisal, training, and selection might be completely new to students, but introducing them and explaining how I/O psychologists have been specially trained to work in these areas of organizational life will help students understand what I/O psychology is all about.

Websites are listed later in this chapter to facilitate web-based classroom environments and to supplement the chapter material. These websites can also be incorporated into assignments in which students can explore the sites and create brief reports about the information they have learned. The SIOP and Academy of Management websites contain helpful resources to facilitate student learning. Some *HR Magazine* articles that are frequently relevant to course topics can be viewed on the Society of Human Resource Management website. Illustrating the relevance of I/O psychology to issues in the popular press is a very powerful way of reinforcing the concepts and principles that students will learn in this class.

■ Suggested Exercises and Assignments

Ice Breaker

Purpose The main objective of this exercise is to introduce students to one another and to the larger class. It will also identify and form class teams that will meet during class time throughout the semester. These teams can engage in discussion of class topics or work on in-class exercises.

Instructions

Ask students to pair up with someone they did not know prior to coming to class. Each pair should then introduce themselves to each other. Inform students that they will be responsible for introducing their classmate to the rest of the class in about 5 to 10 minutes. Ask students to gather the following information about each other:

- First name
- Hometown
- Year in school
- Major
- Why they are taking this class
- Best job they have had and why it was the best
- Worst job they have had and why it was the worst

After 5 to 10 minutes have passed, ask partners to introduce each other to you and to the rest of the class. If your class has more than 20 students, this exercise could extend beyond a single class period. Thus, you may want to consider (1) placing a time limit on partner introductions or (2) forming groups of pairs and having each pair introduce each other in the smaller group.

To extend this activity (if time permits), have pairs form into larger groups (4–8 students) and assign each group an I/O topic that will be discussed later in the book (e.g., interviews, training, motivation, recruitment). Give groups 10 to 20 minutes to discuss the following questions with regard to their topic and ask them to present their ideas at the end of the time period:

- How would you define this topic?
- What work experiences have group members (or others they know) had that are relevant to this topic?
- What are examples of good practices regarding this topic?
- What are examples of bad practices regarding this topic? What do they believe could have been done differently by the organization?

I/O Taboo

I/O Taboo is a simple, yet fun, game that can be played in class (facilitated by the instructor) and used as a learning tool for students to study and review important concepts and key words. Students may also be encouraged to play this game with other students outside of class in preparation for exams.

The object of the game is for a team member to get his/her team to say the I/O word (in **bold type** in the following example) by giving clues about the word without mentioning the other words on the card—they are "taboo." One member of the opposing team referees the clues given by the clue-giving team to ensure that the team does not earn points if a taboo word is spoken. As the clue-givers provide clues, their teammates should shout out what they think the I/O word is until they guess it correctly.

Example *I/O Taboo* game cards are shown below. Using the Key Terms from each chapter of this book, you can create your own game cards with words most relevant to each chapter's topics and to your own lectures.

Chapter 1: Example *I/O Taboo* Cards

Organizational Psychology	Scientist/Practitioner Model	Dissertation
"O" Side	Graduate Training	PhD
Motivation	SIOP	Research
Work Attitudes	Knowledge	Graduate School
Groups	Consumers	Literature Review

I/O Syllabus Hunt

This activity can be used to help students become acquainted with the textbook, the syllabus, or both. Have students form small groups (2 to 3 students) and come up with a problem they have encountered in the workplace. Once they have described the problem, have them look at the book or your syllabus and discuss where they believe they might find a solution to this problem. In smaller classes, you might have groups compete against one another to see who can most quickly find the chapter or class period that sounds most relevant to the problem. Ask students to share some examples so that classmates can begin to think about problems they might be able to solve after completing the course.

SIOP Scavenger Hunt

Purpose Students will have an opportunity to review siop.org, a useful resource for I/O psychologists and interested students.

Instructions

Provide students with computers that have access to the Internet. If you are limited in the number of computers, students can participate in teams. Ask them to use the website to find the following:

- Find a company that is currently hiring someone with a PhD in I/O psychology.
- Find a school that offers a master's degree in I/O psychology.
- Find out when and where the next SIOP conference is.
- Find a consultant who works in your state (or a neighboring state).
- Find out when the graduate student scholarship application materials are due.
- Find the latest edition of *TIP* (the official SIOP publication).

The group that finds all of this information first wins.

What Topic Is Most Interesting?

Purpose Students will be able to discuss what they have read in the book and consider which topics they might find most interesting in the course.

Instructions

In the book, it is mentioned that there are five major areas where an I/O psychologist is apt to spend his/her time: selection, training/development, organizational development, performance appraisal, and quality of work life. Ask students to discuss which of these topics they find most interesting and/or important. You may wish to use the following discussion prompts:

- Why do you believe this particular topic is so important?
- How do your own personal experiences with work affect your opinion?
- What outcomes do you think these topics might affect (e.g., motivation, performance)?
- How do you think this topic might change in the 21st century?

■ Evaluating "Taking It to the Field"

In this chapter, the "Taking it to the Field" activity asks students to explain what an I/O psychology firm does and how it might help Chris, a restaurant owner, with his problematic cooks. There are many possible responses to the scenario, but the points below are suggestions for what poor, good, and excellent responses should look like.

Poor responses . . .	• Contain spelling and grammatical errors, which will not impress a potential client. • Fail to explain I/O psychology OR use complex terminology that a layperson would not understand. • Do not address the specific problems Chris is experiencing in his restaurant. • Are too short to be helpful OR are very long-winded. • Are missing a salutation (e.g., "Hello, Chris"). • Are missing a sign-off (e.g., "Looking forward to speaking with you more! Susan").
Good responses . . .	• Use proper spelling and grammar. • Explain what I/O psychology is in a relatively concise and straightforward manner. • Have some vague suggestions for Chris's specific problems (e.g., "Maybe you need to do more training with your cooks?"). • May be slightly wordy or a little bit too sparse but nonetheless get the main idea across and demonstrate understanding of the chapter. • Should have a salutation. • Should have a sign-off.

Excellent responses . . .
- Use flawless spelling and grammar.
- Provide a short, pithy statement about what topics are encompassed by I/O psychology; a description that goes beyond what Chris mentions as problems can help open the door for future work with him.
- Specifically address how they might help Chris with his problem in a way that shows they have paid attention to the chapter and perhaps have looked at the topics in the table of contents. Students might mention doing a better job of selecting and training cooks. They may also indicate problems with motivation or Chris's own management/leadership skills. Students should not go into too much depth in their suggestions.
- Should suggest a follow-up meeting or phone call so that they can start working with Chris and coming up with a solution to the problem.
- Contain a salutation.
- Contain a sign-off.

■ Evaluating "Application Questions"

1. Go to www.siop.org and find a university that offers an MA, a PsyD, or a PhD in I/O psychology. Visit that university's I/O psychology page and read about the program. What are some aspects of that program that seem appealing to you? What aspects seem unappealing? If you wanted to apply to this school, what would you need to do?

   Evaluation Guide: Students rarely have a good sense of how to evaluate different programs for graduate training. Here are some suggestions for providing feedback or prompting discussion:
   - If students focus on superficial aspects of the website ("The website looks nice"), you can prompt them to think carefully about what this says about a school: Does a nice-looking website indicate anything about what they will learn or whether they will enjoy what they are learning?
   - If students say things that make it clear they do not understand what graduate training is like ("This program looks too hard!"), you can provide them with a more realistic preview of graduate school and the demands that are involved. You may also share helpful resources for learning about graduate training, such as Robert Peters's excellent book *Getting What You Came For.*
   - If students focus on aspects of the program itself, encourage them to think of different aspects of the program that might be indicators of quality (e.g.,

what classes they will take, student satisfaction, graduation or placement rates).

- Students often do not realize the importance of there being a faculty member who is conducting research they find interesting. Encourage them to look at faculty profiles to see what types of research they might be doing if they attend that school.

2. Your book mentions five main topics that I/O psychologists investigate— selection, training, organizational development, performance appraisal, and quality of work life. Which of these topics seems most interesting to you? Write a question about that topic that you think I/O psychology could answer.

    Evaluation Guide: This activity serves two purposes. First, it allows students to imagine themselves in the role of an I/O psychologist and to seriously consider what types of issues interest them. Second, it allows for a discussion of what questions are appropriate in terms of scientific investigation. Here are some suggestions for providing feedback or prompting discussion:

    - If a student brings up a question that is not testable because it deals with opinion rather than fact ("Men are better leaders than women"), you can discuss the importance of being objective and specific in science, emphasizing the need to ask questions that can be answered. You can also guide the student in changing the question so that it is testable ("Men tend to work longer hours than women").
    - A student might bring up a question that fits under a different topic than he/she has indicated or that fits under two topics ("Does a webinar actually improve performance?"). You can use this situation to discuss how many questions in I/O psychology bridge different topic areas and how it is helpful for an I/O psychologist to know about many different areas so he/she can be prepared to investigate a number of different questions.
    - A student might bring up a question that also connects with a different area of psychology ("What prejudices do African Americans face at work" might also connect to social psychology). You can use this situation to indicate that I/O psychology often uses theories that have been developed in other fields of psychology or business to answer new questions.

3. Your book discusses the importance of understanding diversity in the workplace. One currently popular topic is the issue of generational differences. How does your attitude toward work differ from that of people who are older than you (e.g., your parents or grandparents)? What kinds of problems might arise out of those differences?

    Evaluation Guide: Students tend to be particularly interested in this topic because it is a fairly common topic in the popular media. Students may hone in on a number of stereotypes or generalizations they have heard about their own generation; they may be interested in a discussion of why these generalizations occur and what some consequences of the generalizations might be.

- Younger generations are often stereotyped as feeling entitled as well as being impatient or spoiled. If a student brings up this point, you can discuss differences in how the generations were raised and behaviors of younger people (e.g., not using proper titles like Mr. or Ms.; texting during meetings) that might lead to these perceptions.
- Younger students may also mention that they have different expectations about their work environment (e.g., more flexible work schedules, telecommuting). You might discuss differences between more traditional work environments and changes that are occurring due to new technology. You might also discuss ways that technology can change the way we think and work (e.g., younger students tend to rely on their memory less because it is easy to look up information if it is forgotten; prior to search engines, however, forgetting information cost workers a lot of time).
- Students may also bring up their own negative generalizations about older workers (e.g., crabby, traditional, resistant to change). This can provide an opportunity to discuss some of the problems they might encounter because of these generalizations (e.g., if they come up with an idea, they may need to persuade others to buy into the idea rather than having it adopted immediately).

4. Your book discusses the scientist/practitioner model. One common problem in I/O psychology is what is called a scientist/practitioner gap; that is, scientists often complain that practitioners don't always use techniques that have empirical support, while practitioners often complain that scientists don't conduct studies that have practical applications in the workplace. What are some steps that the field of I/O psychology could take to ensure that scientists and practitioners can benefit from one anothers' work?

Evaluation Guide: This is a point of contention among many I/O psychologists, and it may be interesting for students to learn that controversies exist even among I/O psychologists. Scientists and practitioners have tried a number of approaches that you can discuss in class:

- If students mention providing a forum for scientists and practitioners to talk, you can indicate that some forums exist at SIOP conferences but ask them to consider other places and times this could happen.
- If students mention having researchers and practitioners collaborate on studies, spend some time discussing some potential barriers to this (e.g., confidentiality of data, finding results that contradict what the

practitioners are doing, disagreements about which research questions are important).

- If students indicate that scientists are out of touch with what workers experience, ask for some examples of how scientists could get a better sense of current issues and keep up with current concerns.

5. Consider a problem that you are facing either at work or at school. How might I/O psychology be able to help you solve this problem?.

Evaluation Guide: Students can come up with a variety of answers. Some common examples might include the following:

- Arguments or difficulties with roommates (I/O psychology can help you communicate better or select better roommates)
- Having problems getting others to go along with ideas or plans (I/O psychology can help you learn to lead or persuade other people)
- Getting other people to contribute more on class projects or housework (I/O psychology can teach you about how to get teams to work together effectively, or how to motivate other people to do tasks, or how to organize work more effectively)
- Feeling dissatisfied with a job or major (I/O psychology can help you determine what aspect is dissatisfying or what job/major would fit you better)
- Struggling with difficult coursework (I/O psychology provides training principles that can help motivate students and ensure that they retain what they learn)

6. As you have probably noticed in reading the textbook, the topics explored by I/O psychology have changed over the years. What topics do you believe are going to be important for I/O psychology to address over the next decade? Why do you think these topics will be so important?

Evaluation Guide: Again, students may have a wide variety of answers. The book mentions leadership development, compensation and benefits, executive compensation, work–life issues, retirement of baby boomers, attitudes toward aging, work intensification, talent management, culture transformation, managing change, increasing diversity, globalization, and ethics and ethical leadership. Encourage students to come up with specific examples of these topics or to think of additional problems they believe will develop soon. Examples of discussion points might include the following:

- Finding a way to keep employees constantly up-to-date as technology undergoes rapid changes
- Helping workers become fluent in more than one language/culture as globalization expands
- Addressing CEO's pay compared to what others in an organization are paid
- Addressing intergenerational conflicts

■ Highlighted Study for Discussion

SIOP Member Survey

Although it is not a journal article, having students read a SIOP member survey (http://www.siop.org/surveys.aspx) can help them get a sense of what types of jobs exist for SIOP members and what the pay is for different types of jobs. This report is 66 pages long (though most of the pages contain tables, so there are only about 18 pages of text for students to read). Some key points of the 2009 survey results are as follows:

- Salaries appear to be getting higher over time (i.e., the median reported salary in 2009 was higher than it was in 2006).
- Salaries tend to be higher in areas that have a high cost of living, such as Manhattan, Los Angeles, and Boston.
- The median income of women was 16.4% lower than that of men; the report suggests that this may be partially due to the higher number of women earning MA degrees instead of PhDs, the fact that women work fewer hours, and the fact that women are less likely to own their own consulting business; however, this can be a good place to discuss whether the pay difference is fair.
- Respondents who were older and had earned their degree a long time ago tended to make more than young and new I/O psychologists. This finding may provide an interesting discussion point in terms of why this might be the case (e.g., a higher cumulative number of raises, more experience leading to higher pay).
- The majority of I/O psychologists work in consulting organizations or in colleges/universities. However, there are a variety of other organizations where I/O psychologists work (e.g., pharmaceutical companies, government entities, the military, nonprofits, IT companies).
- The highest salaries are earned by self-employed consultants, followed by those employed by pharmaceutical companies and hospitality organizations. The lowest-paying jobs appear to be in colleges/universities, publishing, and transportation organizations. You could have a discussion about why some positions are so well paid and how we might determine the value of a job (e.g., people tend to be paid more for high-risk positions, in companies that make good profits, etc.).
- The starting salary for someone with a PhD is about $20,000 more than for someone with an MA degree. You may want to discuss the pros and cons of getting a master's degree compared to a PhD (e.g., lower earnings, less time in school, fewer student loans, more difficulty moving up in a company).

■ Web Learning

Title	Address
Society for Industrial and Organizational Psychology (SIOP)	http://www.siop.org
Academy of Management (AOM)	http://www.aomonline.org
Society for Human Resource Management (SHRM)	http://www.shrm.org
American Psychological Association (APA)	http://www.apa.org
American Psychological Society (APS)	http://www.psychologicalscience.org
International Association of Applied Psychology (IAAP)	http://www.iaapsy.org
Archives of the History of American Psychology	http://www3.uakron.edu/ahap
Professional Industrial-Organizational Psychologist Network	http://www.piop.net

CHAPTER 2

Research Methods in I/O Psychology

LEARNING OBJECTIVES

This chapter should help students understand:

- The scientific method and its goals and assumptions
- The importance of theory to science and psychology
- Internal and external validity
- The complex interplay among experimental variables
- How research is conducted, with an emphasis on induction and deduction as well as the five steps involved in the process
- A variety of measurement issues such as reliability and validity
- Basic-level statistics ranging from descriptive statistics to correlation and regression

CHAPTER SUMMARY

Research methods are important to I/O psychology—and all scientific endeavors, for that matter—because research conducted without care is unreliable and worthless. But when we are careful to base our theories on data and to use these data to test and revise the theories, the science of I/O psychology can make a meaningful contribution to the world of work. This science is more than just a matter of commonsense predictions and beliefs. Among its goals are to describe, explain, predict, and control human behavior at work. It is also important to realize that theories are the domain not just of basic science but also of applied scientific disciplines such as I/O psychology. In fact, it is only through careful theoretical development, testing, and revision that we can use our knowledge to describe, explain, predict, and control organizational behaviors and environments.

A major goal of most research in I/O psychology is to be able to draw causal inferences about the relationship between two or more variables. Thus, we must design our studies with an emphasis on internal validity, attempting to control for extraneous variables that could provide alternative explanations for our results. In addition to internal validity, we must concern ourselves with external validity, or the generalizability of our findings.

There are many ways in which I/O psychologists go about collecting data, but the survey is perhaps the one most frequently used. Surveys are very useful in gathering information about attitudes and beliefs. Technological advancements such as the Internet have provided new alternative approaches to survey administration. We may also use observational approaches to measure and record frequency or incidents of particular behaviors or interactions. Archival research is a popular approach as well, given our access to the numerous large-scale data sets that have been collected by the government and private organizations. I/O psychologists often combine these and other data collection techniques in any given study to better examine their research questions.

Without reliable and valid measurement, the research conducted by I/O psychologists would have very little to offer. Researchers must work very hard to eliminate sources of measurement error and to ensure that their measures are tapping the constructs that they were intended to tap. There are a few different approaches to estimating reliability, and each is important for demonstrating the soundness of any particular measure. Validity is important as well, but to talk of validity in general is not very helpful, as the term can mean several different things. In I/O psychology, when we speak of the validity of a test or predictor, we are usually referring to the extent to which the test predicts job performance or some other criterion.

After we have collected our data, the next step is to describe and summarize those data using descriptive statistics such as measures of central tendency and dispersion. Because I/O psychologists are usually interested in the relationships among variables and the prediction of one set of variables from another set, correlation and regression are statistical techniques that are very useful to us. Ultimately, we complete our five-step research process with a written report that summarizes the research project.

In the remainder of this text, we will discuss various content areas of I/O psychology and the research that is conducted in those areas, along with their implications for organizational functioning.

■ Teaching the Chapter

Mastery of research methods and statistical concepts is a requirement for practicing I/O psychology. As such, it is important that the basic principles in this second chapter be presented clearly and effectively so that students have a solid foundation for understanding the material in the remainder of the textbook. Students are often uncomfortable and apprehensive about approaching statistics and research methods. Thus, clearly presenting this chapter's material and providing opportunities for students to engage in exercises that demonstrate the applicability of I/O research to real organizational issues is vital to ensuring that they will comprehend subsequent material in this book.

Instructors face at least four major challenges when teaching the material in this chapter. First, it may be difficult for students to comprehend that science is, according to Karl Popper, all about ruling out alternative explanations so that we can support a theory. Everyone is more comfortable when we can "prove" something, but, as you well know, in I/O psychology and in science, we cannot really prove anything. Thus, it may be worth pointing out to students that in many studies "significant" findings can explain as little as 10% of the variance in a dependent variable. So, even though 90% of variance remains unexplained, the results can be very important for theory building. As social scientists, we must continually refine and adapt our research questions to modern settings, a process that keeps us engaged in interesting and important research.

A second major issue for students in this chapter surrounds confusion about causal relationships and correlational relationships. When first introduced to research design and statistics, many students misinterpret large correlations between independent and dependent variables (IVs and DVs, respectively) as a causal relationship. Thus, it is important to clearly explain the importance of research design, the roles of IVs and DVs, and the concept of experimental control. Some of the chapter exercises have been designed to address this very issue by clarifying these concepts. You may want to select research studies using organizational samples that have been published in reputable journals (e.g., *Journal of Applied Psychology*, *Academy of Management Journal*) to illustrate and clarify the topics of research control and causal inference.

Third, understanding the important concepts of reliability and validity of measures in I/O psychology is critical because they reemerge in subsequent chapters dealing with selection, predictors, and performance appraisal. The earlier in the course that students comprehend the importance of reliable and valid construct measurement, the greater the benefit and understanding they will have when these topics are discussed later in the semester. Before drilling down into statistical issues, consider helping students focus on the conceptual meaning and significance of *reliability* (measurement consistency) and *validity* (measurement precision).

Finally, though some of the statistical concepts presented in the chapter should be familiar to students, they will undoubtedly benefit from a comprehensive review of the concepts of central tendency, the properties of dispersion, and a reminder of what the correlation coefficient means to research.

The following suggested exercises have been designed to help you encourage students to apply their thinking and discuss research methods. Any review of research methods should contain considerable discussion about research design and relevant considerations when setting up a research study. The first exercise involves designing a training study to improve the test scores of students in a class. Aside from providing a wonderful opportunity to discuss and clarify IVs and DVs and to consider the consequences of different research designs, this exercise can also supplement student learning by promoting an active discussion about the ethics of using a control group in the study.

We also encourage you to assign students to use a library database to identify a research study from an I/O journal and present its key points to the class. This exercise can help students identify the important points to take away from research studies and provide valuable practice in reading I/O literature. Alternatively, you can assign students to locate an article on a given course topic, ensuring that all course topics are covered. Then, on the day that topic is discussed, have one or more students present an article on it. This can help break up the monotony of lectures, help students sharpen their presentation skills, and give the class additional exposure to research on I/O topics.

■ Suggested Exercises and Assignments

Design an Experiment: Improving Test Performance

Purpose The objective of this exercise is to provide students with an opportunity to apply research method concepts from the textbook and lecture by creating their own research study. Students should find this exercise interesting because they are often concerned with their test scores and how they can improve them.

Instructions

- Divide the class into groups of four to six and ask them to develop a study designed to improve the test scores of students in the class.
- The intervention (training) can focus on improving study habits, increasing class attendance, or anything else that students can think of. Groups should identify:
  - The intervention (training) they will use to improve course grades
  - The hypothesis of the experiment
  - The independent variable
  - The dependent variable
  - The research design
  - Any potential extraneous variables

Discussion Questions

- What steps could be taken to control for extraneous variables?
- What other related dependent variables might we want to examine?
- What steps could be taken to ensure that this experiment is conducted in an ethical manner?

Article Retrieval

Purpose The objective of this exercise is to give students an opportunity to locate and read published research articles in the I/O literature and to increase their comfort level in reading scholarly work.

Instructions

- Students will need to use the library database to locate an article in an I/O journal on a topic that you designate or one that is of interest to them.
- At the start of the semester, you might want to consider assigning individual students (or groups of four to six) an article that is relevant to each course topic. Then have each student (or group) present the article on the day you teach the given topic.
- Students should identify and report the following information from the article(s):

- Author, title, and publication date
- Purpose of study
- Hypotheses
- Type of research method used
- Statistics used
- Sample population
- Independent and dependent variables
- Summary of research findings
■ Suggested journals:
  - *Journal of Applied Psychology*
  - *Personnel Psychology*
  - *Academy of Management Journal*
  - *Journal of Management*
  - *Organizational Behavior and Human Decision Processes*
  - *Leadership Quarterly*

Discussion Questions

■ Why is this research important to the practice and science of I/O psychology?

■ What, if anything, could the researcher(s) have done to improve the study?

Becoming an Observer

Purpose The objective of this exercise is to give students the opportunity to practice and exercise observational skills and to report observations.

Instructions

■ Ask students to observe and document the events that occur during a situation typical of their daily life.
  - *Suggested situations suitable for observation*: standing at a bus stop, sitting in the library, eating dinner, going to the gym

■ Work together in class to identify one situation that all students will observe before a designated class period. Then identify all of the important variables that you want them to collect data on (e.g., numbers of people, topics of conversations).

■ Once students have made their observations and documented the behaviors, have them present their findings to the class (or in small groups).

Discussion Questions

■ What are the main similarities in your observations? The main differences?

■ Why do you think there were differences in your observations?

■ What, if any, difficulties did you encounter when observing the situation?

■ What could be done to make your reports more consistent?

Debate

Purpose The objective of the exercise is to give students the opportunity to debate issues relating to survey research in organizations.

Instructions

- Inform students that they are a team of I/O psychologists interested in surveying employees to learn about the effects of Internet use on employee work performance.
- Divide the class into several small groups of four to six students.
- Assign groups to the following positions:
  - In favor of web-based surveys
  - In favor of mail surveys
  - In favor of interviews
- Have the groups outline the benefits of their assigned survey type. They should also be prepared to defend the drawbacks of their survey type.

Discussion Questions

- How does the cost of administering the survey affect the type of survey you would give?
- What (if any) ethical concerns might there be in this type of research?

Archival Research

Purpose The objective of this exercise is to give students an opportunity to carry out archival research that relates directly to I/O concepts.

Instructions

- Ask student to consider what skills, traits, or abilities might be required in the workplace. Divide students into groups and ask them to create a short list (e.g., five to seven items) of qualifications they believe organizations will expect of their applicants.
- Ask groups to examine a source where job opportunities are listed (e.g., an online resource such as craigslist.com or monster.com or a newspaper). Ask them to randomly choose 20 ads and put a checkmark next to each qualification when they see it mentioned in these ads.
- When students have had enough time to complete the task, ask them to come back together into a larger group.

Discussion Questions

- What characteristics seemed to be most important to organizations? Least important?
- Is this a representative sample of organizations? Why or why not?

- Do you think you will have these commonly requested skills/abilities when you complete college? If not, what can you do to acquire them?

Observational Research

Purpose In this exercise, students will both learn a method of research and become aware of some of the difficulties with this approach.

- Obtain a short television episode or a short movie clip. Prior to class, view the clip and identify a construct that is potentially tricky to operationally define but possible to observe. For example, you can ask students to identify an act of aggression in a children's cartoon. Or you can ask students to identify acts of sexism, leadership, harassment, or something similar in an episode of a workplace sitcom (such as *The Office* or *Better Off Ted*).
- Ask students to observe the clip you have selected and briefly jot down a note about each instance of the target construct.
- Once the clip has ended, ask students to turn to a nearby student to compare notes.
- Students are likely to note that there are some differences in what they have identified. For example, if one character says something mean to another character, some students may not have identified that behavior as aggressive. Or if a female character tells a male character to "be a man" about something, some students may not identify this as sexist behavior.

Discussion Questions

- How did you operationally define your variable?
- Did you find it difficult to determine whether any behaviors you saw should be included as examples of the target construct? Why was this difficult?
- What does this exercise demonstrate about operational definitions and constructs?

■ Evaluating "Taking It to the Field"

This chapter's "Taking It to the Field" exercise dealt with an e-mail from Kendall Phillips, the HR manager of the law firm MacLaughlin & MacDougal. She designed a new selection measure for her firm and needs some feedback from someone who knows more about reliability and validity. There are many possible responses to the scenario, but the points below are suggestions for what poor, good, and excellent responses should look like.

Reliability

Poor responses . . .	• Are based primarily on the student's gut feelings or impressions and demonstrate little critical thinking (e.g., "I think that you did a great job making your test!").
	• Fail to indicate which types of reliability are covered or use terms inappropriately (e.g., referring to test–retest reliability as internal consistency).
	• Suggest that Kendall must establish interrater reliability. In this case, there is no real need for interrater reliability because there are no observations/ratings taking place.
Good responses . . .	• Clearly indicate that the test has .89 test–retest reliability and indicate that this is above the usual .70 minimum.
	• Indicate that Kendall does not have any measure of internal consistency and that she should consider assessing this.
Excellent responses . . .	• Clearly indicate that the test has .89 test–retest reliability and that this is above the usual .70 minimum.
	• Indicate that Kendall does not have any measure of internal consistency and suggest that she use her existing data to calculate this (using split halves, Cronbach's alpha, or the Kuder-Richardson 20).
	• Suggest that Kendall also consider creating an alternate version of the test (so that if there is a mistake, someone can retake it) and encourage her to establish parallel forms reliability.
	• Do NOT suggest establishing interrater reliability (as there are no raters in this scenario).

Validity

Poor responses . . .	• Are based primarily on the student's gut feelings or impressions and demonstrate little critical thinking (e.g., "I think that you did a great job making your test!").
	• Fail to indicate which types of validity are covered or use terms inappropriately (e.g., referring to content validity as construct validity).
	• Fail to clearly demonstrate knowledge of which statistical evidence relates to each type of validity if specific types of validity are mentioned (e.g., telling Kendall that she has adequate divergent validity without indicating which statistic refers to that validity).

Good responses . . .
- Discuss whether Kendall has established content validity. There can be some debate here—students may argue that because she has consulted with experts and looked at similar tests, she has done what she can to establish this. Alternatively, students might ask to see the test items or suggest that Kendall have one of her experts look over the test to ensure that it covers all aspects of neuroticism.
- Indicate that Kendall has partially satisfied the requirements for criterion-related validity. The correlation between the NAF and performance ($r = .30$) represents concurrent validity.
- Indicate that Kendall has provided both convergent validity ($r = .75$) and divergent validity ($r = .34$). Because the convergent validity is relatively high and the divergent validity is relatively low, she has demonstrated that her instrument appears to measure neuroticism, not some other construct. Note that students are often confused about divergent validity, so it will be helpful to provide feedback if they make a mistake on this point.

Excellent responses . . .
- Discuss whether Kendall has established content validity. There can be some debate here—students may argue that because she has consulted with experts and looked at similar tests, she has done what she can to establish this. Alternatively, students might ask to see the test items or suggest that Kendall have one of her experts look over the test to ensure that it covers all aspects of neuroticism.
- Indicate that Kendall has partially satisfied the requirements for criterion-related validity. The correlation between the NAF and performance ($r = .30$) represents concurrent validity. Excellent responses will also note that she does not have predictive validity and may suggest that she begin administering this measure to job applicants to see if it also predicts performance.
- Indicate that Kendall has provided both convergent validity ($r = .75$) and divergent validity ($r = .34$). Because the convergent validity is relatively high and the divergent validity is relatively low, she has demonstrated that her instrument appears to measure neuroticism, not some other construct.
- Mention construct validity. Students should indicate that the above components (content validity, criterion-related validity, convergent and divergent validity) indicate whether the measure has construct validity. Because construct validity is somewhat subjective, students can either agree or disagree that the measure is valid, as long as they indicate why they believe so.

■ Evaluating "Application Questions"

1. Imagine that a fellow student says to you, "I don't need a study to tell me that lecturing is a bad way to teach students. I know from my own experience that it never works!" How would you convince this student of the value of research? What might be an example of a study you could conduct to see if this student's belief is accurate?

   Evaluation Guide: Students may have a variety of responses to this statement. Some examples might be:
   - Students may note that this student's experience may not be accurate or relevant to other students (e.g., this student may not take classes where lecture is effective; this student may have had unskilled lecturers; some people may learn better from lectures than from other methods).
   - Students may also note that this student's statement is not precise. What does the student mean by "a bad way to teach"? Does this mean that lectures are boring? That most students don't remember what they hear?
   - Students may also note that this student is not precise about what he or she means by "lecture"—some lectures incorporate interesting examples and discussions, while others simply restate content from the book.
   - Finally, students may point out that "never" is an overgeneralization. Lectures may work sometimes, in some situations, for some people, and for some topics.
   - Students will likely have a number of ideas for research, but probably the best option is to conduct an experiment in which students are taught about a topic in a lecture versus another method (e.g., group activity, video, or discussion). Depending on how well the students perform on a test assessing whether they have learned and understood the content, we can determine whether one method of teaching is more effective than another.

2. Think about a behavior you have observed among fellow students. What do you think causes that behavior, and what might be a theory you can develop to explain why that behavior occurs?

   Evaluation Guide: Students may come up with a variety of interesting observations and theories. It may help to address the following topics:
   - Does the theory describe the behavior? If not, how can students be more specific in describing a behavior? For example, if a student observes that men and women listen to music "differently," ask for a more detailed explanation of what is meant by "differently" (e.g., different types of music, different volume, use of earphones versus speakers).
   - Does the theory explain why a behavior occurs? If a student states that women are more likely to wear earbuds to listen to music, while men are more likely to use headphones, ask why might this be. What is it that might

make women prefer earbuds (e.g., better fit for smaller ears, doesn't interfere with hairstyles)?
- Does the theory help predict what someone might do? For example, if
I own an electronics store, how might this theory help me decide what
types of inventory to carry if a lot of women shop there?

3. A researcher has been asked to find a way to help construction workers put
on their helmets. Describe a survey study she could conduct. What information would she get from that study? Describe an experimental study she
could conduct. What information would she get from that study?

Evaluation Guide: Students may come up with a variety of ideas.
However, strong responses will address the following issues:
- For the survey study, students should identify questions they might ask the
construction workers (e.g., "What are some reasons why you do not wear
your hard hat? How often do you forget to wear your hard hat? Is your
hard hat comfortable?"). However, students should also recognize that
because construction workers are reporting on their own behavior, their
judgments may or may not be accurate.
- For the experiment, students should suggest changing something to
see if that encourages the construction workers to wear their hard hats
(e.g., putting up signs, making hats more comfortable). The researcher
then might measure whether construction workers wear their hard hats
more after she has implemented the change (or, alternatively, students
might suggest she change something at one site and not at another, so
she can compare the two groups of construction workers). Students
should recognize that this would allow the researcher to assume causality
(e.g., putting up signs causes construction workers to remember to put
on their hard hats).

4. Reliability and validity are two separate characteristics of a measurement,
but they are related. The chapter notes that you must have reliability (consistency) before you can have validity (accuracy). Provide an example of a
measure that is consistent but inaccurate.

Evaluation Guide: Students often find this topic to be quite difficult, so
this allows you to identify confusion or misunderstandings. Common examples might include the following:
- A clock might be set to the wrong time. This clock is consistent (it can
still tell you how long a minute is), but it is inaccurate (it is telling you
the wrong time).
- A scale might be calibrated incorrectly. This scale is consistent (you can
step on it every day, and every day the scale will read 180 pounds), but it
is inaccurate if you actually only weigh 120 pounds.
- Many women's and men's magazines have quizzes that purport to measure
personality by asking questions about how you decorate or what foods

you like. These measures might be consistent (you can get the same score each time you take it), but they are probably not accurate (liking cheese-cake probably does not say anything much about your personality).

5. Correlation coefficients can help us understand how two variables are related. What are two variables that might have a strong, positive correlation? A strong negative correlation? A correlation of 0?

Evaluation Guide: Students typically can easily come up with a few examples of each. Some topics that emerge might be:

- If one student expects a positive relationship between two variables, and other students disagree, you can discuss the importance of theory. For example, one student might believe that if a boss is rude, there will be less cooperation among team members (because team members take out their frustrations on one another); another student might believe that the oppo-site result is likely (because the coworkers see the boss as a common enemy, they will be more supportive of and cooperative with one another). This might lead to a discussion about how many theories can contradict one another and how empirical investigation can determine which one is likely to apply in a certain situation.
- Students may struggle to think of examples in which there is no relation-ship between variables. Sometimes choosing silly variables can help (e.g., there is no correlation between how many hours you spend in a car per day and how many pairs of scissors you own). This can also help demon-strate that variables that aren't correlated typically are not very interesting to most scientists!

■ Highlighted Study for Discussion

Fine, M. A., & Kurdik, L. A. (1993). Reflections on determining authorship credit and authorship order on faculty–student collaborations. *American Psychologist, 48,* 1141–1147.

This article discusses a number of the concerns that faculty and students might con-sider when publishing a paper together. The article provides some nice insight into some of the issues at hand in research that may not always be considered by research-ers at the outset. It provides several scenarios, as well as the authors' opinions on how credit should be awarded. The scenarios are as follows:

- *Case 1:* A student develops an idea with his practicum supervisor. The student, his practicum supervisor, and the dissertation committee chair agree to publish the paper, with the student as first author, the practicum supervisor as second author, and the committee chair as third author. However, after several drafts, the student loses interest, and ultimately the committee chair takes over the paper and conducts extensive reanalysis of the data.

- *Case 2:* An undergraduate student and her advisor work together on an undergraduate honors thesis. The student comes up with the initial idea, collects the data, and writes drafts of the paper. The advisor clarifies the research methodology, conducts the statistical analysis, and edits the final paper. One-third of the final paper is made up of portions of the student's thesis.
- *Case 3:* A psychologist and a psychiatrist designed a study and invited a master's student to help with the paper. The student finds several additional articles, collects and analyzes the data, and writes a thesis under the supervision of the psychologist. After the defense, the paper requires some reanalysis and writing to be ready for publication. The student is not asked to help with this part.
- *Case 4:* An undergraduate and faculty member work together on an undergraduate thesis project. The student and faculty member design a measure together. The student collects the data and writes the paper. The faculty member helps with the statistical analyses. The paper needs revisions to become an empirical article, which is done by the professor. In the revision, they need to use aspects of the study not included in the original thesis, and it will require a major rewrite.
- The authors present their perspective on considerations for deciding authorship and suggest the following for each case:
  - In Case 1, the student deserves authorship because of his contribution to the paper, but perhaps not first authorship if he drops out of the project. The supervisor's contribution should also be carefully considered when deciding authorship.
  - In Case 2, the student should be given first authorship if she continues to work on the paper to make it into a publishable article. If not, she should still receive second authorship, with a note in the article that it was based on her honor's thesis.
  - In Case 3, the student should be given third authorship, as he contributed what was expected and to the utmost extent of his professional capabilities.
  - In Case 4, the student should be offered an opportunity to participate in the rewrite; if she accepts, she should be given first authorship.
- Additional discussion points with your class might center around what constitutes "work" and reward in these contexts. It might also be helpful to ask students not to read the authors' recommendations and instead to consider what they think would be fair in each scenario. Students can then discuss how they define "fair" and consider the implications of their definitions on both the student and the faculty member or supervisor.

▪ Web Learning

Title	Address
APA Ethical Principles of Psychologists and Code of Conduct	http://www.apa.org/ethics/code2002.html
Academy of Management Research Methods Division	http://division.aomonline.org/rm/joomla
American Statistical Association (ASA)	http://www.amstat.org
Electronic Textbook: StatSoft	http://www.statsoft.com/textbook/stathome.html
Statistics for Psychologists	http://www.psychwww.com/resource/bytopic/stats.html
Hyperstat Online: An introductory statistics book	http://www.davidmlane.com/hyperstat/intro.html
Web Center for Social Research Methods	http://www.socialresearchmethods.net
Organizational Research Methods (journal, requires subscription)	http://orm.sagepub.com
A survey design tutorial	http://www.surveysystem.com/sdesign.htm

CHAPTER 3

Job Analysis

LEARNING OBJECTIVES

This chapter should help students understand:

- How important job analysis is to HR functioning

- The common terminology used in the area of job analysis

- How to differentiate between job-oriented and worker-oriented job analysis techniques

- How to conduct a job analysis using the Task Inventory Approach, Functional Job Analysis, Job Element Method, Position Analysis Questionnaire, and Common-Metric Questionnaire

- What's included in the *Dictionary of Occupational Titles* and how it has been improved through the development of the Occupational Information Network (O*NET)

- What a job description is and how it is used in human resource practices

- What job specifications are and how they are used in human resource practices

- The variety of human resource functions for which job analysis is of great importance

- The newly developing role of technology in the analysis of jobs

- The role of job evaluation in setting compensation levels

- The doctrine of comparable worth and the wage gap

CHAPTER SUMMARY

Although job analysis tends to receive little empirical attention, it is among the most important areas of I/O psychology, providing the foundation on which all other HR processes are built. This chapter was largely structured around Figure 3.1, which shows the interrelationships among job analysis, job descriptions, job specifications, job evaluation, and the HR functions that are built on these processes. It should be clear by now that without a carefully designed and executed job analysis, HR practitioners and I/O psychologists would have very little to go on in making HR decisions.

Both job-oriented and worker-oriented approaches to job analysis were presented in this chapter, along with a discussion of different methods within each category. Also discussed were the advantages and disadvantages of each approach, the choice of which should depend on the job analyst's purpose. Some developments in the area of job analysis were considered as well. First, although the DOT has been of great importance to the I/O field for many years, the Department of Labor's current undertaking, the O*NET, should provide more updated, useful, and accessible data on occupations and jobs. Second, the CMQ was presented as one of the newer job analysis instruments with great potential to serve the purposes of worker-oriented job analysis methods while avoiding criticisms regarding reading level and work behaviors that are too general.

Job descriptions and job specifications are derived either directly or indirectly from the job analysis and are directly or indirectly connected to a myriad of HR functions. This chapter provided a brief discussion of the links between job analysis and these HR functions; the remainder of the second part of the text will cover these HR functions at length. Finally, the role of job analysis in job evaluation was considered. The Equal Pay Act of 1963 mandates that individuals who do equal work should receive equal pay, but it does not speak to wage gaps between "male-typed" and "female-typed" jobs. The emergence of the doctrine of comparable worth suggests that organizations and society need to do a better job in setting compensation for jobs while taking gender-based job classes into account.

■ Teaching the Chapter

Job analysis is the foundation for the "I" (industrial) component of I/O psychology. I/O psychologists rely on job analysis data to design selection systems, performance appraisal instruments, and training programs and to select criteria for measuring work performance. For this reason, ensuring that students understand the material in this chapter is paramount to their comprehension of subsequent topics discussed in this book. From their reading, your lecture, and the class exercises, students should gain an understanding of the components of job analysis as well as the types of information collected and recorded during the process.

In this chapter, the technical issues, approaches, and methodologies involved in job analysis are discussed thoroughly. As an instructor, you can choose to emphasize either job-oriented or worker-oriented methodologies (or both) in class assignments. But regardless of the methodology you emphasize in class activities or assignments, this chapter provides the foundation for explaining the use of job analysis for I/O psychologists, HR functioning, and organizational effectiveness.

To supplement chapter reading and lectures, students should be engaged in activities and assignments that focus on applying their knowledge to an actual job analysis project. The following section provides several activities designed to enhance textbook material. The activities will also help to develop students' practical knowledge and experience in the classroom and extend it toward a larger assignment that can be used throughout the semester as a resource for class exercises.

The first exercise is designed to get students thinking about the types of KSAOs and the level of investigatory work necessary for conducting a job analysis. By working to identify the knowledge, skills, abilities, and other requirements of psychology professors and students, your class will learn about the details that an effective job analysis should capture. This exercise also may stimulate a lively class discussion about academic responsibility. The remaining exercises/assignments can be conducted in class or given as assignments to provide your students with applied job analysis experience. Because job analysis is the basis for so many other I/O activities, the job analysis assignment should be framed with a semester-length scope, requiring students to reference the data they collect in the job analysis for forthcoming projects (e.g., designing a job advertisement and a performance appraisal instrument).

■ Suggested Exercises and Assignments

KSAOs for College Students and Psychology Professors

Purpose Through this exercise, students will gain insight into the jobs of students and professors in the academic environment as well as what each party must bring to the class in order to create an effective educational experience.

Instructions

- *Prior to class:* Visit the O*NET website (http://online.onetcenter.org) and look up the listing for a psychology professor (SOC code: 25-1066.00: "Psychology Teachers, Postsecondary"). Using the "Occupation Quick Search" field, enter "Psychology Professor" to quickly go to the listing. If your classroom has multimedia (i.e., Internet access), you could bookmark the page so you can show it to students after they have completed this activity. Otherwise, you could print the classification's "Summary" page to show the class.
- Break the class into small groups and ask them to brainstorm about the KSAOs that are required to be a college student and a psychology professor. Also, time permitting, they should brainstorm task requirements for each job.
- Ask groups to share the KSAOs and tasks that they identified for each role. Create a class list that contains the unique KSAOs and tasks for each role. Each group will likely have unique contributions to these lists.
- After students have generated their lists and shared them with the class, share the O*NET list of the KSAOs and task requirements of a psychology professor.

Discussion Questions

- To what extent have we adequately described our roles as professor and students?
- Does the O*NET adequately describe the professor's role? Are there any areas of a professor's job that this description has omitted?
- Since the O*NET already contains so much information, why do I/O psychologists conduct job analyses instead of simply referring to this comprehensive database?
- How could an I/O practitioner use the information from the O*NET?

Developing Questions to Gather Job Analysis Information

Purpose In this exercise, students will consider the questions they would use when interviewing job incumbents to collect job analysis information and to generate a set of questions they can use in their own job analysis assignments.

Instructions

- *Prior to class:* Create a handout that outlines the critical information that must be collected in a job analysis:
  - A definition of knowledge, skills, abilities, and other characteristics along with an explanation of how each K, S, A, or O is different from the others
  - A definition of task requirements and work environment characteristics
  - A way to differentiate between essential and nonessential tasks
- Consider dividing the class into small groups. Or simply conduct this as an open class discussion if your class is not too large.
- Provide the handout outlining the necessary information to students.
- To ensure that students understand the differences between knowledge (K), skills (S), and abilities (A), you might provide examples and ask the class to identify each as a K, S, or A. For example, is being fluent in a second language a knowledge, skill, or ability? One must have knowledge of the language but must also be able to speak it well. Are skills manual-type activities (like typing or digging), or can speaking another language also be a skill? Stimulate class thinking about the challenges in classifying behaviors as K, S, or A.
- Have students brainstorm a set of approximately 10 questions, including any necessary follow-up questions they would use when interviewing a job incumbent.
- Have individuals/groups turn to other individuals/groups and share their list of questions to receive feedback on its comprehensiveness and effectiveness.
- As an outcome of this exercise, a "job analysis questions" handout can be generated for students' use in conducting their own job incumbent interviews.

Discussion Questions

- Did you receive any surprising feedback from other groups? What are some examples?
- What were some aspects of the job that you overlooked?
- What did you find more challenging than you expected during this exercise?
- How do you think answers to these questions might differ if you interview a supervisor instead of a job incumbent?

Job Analysis

Purpose Students will conduct an abbreviated version of a job analysis in a "safe" environment (i.e., they interview a friend or family member and write up the results for class instead of an organization).

Instructions

- Ask students to conduct a job analysis by interviewing a friend or family member who is currently employed. Information should include (but not be limited to) the following:
  - An overall description of the job
  - An explanation of how the job is classified in the O*NET (including the occupational code and task requirements)
  - A description of the knowledge, skills, abilities, and other characteristics that are essential to job performance (based on student findings, not the O*NET)
  - A description of the work environment, including a description of the physical work environment, supervisory controls, physical demands, typical amount of interpersonal contact, amount of expected teamwork, job complexity, and amount of direction (supervision) typically required to get the job done (again, based on student findings, not the O*NET)
  - A brief summary of the organization's culture and competitive environment
- Have students write their job analysis, including the information presented above. They should also outline any challenges they faced in interviewing the incumbent and writing the job analysis. Write-ups can be anywhere from two to five pages in length.
- If feasible, have students present their job analysis findings to the class.

Discussion Questions

- Were there any aspects of the job that you were surprised by? What are some examples?
- What challenges did you face while you were working on this assignment?
- How do you think your results might have differed if you interviewed a different person in this position at this organization?
- What would differ if you interviewed someone in the same position in a different organization?
- Why is accuracy so important in job analysis? What are some barriers to obtaining accurate responses from your interviewee?

Design a Job Advertisement

Purpose Students will apply information from their job analysis to a real-world application.

Instructions

- *Prior to class:* Prepare a sample job analysis before class to present to students (this can be the psychology professor O*NET description). Or have students bring a copy of their job analysis to class.
- Divide students into groups of three or four.
- Have students select one group member's job analysis to use in writing a job advertisement. Once they have selected the job, they should generate a fictional organization where the job is located.

- Have students create a brief advertisement for the job, including the following:
  - An accurate description of the task requirements for the job
  - A brief list of applicant requirements
  - Something that "sells" the organization to potential applicants
- Have students share their job advertisements with the class. You might consider having students vote on the most desirable job based on the advertisements.

Discussion Questions

- Was there any information that you would have liked to have, but was not available, when you created the job description?
- Would you apply for a job like the one you are advertising based on the advertisement you created? Why or why not?
- What job advertisements have you seen that attracted you to apply for a job?

Conduct a Job Evaluation

Purpose Students will consider what types of factors lead to different pay in organizations.

Instructions

- *Prior to class:* Consider an organization with which students are likely to have had experience. For example, they can consider jobs on a college campus or in an organization for which they have worked or been a customer (e g , a grocery store, restaurant, or a retail outlet).
- Divide students into groups of three or four. Ask them to think of three jobs in the target organization and consider the following:
  - How much *effort* is involved in each job?
  - How much *skill* is required by the job?
  - How much *responsibility* is required by the job?
  - What are the *working conditions* of the job?
- Ask students to use their answers to these questions to estimate the annual salary for each position (these will likely be rather high compared to what would be realistic).
- Have students share the jobs they considered and their estimated salaries.

Discussion Questions

- How important did you consider each component when deciding how much to pay each person? Did you tend to weight one aspect more heavily than others when you were estimating salaries?
- What information would you have liked to have? How might you go about getting that information?

■ Evaluating "Taking It to the Field"

The Chapter 3 activity involves having students interview college employees to learn more about what characteristics are required to be effective at a certain job. We use this approach so that students can also learn more about their college/university. However, if you have concerns about receiving a number of varied responses, you can also ask the students to do a job analysis for an employee they all have access to (e.g., a college professor) or you can ask them to create a job description for a position they are likely to be familiar with (e.g., a fast-food cook, a server in a restaurant).

Below is a general rubric for what poor, good, and excellent responses look like.

Poor responses . . .	• Contain spelling and grammatical errors • Are copied directly from O*NET • Use inconsistent verb tense (e.g., *Listens, Observed*) • Are too vague to provide useful information about the job (e.g., "Knows how to clean") • Provide the response in an essay-style format • Focus on job tasks (e.g., "Cleans tables properly") • Are too short (e.g., less than a half a page) or too long (over two pages)
Good responses . . .	• Use proper spelling and grammar • Use consistent verb tense (e.g., *Listens, Observes*) • Provide adequate detail for an applicant to understand a position (e.g., "Knows how to properly disinfect a food preparation area") • Effectively use bullet points • Are an appropriate length (one to two pages)
Excellent responses . . .	• Use flawless spelling and grammar • Use consistent verb tense • Provide adequate detail for an applicant to understand a position (e.g., "Knows how to properly disinfect a food preparation area") • Effectively use bullet points • Are an appropriate length (one to two pages) • Note details about workers that other students may take for granted (e.g., whether speaking English is necessary, whether good vision is required for the job)

■ Evaluating "Application Questions"

1. Find a job ad in the newspaper or online. According to this ad, what are some KSAOs required for that position? Are there any KSAOs you believe might be expected but are omitted from this ad? What might be the consequences of that omission?

Evaluation Guide: Responses from students may vary a great deal in this activity. So you might ask to see the ad as well as students' responses so you can better evaluate how well they have identified key points. Here are some points you might consider making:

- There may be some expectations that are assumed on the part of the HR department and thus are not mentioned in the job ad. For example, sometimes job ads omit information about being able to work with others, having writing skills, or being able to work with ambiguous or poorly defined problems.
- There are some KSAOs that are likely to be common across ads. This might be a good opportunity to connect students' college experiences with these ads. For example, if many ads stipulate the importance of having good interpersonal skills, you might discuss with students how they can work on building these skills during their time in college.

2. Consider three potential sources of job information—incumbents, supervisors, and I/O psychologists. What are some advantages and disadvantages of using each source for information about a job?

Evaluation Guide: Responses may include the following:

- Advantages of using job incumbents include that they may know a lot of details about the job, they may recognize behaviors or skills that are necessary but may not be apparent to an observer, and they are likely to know about tasks or duties that are rarely needed but important. Disadvantages include that incumbents may believe they know a lot about a job but are actually ineffective workers, they may not see how their role compares to other jobs in an organization, and they may not be honest if they have concerns about losing their jobs.
- Advantages of using supervisors include that they may have a good sense of which KSAOs are most important to the mission of the organization, and they may be more objective than job incumbents about which KSAOs are important. Some disadvantages include that they may not be aware of some of the day-to-day minutiae, and they may not know about KSAOs that are rare or not easily observable.
- Advantages of using I/O psychologists include that they may have a good sense of how a job differs between organizations because they know about many different jobs, and they may have more experience identifying KSAOs. Disadvantages include that they cannot identify tasks that are unobservable or rare, they are unaware of day-to-day minutiae, and they may not be aware of idiosyncrasies within a certain organization.

3. Competencies tend to involve broader skill sets than are typically described in a job analysis. One advantage to this approach is that a competency model can generalize to many different roles within an organization. What broad competencies can be used to describe what is necessary to be an effective student in any class, in any college/university? What are some aspects of student competencies that you believe are unique to this specific class?

Evaluation Guide: Responses to this item may vary, but students should be able to identify competencies that are fairly broad in nature. Example responses may include the following:

- With respect to any class in any college/university, competencies might include effective communication, effective writing, effective study skills, leadership skills, and ability to engage in teamwork. Encourage students to use broader competencies (e.g., effective communication) rather than specific tasks or characteristics (e.g., being proactive in asking an instructor for help).
- With respect to competencies that might be unique to the student's institution, there may be unique skills or beliefs that are important for student success or self-esteem. For example, in religious institutions, demonstrating strong faith may be part of the student experience. In a school where volunteerism is a focus, interests and skills in this area may be relevant.
- It is helpful to draw students' attention to the difference between competencies (which can be quite general) and a more task-oriented job analysis approach (which is quite specific)

4. What are some jobs that have a significant need for strategic job analysis? Why is this so?

Evaluation Guide: Students may have a broad array of responses for this question. If they need prompting, you could encourage them to think about what jobs might be more important in the future work environment or how the changing nature of work and technology might affect the skills that are necessary. Here are some additional points to consider:

- Students are likely to identify jobs where technology is a focus. It can be helpful, however, to emphasize that many jobs are not immediately identifiable as highly dependent on technology. For example, many manufacturing jobs are becoming more technical because of advanced equipment.
- Students should also consider jobs that are changing because of telecommuting, globalization, or other changes to the workplace setting or expectations.

■ Highlighted Study for Discussion

Landrum, R.E., Hettich, P.I., & Wilner, A. (2010). Alumni perceptions of workforce readiness. *Teaching of Psychology, 37,* 97–106.

Although not strictly about job analysis, this article provides an interesting example of a mismatch between individuals' skills and the jobs they hold. The article may also provide students some insight into how college can prepare them for the workforce and why instructors may make decisions about including particular projects or policies in the classroom. Key points in the article include the following:

- Several national surveys indicate that current employers are generally unsatisfied with the level of preparedness among recent college graduates.

- Three hundred and six Boise State University psychology alumni were mailed a survey regarding which skills they believed they gained in college and which they gained in the workplace. Seventy-eight of these were returned with usable data.
- The top 10 skills in terms of importance were the following:

    1. Possessing self-discipline (punctuality and responsibility)
    2. Acting responsibly
    3. Working with others
    4. Meeting the needs of others
    5. Setting priorities and managing time effectively
    6. Identifying and solving problems
    7. Making appropriate decisions
    8. Working without supervision
    9. Working independently
    10. Managing several tasks at once

- The authors also noted personality characteristics of alumni that changed a great deal after graduation. These included being more confident, independent, mature, and assertive as well as being less shy, resentful, and defensive.
- The authors also collected open-ended comments from alumni. Many of the comments related to how professors should use classroom assignments to help build needed skills. For example, respondents suggested that professors should be more stringent with deadlines and assignment completion because these qualities are expected in a work environment. Similarly, respondents noted the importance of group work in developing skills for working with other people.

■ Web Learning

Title	Address
O*NET online	http://online.onetcenter.org
Dictionary of Occupational Titles, 4th edition	http://www.oalj.dol.gov/libdot.htm
HR-Guide.com	http://www.hr-guide.com
R. J. Harvey's job analysis and personality research website (O*NET knowledge, skills, and abilities questionnaires are presented here)	http://harvey.psyc.vt.edu
U.S. Department of Labor website	http://www.dol.gov
Job evaluation website (from HR-Guide.com)	http://www.hr-guide.com/jobevaluation.htm
Job classification website (from HR-Guide.com)	http://www.job-analysis.net/G010.htm
Equal Pay Act of 1963	http://www.eeoc.gov/policy/epa.html

CHAPTER 4

Criterion Measurement

LEARNING OBJECTIVES

This chapter should help students understand:

- What the criterion problem is
- How criteria are defined in I/O psychology
- What the criteria for the criteria are
- The difference between the ultimate criterion and the actual criterion
- How to differentiate between criterion contamination and criterion deficiency
- The important issues that revolve around multiple criteria
- Different ways to weight criteria to arrive at a composite criteria
- What dynamic criteria are and how they can affect HR functioning
- The differences between objective and subjective criteria
- The potential role of contextual performance (including counterproductive behavior) in criterion development

CHAPTER SUMMARY

Traditionally, I/O psychologists have emphasized predictors at the expense of criteria. But this is less the case now that more and more scientists and practitioners have recognized the great importance of developing valid criteria and understanding their role in organizations. Consistent with this observation is the fact that all the HR functions to be discussed in the remainder of the text depend completely on adequate criteria.

In this chapter, the criterion problem was discussed at length and identified as a potential stumbling block to advancing research in I/O psychology. The measurement of performance criteria is as complex as it is important, which is why we speak of the criterion problem. Nevertheless, we are making progress in the process of presenting generally accepted definitions of criteria, examples of criteria, and evaluative standards for criteria, such as relevance, reliability, sensitivity, practicality, and fairness. The ultimate criterion and the actual criterion were defined and discussed, and the traditional view of criteria was explained in detail; also discussed were more recent concerns about the impression that this view can give about the nature of criteria. An actual criterion that does not cover a representative sample of the ultimate criterion was described as deficient, and one that measures things other than what is in the ultimate criterion was described as contaminated.

In discussing the criterion problem, the chapter highlighted two major issues that contribute to that problem. First, the debate regarding multiple criteria versus a composite criterion was considered; the text suggested that even though, from an applied perspective, a decision needs to be made based on some score or number, the variety of information that comes from using multiple criteria must not be ignored. Performance is surely multidimensional, and multiple criteria are needed to measure it well. Campbell's work in the area of performance modeling and approaches to criteria was highlighted as providing a model for how to proceed in this arena (Campbell, 1990; Campbell et al., 1993). Second, the common belief that criteria are dynamic was addressed. This belief is reflected in the relative changes in an individual's performance over time; issues of measurement and prediction were also considered in this context.

The differences between objective and subjective criteria were also examined, and attention was given to various examples of each (e.g., measures of productivity, absenteeism, and lateness) as well as to supervisor ratings of employees' performance. (The latter are discussed in the next chapter.) In addition, the chapter presented a newer component of performance criteria called contextual performance and considered a great deal of recent research in this area identifying the various antecedents of contextual performance and considering this new line of work within an international context. Finally, counterproductive work behaviors were discussed as conduct that has a negative impact on the organization and other employees.

■ Teaching the Chapter

Defining criteria and describing important standards with which to assess a criterion are the key issues addressed in this chapter. In the first part of the chapter, students are presented with a description of the criterion problem to highlight the difficulty that is inherent in determining how to measure individual, organizational, or process-oriented performance.

The first exercise brings the issue of criteria selection to the forefront through a discussion of grading procedures used in elementary, secondary, and undergraduate coursework. Specifically, you will lead a discussion with your class about the criteria used in academic settings to measure success—*GRADES!* While only brave-hearted instructors may choose to have a class discussion on this issue, the conversation will give students insight into how instructors select criteria for performance. Most students should be able to easily relate to this issue, as they should be to some extent experts at being students and adapting to academic environments. Help your students apply this experience to emphasize some of the major points about criteria that are presented in this chapter.

The last part of the chapter distinguishes between objective and subjective criteria. It also introduces contextual performance, including counterproductive behavior. The next chapter is focused on performance appraisal and will present many more opportunities to examine objective and subjective criteria. However, in this chapter you may want to discuss contextual performance in greater detail as it is becoming a larger part of what I/O psychologists consider when designing selection, performance appraisal, and training programs. In the section that follows, a group simulation exercise is outlined. It may be a fun way for students to observe and think about the effects of contextual performance-related behaviors on perceptions of objective performance and performance criteria in the workplace.

While this is one of the shorter chapters of the book, it has been placed carefully so that it sets up the remaining chapters on performance appraisal, selection, and training.

■ Suggested Exercises and Assignments

College Course Criteria Selection

Purpose The main objective of this exercise is to stimulate students' discussion of the criterion problem by using their firsthand experiences with course grades.

Instructions

- Divide students into small groups to generate responses to the following questions:
  - What is the ultimate criterion within the context of a college education?
  - In your college classes, what criteria have been most often used in evaluating your performance?
  - In your opinion, were these criteria highly relevant to the ultimate criterion?
  - Do you agree with how academic performance is assessed in college? If not, what would you use as actual criteria?
  - What is the best way to go about determining "good" criteria in an academic setting?
- Ask each group to share their answers with the class to generate conversations about how grades are determined, as well as what alternatives exist, and to gather your students' opinions on this issue.

Discussion Questions

- To what extent do you feel the criteria for this class are relevant to the ultimate criterion?
- To what extent are you aware of the grading criteria used in your classes?
- How do you use this awareness to enhance your class performance?

Instructor Evaluations

Purpose The main objective of this exercise is to provide students with a concrete example of how performance is measured and to give them an opportunity to critique it.

Instructions

- Obtain copies of the measure your institution uses to evaluate instructor performance.
- Divide students into small groups to generate responses to the following questions:
  - What items measure information unrelated to instructor performance (i.e., criterion contamination)?
  - What items might you add that you believe are missing (i.e., criterion deficiency)?
  - What else might be important to measure to assess a professor's/instructor's performance unrelated to classroom performance (e.g., research or service work)?
- Ask each group to share their answers to generate a discussion about problems and concerns they have with the measure.

Discussion Questions

- Do you believe students provide honest and accurate ratings on this form? Why or why not?
- How do you believe these ratings should be used? Is it appropriate to use these to determine which professors should receive promotions or be allowed to keep their jobs? Why or why not?

Job Analysis and Criteria Development

Purpose This exercise allows students to apply their job analysis data completed from the exercise in Chapter 3 and engage in identification of criteria.

Instructions

- *Prior to class:* If this exercise is to be conducted during class time, ask students to bring a copy of their job analysis to class. This activity can also be given as a course assignment.
- Ask students to use the information they obtained during the job analysis to help them identify and define several criteria important for success on the job. The criteria should be clearly linked to job success and organizational value.
  - How are these criteria related to compensation or salary for this job?
- Have students share their criteria and why they identified them as important.

- Through this discussion, students can hear different rationales for selecting criteria (e.g., most frequently performed behaviors, value of criteria to the organization). It is important for students hear other perspectives on this issue in order to maximize their learning.

Discussion Questions

- How did you go about selecting the most important criteria?
- What seem to be the key considerations when selecting criteria for job success?
- Are the most important criteria associated with the employee's salary?
- Have you had any work experiences in which you were evaluated on criteria that had a high degree of relevance (i.e., overlap between the actual and ultimate criteria)?

Job Analysis and Contextual Performance

Purpose The main objective of this exercise is to have students apply their job analysis data and recognize contextual performance.

Instructions

- *Prior to class:* As in the previous exercise, ask students to bring a copy of their job analysis to class if this exercise will be conducted during class time.
- Have students identify at least one example for each of the five categories of contextual performance:
  1. Working with extra enthusiasm to get the job done
  2. Volunteering to do things that aren't formally part of the job; taking on extra responsibility
  3. Helping others with their jobs (sportsmanship or organizational courtesy)
  4. Meeting deadlines and complying with organizational rules and regulations (civic virtue or conscientiousness)
  5. Supporting or defending the organization for which the employee works
- Have students share their examples with one another. Then, as a class, use the discussion questions below to guide your conversation about contextual performance and how it is differentiated from task performance.

Discussion Questions

- How does contextual performance differ from task performance?
- Could contextual performance overlap with task performance? If so, how?
- Have you engaged in contextual performance at work? If so, what did you do?
- Do you think that contextual performance should be rewarded? Why or why not?

Organizational Citizenship Behaviors (OCBs)

Purpose This exercise demonstrates how OCBs can affect work group performance and perception of an individual's performance.

Instructions

- *Prior to class:* While any group game can be used for this exercise, one that involves making decisions and identifying actions for survival is most conducive to illustrating the point of this exercise. Games involving a group that must decide what to do if they were stranded on a deserted island, lost in the mountains, or lost in the desert are suggested examples.
  - Generate a list of steps or items that will enable the group to survive. Provide copies of the list to all group members.
  - For each role listed below, write the instructions for the role on a separate piece of paper to be given to a designated group member.
    - *Participant 1:* You are concerned with time pressure and need to focus only on keeping the team on task and making decisions as quickly as possible. Do not contribute much to the discussion of the issues. Instead, frequently mention that time is important for survival.
    - *Participant 2* (this individual will receive the correct rankings of the top five or so items for survival): Your role is to provide the group with the correct answers and do so without showing any consideration for the views of your team. You know the right answers (but do not be too obvious about that fact with your teammates), so you are not interested in discussing ideas. Instead, you just want the team to agree with your decisions—the less discussion and explanation, the better.
    - *Participant 3:* You are focused only on OCBs. You should not add anything of value to the discussion of the rankings of the items. However, you should spend the meeting time ensuring that everyone is "doing all right." Specifically, you should be helpful to others, provide encouragement and support, stick up for others, and volunteer to do anything for the group based on its decisions. However, be careful not to contribute any ideas to the actual decision making that takes place.
    - *Participant 4:* You are to be actively involved in the task, but watch out for someone who acts like a "know-it-all." If other participants try to dominate the decision-making process by acting like they have all the answers, be sure to step in and question everything those individuals say.
- *In class:* Select four volunteers to participate in a group role-play.
  - Explain the goal of the exercise to the volunteer group: to rank the items on the list (hand out the list of items) that will facilitate the group's survival while stranded.
  - Explain that the two criteria critical for success are: (1) speed of decision making and (2) decision-making accuracy (ability to correctly rank the items).

- Hand out the role instructions (prepared in a previous step) to the volunteers and instruct them to play their designated roles to the bet of their ability. Also, you may want to instruct each volunteer not to share his or her role with the other team members.
- Tell the group they will have eight minutes to play the game and to work on their list. Begin timing the exercise as soon as the group begins discussion.
- Tell the rest of the class to observe the group and be ready to evaluate each member's performance on a scale of 1 (least effective) to 9 (highly effective) on the following criteria:
  - Contribution to the group goal of survival
  - Effort
  - Cooperation
  - Leadership
  - Anything else that seems relevant to group performance
- After the role-play has concluded, have the class rank the performance of each group member. This exercise is intended to result in Participant 3 (the OCBer) being rated very highly even though he or she contributed very little to the group goal of successful survival decisions.
- Be sure to explain to the class the prescribed roles of each volunteer participant.

Discussion Questions

- Why did the OCB participant receive such high ratings (if relevant to the class's ratings)?
- What other criteria were used in evaluating the performance of the participants?
- What might the findings in our simulation say about how employee evaluations are made in organizations?
- Are there other criteria that we could have used in order to obtain greater accuracy and fairness in our ratings?

■ Evaluating "Taking It to the Field"

The Chapter 4 activity involves providing a critique of metrics used to assess performance among gardeners. This activity is intended to get students thinking about some of the difficulties associated with defining and measuring criteria. As such, the important part of this assignment is that students be effective in critiquing the current metrics provided by Stacia. Students who simply state that all the metrics are adequate are not thinking carefully about why certain metrics might be different among gardeners.

Below are some potential responses you may receive from students.

Poor responses . . .	• Demonstrate little critical thinking (e.g., "Your performance measures are great!").
	• Fail to specifically discuss each potential performance measure.
	• Fail to provide Stacia with any potential new performance measure metrics.
Good responses . . .	• Demonstrate that the student has carefully considered what each metric may measure. The student should explain to Stacia some of the more obvious shortcomings of each metric. For example, students could note that some clients may want certain plants even if they die easily; if these plants fail to survive, it may not be the fault of the gardener.
	• Provide reasonably effective suggestions for measuring performance, such as supervisor evaluations, peer evaluations, and the like.
Excellent responses . . .	• Demonstrate that the student has carefully considered what each metric measures. Students should explain to Stacia some of the more complex shortcomings of the measures (e.g., some plants may be more vulnerable to diseases and insect infestations in particular geographic regions).
	• Provide effective and interesting suggestions for measuring performance, such as how much profit the gardener generates, how many new contracts the gardener sells each year, and so on.

Possible Critiques

Number of plants that die: The number of plant deaths may not necessarily indicate the gardener's skill. For example, some clients ask for plants that are difficult to care for; some clients have children or pets that kill the plants; drought, disease, or other problems can also cause plants to die. Furthermore, larger plants (e.g., trees) may be more serious problems if they die, compared to smaller plants (e.g., tulips).

Number of houses visited per week: Some large properties may take a long time to care for; gardeners who visit a large number of houses per week may be doing poor-quality work; if gardeners are in an area where clients are more separated (e.g., more rural areas) or where traffic is difficult (e.g., populous urban areas), it may take them a long time to get from one client to another.

Satisfaction ratings from the gardener's customer: Skilled gardeners may not always be well liked by their clients; clients may also have unreasonable expectations or may imply they are dissatisfied in the hope that they will receive discounts or compensation.

■ Evaluating "Application Questions"

1. Consider some of the ways your performance as a student is evaluated (e.g., exams, papers, projects). What might be some examples of criterion deficiency (i.e., what are some aspects of student performance that are not well assessed using these types of measures)? What might be some examples of criterion contamination (i.e., what are some aspects students might be judged on that are not relevant to student performance)?

   Evaluation Guide: Students are apt to come up with a number of examples for this. If you have a group of students who have more work experience, you can tailor this question to discuss their experiences in the workplace as well and contrast how work performance measures differ from exams and papers students complete in school. Common responses may include the following points:
   - Criterion deficiency may include aspects of performance that teachers are unable to observe, such as time spent studying, time spent helping and mentoring other students, time spent on schoolwork despite having important personal concerns or tragedies, and individual effort put forth on group projects.
   - Criterion contamination may exist when teachers display favoritism toward students they like or when teachers give lower grades to students who don't share their opinion or students who experience test anxiety.
   - This question may lead to some interesting discussions that can help students understand the instructor's position on some issues. For example, you might ask students to consider a professor who will not let students hand in papers if they are unstapled or not printed on time: Is that a valid measure of performance? Why or why not? Discussing issues that might get in the way of accurately assessing someone's knowledge (test anxiety, being ill) could also prove interesting.

2. In the United States, there is a great deal of debate about how to distinguish good teachers from poor teachers in public schools. Some people advocate using student scores on standardized tests to determine which teachers are doing well. Other people advocate using student ratings of teachers. What are the pros and cons of each approach?

   Evaluation Guide: This is a particularly complex issue, and students will likely have strong and varied opinions about the topic. Here are some potential issues that might come up:
   - Using standardized test scores to determine which teachers are doing well has a number of advantages; for example, using such scores makes it easier to compare teachers across schools, and they are easy to operationalize and measure. One problem with this approach is that some teachers may have more resources than others as well as students with different ability levels, making it appear as though there is a difference in teaching when it is actually a

difference in student performance. Other potential problems are that teachers will teach to the test or that cheating will occur to ensure good test scores.

- Using student ratings has a number of benefits as well. Student ratings can indicate how enjoyable and engaged the instructor is, and they are easy to measure. Some potential problems are that when students are having fun, they are not necessarily learning the content; that students who receive poor grades may retaliate by giving poor evaluations; and that some teachers in unpopular subject areas, such as math, might be penalized unfairly.

3. What are some examples of contextual performance that you might have engaged in at your job or in your classes? When were you most likely to perform those behaviors?

Evaluation Guide: Students will likely name a number of these behaviors, including talking well of their organization, helping coworkers with difficult tasks, or cleaning up communal areas. Possible discussions might include the following issues:

- Students tend to be more likely to engage in contextual behaviors when they have time, feel confident they will be successful in helping others, and like their organization. You could discuss how organizational climate and the way in which work is organized might prompt employees to engage in more of these behaviors.

- You could also discuss whether these behaviors are really part of performance if they are not explicitly stated in the job description, examining some of the advantages to considering them as performance (encourages people to perform these behaviors; gives people credit for taking time out of their day to help) and some of the disadvantages (busier people may not have as much time for such behavior; if they are not required, it is unfair to use them in performance reviews).

4. Imagine that you have a subordinate who has shared something negative about one of his clients using social media (e.g., on Twitter or Facebook). Do you believe this behavior is a part of performance that should be considered during his performance review? Why or why not?

Evaluation Guide: This is a helpful thought experiment to help students consider their own behaviors from the point of view of a supervisor. Some topics to discuss might include the following:

- Is it appropriate to consider things an employee does outside of work as part of job performance? On the one hand, employers cannot dictate what employees can do outside the workplace; on the other hand, sharing something like this can have important ramifications at work, on coworkers, and on how that person is regarded in the organization.

- What might be some consequences at work if colleagues or clients see the insulting post?

- What are some more appropriate and constructive ways for employees to "vent" when they are frustrated with their jobs or clients?

■ Highlighted Study for Discussion

Sackett, P.R., Zedeck, S., & Fogli, L. (1988). Relations between measures of typical and maximum job performance. *Journal of Applied Psychology, 73,* 482–486.

This important article helped to demonstrate the importance of understanding the difference between typical and maximum performance in the selection context. Although this is a relatively dated article, it is clearly written and includes measures that are easily understood by most students. It is also quite short and manageable, even for students who have little experience reading articles from scholarly journals. Key points in the article include the following:

- Maximum performance occurs when (1) subjects know they are being evaluated, (2) subjects recognize (either implicitly or explicitly) that they are to attempt to maximize their performance, and (2) measurement of performance takes place over a relatively short time. Typical performance, in contrast, occurs when these conditions are not present and better reflects how individuals are apt to perform most of the time.
- Comparing typical and maximum performance has important implications for understanding why different measures of performance may not converge if they measure different types of performance.
- Participants in the study were store cashiers. Maximum performance was measured by having the participants scan 25 standard items from shopping carts as quickly as possible; this was tested by scanning items from two of these shopping carts one after another, and then again after 15 days. Typical performance was assessed by measuring items scanned per minute and the accuracy of scans over the course of four weeks.
- Results indicated that typical and maximal performance demonstrate only moderate correlations with each other (.16 in one sample and .36 in another). This suggests that measures of maximal versus typical performance assess different constructs. This finding presents an excellent opportunity to discuss some problems that might occur with certain selection measures (e.g., just because someone does well on a job simulation does not necessarily predict that that person will have high typical performance). Students can be encouraged to think of times they have been measured on typical versus maximum performance and to discuss how these performances differed for them.

■ Web Learning

Title	Address
Academy of Management Journal	http://journals.aomonline.org/amj
Academy of Management: Research Methods Division	http://division.aomonline.org/rm/joomla
O*NET	http://online.onetcenter.org
Statistics for Psychologists: Resources on the web	http://www.psychwww.com/resource/bytopic/stats.html
American Statistical Association (ASA)	http://www.amstat.org
Principles for the Validation and Use of Personnel Selection Procedures, 4th edition	http://www.siop.org/_Principles/principles.pdf
Presentation on citizenship behavior and organizational performance by Walter Borman, University of South Florida and Personnel Decisions Research Institutes (1999 IPAC conference)	http://www.ipacweb.org/conf/99/borman.pdf
Counterproductive Behavior at Work	http://chuma.cas.usf.edu/~spector/counterpage.html

CHAPTER 5

Performance Appraisal

LEARNING OBJECTIVES

This chapter should help students understand:

- The purposes of performance appraisal
- The various formats used in the evaluation of performance
- The effect of rating errors on the appraisal process
- How the broader context in which performance appraisal takes place has various and diverse implications for performance appraisal and organizational functioning
- The role of employee development in the performance management process
- The important role played by legal issues in the performance appraisal process
- The complexities involved in giving and receiving performance feedback

CHAPTER SUMMARY

Performance appraisals are used to make personnel decisions, to provide employees with important job-related feedback, and to document employee performance as a way of protecting the organization from potential legal suits. Industrial/organizational psychologists often play an active and important role in the performance management systems of organizations.

Performance appraisals are available in many formats, including graphic rating scales, behaviorally anchored rating scales (BARS), checklists, and employee comparison procedures. Each format has advantages and disadvantages (see Table 5.1); none have clearly been identified as the single best approach. The process of appraising an individual's performance is very complex and can result in rating errors such as halo, leniency, central tendency, and severity. Two types of rater training, Rater Error Training (RET) and Frame of Reference (FOR) Training, have been established as potentially useful in reducing these errors and/or improving accuracy.

Contemporary performance appraisal research continues to focus on the social-psychological context in which the appraisal takes place. This research indicates that ratee and rater reactions toward the appraisal process are important in measuring the success of an appraisal system. Also relevant to the appraisal process are the relationship between the supervisor and subordinate, the political climate within the organization, the rater's motivation and accountability, and the degree of trust among raters.

Participation is another integral element in the appraisal process. One interesting development in this area is the 360-degree feedback system, in which employees receive performance feedback from peers, subordinates, supervisors, and clients/customers. Self-ratings are commonly included in this system, especially when the only other participant is the supervisor. Although 360-degree feedback is relatively new, early research indicates not only that many employees like it but also that it has a great deal of potential for improving the feedback process in general. Employee development continues to grow in importance as both employees and organizations recognize the benefits of employee growth and learning. Employee development not only benefits individual workers but also functions as a source of competitive advantage for organizations that encourage and provide opportunities for development.

Adherence to legal guidelines is also critical to the performance appraisal process. Recent work has identified fairness as important not only to ratees but also to the courts, which appear to weight it quite heavily in making judgments for or against plaintiffs.

As we have seen, performance appraisal has widespread implications for organizations because appraisal information is used for such important personnel decisions as promotions, demotions, layoffs, dismissals, and raises. Obviously, invalid performance appraisal information is likely to result in poor organizational decisions. Our understanding of the appraisal process is thus enhanced by our appreciation of the context in which it takes place.

■ Teaching the Chapter

The concept of criterion development in Chapter 4 is directly applied and reinforced in Chapter 5 by considering issues regarding the design and implementation of performance appraisals. The purposes of performance appraisal are discussed, with emphasis on its ability to collect data for personnel decisions, employee development, and documentation of employee performance to protect against legal action. The material in Chapter 5 also lends itself to applying data from the job analysis assignment given earlier in the course in Chapter 3. Specifically, the first activity involves creating a performance appraisal format that best evaluates performance.

This is a relatively comprehensive chapter and can be somewhat difficult to teach; numerous facets of the appraisal process are covered, so there is a lot of material to cover. If you have access to sample performance appraisals that use different types of rating formats, it might be helpful to bring these to class to give students a better understanding of what performance appraisals look like in the real world.

You might want to devote an entire class period to reviewing student performance appraisals. During the review, you should discuss the extent to which students' job analyses and the chapter information facilitated their ability to complete the assignment. When students apply their job analysis to other projects, they often find that they might have approached it differently (e.g., sought different information or covered other areas of the job). However, the lessons students learn can be quite interesting and can contribute to effective classroom discussion.

■ Suggested Exercises and Assignments

Performance Appraisal Development

Purpose In this exercise, students apply previously generated job analysis data and use this information to create a performance appraisal instrument.

Instructions

This assignment contains two parts: (1) rater instructions for the appraisal of the target job and (2) development of an abbreviated performance appraisal.

Part I: Rater Instructions Students should consider some of the problems that occur (i.e., rating errors) when evaluating performance, the legal issues related to performance appraisal, and how their performance appraisal instrument is designed to minimize error and improve accuracy. These instructions should address the following questions:

- How often are subordinates evaluated?
- What types of rating scales are used and why?
- What behaviors are most relevant to the appraisal?
- How often should the rater collect performance information?
- What can the rater do to minimize the chances of creating biased ratings?
- How does this system address any potential legal concerns?

Part II: Performance Appraisal Instrument Students should revisit the criteria they identified in the Chapter 4 assignment "Job Analysis and Criteria Development" and select two to four criteria. For each criterion (or dimension), they should create a rating scale (with a format type of their choosing). The instrument should address the following questions:

- Does the instrument focus on results or behaviors?
- To what degree are the criteria subjective or objective? What advantages or disadvantages do they present for the appraisal's effectiveness?
- Are the scales easy to use (from a rater's point of view)? Do they differentiate between high- and low-performing individuals?
- Does putting the criteria (or dimensions) in performance appraisal format affect how ratings are made?

Discussion Questions

- Describe your ratings scale. What issues did you consider when you were designing your measure?

- What might be some strengths and weaknesses of your scale?
- Do you believe your raters would answer accurately on your scale? Why or why not?

Performance Appraisal in the Courtroom

Purpose The objective of this exercise is to make students aware of the consequences of poorly designed/implemented performance appraisal systems.

Instructions

Either have students identify a legal case involving a performance appraisal system *or* designate a particular legal case for them to review. Students should research the case and then write and turn in a summary of the case. Alternatively, this assignment could be carried out in a variety of other ways—class discussion, class presentation, take-home assignment, or a combination of these methods. The written summary and/or class presentation should include the following:

- Who was the plaintiff in the case? Who was the defendant?
- What was the main reason why the plaintiff sued the defendant?
- Describe the performance appraisal that was used by the defendant.
- Who created the performance appraisal? The defendant or an outside company? Did this make a difference?
- Was a job analysis mentioned?
- How did the court rule in this case? What was the outcome?
- What is your opinion on this case? Do you agree with the verdict and the outcome for the winning party?
- What might be some challenges associated with implementing a new performance appraisal system in this organization?
- What could you do to establish trust between the organization and its employees with regard to the performance appraisal system?

Discussion Questions

- Have you ever experienced a performance appraisal you thought was unfair or illegal? What was the system? Why was it problematic?
- Were there any parts of the legal case that surprised you? Why?
- Do you think the final verdict was fair? Why or why not?

Current Research in Performance Appraisal

Purpose The objective of this exercise is to make students aware of current research issues in performance appraisal.

Instructions

Either have students identify a recent (within the last five years) research article related to a contemporary issue in performance appraisal research *or* designate a particular research article for them to review. Students should review the article and then write and turn in a summary of the article. Alternatively, you could distribute copies of the article to the class (depending on the size of your class) to facilitate an in-class discussion. Here is a list of suggested journals from which to choose an article:

- *Journal of Applied Psychology*
- *Personnel Psychology*
- *Academy of Management Journal*
- *Journal of Management*
- *Organizational Behavior and Human Decision Processes*

Students should answer the following questions about the article:

- What year was the article published?
- Who is/are the author(s)?
- What are the hypotheses?
- What type of research method was used?
- What did the author(s) find?
- How does this article relate to the social-psychological context?
- What are the implications of this research for organizations?

Discussion Questions

- How might an organization use the findings in the article to improve their performance appraisal system?
- What are some weaknesses or flaws in the study? How might researchers address this weakness in a future study?
- If you were a researcher, what hypotheses would you propose for a future study?

Examining Rater Errors

Purpose The objective of this exercise is to provide a concrete example of how raters use rating scales, mistakes they make, and ways these mistakes can be prevented.

Instructions

- *Prior to class:* Design a survey for assessing your teaching performance. The measure should include a number of constructs students have had an opportunity to observe (e.g., speaks with a clear voice; presentation quality; provides helpful examples) and some that students have not likely observed (e.g., works well with colleagues, conducts rigorous research, engages in professional development). You might also incorporate some items over which you have no control (e.g., having to do with the quality of the classroom, the size of the class, the time the class is offered).
- If you have a relatively large class (40+ students), you could introduce a manipulation, telling some students that the evaluation is to help you develop

as a professor and others that it will be used to determine whether you will be rehired/allowed to teach the I/O course again.

■ Distribute this assessment before the day you intend to discuss performance appraisal so you have enough time to collect and analyze student responses. You will likely find the following responses:

• In general, if you performed the manipulation mentioned above, students who received a version implying that their feedback will affect your job status will be more lenient in their ratings than students who believe the ratings will be used for development purposes.

• Students also typically provide ratings for items they have not actually observed. These ratings often reflect either halo or central tendency errors.

■ Provide students with an overview of some of your ratings. You can break down the overview by question, or you can divide it into ratings of items students have and have not been able to observe.

Discussion Questions

■ You likely had a hard time answering some of these items because you have never observed your instructor using these skills. On what did you base your ratings? How is this relevant to performance appraisal?

■ Consider a website such as www.ratemyprofessor.com. Do you think these ratings truly reflect professors' performance? Who is likely to evaluate professors on this site?

Developing BARS to Evaluate Customer Service

Purpose The objective of this exercise is to give students experience in developing a type of appraisal format and to see firsthand the benefits and drawbacks of using the behaviorally anchored rating scale (BARS) format.

Instructions

■ Divide the class into groups of four to six.

■ Have students create a 9-point BARS for evaluating a retail salesperson, where 1 is low effectiveness and 9 is high effectiveness.

• Step 1: Generate behavioral examples related to customer service. Students will likely have some horrific and some great stories that illustrate various levels of customer service they have experienced when shopping. These will serve as critical incidents and should illustrate extremely effective to extremely ineffective performance.

• Step 2: Rate each example on effectiveness (1 is low, 9 is high).

• Step 3: Have the group choose nine items as behavioral anchors for the final scale.

• Step 4: Have the group draw their BARS so they can share it with other groups. A chalkboard or flipchart can be used to facilitate this step.

Discussion Questions

- Are there any noticeable differences between each group's scales?
- What are some common behaviors that appear on all the scales?
- Was it difficult to evaluate the behaviors on a continuum of effectiveness? Are there any numbers on your rating scale that do not have examples? If so, why do you think that is so?
- Do you think that your rating scale is a fair assessment of customer service? Why or why not?
- What are the main strengths and weaknesses of the scale you developed?

■ Evaluating "Taking It to the Field"

In this activity, a director of institutional research at a college asks for feedback on a measure she uses to assess professors' performance and also asks what the BARS rating system is all about. Student responses are likely to vary widely on this assignment. Below are some possible guidelines for grading student responses.

Poor responses . . .	• Fail to demonstrate careful thought about the items on the measure (e.g., "Your evaluation looks great the way it is!"). • Fail to provide specific or clear suggestions for Pai. • Overlook the possibility that Pai could use an alternative format for her evaluation (e.g., the possibility of open-ended questions, BARS, etc.). • Offer impractical solutions (e.g., rater training for all students).
Good responses . . .	• Note that the scale she uses fails to capture negative responses. • Note areas of criterion deficiency (e.g., an item measuring the instructor's speaking skills would be a reasonable suggestion). • Note areas of criterion contamination (e.g., instructors do not have control over the room they teach in or whether students come to class). • Provide some suggestions for additional questions; these suggestions should be carefully worded and should assess aspects that are relevant to teaching in a classroom (e.g., getting students involved, using class time effectively). • Provide information on BARS and a suggestion as to whether Pai should use this instrument. Students can argue either way—BARS do help improve the accuracy of ratings, but they are also expensive and time-consuming to develop.

Excellent responses . . .	• Note that the scale she uses fails to capture negative responses.
	• Note areas of criterion deficiency (e.g., an item measuring the instructor's speaking skills would be a reasonable suggestion).
	• Note areas of criterion contamination (e.g., instructors do not have control over the room they teach in or whether students come to class).
	• Indicate which items may be vaguely worded (e.g., what is meant by "responses to e-mails"? By "timeliness"? By "quality"?).
	• Address whether items are actually measuring what they are intended to measure (e.g., whether the class was interesting may depend on whether it is in the students' majors; whether students liked the instructor, or felt the grading was fair may be affected by their grade in the course).
	• Provide feedback for the last item—because it implies that their feedback may be used to lay off an instructor, students will tend to be lenient on this item.
	• Provide some suggestions for additional questions; these suggestions should be carefully worded and should assess aspects that are relevant to teaching in a classroom (e.g., getting students involved; using class time effectively).
	• Provide information on BARS and an illustrative example as well as a suggestion as to whether Pai should use this instrument. Students can argue either way—BARS do help improve the accuracy of ratings, but they are also expensive and time-consuming to develop.

■ Evaluating "Application Questions"

1. Imagine that when using a 360-degree performance appraisal system, an employee receives a rating of 3.5/5 from his supervisor, 4.2/5 from his peers, and 2.25/5 from his subordinates. What might be some reasons for these discrepancies? What would you recommend that this individual's supervisor do to gain a better understanding of what these ratings indicate about the employee's performance?

   Evaluation Guide: Students should note that the differences in ratings could be due to rater error or could reflect actual differences in that employee's skill in dealing with different groups of people. Some points to consider:
   • Students might note the discrepancy between the supervisor's and the peers' ratings. First, this difference may be due to rater errors. For example,

the supervisor might not be around to observe some of this employee's skill in negotiating and working with his peers. Alternatively, perhaps this individual's peers are providing lenient ratings because they don't want to hurt their relationships with him. These differences may also reflect meaningful differences in his performance; perhaps he is quite effective at managing teamwork but not very effective at higher-level functions or functions that are more related to the organization's goals (which would be more relevant to the supervisor).

- Students might also note the discrepancy between the high supervisor/peer ratings and the low subordinate ratings. Once again, this could be due to rater error—perhaps the subordinates are upset about a policy change or some of the work they are completing and are retaliating by providing harsh ratings. Alternatively, perhaps these ratings reflect a meaningful performance issue—maybe the subordinates know that this person is incompetent, and they constantly need to fix his work (and his supervisor is not aware of this issue). Perhaps this employee is also abusive or unreasonable toward his subordinates, a fact he hides from his peers and supervisor.

- In terms of next steps, students should indicate that more information would be helpful. For example, the supervisor could solicit ratings on what parts of his performance are adequate and inadequate, meet with the raters to learn more about the reasoning behind their ratings, or meet with the employee to see if he has thoughts on why his ratings are different. Students may also suggest that it would be helpful to ensure that all parties are using the rating scale in the same way in case the differences are due to rater errors.

2. Imagine that, in order to assign grades on a group project, your professor requires all group members to provide ratings for one another, which he will consider in grading the project. One group member has been particularly troublesome—she has been argumentative, refuses to accommodate other group members' schedules, and completes the bare minimum amount of work. Would you feel comfortable giving her a poor performance appraisal? Why or why not?

Evaluation Guide: This scenario often evokes considerable interest among students, as most of them have had some frustrating experiences with group projects. Whether students would be comfortable giving this student a low score is a subjective issue, but some potential discussion topics might include the following:

- If students are unwilling to give this student a poor rating, ask them why it is difficult to do so. Students may indicate that they would have concerns about the rating affecting their own grades, that they don't want to make this person mad (and perhaps even more difficult), or that they feel badly about the consequence this might have on her grades. You could further prompt students to consider why it might be important for the professor to know about problems with this group member.

- If students say they would give the student a low rating, ask them what grade they would give the student. In many cases, students are willing to give a poor grade (C) but not a failing one. This may lead to further discussion about the difficulty in giving honest feedback when you know it may have a serious consequence (e.g., getting someone fired).
- It might also be fruitful to discuss what students could do to avoid the situation (e.g., talk to the teacher ahead of time, have a feedback session with the problematic student).

3. Once again, imagine that your professor has asked for your feedback on your fellow group members' performance on a project. This time, you have a group member who is very proactive in volunteering and takes an active role; however, even though she tries very hard, she has a lot of trouble understanding concepts introduced in the class; as a result, often the work she does is not usable for the project. Would you feel comfortable giving her a poor performance? Why or why not?

   Evaluation Guide: This can sometimes be a tough discussion for students, as they likely feel some sympathy for this student but also recognize that her performance is not effective. Potential discussion topics include the following:

   - If students are unwilling to give this student a poor grade, discuss why that might be. It is possible that they want to give her credit for her effort. If this is the case, have them discuss some of the eventual consequences of giving her her an acceptable rating when her performance is not acceptable.
   - If students do decide to give this student a low rating, discuss some steps that can be taken to help her do a better job. For example, students might suggest switching around tasks in the group to give this student simpler tasks that she can perform more effectively or having another student work with her to help her when she is struggling. Students may also suggest ways of getting support from the instructor to help them with this student.

4. In many work environments, employees can engage in organizational citizenship behaviors (acts that help coworkers or the organization, even though they are not part of their job), such as staying late to work on a project they are not normally a part of or speaking positively about the organization to other people. Should these behaviors be considered in a performance appraisal? Why or why not?

   Evaluation Guide: Although the concept of contextual performance/OCBs was covered in Chapter 4, it is often helpful to reconsider it when discussing performance evaluation, as the realities of having contextual performance incorporated into performance measures are not always immediately evident.

Students often make a snap judgment on this topic without thinking through the implications. Consider addressing the following issues:

- If employees are now required to do "extra" things like helping other teams and speaking well about the organization, what might be some effects on employee morale? Who will be more excited about this type of change, employees who feel connected to the company or employees who feel frustrated by the company?
- If employees are required to do "extra" things, how will that change what a person thinks and feels when someone else does something extra?
- What are some other ways in which OCBs can be recognized outside of a performance appraisal context? Awards, certificates, or other recognition ceremonies might be one approach students can consider.

5. Think of a time when you worked with someone who did not perform as well as you believed he or she should. What sorts of things did this person do/not do that led to a poor performance? If you were asked to deliver feedback to this person, what would you say?

   Evaluation Guide: Student responses will vary a great deal on this question. However, keep in mind the following points as you discuss this issue:

   - Effective feedback should be focused on the individual's behavior, not on the individual him- or herself. For example, a student should not say "I would tell this student he needed to stop being so lazy"—a better response would be "I would tell this student that when he is late to meetings, it makes it difficult for our group to get our work completed on time."
   - Although students have not learned about justice theory yet, you can incorporate pieces of this concept into your discussion—for example, emphasizing the importance of being respectful and providing specific examples and information about the problematic behavior.

■ Highlighted Study for Discussion

As an alternative to an empirical study, a series of three blog posts by Rod McCloy and Andrea Sinclair of HumRRO are the topic for discussion. These posts examine the difficult question of teacher evaluation and ask why I/O psychologists have not played a larger part in the debate. These three series can be reviewed in class individually or together:

Part 1: Performance or Effectiveness? A Critical Distinction for Teacher Evaluation: http://blogs.edweek.org/edweek/on_performance/2011/10/performance_or_effectiveness_a_critical_distinction_for_teacher_evaluation.html

Part 2: Ramifications of the Performance/Effectiveness Distinction for Teacher Evaluation: http://blogs.edweek.org/edweek/on_performance/2011/11/ramifications_of_the_performanceeffectiveness_distinction_for_teacher_evaluation.html

Part 3: Reccomendations for Developing Teacher Evaluation Systems: http://blogs.edweek.org/edweek/on_performance/2011/11/recommendations_for_developing_teacher_evaluation_systems.html

- In Part 1, the authors discuss the controversy over teaching evaluations and introduce the concept of I/O psychology. They provide a definition of performance and emphasize that it is not the same thing as effectiveness. The authors then argue that using standardized test scores (a measure of effectiveness) rather than a performance measure (an evaluation of teacher behaviors) can cause a number of problems. They particularly focus on the idea that some issues are not under teacher control and thus are not something the teacher can change.

- In Part 2, the authors are more specific about why measuring effectiveness, not performance, is problematic. Specifically, high-performing teachers may not be effective, teachers who are effective in one location may not be effective in another, and focusing on performance can ultimately lead to effectiveness. The authors also discuss shortcomings of value-added modeling (VAM).

- In Part 3, the authors provide several suggestions for evaluating teachers, which include the following:
  - Creating comprehensive, multidimensional performance measures
  - Keeping performance and effectiveness ratings separate and evaluating only on performance (not effectiveness)
  - Realizing that teachers perform other tasks in addition to classroom teaching, such as motivating students, managing dangerous students, and the like

■ Web Learning

Title	Address
U.S. Office of Personnel Management: Performance Management	http://www.opm.gov/perform/overview.asp
Online Performance Appraisal and 360-Degree Feedback Forms	http://www.hr-guide.com/data/133.htm
Manager's Guide to Performance Appraisal	http://www.hr-guide.com/data/132.htm
Free Performance Measurement Resources (registration required)	http://www.zigonperf.com/freeresources.asp
Society for Human Resource Management (SHRM)	http://www.shrm.org
Links to 360 Degree Feedback websites	http://www.hr-software.net/pages/215.htm
Performance Management and Appraisal Help Center	http://performance-appraisals.org/
Community for Human Resource Management (CHRM)	http://www.chrmglobal.com/index.php
Performance Appraisal Software links	http://www.hr-guide.com/data/209.htm

CHAPTER 6

Predictors

LEARNING OBJECTIVES

This chapter should help students understand:

- The definition of a test and how to find existing tests used for personnel selection

- The difference between various types of tests, such as speed versus power tests, individual versus group tests, and paper-and-pencil versus performance tests

- The importance of validity coefficients to employee selection

- Definitions, estimates of validity, and examples of the following types of predictors: cognitive ability (both general and specific) tests, psychomotor tests, personality tests, integrity tests, work samples, assessment centers, biographical information, and interviews

CHAPTER SUMMARY

In this chapter, tests were classified in terms of form as well as the predictor type they represent. The most frequently used selection instruments—cognitive ability tests, psychomotor tests, personality tests, integrity tests, work sample tests, ACs, biographical information, and interviews—were discussed in the context of their role in employee selection. The validity coefficients of these selection instruments are listed in Table 6.4. Note that the variability of these coefficients may be due to the diversity of the studies included in the meta-analyses (e.g., Hunter & Hunter, 1984, versus Schmitt et al., 1984) as well as to differences among the predictors and criteria.

We can draw a few general conclusions. First, it is clear that ability measures (e.g., general cognitive, specific cognitive, and psychomotor) are among the most valid predictors of performance criteria in an employment setting. Second, the validity coefficients for personality tests are not as high as those for most of the other predictors included in our review. Third, nontraditional predictors, such as integrity tests, biodata, work samples, and ACs, are consistently valid predictors of on-the-job performance. And structured interviews tend to be better predictors of job performance than unstructured interviews. In Chapter 7, we will discuss the actual selection process, focusing also on the legalities involved in how organizations use these predictors to hire employees.

■ Teaching the Chapter

Selecting predictors along with designing assessments for applicant selection and employment evaluation are two of the most important applications of I/O psychology. This area of the field will be the most recognizable to most students, as they have likely been involved in filling out job applications, taking employment tests, and/or taking part in job interviews. It is particularly important to clearly convey the material in this chapter and to reinforce that predictors should be derived from the job analysis. The exercises and activities for this chapter were designed with this in mind. All of them require students either to apply their job analysis assignment from earlier in the course or to use the suggestions from Chapter 6 for providing explicit KSAO information when selecting predictors, designing applications, and developing questions for structured interviews.

When reviewing the different kinds of tests, note that the book uses the SAT and ACT as examples; students may want to contribute their own college entrance exam experiences. Further, if you are working with more senior students, you may want to facilitate a discussion around the GRE and its adaptation from paper-and-pencil format to a computer adaptive format. You may find http://www.gre.org to be a useful resource in guiding discussion on computer testing, especially with regard to the accuracy of these computerized tests.

You will notice that a considerable part of this chapter is dedicated to describing the different types of predictors used for selection purposes in organizations. As mentioned previously, students should have some familiarity with many of these predictors. Discussing and sharing these experiences with one another will likely be a valuable complement to the lecture on these topics. Conversations around students' experiences (good and bad) with interviews, integrity tests, and biodata may elicit some interesting stories. The majority of the exercises outlined below are designed to demonstrate the importance of using job analysis data as the starting point for predictor selection and assessment design.

■ Suggested Exercises and Assignments

Identifying Predictors

Purpose The objective of this exercise is for students to apply their job analysis data from the Chapter 3 exercise and to identify the most effective predictors to use when selecting a job candidate.

Instructions

- You might begin teaching the chapter with this exercise and then have students revisit their predictor choices from Chapter 3 after you have presented all of the predictors during lecture.
- Students should have read the chapter before this class exercise, but they may need to use their book to help them identify and describe the predictors they would select for their job. Alternatively, you can show a slide or provide a handout listing of all the possible predictors.

- Inform students that they are I/O psychologists hired by a company to develop a cost-effective method for selecting candidates for the job they analyzed (during the job analysis exercise). Because the company has limits on costs (time and money), they can choose only three types of predictors. Give students 10 minutes to do the following:
  - Review their job's KSAO list
  - Identify the three most effective predictors for selecting a candidate for their job and the rationale for these choices
  - Share their choices with classmates (individually or in groups)
- After you have discussed all the predictors outlined in the chapter, open up discussion on how students chose their predictors. Ask if they would make any changes to their three predictors based on what they have learned.
- To challenge students and engage them further, tell them they have to replace at least one of their predictors with a different one.
- As an out-of-class exercise, you might have students write up their three predictors and their rationales (based on the job and the characteristics of the predictors).

Discussion Questions

- What are the most frequently chosen predictors?
- Why were these predictors chosen over others?
- Which predictors were replaced and why?

Developing an Application Blank

Purpose The objective of this exercise is to have students design an application blank, apply their own experience, and learn the importance of using applications that are legally defensible.

Instructions

- Divide students into groups of four to six and have them select one student's job analysis data for this exercise. As an alternative, predetermine the job that will be used for this exercise (e.g., Customer Service Representative, O*NET code: 43-4051.00; Retail Sales Person, O*NET code: 41-2031.00).
- Have students refer to the KSAOs derived from the job analysis (or the O*NET) to guide this exercise.
- In their groups, have students design a 10- to 15-item application blank for the job. They should provide justification for each item they include on the application blank.

Discussion Questions

- What did you think were the most important KSAOs for selection?
- How did you select the items for your application blank? Was there any disagreement in your group about what to include on the application blank?

- Are all of your items legally defensible?
- Is there anything you wanted to include but could not defend?

Using Biodata to Hire an Auto Mechanic

Purpose Many students own a car, so they should have some firsthand knowledge about the importance of finding a good mechanic. In this exercise, students will apply their experiences to create biodata questions for the assessment of an auto mechanic.

Instructions

- *Prior to class:* Look up the O*NET description for auto mechanic at http://online.onetcenter.org (Automotive Body and Related Repairers, O*NET code: 49-3021.00).
- Have the entire class brainstorm approximately 10 KSAOs that define the job requirements, or refer to the O*NET information.
- Divide the class into as many groups as there are KSAOs for the job. Ask each group to generate five biodata items to use for selection purposes. Refer them to Table 6.2 for examples of biodata items for a customer service job.
- Have groups share their items and the rationales behind their use with the rest of the class. Facilitate the group presentations to ensure that they do not take up too much time. If you become short on time, you may want to have groups share only their best biodata items.

Discussion Questions

- Was creating these items harder or easier than you thought it would be?
- Would these items be perceived as valid by job applicants?
- Are these items content-valid?
- Would you hire an auto mechanic based on these biodata items alone?

Structured Interview Development

Purpose The objective of this exercise is to have students apply job analysis data and information in developing structured interview questions.

Instructions

- *Prior to class:* You may want to print out a white paper titled "The Validity of Behaviorally Based Interviews" (at www.ddiworld.com/pdf/ddi_selection_ts_wp.pdf) to share with students.
- Have students work on this brief exercise individually or in small groups.
- Inform students that their assignment is to develop three questions that could be used in a structured interview. Each question should address the following concerns:
  - To what job task does this question link?
  - What competencies/KSAOs are tapped by the question?

- What are some examples of effective versus ineffective responses to this question?
- What could an interviewer ask as a follow-up question if the applicant does not initially provide sufficient information?
■ Have individuals (or groups) present their questions to the class and ask for feedback.

Discussion Questions

■ Was it easy to create these questions?
■ If you have performed this job in the past, were you asked similar questions during your interview?
■ Is it possible for a candidate to fake an interview? How might you address this problem?

Mock Interviews

Purpose The objective of this exercise is to have students experience what it is like both to undergo and conduct a structured interview.

Instructions

■ Create two versions of a structured interview with a few typical interview questions (e.g., "Tell me about a time you had to resolve a conflict" "What would you do if a coworker took credit for your work?").
■ Have students pair up and take turns role-playing interviewer and candidate. They should take brief notes when they are the interviewer so that they can report back to the rest of the class.
■ Bring students back together to share examples of responses and impressions they had about the activity. It can be particularly helpful to illustrate how interviewers can use responses to understand what the applicant is like. For example, if a candidate talks about going to a boss to resolve a conflict rather than dealing with the person with whom he or she had the conflict, what might that say about how that person will function on the job?

Discussion Questions

■ What was difficult about being the applicant?
■ What could you do to prepare for an interview if you were an actual applicant?
■ What was difficult about being the interviewer?
■ What might you do as an interviewer to ensure you are being fair to all applicants? What might make that difficult?

How Predictors Are Selected in the Real World

Purpose By interviewing a supervisor, students will better understand the selection and use of predictors in real-world settings and be able to review this information in light of what they have learned in class.

Instructions

- This exercise works best as a written assignment.
- Have students identify a first-line supervisor or manager of any particular job (although the job they analyzed in the initial class assignment would be preferable). They should briefly interview the supervisor/manager face-to-face or over the phone.
- Interviews should address the following questions:
  - What is the typical selection process for this job?
  - Approximately how many candidates go through this process each month? Each year?
  - Do candidates fill out an application? If so, what does it look like?
  - Do you think your selection process has been successful in identifying good employees?
  - Is there anything you would change about the process? If so, what?
- Have students write up the results of their interview.
- You may want students to include answers to the discussion questions in their write up if you do not have time to incorporate them into class discussion.

Discussion Questions

- Were you surprised at what you learned from the supervisor? If so, what was most surprising about the selection process?
- Is any part of the supervisor's selection process *not* in line with the methods described in class? If so, explain.
- How much does the real-world process differ from what you proposed in the earlier assignment (if "Identifying Predictors" was assigned)? Explain how the two processes are different and how they are the similar.

■ Evaluating "Taking It to the Field"

The Chapter 6 activity involves a fireworks company that is asking for help with its selection battery. There are many possible critiques of and solutions to Pierce's problems. Below are some examples you might receive from your students.

Poor responses . . .	<ul><li>Fail to provide evidence for any assertions the student makes.</li><li>Do not critique the current selection system or note only the most glaring problems.</li><li>Do not provide any suggestions for improving the test battery or provide suggestions that will not improve prediction of performance or that are impractical (e.g., work sample, role-plays, assessment centers).</li></ul>

Good responses . . .
- Note that the off-the-shelf application blank is problematic because it does not necessarily ask questions pertinent to the job and because some of the questions may be illegal.
- Note that the interview is unstructured, giving it less predictive power compared to structured interviews.
- Provide suggestions for assessing the applicant's ability to interact with customers, such as measures of extraversion, agreeableness, and emotional intelligence.
- Provide suggestions for identifying applicants with good attention to detail. Common suggestions may include conscientiousness tests, a work sample, or a test similar to the clerical test mentioned in the textbook. Cognitive ability tests may also be suggested; if so, students should explain how cognitive ability relates to detail orientation (e.g., those with higher cognitive ability are less prone to mistakes).
- Provide suggestions for identifying individuals who are cool under pressure. Common suggestions might include tests of neuroticism, cognitive ability, or integrity.

Excellent responses . . .
- Note that the off-the-shelf application blank is problematic because it does not necessarily ask questions pertinent to the job and because some of the questions may be illegal.
- Note that the interview is unstructured, giving it less predictive power compared to structured interviews. Students may also note that the questions managers ask during these interviews could potentially be illegal. Students might also provide some examples of interview questions. Most students are not particularly skilled at writing interview questions without some specific direction, so you may see interview questions such as "Will you panic if something goes wrong?" Feedback on asking less obvious questions—such as "Tell me about a time you had to deal with an emergency"—will be helpful to those students.
- Provide suggestions for assessing the applicant's ability to interact with customers, such as measures of extraversion, agreeableness, and emotional intelligence.
- Provide suggestions for identifying applicants with good attention to detail. Common suggestions may include conscientiousness tests, a work sample, or a test similar to the clerical test mentioned in the textbook. Cognitive ability tests may also be suggested; if so, students should explain how cognitive ability relates to detail orientation (e.g., those with

higher cognitive ability are less prone to mistakes).
- Provide suggestions for identifying individuals who are cool under pressure. Common suggestions might include tests of neuroticism, cognitive ability, or integrity.
- Indicate that the strength test does not do a good job of simulating the actual requirements for the job (e.g., at the shoot, there is no need to hold 80 pounds overhead, just to lift it out of a truck). Students should suggest establishing a strength test that better simulates the actual activities required on the job.

■ Evaluating "Application Questions"

1. Many managers look for indications about how someone behaves outside of an interview and testing context. For example, if a candidate shows up late, is dressed in a sloppy way, or fails to send a thank-you note, the manager may no longer consider that person for the position. Do you think this is a valid predictor of performance? Should managers use information like this in making a hiring decision?

   Evaluation Guide. Student responses to this question will likely vary. Common responses might include the following:
   - Using something like lateness might screen out people who would actually be good at the job. For example, they could have been in an accident or encountered some other unavoidable delay. It would be unfair to penalize them for something out of their control.
   - In some jobs, dressing professionally may not be relevant (e.g., people in tech support do not typically deal with clients and thus may not need to look as professional). However, how people are dressed may indicate how professional they are in other respects, which may be relevant.
   - Make sure that students understand the difference between questions that prompt information about protected classes versus performance-relevant information. Also, indicate that all applicants should be judged equally, so if clothing for one applicant is considered relevant, it needs to be noted for all applicants. In addition, call students' attention to potential problems with judging aspects like grooming that might differ according to gender (e.g., expecting women to be more formally dressed than men for an interview) or race (e.g., deeming an Afro an unprofessional hairstyle, which would be discriminatory) as well as to other issues that could be problematic if used against a protected class.

2. There has been some recent debate about looking at job applicants' social media information (e.g., Facebook pages, Twitter accounts). Do you believe it is appropriate for managers to look at this type of information about a candidate? Why or why not?

Evaluation Guide: Students will likely have some strong opinions. Some issues to note include the following:

- How an individual behaves on his or her personal pages may not represent how that person behaves in the workplace. Organizations should be careful not to discount strong candidates based on ambiguous information presented in these types of media.
- Organizations need to be cautious about viewing information about protected classes (e.g., marital status, age). Making decisions based on such information could lead to a lawsuit.
- Organizations need to treat all applicants equally, so they need to carefully look at these types of accounts if not all applicants have them.
- Students may benefit from a discussion about avoiding having inappropriate information or material on their Facebook pages and the like. For example, photos of people drinking or doing illicit drugs as well as negative posts about their organizations can prevent individuals from being hired or cause them to be fired. A discussion about ways to keep their professional and personal personas separate may be useful (e.g., using an altered name on their Facebook page so they are more difficult to find).

3. Imagine you are applying for a job and you know the company is looking for a candidate who is very conscientious and extraverted. Do you believe you would be able to fake these traits on a personality test? If so, do you think that personality tests should be used for selection? If not, why do you believe it would be hard to fake these traits on a personality test?

Evaluation Guide: This topic is controversial among I/O psychologists, so it might generate some interesting discussion among students. Here are some points worth making:

- Since students in this class are psychology students, they may have a better sense of what questions relate to what personality variables than do other people.
- If students believe they could fake traits on a test, ask whether they find it easy in most interviews to determine what types of answers managers are looking for—note that it is not always transparent what employers are looking for.
- If students believe faking is easy, ask them whether this affects their opinion on whether these tests are effective for selection. Often, if students believe they can fake their way through tests, they also believe that other people can and will do so and thus think that organizations are making a poor choice by using personality tests.

4. Have you ever had a job that was described differently from what it actually turned out to be? What happened? What could the organization have done to better prepare you for the actual job?

Evaluation Guide: Students may have a variety of stories to share for this example. You might bring up the following points:

- In some cases, the organization might have unintentionally misrepresented a job—the position might have changed, or the person in charge of hiring might not have been aware of some of the minutiae of the job. In other cases, the organization might have intentionally misrepresented a job to get an applicant to join the organization. You might prompt students about the problems this could cause.
- Organizations could better prepare applicants for a job by, for example, preparing a good job analysis so as to describe the job accurately, giving applicants an opportunity to ask questions during their interviews, and allowing applicants or new hires to do some job shadowing.

5. Some workplaces conduct drug testing to ensure that their employees are not using recreational drugs. Do you agree with this practice? When might this practice be justified?

   Evaluation Guide: Student responses may vary. You could pose the following questions to generate discussion:
   - Is illegal drug use related to performance on a job? What about jobs where fine motor skills or mental clarity are important for keeping people safe?
   - Is it fair for organizations to judge employees on behaviors they engage in outside of work?
   - How might this affect employee attitudes about the workplace?

■ Highlighted Study for Discussion

Sachau, D., Congemi, P., Meyer, J., & Blackhurst, E., Should you hire BlazinWeedClown@Mail.com? Available at http://www.siop.org/tip/oct11/05sachau.aspx

Many articles on predictor measures are highly technical. If your students tend to be advanced, the recommended sources in the book are excellent for reviewing. However, for students with less experience with scholarly articles, this publication in *The I/O Psychologist* (TIP) is more accessible and might be better able to help them understand how researchers explore a potential predictor variable.

- In this study, the authors obtained applicant scores on personality and cognitive tests as well as e-mail names.
- The authors then coded e-mail names into three categories, with a number of subcategories: (1) inappropriate (e.g., armpitfart), (2) of questionable appropriateness (e.g., bballstud_23), and (3) appropriate (e.g., Jim.Johnson).
- Results indicated that individuals with inappropriate e-mail names scored lower on conscientiousness, professionalism, and work-related experience compared to those with appropriate names.
- One surprising finding was a lack of differences on cognitive ability. This would be a good opportunity for students to consider why someone who is very smart might have an inappropriate e-mail name. Students could also

discuss whether there might be other problems with considering applicant e-mail names when making a hiring decision (e.g., would there be potential for discrimination unrelated to performance?).

■ Web Learning

Title	Address
Online HR Guide: Personnel Selection	http://www.hr-guide.com/selection.htm
APA Information: Assessment Centers	http://www.psychologymatters.org/assessmentcenter.html
Assessment and Development Center Information	http://www.psychometrics.co.uk/adc.htm
Hogan Personality Inventory	http://www.hoganassessments.com/hogan-personality-inventory
SIOP: Types of Employment Tests	http://www.siop.org/Workplace/employment%20testing/testtypes.aspx
U.S. Office of Personnel Management: Assessment Decision Guide	https://apps.opm.gov/ADT/Content.aspx?page=TOC
International Personnel Assessment Council (IPAC)	http://www.ipacweb.org
Information on the Five-factor Model of Personality	http://www.personalityresearch.org/bigfive.html
The Personality Project	http://www.personality-project.org
Developmental Dimensions International (DDI)	http://www.ddiworld.com

CHAPTER 7

Selection Decisions and Personnel Law

LEARNING OBJECTIVES

This chapter should help students understand:

- The steps involved in validating a selection battery
- Some of the best recruitment strategies used by organizations to recruit individuals to apply for jobs
- The differences between predictive validation and concurrent validation and the steps involved in each
- The importance of cross-validation
- What validity generalization is and how important it has become to I/O psychology
- The three main approaches to selection (multiple cutoff, multiple hurdle, and multiple regression) and the differences among them
- The importance of the utility concept for I/O selection
- The factors that affect the utility of a selection battery (namely, validity, base rate, selection ratio, and cost)
- Important related concepts such as employment at-will, adverse impact, and affirmative action
- What has been rendered illegal by certain U.S. employment laws
- The different forms of sexual harassment
- How the courts seem to be interpreting reasonable accommodation, essential functions of the job, and undue hardship under the Americans with Disabilities Act

CHAPTER SUMMARY

Whereas Chapter 6 discussed the many types of predictors used in employee selection, this chapter presented information about how to use those predictors in making selection decisions. Predictive validation, concurrent validation, validity generalization, and synthetic validation were examined in light of how important they are for employee selection. Recruitment was also discussed as an important precursor to employee selection, and the recent role of social media in this process was examined.

Various approaches to the selection process were discussed, including the multiple cutoff, multiple hurdle, and multiple regression techniques. This part of the discussion provided both a how-to guide and an overview of the differences among these approaches. A lengthy discussion of utility followed; here it was noted that if a selection battery is not viewed as useful for an organization, the organization is unlikely to be interested in it. The chapter also looked at two ways in which decision accuracy can be operationalized: decision accuracy for hires and overall decision accuracy. Validity, base rate, selection ratio, and cost were identified as important factors affecting the utility of a new selection battery.

The last half of the chapter was devoted to legal issues in industrial psychology. The emphasis was on selection, as it is in this area that legal issues tend to emerge most often. First, the history of the EEOC was discussed. Next, employment at-will, adverse impact, and affirmative action were examined, as these are among the most important concepts one must understand in order to appreciate the context and procedures involved in personnel law. Finally, the major employment laws currently in place (see Table 7.8) were considered. Distinctions were drawn between disparate treatment and disparate impact, between *quid pro quo* harassment and hostile work environment harassment, between BFOQ defenses and job-relatedness defenses, and between reasonable accommodation and undue hardship.

■ Teaching the Chapter

There are three interrelated topics presented in this chapter: recruitment, selection decisions, and employment law. The recruitment portion of the chapter presents an opportunity to stimulate class conversation about what types of things attract people to apply for a job in an organization. Do they look at how nice the recruitment material appears, do they focus on certain types of information, or do they simply look for a name brand that they recognize? The dramatic increase in the role of the Internet in recruitment efforts also takes center stage in this chapter and is worth discussing with students. Who is the primary audience for online recruiting efforts? What are the legal implications of using the Internet to recruit and attract employees?

The second part of the chapter is dedicated to a discussion of selection decisions. Specifically, validation and regression approaches to selection are discussed—though they should be a review of information presented in Chapter 2. However, this chapter further offers students the opportunity to integrate that material into the practical application of making a selection decision. In addition, the second exercise presented below is designed to allow you to demonstrate the complexity of selection decisions as well as how decisions may differ depending on predictor weighting and how cut-offs are used. Discussion around the value of I/O and HR in organizations may result from the chapter's coverage of utility.

The chapter concludes with a primer on employment law, which is important to organizations, I/O psychology, and society as a whole. Personnel laws have been established, and currently are used, to help level the organizational playing field for groups that have historically experienced discrimination in employment and society. Laws are also designed to give certain protections from overzealous corporate interests. Therefore, students are likely to be very engaged in discussing the legal implications of employment decisions even if they do not plan to become an employment litigator. One of the exercises below was developed to help students gain exposure to employment law and legal research. Mainstream media outlets, such as major newspapers and magazines, also may be fruitful sources of legal issues pertaining to employment decisions. You may want to consider integrating such current articles into your classroom discussions to give students a glimpse of how these laws affect employees and organizations in real time.

■ Suggested Exercises and Assignments

The Internet and Recruitment

Purpose The main objective of this exercise is to examine a variety of employers' websites and determine the factors that make the employers and their respective websites attractive to potential applicants.

Instructions

- Have students identify a job and an industry they are interested in researching. This may be the job/industry for which they conducted their earlier job analysis in Chapter 3.
- Ask students to go to a major Internet job board (e.g., monster.com, hotjobs.com, or careerbuilder.com) and enter their target job.
- Ask students to identify as few as two or three companies (or as many as eight to ten) that have posted jobs on the job board. They should use the links to the employers' websites to examine the employers' recruitment pages. Have students report (in written or presentation format) on the characteristics of these sites, guided by the following questions:
  - What are the major differences and similarities between the sites?
  - Can you tell by the website's presentation what target audience the company is trying to attract?
  - What kind of information is presented on each site (e.g., salary ranges, workplace diversity, realistic job previews)?
  - What aesthetic aspects of the websites are attractive to you (e.g., animation, pictures, interactivity)?
  - To what extent is it easy to get information about the job from the website? Does it seem easy to contact someone at the organization?
  - Can an applicant apply online?

Discussion Questions

- What stood out as the major similarities and differences across these websites?
- Were there any sites that definitely would have/would not have led you to apply for a job?
- Aside from using the employers' recruitment web pages, how else might job applicants use the Internet in their job search?
- How might employers use the Internet to learn more about potential applicants (Facebook, LinkedIn, etc.)?

Making Selection Decisions for a Bookstore

Purpose This exercise will give students experience in applying the principles learned in the chapter regarding selection decisions (multiple scores, multiple cutoffs, multiple regression) to a practical example.

Instructions

- *Prior to class:* Copy the table below into a format you can present to students during class (reproduce in an electronic file if a virtual classroom is used, or on your classroom board). You will not reveal the entire table at first.
- Begin by informing students that you will be staffing a bookstore with one manager, three sales clerks, and two warehouse workers.
- Next, show students the first row of the table, which illustrates all of the various predictors to be used. Ask the class which two predictors in the table they would use to make a selection decision for hiring a bookstore manager. Then have the class calculate scores to demonstrate who should be chosen for the job.
- Ask students what they feel is absolutely necessary to perform the manager job and create a cutoff score (note that all scores range from 1 to 10).
- Then have students run through a variety of scenarios for hiring sales clerks and warehouse workers. Have the class note how the different equations and combinations of cutoff scores change the composition of who should be hired for which job.
- Feel free to use the information in the table in as many different ways as you would like, depending on what issue and element you would like to highlight.

Discussion Questions

- What is your impression of the challenges facing organizations when making selection decisions?
- Would you implement a multiple hurdle approach for any of the three jobs? Why or why not?

					Sit.	Cog.		Regression	Regression
Applicant	Gender	Big 5	Exp.	Intrvw.	Judgment	Abil.	Total	Equation$_1$	Equation$_2$
Donald	M	Hi E, Lo C	8	8	6	7	29	19.96	23.40
Terry	F	Hi A, Lo C	1	7	4	4	16	7.44	20.44
Brian	M	Lo E, Hi C	6	8	10	7	31	18	23.44
April	F	Hi N, Hi C	4	6	4	10	24	14.04	18.62
Peter	M	Hi E, Lo C	2	2	1	4	9	6.67	7.52
Anita	F	Hi E, Lo C	5	10	8	7	30	16.58	25.88
Jim	M	Lo E, Hi C	3	7	3	8	21	11.78	18.79
Diane	F	Lo O, Hi A	2	9	7	3	21	9.92	20.79
Cut Scores									
Manager		Hi E	4	7	5	4	20	12.20	18.21
Sales		Hi A	3	6	4	4	17	10.14	15.72
Inventory		Hi C	2	2	1	4	9	6.67	7.52

Table for use with this exercise:

Regression Equation$_1$ = 1.2 + 1.5 (Experience) + .3 (Interview) + .26 (Sit. Judgment) + .4 (Cog. Abil.)

Regression Equation$_2$ = 1.2 + .5 (Experience) + 1.73 (Interview) + .26 (Sit. Judgment) + .4 (Cog. Abil.)

Gratz v. Bollinger Case

Purpose This exercise will provide students with an example of a case that had an important impact on selection of students at Michigan State.

Instructions

- Introduce the *Michigan State v. Gratz* case. There are several videos available of the case; for example, *Tom Brokaw Reports: Affirmative Action Hour* provides a good overview of the case. Alternatively, you can provide a handout with the details of the case.

- After the case has been presented, you could take an anonymous poll to see where students stand on the case (or on affirmative action in general) or divide the class in half and ask them to argue one side versus the other.
- Debrief by talking about any updates to selection law that have occurred since the video; indicate to students that the laws change frequently, so it can sometimes be difficult to navigate selection unless one is up-to-date on cases.

Discussion Questions

- Do you believe that there will ever truly be equality between races in the United States?
- What do you think it means to be "fair"?
- What are some arguments for affirmative action? Against affirmative action?
- Is diversity important for the workplace? Why or why not?

What Is Reasonable?

Purpose The point of this exercise is to help students think about some of the intricacies involved in determining what changes to an organization or job seem reasonable to accommodate an employee with a disability.

Instructions

- Pair up students. Ask students to consider a position they have had in the past or one that they are relatively familiar with in terms of its core tasks. Ask them to think of a disability someone might have (e.g., hearing impairment, visual impairment, mobility issues).
- Have the pairs discuss which of the position's tasks might be difficult for someone with a disability to perform. How difficult would it be for the organization to change the job to accommodate this disability? What tools and technology might help to accommodate a disabled employee?
- Have the pairs share with the class some key points of their discussion.

Discussion Questions

- What are some examples of changes you believe are reasonable? Which changes seem like they might cause an organization undue hardship?
- Why is it important for organizations to accommodate people with disabilities?
- What steps can organizations take to be proactive about welcoming people with disabilities into the workforce?

Employment Law

Purpose The objective of this exercise is to give students exposure to the many legal decisions involving employment issues.

Instructions

You should conduct this exercise after lecturing about the major employment laws. This exercise is best suited for a classroom that includes computer technology for all students. However, if you do not have this type of classroom, you may want to identify a particular case or cases in advance for students to review and discuss.

- Divide students into small groups.
- Assign each group to one of the major employment laws discussed in class: the Civil Rights Act (1964, 1991), Equal Pay Act, Americans with Disabilities Act (ADA), Age Discrimination in Employment Act (ADEA), or Family and Medical Leave Act (FMLA).
- Provide students with the following Internet resources for this exercise:
  - http://www.hr-guide.com
  - http://www.supremecourtus.gov
  - http://www.dol.gov/elaws
  - http://hrmgt.com/hrlaw.htm
- Have each group report the following to the rest of the class:
  - A brief overview of the law (this should be a review, since it was already discussed in class)
  - A general statement of why the law is important to organizations and employees
  - An example of a case that is based on that law, including the following information:
    - Who were the parties involved? Plaintiff(s)? Defendant(s)?
    - What was the key issue brought by the plaintiff(s)?
    - What was the final outcome (i.e., the legal decision)?
    - What was the implication of this case for upholding the law?
- As can be seen, this is a very involved exercise, which may take close to an entire class period. Alternatively, you may want to identify one of the primary laws and a relevant case in advance. Also, at the time of teaching this class, there may be an important case being reviewed in the court system that will serve as an effective example.

Discussion Questions

- In the case that you reviewed, what did the judges rely on most when making their decision?
- As an I/O psychologist or HR manager, how would you stay current on court decisions affecting employment laws?

■ Evaluating "Taking It to the Field"

This activity asks students to do a number of things. First, it asks them to indicate whether adverse impact is occurring at John Marshall's pork-processing plants. Second, it asks them to consider whether the company's current selection processes are legal and, if not, what needs to be done to make them legal. Student responses may vary, but guidelines for responses are below:

Adverse Impact Calculations*			
Comparison	Majority Group Ratio	Minority Group Ratio	Adverse Impact Calculation
African American and Caucasian American	300/400 = .75	120/200 = .60	.80
Latino American and Caucasian American	400/500 = .80	120/200 = .60	.75
Latino American and African American	400/500 = .80	300/400 = .75	.94

*Because there are no Asian Americans applying for the job, we are unable to calculate a ratio for that group.

Poor responses . . .	• Provide only a blanket response (e.g., "Yes, it is legal") without explaining how they have come to that conclusion. • Fail to provide any information *or* calculations on adverse impact *or* provide incorrect calculations for adverse impact. • Do not critically evaluate each selection component *or* provide only very general critiques that will not be useful to the client.

Good responses . . .	• Provide correct (or mostly correct) adverse impact calculations and indicate that there is adverse impact when comparing the Caucasian Americans and Latino Americans (with the Latino Americans as the majority group).
	• Should note that the neuroticism test is legal because it measures performance and is not likely to be different among the racial groups.
	• Should note that the strength test is potentially one test that is causing the differences among the hiring rates for each race. Students should note that adverse impact is not automatically illegal, and they can make one of two arguments:
	  • Because hand strength is job-relevant, as indicated by the validation evidence, this qualification is a BFOQ and is therefore legal despite the adverse impact it causes.
	  • The organization can make reasonable accommodations so that the hand strength requirement is loosened.
	• With respect to the work experience component, note that this is another likely source of the

adverse impact. Students should indicate that there is no validity evidence for this component, so it is not clear whether this predictor is actually related to job performance.

Excellent responses . . .
- Provide correct adverse impact calculations, and indicate that there is adverse impact when comparing the Caucasian Americans and Latino Americans (with the Latino Americans as the majority group). Students may also mention that because the African American and Caucasian American comparison is right at the .80 cutoff, the organization may want to consider implementing an affirmative action program to head off any potential problems.
- Indicate that whichever group has the highest hiring rate is considered the majority in a selection context, even if it is a race that is typically referred to as a minority (e.g., Latinos).
- Note that because no Asian Americans applied, there is no way to calculate an adverse impact ratio for that group. Students could mention that the organization may want to consider initiating an Affirmative Action Plan to get some qualified Asian American applicants into the hiring process.
- Note that the neuroticism test is legal because it measures performance and is not likely to be different among the racial groups
- Note that the strength test is potentially causing the differences among the hiring rates for each race. Students should note that adverse impact is not automatically illegal, and they can make one of two arguments:
  - Because hand strength is job-relevant, as indicated by the validation evidence, this qualification is a BFOQ and is therefore legal despite the adverse impact it causes.
  - The organization can make reasonable accommodations so that the hand strength requirement is loosened. Students may suggest that the jobs could be rearranged so that hand strength is not integral to some positions or that workers could work to improve their hand strength after they have been hired.
- With respect to the work experience component, note that this is another likely source of the adverse impact. Students should indicate that there is no validity evidence for this component, so it is not clear whether this predictor is actually related to job performance. Students should suggest implementing a validity study to evaluate whether experience predicts performance.

■ Evaluating "Application Questions"

1. The book mentions person–environment fit. When you are looking for a job, what are some cues that indicate an organization is a "good fit" for you? Have you ever been in an organization that wasn't a good fit for you? What happened?

   Evaluation Guide: Students will likely have good stories about organizations that did not fit them. Some points to make during the discussion:
   - Fit is subjective; for one person, a very casual work environment may be enjoyable, while other people prefer more professional environments.
   - When people don't fit in, there are a number of consequences. First, people may find that they are unable to assimilate well—they may not be invited out to socialize, other workers may avoid them, or they may end up feeling lonely and unsupported. Second, people are much more likely to quit when they don't fit in.
   - Students may have some good ideas for helping people to feel that they fit in—for example, making sure that everyone is introduced to a coworker or praising and supporting coworkers will often help them feel more accepted by their peers, even if they don't see eye to eye on some issues in the workplace.

2. Refer to Figure 7.2. Imagine that you are working for a company and a change in federal regulations leads you to require a higher score on the predictor battery. What will happen to the number of false alarms? To the number of false misses? In what other situations might you choose to raise your cutoff score on a predictor battery?

   Evaluation Guide: This is a fairly straightforward question, but providing some examples on slides or on the board may help. Some ways to approach this include the following:
   - Draw a scatterplot on the board showing a positive relationship between a predictor score and performance. Draw lines to indicate a cutoff score as well as a minimal "acceptable" performance.
   - Show students that, even with very valid measures, there are bound to be some false positives and false negatives.
   - Next, redraw the cutoff score higher, and examine what this does to false positives and false negatives (false positives go down, but false negatives go up). Discuss with students when we might want to have fewer false positives (e.g., surgeons or other jobs where poor performance is dangerous; when you have a large applicant pool).
   - You may also wish to show what happens when a cutoff score is dropped (false positives go up, but false negatives go down). Discuss with students the types of situations where this would be useful (e.g., when you are worried about missing out on good applicants because they don't test well, or if you have a smaller applicant pool). These occasions tend to be much rarer than the opposite.

3. How common are BFOQs? Interview five people about their jobs and determine whether someone in a protected class (race, color, religion, national origin, sex, age, disability) would be unable to perform an essential job function.

    Evaluation Guide: Students may have a variety of interesting examples. Issues related to disability tend to be most evident to students, as many of them have been engaged in types of manual labor (e.g., roofing or housepainting). However, encourage students to also think about what types of jobs might require characteristics that could be related to protected classes, such as the following:
    - Janitors, dressing room attendants, or security officers may need to be a certain gender in order to perform their duties (e.g., patting down a female offender).
    - Some jobs may have a height requirement. Women and some racial/ethnic groups may tend to be shorter, which can lead to discrimination based on a BFOQ.
    - Jobs in religious institutions can sometimes be exempt from many of these requirements. Currently, religious institutions are allowed to refuse to hire people who are of a different religion. Recent cases have also supported religious institutions in not hiring people with disabilities if it is deemed that they are unable to complete aspects of their job because of it.

4. Consider a job you have had. Provide one example of a reasonable accommodation that could be made so an applicant with a disability could do the job. What types of changes do you believe would be unreasonable (i.e., cause undue hardship for the company)?

    Evaluation Guide: It is important to emphasize that what is considered reasonable is fairly complex, and lawyers and other experts would likely be consulted. However, it is a good thought experiment to have students balance the needs of the employee against the needs of the organization. Some potential accommodations that students may discuss include the following:
    - Putting in ramps (which is likely reasonable).
    - Putting in an elevator (unlikely to be reasonable for some organizations).
    - Putting up Braille signs (likely to be reasonable).
    - Changing a job so that a small component is completed by someone else. For example, if filing is part of the job and someone in a wheelchair is unable to access some of the drawers, this would likely be reasonable. However, if a job requires this behavior quite a bit, it may be deemed unreasonable to completely change the job to accommodate a person who is disabled.

5. Typically races other than Caucasians are considered to be minorities. Are there any jobs where one might expect a different racial group to be hired more often than Caucasians? In these cases, would you recommend that the organization enact an AAP? Why or why not?

Evaluation Guide: This may be a rather controversial question for some students. Some issues to consider:

- In I/O psychology, "minority" is typically discussed in terms of the number of people who are least selected. So in some positions, Caucasians may be considered a minority. Be aware, however, than many other approaches to racial differences define "minority" less by numbers and more by privileges or social status. Explaining that different philosophies and approaches exist will be helpful to students.

- In the United States, there have been instances of Caucasian individuals successfully suing an organization that selects a higher proportion of other races (what is sometimes referred to as "reverse discrimination"), so organizations need to be aware of this possibility.

- If students come up with jobs that tend to be highly populated by minority members (e.g., in the food industry and in manufacturing), it may be helpful to talk about why that is the case (e.g., different access to education and jobs for different groups of people).

- Students are likely to have many opinions on whether an AAP is appropriate. This is an important point for gauging whether students understand key concepts from the chapter, including that AAPs are not quota systems and there are a variety of noncontroversial ways to enact them, that AAPs should not result in unqualified workers being hired, and that sometimes AAPs can have important effects on how hired minorities are viewed in the organization.

6. In the United States, new mothers are given 12 weeks of unpaid leave. Some countries provide paid maternity leave (e.g., Portugal), paternity leave (e.g., Sweden), or longer periods of unpaid leave (e.g., Japan). What are some advantages and disadvantages of the U.S. policy? What changes (if any) would you make to the U.S. policy?

Evaluation Guide: Many students are unaware of some of the policies in other countries, including forced maternity/paternity leave, longer leaves, and paid leave. You may want to indicate the following points:

- The United States tends to have a longer workweek and less vacation time than other countries. As a result, the United States tends to be quite productive and rich as a country.

- In countries (such as Germany) where women are given a great deal of leave, it can sometimes be difficult to convince companies to hire women because of the risk of losing them. If protection is not offered for this type of discrimination, it can be difficult for women to obtain work.

- In terms of disadvantages, U.S. women may be discouraged from working or from having both children and a career. In addition, it can difficult for women to obtain prestigious positions in the organization. You may wish to discuss with students what women can offer in the workplace and why it might be problematic to discourage them from moving up.

- You can also note that 12 weeks of unpaid maternity leave is what is legally required, but organizations can also implement their own policies that are more generous. You could ask students what organizations can do to help working mothers (e.g., implementing paternal leave, providing lactation rooms, helping women reenter the workforce after their leave).

■ Highlighted Study for Discussion

Resendez, M. G. (2002). The stigmatizing effects of affirmative action: An examination of moderating variables. *Journal of Applied Social Psychology, 32,* 185–206.

This article is a two-part study exploring the effects of stigma on minorities in affirmative action (AA) hiring situations. For the most part, the article is short and accessible, but it may be helpful to point out to students that the variables are coded in a way that may not be intuitive (higher scores indicate more negative attitudes). Main points of the article include the following:

- Study 1 was a 2 × 3 factorial design, where qualification (high versus moderate) and race (Black, White, and affirmative action Black) were manipulated in a hiring scenario. Participants rated competence, projected career progress, hiring as a result of qualifications, activity, potency, perceived early deprivation, and perceived difficulty in obtaining employment.
- Results indicated that qualified applicants were seen as more competent, had better projected career success, were more likely to be hired due to qualifications, were more active, were less potent, and faced fewer obstacles.
- In terms of race, affirmative action hires were seen as less competent (compared to both Black and White applicants), were less likely to be hired due to qualifications (compared to both Black and White applicants), and faced more obstacles (compared to Black applicants).
- The second study manipulated qualifications (superior versus equal to another candidate) and race/status (White, Hispanic, Hispanic hiree with elimination of discrimination Affirmative Action Plan, and Hispanic hiree with preferential treatment Affirmative Action Plan).
- Participants read scenarios and rated the hiree on how well they thought the hiree would do compared to other employees, on the hiree's projected career progress, and on the fairness of the hiring procedure.
- Results indicated that Hispanics on AAPs were rated as less competent than both Hispanics without an AAP and White hires. Hispanic hires in both AAP conditions were also expected to experience less career progress than Hispanics without an AAP and Whites. Finally, Hispanics in both AAP conditions were believed to have been hired for reasons other than their qualifications.
- Results also indicated that participants' attitudes toward AAPs affected their judgments of hires. Specifically, participants who believed AAPs were unfair

were more likely to feel negatively about an AAP hire's competence, career progress, and hiring based on qualifications. Students may have a number of interesting opinions about this finding.

■ The authors indicate that applicants who are hired under Affirmative Action Plans experience a sense of stigma, even when their qualifications are superior to those of other applicants. The authors suggest that, rather than eliminating AAPs, the public should be better informed about them. They also suggest that more education about institutional discrimination may prevent this stigma from forming. These opinions may provide a segue for fruitful discussion about I/O psychologists' role in educating the public about AA and AAPs so that AAP hires can be more effective in the workplace.

■ Web Learning

Title	Address
HR Guide: Personnel Selection	http://www.hr-guide.com/selection.htm
HR Recruitment: Toolbox for the HR Community	http://recruiting.hr.toolbox.com/groups/?reftrk=no&cid=39924779
Workforce Management Website	http://www.workforce.com
StatSoft.com: Multiple Regression	http://www.statsoft.com/textbook/stmulreg.html
LegalWorkplace.com, HR Compliance Information Specialists (from the Alexander Hamilton Institute)	http://www.legalworkplace.com
HR Law "Megalinks"	http://www.hrmgt.com/hrlaw.htm
Employment Law Watch	http://www.employmentlawwatch.com
Americans with Disabilities Act (ADA) Home Page	http://www.ada.gov
University of Michigan Documents Center: Affirmative Action in College Admissions (1997–2003)	http://www.lib.umich.edu/govdocs/affirm.html
U.S. Supreme Court: Recent Opinions	http://www.supremecourtus.gov/opinions/08slipopinion.html
U.S. Equal Employment Opportunity Commission (EEOC)	http://www.eeoc.gov
Employment Law Information Network	http://www.elinfonet.com

CHAPTER 8

Training and Development

LEARNING OBJECTIVES

This chapter should help students understand:

- How important training is to both organizations and employees

- How to diagnose an organization's training needs through the use of organizational, task, person, and demographic analyses

- The basic principles of learning that affect training success, such as meaningfulness, practice, overlearning, and feedback

- What makes an organization's learning context conducive to successful training

- Each of the various training techniques, as well as their strengths and weaknesses

- The key elements of transfer of training

- The traditional criteria used in training evaluation, along with a newer perspective on these criteria

- How to design a training evaluation study in a number of different ways

- The increasing importance and prevalence of both sexual harassment training and diversity training

CHAPTER SUMMARY

This chapter was structured around five major areas. First, there was a discussion of how organizations are diagnosed with respect to training needs. The organizational analysis identifies where training is needed in the organization, the task analysis identifies which behaviors or duties have to be improved through training, and the person analysis identifies those employees who need to be trained. In addition, demographic analysis may indicate the training needs of particular employee populations.

Second, the learning context and its role in training effectiveness were considered. Some learning principles were defined and then applied to specific training issues. As discussed, these principles can play a critical role in the success of a training program. For instance, trainees may fail to learn effectively if the material to be learned is too large and cumbersome; if the material is not meaningful; if practice is rarely used or done poorly; if the desired behaviors are not overlearned; and if immediate, specific feedback is not provided. In addition, the transfer of learned behaviors and skills back to the workplace is contingent on many factors that make up the learning context.

Third, training delivery methods—categorized as traditional, technology-based, or employee development–focused—were discussed. Many of the most frequently used specific techniques within each category were considered, along with examples and empirical evidence.

Fourth, the evaluation of training programs was examined. The chapter addressed Kirkpatrick's four levels of criteria (reaction, learning, behavioral, results), as well as the augmented framework presented by Alliger and his colleagues. In addition, a few commonly used training evaluation designs were discussed.

Finally, some time was spent considering a recent trend in the training literature—diversity. In particular, there was a discussion of issues related to both sexual harassment training and general workplace diversity training, with a consideration of the role these play in today's organizations.

■ Teaching the Chapter

Training, one of the more dynamic topics in I/O psychology, is covered in Chapter 8. An ironic aspect of covering this topic is that you will be discussing training in one of the most common training environments—the classroom. There are many options you can use to make this material interesting and bring it to life for your students. In addition, to complement your lecture, students are likely to have experience participating in some form of job training and will be able to share stories about their experiences. In fact, one of the exercises below capitalizes on students' personal experiences with job training to help reinforce the material about training evaluation.

In addition to the exercises provided below, there are numerous training websites on the Internet. These can be used during class to help students gain practical insight into the fundamentals of training (see links below). Also, the increasing use of, popularity of, and generally positive reactions to multimedia/video training presentations are discussed in this chapter. Hundreds of training videos are available, and you may find that companies will provide you with demo copies for educational purposes. One website that may be particularly useful is http://www.trainingabc.com/johncleese.htm, which demonstrates and sells training videos. The Video Arts series featuring *Monty Python's* John Cleese is sure to be entertaining for any class.

Finally, you can stimulate class discussion by holding a debate about a very fast-growing training phenomenon—online training. Many Fortune 500 companies as well as many universities and colleges are using online training techniques. In fact, entire universities are now located only on the Internet. You may want to focus a debate on the pros and cons of online training (from the both the trainees' and the organization's perspective), the potential ethical issues regarding online training, whether online training is more efficient for student or employee learning, and who benefits most from this training format.

■ Suggested Exercises and Assignments

Using Job Analysis Data to Inform Training Needs Analysis

Purpose Students will examine and apply their job analysis data to devise a training needs assessment.

Instructions

- *Prior to class:* Give this assignment to students prior to class, then discuss it at the beginning of the class period after the assignment is turned in.
- This assignment involves conducting a training needs assessment for the job they analyzed earlier in the course.
- Students' assignments should include the following sections:
  - *Brief summary of job analysis:* Include a list of tasks that are performed on the job, the KSAOs that are necessary for successful performance, and the current training that an employee in that position must complete.
  - *Identify and distinguish KSAOs:* Identify which KSAOs are needed for an employee to be selected, which must be performed on the first day of the job, and which can be taught once a person is hired by the organization.
  - *Recommend which KSAOs and tasks should be the focus of training* in order for the employee to be deemed competent in the current job.
  - *Recommend training* that can be provided to prepare employees for long-term success in the company.

Discussion Questions

- Do you think that employees for your job receive adequate training based on what you learned during your job analysis and your overall experience with people in this job?
- Was it difficult to distinguish the KSAOs needed on the first day from the ones that could be taught?

Designing a Training Program

Purpose Students will consider and practice designing a training program.

Instructions

- Divide students into groups of four to six.
- Have students design a training program for one of the following activities (you may need to provide a larger number of activities depending on your class size):
  - Throwing a party
  - Cleaning an apartment

- Studying for a test
- Going grocery shopping
- Taking the SAT
- Giving a speech
- Grooming a dog
- Cooking a meal

■ Have each group identify critical behaviors/tasks that lead to effective performance, explain how those behaviors/tasks will be taught, specify why they will be using the methods they selected, and provide a clear description of criteria for successful performance.

■ Give groups 15 to 25 minutes to design their training programs. Then, for the remainder of the class period, have groups share their training programs with the other students.

Discussion Questions

■ Did your group encounter any difficulties agreeing on criteria for successful performance?

■ How would you measure whether your training program was a success?

■ Will the training program you designed help you perform the task better than before? Why or why not?

Instructional Designer/Trainer for the Day

Purpose In this exercise, students will apply their new knowledge about learning principles and consider ways to effectively train an employee given practical considerations.

Instructions

■ Divide students into groups of four to six.

■ Have groups design the curriculum for a one-day training session for entry-level retail salespeople. If you would like the formal description of tasks and KSAOs necessary for this job, visit O*NET Online, job code #41.2031.00, at http://online.onetcenter.org/link/summary/41-2031.00.

■ The following parameters should guide this assignment:

- Trainees have limited job experience and will begin working in a retail store tomorrow, which is the first day of the holiday shopping season.
- Your store has a strong reputation within its industry for excellent customer service and low prices. Salespeople do not receive commission on sales, and the work environment is characterized as highly collaborative and cooperative.
- The following tasks and KSAOs must be addressed during a training session that will last approximately eight hours (9:00 A.M. to 5:00 P.M.):
  - Customer service
  - Cash register operation

- ○ Organizational culture
- ○ Inventory management
- For each component of training, have groups explain why they chose a specific methodology to train the employees. Also, instruct them to clearly link the training components to the KSAOs/tasks that are necessary for successful performance on the job.
- The trainees are likely to be between the ages of 18 and 25, and it is crucial to keep them engaged. Tell students that the company wants them to be creative and consider things like multimedia videos, simulations, and so on.
- Tell students that the product of their work should look like a schedule or agenda for the training day. It should include a timeline, a description of the training activities, and explanations of why they chose the activities/methods they did.

Discussion Questions

- Do you feel like you could accomplish all of the required tasks/KSAOs in the time you have for training? Do you think one day is enough time to prepare the person for the job?
- Have you ever attended a similar training? What was the experience like? What made the training interesting (or not interesting)?
- How would you gauge trainees' reactions to this training?

Organizational Socialization

Purpose The objective of this exercise is to discuss the importance of, and informal methods for, organizational socialization.

Instructions

- This exercise can be conducted as a class discussion or in groups.
- Ask students to discuss examples of instances when they felt they were socialized into an organization (it can be a work organization or a social organization). Specifically, how did they obtain the information (attitudes, behaviors, knowledge) that they needed to be an organizational member?
- The discussion should focus on the informal techniques they used, not necessarily on formal training programs.

Discussion Questions

- Facilitate students' reactions and responses to their experience with socialization. Did students feel they were adequately socialized into their organization's culture? Was socialization necessary to perform the job or role? How did the socialization process affect their view of the organization?
- Is there a socialization process that happens upon entering college? If so, how does it happen and how does it differ from the socialization process an employee might experience?

The Value of Active Learning

Purpose This exercise will provide students with a simple illustration of the importance of active learning and practice in training.

Instructions

- Devise a moderately complex task to teach students. For example, you might teach them how to make an origami crane or how to execute a magic trick. Whatever you choose, be certain it requires some physical movement and several steps that must be done in succession.
- Divide the class into two groups. One group should receive the materials you use so they can follow along step-by-step; the other group should not receive the materials.
  - If you have a larger class, you could add a third condition, such as a group that hears the instructions several times before attempting to replicate the task or a group that takes notes on the task.
- After you are done teaching the students how to complete the task, give them an opportunity to replicate it.
- If some students struggle with the task, have students who were successful help their classmates.

Discussion Questions

- Which group appeared to have the most success in completing the task? Why?
- How does this translate to the workplace? What steps can we take to help trainees be actively engaged in what they are learning?
- How can you also apply this to school? What steps can you take to be engaged in classes and to actively learn material?

Evaluating the Effectiveness of Training

Purpose The objective of this exercise is to have students apply their own work experiences to learn about the application of training criteria in practice.

Instructions

- Divide students into groups of four to six.
- Have groups design a training evaluation form to assess the training experienced by one of the group members. Thus, one of the group members needs to describe an employee training perience. Based on this experience, groups should create an evaluation form that is one page in length.
- Items/methods included in the evaluation should measure the following training criteria:
  - Affective reactions
  - Utility reactions

- Immediate posttraining learning
- Behavioral demonstration
■ Groups should also describe how the long-term effectiveness of the training would be evaluated and what could be done to reinforce the training going forward.

Discussion Questions

■ How effective was the assessment of the actual training experienced by the person in the group? Was there any attempt to evaluate training at the time it took place, or did the evaluation come later?

■ What do most training evaluations seem to measure? Do these seem to be useful constructs/criteria?

■ Why do you think organizations might not follow up on training?

■ Evaluating "Taking It to the Field"

For the Chapter 8 activity, a Florida bar is requesting help designing a training program for servers that is quick, cheap, and effective. The owner also asks for help determining how to address problems with training transfer and behaviors. A general guide to responses is provided below.

Poor responses . . .	• Provide feedback that is too vague to be helpful (e.g., "You need to do a better job of training servers") • Propose large changes to the job itself (e.g., "Servers shouldn't be required to enter their own orders into the cash register"). • Provide suggestions that are impractical or go against what Imani has requested (e.g., day-long training programs, comments about Imani's leadership ability).
Good responses . . .	• Suggest that Imani more carefully select which servers the new hires shadow. Some servers may be teaching a number of bad habits to new employees, which could be part of the problem. • Identify different ways that Imani could organize and deliver the training. Most of the suggested techniques should rely on empirically supported techniques, such as distributed practice or active learning. • Should identify opportunities for servers to receive timely and relevant feedback on their performance; for example, having the trainer shadow the new server. • Should avoid the use of expensive or time-consuming techniques, such as lectures, self-directed training, or e-learning.

Excellent responses . . .
- Suggest that Imani select which servers are shadowed so that new servers are learning from individuals who demonstrate strong job performance. Students may also suggest incentivizing the role of a trainer.
- Suggest ways for servers to learn off the job (e.g., giving servers a menu to review outside of work) or ways to distribute practice (e.g., having servers focus on smaller portions of the menu throughout their training).
- Suggest ways for servers to practice their knowledge and receive feedback (e.g., short quizzes on the menu; entering fake tickets into the cash register).

■ Evaluating "Application Questions"

1. Consider some of the different ways you have learned content throughout your college career (e.g., online classes, class activities, lectures). Which methods have you found most effective? Why do you think that is so? What are some things you remember most vividly from some of your classes, and what made them memorable?

   Evaluation Guide: Students may vary in their responses. However, you can identify some of the following aspects that help people retain knowledge:
   - Illustrations that are particularly relevant or memorable can help people remember information. Students might note memorable videos or examples that helped them remember something. Discuss how organizations could devise memorable examples for their trainees.
   - Cognitive tools such as mnemonics can also aid memory. Discuss how trainers can come up with helpful acronyms, visuals, and similar content to aid training.
   - Connecting information to existing knowledge can also help. You could mention how psychology classes often build on and connect to one another and suggest this as a helpful way to learn content. You can also discuss ways in which trainers might be able to build such knowledge structures for employees.

2. Imagine that a friend complains that he has been having trouble learning the menu at the restaurant where he works as a cook. He has the menu, and he looks it over every night right before work to refresh his memory, but he can't seem to keep items and their ingredients straight. What would you suggest he do to help him remember his training?

   Evaluation Guide: Students may offer a variety of suggestions, including the following:
   - He should spend some time throughout the week working on memorizing the menu; cramming right before work is not an effective practice.

- Tracking his mistakes might help him identify where his knowledge is deficient. It could also help him process the information more deeply.
- Finding ways for him to actively learn might help. Practicing at home or visualizing the ingredients might help him learn the material more effectively.
- Asking for feedback from others could also help him identify areas that need more work.

3. Think of a time when you overlearned something. How did it happen? How did that overlearning come in useful?

   Evaluation Guide: Students will have a variety of ideas, but the following examples might help prompt them if they have trouble getting started:
   - Driving a car is something that most people have overlearned. This usually happens because they get a great deal of practice and because most driving actions are fairly routine. This is useful because we can talk and think about other things while driving.
   - Some people have overlearned typing to such an extent that they can type and talk at the same time. People who do this can work more quickly; they are also able to plan what they will write because they don't need to concentrate on their typing.
   - Data entry can also be overlearned; when people have to type in the same information over and over again, they can often hold conversations or think about other tasks because they don't need to concentrate as much.
   - It might also be worthwhile to distinguish between multitasking and overlearning. Often we think we are effective at doing many things at once, like studying and playing on a computer, but research suggests this is not the case.

4. Talk with another student about a time when he or she was not able to transfer training to the job. What got in the way? What could the organization have done better to help him or her use the training?

   Evaluation Guide: Student responses may include some of the following issues:
   - Students may be unable to transfer their new knowledge because the environment they learned it in was not similar to their work environment. A good discussion point here is that many of the skills they learn in college (communication skills, teamwork skills) can translate to a work environment, but it may be difficult to identify opportunities for this because school can be quite different from a work environment.
   - Students may not have had a chance to actively practice their skills. It can be dangerous or problematic to make mistakes on some skills; this can make it difficult for workers to practice such skills without fearing failure or mistakes.
   - Students may have been unable to use their skills due to lack of social support, time pressure, or an environment where there is a poor transfer

climate. A school example may be relevant here: Many children fear that showing that they know something will make them seem "nerdy," so they intentionally make mistakes or refuse to answer a teacher's question so they can maintain their status among peers.

■ Highlighted Study for Discussion

Truxillo, D. M., Paronto, M. E., Collins, M., & Sulzer, J. L. (2004). Effects of subject matter expert viewpoint on job analysis results. *Public Personnel Management, 33,* 33–46.

This article investigates how different sources of job analysis information (job incumbents versus consumers) differ in how they rate task importance. This is a good article for students to read because it is relatively short and straightforward in its methodology and statistics. Main points include the following:

- The researchers sampled ratings of a number of writing skills on police reports. As SMEs, they used police officers (the job incumbents) and district attorneys (who ultimately consume the police reports while building a case in court). It may be useful to initially present only the introduction and method to students so that you can discuss what they think will happen: Why might ratings differ for police officers and DAs?
- The researchers sampled 72 training officers and 33 DAs. The researchers asked participants to rate how critical 16 different writing skills are for writing effective police reports. These 16 skills were broken down into two dimensions: grammatical skills (such as using appropriate sentence structure) and content skills (such as recording all pertinent details).
- Using a 2 (occupation) × 2 (dimension) ANOVA indicates a main effect of occupation, a main effect of dimension, and an interaction between the two variables. Specifically, both DAs and police officers tend to consider content to be quite important; however, police officers believe that grammatical correctness is more important than do DAs.
- It would be useful to discuss the concept of accuracy: When ratings differ, how can we determine which is more accurate? It might also help to discuss more recent research that suggests that the SMEs' own experiences and personality can tint their view of job tasks.

■ Web Learning

Title	Address
American Society for Training and Development	http://www.astd.org
Training magazine	http://www.trainingmag.cozm/msg/index.jsp
Training Time: Portal to training links	http://www.trainingtime.com
Training ABC: Training video/book store	http://www.trainingabc.com/xcart/home.php
Workforce Diversity Network	http://www.workforcediversitynetwork.com
HR Guide: Training Needs Analysis	http://www.hr-guide.com/data/G510.htm
Workforce Management magazine: Training and development community	http://www.workforce.com/index.html
McDonald's Hamburger University	http://www.aboutmcdonalds.com/mcd/careers/hamburger_university.html
Instructional Design website	http://www.instructionaldesign.org
International Coach Federation	http://www.coachfederation.org
International Journal of Training and Development	http://www.wiley.com/bw/journal.asp?ref=1360-3736

CHAPTER 9

Motivation

LEARNING OBJECTIVES

This chapter should help students understand:

- The importance of work motivation to organizational psychology
- How the three major categories of motivation theories differ from each other
- The similarities and differences among the various need–motive–value theories of motivation
- How cognitive choice theories emphasize the rationality of human behavior
- The similarities and differences between equity theory and expectancy theory
- How important self-regulatory processes are to work behavior
- The major principles and findings with respect to goal-setting theory
- Why discrepancies are so important to goal-directed behavior
- The widespread use and success of organizational behavior management programs for improving motivation and performance
- How successful goal setting (including management by objectives) is as an applied technique for improving motivation and performance
- What job enrichment approaches have to offer organizations and the various ways in which enrichment can be employed
- The current trends with respect to job crafting and how individuals change and create jobs to better fit their needs and to serve the organization

CHAPTER SUMMARY

Few topics in I/O psychology have been as thoroughly explored as work motivation. The first part of this chapter presented the most commonly cited theories of work motivation; the second part focused on applications of these theories to organizational problems. Three sets of theories were considered: need–motive–value theories, cognitive choice theories, and self-regulation theories. Although need–motive–value theories are no longer as well accepted by researchers and academics as they were 40 years ago, they are still popular in business settings. After a discussion of Maslow's hierarchy of needs, the chapter examined two approaches that are related to Maslow's work: ERG theory and two-factor theory. Job characteristics theory and cognitive evaluation theory were also considered in this category, as they clarify the different motivational potentials that are inherent in jobs and people.

Cognitive choice theories, which view motivation and behavior as rational processes rather than as a function of inherent needs or values, were discussed in terms of two important theories: equity theory and expectancy theory. The latter—presented in the context of VIE theory—was described as the most rational theory of them all. Each of its three components was discussed in terms of recent meta-analytic research on expectancy theory. The conclusion drawn was that these three components seem related to motivation, though not always in the multiplicative manner predicted by the theory.

Self-regulation theories were discussed last. In this context, goal-setting theory was presented as one of the simplest and most empirically supported models of work motivation. Social cognitive theories were described as extensions of goal-setting theory that provide potential explanations for why goals are so important to individual motivation and performance. All three sets of theories have received a great deal of attention in the literature, some of which was reviewed in the text.

The second part of the chapter presented applications of motivation theories to organizations. OBM was discussed as a very successful technique (particularly in the area of improving organizational safety) that stems from reinforcement theory. A similar approach was followed with respect to goal setting and management by objectives. There appears to be a great deal of support for these goal-based interventions as well. Finally, job enrichment and its potential for organizational improvement were discussed. In addition, some of the more cutting-edge thinking around job crafting and idiosyncratic deals was presented, and a series of questions that could drive future research were generated.

■ Teaching the Chapter

Various theoretical perspectives on motivation are presented in the first part of this chapter. These perspectives should be somewhat familiar to students, who have likely been introduced to this information in a general-level psychology course. Students should find this material interesting because many of these theories have an intuitive appeal. However, this can also be a liability, as students may gloss over the material when studying for exams, believing that they are already familiar with the concepts. On the other hand, their familiarity with this material can be an advantage in terms of class discussion and debate. For example, a debate that may stimulate lively conversation could focus on why there is not more empirical support for many of these theories (which is also discussed in the chapter).

Be sure that you clearly present and discuss the pros and cons of these motivational theories, including why using theoretical frameworks with mixed empirical support might impact organizational practice (e.g., discuss with students how such frameworks might be problematic or advantageous). The exercises and assignments included in this section can help students apply this chapter's lessons after they are clear on the theories and related concepts presented in the first part of the chapter.

Applying motivational theories to organizational problems is the central theme of the second part of the chapter. Numerous cases that demonstrate the application of these perspectives are presented in the chapter. For more information, especially related to organizational behavior management, you may want to view these online references: http://www.safetyperformance.com (Safety Performance Solutions, a consulting firm led by Scott Geller, who has been involved in safety-based behavioral interventions, including the pizza delivery driver studies mentioned in the chapter) or http://www.ishn.com (Industrial Safety and Hygiene News, an excellent resource for current articles related to applications of organizational behavior management).

The exercises below will guide students in applying theoretical concepts to workplace problems and their own experiences. One exercise involves examining the link between job characteristics theory and a job description to determine how motivation and performance can be improved. Students will also consider how a need theory applies to a highly complex job—that of president of the United States. They also will examine their experiences with goal setting in light of what was learned from expectancy theory. In addition to these exercises, another way to expose students to an organizational motivation problem is to use case studies in course discussion; case studies might come from a source such as the *Harvard Business Review*. You can also identify a current issue in the popular press where employee motivation might be an issue (e.g., company-wide layoffs).

■ Suggested Exercises and Assignments

Job Characteristics Theory and TSA (Transportation Security Administration) Officers

Purpose Students will analyze the job of an airline security officer within the framework of Hackman and Oldham's job characteristics theory and then develop ways to improve the job by considering its core job dimensions, improvements in employee motivation, and the overall attractiveness of this job.

Instructions

- Divide the class into groups of four to six.
- The tragic events of September 11, 2001, led to an intense debate about the effectiveness of airport security around the world. At the center of this debate was the state of airport security personnel's qualifications and what could be done to increase their competence. In this exercise, students will consider this question themselves.

- Groups should be instructed to brainstorm the results of a job analysis for a TSA officer. They should generate a list of KSAOs and job tasks that are necessary for the performance of a typical TSA officer, based on their own experience traveling through airports. Because some students may not have had such experiences, make the O★NET Transportation Security Screener description available (go to O★NET Online, job code #33-9099.01, at http://online .onetcenter.org/link/summary/33-9099.01). Groups may also want to include a general description of the security screening process to assist in job redesign conversations.
- After the groups have generated their job analysis information, they should consider how this job fits (or does not fit) with job characteristics theory. Textbook Figure 9.3 illustrates the framework of the theory. Students should consider the extent to which a TSA officer experiences the following:
  - *Skill variety:* the extent to which an employee would perform the same functions during and across workdays
  - *Task identity:* the extent to which an employee can point to something from his or her work as being generated by personal effort
  - *Task significance:* the extent to which work tasks are perceived as important to coworkers and society
  - *Autonomy:* the extent to which an employee can make decisions and perform the job without approval or intrusion from supervisors
  - *Feedback:* the extent to which an employee receives information about the quality of work performance
  - *Experienced meaningfulness:* the extent to which an employee perceives the outcomes of his or her job as meaningful
  - *Responsibility for outcomes:* the extent to which the job generates a feeling of accountability in an employee
  - *Knowledge of results:* the extent to which an employee is aware of the outcomes of his or her efforts
- Students should prioritize the job characteristics according to the extent to which they need to be changed or not changed. They should provide the rationale behind the order of their rankings.
- Post the groups' rankings of the job characteristics and base your class discussion on these rankings. Are there any similarities or differences between groups?

Discussion Questions

- Do you see any issues with this job that fall outside the scope of job characteristics theory?
- How practical are the changes that you have proposed?
- Would you make the same changes to improve *performance* as you would to improve *motivation*?
- Is there anything that passengers could do that would improve the motivation of TSA officers?

Self-Actualization and the Commander-in-Chief

Purpose Students will consider the job of president of the United States (or leader of another country, if applicable) in light of Maslow's hierarchy of needs. In doing so, they will also find themselves discussing the positive and negative facets of a job that holds great power, prestige, and responsibility.

Instructions

- Current articles available in popular magazines (e.g., *Newsweek, Time*), presidential biographies, or television shows may provide valuable information for this exercise.
- This exercise is well suited for use with the entire class.
- Have the class discuss the job of president and its potential for personal need fulfillment.
  - Remind students that Maslow's hierarchy proposes that one can self-actualize only after lower-level needs are fulfilled. You may want to direct students to Figure 9.1, which depicts the five levels of the hierarchy.
  - Keep students focused on the need levels: physiological, safety, love, esteem, and self-actualization.
- After the class has discussed the potential for self-actualization, you could split the class into two groups—one that believes the presidency can lead to self-actualization and one that believes it cannot. Ensure that the discussion includes the reasons why students feel one way or the other.

Discussion Questions

- How well does Maslow's hierarchy apply to a job as complex as that of president?
- Would our debate differ if we were using Alderfer's ERG framework as the basis of our analysis? If so, how?
- What historical figures do you believe achieved self-actualization? What makes you think so?

Explaining Behavior Using Expectancy Theory

Purpose This exercise will allow students to consider how their own values, instrumentalities, and expectancies have interacted and played a role in motivating past actions or inactions.

Instructions

- Give students 10 minutes to recall and write down one example of attaining a goal and one example of failing to attain a goal. (The goal could be anything that is personally meaningful—academic, sports-related, etc.) For both examples, they should analyze how their values, perceptions of instrumentality, and expectancies interacted to affect their success (or lack of success).
- Divide the class into groups of four to six to discuss their experiences.

- Have groups attempt to identify which component of expectancy theory seemed to be most significant overall in group members' goal attainment and failure to achieve their goals.
- Facilitate discussion of the three components of goal attainment and how they may influence behavior.

Discussion Questions

- Do the components of expectancy theory seem to affect people at the same stage of the decision-making processes related to goal attainment?
- Would knowledge of expectancy theory have helped you reach a goal that you did not achieve? If so, how?

Learning How to Set Goals

Purpose Students will apply goal-setting theory to a behavior relevant to their own lives.

Instructions

- Have students work with a partner to create a goal that is relevant to them. This goal may be related to school or work (e.g., studying more for class or learning something new) or to something in their personal life (e.g., exercising more).
- Give students a few minutes to write down an initial goal. Next, discuss aspects of an effective goal; a common acronym to help design goals is SMART—goals should be specific, measurable, attainable, relevant, and timely (Doran, 1981; see Chapter 11).
- Have students trade statements with their partner to get feedback. You may also want to check in with students to see how they are doing. For example, you could prompt a student who writes down "Exercise more" to be more specific, such as "Exercise for 30 minutes at least three times a week."
- You might check in with students later on to see whether this approach was effective for them.

Discussion Questions

- When you create a specific goal for yourself, does this specificity make it seem easier to achieve? Why or why not?
- What are some ways you can remind yourself of your goal? What can you do if you fail to reach your goal or if you fall behind in your progress?
- What are some other examples of goal setting that you or others have used to achieve something?

Looking Back: How Do We Improve Secondary Education?

Purpose Students will use their educational backgrounds to consider what might enrich the experiences of the next generation of high school students.

Instructions

- Divide the class into small groups and lead them through this exercise by following these steps:
  - Describe your typical high school educational environment.
  - What parts of your high school education were particularly motivating? What was lacking in this regard? Consider these questions within the context of the motivational theories that were just presented to you.
  - Based on your experiences, the motivational theories, and the principles of learning you have reviewed, how would you enrich the high school education you described in the first step of this exercise? Any suggestions you offer should be supported by motivational theories and principles of learning.

Discussion Questions

- What did you learn from one another about different styles of high school education? What were the noticeable differences in your fellow students' educational backgrounds?
- What educational experiences were common to most of you?
- Were there any motivational areas that all of you agreed needed some type of change? If so, what were they?
- In your opinion, what are the most important characteristics in a motivational environment?

■ Evaluating "Taking It to the Field"

Poor responses . . .	• Provide a superficial response to Hollister Consultants' suggestions (e.g., "These sound great!"). • Indicate that the suggestions are not good but fail to clearly critique the problems with the suggestions. • Provide a critique of only one of the suggestions. • Fail to provide an additional suggestion for motivating employees or provide an approach that has little empirical support (e.g., Maslow's hierarchy of needs) or misapplies an approach.

Good responses . . .	• Identify at least one mistake in the way Hollister Consultants is applying the job characteristics model:
	   • Hollister Consultants suggests reducing task variety; in fact, the job characteristics model suggests that increasing task variety will increase motivation.
	   • Hollister Consultants also suggests adhering strictly to a set guidebook. This also goes against the job characteristics model of autonomy; tour

guides will likely be more motivated if they have some control over how they do their job and if they can change their approach based on their tour group.

- Part of the job characteristics model is concerned with whether an individual has high growth need strength. It might be helpful for Blues Bus Tours to provide tour guides with high growth need strength by means of more opportunities to make the work feel meaningful. For example, tour guides could receive feedback from their tour group, be given more autonomy in how they conduct tours, or be offered a variety of tours they could lead to keep things interesting for them.
- Identify at least one mistake in the way Hollister Consultants is applying equity theory:
  - Equity theory is based on the individual's input/output ratio compared to other people's input/output ratio; in the example provided, there is no comparison between coworkers, so equity theory is being applied incorrectly.
  - Equity theory also suggests that overpayment will make people feel guilty and lead them to work harder, but empirical evidence has failed to support this proposition.
  - Although this is not presented in conjunction with equity theory, the overjustification effect suggests that higher pay may not help with intrinsic motivation, so, in the end, the workers may not be more motivated to do their jobs despite the higher pay.
  - Finally, as suggested by equity theory, rewarding those who are unmotivated (and who are likely doing a poor job) can disrupt feelings of organizational justice among tour guides who are motivated—it will seem as though lazy tour guides are being rewarded for their laziness.
- Suggest an additional approach, but it may have mixed empirical support (e.g., Herzberg's two-factor theory) or may not provide enough detail to demonstrate that the student has a strong understanding of how to apply the theory.

Excellent responses . . . • Identify several issues in the way Hollister Consultants is applying the job characteristics model:
  - Hollister Consultants suggests reducing task variety; in fact, the job characteristics model suggests that increasing task variety will increase motivation.

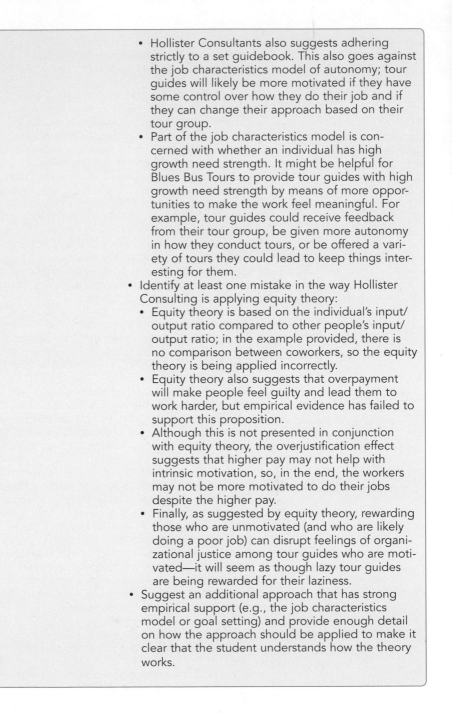

- Hollister Consultants also suggests adhering strictly to a set guidebook. This also goes against the job characteristics model of autonomy; tour guides will likely be more motivated if they have some control over how they do their job and if they can change their approach based on their tour group.
- Part of the job characteristics model is concerned with whether an individual has high growth need strength. It might be helpful for Blues Bus Tours to provide tour guides with high growth need strength by means of more opportunities to make the work feel meaningful. For example, tour guides could receive feedback from their tour group, be given more autonomy in how they conduct tours, or be offered a variety of tours they could lead to keep things interesting for them.
- Identify at least one mistake in the way Hollister Consulting is applying equity theory:
  - Equity theory is based on the individual's input/output ratio compared to other people's input/output ratio; in the example provided, there is no comparison between coworkers, so the equity theory is being applied incorrectly.
  - Equity theory also suggests that overpayment will make people feel guilty and lead them to work harder, but empirical evidence has failed to support this proposition.
  - Although this is not presented in conjunction with equity theory, the overjustification effect suggests that higher pay may not help with intrinsic motivation, so, in the end, the workers may not be more motivated to do their jobs despite the higher pay.
  - Finally, as suggested by equity theory, rewarding those who are unmotivated (and who are likely doing a poor job) can disrupt feelings of organizational justice among tour guides who are motivated—it will seem as though lazy tour guides are being rewarded for their laziness.
- Suggest an additional approach that has strong empirical support (e.g., the job characteristics model or goal setting) and provide enough detail on how the approach should be applied to make it clear that the student understands how the theory works.

■ Evaluating "Application Questions"

1. Imagine you have a friend who is currently dissatisfied with her job. She feels that she puts a great deal of effort and time into her job yet is passed over for promotions and awards. What would you suggest she do to feel better about her job?

   Evaluation Guide: Students are likely to have a number of suggestions. You are likely to see some of the following responses:
   - Your friend could stop putting so much effort into her work or find other ways to limit her input (e.g., not offering as much of her expertise).
   - Your friend could change her outcomes by asking for a raise, a promotion, or some other valuable reward.
   - Your friend could change her comparison group. If people who are getting promoted are much older and more experienced than she is, she may be unreasonable in her expectations and should examine her input/outputs vis-à-vis a group that is more similar to her.

2. Consider a job you held in the past. What were examples of what Herzberg calls motivators? What were examples of hygienes? What were some hygienes that you overlooked or took for granted?

   Evaluation Guide: Students often find that Herzberg's theory makes intuitive sense, although they sometimes overlook examples of hygienes. Example responses may include the following:
   - Depending on the job, students may think that some motivators they've experienced include recognition, interesting work, additional responsibilities, learning opportunities, promotions, commissions, discounts on products, or other perks.
   - Depending on the job, students may think that some motivators they've experienced include basic supervision, fair wages, a safe work environment, lack of sexual harassment, fair treatment, and other similar workplace attributes. Students often take hygiene factors for granted. For example, because most students have experienced relatively safe work environments, they may overlook the fact that some work situations can be quite dangerous and may have very high accident or fatality rates.

3. Consider the job of a babysitter. How might expectancy theory apply to this job? What is an example of expectancy in this context? Of instrumentality? Of valence?

   Evaluation Guide: Students may think of many examples of how expectancy theory can play out for a babysitter. Examples include the following:
   - *Expectancy:* A babysitter who has very badly behaved children may work hard to keep them under control but may not be successful.
   - *Instrumentality:* A babysitter who thinks the parents are overly strict or unfair may believe that even if the children are well behaved, the parents may try to reduce her pay or find problems with her work.

- *Valence:* A babysitter who does not need money may not be interested in the money he receives from the parents; alternatively, a babysitter who is offered something she doesn't want (e.g., free food instead of pay) may also experience a low level of valence.

4. Imagine you have a friend who has decided he wants to do better at his job as a salesman in a retail store. He decides he is going to set a goal for himself: "I will get a promotion within the next three months." What are some problems with his goal? What would you suggest as a more effective goal?

Evaluation Guide: As noted in the text, goals are best when they are specific and difficult (but achievable) and when you receive feedback about progress. Thus, responses may include the following:

- This goal is not very specific—it does not relate to a behavior that the friend has control over. Instead of making the goal about getting a promotion, it could be about selling a certain number of items each week or about making sure to check in with at least one customer every 15 minutes.
- This goal is also not necessarily achievable—getting a promotion within three months may be too difficult. Your friend should attempt a goal that is difficult but reasonable. Again, one example might be to sell a certain number of items per week.
- Finally, it will be difficult for your friend to receive feedback along the way—he will only know if he's met his goal if he receives the promotion at the end of three months. Having a more specific goal with smaller intermediary steps will help him adjust his behaviors along the way.

5. Job crafting is a relatively new idea in the field. What are some advantages of allowing employees to customize their own jobs? What are some disadvantages?

Evaluation Guide: Because research is still developing in this area, students may come up with a number of ideas for which we have not yet found empirical support. Example answers may include the following:

- *Advantages:* People can focus on tasks they enjoy and are good at; people can work on their own to match the work to their values and interests; people can work to develop their self-efficacy; people can set their own goals and pace, which may help them feel more satisfied.
- *Disadvantages:* People who are not motivated may craft their job in such a way that they can expend minimal effort to meet the requirements; some people may feel anxious when faced with such an ambiguous job; some people may not have a good understanding of what behaviors contribute to the goals of the organization.

■ Highlighted Study for Discussion

Latham, G. P., & Baldes, J. J. (1975). The "practical significance" of Locke's theory of goal setting. *Journal of Applied Psychology, 60,* 122–124.

Although this is quite an old article, it is an excellent example of bridging the scientist/practioner gap. It also is short and accessible to students with little experience in reading psychology research articles. The main points of the article are as follows:

- The authors set out to demonstrate the practical value of goal setting in a field setting. Weyerhauser Company, a paper mill, was experiencing problems with the way that logging trucks were loaded—many trucks were being loaded well below capacity, causing the trucks to take more trips, which was a waste of time, wages, and fuel.
- Prior to the experiment, when the truckers were asked to "do their best" at loading trucks as close to the maximum weight as possible, they were loading trucks to only about 60% of capacity.
- The authors set the difficult but attainable goal of having trucks loaded to over 90% capacity. Almost immediately, trucks were being loaded to about 80% capacity, which increased over time to about 94% capacity. This high performance was maintained even after the researchers ended their observations. Ultimately, this change in behaviors saved the company $250,000 over the course of nine months.

■ Web Learning

Title	Address
Abraham Maslow: Information and publications	http://www.maslow.com
Changing Minds.org: Motivation theories	http://changingminds.org/explanations/theories/a_motivation.htm
Job Motivation Indicator: Motivation questionnaire	http://www.myskillsprofile.com/tests.php?test=20
General Overview of Motivation	http://www.geocities.com/Athens/Forum/1650/htmlmotivation1.html
Expectancy Theory of Motivation	http://www.geocities.com/Athens/Forum/1650/htmlexpectancy.html
Inc. Magazine Guide to Motivating Employees	http://www.inc.com/guides/hr/20776.html
Organizational Behavior Division of the Academy of Management	http://www.obweb.org
Academy of Management: Organization and Management Theory	http://division.aomonline.org/omt
Organization Development Network	http://www.odnetwork.org

CHAPTER 10

Job Attitudes: Antecedents and Consequences

LEARNING OBJECTIVES

This chapter should help students understand:

- The role played by attitudes in predicting behavior
- Why attitudes are sometimes unrelated to behavior
- What job satisfaction is and how it is measured
- What determines a person's level of job satisfaction
- How job satisfaction affects important organizational outcome variables
- The three major components of organizational commitment
- What determines a person's commitment to his or her organization
- How organizational commitment affects important organizational outcome variables
- What types of withdrawal behaviors are important to organizations
- What types of counterproductive behaviors are concerns for organizations
- The role played by emotional labor in organizations
- The effect that perceived organizational support has on employee attitudes and behaviors

CHAPTER SUMMARY

This chapter is divided into four sections. The first section presented some background information on attitudes, behaviors, and the relationship among them. At the outset, a popular model of this relationship was discussed and then referred to throughout, with an emphasis on the links between work-related attitudes and organizational outcomes. The work of Ajzen and Fishbein provided a nice foundation for the more work-specific issues that were discussed later in the chapter.

Second, after a consideration of various reasons why I/O researchers and practitioners are interested in job attitudes, a detailed overview of job satisfaction was presented, using Figure 10.2 as a basis for discussion. Research dealing with the four main classes of antecedents to job satisfaction was cited: job characteristics, individual/personal characteristics, social factors, and growth opportunities. All of these antecedents appear to make important contributions to employees' levels of job satisfaction. A few scales that measure job satisfaction were discussed, examples of those scales were included, and the multidimensional nature of job satisfaction was considered. In the conclusion to this section on job satisfaction, three classes of organizational outcome variables (consequences) that appear to be substantively linked to job satisfaction were discussed at length: performance, withdrawal behaviors, and counterproductive behaviors.

In the third section, Figure 10.10 was presented as a working heuristic for the discussion of organizational commitment. Throughout, the text reviewed Meyer and Allen's three-component model: affective commitment, continuance commitment, and normative commitment. The antecedents of organizational commitment were classified as organizational, individual, or social in nature. Each of these sets of variables seems to have potential effects on organizational commitment. Indeed, recent research in this area demonstrates that performance, withdrawal behaviors, and counterproductive behaviors are all influenced by organizational commitment. Finally, in the context of other work attitudes, there was a discussion of the role played by job involvement, work centrality, perceived organizational support, and emotions in the workplace.

■ Teaching the Chapter

As discussed in this chapter, the study of work attitudes is important for a number of reasons. Work attitudes are related to a variety of organizational outcomes and are an appropriate focus for I/O psychologists who select, train, and evaluate employees. In addition, work attitudes affect our professional lives as well as our personal lives and well-being. Work attitudes can make the work environment a better place. Job satisfaction and organizational commitment are the two primary work attitudes discussed extensively throughout this chapter. Facilitating discussion of these issues and soliciting examples from students whose work experiences should easily illustrate these concepts will nicely complement your lecture materials. A common assumption is that I/O psychology is the study of what makes people happy at work, and many people enter the field to research this topic and make a difference in society. In the business sections of libraries and bookstores, self-help books and various publications that deal strictly with job satisfaction, organizational commitment, and other specific work attitudes offer evidence for a general interest in work attitudes. This chapter is well suited to individuals with such interests.

Like many issues studied in psychology, attitudes are not directly observable. One may be able to infer an attitude from someone's behavior, but it is difficult to say with absolute certainty that an individual is committed to or satisfied with his or her job. Therefore, we use surveys to capture and understand these phenomena. This chapter includes some sample items from popular measures that have been used in practice and research. In the section that follows, there are some websites you may want to use as a background for a discussion on surveys. Be sure to reinforce the previous class lessons about the importance of *reliability* and *validity* in assessing job attitudes, as well as the importance of asking questions that measure a single construct (e.g., affective commitment).

■ Suggested Exercises and Assignments

Are We Happy and Committed Employees? A Qualitative Investigation

Purpose The objective of this exercise is to have students explore the job characteristics they find important for determining their job satisfaction and organizational commitment.

Instructions

This exercise is meant to stimulate class discussion based on as many ideas and experiences as possible. Thus, it is recommended that you do not divide the class into groups (unless you have a very large class).

- Solicit suggestions from students about the aspects of a job that they have found make them:
  - Happy with the job
  - Unhappy with the job
  - Committed to their organization
  - Not committed to their organization
- After generating a list of job characteristics that have contributed to their job satisfaction/dissatisfaction and commitment/lack of commitment, categorize the characteristics with regard to the frameworks for job satisfaction (Figure 10.2) and organizational commitment (Figure 10.10) provided in the text.
- What themes emerged during the discussion? Discuss what they mean for students when they are searching for a job; also discuss what students look for in organizations when they are considering the requirements and retention policies for jobs.

Discussion Questions

- Why do we pay attention to the factors that make us unhappy? Why not just pay attention to the ones that make us happy? Do you recall what motivation theory also makes this distinction?
- What job characteristics seem to affect both job satisfaction and organizational commitment?
- Are there factors that seem to affect job satisfaction more than organizational commitment? Organizational commitment more than job satisfaction?

Are We Happy and Committed Employees?
A Quantitative Investigation

Purpose The objective of this exercise is to have students explore the job characteristics they find important for determining their job satisfaction and organizational commitment. It can be used in place of the previous qualitative exercise or in conjunction with it to show the value of quantitative versus qualitative data.

Instructions

- Prior to class, ask students to fill out some measures of job satisfaction as well as any other outcomes that might relate to satisfaction. Some possible measures could include the following:
  - The Job Descriptive Index (JDI), which is available for free from http://www.bgsu.edu/departments/psych/io/jdi/index.html and measures facets of satisfaction
  - The Job in General scale (JIG), available from the same website, which measures overall satisfaction
  - Other available measures that assess motivation, happiness, stress, or other relevant outcomes
- Score the tests, and calculate correlations between each facet and overall satisfaction as well as any other outcome variables you assessed.
- Share the results of these analyses with students. In small classes, you may need to note that the small sample size makes the estimates unstable; in larger classes, typically satisfaction with work itself is most strongly related to overall satisfaction. In addition, satisfaction with pay as well as with opportunities for promotion are typically quite low among students.
- If you also used the previous exercise, you could compare the results of the empirical evidence with students' qualitative responses. Often, what students believe is most important to their satisfaction is not what actually relates to overall performance once the different facets are assessed.

Discussion Questions

- What facets appear to be most important to overall satisfaction? Why might that be?
- What facets appear to be low for this sample? Why might this be the case? Is this problematic, or is it simply a fact of life for college students?
- Which of these facets would likely be the easiest to change? The hardest?
- How do these results match qualitative results? How do they differ?

Are Work Attitudes Important in Organizational Life?

Purpose The objective of this exercise is to have students consider the importance of work attitudes in organizational life.

Instructions

- This exercise can be used in place of lecture to emphasize the importance of work attitudes.

- *Prior to class:* Have students search popular press (newspapers, newsmagazine, etc.) websites for information about an organization. The organization should be one that students think is doing a good/poor job in keeping employees satisfied and/or committed.
- During class, ask students to discuss the following questions:
  - What made you select this organization?
  - Do you think that job attitudes such as job satisfaction and organizational behavior influence work behavior in this organization?
  - How does this organization affect its employees' attitudes? If the organization is doing a poor job of keeping its employees satisfied/committed, what costs may it face if it fails to consider worker attitudes?
  - Did you find information about the organization that demonstrates it promotes job satisfaction or encourages commitment?
  - Do you think our job-related attitudes affect our overall attitudes about life outside of the workplace (e.g., attitudes about friends, family)?
- Have students lead the class discussion by presenting their answers to these questions in a way that builds a case for the importance of work attitudes in organizational functioning.

Discussion Questions

- Overall, do you think that attitudes are important to organizations?
- What do you think happens when employees collectively are dissatisfied with their job/the organization? What are the positive outcomes for an organization with satisfied employees?
- How would you build job satisfaction in employees working in this organization? How would you improve organizational commitment?

Hiring a Capable Airline Ticket Counter Agent

Purpose The objective of this exercise is to have students design a screening system for a job that requires a high level of customer service and the ability to regulate emotions.

Instructions

- Divide the class into small groups of four to six students.
- Ask groups to design a system that effectively screens airline ticket counter agents based on their emotion regulation ability.
  - You may find it helpful to have the O*NET job description for Reservation and Transportation Ticket Agents and Travel Clerks available (go to O*NET online, job title #43-4181.00, at http://online.onetcenter.org/link/summary/43-4181.00).
  - The primary job task for this position is to interface with the public, which makes it an ideal candidate for an exercise involving emotion regulation.
- Giving students very few guidelines should enhance their creativity in this exercise. Remind them of the information they have learned thus far in the

course (e.g., recruitment, selection, training). Assessment tools may include anything from a paper-and-pencil test to an assessment center to any other instrument that may effectively differentiate candidates who can regulate their emotions from those who cannot.

- Have groups justify their chosen selection tool by linking its use to the job. Also, ask students to indicate how their assessment would be scored (and weighted, if using more than one methodology).
- Have groups present their selection systems to the class.

Discussion Questions

- Did you encounter any difficulty trying to assess emotion regulation?
- What role does training play in how employees perform emotional labor on the job?
- Does your selection system apply to other customer service–oriented jobs or is this job unique?

Job Characteristics

Purpose The objective of this exercise is to have students connect what they have learned about Hackman and Oldham's job characteristics model from Chapter 4 to job attitudes.

Instructions

- Ask students to consider a job they are familiar with or one that is likely to have a number of dissatisfied employees. Some examples might include the following:
  - A factory worker who does the same monotonous task all day, every day
  - A social worker who never finds out what happens to the people she helps
  - A dog trainer who never knows whether his clients continue to work with the dog after he finishes with them
  - A pizza delivery driver who works in a town where people don't tip well
- Ask students to use the job characteristics model to determine ways they might change the job itself to increase satisfaction. For example, students might suggest ways that organizations can show workers how their efforts matter.

Discussion Questions

- Which job characteristics seem easiest to change? Most difficult?
- Which job characteristic do you believe is most important to worker satisfaction? Why?
- Do you believe we always have control over job characteristics? Why or why not?

■ Evaluating "Taking It to the Field"

The Chapter 10 activity involves a decrease in morale among bank employees who have experienced a layoff at another location. The client, Karen Strazinski, believes the employees are afraid for their own jobs, even though she has assured them they are safe. She also believes some of the employees at the recently closed North branch who transferred to her South branch are spreading rumors and making other employees anxious. Students can have a variety of effective responses to the prompt. Below are some suggestions for grading the responses.

Poor responses . . .	• Suggest that Karen continue to do what she is doing, or suggest that she send a sharp e-mail to employees about their performance. • Fail to provide Karen with specific actions she can take to help increase morale for employees. • Overlook the problem of withdrawal among employees. • Provide only one or two suggestions to Karen, and do not recognize that satisfaction relates to more than just the closure of the branch. • Assert that it is now too late to address the problem.
Good responses . . .	• Use proper spelling and grammar. • Indicate that employees are engaging in withdrawal behaviors, which indicate dissatisfaction with the job. • Recognize that job satisfaction can be approached in several ways—for example, a good response might note that perceived organizational support may be lacking and that job characteristics may also be influencing worker satisfaction. • Provide concrete suggestions for how Karen can handle the situation—for example, having a discussion with employees explaining the closure of the North branch and why this does not mean the South branch will also be closed. • Recommend that Karen *not* send a sharp e-mail and instead communicate face-to-face with her employees in a friendly manner.
Excellent responses . . .	• Use flawless spelling and grammar. • Recognize that employees are engaging in withdrawal behaviors, and connect that to both a lack of satisfaction and to issues of motivation. • Connect their recommendations with what they have learned in both Chapter 9 and Chapter 10. For example, an excellent response might note that employees may feel that they are being treated unjustly, so Karen might provide informational and interactional justice in her discussions about the closure of the North branch. • Identify several ways that Karen can approach job satisfaction, including examining how job characteristics, social factors, growth opportunities, commitment, involvement, positive organizational support,

> and/or emotional labor might be affecting attitudes.
> - Recommend that Karen *not* send a sharp e-mail and instead communicate face-to-face with her employees in a sensitive manner.
> - Suggest that Karen target the transfer employees in particular. They are likely still acclimating to the new branch and likely have a great deal of anxiety about whether they will also lose this job. Karen should find ways to help them socialize with fellow employees and work hard to ensure that they feel supported by their new organization.

■ Evaluating "Application Questions"

1. Compare two jobs you have held and your overall satisfaction with those jobs. Was your satisfaction similar in both jobs? If so, why do you think that is? If not, what affected your satisfaction?

   Evaluation Guide: This question gets at the heart of whether job satisfaction is related to the individual or the workplace. Your students will likely express a variety of responses. Discussion points might include the following:
   - Many students will have had temporary jobs that paid poorly and offered little in the way of promotion. Thus, if they find they have similar attitudes across jobs, it may be useful to discuss whether they feel they are currently building a career versus just working at a series of unrelated and unimportant jobs.
   - Because affectivity is related to job attitudes, students who have strong positive or negative affect will likely have similar attitudes across jobs. So it might be useful to gauge students' attitudes toward a variety of topics to see if they are consistent in their attitudes in many arenas.
   - Students may say that their attitudes come from a particular aspect of a job—for example, they may discuss how they did not fit in a particular organization or how they had great coworkers and managers. This is a good opportunity to discuss how facets of job satisfaction relate to overall satisfaction as well as other outcomes, such as citizenship behaviors or counterproductive work behaviors.

2. It is common in consulting work to encounter managers who believe that job attitudes do not matter—if someone quits, they will just hire another person to replace the departing employee. What might you say to these types of managers?

   Evaluation Guide: This question gives students an opportunity to connect with other topics in the book. The following points may be relevant:
   - Recruiting, selecting, and training new employees is expensive; if an organization can retain a good employee, this will save it money in the long run.

- In an unpleasant job, the organization may lose high-performing employees because they have more alternatives than low-performing ones. Thus, replacing a lost employee with a new employee will not guarantee that the new employee will be as good as the one who left.
- When an organization has high turnover, it is difficult to develop employees over time for promotion. As a result, upper-level managers may be external hires who will need training to learn about the organization and its culture.

3. Imagine you have to tell one of your best employees that she will not be getting her expected bonus check this year due to financial problems in the company. What might you tell her to ensure that she still feels satisfied with her job, even though she will be disappointed about her bonus check?

   Evaluation Guide: This question is well addressed using the justice approach. Suggestions include the following:
   - Providing this employee with a clear explanation for why she is not getting the bonus is key.
   - Providing interactional justice is also helpful—expressing regret over the lost bonus will help her feel more supported.
   - Finding ways to thank her for her work other than through monetary incentives may also help; for example, giving her an extra day off or giving her an award or some other recognition may help her feel valued and supported by the organization.

4. The chapter discusses emotional labor (when employees must fake positive emotions or hide negative emotions). Provide an example in which you had to engage in emotional labor and how that experience made you feel about that situation.

   Evaluation Guide: Naturally, students will have a variety of stories to tell in response to this question. Some of the following points can be addressed:
   - Many students work in service industries, where they are required to be kind to rude customers. You could ask them to discuss how they feel after dealing with a rude customer and how they might blow off steam afterwards (e.g., complaining to coworkers).
   - You could also ask about situations in which students had to do the opposite of typical emotional labor—that is, fake negative emotions or hide positive emotions. For example, police officers, property repossessors, and the like may need to act aggressively even when they are in a good mood. Similarly, people who work with children may need to respond sternly when children engage in misbehavior even when it is amusing.
   - It is also worth discussing what happens if someone has had to engage in emotional labor constantly over a long period of time. What strategies do people use to make this process easier (e.g., attempting to actually experience the faked emotion rather than just faking it)?

5. If you were to win enough money in a lottery so that you would never need to work again if you didn't want to, would you still work? Why or why not?

Evaluation Guide: Students often like discussing this topic and have varying opinions about it. Essentially, this question is about work centrality—individuals who believe that work is a key part of their identity will continue to work despite not needing the money. Some potential discussion points might include the following:

- If some students would opt not to work, what do they think they would do with their free time? How would they meet new people and find ways to socialize if they don't have a job?
- Discuss what it is like to be out of work for a long time. Most students have not experienced a long period of unemployment and thus may not realize that they could become quite bored. Students who have had that experience may have interesting points to share with others.
- It could also be valuable to discuss how students might change their career plans if they did not need to work for the money. Would they choose a different, less lucrative career? How might they incorporate the skills and activities of that alternative career into their life now, given that they have not actually won the lottery?

■ Highlighted Study for Discussion

Yannis, G., Lange, T., & Tabvuma, V. (2012). The impact of life events on job satisfaction. *Journal of Vocational Behavior, 80,* 464–473.

This recent article examines the effect of life events (e.g., marriage, childbearing) on job satisfaction. It also complements the content of the book, in that the text indicates that the job itself affects satisfaction, as do individual differences. This article suggests that life events can affect job satisfaction above and beyond how stable individual differences affect satisfaction. The article can be particularly valuable for students who are inexperienced with research articles, as the results are presented in an easy-to-understand graphical form. Key points include the following:

- The authors assessed only first marriage and birth of the first child as "life events" that affect job satisfaction. You could ask students to come up with additional life events they believe are worth investigating (e.g., getting a divorce, buying a house, sending the first child to college). You might also have a discussion about the narrow definition of "life events" for this study—note that unmarried and childless individuals could not be included in this study because of the way life events are defined.
- The authors measure lead and lag variables: They have several lead variables that assess satisfaction up to four years prior to the life event. Likewise, they assess satisfaction up to five years and more after the life event.
- The authors control for a number of demographic variables, such as age, occupation, education, and the like. You could discuss with students what it means to "control" for variables and why certain variables are chosen to be controlled for. The authors also separate private- versus public-sector employees, as well as

men and women—it could be helpful to discuss with students why these two variables might affect the findings.

- The results on marriage indicate that both men in the public sector and women in the private sector experience a boost in job satisfaction prior to marriage; men in the private sector and women in the public sector, meanwhile, experience a marked drop in satisfaction after marriage. It might be fruitful to discuss why this occurs.

- The results for the birth of a first child are more obvious; women in both the private and public sectors experience a notable drop in job satisfaction that can last more than five years. Men in the private sector also experience a gradual decrease in satisfaction over the course of five years.

- The results likely illustrate the difficulties associated with work–family conflict. Although marriage and the birth of children are often considered positive events, it is clear that they have a negative impact on satisfaction in the workplace. You could discuss with students what workplaces can do to help with this issue (or whether it is inevitable). It could also be interesting to discuss the differences between men and women, particularly with respect to child rearing, and why these differences might exist.

■ Web Learning

Title	Address
Mayo Clinic: Strategies to make work more gratifying	http://www.mayoclinic.com/health/job-satisfaction/wl00051
HRM Guide: Results from their job satisfaction survey	http://www.hrmguide.com/commitment/job-satisfaction.htm
SIOP: Job Attitudes Learning Module	http://siop.org/Instruct/JobAttitudes/JobAttitudes.ppt
Emotions in Organizations Network (EMONET)	http://www.uq.edu.au/emonet
Perceived Organizational Support	http://pos.psych.udel.edu/theory.asp
HRhero.com: Legal issues in absenteeism and attendance	http://www.hrhero.com/topics/absentee-ism.html
WebMD: Workaholism feature article	http://www.webmd.com/mental-health/features/workaholism
Bureau of Labor Statistics: Job Openings and Labor Turnover Survey	http://www.bls.gov/jlt/home.htm
University of Michigan Institute for Social Research: Survey Research Center	http://www.src.isr.umich.edu
Expert Survey Systems	http://www.expertss.com

CHAPTER 11

Stress and Worker Well-Being

LEARNING OBJECTIVES

This chapter should help students understand:

- The difference between stress and strains
- Why so many Americans are "working scared" and how best to deal with this situation
- How coping skills help individuals handle stress
- Warr's environmental determinants of well-being
- Many of the important issues that are involved in work–family conflict
- The importance of family-friendly employee benefits
- The ways in which companies are helping employees balance their work and family lives with as little stress as possible
- The particular complexities faced by dual-earner couples
- Why job loss is one of the most severe sources of stress that individuals ever experience
- The factors that trigger workplace violence in the United States today

CHAPTER SUMMARY

The purpose of this chapter was to discuss stress as it manifests itself in the workplace. The chapter began with a look at stress, strains, and coping. After these important terms were defined and stress in general was briefly considered, a model indicating various sources and outcomes of job-related stress was presented. In the second section, Warr's model of environmental determinants of well-being was highlighted as a way of thinking about how employees' jobs can affect their well-being. (Later in the chapter the same model was used to show how job loss can result in anguish.)

The third section focused extensively on work–family conflict because of the importance of this area to both employees and organizations. In particular, work–family conflict and enrichment were defined, a conceptual model demonstrating how work and family interact with each other and related variables was presented, and the various struggles faced by people who are working and nurturing a family at the same time were emphasized. The benefits that some organizations currently provide employees to help them deal with this conflict were then discussed—benefits such as family-leave policies, child care, and elder care. Because more and more married people are dual-earner couples, some of the issues that make this situation stressful were considered, followed by an investigation of how companies can help reduce the stress associated with juggling multiple careers and family responsibilities. Throughout this section, specific companies' work-life supports were highlighted to provide a sense of the many family-friendly benefits and services being offered to help reduce employees' stress.

The last two sections took a darker serious turn. First, there was a discussion of the psychological effects of job loss in light of the increased number of layoffs at major U.S. corporations and the perceived threat of being laid off experienced by so many employees in the 21st century. Then the rise of workplace violence was addressed. In this context, employees at risk of becoming perpetrators were profiled, some recent research was reviewed, and a discussion was presented of two recent theoretical works that attempt to model the process through which workplace aggression and violence occur.

■ Teaching the Chapter

Because students are beginning to prepare to embark on their professional careers, this chapter discusses several complex and relevant concerns. The first portion of the chapter deals with a topic that is very familiar to college students—stress. However, the chapter will provide students with a theoretical framework for understanding this well-known concept along with research that is likely new to them. In addition to introducing students to stress-related theory and research, this chapter also discusses various coping strategies and techniques to alleviate stress. The accompanying exercises are meant to help students consider how the stress in their lives will likely change as they transition from college to the world of work and as they create their own families. Students also should have the opportunity to discuss various coping strategies that they have used, how their own strategies fit with the ones described in the chapter, and how this knowledge can be applied in the future.

The next section of the chapter discusses the sensitive issue of job loss, which is particularly relevant given the recent economic downturn. This is clearly an especially important topic, as we have seen tremendous job losses through layoffs, downsizing, and bankruptcies. Unfortunately, many of us are likely to experience job loss at some point during our career. Class discussion may focus on how job loss affects internal and external perceptions of organizations with regard to financial health, competitive advantage, and organizational trust. You may want to consider comparing case studies of organizations that have been adversely affected by mass layoffs versus organizations that have been able to maintain their competitive advantage year after year.

This chapter concludes with a complex and highly emotional topic—workplace violence. Every year, horrendous acts of workplace violence are in the headlines. A poll of 1,000 employees indicated that 25% believed their employers were unprepared to handle an incident of workplace violence (Foran, 2001). An article that describes workplace violence incidents in the 1990s and the resulting pressure on management and surviving employees is suggested below as a complement to the chapter. Class discussion may revolve around the handling of such situations. For example, how would you help a company move forward in the wake of a traumatic event such as a workplace shooting? The chapter also discusses research on aggression in the workplace, which may not be as headline-grabbing as shootings but is more typical in organizations.

■ Suggested Exercises and Assignments

Removing Stressors for a Day

Purpose The objective of this exercise is to have students figure out how to eliminate activities they engage in that contribute to stress.

Instructions

During the class prior to this activity, ask students to list three discretionary activities they engage in regularly that they believe contributes to their stress levels. Examples of stressful activities they might discuss could include the following:

- Talking with a friend who is always having a crisis
- Taking on too many volunteer activities
- Spending time on the Internet
- Procrastinating on schoolwork
- Getting into arguments about unimportant topics

Ask students to spend a day or two avoiding these stressful activities. For example, if a student is always getting into intense discussions on Facebook, suggest that the student avoid doing so for a day or two.

Discussion Questions

- How difficult was it to avoid these activities?
- Why do you think you engage in these activities? Is it out of force of habit? Boredom?
- What are some other behaviors you engage in that contribute to your stress levels? How could you avoid these activities?
- Is it always helpful to avoid stressful activities? What are some negative consequences of doing so?

Get the Stress Out!

Purpose The objective of this exercise is to have students consider how they cope with daily stress and what they can do to improve their coping strategies.

Instructions

- Ask students to make a list of the five biggest stressors they are facing right now, the five biggest stressors they faced 10 years ago, and what they believe will be their five biggest stressors 10 years from now. For each list, have the students identify coping strategies they use, used, and might use to mitigate the stressors. Tell them that they can use the text to help them identify coping strategies to be used in the future.
- Divide the class into groups of four to six.
- Have students discuss their lists and then create a master group list of the five biggest stressors of the present, past, and future. For each stressor, have students identify the coping strategies they use, used, and might use and how effective they believe those strategies are, were, and will be.
- If technology is available in the classroom, have students look at websites that deal with stress management. Then ask them to develop ways to improve their current stress management and think about how they might manage stress in the future. (There are many websites listed at the end of the chapter that might be useful for this exercise.)
- Groups should outline their findings in the following manner to share with the class:
  - Top five stressors: past, present, and future
  - Popular coping strategies: past and present only
  - Plans for stress management: present and future only

Discussion Questions

- How have your perceptions of stressful events changed throughout your life?
- Were these changes similar among your group members?
- How do you think your stress will change in the future?

Critical Incident for the Vice President of Human Resources

Purpose The objective of this exercise is to have students think about the complexities of ambiguous organizational situations.

Instructions

- *Prior to class:* You might want to copy the text below into a document that students can use during class. It is a brief description of a case that they can discuss and consider.

  You are the Vice President of Human Resources for a large midwestern automaker that has fallen on tough economic times. Over the last 12 months, to keep your operation running, you have implemented a hiring freeze, eliminated all bonuses, and begun laying off employees. The labor union that represents your line employees has become increasingly hostile due to these changes, which does not help your already adversarial relationship with it. At this point, your margin for operating error is slim because your current contracts are the only thing keeping your company from falling into bankruptcy.

Last week a worker who was recently laid off arrived at the manufacturing plant, stormed into the main office, and demanded to see the management team responsible for laying him off. Before security could arrive on the scene, he opened fire with a shotgun, killing an administrative assistant, a foreman, and six line workers. In the end, he also took his own life.

■ Ask students to develop an action plan to respond to this situation. For help, they can go to the websites on workplace violence listed at the end of the chapter. Ask them to address the following questions in their plans:
  • How would you handle notifying medical personnel, the victims' families, the news media, customers, employees, and the union?
  • Given the circumstances, should you close down the plant? If so, for how long? What would guide your decision?
  • What can you do to assist surviving employees?
  • How do you continue to meet customer obligations on such a slim budget and margin?
  • What policies and/or procedures could you put into place that might help prevent a similar incident? Is there anything in the selection process that could have screened out this individual?
  • How do you handle your own stress (as Vice President of Human Resources) given the added pressure you are now experiencing?

Discussion Questions

■ Have you ever encountered aggressive behavior in the workplace? What happened?
■ What actions do you believe the organization could have taken prior to the incident to help decrease stress and increase communication between employees and management?
■ What, as a coworker, would you do if you heard someone making threats about bringing a gun to work?
■ Do you think smaller acts of aggression (e.g., throwing a stapler) are problematic in the workplace? What would you do about them if you were a coworker? A manager?

Reframing Activity

Purpose One easy way to address workplace stress is to reframe situations. This activity provides students with a demonstration of how they can view situations differently and in a more positive light.

Instructions

You might want to copy the list below or develop some additional scenarios for students to consider. Present each situation, and ask students to come up with another way for the character to think of the situation that will make it seem less intimidating. You could also ask students to suggest ways that the individual can proactively cope with the scenario.

- Melissa, a social worker who has only been at her job for a year, has just been asked to step into a management position. She is much younger than any of the other managers, and she is worried that she does not have enough experience to perform the job effectively.
- Kendra is presenting her project proposal to her team. Typically, her presentations get a positive response, but one of her colleagues, Dean, seems irritated by her presentation. Afterwards, Dean says to Kendra, "I know you mean well, but you obviously don't understand anything. This plan will be a disaster for our team!" Kendra feels like Dean does not respect her work or her position in the team and is considering asking to be transferred to a different team.
- Ricardo worked all night on a project to complete it by the deadline for a particularly difficult client. Ricardo is proud of his work, but neither his boss nor his client thanks him for his extra effort. As a result, he feels like he is unappreciated and is considering leaving his position.
- Benton has been trying to get in touch with a colleague, Layla, about a project they are supposed to work on. He has sent her several e-mails and voice mails. He knows she is in the office today, and he is still waiting to hear back from her. He feels as if she is a particularly irresponsible and disrespectful coworker.

Discussion Questions

- In these scenarios, are the characters making some assumptions? What are some examples?
- In these scenarios, the characters seem to think that they are unable to deal effectively with the stressor. Do you believe these are reasonable perspectives? Why or why not?
- What are some different ways these characters can deal with the problem? Why might these alternative approaches be more effective?

Worker Stress and Well-Being in the Movies

Purpose A number of movies include themes that directly apply to the concepts discussed in this chapter—job stress, work–family conflict, job loss, and workplace conflict/violence. This activity will give students the opportunity to see the class material come to life and to discuss the issues in specific detail.

Instructions

Screen one or more of the following movies in class or assign them for home-work. Follow up with a class discussion. Alternatively, you could show segments of the movies during class lectures to illustrate concepts. This list is by no means exhaustive.

- Work–family conflict/roles
  - *Mr. Mom* (1983): Starring Michael Keaton, who trades in his career to take over home responsibilities so that his wife can pursue her career goals.
  - *Baby Boom* (1987): Starring Diane Keaton, who plays a high-powered ad executive who is working her way to the top of a male-dominated corporate hierarchy when the will of a recently departed cousin names her guardian of a 13-month-old baby girl.
  - *One Fine Day* (1996): Starring Michelle Pfeiffer and George Clooney as single parents trying to juggle their career demands with caring for their young children.
  - *Raising Helen* (2004): Starring Kate Hudson as a young, career-oriented woman who unexpectedly becomes the guardian of her sister's three young children, which derails her own career ambitions.
- Work/job stress
  - *Falling Down* (1993): Starring Michael Douglas, who is having one of the worst days a person can have. This entertaining, yet disturbing, movie examines work pressures and family pressures as well as how mounting stress can push a person over the edge.
  - *The Devil Wears Prada* (2002): Starring Anne Hathaway, who plays a stressed-out assistant to a fashion magazine editor (as performed by Meryl Streep) who is overly demanding and controlling.
  - *North Country* (2005): Starring Charlize Theron, who deals with many stressors (including sexual harassment) as a woman working in a coal mine.
- Job loss
  - *Roger & Me* (1989): A documentary by Michael Moore chronicling General Motors plant closings in Flint, Michigan, and the resulting effects of job loss on the town and GM employees.
  - *Glengarry Glen Ross* (1992): Real estate salesmen are faced with job loss and a decision that will either make or break them.
  - *Office Space* (1999): The classic I/O film depicting employees who are downtrodden in their jobs and the measures they take when consultants are brought in to implement downsizing.
  - *Fun with Dick and Jane* (2005): Starring Jim Carrey as an executive who unexpectedly loses his job and makes numerous attempts at crime to maintain his lifestyle.
- Workplace conflict
  - *American Dream* (1992): A documentary by Barbara Kopple that depicts the six-year labor dispute at a meat-packing plant in Minnesota.
  - *Employee of the Month* (2006): Starring Dane Cook as an otherwise lazy employee who engages in a heated competition with a coworker to become employee of the month.

Discussion Questions

- What were the major themes depicted in these movies?
- Did the characters meet the demands they faced? Were their coping strategies effective? What other coping strategies could they have used?
- Do you believe these are accurate portrayal of stress/conflict/job loss?
- How were others affected by the main characters' situations in the movie?

■ Evaluating "Taking It to the Field"

The Chapter 11 activity involves Michael Yurttas of the Dutler Accountancy Firm, who is concerned about satisfying working mothers despite needing them to work 60–70 hour a week for two months of the year. Students may have a variety of suggestions for Michael; below are some guidelines for evaluating their responses.

Poor responses . . .	• Fail to provide concrete solutions for Michael. • Argue that focusing on retaining women at the organization is unimportant. • Suggest any illegal approaches (e.g., hiring only unmarried women or women without children).
Good responses . . .	• Acknowledge the importance of retaining female workers. • Provide concrete and helpful suggestions, such as providing onsite day care and offering other incentives (such as providing telecommuting or flextime during other times of the year).
Excellent responses . . .	• Acknowledge the importance of retaining women in the company. • Note the point that sometimes work is slow, and leverage that point in the recommendations (e.g., offering reduced hours during the summer, asking women who have left the company whether they would be willing to come in part time during the busy season to help other employees). • Identify additional approaches or policies that might make the work easier and more enjoyable for everyone, not just working mothers. For example, students might suggest changing incentives, since other workers might not be interested only in overtime pay as a reward. Students might also suggest some of the work arrangements suggested in the text, including telecommuting, paid sabbaticals, and child-care benefits.

■ Evaluating "Application Questions"

1. Consider a recent stressful event you experienced at work. What types of job-related, emotional, and physiological strains did you experience as a result of this event? What are some problem-focused and emotion-focused coping strategies you might have used?

   Evaluation Guide: Because this question relates to student experiences, responses will vary. However, the following guidelines will help ensure that students are answering the questions appropriately and understand concepts appropriately:
   • Job-related strains encompass responses such as "I don't feel like working hard" or "I call in sick to work more, even when I'm not sick."
   • Emotional strains encompass responses such as "I feel angry or sad at work."
   • Physiological strains encompass responses such as "I have headaches and stomach aches" or "I get sick more often."
   • In terms of coping strategies, students should clearly recognize the difference between problem-focused and emotion-focused coping. For example, a student who felt disrespected by his or her boss and therefore had a frank discussion with the boss about the situation would be engaged in problem-focused coping. Alternatively, a student who went for a run after work to blow off steam would be engaged in emotion-focused coping.

2. Telecommuting is becoming more popular in a number of different companies. Consider your own schoolwork and how productive you are when you are working at home or in your dorm room, compared to when you are in a computer lab or a library. What are some benefits you have found to working at home? What are some difficulties? Given the choice, would you prefer to always work from home or never work from home?

   Evaluation Guide: This question allows students to consider their own current work habits and what is best for them. If students have difficulty coming up with responses, you could consider the following points:
   • Students may encounter different distractions in different environments. For example, when working at home or in their dorm room, they may get distracted by the Internet, friends stopping by to visit, pets, children, phone calls, and a number of other interruptions. They may also lose access to helpful resources that are available at the library or elsewhere on campus (including tangibles such as books and articles as well as advice and support from fellow students). Alternatively, they may benefit from working at home by having a more comfortable chair or desk area, a quieter work environment, or more freedom about when to take breaks.
   • Many students might immediately indicate that they would prefer to work from home all the time. It can be helpful to ask them whether it would be difficult for them to set scheduled work times, to find opportunities to socialize with other people, and to prevent work and leisure time from

bleeding into each other. Discussing this may also help students to consider how to change their own work habits to avoid wasting time by studying in front of the TV and similar types of behaviors.

3. Some jobs, such as being a police officer or a social worker, involve a great deal of stress nearly every day. Imagine yourself in such a stressful occupation. What could the organization do to help you feel less stress?

    Evaluation Guide: Students will likely have a number of suggestions, but it could be helpful to draw parallels between their suggestions and suggestions offered by the book. The following points are examples of how this can be done:
    - Allowing these workers more personal control over their work can be helpful. For example, allowing social workers some control over what territories to cover and when, as well as providing them with good information about their clients, can help them prepare more effectively for encountering difficult cases.
    - Appreciating employees' efforts can also be helpful, as it will make them feel valued and respected.
    - Providing supportive leadership and good feedback can also reduce role ambiguity—workers will spend less time worrying about their performance and can focus on the job at hand.
    - Providing workers with an opportunity to vent and share strategies can also increase social support and ensure they are learning new ways to address problems.

4. Imagine that a friend talks about a coworker who has recently been acting aggressively at work, such as throwing objects when she gets frustrated and yelling at other people. What advice would you offer this friend?

    Evaluation Guide: Most students will not have encountered any issues like this, so it may be a useful exercise to walk them through good responses to this type of situation. Students may generate these answers on their own; if not, you should prompt them to consider these actions. In general, student answers should reflect the seriousness of the problem. In most cases, it is appropriate to bring this concern to the attention of the HR department or one's supervisor. The friend should probably not directly confront this coworker unless he has a friendly relationship with her.

5. Imagine that a friend was recently laid off. He has only been unemployed for a few weeks, but already he is feeling depressed and hopeless about finding another job. What might you do to help him? What advice would you offer him?

    Evaluation Guide: As noted in the text, there is a fair amount of research on unemployement and stress. Some potential discussion points include the following:
    - Your friend may benefit from adding additional structure to his day. For example, he should set aside specific times to conduct his job search as well as to engage in some stress-relieving activities such as exercising, spending time with friends, and so on.

- Finding opportunities to receive social support may also help. For example, joining a job search group would bring him into contact with people who have similar problems who can listen and suggest solutions. The more he can stop thinking about the job loss and start thinking about a new opportunity, the lower his stress will be.
- Your friend can also find a number of ways to engage in problem-focused and emotion-focused coping. For example, if he feels that he does not have the skills necessary to be employable, he could take some classes or practice his skills to increase his confidence. Additionally, he could make sure to spend some time doing enjoyable activities during the day to help him feel better so that he can continue to focus on his job search.

■ Highlighted Study for Discussion

Shimazu, A., Shaufeli, W. B., & Taris, T. W. (2010). How does workaholism affect worker health and performance? The mediating role of coping. *International Journal of Behavioral Medicine, 17,* 154–160.

In this article, the authors define workaholism and examine whether it has deleterious effects on worker health and performance. Short and straightforward, it can serve as a helpful introduction to structural equation modeling (SEM) for students who are not familiar with the technique. The main points of the article are as follows:

- Previous studies had established a negative relationship between workaholism and health. This study examined whether coping skills mediate the relationship between workaholism and health as well as between workaholism and performance.
- Participants in the study were employees of a construction machinery company in Japan. You could discuss with students whether this population might differ from others (given that Japan tends to have long workweeks and a strong work ethic compared to many other countries).
- The authors assessed workaholism, active coping (analyzing information to solve problems), emotional discharge (taking out frustrations on others), psychological distress, physical complaints, and self-rated job performance. It could be helpful to discuss the problem with having the job incumbent provide ratings on all of these scales, particularly the job performance scale.
- The results indicated that workaholism had a strong direct link with ill health (.63). It also had indirect links, such that workaholism led to more active coping, which led to ill health. Workaholism also led to more emotional discharge, which led to more ill health. Meanwhile, workaholism was not directly related to higher performance; it was, however, indirectly related through active coping. Many of these findings would be fruitful topics for discussion—for example, why workaholism is not directly related to performance.
- In sum, workaholics spent more time thinking about problems they were facing and dealing with their emotions through other people, tendencies that had

mixed results: Active coping led to higher levels of performance and ill health. Emotional discharge was related to ill health but appeared to be unrelated to performance. The authors suggest that if organizations want to ensure healthy employees, they should attempt to reduce workaholism among them.

■ Web Learning

Title	Address
National Institute for Occupational Safety and Health (NIOSH)	http://www.cdc.gov/niosh/topics/stress
Stress management resources from Mind Tools	http://www.mindtools.com/smpage.html
Discovery Health: Stress Management Center	http://health.discovery.com/centers/stress/stress.html
Sloan Work and Family Research Network: Resources for Workplace Practice	http://wfnetwork.bc.edu/business.php
U.S. Department of Labor: Economy at a Glance (includes unemployment numbers)	http://www.bls.gov/eag/eag.us.htm
U.S. Department of Labor, OSHA: Workplace Violence	http://www.osha.gov/SLTC/workplaceviolence/index.html
NIOSH Risk Factors and Prevention Strategies: Violence in the Workplace	http://www.cdc.gov/niosh/violcont.html
The National Institute for the Prevention of Workplace Violence	http://www.workplaceviolence911.com
U.S. Department of Health and Human Services: Eldercare Locator	http://www.eldercare.gov/Eldercare.NET/Public/Home.aspx
Fortune 100 Best Companies to Work For (2009): Child-care benefits	http://money.cnn.com/magazines/fortune/bestcompanies/2009/benefits/child_care.html
Portland State University: Dual Earner Couples in the Sandwiched Generation	http://www.sandwich.pdx.edu
The Riley Guide: Coping with Job Loss	http://www.rileyguide.com/cope.html

CHAPTER 12

Group Processes and Work Teams

LEARNING OBJECTIVES

This chapter should help students understand:

- How social influence affects group behavior
- Group cohesion and its importance in group processes
- The stages of group development
- The implications for work groups of social loafing and free riding
- The stages of effective decision making
- Why groups don't always make good decisions
- What groupthink is and how it can affect organizations
- Why one current trend in organizational processes is the use of work teams
- How to differentiate among the various types of work teams
- What self-managed work teams are, along with some of the processes involved in their success
- How to measure work-team effectiveness and what factors affect it
- The implications that work teams have for employee selection and placement

CHAPTER SUMMARY

This chapter introduced the concepts of work groups and work teams and discussed the processes involved in the use of such groups in organizations. The chapter began with a definition of work groups and a review of group processes. It then discussed social influence in groups in the context of norms, roles, cohesion, and social loafing, applying those elements to organizational functioning. Tuckman's model of group development and the popular punctuated equilibrium model were then presented.

Group decision making was another area emphasized in this chapter. Because groups are entrusted with important organizational decisions, considerable time was spent discussing a process that, when followed, is likely to result in effective decision making. This five-step process emphasizes the quality of the social interaction among group members—an issue that was discussed in connection with some of the common mistakes made at certain points in the process. This topic led logically to ineffective decision making, with a particular emphasis on groupthink. Here the chapter presented historical examples of groupthink and discussed its antecedents and symptoms in light of organizational situations.

The last section focused on work teams, which have become incredibly popular in modern-day organizations. The chapter discussed various types of work teams and gave examples of each, placing particular emphasis on self-managed work teams both because of their prevalence in organizations and because of their inherent complexities. A few examples of organizations currently using work teams were provided, the idea of shared mental models was introduced, and the determinants of work-team effectiveness were identified. The chapter concluded with a discussion of current trends, such as the growth of virtual teams and the recent focus on selection for teams.

■ Teaching the Chapter

Almost all students will have had some experience with teams—likely from involvement with athletic, academic related, or community organizations. If students have not had these experiences, they may relate to teams they have seen on TV or observed in their own family life. Therefore, the subject matter in this chapter should come easily to students, and a great deal of discussion should emerge based on their experiences. The only potential "sticking point" that students may have is differentiating between *groups* and *teams,* terms that are used interchangeably in the text and that are even confused a great deal in the team/ group literature.

The exercises below are designed to help students consider issues regarding groups in a variety of situations. The first exercise draws on students' experience with teams and encourages them to consider and analyze what makes a team successful or unsuccessful. The next exercise simulates a self-managed work-team environment and introduces some team competition to reinforce the chapter material on team development and decision making. The third exercise focuses on groupthink, offering students a glimpse of this concept in action.

Many team-building exercises and activities are available online and in other publications, and you may find these to be valuable sources for reinforcing the concepts in the chapter. An exercise that has been well received in classes and training seminars is the "lost in the desert/mountains/ocean/arctic" exercise, which involves comparing individual judgment/processing with that of a group. Another interesting topic for students to discuss is the future of organizational teams and the use of virtual teams. One of the Internet website links provided at the end of this chapter focuses on research and practice regarding virtual teams. Addressing the pros and cons associated with the use of virtual teams in organizations, as well as how technology may impact students' future teamwork in their careers, should stimulate lively class discussion.

■ Suggested Exercises and Assignments

The Group That Sticks Together . . .

Purpose Students will discuss effective and ineffective teams and the role that cohesiveness plays in team success.

Instructions

- After presenting the chapter material related to group cohesion, divide the class into groups of four to six.
- *Exercise Option 1:* Ask each group to focus on one of the categories of teams listed below:
  - Business (famous management teams)
  - Athletics (professional, collegiate)
  - Entertainment (television or movies)
  - A personal experience
- *Exercise Option 2:* In class, show an episode of a reality TV show that involves teamwork. Examples of shows that have worked well in class include scenes from *The Apprentice, Survivor,* and *Real World/Road Rules Challenge.*
- After either exercise option, have students discuss the following questions in their groups and then prepare a brief report to present to the class.
  - Why was your team effective?
  - Could it have been more effective? Did the team encounter any problems? If so, how were they handled?
  - To what extent did the group communicate? Did communication flow freely in the group? Why or why not?
  - How did the group make decisions?
  - Were there social loafers in these groups?
  - Did any symptoms of groupthink emerge?

Discussion Questions

- What elements are common to successful teams? To unsuccessful teams?
- What, if any, common problems did these teams encounter?
- Do you notice any differences in the communication patterns of cohesive and noncohesive groups?

Rope Square

Purpose In this exercise, students must communicate clearly and efficiently with their fellow group members to accomplish a task.

Instructions

- This activity is best for about 12 or fewer people. If your group is larger than this, consider breaking them into several groups or having some students serve as observers. Make sure you have a safe, open place to play the game (e.g., go outside, or move desks and chairs to the edges of the room).

- Ask students to volunteer to be team members. Let them know that they will be blindfolded for this activity, and allow anyone who would find this unpleasant to opt out.
- Ask students to spread out in the room, put their blindfolds in place, and spin around a few times to become disoriented.
- Provide one of the students with a length of rope or string (about 10 yards long). Tell them they must form this rope into a perfect square by working together.
- Supervise the activity (or assign a student to each group to supervise) so that nobody runs into anything or gets hurt. You may also choose to intervene if students become frustrated.
- When students have had about 30 minutes to perform the task, ask them to remove their blindfolds and come together as a group.

Discussion Questions

- How well did you do at the task?
- What prevented you from accomplishing the task quickly? What frustrated you?
- What seemed to work well?
- How does this relate to completing group work, especially in a workplace where some of your colleagues might be working remotely?

Flying the Friendly Skies

Purpose Students will engage in a group exercise that illustrates the steps of team development, as discussed in the text.

Instructions

- *Prior to class:* You will need the following supplies for each group:
  - Sheets of blank paper (with each group receiving the same number of sheets of paper)
  - Measuring tape
  - Markers
  - Scissors
  - *Optional:* You may also consider giving the winning team a prize.
- After presenting Tuckman's five stages of team development (forming, storming, norming, performing, and adjourning), divide the class into four- to six-member groups. To the extent possible, place students in groups with other students they may not know very well.
- Each group must assign one member to serve as the observer/recorder. This member will report the behavior and activities of the group, as well as classify behaviors into one of Tuckman's five stages.
- The group task is to make quality paper airplanes.

- Explain the criteria for successful performance (and announce a prize to the winning team, if applicable). Successful performance is based on the following criteria:
  - *Quantity:* number of airplanes assembled
  - *Quality:* length of flight, design, appearance
- You might want to suggest that each team designate roles to its members (e.g., research and development, assembly, test piloting, decoration design, etc.). Teams may also want to develop an action plan before proceeding with the task and spend time developing a prototype before beginning to assemble airplanes.
- Set a time limit (10 minutes or longer) for the groups to assemble as many airplanes as possible.
- After the time limit has expired, have the observer count the number of assembled airplanes and select the plane to be used in a flight test.
- One representative from each group should explain the design of the plane as well as the meaning behind any decorations on the plane. He or she will also launch the plane to assess its flight performance (this is where a measuring tape comes in handy).
- Select a winning group based on flight length, decoration, and number of planes produced.
- Have observers (and team members) discuss the extent to which their teams moved through Tuckman's five stages.

Discussion Questions

- To what extent did your team follow Tuckman's model? If the team did not follow this model closely, why do you think this happened?
- What problems did your team encounter during this exercise?
- What was the toughest part of this task?
- Do you think your teamwork affected the measures of team performance (quantity/quality of airplanes)? Why or why not?

Culture Shock Activity

Purpose The objective is to give students a simulated experience of working to accomplish a task in a group with a different culture.

Instructions

- This activity is best for smaller classes (20–30 students) and can take up to an hour. However, most students find it to be a fun experience.
- Divide the class into two groups, and place the groups in separate rooms. Each group of students will be from a different culture. The following are suggestions for how each group might behave, but you can replace any rules with different ones that you think would be interesting.

- Group X culture
  - This is a very friendly and warm culture. Members like to stand close to one another, and they touch elbows when they greet each other.
  - Members are also very polite; before they get down to business, they ask one another about what is going on—how everyone is doing, what everyone has been up to.
  - Females are in charge. The oldest female is the leader, and other members of the group show respect for her by shaking their heads back and forth (in a "no" motion") whenever they address her.
  - Whenever a cultural rule is violated, the nearest person says, "Eep eep!" and walks over to the female leader.
- Group Y culture
  - This is a more reserved culture. Members like to have a lot of space between them and other people, and they tug their own ear to greet another person.
  - Members also like to get down to business. Asking others about themselves only takes place after business has been discussed.
  - Males are in charge. The male with the shortest hair is the leader, and other members show respect by rubbing their own stomach when the leader approaches them.
  - Whenever a cultural rule is violated, the leader claps his hands, and all members of the group move away from the person who violated the rule.
- Allow each group a little time to practice these cultural rules among themselves. Inform each group that their task is to determine whether they think they would like to partner with the other culture to form a new technology firm. Send students (in pairs or trios, depending upon the size of your class) to visit the other culture and learn about it. Allow students a couple of minutes to visit the group, and then ask them to return to their original group to share their findings. You may repeat this step as many times as you like with new visitors, potentially until everyone has visited the opposite culture.

Discussion Questions

- Do you think you would want to work with this other culture? Why or why not?
- What do you think are some of the rules in the other culture? What are the actual rules in that culture?
- What could members of Group X/Group Y do to help make working with the other culture easier?
- What might be some potential trouble areas between the two groups?

Groupthink Prevention Strategies

Purpose The objective is to have students think about the occurrence of groupthink and how to prevent it.

Instructions

- After you have presented the material on groupthink, divide the class into groups of four to six.
- Have teams assign each group member to one of the following roles:
  - Strong, biased leader
  - Mindguard
  - Devil's advocate
  - Observer who records the social behavior in the discussion (this person does not participate in the discussion)
  - *Optional role:* Followers who support the leader's position
- In their groups, students should discuss an issue that has recently been in the news. The group must decide on a specific course of action. Once you have given groups sufficient discussion time, ask them to report their decision (if reached). Also, solicit the observer's comments on the decision-making process that occurred in the group as well as any symptoms or consequences of groupthink that may have surfaced.

Discussion Questions

- How difficult was it to maintain the role you were assigned?
- Do you think governmental decision makers face groupthink?
- Do you think groupthink can be eliminated or minimized?

■ Evaluating "Taking It to the Field"

The activity for Chapter 12 involves a question from Siran Belekdanian at WeldCo, where service people and salespeople have differing viewpoints on how the work should be done. The salespeople are focused on making sales in any way possible, even when it means making promises the service people cannot keep. The service people, meanwhile, are purposely slowing down work to get back at the salespeople. The prompt asks students to think of three suggestions for Siran. Below are some suggestions for evaluating responses.

Poor responses . . .	<ul><li>Provide superficial responses to Siran—for example, suggesting team barbecues or team-building activities without addressing the root problem.</li><li>Provide fewer than three suggestions.</li><li>Fail to include members of both teams in devising a solution.</li><li>Side with only one group (salespeople or service people).</li></ul>

| Good responses . . . | • Identify or speculate about some of the root causes of the mismatch (e.g., salespeople trying to meet unreasonable goals, the service team being understaffed).
• Suggest that Siran bring together both teams to discuss the issue and find solutions together.
• Emphasize that Siran should help WeldCo employees recognize that they have the same ultimate goal—satisfied customers.
• Discuss *one* of the following issues:
  • Inappropriate group norms (e.g., selling more than they can deliver).
  • Roles (e.g., whether any team members have a responsibility to check in with the other team).
  • Cohesion (e.g., finding ways to build better and routine connections between members of each team).
  • Groupthink (e.g., if the teams are too insular, they may not see how some of their decisions, such as slowing down service, are harmful).
  • Tuckman's stages of group development (e.g., the teams appear to be in the storming phase and may need to develop clear overall norms to feel more unity).
  • Social loafing (e.g., ensuring that salespeople who oversell are held responsible for doing so; ensuring that service people who are slowing down service are held accountable).
• Suggest ways that Siran might apply the five steps of good group decision making (found in Table 12.2 in the book) to the issue. |
| Excellent responses . . . | • Identify or speculate about some of the root causes of the mismatch (e.g., salespeople trying to meet unreasonable goals, the service team being understaffed).
• Suggest that Siran bring together both teams to discuss the issue and find solutions together.
• Emphasize that Siran should help WeldCo employees recognize that they have the same ultimate goal—satisfied customers.
• Discuss *two or more* of the following issues:
  • Inappropriate group norms (e.g., selling more than they can deliver).
  • Roles (e.g., whether any team members have a responsibility to check in with the other team).
  • Cohesion (e.g., finding ways to build better and routine connections between members of each team). |

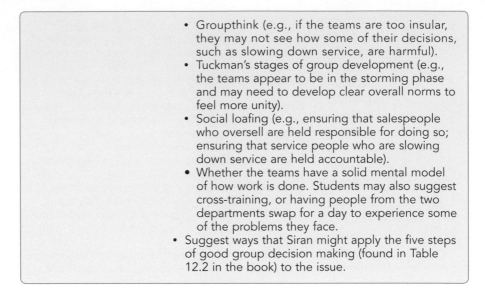

- Groupthink (e.g., if the teams are too insular, they may not see how some of their decisions, such as slowing down service, are harmful).
- Tuckman's stages of group development (e.g., the teams appear to be in the storming phase and may need to develop clear overall norms to feel more unity).
- Social loafing (e.g., ensuring that salespeople who oversell are held responsible for doing so; ensuring that service people who are slowing down service are held accountable).
- Whether the teams have a solid mental model of how work is done. Students may also suggest cross-training, or having people from the two departments swap for a day to experience some of the problems they face.
- Suggest ways that Siran might apply the five steps of good group decision making (found in Table 12.2 in the book) to the issue.

■ Evaluating "Application Questions"

1. What is an example of a group you've been a part of that was highly cohesive. What made it that way? How could some of those qualities be instilled in a workplace team?

   Evaluation Guide: Students will likely come up with a variety of suggestions for this question. The following are common suggestions:
   - If students have difficulty thinking of groups, you could prompt them to think of social groups (hobby clubs, fraternities/sororities, honors societies).
   - Prompt students to think of what sorts of experiences and activities make them feel close to other group members. For example, fraternity/sorority members might be able to discuss the difficult tasks pledges had to accomplish; honors society members might talk about how hard they had to work to be admitted.
   - Discuss with students why having groups face common challenges and difficulties can help people feel more connected (e.g., they know they have all been through the same things; being in a group that is hard to get into makes people appreciate being a part of the group).
2. Consider a time when you experienced social loafing in a group (in a class or at work). What were some aspects of the situation that caused social loafing to occur? What could your instructor or boss have done to decrease social loafing?

   Evaluation Guide:
   - For students who had to do a lot of the work in the group, ask them to explain why other group members did not work. Did they get to

evaluate other group members' work? Was there a way for the instructor/employer to notice individual effort and skill? Were the other members uninterested in the reward (such as effective performance or a good project grade)?

- For students who are brave enough to admit they have engaged in social loafing, ask why they chose to let someone else do the work—was it a purposeful decision? How did they feel after the fact? Would they have behaved differently if they knew they would have to work with the same group members again?

3. Think about a group you are currently a member of. Where in Tucker's stages of development is this group? Give examples to support your opinion.

Evaluation Guide:

- Students who believe their group is in a "forming" stage might mention being on good behavior, trying to make a good impression, not being sure of how to do things the "right" way, and not being sure who to trust or distrust in the group.
- Students who believe their group is in the "storming" stage might mention the emergence of group members' personalities and group conflicts, a jostling for power or status within the group, conflict over jobs or tasks, and the emergence of more disagreement among members about how to do the work or how well to do the work.
- Students who believe their group is in the "norming" stage might mention being able to articulate some of the "rules" of the group (timeliness, what should be accomplished each time they meet) and finding close friends within the group who share their opinions.
- Students who believe their group is in the "performing" stage might mention that most of the conflict is worked out and that they are able to focus on tasks or goals.
- Students who believe their group is in the final stage, "adjourning," might mention finishing a project and dissolving the group, feeling that the group no longer shares a common goal, or feeling sad as the cohesion begins to disappear among group members. It may also be worth asking all students if they ever expect their groups to reach an adjourning stage and, if so, when it might occur.

4. Although brainstorming can be useful, sometimes it prevents groups from thinking creatively about solving a problem. What are some reasons why this might happen, and what are some ways you could avoid those problems?

Evaluation Guide:

- Students may have some difficulty addressing this question, so you might prompt them by asking which members are likely to get the most attention (e.g., extraverts, males, people who repeat themselves or are more assertive). Also discuss whether people who have those qualities will automatically have the best ideas.

- Have students think about ways in which all members of the group can be heard. For example, having group members brainstorm privately and then share their thoughts will ensure that everyone will have something to contribute.
- Have students consider how group members can ensure that they stay on track. For example, setting a timer for discussion and limiting how long any individual can speak may help prevent people from derailing the group. Likewise, assigning roles to group members, such as "devil's advocate," can help the group think critically about ideas without discomfort or conflict.

5. Consider a job you once had or a group project you worked on in a class. In order to work with others, you likely had a shared mental model. Give some examples of what might have been part of this mental model you shared with group members.

Evaluation Guide:

- Students will have a variety of ideas about this question. For example, a student who is thinking about a social group may think about how a group makes a decision; for example, is one person typically responsible for driving? For making reservations? Students who are thinking about a work situation may consider how workers can seamlessly take on one anothers' tasks (e. g., a student who works in a kitchen may be able to describe how cooks cover for one another during bathroom breaks or during the dinner rush).
- If students have difficulty coming up with examples, you could prompt them by asking about cases where a mental model didn't exist and they were unable to anticipate what someone else was going to do. Ask them how they would go about helping others build a common mental model.

■ Highlighted Study for Discussion

Liden, R. C., Wayne, S. J., Jaworski, R. A., & Bennett, N. (2004). Social loafing: A field investigation. *Journal of Management, 30,* 285–300.

This article is an interesting example of moving from lab studies to field studies. It is somewhat long and uses some relatively complex statistical techniques (hierarchical linear modeling), but the method and techniques are clearly described and should be relatively accessible for most college students. It is also a nice example of the interesting questions that are generated when findings don't go as expected.

- The authors provide evidence from lab-based student studies about social loafing in work groups. They argue that there is a need for more data on actual work groups, which they present in the article.

■ Specifically, the authors hypothesize the following:
  • Higher levels of task interdependence will be related to less social loafing.
  • Low task visibility will be related to more social loafing.
  • Work groups in which there is little sense of justice (distributive and/or procedural) will experience more social loafing.
  • Larger groups will experience more social loafing.
  • Highly cohesive groups will experience less social loafing.
  • Individuals who believe there is more social loafing will also engage in higher levels of social loafing.

■ A total of 168 employees and 23 managers completed measures on the variables. Employees reported on task interdependence, task visibility, distributive justice, and procedural justice. Managers completed measures on group size, group cohesiveness, perceived coworker loafing, and social loafing for the participating employees.

■ All of the hypotheses were supported by the data, with the exception of two. First, procedural justice was not related to social loafing. Second, individuals who believed their coworkers engaged in a great deal of social loafing actually engaged in less loafing themselves, contrary to what was predicted. It may be useful to discuss why they believe those two hypotheses were not supported. Were the authors justified in their original hypotheses? Why or why not?

■ It may also be worthwhile to discuss one of the strengths of this article—that social loafing by individuals was rated by the manager instead of the employee. Discuss with students why this might have been an important thing to do in this study.

■ Web Learning

Title	Address
Purdue University: Department of Organizational Leadership and Supervision	http://www.workteams.unt.edu
Virtual Organization: Links to information and articles about virtual teams	http://www.seanet.com/~daveg/articles.htm
University of Michigan: Research Center for Group Dynamics	http://www.rcgd.isr.umich.edu
NASA: Team and Teamwork	http://www.hq.nasa.gov/office/hqlibrary/ppm/ppm5.htm
Center for Media and Democracy: Groupthink (includes recent news examples)	http://www.sourcewatch.org/index.php?title=Groupthink
What is groupthink?	http://www.psysr.org/about/pubs_resources/groupthink%20overview.htm
Psychtests.com: Team Roles Test	http://www.psychtests.com/tests/career/team_roles_access.html
List of research articles relevant to social loafing	http://www.cs.cmu.edu/~kraut/cscw/social-loafing.html
Presentation on teamwork, including Tuckman's model of group development	http://www.dspace.dial.pipex.com/town/estate/dd75/teamwork/tsld001.htm
BusinessWeek: "ManagingYour Team" main page	http://www.businessweek.com/managing/team
Team Building Activities for the Classroom	http://thiagi.com/games.html http://www.teampedia.net/wiki/index.php?title=Main_Page http://www.ultimatecampresource.com/site/camp-activities/team-building-games-and-initiatives.page-1.html

CHAPTER 13

Leadership

LEARNING OBJECTIVES

This chapter should help students understand:

- What leadership is and how the effectiveness of leaders is evaluated
- The various types of power and how they are employed by leaders
- The major elements of the various leadership theories
- The historical development of leadership research and conceptualization
- How to distinguish between leader traits and behaviors
- What kinds of contingencies affect leadership processes
- The most recent theories about leadership, such as leader-member exchange theory, implicit leadership theory, and transformational leadership theory
- The differences between transformational and transactional leaders
- How both gender and culture affect leadership processes
- The role of leader and subordinate emotions in organizational effectiveness

CHAPTER SUMMARY

This chapter provides an overview of leadership, with an emphasis on the theoretical and empirical work done in the field. The chapter began by defining leadership and demonstrating how the concept of power and its different types relate to leadership processes. It then emphasized that leaders use different types of power in different situations and that some leaders rely on some types of power more than other types.

Next, the major theories of leadership were presented, with an eye toward tracing their historical development; the rationale here was to show that history provides clues about how our thinking on leadership has evolved and become more sophisticated. The chapter then described trait theories as the first real systematic approach to leadership, explaining that because no traits consistently emerged as necessary to be a good leader, this approach was largely abandoned (albeit revived later) in favor of research on leadership behaviors. The latter has revealed that some effective leaders exhibit mostly consideration behaviors, whereas others exhibit mostly initiating-structure behaviors. Taking a different direction, the chapter then considered research on situational and individual moderators, as well as contingencies. In particular, Fiedler's theory was presented as an important new approach that eventually came under criticism—with the result that leadership advocates began looking elsewhere for a theoretical orientation.

In a later section, considerable time was spent discussing three contemporary theories—LMX theory, ILT, and transformational leadership theory—that have great potential to help us understand leadership processes. It was also noted that the perspective on leadership taken by both LMX and ILT is very different from that of more traditional theories. At the conclusion of the chapter, three cutting-edge issues in leadership that promise to be relevant in the 21st century were described—gender, culture, and emotions. These issues merit further study, as an understanding of their impact on leadership processes promises to enhance organizational practice.

■ Teaching the Chapter

At some time or another, your students have more than likely asked: What makes an effective leader? On playgrounds, one can observe the emergence of leadership in groups of children. Interestingly, such early perceptions are likely to influence how individuals view leaders and leadership throughout their lives. Many of your students may have recently participated in their very first presidential election. They probably asked themselves this question about effective leadership when deciding whom to vote into office. The question of leadership and the study of leaders are integral and significant parts of our society. Chapter 13 provides the opportunity for you to guide students through the numerous frameworks that have been offered to explain leadership emergence and effectiveness in organizations.

Your class will likely engage in lively discussion based on the content of this chapter. The exercises included below are aimed at getting students to think about their own experiences with leaders and what they expect from a leader when they are in a subordinate role. There is also a dark side to leadership, as it does not always result in positive, humanitarian outcomes. One question you may want to pose to your class is, "How do leaders get people to engage in bad behavior?" You may want to reference infamous leaders such as Hitler or Osama bin Laden. In addition, you may want to encourage debate about gender and leadership by splitting the class into groups of males and females and asking them to take the side of the other gender in the debate.

In the Web Learning section at the end of this chapter, a number of websites contain supplementary reading materials, including essays on leadership and recent news articles related to leadership. These sites include the Leader to Leader Institute, Fast Company, and Forbes.

■ Suggested Exercises and Assignments

What Is a Leader?

Purpose The objective of this exercise is to have students consider what stereotypes or assumptions they have about leaders and what makes them effective or ineffective.

Instructions

- Ask students to write down the first person who comes to mind when they hear the word *leader* (they can use a pseudonym if it is someone that other students might know or if they are uncomfortable sharing someone's name in class).
- Have students write down 10 words that they feel describe that person's leadership.
- When students are done, ask them to pair up with another student and discuss the person that they picked, as well as the 10 words they wrote down.
- Come together as a class and ask students to share some interesting examples.

Discussion Questions

- Are most of the examples of leaders good leaders or bad leaders? Why do you think that is?
- What are some common themes you noticed as people shared their 10 words? Do you think these can be considered the most important characteristics of leaders? Why or why not?
- We often forget that leadership is not always a formal designation. Are there any examples of people who demonstrated leadership even when they were not officially a leader?
- What are some aspects of leadership that did not come up in your discussion? Why might these qualities be overlooked when we talk about leadership?

What Leaders Have in Common

Purpose The objective of this exercise is to have students think about their experiences with leaders, identify the qualities that led them to be perceived as leaders, and consider whether such qualities would generalize to other situations.

Instructions

- Ask students to write down their answers to the following questions:
  - What qualities have the effective leaders in your life had in common?
  - Have any differences existed among those leaders?
  - Why do you think those leaders were different? Were there aspects of the context, organization, people, or job that required different leadership qualities?
- Divide up the class into small groups of six to eight.
- Ask each group to generate a compilation of its members' responses to the above questions and to make sure that they provide the following three lists:
  - Qualities that generalize across most effective leaders in most situations
  - Qualities that seem to be very situation-specific
  - Situational characteristics that require different leadership qualities or skills

Discussion Questions

- What is more important for effective leadership—leader qualities/capabilities or situational characteristics?
- What experience have you had with leaders? Have they been mostly good or mostly poor? Why?
- Did the poor leadership you experienced still lead to positive outcomes?

What's Your Leadership Style?

Purpose This activity that will help students demonstrate their own leadership behaviors and give them new ideas for how to influence others.

Instructions

- *Prior to class:* Purchase enough small plastic or paper cups so that you can divide students into groups of three or four and provide each group with approximately 20–30 cups. You should also have enough blindfolds so that each group can have one.
- Divide the students into groups, give them the cups, and ask them to set a goal for how high they can build a tower of cups. Write each team's goals on the board.
- Tell the students that each group will have one "follower," who will be blindfolded. The follower is the only individual who is allowed to touch the cups. The rest of the group will serve as "leaders" who must help guide the follower in building the cup tower.
- Give the students 20–30 minutes to work on their towers. Walk around and observe how the leaders interact with the follower.
- After time is up, ask each group whether they met or exceeded their goal. Spend some time debriefing by asking the followers how each of their leaders behaved.

Discussion Questions

- How much time did leaders focus on initiating-structure (task-oriented) behaviors? Were these helpful or harmful to your goals?
- How much time did leaders focus on consideration (relationship-oriented) behaviors? Were these helpful to your goals?
- What were some leadership behaviors that seemed to be particularly helpful or harmful?
- What have you learned about your own leadership style through this exercise?

Creating the Prototypical Leader

Purpose Students will consider their expectations of a leader across a variety of situations and think about how their experiences reflect their own traits. They will also consider prototypes of followers and their impact on leader effectiveness.

Instructions

- Divide the class into groups of three or four.
- Instruct groups to create a leader prototype and a follower prototype based on their own expectations about leader qualities, follower qualities, and the behaviors in which both leader and follower should engage.
- Ask groups to present their prototypes to the rest of the class.

Discussion Questions

- How easy was it for your group to develop a leader prototype that everyone agreed on? A follower prototype?
- What influence did your own skills and abilities have when you were developing your leader and follower expectations?
- Across the class, how similar are the prototypes that were created?

Breaking Through the Glass Ceiling

Purpose Students will discuss the issues surrounding women in leadership roles.

Instructions

- Before discussing the role of gender and leadership in class, you may want to assign an article that presents some current statistics about the representation of women in corporate or government leadership roles. Note that www.catalyst.org has a plethora of research papers that report statistics about women in leadership in a clear, easy to read manner. Under "Topics," select "Women in Leadership."
- Alternatively, there may be a current event involving women in leadership that may be worthy of discussion. For example, in August 2009, Sonia Sotomayor became an Associate Justice of the U. S. Supreme Court.
- After presenting the chapter material on gender and leadership, hold a class discussion in one of three ways:
  - Split the class solely by gender to form debate teams (it may be interesting to have them discuss the questions from the opposite gender's point of view).
  - Divide the class into small groups, split evenly by gender, and have them discuss gender and leadership.
  - Hold an open discussion/debate about gender and leadership with the entire class.
- Present students with the following questions, giving ample time between each question for thorough discussion:
  - Can you think of a well-known or famous woman who holds an important leadership position? In what industry does she work? Is this industry female-oriented or male-oriented?
  - How are women leaders portrayed in movies, books, and so on?

- Are women unfairly underrepresented in leadership roles?
- Do you think women and men are held to different standards in order to attain promotions in organizations?
- Are expectations the same for male and female leaders?
- Do you think women make greater sacrifices than men in order to ascend the corporate ladder?
- How would you increase the number of women in leadership positions? Would men perceive these methods as fair?

Discussion Questions

- *If applicable:* Did arguing from the other gender's point of view affect your perspective on the issues?
- What idea was most likely to be implemented by your group to reduce gender inequity?
- Are men likely to feel unfairly treated by interventions designed to give women a better opportunity to achieve leadership positions?
- What, if any, effect do work–life programs (e.g., telecommuting) have on the career and leadership development of men and women?

■ Evaluating "Taking It to the Field"

The Chapter 13 activity involves a game developer and manufacturer that has recently increased its staff. The company has also experienced an increase in turnover, which appears to be related to leadership. The owners, Kyle and Sophie Konig, have received some (rather poor) advice from Hollister Consulting and have asked for a critique of this advice. Below are some suggestions for evaluating responses.

Poor responses . . .	• Provide a superficial response to Hollister Consulting's suggestions (e.g., "These sound great!"). • Indicate that the suggestions are not good but fail to clearly critique the problems with the suggestions. • Provide a critique of only one of the suggestions. • Fail to provide an additional suggestion for changing the company's leadership, or provide an approach that has little empirical support or limited applicability (e.g., Fiedler's contingency theory). • Provide an approach with research support but misunderstand or misapply the approach.

Good responses . . .
- Identify at least one mistake in the way Hollister Consulting is applying the job characteristics model:
  - Hollister Consulting suggests increasing legitimate power; in fact, research shows that prosocial bases of power (reward, referent, and expert) are better for influencing follower attitudes; legitimate and coercive power have been associated with negative attitudes.
  - Hollister Consulting also suggests that LMX theory recommends that the Konigs select favorite employees and give them special privileges. This is a misapplication of LMX theory—instead, the theory suggests trying to develop high-quality relationships with all employees so that they can be treated differently based on their talents and weaknesses. What Hollister suggests here is known as high LMX differentiation, which is associated with high turnover.
  - Finally, Hollister Consulting has suggested that Kyle be designated the leader of the organization because males make better managers. This is not correct; research suggests that men and women are perceived as equally effective as leaders in most contexts, and the "feminine advantage" perspective suggests that women may be more effective than men in leadership positions.
- Suggest an additional approach that has mixed empirical support (e.g., LMX theory) or fail to provide enough detail about the suggestion to demonstrate a strong understanding of how to apply the theory.

Excellent responses . . .
- Identify at least one mistake in the way Hollister Consulting is applying the job characteristics model:
  - Hollister Consulting suggests increasing legitimate power; in fact, research shows that prosocial bases of power (reward, referent, and expert) are better for influencing follower attitudes; legitimate and coercive power have been associated with negative attitudes. Students may also note that a superficial title change is not likely to do much to change attitudes about leadership; the Konigs need to find ways to connect with their employees on a more regular basis.

- Hollister Consulting also suggests that LMX theory recommends that the Konigs select favorite employees and give them special privileges. This is a misapplication of LMX theory—instead, the theory suggests trying to develop high-quality relationships with all employees so that they can be treated differently based on their talents and weaknesses. What Hollister suggests here is known as high LMX differentiation, which is associated with high turnover. Students may connect some of the principles of LMX with the individualized consideration aspect of transformational leadership and use that as a better framework to explain how to motivate the employees.
- Finally, Hollister Consulting has suggested that Kyle be designated the leader of the organization because males make better managers. This is not correct; research suggests that men and women are perceived as equally effective as leaders in most contexts, and the "feminine advantage" perspective suggests that women may be more effective than men in leadership positions. Students may note that because KoniGames has both a manufacturing side and a development side, Kyle and Sophie may be suited for leading particular branches. For example, because manufacturing tends to be more male-dominated, those employees may be more receptive to Kyle's leadership, while employees on the development side may be more receptive to Sophie's leadership.
- Suggest an additional approach with strong empirical support (e.g., transformational leadership theory) and provide enough detail to show a firm grasp of the key concepts.

■ Evaluating "Application Questions"

1. Consider each of the bases of power. How might a college instructor demonstrate each of these? How do you react when instructors use these types of power?

   Evaluation Guide: Students will likely come up with a variety of suggestions for this question. The following are common suggestions:
   - *Legitimate power:* Because instructors have a title and are considered to be in charge in the classroom, often just having a designation such as "professor" can lend them power.
   - *Reward power:* Instructors control course grades and points, so they have the ability to reward students for good work.

- *Coercive power:* Instructors can also deduct points for poor performance, so they can use this basis of power to change student behavior.
- *Expert power:* Instructors should be experts in their field, so students typically trust that what they say is true and accurate.
- *Referent power:* Instructors who are excited about what they are teaching can emphasize the importance of learning to students. This is often important to students, as excitement can be contagious.

2. One aspect of LMX theory that researchers are beginning to explore is the varying quality of relationships within a team. Research demonstrates that when leaders have very strong relationships with only a few team members, it leads to turnover. Have you ever experienced something like this? Were you one of the favorites or one of the "outsiders"? What effect did this have on you?

   Evaluation Guide: Most students will be able to come up with at least a few experiences of being an outsider or being a favorite. Some worthwhile points to make in this conversation include the following:

   - Discuss with students how this affects their motivation. For example, if they are not a favorite, what can that do to their work ethic? It might be helpful to connect this discussion back to expectancy theory or organizational justice to show that many of these principles can apply to several areas of research.
   - If you have students who were a favorite, ask them how it made them feel. Was it a pleasant experience, or was it uncomfortable? How did it affect their relationships with coworkers? Did they feel they deserved to be a favorite?
   - Is it appropriate for a leader to show a preference for an employee who is a hard worker? What would transformational leadership have to say about this? What about transactional leadership?

3. Imagine you have a friend who is interested in becoming more transformational in her leadership style. What behaviors would you suggest she increase in order to become more transformational?

   Evaluation Guide: Students can suggest a number of different ideas for how to become more transformational. It may be useful to discuss what they, personally, can do to be better leaders in their own lives. Here are some discussion points and examples:

   - *Idealized influence and inspirational motivation:* Leaders who are passionate and excited about their work can help get workers excited as well. It is also important for leaders to "practice what they preach" so that they serve as a good role model for followers.
   - *Intellectual stimulation:* Finding "stretch assignments" for followers can help people develop and become more creative. Students may also mention providing time and support for trying something new and making mistakes.
   - *Individualized consideration:* Leaders should get to know their followers and know what sorts of goals and preferences they have. Taking time to connect with followers and provide developmental feedback can be key.

4. Consider some examples of famous female leaders. What are some ways in which female leaders are treated differently than male leaders (by the media as well as by peers and followers)?

Evaluation Guide: Students should be able to think of some prominent female leaders. Some students may get somewhat heated in this discussion, particularly if they feel that sexism and the glass ceiling are not issues. It may also be worth noting that, although liberals tend to be more outspoken about issues of sexism, female politicians from both the left and the right have experienced sexism. Some examples are listed below:

- *Hillary Clinton:* Particularly during her campaign for the Democratic presidential nomination, Clinton had to face a number of negative images in the media. She was often critiqued for being too tough and aggressive; however, after choking up during an interview, she began to be criticized for being too weak. A number of products mocked her toughness, such as a nutcracker designed to look like her.
- *Sarah Palin:* Republican vice-presidential candidate Sarah Palin also received a number of critiques that would be unusual for male candidates. For example, a number of T-shirts and other products with images that were sexual in their overtones and had little to do with her stance on issues surfaced. She was also referred to in the media as a "bimbo" or an "airhead" for some of her mistakes—terms that are not typically applied to male candidates when they make mistakes.
- *Condoleeza Rice:* The secretary of state under President George W. Bush, Rice often had to field questions in interviews about her marital status and whether she planned to have children. She also received widespread criticism when she wore an above-the-knee skirt with knee-high boots. In addition, in the wake of the 2011 Libyan rebellion, she discussed having awkward meetings with Muammar Gadhafi, who made several romantic overtures toward her.
- *Margaret Thatcher:* Called the Iron Lady for her toughness and her approach to the Soviet Union, Thatcher first assumed a position as Great Britain's secretary of state for education and science, and she had difficulty getting Prime Minister Edward Heath to listen to her suggestions (he seemed to consider her a token female whom he had to accept to appear inclusive). She was also asked many questions about whether she would have time to be a leader, given that she had children.
- A number of historical female leaders and political figures (e.g., Cleopatra, Anne Bolyn) often have their sexual exploits discussed as part of their rise to power, an aspect that is rarely discussed with male leaders.

5. Consider implicit leadership theory. People's reliance on stereotypes and prototypes are not just a problem in the study of leadership. What is another example from I/O psychology of people relying on stereotypes to evaluate others?

Evaluation Guide: Students should hopefully recognize the link between ILT and what they have previously learned about performance evaluation and the halo effect—that is, people will sometimes rate behaviors they have never observed because they rely on prototypes and stereotypes. It may also be worthwhile to discuss whether this is an issue that is worth addressing in many other areas of psychology: If people rate according to assumptions, what implication does that have for measurement in general in psychological research?

■ Highlighted Study for Discussion

Falbe, C. M., & Yukl, G. (1992). Consequences for managers of using single influence tactics and combinations of tactics. *Academy of Management Journal, 35,* 638–652.

Although the textbook does not discuss influence tactics, they are strongly related to leadership and how people respond to the influence attempts of others. The main points of the article are as follows:

- The researchers examined three outcomes of an influence attempt: resistance (where the individual refuses to comply with a request), compliance (where the individual carries out a task but shows no initiative or engagement), and commitment (where an individual carries out a request enthusiastically and willingly).
- The researchers also examined the following influence tactics:
  • Inspirational appeals (where the requester appeals to the target's values)
  • Consultation (where the requester seeks the target's help in completing a task)
  • Rational persuasion (where the requester attempts to persuade the target by using facts, statistics, or logical arguments)
  • Ingratiation (where the requester uses flattery or similar behaviors to influence the target)
  • Personal appeals (where the requester appeals to the target's feelings of friendship)
  • Exchange (where the requester offers to trade favors for the target's cooperation)
  • Pressure (where the requester uses threats or demands to get what he or she wants)
  • Legitimating (where the requester uses his or her authority or rules to influence others)
  • Coalition (where the requester enlists endorsements from others to persuade the target)
- Researchers asked MBA students to provide critical incidents describing a time when someone tried to influence them, as well as their response to the tactic. These qualitative responses were coded by researchers.
- The results indicated that rational persuasion was the most common tactic used but succeeded in gaining commitment in only 23% of cases. Inspirational appeals, although rarely used, gained commitment in 90% of cases. Legitimating was best for gaining compliance. Coalition and pressure typically resulted in high rates of resistance.

■ The researchers also compared "soft" techniques (ingratiation, consultation, inspirational appeals, and personal appeals) with "hard" techniques (pressure, legitimating, and coalition) and rational persuasion. Results indicated commitment was most likely when an individual used a combination of soft techniques or combined a soft technique with rational persuasion. Using a combination of hard techniques was most likely to result in resistance or compliance.

■ Web Learning

Title	Address
The Leader to Leader Institute: An extension of the Drucker Foundation	http://www.pfdf.org
Center for Creative Leadership	http://www.ccl.org/leadership/index.aspx
ChangingMinds.org: Leadership theories	http://changingminds.org/disciplines/leadership/theories/leadership_theories.htm
Move the Mountain Leadership Center	http://www.movethemountain.org
Big Dog & Little Dog: The Art and Science of Leadership	http://www.nwlink.com/~Donclark/leader/leader.html
Forbes magazine: Leadership page	http://www.forbes.com/leadership
Fast Company: Leadership page	http://www.fastcompany.com/topics/leadership
Catalyst: Research on women in leadership roles (under "Topics," select "Women in Leadership")	http://www.catalyst.org
Leadership Learning Community	http://leadershiplearning.org/
The Institute for Management Excellence	http://www.itstime.com

CHAPTER 14

Organizational Theory and Development

LEARNING OBJECTIVES

This chapter should help students understand:

- The various organizational theories and how they have developed

- The differences between bureaucratic theory and Scientific Management

- How Theory X differs from Theory Y

- How open-system theory provides a useful framework for thinking about organizations

- What organizational development is and why it is so important for the long-term success of organizations

- The basic premises on which organizational change is based

- The major principles of many organizational development interventions, as well as some benefits of each

- Some of the specifics concerning organizational development interventions, such as total quality management and gainsharing

- Technostructural interventions such as reengineering

- How culture-change interventions and knowledge-management interventions can act to transform organizations profoundly

CHAPTER SUMMARY

This chapter presents information about two related organizational topics: organizational theory and organizational development. These were defined and discussed in terms of their importance to the effectiveness of organizations. Three organizational theories were then presented: classical organizational theory, with its emphasis on Scientific Management and bureaucracy, and the more recent approaches known as humanistic theory and open-system theory.

Before discussing various techniques of organizational development, the chapter spent considerable time highlighting reasons why companies, if they are to be successful, must pursue OD. Examples of companies that have succeeded in part because of OD were presented, as well as examples of companies that did not succeed owing to a lack of flexibility and willingness to change. In this context, the chapter provided a detailed discussion of Lewin's general change model and the more well-developed action research model.

Next, some of the most frequently used OD interventions were discussed, such as survey feedback, team building, total quality management, and gainsharing; empirical support was cited, along with a description of their potential benefits and disadvantages. More recently conceived OD interventions were also introduced, such as reengineering, information technology, and appreciative inquiry. Finally, the chapter discussed organizational transformation in the context of interventions that profoundly change the nature of the organization. Here, culture change and knowledge management were presented as two examples of organizational transformation.

■ Teaching the Chapter

Chapter 14 is devoted solely to the "O side" of I/O psychology. While previous chapters (e.g., Chapter 9—Motivation) covered primarily "O-side" topics, this chapter examines the organization as a whole by presenting material focused on organizational theory and organizational development. Something to keep in mind and share with students is how this theoretical work fits into a historical context. Specifically, Frederick Taylor's theorizing and ideas about Scientific Management were developed during the industrial revolution, when organizations and management were struggling with how to manage people and machines. After World War II, humanistic theories were developed in response to a rapidly growing population, industrial strength, and the emergence of a service economy. For the first time, employees began considering work as more than just a paycheck, growing sensitive to how organizations affected their lives outside the workplace. With the growth and expansion of modern-day organizations, more sophisticated theories such as open-system theory have emerged to help explain organizational production and coordination.

During the last 25 years, the management consulting industry has grown rapidly in response to organizational change and development. Again, the historical context should not be ignored and may supplement class material very well. In the early 1980s, American industry experienced difficult times due to increasing competition from Japanese products and industry. After creating a competitive advantage for the Japanese, total quality management (TQM) practices emerged in the United States by the mid-1980s to improve the product quality and market share of American goods. Today, quality is still an important performance criterion for organizations and is heavily emphasized across industries. Several of the websites listed at the end of the chapter can provide students with further information relating to TQM and other popular organizational development tools such as team building and gainsharing.

Additionally, below is a list of resources you may want to consider for team building and organizational development activities that may be fun yet educational for your class. This is not meant to be an endorsement of these books; this list is *only* for information-sharing purposes.

Harrington-Mackin, D. (2007). *The team-building tool kit: Tips and tactics for effective workplace teams.* New York: AMACOM.

Miller, B. C. (2003). *Quick team-building activities for busy managers: 50 exercises that get results in 15 minutes.* New York: AMACOM.

Newstrom, J. W. (2008). *The big book of team-building: Quick, fun activities for building morale, communication, and team spirit.* New York: McGraw-Hill.

Senge, P. M., Kleiner, A., Roberts, C., Ross, R., & Smith, B. (1994). *The fifth discipline fieldbook.* New York: Crown Publishing.

Sikes, S. W. (1995). *Feeding the zircon gorilla and other team building activities.* Tulsa, OK: Learning Unlimited Corporation.

Sikes, S. W. (1998). *Executive marbles and other team building activities.* Tulsa, OK: Learning Unlimited Corporation.

■ Suggested Exercises and Assignments

Theory X Versus Theory Y

Purpose Students will consider how they think about organizational work and reflect on how their ideas might have changed over the course of the semester.

Instructions

- Find or design a measure to assess whether students tend to agree with Theory Y or Theory X philosophies (you can find some examples at http://www.businessballs.com/freepdfmaterials/X-Y_Theory_Questionnaire_2pages.pdf and at http://www.proprofs.com/quiz-school/story.php?title=are-you-theory-x-manager-theory-y-manager).
- Provide students with their scores (or ask students to score the measure on their own).

Discussion Questions

- Did you find you agreed more with Theory X or Theory Y? What experiences have led you to believe this?
- Do you believe your philosophy has changed over the course of this class? How?
- What are some topics we've talked about in class so far that seem to support the importance of Theory Y?

Overcoming Personal Roadblocks to Success

Purpose Students will simulate business process reengineering relating to their own academic performance via brainstorming and problem solving.

Instructions

- This exercise will likely be covered as students start to think about the end of the semester and final exams. This exercise offers them the opportunity to consider their performance, their satisfaction with that performance, and what they might have done to perform better.
- Ask students to think about their performance in this class throughout the semester. Instruct students to individually answer the following questions:
  - To what extent are you satisfied with your overall performance?
  - What factors acted as roadblocks for you? Specifically, what factors got in the way of achieving better performance? If no roadblocks were encountered, what factors were overcome in order to achieve successful performance in this class?
  - Considering this list of factors, rate each factor (yes/no) on whether it was *within* your control or *outside of* your control.
  - For factors within your control, what could you have done to deal with them more effectively?
    - On a scale of 1 (very easy) to 5 (very hard), how difficult would it be to make these changes? For factors outside of your control, what could you have done to minimize their effects on successful performance in class?
    - You might want to consider using this example as a template for students:

Roadblock	Within Your Control	Change Strategy	Difficulty of Change
Attended too many parties	Yes	Attend fewer weeknight parties	4

- Divide the class into groups of four to six to discuss their roadblocks and strategies for change.
- Instruct each group to develop a list of their top roadblocks and their plans for change. Then have each group present their ideas to the rest of the class.

Discussion Questions

- Will you be able to implement these change strategies in your future classes? Why or why not?
- Were you surprised by the number of roadblocks you identified?
- Were there any surprising roadblocks?
- What was the roadblock that was most difficult to change among your group?

Organizational Development and Management Fads

Purpose The objective of this exercise is to familiarize students with different commercially available interventions and help them understand how they fit into the general types of interventions.

Instructions

- If computers with Internet access are available, this activity can be done in class. If not, during the previous class you can ask students to do some research before the next class session.
- Ask groups of students to gather basic information about trendy (or formerly trendy) interventions. Some examples might include the following:
  - ISO 9000
  - Theory Z
  - Six Sigma
  - Kaizen
  - Knowledge management
  - Quality circles
  - One-Minute Management
  - Reengineering
  - Matrix management
- Have students present their information to one another (either in front of everyone, or create new groups that have one representative from each group).

Discussion Questions

- Do you believe any of these interventions are fads? Why?
- What is the difference (if any) between organizational development and management fads?
- What skills or knowledge would someone need to identify a fad?
- How might you test these interventions to determine if they are actually effective?

Creating Culture Change

Purpose Students will consider what is involved in changing the culture, even within a small organization.

Instructions

- Ask students to spend a few minutes thinking of a way to describe a culture they are part of (e.g., your college/university or your classroom).
- Have students share some of their thoughts, and then ask them how they might change the culture (e.g., if the classroom is typically quiet, ask them how they might change it into a place where people speak up more).
- Have students work in pairs or groups to devise ways in which the culture of the classroom could change.
- Have students share their ideas.

Discussion Questions

- Do you think culture change here is possible? Why or why not?
- Which of these suggestions do you think would be most successful? Why?
- What are some barriers to culture change you can think of?

Organizational Development Interventionist for a Day

Purpose Students will consider the various types of organizational development (OD) interventions and apply them to an organizational scenario.

Instructions

- *Prior to class:* You might want to have copies of the following scenario available for each student/group:

  > You are an organizational development consultant at RPJ Consulting, Inc. You have just been hired by the CompuCool company, which designs and sells "netbooks" (small laptop computers with limited capability that cost less than $300). In the past year, the company has gone from 150 employees with virtually no organizational chart to 1,500 employees working in the areas of research and development, production, sales, marketing, and finance.
  >
  > CompuCool primarily manufactures netbooks, but it also produces small accessories for the netbook (e.g., case, wireless mouse, etc.). The company's sales have gone from $3 million to $15 million in two years. Furthermore, the founders of the company were college roommates, are very laid back, and do not like a lot of rules and procedures. To this point, the company culture has been very informal, with few procedures in place. CompuCool's mission statement, which has existed since the beginning of the company, reads, "Our mission is to produce a cool, accessible netbook computer for all people. In doing so, we want to have fun while making a difference and maybe a profit, too." The company has hired you because they are concerned with the company's overall effectiveness, efficiency, and productivity.

- Divide the class into groups of four to six.
- Instruct the groups to address the following:
  - How would you go about diagnosing CompuCool's problems? What appear to be the main organizational problems?
  - Choose two OD interventions to implement to help the organization achieve its goals. Describe why you chose these methods and draw up detailed plans for how you will go about addressing the OD issues in the organization.
  - What obstacles might you face in implementing these interventions?
  - Who would you involve in your planning?
  - How would you get the two company founders to support your ideas?

Discussion Questions

- How difficult was it to select interventions for this situation?
- To what extent do you believe it would be difficult to conduct an OD intervention in this situation?

- How would you determine if your intervention was effective?
- Have you ever participated in an activity that was part of an OD intervention?

■ Evaluating "Taking It to the Field"

In the Chapter 14 activity, the CEO of another I/O consulting firm is asking for help implementing a survey feedback intervention for his company. He has outlined several problems and asked students to outline a plan for implementing the survey, example items for the survey, and what is needed from him. Responses will vary, particularly depending upon whether your students have taken a research methods class prior to your class. Their responses may also vary depending upon how in-depth you have covered information about measurement and surveying in your class. However, a rough guideline to grading is provided below.

Poor responses . . .	• Provide only superficial steps for implementing the survey (writing it, setting it up on a website, sending the link). • Fail to provide five example items or provide items that are poorly constructed or do not ask important questions. • Do not ask the CEO for any help or support, other than monetary payment.
Good responses . . .	• Refer in a general way to the steps outlined in the chapter (gaining top management support; sending anonymous surveys; compiling results by locations, departments, etc.; providing feedback to the organization; meeting to identify potential changes for implementation). • Provide five example items that seem like they will be useful (e.g., questions about attitudes and perceptions, particularly regarding top management, mid-level management, issues with customers). • Emphasize the importance of the CEO in supporting the survey, communicating the anonymity of the survey responses, and indicating how the results will be used.
Excellent responses . . .	• Explicitly align their plan with the steps outlined in the book (gaining top management support; sending anonymous surveys; compiling results by locations, departments, etc.; providing feedback to the organization; meeting to identify potential changes for implementation) and emphasize that the survey is only the first step in designing a targeted intervention, rather than an end in itself. • Provide five example items that appear to grasp potential issues that may be going on at Arianda

Consulting (e.g., there may be differences in satisfaction with work or management at each separate location; internal hires may indicate that internal promotion is not common; customer satisfaction with service in Philadelphia may be linked with differences in the quality of management).
- Emphasize the importance of the CEO in supporting the survey, communicating the anonymity of the survey responses, and indicating how the results will be used.

■ Evaluating "Application Questions"

1. Think of a time you had had to deal with a bureaucracy. What did you need to do? Did you see any reason for that bureaucracy's existence?

Evaluation Guide: Most students will have experienced some level of bureaucracy. For example, students will commonly express irritation at paperwork they have to fill out for the university/college. This discussion might help clarify the difference between useful and wasteful bureaucracy, and how this can change over time. The following may be helpful points to make:
- Sometimes bureaucracy is important and necessary. For example, students who are taking a course abroad may need to provide a great deal of paperwork for their own safety.
- Sometimes bureaucracy was once important but has now outlived its usefulness. For example, if an administrative assistant requires hard copies of documents that are available online, this would be an example of a bureaucracy that has not appropriately adapted to technology.
- Sometimes bureaucracy is created needlessly because the individual making the decision did not realize the amount of work he or she was creating. For example, if a higher-up official decides to change a form so that it now requires two departments to collaborate to fill it out, rather than having separate documents that each department can fill out independently, that official may have unknowingly created a need for additional meetings between the departments.

2. Have you ever been in an organization that was undergoing an organizational development intervention? What happened? How did employees react?

Evaluation Guide: Some students may not have had any experience in organizations that were experiencing major changes, so even discussing minor procedural changes (e.g., a new sandwich on a menu) can provide them with an idea of what that situation is like. Some points worth making are listed below:
- Frequency of organizational change is important. In organizations where there are always new changes in progress, employees can become jaded,

especially when the changes fail to produce meaningful and practical outcomes.

- Communication is important as well; interventions that are not supported by upper management and that are not well explained and justified also tend to fail.

3. Consider an organization where you have worked. Do you think this organization was a "learning organization"? Why or why not?

Evaluation Guide: Students will have a wide variety of experience on this topic. Some students might have worked in relatively low-level jobs in organizations that tend to promote from within (e.g., Starbuck's, Target, the U.S. military); others might have worked in smaller organizations where entry-level jobs rarely develop into lifelong careers. Below are some points to discuss:

- Learning organizations have a number of benefits. Workers are more likely to stay loyal to the company if they feel they can develop and grow their career there. Workers also may enjoy learning and feel valued if they are compensated for spending extra time learning relevant information. Some organizations may also support employees who go back to school to earn degrees that are relevant to the company.

- Learning organizations also face some difficulties. Workers will sometimes need to be away from work or decrease their workload to engage in these learning activities (employees are unlikely to be willing to use their personal time to take a training course, so someone will need to cover for them while they are gone). Furthermore, if the organization makes continuous learning a requirement, individuals who are not interested in learning more may end up leaving or being fired, which could be a problem.

- In general, most students appreciate a company that supports continuous learning, so discussing their experiences in such an environment will help them understand how common such an appreciation is and some of the ways they were able to develop in the workplace.

4. Consider positive organizational development. Do you believe people should spend more time focusing on using their strengths or addressing their weaknesses? Why?

Evaluation Guide: This is an ongoing controversy in the I/O arena, and students may have strong opinions about this. Here are some points in the debate worth noting:

- Focusing on strengths rather than weaknesses seems inclusive because it assumes everyone has a strength. It also is thought to help people feel more empowered in their work. A number of measures (e.g., StrengthsFinder) focus on finding strengths and leveraging them, and employees seem to like this approach.

- Focusing only on strengths, however, may allow individuals to overlook weaknesses that are actively harming their performance. Some also argue that focusing on strengths removes accountability for some individuals, which can be problematic.

5. Imagine you work for a company that uses gainsharing. Do you think you would like it? Why or why not?

Evaluation Guide: Most students will initially be in favor of gainsharing. In order to generate more discussion, consider splitting the class into a debate of pro versus con, or ask the following questions:

- Think about group projects you have worked on where all members received the same number of points. What were some things you found frustrating about that situation?
- Think about what types of rewards you would prefer: Stocks? Cash? An upgrade to a better office? A group vacation? Keeping in mind that everyone has to receive the same reward, which would you suggest companies use for their reward system?
- How would you solicit employee suggestions for gainsharing, and how would you encourage them to continue to share their ideas in the long run?

■ Highlighted Study for Discussion

Vermeulen, F., Puranam, P., & Gulati, R. (2010). Change for change's sake. *Harvard Business Review, 88,* 70–76.

This article, from the *Harvard Business Review,* provides an interesting opportunity to discuss the importance of empirical support in OD. The main points of the article are as follows:

- The authors make the case that even untroubled organizations should engage in organizational change from time to time. They argue that organizations that are doing well tend to overlook inefficiencies, routines, and silos that have developed over time.
- First, the authors suggest reorienting the organization around a new criterion. They provide the example of Cisco Systems, which created a centralized R&D group to facilitate technical innovation. It may be useful to ask students whether they think this change would work for all organizations and what might prompt an organization to do this.
- Second, the authors suggest that being proactive in changing can help break up routines and typical ways of doing work. They cite GE Healthcare, which changed the organizational structure and created new positions intended to reconnect equipment and service silos. This provides an opportunity to ask students about some of the implications of changing the organizational structure, which are downplayed by the authors.
- Third, the authors suggest that groups within an organization can become too powerful over time and that resource allocation is not done properly. They cite Jones Lang LaSalle, where a new CEO broke up the three divisions and integrated them. The authors note that senior executives left when they lost

their power and influence but that the change eliminated bottlenecks. Asking students to consider what research in I/O might say about this change will help them think critically about the change.

- The article also provides a small test that the authors suggest be handed out to managers to assess whether it is time for a change. This would provide a good opportunity for students to consider and discuss test development and validation. It also might be helpful to discuss what it would mean if managers or CEOs make decisions based on the outcomes of this measure.

■ Web Learning

Title	Address
American Society for Quality	http://www.asq.org
Baldrige National Quality Program	http://www.quality.nist.gov
Deming Electronic Network: Resources	http://deming-network.org/deming_map.htm
HR Guide: Compensation, Incentive Plans, Gainsharing	http://www.hr-guide.com/data/G443.htm
Fieldbook.com: The Fifth Discipline Field Book Project	http://www.fieldbook.com
Organizational Development Portal	http://www.odportal.com
Organizational Development Network	http://www.odnetwork.org
Action Science Network	http://www.actionscience.com
Change Management Toolbook	http://www.change-management-toolbook.com
Open Systems Theory	http://faculty.babson.edu/krollag/org_site/encyclop/open_system.html
Academy of Management: Organization and Management Theory	http://division.aomonline.org/omt
Group Performance Systems: Learning Organization Resources on the Web and on the Net	http://www.gpsi.com/lo.html
Free Management Library: Team Building	http://managementhelp.org/grp_skll/teams/teams.htm